CLASSIC
HOME
COOKING

CLASSIC
HOME
COOKING

MARY BERRY
AND MARLENA SPIELER

DORLING KINDERSLEY
London • New York • Stuttgart

A DORLING KINDERSLEY BOOK

Created and produced by
CARROLL & BROWN LIMITED
5 Lonsdale Road
London NW6 6RA

Editorial Consultant Jeni Wright

Project Editor Vicky Hanson

Editors Jo-Anne Cox, Anne Crane, Trish Shine,
Jo Stanford, Stella Vayne, Madeline Weston

Cookery Consultants Valerie Cipollone
and Anne Hildyard

Art Editors Louisa Cameron and Gary Edgar-Hyde
Designers Alan Watt, Karen Sawyer, Lucy De Rosa

Photography David Murray and Jules Selmes

Production Wendy Rogers and Amanda Mackie

First American Edition, 1995
2 4 6 8 10 9 7 5 3 1

Published in the United States by Dorling Kindersley Publishing, Inc.,
95 Madison Avenue, New York, New York 10016

Published in Great Britain by Dorling Kindersley Limited.
Distributed by Houghton Mifflin Company, Boston.

Library of Congress Cataloging-in-Publication Data
Berry, Mary
  Classic Home Cooking/by Mary Berry and Marlena
  Spieler. – 1st American ed.
  p. cm.
  Includes index
  ISBN 0-7894-0153-3
1. Cookery. I. Title. II. Spieler, Marlena
  TX714. B396 1995   95-2198
  641.5 - - dc20   CIP

Reproduced by Colourscan, Singapore
Printed and bound in France by Partenaires Fabrications

FOREWORD

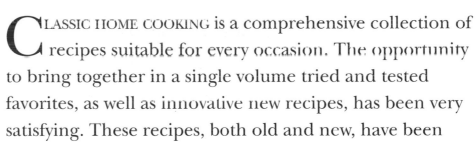

Classic home cooking is a comprehensive collection of recipes suitable for every occasion. The opportunity to bring together in a single volume tried and tested favorites, as well as innovative new recipes, has been very satisfying. These recipes, both old and new, have been assembled in order to meet today's requirements for healthy, quick dishes made with fresh ingredients. The emphasis is on choice and flexibility: our intention has been to make the book the perfect companion for the person who needs to prepare meals for a family each day, as well as for those who find entertaining a pleasure.

Each chapter provides a varied selection of recipes, including both the traditional and the new, and has been designed to accommodate elegant entertaining as well as family meals. There is such a wonderful variety of new ingredients to be found in today's supermarkets – a large selection of fresh herbs, exotic ingredients such as lemongrass, unusual types of fish, and a wide range of meat and poultry – that we have been able to gain inspiration from the recipes and cooking techniques used all over the world. We hope you will enjoy using this book as much as we have enjoyed creating it.

Mary Berry

Marlena Spieler

CONTENTS

INTRODUCTION

Home cooking with fresh ingredients is the best way to ensure that your meals will be well prepared and delicious. Despite the popularity of so-called convenience foods, time spent shopping for and cooking fresh, good-quality ingredients is time well spent.

Home-cooked meals need not be labor intensive – when modern gadgets can save you time, their use has been incorporated in the recipes in this book. Tricky techniques that may be *de rigueur* for professionals, but impractical for everyday cooking, have been avoided. If there's a short cut that gives good results, its use has been explained. By the same token, a well-stocked pantry and a few good tools are important parts of the process as well – saving you precious time.

The aim of this book is to make cooking the enjoyable experience it should be, and to make meals as pleasant to prepare as they are to eat.

THE PANTRY

With a supply of useful ingredients always on hand, you'll never be short of ideas for an impromptu meal. Canned tomatoes, fish such as tuna and anchovies, and ready-cooked beans, such as kidney beans, can be added to a whole host of dishes. Dried pasta and noodles, different types of rice, and a variety of legumes can form the basis of many meals. Olives and capers will pep up numerous dishes, many different oils can be used for cooking and flavoring, and flavored vinegars add distinction to salad dressings and marinades. And of course you should have a good supply of spices and dried herbs. Keep jars of chutneys, pickles, and mustards, and bottles of soy sauce, chili sauce, and Worcestershire sauce for adding spice to savory meals; and use jams, marmalades, and honeys for adding a sweet, fruity note to all kinds of dishes.

With a constant supply of sugars, flours, nuts, and dried fruits, you'll be able to bake cakes at a moment's notice. Dry ingredients, such as flour, dried pasta, and spices, should be kept in a dark cabinet.

You'll find advice on storing different foods in the Know-How pages of the chapters. Be sure to keep an eye on use-by dates, and remember that foods at the back of the cabinet won't last indefinitely – try to rotate goods so that the first to be stored in the cupboard are the first to be used.

BASIC EQUIPMENT

Good equipment makes cooking easy. With high-quality knives, pots and pans, and other utensils, you will be able to cook efficiently and with pleasure. If you are equipping your first kitchen, an investment in a few basic items is all that's required – you don't need many fancy utensils to turn out delicious meals. Then, as your skills and experience grow, you can add to your collection of kitchen equipment, buying more unusual items to prepare the food you like to cook. It's important to buy the best tools and equipment you can afford. High-quality, well-made equipment is a worthwhile investment because it will last for many years, giving good service. The cheaper alternatives will need to be replaced more often, as they will dent, break, or wear out. And using a thin pan in which food always sticks and burns, or trying to chop vegetables with a flimsy knife, can turn cooking into a chore.

YOUR KITCHEN

Although there is no lack of appliances on the market, kitchens vary from being underequipped to overequipped. The basics, of course, are most important, and well-built appliances should last a good long while.

A refrigerator-freezer and conventional oven are all that is really needed, although many homes are now equipped with microwave ovens and free-standing freezers as well. There's advice on microwaving and freezing in the Know-How pages at the beginning of each chapter, and you'll find additional information on pages 492–495.

Traditional ovens are still the norm, whether gas or electric. Ovens are all slightly different, and yours may be hotter or cooler than you expect. Use an oven thermometer for the most accurate reading.

Convection ovens can cook foods quicker than conventional ovens. To compensate, you can reduce the temperature given in a recipe, but it's best to consult the manufacturer's handbook. Convection ovens have an even temperature throughout; in conventional ovens, the heat rises, so that the top of the oven is hotter than the bottom.

MEASURING EQUIPMENT

Even experienced cooks need accurate measuring tools to ensure that ingredients are in correct proportion to one another. The following are essential in the kitchen and can be found in any good kitchenware store. Look for durable equipment:

• **Measuring cups:** for measuring dry ingredients such as flour, sugar, cornmeal, dried beans, and rice. You should have at least one set of $1/8$-cup, $1/4$-cup, $1/3$-cup, $1/2$-cup, and 1-cup measures. A clear glass 2-cup (500-ml) measuring cup with a spout and clearly marked calibrations is also useful. Some ingredients can be measured accurately only by weight, so it's useful to have a small **kitchen scale.**

• **Set of measuring spoons:** $1/4$ tsp (1.25 ml), $1/2$ tsp (2.5 ml), 1 tsp (5 ml), and 1 tbsp (15 ml).

• **Meat thermometer:** to measure the internal temperature of meat and poultry during cooking.

• **Deep-frying thermometer:** to check the temperature of oil. Electric deep-fat fryers usually contain their own built-in thermometers.

• **Oven thermometer:** to check oven temperature; some ovens can exceed or fall short of the desired temperature.

POTS & PANS

Pans used on top of the stove must be heavy enough to sit securely on the burner without tipping, yet not so heavy that you have trouble lifting them. A heavy base is particularly important for gentle, even heat distribution. Pots and pans should also have lids that fit tightly and sturdy handles that stay cool. Ovenproof handles make it easy to transfer pots and pans from the stove top to the oven, when necessary.

- **Three straight-sided saucepans:** 1 quart (1 liter), 2 quart (2 liter), and 3 quart (3 liter) capacity with tightly fitting lids.
- **Two nonstick skillets:** one 8 in (20 cm) in diameter and the other 12 or 14 in (30 or 35 cm) in diameter, preferably with lids so that foods can be covered and allowed to simmer.
- **Large, heavy, flameproof casserole:** preferably cast iron coated in enamel, which disperses a gentle heat, with a tight-fitting lid. Use for stewing and braising.

- **Wok:** for stir-fries and steaming. A wok with a single long handle is easier to use than a wok with 2 small handles. The more authentic Chinese woks are made from steel, although nonstick models are also available. A wok with a lid is the most versatile.
- **Steamer:** for cooking vegetables and fish. Available as a pan with a perforated base that forms a tier between 2 saucepans, as a folding basket that fits in a saucepan, or as a bamboo steamer to use in a wok.
- **Omelet pan:** 7 or 8 in (18 or 20 cm) in diameter is the most convenient; look for curved sides.
- **Crêpe pan:** with a flat bottom and shallow, sloping side for making crêpes and pancakes.

- **Small, nonstick pot:** with a spout for easy pouring.
- **Large, lightweight stockpot:** for making stock and cooking pasta. The best ones are tall and narrow, in order to contain a large amount of water but to limit the evaporation of water and keep the flavors in.
- **Stove-top grill pan:** used for cooking steaks and chops on top of the stove. The base of this heavy, flat, cast-iron pan is ridged to keep the meat out of the fat – there is also a spout for pouring off the fat. It gives results similar to cooking on a barbecue or broiler.

Uncoated cast-iron pans, omelet pans, and crêpe pans should all be seasoned before using for the first time: cover with a thin layer of oil and heat until very hot, then wipe the oil away with paper towels. The pan need never be washed – simply wipe with paper towels after every use. If you do have to wash it, soak in hot water only and wipe clean, don't use detergent or scouring pads, and season as before.

CUTTING & CHOPPING

A set of sturdy, well-made knives that are kept sharp is essential for efficient food preparation.

- **Chef's or cook's knife:** with a rigid, heavy, wide blade 8 or 10 in (20 or 25 cm) long.
- **Sharp knife:** with a blade 5 or 6 in (12 or 15 cm) long, for cutting fruit and vegetables.
- **Small knife:** with a 3- or 4-in (7- or 10-cm) blade. Use to trim and peel fruit and vegetables.

Knives made of high-carbon stainless steel combine the best of both their components: the carbon enables the knife to take a sharp edge and the stainless steel prevents rusting. Ideally, the metal of the blade should run all the way through the handle and the handle should be well riveted. Keep knives in a knife block or on a magnetic strip; knives lying in a kitchen drawer are dangerous and can become damaged. Use a sharpening steel regularly and have your knives sharpened professionally once or twice a year. Blunt knives cause accidents.

- **Sharpening steel:** to hone or refresh your sharpened knives.
- **Two-pronged carving fork:** some have a guard to protect your hand in case the knife slips.
- **Cutting boards:** these are indispensable, and you should have at least two, keeping one for raw meat and poultry only. Both wooden and plastic boards are good for home use. Clean them thoroughly with hot, soapy water after each use. Dry them well before storing.

OVENWARE

Cooking in the oven requires sturdy pans and dishes that conduct and retain heat efficiently. Baking pans and sheets are now available with nonstick coatings, although these are liable to become scratched if you use metal tools. For added convenience, choose oven dishes – casseroles, baking dishes, and gratin dishes – that are attractive enough to be used for serving at the table too.

- **Roasting pan:** made of heavy stainless steel or aluminum. If possible, have pans in 2 sizes. Roasting in a pan that is too large will cause juices to evaporate and burn; if the pan is too small, it will be difficult to baste the meat or poultry properly.
- **Two flat baking sheets:** for cookies and meringues.
- **Two loaf pans:** for baking breads and cakes, molding mousses and gelatins; and for savory dishes such as pâtés and terrines.
- **12-hole muffin pan:** for baking muffins, vegetable timbales, fruit buns, and Yorkshire puddings.
- **Deep, loose-bottomed cake pan:** 8 or 9 in (20 or 23 cm) in diameter, for large cakes such as fruit cakes.
- **Springform cake pan:** for making cheesecakes, some cakes, and mousses. The sides open out and the bottom is loose, to allow easy removal.

- **Individual soufflé dishes or ramekins:** used for small soufflés, baked puddings such as crème caramel, baked eggs, savory pâtés and terrines, and mousses.
- **Two 8-in (20-cm) sandwich pans:** for making layered cakes such as sandwich cakes.
- **Jelly roll pan:** with shallow sides and a nonstick coating. Jelly roll pans usually measure 9 x 13 in (23 x 33 cm), and are used for both sweet and savory sponge mixtures and roulades.
- **Shallow, fluted tart pan:** 8 or 9 in (20 or 23 cm) in diameter, for making quiches and sweet and savory tarts. Metal tart pans conduct heat more efficiently than ceramic dishes and ensure crisp pastry. The bottoms of the pans are usually loose so that the tarts are easy to remove.
- **Individual tartlet pans:** for sweet and savory tartlets. Available in a variety of shapes, including round, diamond-, and boat-shaped.
- **Straight-sided soufflé dish:** 5 cup (1.25 liter) capacity. The dish can double as a baking dish for crumbles and other desserts.
- **Large gratin dish:** for making vegetable and other gratins. Also useful for desserts and for baking fish.
- **Oval pie dish:** with a wide lip for deep-dish sweet and savory pies.

MATERIALS FOR COOKWARE

Since it is important to have pots and pans in a variety of shapes and sizes, it is important that they be made from a variety of materials. A well-stocked kitchen has some cookware made of each of these materials. Buy the best you can afford.

Copper is an excellent heat conductor. Copper pans lined with nickel, tin, or stainless steel are truly the best, preferred by many professional chefs. Copper pans are very expensive and heavy, however, and have to be kept polished.

Aluminum is another efficient heat conductor, but it has certain disadvantages. It scratches easily and can react with acidic foods, giving them a metallic taste. Since recent research suggests that aluminum may also contaminate foods, it is usually covered with another material, such as stainless steel.

Porcelain pans both hold and conduct heat well.

Stainless steel is lightweight and durable, but not a very good heat conductor. To compensate, the bases of stainless steel pans are usually reinforced with aluminum or copper.

Cast iron can be heated to a high temperature and retains heat well. Plain cast-iron pans should be seasoned before use. Enameled cast-iron pans retain heat well and do not need to be seasoned – perfect for long, slow cooking. Both materials are very heavy.

Nonstick pans are easy to clean and can be used with little or no fat. The coating is easily scratched, however, and will wear off with time.

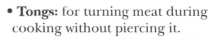

ELECTRICAL EQUIPMENT

The many machines now available take much of the hard work out of food preparation. Though not absolutely necessary, these machines will often speed the cook's progress through a recipe.

• **Hand-held electric beaters:** compact in size and easy to use. An electric beater allows you to whip egg whites or cream in seconds.
• **Stand mixers:** bulkier than hand-held mixers but will quickly mix cake batters and bread doughs.
• **Blenders:** puree soups, sauces, and other liquids. They cannot be used for solids alone.
• **Food processors:** by changing the blade, you can chop, grate, slice, or puree all kinds of ingredients and even mix pastry and bread doughs.
• **Electric grinders:** these will quickly produce freshly ground coffee, spices, and peppercorns. They are also useful for grinding nuts and citrus zest.

UTENSILS

You can get by in the kitchen with relatively few utensils and small pieces of equipment. Here is a list of those used most often. All these tools are readily available.

• **Several wooden spoons and spatulas:** in varying sizes.
• **Two rubber spatulas:** for scraping bowls clean.
• **Long, heavy rolling pin:** 2–3 in (5–7 cm) in diameter. Wooden ones are fine, although marble ones stay cooler for rolling pastry and chocolate.
• **Pastry brush:** for glazing pastry, greasing cake pans, and brushing meats with marinades.
• **Set of at least 4 mixing bowls:** in varying sizes. These can double as gelatin molds.
• **Wire rack:** for cooling cakes, cookies, and breads.
• **Pastry cutters:** plain and fluted, for cookies, biscuits, and tartlets.
• **Piping bag and nozzles:** for piping whipped cream and icing onto cakes and desserts, and shaping meringues and puff pastry.
• **Slotted spoon:** for draining foods and skimming stocks.
• **Large spatula:** for turning and lifting large items of food.

• **Tongs:** for turning meat during cooking without piercing it.
• **Wire balloon whisk:** about 12 in (30 cm) long, for whipping eggs, cream, and sauces.
• **Long-handled ladle:** for transferring liquids such as stocks and soups.
• **Narrow spatula:** with a 10-in (25-cm) blade, for turning and lifting foods.
• **Box grater:** with 3 or 4 different cutting surfaces, from coarse to fine, for grating cheese, citrus zest, and nutmeg.
• **Fixed-bladed vegetable peeler:** for peeling potatoes and other round fruits and vegetables. A swivel-bladed peeler is also useful for straight-sided vegetables such as carrots. (When using a peeler with a fixed blade, draw it toward you; use a swivel-bladed peeler in the opposite way, working it in downward strokes away from your body.)
• **Strainers:** rigid metal mesh for sifting dry ingredients, flexible nylon for straining sauces and purees.
• **Kitchen scissors:** made from stainless steel for easy cleaning.
• **Juice squeezer:** preferably with a guard to catch seeds.
• **Colander:** with legs or a base, so it is freestanding.
• **Mortar and pestle:** ideal for grinding herbs.

AND DON'T FORGET

Here's a reminder of those items that no cook can do without.

• paper towels
• foil
• plastic wrap
• waxed paper
• baking parchment
• fine white string for trussing and tying
• wooden toothpicks
• can opener
• corkscrew and bottle opener
• pepper mill is a must for grinding black pepper
• kitchen timer is useful when baking cakes
• metal skewers for testing cakes, and for meat and poultry
• ice-cube trays

HOW TO USE THIS BOOK

E ACH CHAPTER BEGINS with a COLOR INDEX that provides a color photograph and a clear description of each recipe. The recipes are divided into 3 color-coded categories according to the preparation and cooking time of each dish. Details such as the number of servings, the number of calories, and the page on which the recipe can be found are also included. The KNOW-HOW pages contain practical information relating to the recipes in the chapter and step-by-step pictures explaining some of the more specialized cooking techniques. The RECIPE PAGES that follow make up the bulk of each chapter. Every recipe has a comprehensive list of ingredients and easy-to-follow step-by-step instructions. In addition, every recipe page is packed with special features designed to make your cooking simple, enjoyable, and very successful.

COLOR INDEX

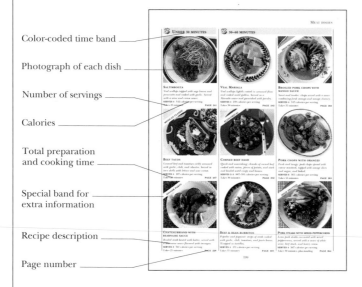

Color-coded time band

Photograph of each dish

Number of servings

Calories

Total preparation and cooking time

Special band for extra information

Recipe description

Page number

KNOW-HOW

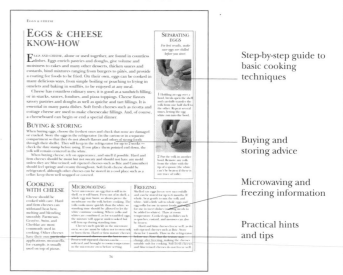

Step-by-step guide to basic cooking techniques

Buying and storing advice

Microwaving and freezing information

Practical hints and tips

RECIPE PAGES

Complete list of ingredients, with American and (metric) measurements

Each stage of the recipe given in concise steps

"Cook's know-how" provides professional tips

Simple variations of the main recipe offer even more choices

Full-color photograph of the finished dish

Additional information about certain dishes

Any special equipment needed is listed with ingredients

Illustrated explanation of specific techniques

1

HOT & CHILLED SOUPS

⏱ UNDER 30 MINUTES

⏱ 30–60 MINUTES

THAI SPICED SOUP

Fresh and chunky: shredded chicken, bean sprouts, and leafy vegetables simmered in coconut milk and stock. Served over noodles.
SERVES 4 238 calories per serving
Takes 25 minutes   **PAGE 37**

ASPARAGUS SOUP

Fresh asparagus blended with stock and potatoes, and richly flavored with garlic. Garnished here with nuggets of butter.
SERVES 6 96 calories per serving
Takes 25 minutes   **PAGE 24**

FRENCH PEA SOUP

Smooth and summery: onion and lettuce blended with fresh peas and stock, and flavored with mint sprigs.
SERVES 4–6 253–169 calories per serving
Takes 35 minutes   **PAGE 22**

WATERCRESS SOUP

Smooth and creamy: blended onion, potatoes, watercress, stock, and milk, lightly flavored with a bay leaf. Can be served hot or cold.
SERVES 6 140 calories per serving
Takes 25 minutes   **PAGE 25**

TOMATO SOUP

Tomatoes, onions, and garlic blended with stock. Enriched with store-bought pesto and flavored with a bay leaf.
SERVES 6–8 134–101 calories per serving
Takes 25 minutes   **PAGE 27**

CUBAN CORN & SEAFOOD SOUP

Hot and spicy: firm whitefish added to corn, squash, potato, stock, and strained tomatoes, and simmered with chili and garlic.
SERVES 4 379 calories per serving
Takes 40 minutes   **PAGE 32**

TASTY MUSHROOM SOUP

Mushrooms, garlic, and onion cooked with stock and white wine, and generously flavored with thyme and marjoram.
SERVES 4–6 109–73 calories per serving
Takes 25 minutes   **PAGE 23**

CHINESE CRAB & CORN SOUP

Blended corn kernels cooked with crabmeat and stock, and flavored with soy sauce, scallions, garlic, and ginger.
SERVES 4 216 calories per serving
Takes 20 minutes   **PAGE 37**

LENTIL & BACON SOUP

Nourishing and hearty: diced vegetables, bacon, and lentils simmered in stock, and richly flavored with garlic and herbs.
SERVES 4–6 301–201 calories per serving
Takes 50 minutes   **PAGE 35**

CLAM CHOWDER

Fresh clams cooked in fish stock, then simmered with milk, onion, and potatoes, and flavored with bacon and bay leaf.

SERVES 4 497 calories per serving

Takes 50 minutes   **PAGE 30**

MULLIGATAWNY SOUP

Vegetables and spices, simmered with garbanzo beans and stock and combined with yogurt, make a rich and piquant soup.

SERVES 4–6 274–182 calories per serving

Takes 50 minutes   **PAGE 28**

WINTER SQUASH SOUP

Nourishing and smooth: blended squash, leeks, and stock enriched with cream and combined with baby peas and spinach.

SERVES 6 329 calories per serving

Takes 50 minutes   **PAGE 34**

GAME SOUP

Rich and aromatic: bacon and mushrooms simmered in game stock, flavored with a citrus and herb bouquet and red currant jelly.

SERVES 4 223 calories per serving

Takes 50 minutes   **PAGE 35**

CURRIED PARSNIP SOUP

Smooth and spicy: parsnips blended with mild curry powder, onion, garlic, and stock, and enriched with light cream.

SERVES 6–8 197–147 calories per serving

Takes 35 minutes   **PAGE 26**

SPICED AUTUMN SOUP

Potatoes, carrots, apples, orange zest and juice, tomatoes, and stock blended with onion, garlic, curry powder, and dried basil.

SERVES 8 171 calories per serving

Takes 50 minutes   **PAGE 29**

BLUE CHEESE & ONION SOUP

Creamy and rich: finely sliced onions combined with stock, blue cheese, bay leaves, and nutmeg make a flavorful soup.

SERVES 6–8 340–255 calories per serving

Takes 50 minutes   **PAGE 29**

WINTER VEGETABLE SOUP

Assortment of seasonal vegetables simmered with stock, seasoned with dill and turmeric, and colored with spinach.

SERVES 6 153 calories per serving

Takes 55 minutes   **PAGE 26**

HOT & SOUR SOUP

Rich and tangy: dried mushrooms, sliced cabbage, tofu, bamboo shoots, and chicken simmered with stock and enriched with eggs.

SERVES 4–6 249–166 calories per serving

Takes 50 minutes   **PAGE 36**

🕐 OVER 60 MINUTES

TZATZIKI SOUP

Cool and refreshing: yogurt, cucumber, and garlic blended with olive oil, white vinegar, and mint and served chilled.

SERVES 4–6 138–92 calories per serving
Takes 15 minutes, plus chilling **PAGE 38**

BORSCHT

Beets, cabbage, potatoes, and tomatoes simmered with stock, vinegar, sugar, and dill for a rich sweet-sour flavor.

SERVES 4 244 calories per serving
Takes 1¼ hours **PAGE 27**

BOUILLABAISSE

Mediterranean favorite: assorted fish and shellfish simmered in stock with vegetables, orange zest, and Provençal herbs.

SERVES 8 337 calories per serving
Takes 1¼ hours **PAGE 33**

GAZPACHO

Tomatoes, red peppers, and garlic blended with stock, olive oil, and red wine vinegar make a rich iced soup. Served with croutons.

SERVES 4–6 249–166 calories per serving
Takes 15 minutes, plus chilling **PAGE 39**

RICH FISH SOUP

Fish fillets blended with stock, dry white wine, and mixed vegetables, and richly flavored with garlic and herbs.

SERVES 4 419 calories per serving
Takes 1¼ hours **PAGE 30**

QUICK SHRIMP GUMBO

Red pepper and tomatoes cooked with chorizo, stock, and okra make a piquant base for shrimp. Served with a rice timbale.

SERVES 4 512 calories per serving
Takes 1¼ hours **PAGE 32**

FRENCH ONION SOUP

Thinly sliced caramelized onions simmered in beef stock and topped with a traditional Gruyère croute: a classic French soup.

SERVES 8 353 calories per serving
Takes 1¼ hours **PAGE 24**

CREAMY CARROT & ORANGE SOUP

Smooth and tangy: carrots and stock mixed with light sour cream, orange zest and juice and flavored with fresh chives.

SERVES 6–8 308–231 calories per serving
Takes 1¼ hours **PAGE 22**

LOBSTER BISQUE

Rich and luxurious: lobster tails, shallots, brandy, wine, stock, and tarragon combined with cream and lemon juice.

SERVES 4 449 calories per serving
Takes 1½ hours **PAGE 31**

OVER 60 MINUTES

CHILLED STRAWBERRY SOUP

White wine sweetened with sugar and blended with strawberries and orange juice, then chilled for a refreshing, sweet soup.

SERVES 4 169 calories per serving

Takes 15 minutes, plus chilling   **PAGE 40**

GOULASH SOUP

Rich and wholesome: beef, roasted red peppers, onions, potatoes, and tomatoes cooked in stock and flavored with paprika.

SERVES 4–6 544–363 calories per serving

Takes 2 1/4 hours   **PAGE 34**

ROASTED TOMATO & GARLIC SOUP

Light and flavorful: roasted ripe tomatoes cooked with onion and stock, accented with garlic and served with pesto.

SERVES 4 127 calories per serving

Takes 40 minutes, plus standing   **PAGE 23**

BLUEBERRY & RED WINE SOUP

Chilled and fruity: cranberry juice, red wine, cinnamon, and sugar simmered with blueberries and enriched with cream.

SERVES 4 364 calories per serving

Takes 30 minutes, plus chilling   **PAGE 39**

VICHYSSOISE

Leeks, onion, and potatoes blended with chicken stock, chilled, then combined with cream result in this renowned velvety soup.

SERVES 4–6 251–167 calories per serving

Takes 45 minutes, plus chilling   **PAGE 38**

VEGETABLE MINESTRONE

Hearty soup: dried beans cooked and added to a tomato sauce with stock, leeks, cabbage, and Arborio rice.

SERVES 4 6 250–167 calories per serving

Takes 1 3/4 hours, plus soaking   **PAGE 25**

CHILLED CURRIED APPLE & MINT SOUP

Apples blended with onion, curry powder, stock, mango chutney, and lemon juice, and combined with yogurt and mint.

SERVES 6 110 calories per serving

Takes 40 minutes, plus chilling   **PAGE 40**

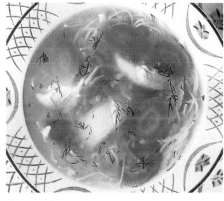

CHICKEN NOODLE SOUP

Rich and warming: simmered chicken, carrots, and stock, flavored with garlic, parsley, and dill and served over noodles.

SERVES 4 391 calories per serving

Takes 2 1/2 hours   **PAGE 36**

SPLIT PEA & HAM SOUP

Green split peas and flavorful ham, simmered with onion, celery, potatoes, and leeks, make a substantial meal.

SERVES 6–8 451–338 calories per serving

Takes 3 3/4 hours, plus soaking   **PAGE 28**

SOUPS KNOW-HOW

HOMEMADE SOUPS are highly nutritious and wonderfully versatile. They may be simple and quick to prepare or cooked gently and slowly to extract maximum flavor from the ingredients. They may be hot and warming or cold and refreshing, light and delicate or rich and hearty. There are even sweet and fruity soups.

First-course soups should stimulate the appetite and not be too filling. Pureed vegetable soups are ideal as first courses, as are clear soups, particularly those with attractive garnishes. Main-course soups are designed to be sustaining, and they normally contain ingredients such as meat, poultry, fish, legumes, and pasta. Some good bread is usually the only accompaniment they need to make a well-balanced meal. Fruit soups, which are often served chilled, can double as delicious desserts.

STOCKS

A well-flavored stock forms the base of many soups, and nothing tastes as good as homemade stock. Stock is economical to make because it is based on meat or fish bones, trimmings, and vegetables. Although it takes time to make stock — several hours of gentle simmering — it is easy to prepare and can be made well in advance and in large quantities. It can then be frozen until needed. Recipes for stocks can be found on pages 104, 148, 209, and 276. If you don't have any homemade stock, you can substitute stock made from bouillon cubes or powder instead. Remember that bouillon cubes are often strong and salty, and some contain artificial colorings and flavorings. Another quick alternative is to use canned broth or consommé, now available in reduced-sodium varieties.

MICROWAVING

For many soups, a microwave oven cannot give the same results as long, slow cooking, but it can produce light vegetable soups in minutes and is useful for thawing frozen stocks and soups and for reheating soups. The most efficient way is to transfer the soup to individual bowls because heating soup in larger containers takes longer in a microwave than in a pan on the stove.

For cooking, use a container that is large enough to allow the soup to rise up slightly during heating. Stir the soup once or twice during cooking, especially just before serving, because microwaving creates "hot spots" in liquids that must be stirred in to equalize temperature throughout. Add any garnish just before serving.

FREEZING

Soups taste best if freshly made, but most can be frozen without impairing flavor or texture. Avoid freezing soups containing ingredients such as pasta, potatoes, and rice since they become mushy. It is always best to underseason, because extra seasoning can be added when reheating. Add any cream, eggs, and milk at the reheating stage; freezing could cause separation or curdling.

To thaw a soup to be served hot, heat from frozen in a heavy saucepan over low heat, stirring occasionally. If the soup appears to be separating, whisk briskly until smooth or work in a blender or food processor for a few seconds. Thaw soup to be served cold in its freezer container in the refrigerator.

PUREEING SOUPS

Soups are often pureed to give a velvety texture. Starchy vegetables or flour helps thicken them.

Blender or food processor
Either of these can be used to process the cooked ingredients in batches. Scrape the sides to ensure there are no solid pieces left unprocessed.

Hand blender
Use this to puree directly in the saucepan, but only for small quantities of soup. It is ideal for blending in a final addition of cream.

Strainer
Work soup through a fine strainer with a wooden spoon. If soup has been pureed in a blender, it can then be strained to make it smoother or to remove any fibers, seeds, or skins.

THICKENING SOUPS

Many smooth soups reach a slightly thickened consistency simply by being pureed. Pureed soups containing starchy ingredients such as rice and potatoes will be even thicker. In some recipes, a little flour is added to the softened vegetables to bind the fat and juices together before pureeing.

Soups that are not pureed may also be thickened with the addition of a little flour before the stock is stirred in. A classic thickening method is to start with a butter and flour mixture called a *roux*, just as you do when making a béchamel sauce.

GARNISHES

Fresh herbs, either chopped or as whole leaves, are widely used to garnish soups — mint, chives, thyme, parsley, basil, tarragon, and cilantro are all popular. Choose an herb that complements or mirrors any herbs in the soup and add it at the last minute so that it retains its freshness.

Other garnishes include grated or crumbled cheese, chopped hard boiled egg, crisp pieces of bacon, shredded or diced meat or poultry, toasted nuts, croutons, chopped scallions, and sliced or diced cucumber.

A spoonful of a sauce such as pesto adds contrast in color and flavor. Or create a pattern on the surface of a smooth soup, using heavy cream for hot or cold soups (see box, below). Plain yogurt can be used instead of cream for cold soups.

SKIMMING SOUPS

As a soup is brought to the boil, foam or scum may form on the surface. This is most likely with soups that contain meat or poultry, particularly on the bone, or root vegetables and legumes. This foam, which contains impurities, should be removed as it forms.

Use a large metal spoon or skimmer (slotted if there are herbs and whole spices in the soup) to skim off foam.

If there is a lot of fat on the surface of a soup, skim it off with a large metal spoon or blot it with paper towels before serving.

Adding cream & yogurt

Heavy cream and crème fraîche can be added to a hot soup and cooked longer, without danger of curdling.

◆

Light cream, sour cream, and yogurt will curdle if overheated, so add them just before serving and warm through over low heat. For chilled soups, add cream or yogurt once the soup has been chilled, before serving.

GARNISHING WITH CREAM

Many attractive garnishes can be added to a soup just before serving. Cream adds a decorative and enriching touch. Whipped cream or sour cream can be simply spooned into the center of a soup, or you can try your hand at one of these simple patterns.

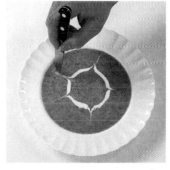

Star
Put a spoonful of cream in the center. Draw the tip of a knife from the center toward the edge of the soup to make 5 points.

Ring of hearts
Drip cream from the tip of a teaspoon to form a circle of drops. Draw the tip of a small knife through the center of each drop.

Flower
Drizzle cream from the tip of a teaspoon to make a circle. Draw the tip of a knife through it outward, then inward.

FRENCH PEA SOUP

 Serves 4–6

2 tbsp butter

1 large onion, coarsely chopped

6 cups (375 g) coarsely chopped lettuce leaves

1 tbsp all-purpose flour

3 cups (1.4 kg) fresh peas, shelled

5 cups (1.25 liters) chicken or vegetable stock

1/2 tsp sugar

2 large mint sprigs

salt and black pepper

shredded fresh mint to garnish

1 Melt the butter in a large saucepan, add the onion, and cook gently, stirring occasionally, for a few minutes until the onions are soft but not browned.

2 Add the lettuce to the pan and cook, stirring constantly, for 2 minutes. Add the flour and stir for 1–2 minutes longer, then add the peas, stock, sugar, and sprigs of mint. Bring to a boil, cover, and simmer, stirring occasionally, for 20 minutes or until the peas are soft.

3 Remove the mint sprigs and discard. Puree the soup in a food processor or blender until smooth.

4 Return the soup to the rinsed-out pan, reheat, and add salt and pepper to taste. Serve hot, garnished with shredded fresh mint.

Cook's know-how

When fresh peas are out of season, substitute frozen peas. Because the pods make up about half the weight of unshelled peas, you will need 1 1/2 lb (750 g) frozen peas.

CREAMY CARROT & ORANGE SOUP

 Serves 6–8

2 tbsp butter

1 onion, coarsely chopped

2 lb (1 kg) carrots, thickly sliced

6 cups (1.5 liters) vegetable stock

grated zest of 1/2 orange (see box, right)

1 1/4 cups (300 ml) orange juice

salt and black pepper

1 1/4 cups (300 ml) light sour cream

3 tbsp snipped fresh chives

1 Melt the butter in a large saucepan, add the onion, and cook gently, stirring occasionally, for a few minutes until soft but not browned. Add the carrots, cover, and cook gently, stirring occasionally, for 10 minutes.

2 Add the stock and bring to a boil. Cover and simmer, stirring occasionally, for 30–40 minutes until the carrots are soft.

3 Puree the soup in a food processor or blender until smooth. Return the soup to the rinsed-out pan and add the orange zest and juice and salt and pepper to taste. Stir in the light sour cream and then gently reheat the soup.

4 Stir in half of the snipped chives; garnish individual servings with the remaining chives.

Grating orange zest

Using the medium holes of a grater, grate the zest, leaving the pith behind.

ROASTED TOMATO & GARLIC SOUP

This soup is light in consistency but full of flavor, making it perfect for late summer, when tomatoes are at their best. Charring the tomato skins under the broiler gives the soup its delicious smoky flavor.

 Serves 4

5 medium ripe tomatoes

2 tbsp olive oil

1 onion, chopped

5 garlic cloves, coarsely chopped

6 cups (1.5 liters) chicken or vegetable stock

salt and black pepper

store-bought pesto to serve

1 Cut the tomatoes in half and arrange them, cut-side down, in a single layer in a baking dish. Place the tomato halves under the broiler, close to the heat, for 3 minutes or until the skins are charred.

2 Roast the tomatoes in a 350°F (180°C) oven for about 15–20 minutes, until they are soft. Remove them from the oven and leave to stand for at least 4 hours.

3 Peel the tomatoes, and squeeze the skins directly into the baking dish to extract all the juice. Discard the tomato skins, then coarsely chop the flesh, adding it to the juices in the baking dish.

4 Heat the oil in a large saucepan, add the onion and half of the garlic, and cook gently, stirring occasionally, for a few minutes until soft but not browned.

5 Add the stock, the tomato flesh and juices, and the remaining garlic and bring to a boil. Lower the heat and simmer for 5 minutes, then add salt and pepper to taste.

6 Serve immediately, with a bowl of pesto so that everyone can stir in a spoonful just before they eat.

MEXICAN ROASTED TOMATO SOUP

Add 1/4 tsp ground cumin and 1/4 tsp crushed dried mild red chilies to the seasoning and proceed as directed. Instead of pesto, serve with a relish made with 3–4 tbsp chopped cilantro leaves, 1 tbsp chopped raw onion, and 1–2 tbsp lime or lemon juice.

SUN-DRIED TOMATO SOUP

Add 2–3 chopped sun-dried tomatoes with the onion and garlic in step 4 and cook as directed. Garnish with finely shredded fresh basil.

TASTY MUSHROOM SOUP

 Serves 4–6

2 tbsp butter

1 small onion, finely chopped

1 garlic clove, crushed

1 lb (500 g) mushrooms, sliced

5 cups (1.25 liters) chicken or beef stock

2/3 cup (150 ml) dry white wine

2 tbsp chopped fresh thyme

2 tsp chopped fresh marjoram

salt and black pepper

1 Melt the butter in a large saucepan, add the onion and garlic, and cook gently, stirring occasionally, for a few minutes, until soft but not browned. Add the mushrooms and cook, stirring occasionally, for 10 minutes.

2 Add the stock, wine, 1 tbsp of the thyme, the marjoram, and salt and pepper to taste. Bring to a boil, cover, and simmer gently for 10 minutes. Taste for seasoning.

3 Serve hot, sprinkled with the remaining fresh thyme.

ASPARAGUS SOUP

 Serves 6

1 large potato, chopped

6 cups (1.5 liters) chicken or vegetable stock

1 lb (500 g) asparagus

2 garlic cloves, crushed

2 tbsp chopped fresh basil (optional)

salt and black pepper

2 tbsp butter (optional)

1 Put the potatoes into a large saucepan, add the stock, and bring to a boil. Cover and simmer for 15 minutes or until the potatoes are tender.

2 Meanwhile, trim the asparagus and discard any tough stalks. Chop into chunky pieces.

3 Add the chopped asparagus and garlic to the pan and cook, stirring occasionally, for about 5 minutes or until the asparagus is tender. Remove 9 tips; reserve for garnish.

4 Puree the soup in a food processor or blender until smooth.

5 Return the soup to the rinsed-out pan and reheat. Add the basil, if using, and salt and pepper to taste. Slice the reserved asparagus tips lengthwise in half. Serve the soup immediately, garnished with the asparagus tips and small nuggets of butter if desired.

ZUCCHINI SOUP

Substitute sliced zucchini for the asparagus, reserving a few slices for garnish. For a lighter soup, omit the potatoes.

ARTICHOKE SOUP

Substitute 13 oz (400 g) canned artichoke hearts or bottoms, drained and diced, for the asparagus, reserving a few dice for garnish.

FRENCH ONION SOUP

 Serves 8

3 tbsp butter

1/4 cup sunflower or corn oil

2 lb (1 kg) large onions, thinly sliced

1 tbsp sugar

1/4 cup (30 g) all-purpose flour

7 1/2 cups (1.8 liters) beef stock

salt and black pepper

8 Gruyère croutes (page 31)

1 Melt the butter with the oil in a large saucepan and caramelize the onions with the sugar (see box, right). Sprinkle the flour into the pan and cook, stirring constantly, for 1–2 minutes.

2 Gradually stir in the stock and bring to a boil. Add salt and pepper to taste, cover the pan, and simmer, stirring occasionally, for 35 minutes.

3 Taste the soup for seasoning, then ladle into warmed bowls. Float a Gruyère croute in each bowl and serve immediately.

Cook's know-how

Cooking with sugar is the key to developing a rich, golden brown color and sweet caramel flavor in onions. It is this process that produces the characteristic taste and appearance of the soup.

Caramelizing onions

Cook the onions in the butter and oil for a few minutes, until soft. Add the sugar and continue cooking over low heat, stirring occasionally, for 20 minutes or until the onions are golden brown.

VEGETABLE MINESTRONE

 **Serves 4–6**

²⁄₃ cup (125 g) dried cannellini or borlotti beans

2 tbsp olive oil

1 onion, chopped

2 celery stalks, chopped

2 carrots, diced

13 oz (400 g) canned plum tomatoes, drained and chopped

1 tbsp tomato paste

1 garlic clove, crushed

salt and black pepper

6 cups (1.5 liters) chicken or vegetable stock

2 cups (250 g) trimmed and finely sliced leeks

1 cup (125 g) finely shredded Savoy cabbage

2 tbsp Arborio rice

grated Parmesan cheese to serve

1 Put the dried beans into a large bowl and cover with cold water. Leave to soak overnight.

2 Drain the beans, put them into a saucepan, and cover with fresh cold water. Boil the beans rapidly for 10 minutes, then simmer until they are soft.

3 Meanwhile, heat the oil in a large saucepan, add the onion, celery, and carrots, and cook over high heat, stirring, for 3 minutes.

4 Add the tomatoes, tomato puree, garlic, and salt and pepper to taste. Cover and cook very gently, stirring occasionally, for 20 minutes. Drain the beans and set aside.

5 Pour the stock into the tomato mixture and continue to simmer, covered, for 15 minutes. Add the leeks, cabbage, rice, and cooked beans and simmer for 20 minutes. Taste for seasoning.

6 Serve immediately, sprinkled with grated Parmesan cheese.

PANCETTA MINESTRONE

Pancetta, Italian unsmoked bacon, is sometimes used in minestrone. Dice 2 oz (60 g) pancetta and fry in the oil over high heat for 5 minutes, then add the onion, celery, and carrots.

WATERCRESS SOUP

 Serves 6

2 tbsp butter

1 onion, finely chopped

2 potatoes, coarsely chopped

1 bunch watercress, tough stalks removed

3²⁄₃ cups (900 ml) chicken or vegetable stock

1¹⁄₄ cups (300 ml) milk

1 bay leaf

salt and black pepper

heavy cream to garnish

1 Melt the butter in a large saucepan, add the onion, and cook gently, stirring occasionally, for a few minutes, until soft but not browned.

2 Add the potatoes and the watercress to the saucepan and cook for about 5 minutes, until the watercress is wilted.

3 Pour in the chicken or vegetable stock and milk and add the bay leaf and salt and pepper to taste.

4 Bring the mixture to a boil, cover, and then simmer very gently for 15 minutes or until the potatoes are tender.

5 Remove the bay leaf and discard. Puree the soup in a food processor or blender until smooth. Return the soup to the rinsed-out pan, reheat, then taste for seasoning

6 Serve immediately, garnished with a little heavy cream.

Cook's know-how

Watercress is a member of the mustard family and has a distinctive peppery flavor. Watercress soup is delicious served chilled in summer. After pureeing, pour the soup into a large bowl, then cover, cool, and chill for at least 3 hours. Taste for seasoning before serving.

CURRIED PARSNIP SOUP

 Serves 6–8

2 tbsp butter

1 1/2 lb (750 g) parsnips, coarsely chopped

1 large onion, chopped

1 large garlic clove, crushed

2 tsp mild curry powder

7 1/2 cups (1.8 liters) chicken or vegetable stock

salt and black pepper

3/4 cup plus 1 tbsp (200 ml) light cream

fresh chives to garnish

1 Melt the butter in a large pan, add the chopped parsnips, onion, and crushed garlic, and cook gently, stirring occasionally, for 5 minutes or until the onion is softened but not browned.

2 Stir in the curry powder and cook for 1 minute, then blend in the stock and add salt and pepper to taste. Bring to a boil, stirring, then cover and simmer gently for 20 minutes or until the parsnips are tender.

3 Puree the soup in a food processor or blender until smooth. Return the soup to the rinsed-out pan, heat gently to warm through, stirring constantly, then taste for seasoning.

4 Stir in the light cream and reheat gently. Serve at once, garnished with fresh chives.

CURRIED CELERIAC SOUP

Substitute 1 1/2 lb (750 g) celeriac, coarsely chopped, for the parsnips and cook as directed.

WINTER VEGETABLE SOUP

Serves 6

3 tbsp butter

1 leek, trimmed and diced

1 onion, chopped

1 celery stalk, diced

1 small potato, diced

1 turnip, diced

1 small carrot, diced

3 garlic cloves, crushed

6 cups (1.5 liters) chicken or vegetable stock

8 cups (250 g) spinach leaves, coarsely shredded (see box, right)

3 scallions, thinly sliced

1/4 tsp dried dill

1/4 tsp turmeric

salt and black pepper

2 hard-boiled eggs, peeled and chopped, to serve

1 Melt the butter in a large saucepan, add the leek, and cook gently, stirring occasionally, for 5 minutes or until softened. Add the onion, celery, potato, turnip, carrot, and garlic and cook for 8 minutes.

2 Add the stock and bring to a boil. Cover and simmer, stirring occasionally, for 25 minutes or until the vegetables are tender.

3 Add the spinach, scallions, dill, and turmeric and cook for 3 minutes or until the spinach is cooked through but still bright green. Add salt and pepper to taste.

4 Serve the soup at once, with a bowl of chopped hard-boiled eggs passed separately.

Shredding spinach

Remove the stalks and stack several spinach leaves. Roll up tightly and cut crosswise into shreds.

TOMATO SOUP

 Serves 6–8

2 tbsp butter

2 onions, coarsely chopped

1 garlic clove, crushed

1 tbsp all-purpose flour

5 cups (1.25 liters) chicken or
vegetable stock

26 oz (800 g) canned tomatoes

1 bay leaf

salt and black pepper

1/4 cup (30 g) store-bought pesto

heavy cream and fresh basil
leaves to garnish

Garnishing with cream

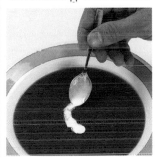

With a teaspoon, quickly swirl the heavy cream in a spiral on each serving.

1 Melt the butter in a large saucepan, add the onions and garlic, and cook gently, stirring occasionally, for a few minutes until soft but not browned.

2 Add the flour to the pan and cook, stirring constantly, for 1 minute.

3 Pour in the stock and add the tomatoes and their juice, the bay leaf, and salt and pepper to taste. Bring to a boil, cover the pan, and simmer gently for 20 minutes.

4 Remove the bay leaf and discard. Puree the soup in a food processor or blender until smooth.

5 Return the soup to the rinsed-out pan, add the pesto, and heat through. Taste for seasoning.

6 Serve at once, garnished with cream (see box, above) and fresh basil leaves.

QUICK TOMATO SOUP

Imported strained tomatoes, from Italy, usually packaged in a box, make a beautiful deep red soup. Substitute 3 1/2 cups (800 g) for the canned tomatoes and then cook as directed.

BORSCHT

 Serves 4

5 beets, peeled

1/2 head of cabbage, coarsely
chopped

2 waxy potatoes, diced

1 medium-large tomato, peeled
(page 39), seeded, and diced

1/2 carrot, chopped

1/4 small onion, chopped

6 cups (1.5 liters) chicken or
vegetable stock, more if needed

3–4 dill sprigs

2 tbsp sugar

2 tbsp red wine vinegar

salt and black pepper

sour cream and dill sprigs
to garnish

Grating beets

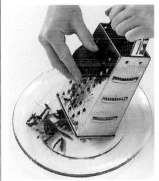

Using the large holes of a grater, grate the beets coarsely onto a plate with firm downward strokes.

1 Dice 4 of the beets, and grate the remaining beets (see box, right).

2 Put the diced beets, cabbage, potatoes, tomatoes, carrot, and onion into a large pan with the stock. Bring to a boil, then simmer for 30–40 minutes, until the vegetables are very tender. Add extra stock if necessary.

3 Add the dill, sugar, and vinegar and simmer for 10 minutes to let the sweet-sour flavors develop. Add the grated beets, salt and pepper to taste, and more sugar and vinegar if necessary.

4 Serve at once, garnished with dollops of sour cream and sprigs of dill.

SPLIT PEA & HAM SOUP

 Serves 6–8

1 lb (500 g) green split peas

1 lb (500 g) ham hock

10 cups (2.5 liters) water

1 large onion, finely chopped

4 celery stalks, finely chopped

3 potatoes, diced

3 leeks, trimmed and sliced

3 tbsp chopped parsley (optional)

salt and black pepper

1 Put the green split peas and the ham hock into 2 separate large bowls and cover with cold water. Leave to soak overnight.

2 Drain the split peas and ham hock, then put them into a large saucepan with the measured water. Bring to a boil, then simmer, uncovered, for about 1 hour.

3 Add the onion, celery, potatoes, and leeks to the pan, cover, and simmer gently for 2 1/2 hours, until the ham is tender and the peas are cooked. Add more water, if needed, during cooking.

4 Skim the surface if necessary. Remove the ham hock from the saucepan and let it cool slightly. Pull the meat away from the bone, discarding any skin and fat.

5 Coarsely chop the meat and return it to the saucepan. Add the parsley, if using, and salt and pepper to taste. Heat the soup gently to warm through, then serve immediately.

SPLIT PEA, HAM, & CHORIZO SOUP

Add 1/4 cup (60 g) sliced chorizo sausage when returning the cooked meat to the pan.

MULLIGATAWNY SOUP

 Serves 4–6

3 tbsp butter

1/2 onion, chopped

1 celery stalk, diced

1 small apple, peeled and diced

1 small carrot, diced

1 small green pepper, cored, seeded, and diced

3–5 garlic cloves, crushed

3 tbsp all-purpose flour

2–3 tsp curry powder

1/4 tsp each ground ginger, cinnamon, and turmeric

5 cups (1.25 liters) chicken or vegetable stock

13 oz (400 g) canned garbanzo beans, drained and lightly mashed

13 oz (400 g) canned chopped tomatoes

1 bay leaf

1 tbsp chopped parsley

1 tbsp lemon juice

3/4 cup (175 g) plain yogurt

chopped parsley and flat-leaf parsley leaves to garnish

1 Melt the butter in a pan, add the onion, and cook gently, stirring occasionally, for a few minutes until soft but not browned.

2 Add the celery, apple, carrot, green pepper, and garlic. Cook, stirring occasionally, for 8 minutes.

3 Add the flour, curry powder, ginger, cinnamon, and turmeric and cook for 2 minutes. Stir in the stock, garbanzo beans, tomatoes, and bay leaf, and bring to a boil. Cover and simmer for 20 minutes, until the vegetables are tender.

4 Remove the bay leaf and discard. Add the chopped parsley and lemon juice to the saucepan. Combine a little of the soup with the yogurt, then stir it back into the hot soup. Serve the soup immediately, garnished with the chopped parsley and parsley leaves.

Mulligatawny

This spiced soup dates from the days of the British Raj and was introduced to the West by nabobs returning from India in the 18th and 19th centuries. The name comes from a Tamil word, milakutanni, *which means "pepper water."*

SPICED AUTUMN SOUP

 Serves 8

4 tbsp butter

2 large onions, coarsely chopped

2 potatoes, coarsely chopped

2 carrots, coarsely chopped

3 garlic cloves, crushed

pared zest and juice of 1 orange

2 tsp mild curry powder

7 1/2 cups (1.8 liters) chicken or vegetable stock

26 oz (800 g) canned chopped tomatoes

2 apples, peeled and chopped

1 tbsp dried basil

salt and black pepper

herb croutes (page 31) to serve

1 Melt the butter in a large saucepan, add the onions, potatoes, carrots, garlic, and orange zest, and cook gently, stirring occasionally, for about 5 minutes.

2 Add the curry powder and cook, stirring constantly, for 1–2 minutes.

3 Add the stock, orange juice, tomatoes, apples, basil, and salt and pepper to taste. Bring to a boil, cover, and simmer gently for 30 minutes or until the vegetables are tender. Discard the orange zest.

4 Puree the soup in a food processor or blender until smooth. Return to the rinsed-out pan, reheat, and taste for seasoning. Serve at once, with herb croutes.

Paring orange zest

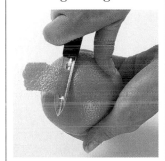

With a vegetable peeler, remove strips of zest, excluding the pith.

BLUE CHEESE & ONION SOUP

 Serves 6–8

2 1/3 cups (600 ml) milk

2 bay leaves

1/4 tsp grated nutmeg

6 tbsp (90 g) butter

2 large onions, finely sliced

9 tbsp (75 g) all-purpose flour

6 cups (1.5 liters) chicken or vegetable stock

salt and black pepper

1 1/4 cups (150 g) crumbled Stilton cheese

light cream to serve (optional)

1 Pour the milk into a saucepan, add the bay leaves and nutmeg, and bring almost to a boil. Remove from the heat, cover, and leave to steep for 20 minutes.

2 Meanwhile, melt the butter in a large pan, add the onions, and cook very gently, stirring occasionally, for 10 minutes or until they are soft but not browned.

3 Add the flour and cook, stirring, for 2 minutes. Strain the milk and gradually blend it into the onion and flour mixture. Add the stock and salt and pepper to taste. Bring to a boil, then simmer, partially covered, for 10 minutes.

4 Add the cheese to the pan and stir over very low heat until it is melted; do not let the soup boil or the cheese will become stringy. Taste for seasoning. If you wish, stir in a little light cream. Serve immediately.

Stilton

This cheese originated in the 18th century in Leicestershire, England, but was first sold at The Bell, a famous inn in Stilton in Huntingdonshire, 30 miles away. Travelers referred to it as Stilton, and the name stuck.

CLAM CHOWDER

 Serves 4

1 lb (500 g) clams in shells, cleaned (page 106)

1 cup (250 ml) fish stock

3 tbsp butter

1 onion, chopped

1/3 cup (90 g) diced salt pork

2 tbsp all-purpose flour

2 potatoes, diced

3 cups (750 ml) milk

1 bay leaf

salt and black pepper

1 Put the clams into a large saucepan, add the fish stock, and bring to a boil. Lower the heat, cover, and cook over medium heat for 5–8 minutes, until the clam shells open.

2 Discard any clams that have not opened. Set aside a few clams in their shells for garnish and keep warm. Remove the remaining clams from their shells. Discard the shells and strain the cooking juices.

3 Melt the butter in a large pan, add the onion, and cook gently, stirring, for a few minutes until soft but not browned. Add the salt pork, and cook for 1 minute. Then add the flour, and cook, stirring, for 1–2 minutes.

4 Add the potatoes, milk, strained clam juices, and bay leaf to the pan. Bring to a boil, then lower the heat and simmer for 15 minutes. Add the shelled clams, and reheat gently for about 5 minutes. Remove the bay leaf and discard.

5 Add salt and pepper to taste. Serve immediately, garnished with the reserved clams in their shells.

Which chowder?

Some people hold very firm views about the best way to make this classic recipe. This version is for New England clam chowder; Manhattan clam chowder omits the milk but adds tomatoes and green peppers.

RICH FISH SOUP

 Serves 4

1/4 cup (60 ml) olive oil

2 leeks, trimmed and chopped

1 celery stalk, chopped

1 potato, chopped

1 carrot, chopped

1/2 red pepper, chopped

3 garlic cloves, chopped

2 medium large tomatoes, peeled (page 39), seeded, and chopped

1 lb (500 g) mixed whitefish fillets, chopped (see right)

1 quart (1 liter) fish stock

2 cups (500 ml) dry white wine

5 basil sprigs

1 tsp chopped parsley

1/4 tsp dried mixed herbs

1/4 tsp cayenne pepper

salt and black pepper

Gruyère croutes (page 31) and basil sprigs to garnish

1 Heat the oil in a large saucepan, add the leeks, celery, potato, carrot, red pepper, and garlic, and cook gently, stirring occasionally, for 5 minutes or until the vegetables are just soft.

2 Add the tomatoes and fish and cook for 3 minutes. Add the stock, wine, basil, parsley, and mixed herbs and bring to a boil. Simmer for 35 minutes.

Cook's know-how

This delicious soup is based on the French soupe de poisson. For an interesting flavor in the finished soup, use several types of whitefish, such as cod, haddock, monkfish, and red and gray mullet. The soup is pureed, so small pieces and scraps of fish are fine.

3 Puree the soup in a food processor or blender until smooth. For a very smooth consistency, work the soup through a sieve after pureeing.

4 Return the soup to the rinsed-out pan and reheat gently. Add the cayenne pepper and salt and pepper to taste.

5 Serve immediately, garnished with Gruyère croutes and basil sprigs.

LOBSTER BISQUE

A bisque is a puree flavored with brandy, white wine, and cream, prepared by a complex process that brings out the maximum flavor. When made with lobster, it is perfect for a special occasion.

 Serves 4

3 tbsp butter

6 shallots, coarsely chopped

1/2 carrot, coarsely chopped

1 live lobster, halved (see Cook's know-how, right)

1 bay leaf

1/4 cup (60 ml) brandy

6 cups (1.5 liters) fish stock

1 cup (250 ml) dry white wine

1/2 cup (125 g) long-grain rice

1–2 tsp chopped fresh tarragon

3/4 cup (175 ml) light cream

1 tbsp lemon juice

pinch of cayenne pepper

salt and black pepper

tarragon sprigs to garnish

1 Melt half of the butter in a large saucepan, add the shallots and carrot and cook gently for 5 minutes until softened. Add the lobster and bay leaf and cook for 5 minutes, or until the lobster turns bright red.

2 Add the brandy and boil until it has reduced to about 2 tbsp, then add the stock and wine. Cook the lobster for another 5 minutes, then remove from the pan and leave until cool enough to handle.

3 Using a mallet, crack the lobster shells, remove the meat (page 107), and set aside. Add the lobster shells, rice, and chopped tarragon to the soup and cook for 15–20 minutes until the rice is tender.

4 Remove the lobster shells and bay leaf from the soup and discard. Cut the cooked lobster into several slices and add half to the soup, reserving the other half for garnish.

5 Puree the soup in a food processor or blender until smooth. Pour the puree through a strainer to make sure that no tiny pieces of lobster shell remain.

6 Return the puree to the pan. Add the cream, lemon juice, cayenne pepper, and salt and pepper to taste, then reheat. Stir in the remaining butter.

7 Serve immediately, garnished with the reserved lobster meat and tarragon sprigs.

Cook's know-how

To kill and cut up the lobster, start by piercing through the cross on the center of the head. Split the lobster in half lengthwise, and remove and discard the intestinal vein and the sack of grit that is found in the head. Scoop out the tomalley (greenish liver) and either discard or reserve for a sauce. Crack the claws, but do not shell them.

CROUTES & CROUTONS

These need not be reserved for special occasions. They can add color, texture, and interest to the most basic everyday soups.

HERB CROUTES

Trim the crusts from slices of bread. Cut each slice into a square or decorative shape. Heat a 1/4-in (5-mm) layer of oil in a skillet, add the bread, and brown all over. Finely chop some parsley or separate into small sprigs. Drain the croutes on paper towels. Roll the edges of the croutes in the parsley or put a leaf on top of each one.

GARLIC CROUTONS

Trim the crusts from slices of bread and cut into 1/2-in (1-cm) cubes. Heat a 1/4-in (5-mm) layer of oil in a skillet. Peel and crush 1 garlic clove and cook for 1 minute. Add the bread cubes and cook, stirring occasionally, until brown all over. Remove and drain on paper towels.

GRUYERE CROUTES

Cut slices from a baguette and toast on one side under the broiler. Remove from the heat and turn the slices over. Grate some Gruyère cheese and sprinkle it evenly on top of the bread slices. Return the croutes to the broiler and cook until the cheese topping has melted and is bubbling softly.

CUBAN CORN & SEAFOOD SOUP

 Serves 4

2 tbsp butter

1 small onion, chopped

2 garlic cloves, crushed

1 lb (500 g) frozen corn kernels

1/4-lb (125-g) piece of pumpkin, peeled and cut into chunks

1 waxy potato, cut into chunks

1 mild, fresh red chili, cored, seeded, and chopped

5 cups (1.25 liters) fish, chicken, or vegetable stock

1 cup (250 ml) strained tomatoes

1 bay leaf

1/4 tsp dried thyme

salt and black pepper

1/2 lb (250 g) firm whitefish, cut into large chunks

lime wedges to serve

1 Melt the butter in a large pan, add the onion and garlic, and cook gently for a few minutes until soft but not browned. Add the corn, pumpkin, potato, and chili, and cook, stirring occasionally, for 5 minutes.

2 Add the stock, tomatoes, bay leaf, thyme, and salt and pepper to taste, and bring to a boil. Simmer, uncovered, stirring occasionally, for 15 minutes or until the pumpkin and potato pieces are just tender.

3 Add the fish to the soup, and heat through gently, cooking just until the chunks become opaque.

4 Remove the bay leaf and discard. Taste for seasoning. Serve the soup immediately, accompanied by wedges of lime.

Cook's know-how

Any firm whitefish or shellfish may be used in this soup. Be careful not to overcook the pieces of fish or they will disintegrate.

QUICK SHRIMP GUMBO

 Serves 4

3 tbsp sunflower oil

1 small onion, diced

1 red pepper, cored, seeded, and diced

1 celery stalk, diced

3 garlic cloves, crushed

2 tbsp chopped parsley

1/4 cup (30 g) all-purpose flour

1/2 tsp paprika

1/4 tsp each ground cumin and dried oregano

4 medium tomatoes, peeled (page 39), seeded, and diced

3/4 cup (175 g) chorizo, sliced

5 cups (1.25 liters) fish stock

1/2 lb (250 g) okra, sliced

1/2–3/4 lb (250–375 g) cooked peeled shrimp

pinch of cayenne pepper

salt and black pepper

rice timbales (see box, right) to serve

large cooked shrimp and scallions to garnish

1 Heat the oil in a pan, add the onion, red pepper, celery, garlic, and parsley, and cook for 8 minutes or until softened. Add the flour, and cook, stirring constantly, for 1 minute.

2 Sprinkle in the paprika, cumin, and oregano and cook, stirring, for 1 minute, then add the tomatoes, chorizo, and stock. Bring to a boil, then simmer, stirring occasionally, for 30 minutes or until the soup has thickened slightly.

3 Add the okra and cook for 5–7 minutes until tender, then add the shrimp and heat through. Add the cayenne pepper, and salt and pepper to taste.

4 Serve the gumbo hot, with rice timbales. Garnish with large cooked shrimp and scallions.

Making a rice timbale

Oil a small bowl, fill with cooked rice, and press down lightly. Turn upside down onto a warmed soup plate and lift off the bowl.

BOUILLABAISSE

Bouillabaisse, the classic fish dish with the authentic flavors of Provence, is one of the most satisfying and delectable dishes you can bring to your table. This rich stew-soup is served with thick slices of toasted bread spread with rouille, a chili-flavored mayonnaise.

 Serves 8

2 tbsp olive oil

2 leeks, trimmed and diced

1 small onion, chopped

1 small fennel bulb, sliced

4 garlic cloves, crushed

1 tbsp chopped parsley

1 bay leaf

1 quart (1 liter) water

2 1/4 cups (600 ml) fish stock

2 medium tomatoes, peeled (page 39), seeded, and diced

1/4 tsp herbes de Provence

5-cm (2-in) piece of orange zest

1/4 tsp fennel seeds

2–3 potatoes, cut into chunks

2 lb (1 kg) assorted fish, cut into bite-sized pieces

2 lb (1 kg) assorted shellfish, shelled

1/2 tsp saffron threads

salt and black pepper

8 slices of baguette, toasted, to serve

ROUILLE

3 garlic cloves

1/2 cup (125 ml) mayonnaise

2 tsp paprika

1 tsp mild chili powder

1/4 tsp ground cumin

3 tbsp olive oil

1 small fresh red chili, cored, seeded, and finely chopped

1 tbsp lemon juice

salt

1 Heat the olive oil in a large, heavy saucepan. Add the diced leeks, chopped onion, fennel, garlic, parsley, and bay leaf and cook, stirring occasionally, for 5 minutes.

2 Pour in the measured water and stock. Add the tomatoes, herbes de Provence, orange zest, and fennel seeds. Bring to a boil and simmer for 30 minutes.

3 Meanwhile, make the rouille (see box, right). Chill until needed.

4 Add the potatoes to the soup and simmer for 10 minutes. Do not stir or the potatoes will break up.

5 Add the fish, shellfish, saffron, and salt and pepper to taste and cook for a few minutes, until the fish becomes opaque.

6 Remove the bay leaf and orange zest and discard. Serve the bouillabaisse with slices of toasted baguette spread with the rouille.

Making rouille

Use a knife blade to crush the garlic. Put into a bowl with the mayonnaise, paprika, chili powder, and ground cumin.

Pour in the olive oil, drop by drop, whisking constantly as the oil is absorbed into the spicy mayonnaise.

Add the red chili and lemon juice to the sauce; add salt to taste and stir well to combine.

Cook's know-how

Bouillabaisse is made with an assortment of firm-fleshed fish, which can include monkfish and halibut, and shellfish, such as mussels, shrimp, and small crab.

WINTER SQUASH SOUP

 Serves 6

3 lb (1.5 kg) winter squash

10 tbsp (150 g) butter

2 leeks, trimmed and sliced

1 quart (1 liter) chicken or
  vegetable stock

1/4 tsp grated nutmeg

salt and black pepper

3 tbsp baby peas

8 cups (250 g) spinach leaves,
  finely chopped

1 1/4 cups (300 ml) light cream

1 Cut out the flesh from the squash, discarding the seeds and fibers. Cut the squash flesh into 3/4-in (2-cm) chunks.

2 Melt 7 tbsp (100 g) of the butter in a large saucepan. Add the leeks, and cook very gently, covered, for 10 minutes or until soft.

3 Add the stock, squash chunks, nutmeg, and salt and pepper to taste. Bring to a boil, cover, and simmer for 30 minutes or until the vegetables are very soft.

4 Meanwhile, cook the baby peas in boiling salted water for 5 minutes. Drain thoroughly.

5 Melt the remaining butter in a saucepan, add the spinach, and cook very gently, covered, for 3 minutes or until soft.

6 Puree the soup in a food processor or blender until smooth, in batches if necessary. Return to the pan and stir in the cream. Stir the baby peas and spinach into the soup, heat through, and serve immediately.

Cook's know-how

For individual servings as illustrated above, use small hollowed-out squash, or a single large squash in place of a soup tureen. When removing the squash flesh, leave a scalloped border to make the container look attractive.

GOULASH SOUP

 Serves 4–6

2 red peppers

2 tbsp sunflower or corn oil

1 lb (500 g) stewing beef,
  trimmed and cut into 1 1/2-in
  (3.5-cm) pieces

2 large onions, thickly sliced

1 tbsp all-purpose flour

2 tsp paprika

6 cups (1.5 liters) beef stock

13 oz (400 g) canned chopped
  tomatoes

2 tbsp tomato paste

1 tbsp red wine vinegar

1 garlic clove, crushed

1 bay leaf

salt and black pepper

3 large potatoes,
  coarsely chopped

dash of Tabasco sauce

sour cream and snipped fresh
  chives to garnish

1 Roast and peel the red peppers (page 354). Cut the flesh into chunks.

2 Heat the oil in a large pan. Add the beef and brown all over. Add the onions, peppers, flour, and paprika and stir over high heat for 1–2 minutes.

3 Add the stock, tomatoes, tomato paste, vinegar, garlic, bay leaf, and salt and pepper to taste. Bring to a boil, cover tightly, and simmer for 1 1/2 hours.

4 Add the potatoes and cook for 30 minutes or until the beef and potatoes are tender. Remove the bay leaf and discard.

5 Add a little Tabasco sauce and taste for seasoning. Serve at once, garnished with sour cream and snipped chives.

Goulash

From a 9th-century nomadic tribal meal of slowly stewed meat, Hungarian goulash has developed into an internationally acclaimed dish, distinctively flavored with paprika, onions, and red peppers and enriched with potatoes, tomatoes, and sour cream.

LENTIL & BACON SOUP

 Serves 4–6

2 tbsp butter

1 onion, chopped

1 carrot, diced

1 celery stalk, diced

3 garlic cloves, crushed

2–3 lean thick slices of bacon, diced

1 cup (175 g) red lentils

2/3 cup (60 g) rutabaga or turnip, peeled and diced

1 small potato, diced

2 bay leaves

1/4 tsp chopped fresh sage

1/4 tsp cumin seeds (optional)

2 quarts (2 liters) chicken or vegetable stock

salt and black pepper

chopped parsley to garnish

1 Melt the butter in a large saucepan, add the onion, carrot, celery, and garlic, and cook, stirring, for 5–6 minutes until soft and lightly browned. Add the bacon, lentils, rutabaga or turnip, potato, bay leaves, sage, and cumin, if using, and cook for 15 minutes.

2 Pour in the stock, bring to a boil, then simmer gently, uncovered, for 20 minutes or until the lentils and vegetables are tender. Add salt and pepper to taste.

3 Remove the bay leaves and discard. Serve immediately, sprinkled with chopped parsley.

LENTIL & FRANKFURTER SOUP

For a hearty main-meal soup, add 1/2 lb (250 g) frankfurters. Chop them into 1/2-in (1-cm) pieces and add to the soup about 5 minutes before the end of cooking, so that they are warmed through but not overcooked. Smoked sausages may also be used in this way.

GAME SOUP

 Serves 4

2 tbsp butter

1/4 lb (125 g) bacon, diced

1 onion, sliced

1/4 lb (125 g) mushrooms, sliced

1 tbsp all-purpose flour

5 cups (1.25 liters) game stock (page 148)

salt and black pepper

1 tbsp red currant jelly

ORANGE & HERB BOUQUET

6 parsley stalks

pared zest of 1 orange

1 bay leaf

1 large thyme or marjoram sprig

1 Melt the butter in a large saucepan, add the bacon, and cook over high heat, stirring occasionally, for 5–7 minutes, until crisp.

2 Lower the heat, add the onion to the pan, and cook gently, stirring occasionally, for a few minutes until softened but not browned.

3 Make the orange and herb bouquet (see box, above) and set aside.

Making a bouquet

Tie the parsley, orange zest, bay leaf, and thyme or marjoram with a piece of white string. Leave a length of string to tie to the saucepan handle so that the orange and herb bouquet can be lifted easily from the pan at the end of cooking.

4 Add the mushrooms to the pan and cook for 5 minutes, then add the flour and cook, stirring constantly, for 1 minute. Add the stock, the herb bouquet, and salt and pepper to taste, then bring to a boil. Cover and simmer for 30 minutes.

5 Remove and discard the orange and herb bouquet, then stir in the red currant jelly. Taste the soup for seasoning, and serve immediately.

CHICKEN NOODLE SOUP

 Serves 4

2 lb (1 kg) chicken pieces

1 lb (500 g) carrots, sliced

1/2 head celery, chopped

1 small onion, peeled but left whole

5 garlic cloves, coarsely chopped

a few parsley sprigs

3 quarts (3 liters) water

2–3 chicken stock cubes

salt and black pepper

1/4 lb (125 g) thin noodles

chopped fresh dill to garnish

1 Put the chicken pieces into a large saucepan with the carrots, celery, onion, garlic, and parsley. Pour in the measured water and bring to a boil. Using a slotted spoon, skim off the foam that rises to the top of the pan.

2 Lower the heat and add the stock cubes and salt and pepper to taste. Simmer gently, covered, for 2 hours, adding extra water if the liquid reduces too much.

3 Meanwhile, break the noodles into 2-in (5-cm) lengths. Simmer in boiling salted water for about 2 minutes or until just tender. Drain and set aside.

4 Skim any fat from the surface of the soup. With a slotted spoon, remove the parsley, onion, and chicken, and discard the parsley, chicken bones, and skin. Chop the onion and chicken and return to the soup. Taste for seasoning.

5 Divide the noodles among warmed soup plates. Ladle the soup over the noodles, garnish, and serve immediately.

Cook's know-how

This soup is best made with chicken thighs and drumsticks; these are more moist and have considerably more flavor than breast meat when cooked for a long time.

HOT & SOUR SOUP

 Serves 4–6

2 dried Chinese mushrooms

1/4 head Chinese cabbage, sliced

6 cups (1.5 liters) chicken or vegetable stock

1/4 8-oz (250-g) package Chinese noodles, such as rice sticks

salt

1/4 lb (125 g) firm tofu, diced

2/3 cup (90 g) sliced bamboo shoots

2/3 cup (90 g) diced cooked chicken

1/4 cup (30 g) bean sprouts

3 tbsp cornstarch mixed with 3 tbsp water

2 eggs, lightly beaten

2 tbsp white vinegar

1 tbsp dark soy sauce

1/4 tsp each white pepper and cayenne pepper

TO SERVE

2 tsp sesame oil

2 scallions, thinly sliced

cilantro sprigs

1 Put the mushrooms into a bowl, cover with hot water, and leave to soak for about 30 minutes.

2 Meanwhile, put the sliced cabbage and stock into a pan. Bring to a boil. Simmer for 15 minutes, then set aside.

3 Break the noodles into pieces. Simmer in boiling salted water for 3–4 minutes, until just tender. Drain and set aside.

4 Drain the mushrooms, reserving the soaking liquid. Pour the liquid through a strainer lined with a paper towel to remove any grit. Squeeze the mushrooms dry, then cut them into thin strips. Reserve the mushrooms and their liquid.

5 Add the tofu, bamboo shoots, chicken, bean sprouts, noodles, and mushrooms and their liquid to the cabbage and stock. Heat until almost boiling, then stir in the cornstarch mixture. Simmer until the soup thickens slightly, then drizzle in the beaten eggs to form strands.

6 Combine the vinegar, soy sauce, white and cayenne peppers and pour into the soup. Taste for seasoning. Drizzle a little sesame oil over each serving, and garnish with scallion slices and cilantro sprigs. Serve immediately.

CHINESE CRAB & CORN SOUP

 Serves 4

12 oz (375 g) frozen corn kernels, thawed

1 quart (1 liter) chicken stock

3 scallions, thinly sliced

1/2-in (1-cm) piece of fresh ginger, peeled and chopped

1 garlic clove, crushed

1 tbsp light soy sauce

1/2 lb (250 g) cooked crabmeat

1 tbsp cornstarch mixed with 2 tbsp water

salt and black pepper

sesame oil and cilantro sprigs to serve

1 Puree the corn with one-quarter of the stock in a food processor or blender until smooth.

2 Pour the remaining stock into a pan and add the scallions, ginger, garlic, and soy sauce. Heat until the liquid bubbles at the edge.

3 Add the crabmeat and the corn puree and continue to heat until bubbles form again. Blend the cornstarch mixture into the soup and cook, stirring occasionally, for 10 minutes or until it thickens slightly. Add salt and pepper to taste.

4 Drizzle a little sesame oil over each serving, garnish with cilantro sprigs, and serve immediately.

THAI SPICED SOUP

 Serves 4

3.75-oz (90-g) package dried Chinese bean thread noodles

salt and black pepper

2 cups (500 ml) chicken stock

13 fl oz (400 ml) canned coconut milk

1/2 carrot, coarsely chopped

1/3 cup (30 g) green beans, cut into 1/2-in (1-cm) pieces

3 scallions, thinly sliced

1 3/4 cups (250 g) shredded cooked chicken

1/4 lb (125 g) mixed greens, such as spinach and bok choy, thinly sliced

1/2 cup (30 g) bean sprouts

2 tbsp fish sauce

1/4 tsp turmeric

2/3 cup (75 g) cucumber julienne and cilantro sprigs to garnish

1 Cook the noodles in boiling salted water for 2–3 minutes or according to package instructions, until just tender. Drain and rinse in cold water. Set aside while preparing the soup.

2 Put the stock, coconut milk, carrot, French beans, and scallions into a large saucepan and bring to a boil.

3 Lower the heat, add the chicken, greens, bean sprouts, fish sauce, and turmeric, and cook for 2 minutes or until the greens are tender. Add salt and pepper to taste.

4 To serve, divide the cooked noodles among warmed bowls. Ladle the hot soup over the noodles and garnish with cucumber strips and cilantro sprigs.

Cook's know-how

For a vegetarian version, omit the cooked chicken and use a vegetable stock instead of the chicken stock. You could also vary the vegetables, but be sure to allow for their different cooking times. Try shredded white cabbage instead of bok choy and snow peas instead of thin green beans. Sliced zucchini, Swiss chard, a small quantity of corn kernels, or even a little diced eggplant would also be good in this soup.

VICHYSSOISE

 **Serves 4–6**

4 tbsp butter

3 large leeks, trimmed and sliced

1 small onion, chopped

2 potatoes, coarsely chopped

5 cups (1.25 liters) chicken stock

salt and black pepper

TO SERVE

2/3 cup (150 ml) light cream

milk (optional)

2 tbsp snipped fresh chives

1 Melt the butter in a large saucepan, add the leeks and onion, and cook very gently, stirring occasionally, for 10–15 minutes until soft but not browned.

2 Add the potatoes, stock, and salt and pepper to taste and bring to a boil. Cover and simmer gently for 15–20 minutes, until the potatoes are tender.

3 Puree the soup in a food processor or blender until smooth. Pour into a large bowl or pass through a strainer for a smoother finish. Cover and chill for at least 3 hours.

4 To serve, stir in the cream. If the soup is too thick, add a little milk. Taste for seasoning. Garnish with snipped chives before serving.

Vichyssoise

This soup is the sophisticated chilled version of a peasant recipe for potato leek soup. It was created in 1917 by the French chef Louis Diat when he was working at the Ritz-Carlton Hotel in New York. Inspired by memories of his mother's cooking, he named it after Vichy, the spa town near his childhood home.

TZATZIKI SOUP

 Serves 4–6

2 1/2 cups (600 g) plain yogurt

1 cup (250 ml) water

1 cucumber, seeded (see box, right) and diced

4 garlic cloves, coarsely chopped

1 tbsp olive oil

1 tsp white vinegar

1 tsp dried mint

salt and black pepper

2–3 tbsp chopped fresh mint and 3 scallions, thinly sliced, to garnish

1 Puree the yogurt, measured water, one-quarter of the diced cucumber, the garlic, oil, vinegar, and mint in a food processor or blender until smooth. Season well with salt and add pepper to taste.

2 Transfer the soup to a large bowl and stir in the remaining cucumber. Cover and chill for at least 1 hour.

3 Taste for seasoning. Sprinkle the soup with chopped mint and scallions before serving.

Seeding a cucumber

Trim the cucumber with a small knife, then cut it in half lengthwise. With a teaspoon, scoop out and discard the seeds from each cucumber half.

Tzatziki

Tzatziki is best known as a cooling Greek salad, but it is even more refreshing when served as a chilled soup. Dried mint is used in the soup because of its intense flavor, although fresh mint is used for the garnish.

GAZPACHO

 Serves 4–6

5 medium tomatoes, peeled
(see box, right) and seeded

1 large Spanish onion

7 oz (200 g) canned roasted red
peppers, drained

2 large garlic cloves

2 1/3 cups (600 ml) cold chicken
stock

4 1/2 tbsp (75 ml) olive oil

4 tbsp red wine vinegar

juice of 1/2 lemon

salt and black pepper

TO GARNISH

1/2 cucumber, diced

1 small green pepper, cored,
seeded, and diced

garlic croutons (page 31)

1 Coarsely chop the
tomatoes, onion, red
peppers, and garlic. Puree in
a food processor or blender
with the stock, oil, and
vinegar until smooth.

2 Turn the mixture into a
bowl and add the lemon
juice and salt and pepper to
taste. Cover and chill for at
least 1 hour.

Peeling tomatoes

Cut the cores from the
tomatoes and score an
"X" on the base. Immerse
the tomatoes in boiling
water for 8–15 seconds,
until their skins start to
split. Transfer at once to
cold water. When the
tomatoes are cool enough
to handle, peel off the
skin with a small knife.

3 Garnish with spoonfuls
of diced cucumber,
green pepper, and garlic
croutons before serving.

BLUEBERRY & RED WINE SOUP

 Serves 4

1 1/2 cups (350 ml) cranberry
juice

1 cup (250 ml) red wine

1 cinnamon stick

2/3 cup (125 g) sugar

2 cups (250 g) blueberries

1 tbsp cornstarch mixed with
2 tbsp water

1/2 cup (125 ml) sour cream

1/2 cup (125 ml) light cream

1 Put the cranberry juice,
wine, and cinnamon stick
into a large saucepan. Add
the sugar (the amount
depends on the sweetness
of the fruit), bring to a boil,
and simmer for 15 minutes.

2 Stir the blueberries into
the pan, reserving a few
for garnish, and cook for
5 minutes. Add more sugar
to taste if necessary.

3 Gradually blend the
cornstarch mixture into
the soup and return to a
boil. Cook for 3 minutes or
until the soup thickens
slightly. Remove the pan
from the heat and discard
the cinnamon stick. Pour the
soup into a bowl and leave to
cool for about
30 minutes.

4 Combine the sour cream
and light cream and stir
into the soup. Cover and
chill for at least 3 hours.
Garnish with the reserved
blueberries before serving.

Cook's know-how

*Red wine adds a richness and
depth of flavor to this creamy
soup and prevents it from
tasting too sweet. Choose
a robust red wine, such as a
California Zinfandel or
a Cabernet Sauvignon. If
blueberries are not available,
use dark sweet cherries instead.*

CHILLED CURRIED APPLE & MINT SOUP

 Serves 6

2 tbsp butter

1 onion, coarsely chopped

1 tbsp mild curry powder

3 2/3 cups (900 ml) vegetable stock

4 medium cooking apples, peeled, cored, and coarsely chopped

2 tbsp mango chutney

juice of 1/2 lemon

7–8 sprigs of fresh mint

salt and black pepper

1/2 cup (100 g) plain yogurt

a little milk if needed

1 Melt the butter in a large saucepan, add the onion, and cook gently, stirring occasionally, for a few minutes until soft but not browned. Add the curry powder and cook, stirring constantly, for 1–2 minutes.

2 Add the stock and chopped apples and bring to a boil, stirring. Cover and simmer for 15 minutes or until the apples are tender.

3 Puree the apple mixture, mango chutney, and lemon juice in a food processor or blender until very smooth.

4 Strip the mint leaves from the stalks, reserving 6 small sprigs for garnish. Finely chop the mint leaves.

5 Pour the soup into a large bowl, stir in the chopped mint, and add salt and pepper to taste. Cover and chill in the refrigerator for at least 3 hours.

6 Whisk in the yogurt, then taste for seasoning. If the soup is too thick, add a little milk. Garnish with the reserved mint before serving.

Cook's know-how

This soup is equally delicious served hot. After pureeing, reheat the soup. Stir in the chopped mint, whisk in the yogurt, and heat through gently. Serve immediately.

CHILLED STRAWBERRY SOUP

 Serves 4

1 cup (250 ml) dry white wine

1/3 cup (90 g) sugar

very small piece of lime zest (optional)

2 cups (250 g) strawberries

1 cup (250 ml) orange juice

mint sprigs to garnish

1 Put the wine and sugar into a saucepan; bring to a boil and boil for 5 minutes. Remove the pan from the heat, add the lime zest, if using, and let cool.

2 Remove the lime zest from the pan. Hull and chop the strawberries, reserving 4 for garnish.

3 Puree the wine syrup and strawberries in a food processor or blender until very smooth.

4 Pour the puree into a large bowl and stir in the orange juice. Cover and chill for at least 3 hours.

5 Garnish with the reserved strawberries and mint sprigs just before serving.

STRAWBERRY & CHAMPAGNE SOUP

Omit the white wine and lime zest. Puree the strawberries, reserving a few for garnish, with the sugar and orange juice. Divide the mixture between chilled glass serving bowls, and top with chilled Champagne or dry sparkling wine. Garnish and serve.

STRAWBERRY & WATERMELON SOUP

Substitute a 2-lb (1-kg) piece of watermelon for the orange juice. Remove and discard the seeds, scoop out and puree the melon flesh until smooth, then combine with the wine syrup, strawberries, and a little lime juice.

2

FIRST COURSES

🕐 UNDER 30 MINUTES

RUSSIAN FISH SALAD

Rich creamy salad of whitefish fillets, sour cream, hard-boiled egg, mayonnaise, and parsley. Served on tomato quarters.

SERVES 4 213 calories per serving

Takes 10 minutes   **PAGE 64**

AVOCADO WITH TOMATOES & MINT

Light and refreshing: chopped tomatoes combined with mint and vinaigrette dressing and piled into avocado halves.

SERVES 4 232 calories per serving

Takes 15 minutes   **PAGE 68**

COQUILLES ST. JACQUES

Rich and luxurious: scallops poached with white wine and bay leaf, then stirred into a Mornay sauce flavored with Gruyère cheese.

SERVES 4 297 calories per serving

Takes 25 minutes   **PAGE 60**

WHITE BEAN PATE

Smooth and summery: cannellini beans blended with rosemary, olive oil, and lemon juice, and richly flavored with garlic.

SERVES 6 150 calories per serving

Takes 10 minutes   **PAGE 57**

CHEVRE CROUTES

Goat cheese and pesto on toasted baguette slices and sprinkled with olive oil give a tangy flavor to this inviting appetizer.

SERVES 4 450 calories per serving

Takes 20 minutes   **PAGE 48**

SARDINES WITH CORIANDER

Lightly broiled fresh sardines, flavored with a butter combining coriander and shallot with lime juice, make a refreshing appetizer.

SERVES 4 511 calories per serving

Takes 25 minutes   **PAGE 62**

SPICY SHRIMP

Shrimp in a dressing of mayonnaise, horseradish, and tomato puree, spiked with lemon juice and Tabasco sauce.

SERVES 4 338 calories per serving

Takes 10 minutes   **PAGE 63**

JUMBO SHRIMP WITH AIOLI

Stir-fried jumbo shrimp served with a Provençal mayonnaise combining garlic, egg yolks, mustard, olive oil, and lemon juice.

SERVES 4 482 calories per serving

Takes 20 minutes   **PAGE 62**

ASPARAGUS WITH QUICK HOLLANDAISE

Tender spears of fresh asparagus served with a simple version of hollandaise sauce and garnished with lemon twists.

SERVES 4 384 calories per serving

Takes 20 minutes   **PAGE 66**

UNDER 30 MINUTES

BRIOCHES WITH WILD MUSHROOMS & WATERCRESS

Light-textured rich bread filled with a mixture of mushrooms, watercress, and cream.
SERVES 6 295 calories per serving
Takes 20 minutes **PAGE 66**

WARM SALAD WITH BACON & SCALLOPS

Light and crunchy: bacon and scallops with salad greens tossed in walnut oil. Dressed with shallots and hot white vinegar.
SERVES 4 276 calories per serving
Takes 20 minutes **PAGE 65**

SPICY MEATBALLS

Tiny warm meatballs seasoned with garlic, onion, paprika, cilantro, and tomato paste. Served with a sesame dip.
SERVES 6 481 calories per serving
Takes 25 minutes **PAGE 17**

SMOKED CHICKEN SALAD WITH WALNUTS

Sliced smoked chicken tossed in an orange dressing and served on a bed of salad greens, orange sections, and walnuts.
SERVES 6 472 calories per serving
Takes 15 minutes **PAGE 65**

MOULES MARINIERE

Traditional French dish: mussels cooked in dry white wine, onion, garlic, parsley, thyme, and bay leaf. Served in a light sauce.
SERVES 6 302 calories per serving
Takes 25 minutes **PAGE 60**

CHEESE PUFFS

Warm nuggets of puff pastry, flavored with aged Cheddar cheese, then deep-fried and served warm.
SERVES 10–12 238–198 calories per serving
Takes 25 minutes **PAGE 49**

30–60 MINUTES

SALMON & SHRIMP PHYLLO PURSES

Bite-sized pieces of salmon combined with shrimp in light textured phyllo pastry purses. Served with a wine, cream, and dill sauce.
SERVES 8 448 calories per serving
Takes 55 minutes **PAGE 53**

CANAPES

Lightly toasted bread served with a selection of toppings: anchovy and shrimp, cheese and scallion, salami, and asparagus.
SERVES 4 251 calories per serving
Takes 40 minutes **PAGE 47**

CHEESE & OLIVE BITES

Pimiento-stuffed olives wrapped in cheese pastry flavored with paprika and mustard. Baked, then served warm or cold.
SERVES 4 317 calories per serving
Takes 40 minutes **PAGE 48**

WARM SALAD WITH PEARS & BLUE CHEESE

Blue cheese toasts on a bed of watercress and pears served with a warm spicy dressing.

SERVES 4 563 calories per serving

Takes 35 minutes   **PAGE 70**

MEXICAN CLASSIC

NACHOS GRANDE

Spicy and nourishing: refried beans, tomatoes, chili, onion, garlic, and green pepper. Topped with cheese and surrounded by tortilla chips.

SERVES 4–6 594–396 calories per serving

Takes 45 minutes   **PAGE 52**

PAN-FRIED PATES

Blended chicken livers with bacon, spinach, shallots, parsley, garlic, and sage, molded into ovals and wrapped in bacon.

SERVES 4 392 calories per serving

Takes 60 minutes   **PAGE 57**

SARDINE PATE

Individual pâtés of sardines blended with butter, low-fat soft cheese, and lemon juice, seasoned with black pepper, then chilled.

SERVES 8 197 calories per serving

Takes 10 minutes, plus chilling   **PAGE 54**

LEEK BUNDLES WITH PROVENÇAL VEGETABLES

Layers of eggplant, pesto, red pepper, zucchini, and tomato, wrapped in leek strips.

SERVES 4 283 calories per serving

Takes 40 minutes   **PAGE 59**

LOW CALORIE

SUMMER MELONS

Contrastingly colored melon balls mixed with tomato strips, dressed in vinaigrette, chilled, and served with mint.

SERVES 4 282 calories per serving

Takes 15 minutes, plus chilling   **PAGE 68**

ITALIAN CLASSIC

ANTIPASTI

Two popular Italian appetizers: crostini, made from thin slices of baguette brushed with garlic and olive oil and baked until crisp,

SERVES 8 311 calories per crostini serving

Takes 45 minutes

then topped with sun-dried tomato paste; and mozzarella, tomato, and basil salad, dressed with olive oil and balsamic vinegar.

180 calories per salad serving

PAGE 69

EGG PATE

Hard-boiled eggs mixed with light sour cream, consommé, and whipped heavy cream, and garnished with large shrimp.

SERVES 8 243 calories per serving

Takes 45 minutes, plus chilling   **PAGE 59**

⏱ OVER 60 MINUTES

GRAVLAX

Scandinavian specialty: fresh salmon fillets pickled in sugar, sea salt, dill, and black pepper, sandwiched together and chilled. Served *in slices, with a rich sauce combining mustard, sugar, white vinegar, egg yolk, sunflower oil, and dill.*

SERVES 16 395 calories per serving
Takes 30 minutes, plus chilling **PAGE 63**

CAPONATA

Eggplant cooked with celery, onions, tomato paste, sugar, and vinegar, then mixed with olives, garlic, and parsley.

SERVES 4–6 297–198 calories per serving
Takes 35 minutes, plus standing **PAGE 70**

SALMON QUENELLES

Little dumplings of salmon, egg whites, and cream, shaped and poached and served with a luxurious asparagus sauce.

SERVES 4–6 766–511 calories per serving
Takes 30 minutes, plus chilling **PAGE 61**

LIGHT CHICKEN PATE

Diced chicken breast combined with wine, olives, garlic, bread crumbs, and egg. Baked in a dish lined with bacon.

SERVES 6 277 calories per serving
Takes 1¼ hours, plus chilling **PAGE 56**

CARROT MOUSSE

Fresh and creamy: carrots blended with tomatoes, cumin seeds, and farmer cheese. Served with a tomato salsa.

SERVES 6 124 calories per serving
Takes 45 minutes, plus chilling **PAGE 58**

SHRIMP BLINI

Russian pancakes made with yeast and buckwheat flour. Served with red and black lumpfish caviar, shrimp, and light sour cream.

SERVES 6–8 369–277 calories per serving
Takes 35 minutes, plus standing **PAGE 64**

THREE-FISH TERRINE

Layers of smoked fish pâtés – trout with cream cheese and lemon juice; salmon with lemon juice, tomato paste, cream cheese, and *dill; and mackerel with cream cheese and lemon juice – wrapped in smoked salmon slices. Served here on a bed of watercress.*

SERVES 10 424 calories per serving
Takes 40 minutes, plus chilling **PAGE 55**

⏱ OVER 60 MINUTES

SMOKED SALMON PINWHEELS

Savory spinach roulade layered with smoked salmon, a mixture of cream cheese, yogurt, scallions, and tomatoes.

SERVES 4–6 407–271 calories per serving

Takes 45 minutes, plus chilling **PAGE 67**

DINNER PARTY

INDIVIDUAL FISH PATES

Rich and delicate: haddock blended with smoked salmon, white sauce, mayonnaise, and cream and flavored with white wine.

SERVES 8 176 calories per serving

Takes 50 minutes, plus chilling **PAGE 54**

MEDITERRANEAN DIPS WITH CRUDITES

Three popular dips: bagna cauda, a warm anchovy and garlic dip; taramasalata, a chilled mixture of smoked fish caviar, lemon *juice, garlic, and oil; and an eggplant dip, in which eggplant, shallots, and garlic are mixed with parsley and tahini paste.*

SERVES 12 120 calories per serving

Takes 1¹/₂ hours, plus chilling **PAGE 49**

PARTY FARE

SPICY CHICKEN WINGS

Crispy finger food: chicken wings marinated in oil, lemon juice, and spices, then baked. Served with blue cheese dressing.

SERVES 4–6 206–137 calories per serving

Takes 60 minutes, plus marinating **PAGE 52**

BROCCOLI TERRINE

Broccoli florets blended with milk and egg yolk, flavored with grated nutmeg, and set with gelatin and heavy cream.

SERVES 4–6 236–157 calories per serving

Takes 50 minutes, plus chilling **PAGE 58**

PREPARE AHEAD

BRANDIED CHICKEN LIVER PATE

Chicken livers blended with bread, bacon, thyme, egg, and nutmeg and flavored with brandy. Baked, then chilled.

SERVES 8 268 calories per serving

Takes 1¹/₄ hours, plus chilling **PAGE 56**

CANAPES

Homemade canapés are an excellent accompaniment for drinks, or they can be served as an appetizer before dinner. The toasted-bread bases make these canapés satisfyingly crunchy – great for guests any time of day.

 Serves 4

4 slices of white bread, crusts removed

ANCHOVY TOPPING

1 tbsp mayonnaise

1 or 2 scallion tops

8 anchovy fillets, drained

4 cooked peeled shrimp

CHEESE & SCALLION TOPPING

2 tbsp cream cheese

2 scallion tops, very finely sliced

4 capers

SALAMI TOPPING

1 tbsp butter

2 slices of salami

4 slices of dill pickle

ASPARAGUS TOPPING

1 tbsp mayonnaise

6 asparagus tips, cooked and drained

2 slices of radish

a few parsley leaves to garnish

1 Make the canapé bases: toast the white bread lightly on both sides. Remove from the heat and leave to cool.

2 Make the anchovy topping: spread 1 piece of toast with mayonnaise and cut into 4 squares. Cut the scallion tops into 4 pieces, then make vertical cuts to separate each piece into strands. Cut the anchovies in half and arrange in a lattice pattern on each square. Place a shrimp on top, and insert a scallion tassel through each shrimp.

3 Make the cheese and scallion topping: spread 1 piece of toast with cream cheese and cut into 4 squares. Arrange the scallion slices diagonally across the cream cheese. Place a caper on each square.

4 Make the salami topping: butter 1 piece of toast and cut into 4 rounds with a pastry cutter.

5 Make the salami cones (see box, below). Put 1 cone and 1 piece of pickle on each canapé.

6 Make the asparagus topping: spread 1 piece of toast with mayonnaise and cut into 4 squares. Halve the asparagus tips lengthwise. Halve the radish slices and cut away the centers to form 4 crescents. Put 3 halved asparagus tips on each square, arrange the radish on top, and garnish.

Making a salami cone

Cut each slice of salami in half, using a chef's knife. Roll each half to form a point at the straight end. Press to seal.

SPICY MEATBALLS

 Serves 6

2 lb (1 kg) lean ground beef

1 small onion, grated

2 garlic cloves, crushed

1 egg, beaten

1½ cups (90 g) fresh bread crumbs

2 tbsp tomato paste

2 tbsp paprika

2 tbsp chopped fresh cilantro

salt and black pepper

3 tbsp olive oil for frying

chopped parsley to garnish

crudités to serve

SESAME DIP

2 tbsp soy sauce

2 tbsp dark sesame oil

1 tbsp rice wine or sherry

1 scallion, thinly sliced

1 tbsp sesame seeds, toasted

¼ tsp ground ginger

1 Make the sesame dip: whisk all the ingredients together and set aside.

2 Combine the meatball ingredients in a bowl. Using your hands, roll the mixture into little balls.

3 Heat the oil in a skillet, and cook the meatballs, in batches, over medium heat for 5 minutes or until firm and cooked through. Garnish, and serve warm with the dip and crudités.

CHEVRE CROUTES

 Serves 4

1/2 8-in (20-cm) baguette

about 2 tbsp store-bought pesto

1 log-shaped goat cheese

olive oil for sprinkling

black pepper

*radicchio and curly endive
  leaves to serve*

chervil sprigs to garnish

1 Cut the baguette into 8 slices, 1/2 in (1 cm) thick, and toast under a hot grill on one side only. Lightly spread the untoasted sides of the baguette slices with the store-bought pesto.

2 Cut the goat cheese into 8 slices, 1/2 in (1 cm) thick, and arrange on top of the pesto. Toast the topped croutes under the broiler, about 3 in (7 cm) from the heat, for 3 minutes or until the cheese is just begining to soften. Remove the broiler pan from the heat.

3 Lightly sprinkle a little olive oil and grind a little pepper over each cheese croute. Return the croutes to the broiler, close to the heat, for 3 minutes or until the cheese begins to bubble and is just tinged golden brown.

4 Line a serving platter with radicchio and curly endive leaves, arrange the croutes on top, and garnish with chervil sprigs. Serve immediately.

CHEVRE CROUTES ITALIAN STYLE

Substitute 8 slices of Italian bread for the French. After toasting the topped croutes, sprinkle chopped black olives over each croute before lightly sprinkling with olive oil, and proceed as directed.

CHEESE & OLIVE BITES

 Serves 4

*1 1/2 cups (175 g) grated aged
  Cheddar cheese*

2/3 cup (90 g) all-purpose flour

*1 tbsp butter, plus extra for
  greasing*

1 tsp paprika

1/2 tsp dry mustard

20 pimiento-stuffed green olives

*cayenne pepper and parsley
  sprigs to garnish*

1 Work the cheese, flour, butter, paprika, and dry mustard in a food processor until the mixture resembles fine bread crumbs.

2 Flatten the dough mixture, and wrap around the olives (see box, right).

3 Butter a baking sheet. Place the wrapped olives on the baking sheet and bake in a 400°F (200°C) oven for 15 minutes, until the pastry is golden.

4 Remove the cheese and olive bites from the baking tray and leave to cool slightly.

5 Serve warm or cooled, sprinkled with cayenne pepper and garnished with parsley sprigs.

Wrapping the olives in the dough

Take a thumb-sized piece of the dough mixture and flatten on a work surface.

Place an olive in the middle of the dough. Wrap the dough around the olive, pressing to make it stick. If the pastry is too crumbly and will not stick, add a little water. Repeat with the remaining dough and olives.

MEDITERRANEAN DIPS WITH CRUDITES

EGGPLANT DIP

 Serves 4

1¹/₂ lb (750 g) eggplant
salt and black pepper
2 shallots, halved
1–2 garlic cloves
4 tbsp lemon juice
4 tbsp olive oil
4 tbsp chopped parsley
2 tbsp tahini paste

1 Cut the eggplant in half lengthwise. Score the flesh in a lattice pattern, sprinkle with salt, and leave to stand for 30 minutes.

2 Rinse the eggplant halves with cold water, and pat them dry with paper towels. Place on a baking sheet and bake in a 400°F (200°C) oven for 20 minutes.

3 Add the shallots and garlic to the baking sheet, and bake for 15 minutes.

4 Puree the eggplant, shallots, and garlic with the lemon juice, oil, parsley, tahini paste, and salt and pepper to taste in a food processor until smooth.

5 Turn the dip into a bowl. Cover and chill for at least 1 hour before serving.

TARAMASALATA

 Serves 4

1 lb (500 g) smoked fish roe, skinned and coarsely chopped
4 small slices of white bread, crusts removed
4 tbsp lemon juice
1 large garlic clove, coarsely chopped
1¹/₄ cups (250 ml) olive oil
salt and black pepper

1 Puree the fish roe in a food processor or blender until smooth.

2 Break the bread into a bowl, add the lemon juice, and let the bread soak for 1 minute. Add to the roe with the garlic, and puree until smooth.

3 Pour the oil into the mixture, a little at a time, and puree until all the oil has been absorbed. Add salt and pepper to taste.

4 Turn the taramasalata into a bowl. Cover and chill for at least 1 hour before serving.

BAGNA CAUDA

 Serves 4

³/₄ cup (150 ml) olive oil
3 tbsp butter
2 garlic cloves, crushed
2 oz (60 g) canned anchovy fillets, drained and chopped
black pepper

1 Heat the oil and butter in a skillet, add the garlic, and cook gently, stirring occasionally, for a few minutes until soft but not browned. Add the anchovies and cook over very low heat until they dissolve in the oil. Season with black pepper.

2 To serve, transfer the bagna cauda to an earthenware pot placed on a chafing dish, or to a fondue pot.

CHEESE PUFFS

 Serves 10–12

1¹/₄ cups (300 ml) water
4 tbsp butter
1 cup (125 g) self-rising flour
2 egg yolks
2 eggs
1 cup (125 g) grated aged Cheddar cheese
salt and black pepper
oil for deep-frying

1 Put the water and butter into a saucepan and bring to a boil. Remove from the heat and add the flour. Beat well until the mixture is smooth and glossy and leaves the side of the pan clean. Leave to cool slightly.

2 In a bowl, lightly mix the yolks and eggs, then beat into the flour mixture a little at a time. Stir in the cheese. Add salt and pepper to taste.

3 Heat the oil to 375°F (190°C). Lower the mixture a teaspoonful at a time into the oil and cook very gently until golden brown. Lift out and drain on paper towels. Serve warm.

Puffs

Cheese is the the most common flavoring ingredient for these little deep-fried puff pastry treats, but chopped anchovies may also be used.

TAPAS

Tapas are Spanish hors d'oeuvres: little plates of savory foods traditionally served in bars and accompanied by glasses of wine and good conversation. All sorts of hot or cold dishes make excellent tapas – just make sure they can be eaten with the fingers or a fork.

VEGETABLES WITH GARLIC DIPS

 Serves 4

$1^1/_2$ lb (750 g) small new potatoes

1 eggplant, thinly sliced lengthwise

olive oil for brushing

1 red pepper, roasted and peeled (page 354)

small bunch of watercress to serve

rouille and aïoli (pages 33 and 62) to serve

1 Boil the potatoes for 10–15 minutes, until just tender. Drain and leave to cool or keep warm as desired.

2 Arrange the eggplant slices on a baking sheet and brush with olive oil. Cook under the broiler, 4 in (10 cm) from the heat, for 10 minutes or until lightly browned on each side. Cut the pepper into strips.

3 Arrange the vegetables on a serving plate, garnish with the watercress, and serve with rouille and aïoli.

GARBANZO BEAN & RED PEPPER SALAD

 Serves 4

13 oz (400 g) canned garbanzo beans, drained

$^1/_2$ red onion or 3 scallions, chopped

3 garlic cloves, crushed

3 tbsp olive oil

2 tbsp white vinegar

salt and black pepper

few sprigs of flat-leaf parsley

1 red pepper, roasted and peeled (page 354)

25 pimiento-stuffed olives

1 Combine the garbanzo beans with the onion, garlic, oil, vinegar, and salt and pepper to taste. Remove the parsley leaves from the stems and stir in.

2 Cut the red pepper into strips. Stir into the garbanzo bean mixture with the olives until evenly mixed.

TUNA TOSTADAS

 Serves 4

$^1/_2$ baguette, cut diagonally into thin slices

1 garlic clove, crushed

3 tbsp olive oil

2 ripe tomatoes, thinly sliced

2 tbsp drained tuna

3 oz (90 g) Gouda or Cheddar cheese, thinly sliced

1 tbsp chopped flat-leaf parsley

1 Under the broiler, lightly toast the bread on both sides. Meanwhile, combine the garlic with the olive oil.

2 Brush each slice of toasted bread with a little of the garlic oil, then top with a thin slice of tomato. Place a little tuna on each, then top with a slice of cheese and a sprinkling of parsley.

3 Return to the broiler and cook, 4 in (10 cm) from the heat, for 2–3 minutes, until the cheese has melted.

Traditional tapas

An appetizing selection of tapas need not involve a whole day in the kitchen. The following authentic dishes require little or no preparation:

- panfried and salted almonds
- black or green olives
- Manchego cheese
- potato omelet (page 81)
- slices of chorizo (spicy sausage)
- chunks of crusty bread
- jumbo shrimp

ANDALUSIAN MUSHROOMS

 Serves 4

$^1/_2$ lb (250 g) mushrooms

2 tbsp olive oil

2 tbsp butter

6 shallots, chopped

3 garlic cloves, crushed

1 oz (30 g) serrano ham or prosciutto strips

$^1/_4$ tsp mild chili powder

$^1/_4$ tsp paprika

$^1/_4$ cup (4 tbsp) water

1 tsp lemon juice

6 tbsp (90 ml) dry red wine

$^1/_4$ cup (30 g) chopped fresh cilantro or parsley to garnish

1 Pull the mushroom stems from the caps. Heat the olive oil and butter in a skillet. When the butter is foaming, add the shallots and half of the garlic, and cook, stirring, for about 5 minutes until soft but not browned. Add the mushroom caps and stems, and cook, stirring, for 3 minutes, until lightly browned.

2 Add the serrano ham, chili powder, and paprika and cook, stirring constantly, for 1 minute.

3 Add the water and lemon juice, and cook over high heat for a few minutes, until the liquid has almost evaporated and the mushrooms are just tender.

4 Add the red wine and continue to cook over high heat until the liquid is reduced and flavorful. Stir in the remaining garlic, sprinkle with the chopped cilantro or parsley, and serve immediately.

Clockwise from top: *Vegetables with Garlic Dips, Aïoli, Andalusian Mushrooms, Tuna Tostadas, Rouille, Garbanzo Bean & Red Pepper Salad.*

SPICY CHICKEN WINGS

 Serves 4–6

1 lb (500 g) chicken wings

2 tbsp sunflower or corn oil

1 tsp lemon juice

1 tsp onion salt

1 tsp garlic powder

1 tsp ground cumin

1/2 tsp dried oregano

1/2 tsp mild chili powder

1/2 tsp paprika

1/4 tsp cayenne pepper

black pepper

parsley sprigs and radish sprouts (optional) to garnish

TO SERVE

1/2 red pepper, cut into strips

1/2 head celery, cut into sticks, plus leaves

blue cheese dressing (page 338)

1 Cut the chicken wings in half (see box, right). Arrange in a shallow dish.

2 In a large bowl, combine the oil, lemon juice, onion salt, garlic powder, cumin, oregano, chili powder, paprika, cayenne pepper, and black pepper to taste. Brush the mixture over the chicken, cover, and leave to marinate in the refrigerator, covered, for at least 1 hour.

Cutting a chicken wing in half

Tilt the chicken wing, raising the double end slightly off the cutting board. Using a chef's knife, cut the chicken wing into 2 pieces at the main joint, making a drumsticklike piece and a miniwing.

3 Line a large baking sheet with foil and place a rack on top. Arrange the chicken wings in a single layer on the rack, and cook in a 400°F (200°C) oven for 40 minutes, or until browned, sizzling hot, and crispy.

4 Remove the chicken from the rack and drain on paper towels. Serve with red pepper strips, celery sticks, and blue cheese dressing and garnish with parsley, and radish sprouts if desired.

NACHOS GRANDE

 Serves 4–6

2 tbsp sunflower or corn oil

1 onion, finely chopped

1/2 green pepper, chopped

3 garlic cloves, crushed

1/2 cup (125 g) canned chopped tomatoes

1/2 –1 fresh green chili, cored, seeded, and finely chopped

1/2 tsp chili powder

1/2 tsp paprika

13 oz (400 g) canned refried beans

5 tbsp (75 ml) water

2 cups (75 g) tortilla chips

1/4 tsp ground cumin

1 1/2 cups (175 g) grated Cheddar cheese

paprika to garnish

1 Heat the oil in a skillet, add the onion, green pepper, and garlic, and cook gently, stirring occasionally, for 5 minutes or until soft but not browned.

2 Add the tomatoes and chili and cook over medium heat for 5 minutes, or until most of the liquid has evaporated.

3 Stir in the chili powder and paprika and cook for 3 minutes, then add the refried beans, breaking them up with a fork. Add the measured water and cook, stirring occasionally, for 8–10 minutes, until the mixture thickens.

4 Spoon the beans into the middle of a baking dish, arrange the tortilla chips around the edge and sprinkle with cumin. Sprinkle the cheese over the beans and tortilla chips.

5 Bake in a 400°F (200°C) oven for 15–20 minutes until the cheese has melted. Sprinkle the paprika in a lattice pattern on top and serve immediately.

Tortilla chips

These are traditionally made from round, flat, soft tortillas that are cut into segments and deep-fried. When covered with melted cheese and perhaps refried beans, salsa, or other toppings, the dish is known as nachos.

SALMON & SHRIMP PHYLLO PURSES

These crisp, golden purses and their creamy sauce are ideal for a party since they can be prepared up to 24 hours ahead, kept covered with a damp cloth in the refrigerator, and cooked at the last minute. For a different and delightful flavor, use scallops instead of shrimp.

 Makes 8 purses

1 lb (500 g) salmon fillet, boned, skinned, and cut into bite-sized pieces

1/2 lb (250 g) cooked peeled shrimp

lemon juice for sprinkling

8-oz (250-g) package phyllo pastry

4 tbsp butter, melted, plus extra butter for greasing

salt and black pepper

lemon slices and dill sprigs to garnish

WHITE WINE SAUCE

7 tbsp (100 ml) dry white wine

1 1/2 cups (300 ml) heavy cream

1 tsp chopped fresh dill

1 Combine the salmon pieces and shrimp. Sprinkle with lemon juice and add salt and pepper to taste. Set aside.

2 Cut the phyllo pastry into sixteen 7-in (18-cm) squares. Brush 2 squares with the melted butter, covering the remaining squares with a damp kitchen towel. Make a phyllo purse (see box, right). Repeat to make 8 purses.

3 Butter a baking sheet. Add the phyllo purses, lightly brush with the remaining melted butter, and bake in a 375°F (190°C) oven for 15–20 minutes, until crisp and golden.

4 Meanwhile, make the white wine sauce: pour the wine into a saucepan and boil rapidly until it has reduced to about 3 tbsp. Add the heavy cream and simmer until it reaches a light coating consistency. Remove the pan from the heat and add the dill and salt and pepper to taste.

5 Pour the sauce into a small bowl and garnish with a dill sprig. Garnish the purses with the lemon slices and dill sprigs and serve with the warm sauce.

VEGETABLE & GARLIC PHYLLO PURSES

Heat 1 tbsp sunflower oil in a skillet, add 3 carrots, 1 1/2 large celery stalks, and 4 large scallions, all cut into matchsticks. Stir-fry over high heat for 2–3 minutes. Add salt and pepper to taste and leave to cool slightly. Prepare the purses as directed, filling them with the vegetable mixture and 1/4 lb (125 g) soft garlic cheese. Proceed as directed.

Making a phyllo purse

Place one-eighth of the salmon and shrimp mixture in the middle of one buttered square.

Fold 2 sides of phyllo pastry over the mixture to form a rectangle. Take the 2 open ends and fold one over the filling and the other underneath.

Place this package on the second buttered phyllo square and pull up the edges. Squeeze the phyllo together at the neck to seal the purse.

INDIVIDUAL FISH PATES

Rich in flavor, these little pâtés make an ideal appetizer for a special occasion. With the gelatin, they are firm enough to be sliced. For softer pâtés, omit the gelatin and wine and serve in ramekins.

 Serves 8

1/2 lb (250 g) haddock fillets

2/3 cup (150 ml) milk

4 tsp butter

3 tbsp all-purpose flour

1 tsp gelatin

4 tbsp dry white wine

1/2 lb (250 g) smoked salmon pieces

2 tbsp mayonnaise

4 tbsp heavy cream

dash of lemon juice

black pepper

oil for greasing

smoked salmon petals (see box, right), lemon slices, and dill sprigs to garnish

1 Put the haddock into a saucepan and add the milk. Bring almost to a boil, then simmer gently for 10 minutes or until the fish is opaque and flakes easily.

2 Lift the haddock out of the pan; remove the skin and bones and discard. Flake the fish and leave to cool. Reserve the cooking liquid.

3 Melt the butter in a small pan, add the flour, and cook, stirring, for 1 minute. Gradually blend in the reserved cooking liquid, and bring to a boil, stirring constantly, until the mixture thickens. Place a piece of damp waxed paper over the surface of the sauce to prevent a skin from forming and leave to stand until cold.

4 Sprinkle the gelatin evenly over the wine in a small bowl. Leave to stand for 3 minutes or until the gelatin is softened.

5 Put the bowl into a saucepan of gently simmering water for 3 minutes or until the gelatin has dissolved. Leave to cool slightly.

6 Puree the haddock, cold white sauce, smoked salmon pieces, and mayonnaise in a food processor or blender until almost smooth. Gradually add the gelatin mixture, processing between additions. Add the cream, lemon juice, and pepper to taste, then puree briefly.

7 Grease 8 small molds. Spoon the pâté into the molds, cover, and chill for at least 2 hours.

8 To serve, unmold each pâté and garnish with smoked salmon petals, lemon slices, and dill sprigs.

Making smoked salmon petals

Cut the salmon into strips 3/4 in (2 cm) wide, using a chef's knife.

Cut diagonally across the strips to make diamond-shaped pieces to represent petals.

SARDINE PATE

 **Serves 8**

8 oz (250 g) canned sardines in oil, drained, bones removed

1/2 cup (125 g) butter, softened

1/2 cup (125 g) low-fat cream cheese

3 tbsp lemon juice

black pepper

lemon twists and parsley sprigs to garnish

1 Puree the sardines, butter, soft cheese, and lemon juice in a food processor until almost smooth. Add pepper to taste and a little more lemon juice if needed.

2 Divide the sardine mixture among 8 small ramekins (or put into 1 large bowl) and level the surface. Cover and chill in the refrigerator for at least 30 minutes.

3 Serve chilled, garnished with lemon twists and parsley sprigs.

SHRIMP PATE

Substitute 1/2 lb (250 g) cooked peeled shrimp for the sardines, and proceed as directed.

THREE-FISH TERRINE

Three smoked fish pâtés, made from trout, salmon, and mackerel blended with soft cheese, are arranged in layers and then wrapped in slices of smoked salmon, providing a subtle variety of flavors and colors. The finished terrine can be frozen for up to 1 month.

 Serves 10

sunflower or corn oil for greasing

6–8 oz (175–250 g) smoked salmon slices

salt and black pepper

watercress to serve

TROUT PATE

6 oz (175 g) smoked trout

6 tbsp (90 g) butter

3-oz (90-g) package cream cheese

1¹/₂ tbsp lemon juice

SALMON PATE

4 oz (125 g) smoked salmon pieces

4 tbsp butter

¹/₄ cup (60 g) cream cheese

1¹/₂ tbsp lemon juice

1 tbsp tomato paste

1 tbsp chopped fresh dill

MACKEREL PATE

6 oz (175 g) smoked mackerel

6 tbsp (90 g) butter

3-oz (90-g) package cream cheese

1¹/₂ tbsp lemon juice

✭ *8- x 1- x 2-in (20- x 10- x 5-cm) loaf pan or terrine*

1 Make the trout pâté: remove the skin and bones from the trout and puree with the butter, cream cheese, lemon juice, and salt and pepper to taste in a food processor until smooth and well blended. Transfer to a bowl, cover, and chill.

2 Make the salmon pâté: puree the smoked salmon pieces, butter, cream cheese, lemon juice, tomato paste, dill, and salt and pepper to taste in a food processor until smooth and well blended. Transfer to a bowl, cover, and chill.

3 Make the mackerel pâté: remove the skin and bones from the mackerel and puree with the butter, cream cheese, lemon juice, and salt and pepper to taste in a food processor until smooth and well blended. Transfer to a bowl, cover, and chill.

4 Assemble the terrine (see box, right). Cover and chill overnight.

5 To serve, carefully turn out the terrine, cut into thick slices, and arrange on beds of watercress on individual serving plates.

Terrine

Named after the long, narrow container in which it was traditionally made, a terrine may be made from fish and seafood, a variety of meats, or even vegetables. Once firm, the mixture is either removed from the container in slices or turned out of the mold and then sliced.

Assembling the terrine

Oil the loaf pan and line with overlapping slices of smoked salmon, arranging them crosswise and allowing 1¹/₂–2 in (3.5–5 cm) to hang over the sides of the pan.

Turn the trout pâté into the loaf pan, spreading it evenly with a narrow spatula and leveling the surface. If necessary, wet the knife to prevent sticking. Add the salmon pâté, then the mackerel pâté in the same way.

Fold the smoked salmon over the mackerel pâté, tucking in the ends.

LIGHT CHICKEN PATE

 Serves 6

2 whole medium boneless chicken breasts, skinned and diced

1 cup plus 2 tbsp (275 ml) dry white wine

2-oz (60-g) can pitted black olives

4 garlic cloves, crushed

salt and black pepper

3 tbsp fresh bread crumbs

1 egg, lightly beaten

6 oz (175 g) bacon slices

★ 9-in (23-cm) round ovenproof dish, 2 1/2 in (6 cm) deep

1 In a bowl, combine the diced chicken with the wine, pitted black olives, garlic, and salt and pepper to taste. Stir in the fresh bread crumbs and egg.

2 Line the base and side of the dish with the bacon slices. Add the chicken mixture, then cover tightly with foil.

3 Place the dish in a roasting pan, pour in boiling water to come about halfway up the sides of the dish, and bake in a 350°F (180°C) oven for about 1 hour until the pâté is firm. Leave to cool.

4 Remove the foil from the pâté and pour off the cooking juices and fat. Replace the foil and put a plate on top that fits inside the rim of the dish. Weigh down with kitchen weights or heavy cans and chill overnight. To serve, cut the pâté into slices.

Cook's know-how

Fat is used as much for preserving as for flavoring, so a low-fat pâté such as this one does not have the keeping qualities of one encased in fat. Keep this pâté, covered, in the refrigerator and use within 3 days.

BRANDIED CHICKEN LIVER PATE

 Serves 8

5 slices white bread, crusts removed

1 garlic clove, coarsely chopped

4 thick bacon slices, coarsely chopped

2 tsp chopped fresh thyme

1 lb (500 g) chicken livers, trimmed

1 egg

4 tbsp brandy

1/2 tsp grated nutmeg

salt and black pepper

4 tbsp butter, melted

★ 8- x 4- x 2-in (20- x 10- x 5-cm) loaf pan or terrine

1 Line the loaf pan with foil, leaving 2 in (5 cm) foil hanging over on each side.

2 Cut the bread into thick chunks and work them with the garlic in a food processor to make fine bread crumbs. Add the bacon and thyme, and work until finely chopped.

3 Add the chicken livers, egg, brandy, grated nutmeg, and salt and pepper to taste, and puree until smooth. Add the melted butter and puree again.

4 Put the pâté mixture into the prepared loaf pan, level the surface, and fold the foil over the top. Place in a roasting pan, pour in boiling water to come about halfway up the sides of the loaf pan, and bake in a 325°F (160°C) oven for 1 hour.

5 Test the pâté for doneness (see box, below). Leave the pâté to cool completely, then cover, and leave to chill in the refrigerator overnight.

6 To serve, cut the pâté into slices.

Testing the pâté

Insert a skewer into the pâté at the end of cooking time. If it comes out clean, the pâté is cooked.

PAN-FRIED PATES

These little bacon-wrapped chicken liver and spinach pâtés are a specialty of Burgundy. They are easy to make and at their most delicious when served with a tangy salad of sliced tomatoes and chopped onions in an herb vinaigrette dressing.

 Serves 4

2 tbsp butter

1/4 lb (125 g) chicken livers, trimmed

5 shallots, coarsely chopped

4 thick lean bacon slices, coarsely chopped

2 cups (60 g) spinach leaves, shredded

2 tbsp chopped parsley

1 garlic clove, chopped

1 tsp dried sage

1/2 tsp chopped fresh thyme

1/4 tsp ground cloves

salt and black pepper

8 bacon slices

1 Melt half of the butter in a skillet, add the chicken livers, and cook gently, stirring occasionally, for 3 minutes or until they are browned on the outside but still pink inside.

2 Puree the chicken livers in a food processor until smooth. Transfer the pureed livers to a large bowl and set aside.

3 Melt the remaining butter in the skillet, add the shallots, and cook gently, stirring occasionally, for a few minutes until soft but not browned.

4 Add the shallots to the chicken livers with the chopped bacon, spinach, parsley, garlic, sage, thyme, cloves, and salt and pepper to taste. Puree half of this mixture until smooth, then stir it into the remaining mixture in the bowl.

5 Shape and wrap the chicken liver pâtés (see box, right).

6 Heat a skillet, add the pâtés, and cook them gently until browned all over. Lower the heat, cover, and cook over very low heat for 35–40 minutes.

7 Serve the pan-fried pâtés either warm or at room temperature.

Cook's know-how

To trim the chicken livers, use a small sharp knife to cut away any membranes.

Shaping and wrapping the pâtés

Mold the pâté into 8 ovals, using your hands or 2 tablespoons.

Place a bacon slice on a work surface and roll it around one oval.

Twist the bacon around the ends to cover the pâté. Tuck it in to secure. Roll a slice of bacon around each of the remaining ovals.

WHITE BEAN PATE

 Serves 6

26 oz (800 g) canned cannellini beans, drained

2–3 garlic cloves, coarsely chopped

1 tbsp chopped fresh rosemary

3 tbsp olive oil

juice of 1 lemon

salt and black pepper

TO GARNISH

6 rosemary sprigs

1 red pepper, cored, seeded, and cut into strips

12 small black olives

1 Puree the cannellini beans, garlic, rosemary, oil, and lemon juice in a food processor or blender until smooth.

2 Add salt and pepper to taste, then spoon the mixture into 6 small dishes, and level the surfaces.

3 Garnish each pâté with a rosemary sprig, strips of red pepper, and 2 olives.

Cook's know-how

Before chopping fresh rosemary, strip the leaves from the woody stems and discard the stems.

CARROT MOUSSE

 Serves 6

4 carrots, sliced

salt and black pepper

1/2 vegetable bouillon cube

1 1/2 tsp unflavored gelatin

2 tbsp olive oil, plus extra for greasing

1 onion, chopped

3 garlic cloves, chopped

2 ripe tomatoes, peeled (page 39), seeded, and diced

1 tsp cumin seeds

5 tbsp (75 ml) fromage blanc or farmer cheese

cilantro leaves and watercress to garnish

TOMATO SALSA

2 ripe tomatoes, peeled (page 39), seeded, and diced

1/2 onion, finely chopped

1 tbsp olive oil

1 tsp balsamic or wine vinegar

1 tbsp chopped cilantro

☆ 6 small ramekins

1 Make the tomato salsa: combine the tomatoes, onion, oil, vinegar, and cilantro. Cover and chill.

2 Cook the carrots in boiling salted water until tender. Drain, reserving 1/2 cup (125 ml) of the cooking liquid in a bowl.

3 Crumble the 1/2 bouillon cube into the reserved cooking liquid and stir to dissolve. Sprinkle the gelatin over the top. Leave to stand for 3 minutes or until the gelatin has softened.

4 Put the bowl into a pan of simmering water and heat for 3 minutes or until the gelatin has dissolved.

5 Heat the oil in a skillet, add the onion and garlic, and cook gently, stirring occasionally, for a few minutes until soft but not browned. Add the tomatoes and cumin seeds and cook for 5–7 minutes, until the mixture is thick.

6 Puree the carrots and the tomato mixture in a food processor until smooth, then add the fromage blanc and salt and pepper to taste, and puree again. Add the gelatin mixture and puree once more.

7 Oil the ramekins and spoon in the carrot mixture. Cover and chill for at least 3 hours.

8 Garnish with the cilantro leaves and watercress and serve with the tomato salsa.

BROCCOLI TERRINE

 Serves 4–6

2 lb (1 kg) broccoli, in florets

salt and black pepper

1 tbsp unflavored gelatin

1/2 cup (125 ml) milk

1 egg yolk

pinch of grated nutmeg

1/2 cup (125 ml) heavy cream

oil for greasing

carrot julienne salad (page 357) to serve

☆ 8- x 4- x 2-in (20- x 10- x 5-cm) loaf pan

1 Cook the broccoli in boiling salted water for 6 minutes or until just tender. Drain, reserving 5 tbsp (75 ml) of the cooking liquid. Rinse in cold water.

2 Pour the reserved cooking liquid into a small bowl, leave to cool slightly, then sprinkle the gelatin over the top. Leave to stand for 3 minutes or until the gelatin is softened. Put the bowl into a pan of gently simmering water for 3 minutes or until the gelatin has dissolved.

3 Put the milk and egg yolk into a small saucepan and beat together. Heat gently, stirring, until the mixture thickens enough to coat the back of the spoon. Leave to cool slightly.

4 Reserve a few broccoli florets for garnish. Roughly chop half of the broccoli and puree the remainder with the milk and egg mixture in a food processor until smooth. Pour the pureed broccoli mixture into a large bowl, add the chopped broccoli, gelatin mixture, nutmeg, and salt and pepper to taste, and mix together.

5 Whip the cream until it forms firm peaks, then fold it into the broccoli mixture. Oil the loaf pan and pour in the broccoli mixture. Cover and chill for at least 3 hours.

6 Turn out the terrine and cut into slices. Garnish with the reserved broccoli florets and serve the terrine with the carrot julienne salad.

LEEK BUNDLES WITH PROVENÇAL VEGETABLES

In this appealing appetizer, the addition of pesto to the dressing, with its delicious flavors of basil, pine nuts, garlic, and Parmesan cheese, complements the pesto inside the parcels, where it enhances the eggplant slices.

 Serves 4

1 large leek, green part only, trimmed and cut in half lengthwise

1 eggplant, cut into 8 slices

1 zucchini, sliced

olive oil for brushing

1/2 tsp herbes de Provence

salt and black pepper

1 red pepper, cored, seeded, roasted, and peeled (page 354)

8 oz (200 g) canned tomatoes, drained

3 tbsp store-bought pesto

2 garlic cloves, chopped

carrot julienne to garnish

PESTO DRESSING

3 tbsp olive oil

3 tbsp white vinegar

1 tsp store-bought pesto

1 Blanch the leek for 1 minute. Drain and rinse. Separate the green layers to get 13 strips.

2 Brush the eggplant and zucchini slices with the oil, sprinkle with the herbs, and season. Cook under the broiler, 4 in (10 cm) from the heat, for 5 minutes.

3 Cut the red pepper and tomatoes into chunks. Brush the slices of eggplant with pesto.

4 Cut one of the strips of leek into 4 long strands and set aside. Take 3 strips of leek and place them on top of one another in a star formation. Assemble the leek bundles (see box, right).

5 Put the bundles on a baking sheet and bake in a 350°F (180°C) oven for 10 minutes.

6 Make the pesto dressing: whisk the oil, vinegar, and pesto. Spoon the dressing onto 4 serving plates, place a bundle on top, garnish, and serve immediately.

Assembling the leek bundles

Place a slice of eggplant where the strips of leek cross. Place a piece of red pepper on top, then 1–2 slices of zucchini, a little of the chopped garlic, a piece of tomato, and finish with another slice of eggplant.

Fold the ends of the leek strips up over the filling so that they meet in the middle and enclose the vegetable filling.

Tie the bundle with one of the long strands of leek or with a length of string. Repeat the assembling steps with the remaining leek strips and vegetables to make 4 bundles.

EGG PATE

 Serves 8

1 tbsp unflavored gelatin

2 tbsp water

13 oz (400 g) canned consommé

2/3 cup (150 ml) heavy cream

6 hard-boiled eggs, peeled and chopped

2/3 cup (150 ml) light sour cream

salt and black pepper

8 large cooked shrimp, lemon slices, and dill to garnish

1 Sprinkle the gelatin over the water in a bowl. Leave to stand for 3 minutes or until the gelatin is softened. Put the bowl into a saucepan of simmering water for 3 minutes or until the gelatin has dissolved.

2 Pour the consommé into a pitcher and stir in the gelatin liquid.

3 Whip the cream in a large bowl until it forms soft peaks. Fold in the eggs, crème fraîche, and three-quarters of the consommé. Add salt and pepper to taste.

4 Divide the mixture among 8 ramekins and level the surfaces. Leave to stand for about 30 minutes until set. If it has already set, reheat the remaining consommé gently. Spoon it over the pâté. Chill for at least 3 hours.

5 To serve, unmold the pâté, and garnish with the shrimp, lemon slices, and dill.

COQUILLES ST. JACQUES

 Serves 4

8 sea scallops or 24 bay scallops

2/3 cup (150 ml) water

4 tbsp medium-dry white wine

1 bay leaf

salt and black pepper

lemon wedges and bay leaves to garnish

MORNAY SAUCE

3 tbsp butter

3 tbsp all-purpose flour

4 tbsp light cream

1/4 cup (60 g) grated Gruyère cheese

★ *4 scallop shells*

1 Cut each sea scallop into 2–3 pieces. Put the water, wine, and bay leaf into a small pan and season to taste. Bring to a boil, then lower the heat and add the scallops.

2 Poach for 1 minute or until the scallops are just tender when tested with the tip of a knife. Lift out the scallops with a slotted spoon, strain the cooking liquid, and reserve.

3 Make the Mornay sauce: melt the butter in a saucepan, add the flour, and cook, stirring, for 1 minute. Gradually stir in the reserved cooking liquid and bring to a boil, stirring constantly until the mixture thickens. Simmer gently for about 5 minutes. Lower the heat and stir in the cream and half of the grated cheese. Taste for seasoning.

4 Stir the scallops into the sauce, divide among the shells, and sprinkle with the remaining cheese.

5 Place the filled shells under the broiler 3 in (7 cm) from the heat, for about 5 minutes until the cheese has melted and the sauce is golden and bubbling. Garnish with lemon wedges and bay leaves.

MOULES MARINIERE

 Serves 6

6 tbsp (90 g) butter

1 small onion, finely chopped

1 garlic clove, crushed

6 lb (3 kg) mussels, cleaned (page 106)

1 3/4 cups (450 ml) dry white wine

6 parsley sprigs

3 thyme sprigs

1 bay leaf

salt and black pepper

1 tbsp all-purpose flour

3 tbsp chopped parsley to garnish

1 Melt 4 tbsp (60 g) of the butter in a large saucepan, add the onion and garlic, and cook gently, stirring occasionally, for a few minutes until soft but not browned.

2 Add the mussels, wine, parsley, thyme, bay leaf, and salt and pepper to taste. Cover the saucepan tightly and bring to a boil.

3 Cook, shaking the saucepan frequently, for 5–6 minutes or until the mussels open.

4 Throw away any mussels that have not opened: do not try to force them open. Transfer the remaining mussels to a warmed tureen.

5 Strain the cooking juices into a small saucepan. Boil until reduced by about one-third.

6 Work the remaining butter and the flour together on a plate until a paste is formed.

7 Whisk the kneaded butter into the cooking liquid and bring to a boil, stirring constantly. Taste the sauce for seasoning and pour over the mussels. Garnish with the parsley, and serve immediately.

Marinière

Derived from the French word marin, *which means "sailor," the term* marinière *may refer to any type of seafood cooked with white wine and herbs.*

SALMON QUENELLES

Quenelles are delicate little dumplings, traditionally oval but sometimes round, that can be made with fish, meat, or chicken. The name comes from Knödel, the German word for dumpling. They look difficult to make, but in fact they are quite simple and make a most elegant appetizer.

 **Serves 4–6**

1 lb (500 g) salmon fillet, boned, skinned, and cut into chunks

2 egg whites

salt and white pepper

2/3 cup (150 ml) heavy cream

lemon slices and flat-leaf parsley sprigs to garnish

ASPARAGUS SAUCE

6 tbsp (90 ml) dry white wine

1/2 lb (250 g) young asparagus, trimmed, tough parts removed

1 1/4 cups (300 ml) heavy cream

1 Make the quenelles: puree the salmon, egg whites, and salt and pepper to taste in a food processor until completely smooth.

2 With the machine still running, pour in the cream in a steady stream until it is thoroughly blended. Transfer the mixture to a large bowl, cover, and chill for about 2 hours.

3 Bring a saucepan of salted water to a simmer. Shape and cook the quenelles (see box, right). Keep the quenelles warm while you make the sauce.

4 Make the asparagus sauce: pour the wine into a saucepan and boil rapidly for about 2 minutes until it is reduced to a thin syrup.

5 Cook the asparagus in a pan of boiling salted water for 3–5 minutes, until tender. Drain, then cut off the asparagus tips and reserve them for garnish.

6 Puree the reduced wine and the asparagus stalks until very smooth.

7 Boil the cream in a saucepan for 4 minutes or until it is thick enough to coat the back of a metal spoon. Stir in the puree and taste for seasoning.

8 Pour the sauce onto warmed plates, arrange the quenelles on top, and garnish with the reserved asparagus tips, lemon slices, and parsley sprigs.

Cook's know-how

When blending the quenelle mixture, be careful not to overprocess the puree or the cream may curdle.

Shaping and cooking the quenelles

Dip a soup spoon into the simmering water, then take a spoonful of the chilled quenelle mixture. Using a second warm wetted soup spoon or your fingers, mold into an oval. Repeat with the remaining mixture.

Lower some quenelles into the simmering water and cook for 6–10 minutes, until they are firm when pressed with a finger. Do not put too many into the pan at one time.

Remove the quenelles with a slotted spoon, drain well, and keep them warm while you cook the remainder.

SARDINES WITH CORIANDER

 Serves 4

12–16 large fresh sardines

olive oil for brushing

salt and black pepper

lime wedges and flat-leaf parsley sprigs to garnish

CORIANDER LIME BUTTER

1 tsp ground coriander

4 tbsp unsalted butter, at room temperature

1½ tsp lime juice

1 shallot, finely chopped

¼ tsp finely grated lime zest

1 Scale the sardines with the back of a kitchen knife. With a sharp knife, cut the stomachs open and scrape out the contents, particularly any dark blood.

2 Rinse the sardines inside and out and pat dry. Brush all over with oil and sprinkle with salt and pepper.

3 Prepare the coriander lime butter: heat a heavy pan, add the coriander, and toast lightly. Transfer the coriander to a bowl and leave to cool slightly.

4 Add the butter and lime juice to the coriander and whisk until thick. Stir in the shallot and lime zest and salt and pepper to taste.

5 Place the sardines under the broiler, 4 in (10 cm) from the heat, and grill for 1½–2 minutes on each side until they begin to feel firm.

6 Transfer the sardines to a platter, and spread a little coriander lime butter on each one. Garnish with lime wedges and flat-leaf parsley sprigs, and serve immediately.

JUMBO SHRIMP WITH AIOLI

 Serves 4

2 tbsp olive oil

12 uncooked jumbo shrimp in their shells

1 tbsp chopped parsley

lemon wedges and flat-leaf parsley sprigs to garnish

AIOLI

2 garlic cloves, coarsely chopped

salt and black pepper

1 egg yolk

1 tsp dry mustard

⅔ cup (150 ml) olive oil

1 tbsp lemon juice

1 Make the aïoli: in a small bowl, crush the garlic with a pinch of salt until it forms a smooth paste. Add the egg yolk and dry mustard, and beat well. Beat in the oil, drop by drop, whisking constantly until the mixture is thick and smooth and all the oil has been absorbed. Beat in the lemon juice and add pepper to taste.

2 Heat the oil in a large skillet, add the shrimp, and toss over high heat for 4–5 minutes until the shells turn bright pink. Remove the shrimp from the skillet and drain on paper towels.

3 To serve, arrange the shrimp on warmed plates, sprinkle with chopped parsley, and garnish with lemon wedges and parsley sprigs. Serve with individual bowls of aïoli.

Aïoli

This is a garlic-flavored mayonnaise from Provence, where it is served with cold fish, hard boiled eggs, cold meats, and fish soups.

GRAVLAX

This is a Scandinavian method of pickling fresh salmon, and a lovely recipe for a party. Serve it with thin slices of dark rye bread. You will find the fish easier to slice if it has been frozen for about 4 hours beforehand.

 Serves 16

4¹/₂ lb (2.25 kg) whole fresh
  salmon, boned and cut into
  2 fillets

dill sprigs and lemon wedges
  to garnish

PICKLING MIXTURE

5 tbsp (75 g) sugar

¹/₄ cup (60 g) coarse sea salt

¹/₄ cup (30 g) chopped fresh dill

MUSTARD DILL SAUCE

3 tbsp Dijon mustard

2 tbsp sugar

1 tbsp white vinegar

1 egg yolk

²/₃ cup (150 ml) sunflower oil

salt and black pepper

2 tbsp chopped fresh dill

1 Make the pickling
mixture: put the sugar,
sea salt, and chopped dill
into a small bowl, season
generously with black
pepper, and stir to mix
thoroughly.

2 Sandwich together
the salmon fillets
(see box, right).

3 Wrap the fillets in a
double thickness of foil
and place in a large dish.
Put a plate on top, weigh
down with heavy cans, and
chill in the refrigerator for
1–3 days, turning the salmon
over every day.

4 Make the mustard dill
sauce: in a medium bowl,
whisk together the mustard,
sugar, vinegar, and egg yolk,
then whisk in the oil a little
at a time. The sauce should
have the consistency of
mayonnaise. Add salt and
pepper to taste and stir in
the chopped dill.

5 Unwrap the gravlax.
A lot of sticky, salty liquid
will drain from the fish when
it has been pickled: this is
normal. Remove the fish
from the pickling liquid and
pat dry with paper towels.
Separate the salmon fillets.

6 To serve, slice each fillet
on a diagonal, cutting
the flesh away from the skin.
The slices should be a little
thicker than for smoked
salmon, and each one
should have a fringe of dill.
Garnish with dill sprigs and
lemon wedges and serve with
the mustard dill sauce.

Sandwiching
the salmon

Put one salmon fillet
skin side down on a
board, cover the surface
with the pickling mixture,
and place the second fillet
on top, skin side up.

SPICY
SHRIMP

 Serves 4

²/₃ cup (150 ml) mayonnaise

2 tbsp horseradish

1 tbsp lemon juice

1 tsp Worcestershire sauce

1 tsp tomato paste

¹/₄ tsp sugar

few drops of Tabasco sauce

black pepper

¹/₂ lb (250 g) cooked peeled
  shrimp

salad greens to serve

thin lemon wedges, parsley
  sprigs, and 4 large cooked
  shrimp in their shells to
  garnish

1 Make the dressing: in a
medium bowl, mix
together the mayonnaise,
horseradish, lemon juice,
Worcestershire sauce,
tomato paste, sugar, and
Tabasco sauce and season
with a little black pepper.

2 Add the peeled cooked
shrimp and stir to coat
with the dressing.

3 Line 4 individual glass
serving bowls with the
salad greens and top with
the shrimp mixture. Garnish
each serving with a thin
lemon wedge, a parsley
sprig, and a large shrimp.

RUSSIAN FISH SALAD

 Serves 4

2 hard-boiled eggs

10 oz (300 g) firm whitefish fillets, cooked

3 tbsp sour cream

3 tbsp mayonnaise

1 tbsp chopped parsley

salt and black pepper

2 large tomatoes, quartered

lemon twists, flat-leaf parsley sprigs, and celery leaves to garnish

1 Remove the yolk from one egg and reserve. Chop the white and the remaining egg.

2 Put the fish into a bowl and flake with a fork. Stir in the chopped egg, sour cream, mayonnaise, parsley, and salt and pepper to taste.

3 Arrange the tomatoes on 4 plates and top with the fish mixture. Push the egg yolk through a strainer and sprinkle over the mixture. Garnish with lemon twists, parsley, and celery leaves.

SHRIMP BLINI

Blini are small traditional Russian pancakes made with yeast and buckwheat flour. Buckwheat flour is available at health food stores, but if you cannot find any, use whole-wheat flour instead. This mixture makes about 24 blini.

 Serves 6–8

BLINI

1 cup (125 g) all-purpose flour

1 cup (125 g) buckwheat flour

1/2 tsp salt

1/2 tsp quick-rise dried yeast

1 3/4 cups (450 ml) milk, warmed

1 egg, separated

sunflower or corn oil for frying

TO SERVE

2 2 1/2-oz (75-g) jars lumpfish caviar (1 red, 1 black)

1/4 lb (125 g) cooked peeled shrimp

1/2 cup (125 ml) light sour cream

lemon wedges and fresh chives to garnish

1 In a large bowl, mix together the plain and buckwheat flours, salt, and quick-rise dried yeast.

2 Gradually beat in the warm milk to make a smooth batter. Cover and leave in a warm place for about 40 minutes until the mixture is frothy and has doubled in volume.

3 Beat the egg yolk into the flour and yeast mixture. In a second bowl, whisk the egg white until stiff but not dry, then fold into the mixture.

4 Heat a large nonstick skillet or griddle, brush with oil, and heat until the oil is hot. Spoon about 2 tbsp batter into the pan for each blini; you should be able to cook 3 or 4 at a time. Cook the blini over medium heat for 2–3 minutes, or until bubbles rise to the surface and burst.

5 Turn the blini over with a spatula and cook for 2–3 minutes longer, until golden on the other side. Wrap the cooked blini in a dish towel and keep them warm.

6 Cook the remaining batter in batches until all the batter is used up, lightly oiling the pan between batches.

7 To serve, arrange the blini on warmed plates, with spoonfuls of red and black lumpfish caviar, shrimp, and light sour cream. Garnish with lemon wedges and fresh chives.

SMOKED CHICKEN SALAD WITH WALNUTS

 Serves 6

1 smoked chicken, weighing about 2¹/₂ lb (1.25 kg)

7 tbsp (100 ml) sunflower oil

2 tbsp walnut oil

5 tbsp (75 ml) orange juice

¹/₄ tsp ground coriander

¹/₄ tsp sugar

salt and black pepper

8 cups (375 g) mixed salad greens

4 oranges, peeled and sectioned

¹/₂ cup (60 g) walnut pieces

1 Remove the meat from the chicken carcass and discard the skin and any gristle. Cut the meat into thin, neat slices. Put the chicken slices into a shallow nonmetallic dish.

2 In a small bowl, combine the sunflower and walnut oils, orange juice, ground coriander, sugar, and salt and pepper to taste. Pour the mixture over the chicken slices and toss them gently until coated evenly.

3 Arrange the salad greens, orange sections, and chicken slices on individual plates, scatter the walnut pieces over the top, and serve immediately.

Smoked chicken

In the past, foods were smoked to preserve them, but flavor is now one of the prime reasons for smoking foods. The chicken is first cold-smoked, then briefly hot-smoked, before being rested to let the flavor mature. It is darker than fresh chicken.

WARM DUCK SALAD

Substitute ³/₄ lb (375 g) smoked duck or turkey breast for the chicken. Gently heat the poultry slices in the dressing and add warm croutons (page 31) to the salad.

WARM SALAD WITH BACON & SCALLOPS

 Serves 4

8 cups (375 g) mixed salad greens, such as radicchio, mâche, curly endive, and arugula

8 shallots, finely chopped

1 tbsp sunflower or corn oil

¹/₂ lb (250 g) lean bacon, diced

12 scallops, halved

3 tbsp white vinegar

2 tbsp walnut oil

salt and black pepper

1 Put the salad greens into a large bowl and sprinkle with half of the shallots.

2 Heat the oil in a skillet, add the bacon, and cook quickly, stirring occasionally, for 5 minutes or until crisp. Add the scallops and cook quickly for 1–2 minutes, until just opaque. Remove the bacon and scallops from the pan and keep warm.

3 Add the remaining shallots to the pan and cook for 1 minute. Add the vinegar and boil rapidly, stirring to incorporate the pan juices.

Tossing a salad

Pour the oil over the salad leaves. Lift a portion of the leaves and turn them over as you drop them back into the bowl. Repeat until all the leaves are coated evenly.

4 Toss the salad with the walnut oil (see box, above). Add the bacon and scallops, hot vinegar and shallots, and season to taste.

Cook's know-how

Stirring vinegar into the skillet loosens and dissolves the flavorful juices on the bottom of the pan so they are not wasted. This is called deglazing.

ASPARAGUS WITH QUICK HOLLANDAISE

 Serves 4

1 1/4 lb (625 g) asparagus

salt and black pepper

lemon twists to garnish

QUICK HOLLANDAISE

2 1/3 cups (600 ml) hot water

1 tbsp lemon juice

1 tbsp white vinegar

4 egg yolks, at room temperature

10 tbsp (150 g) unsalted butter, melted

1 Trim the asparagus, cut off the woody ends, and tie into 4 bundles with string.

2 Stand the asparagus upright in a deep pan with enough boiling salted water to come halfway up the stems, allowing the tips to steam rather than boil. Cover and cook for 8–10 minutes, until the asparagus is tender but still firm.

3 Meanwhile, make the quick hollandaise: put the measured hot water into a food processor or blender and process briefly to warm the bowl. Discard the water and dry the bowl.

4 Put the lemon juice and vinegar into the food processor, add the egg yolks, and process briefly. With the machine running, gradually pour in the melted butter, and process until thick and creamy. Season to taste.

5 To serve, drain and untie the asparagus. Ladle the hollandaise sauce onto warmed plates, arrange the asparagus on top, and garnish with lemon twists.

Asparagus

One of the most prized of all vegetables, asparagus is a harbinger of spring in supermarkets across the country. Select spears with a good color, that are crisp, straight, and firm with tightly closed tips. Ideally, asparagus should be cooked and eaten on the day it is bought, but if you need to keep it longer than 12 hours, wrap the bottoms of the stalks in wet paper towels, seal tightly in a plastic bag, and store in the refrigerator. Use within 4 days.

BRIOCHES WITH WILD MUSHROOMS & WATERCRESS

 Serves 6

2 tbsp butter

1/2 lb (250 g) wild mushrooms, trimmed and sliced

1/2 bunch watercress, finely chopped

1/4 cup (60 ml) heavy cream

squeeze of lemon juice

salt and black pepper

6 brioches (page 380)

watercress sprigs to garnish

1 Melt the butter in a large skillet, add the mushrooms, and cook gently, stirring occasionally, for 3 minutes or until tender. Add the watercress, cream, lemon juice, and salt and pepper to taste and cook until the watercress is just wilted.

2 Remove the tops and insides from the brioches (see box, right). Spoon in some of the mixture.

Preparing brioches

Remove brioche top and set aside. Using your fingers, pull out the soft inside, leaving a 1/4-in (5-mm) crust. Repeat with the remaining brioches.

3 Transfer the brioches to warmed serving plates, replace the brioche tops, and spoon the remaining mushroom and watercress mixture onto the plates beside the brioches. Garnish with watercress sprigs and serve immediately.

SMOKED SALMON PINWHEELS

The pinwheel pattern of the roulade is almost as delightful as its flavor. Since both the cream cheese and smoked salmon layers are quite rich, the inclusion in the roulade of a very thin layer of tomatoes provides a fresh contrast.

 Serves 4–6

1 tbsp butter

1 garlic clove, crushed

5 cups (150 g) spinach leaves, cooked, squeezed, and chopped

4 eggs, separated

1 tsp chopped fresh rosemary

pinch of grated nutmeg

salt and black pepper

salad greens and lemon slices to garnish

FILLING

³/4 cup plus 2 tbsp (200 g) cream cheese

3 tbsp yogurt

4 scallions, thinly sliced

¹/4 lb (125 g) smoked salmon

2 ripe tomatoes, thinly sliced

★ 13- x 9-in (33- x 23-cm) jelly roll pan

1 Line the jelly roll pan with a sheet of baking parchment, cutting the corners so that it fits snugly.

2 Put the butter into a saucepan, add the garlic, and cook gently until the butter melts. Remove from the heat. Stir in the spinach.

3 Add the egg yolks, rosemary, and nutmeg, season to taste and beat into the spinach mixture.

4 In another bowl, whisk the egg whites until stiff but not dry. Fold 2–3 spoonfuls into the spinach mixture, then fold in the remainder.

5 Spread the mixture in the jelly roll pan, and bake in a 375°F (190°C) oven for 10–12 minutes, until the mixture feels firm. Remove from the oven, cover with a damp dish towel, and leave to cool.

6 Meanwhile, make the filling: in a medium bowl, beat together the cream cheese and yogurt until smooth, then stir the scallions into the mixture.

7 Turn out the cooled roulade and peel off the paper. Fill and roll the roulade (see box, right).

8 Wrap the roulade in foil, then overwrap with a damp dish towel and chill overnight.

9 To serve, trim off the hard edges of the roulade, cut into thick slices, and arrange on a serving platter. Garnish with salad greens and lemon slices.

PROSCIUTTO PINWHEELS

Substitute 2 cups (150 g) broccoli florets, cooked and pureed, for the spinach, and 4 oz (125 g) thinly sliced prosciutto for the smoked salmon. Proceed as directed.

Filling and rolling the roulade

Arrange the slices of smoked salmon on top of the roulade, leaving a 1-in (2.5-cm) border on each side.

Spread the cream cheese filling over the smoked salmon, using a spatula. Arrange the tomato slices over half of the cream cheese filling.

Roll up the roulade, starting from the end where the tomato slices have been placed.

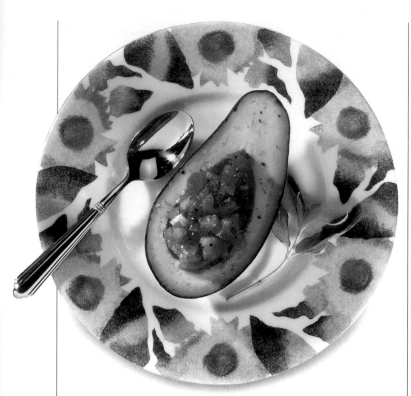

AVOCADO WITH TOMATOES & MINT

 Serves 4

4 small firm tomatoes

2 ripe avocados

1 tbsp chopped fresh mint

mint sprigs to garnish

DRESSING

2 tsp white vinegar

1 tsp Dijon mustard

2 tbsp olive oil

1/4 tsp sugar

salt and black pepper

1 Peel the tomatoes: cut out the cores and score an "X" on the base of each, then immerse in boiling water until the skins start to split. Transfer immediately to a bowl of cold water. Peel, seed, and then coarsely chop the tomato flesh.

2 Make the dressing: in a small bowl, whisk together the vinegar and mustard. Gradually whisk in the oil, then add the sugar, and salt and pepper to taste.

Pitting an avocado

Cut the avocado in half lengthwise, through to the pit. Twist the halves and then pull them apart. Embed the blade of a chef's knife in the pit and lift it out.

3 Halve and pit the avocados (see box, above). Brush at once with a little dressing to prevent discoloration.

4 Combine the tomatoes, chopped mint, and dressing. Pile the tomato mixture into the avocado halves, garnish with mint sprigs, and serve at once.

SUMMER MELONS

 Serves 4

2 1/2-lb (750-g) ripe melons with different-colored flesh

3 medium tomatoes

1 tbsp chopped fresh mint

mint sprigs to garnish

DRESSING

6 tbsp (90 ml) sunflower oil

2 tbsp white vinegar

1/4 tsp sugar

salt and black pepper

1 Cut the melons in half and remove and discard the seeds. Using a melon baller, cut balls from the flesh of each half into a bowl or cut into neat cubes.

2 Peel the tomatoes: cut out the cores and score an "X" on the base of each one, then immerse in a bowl of boiling water until the skins start to split. Transfer immediately to a bowl of cold water. Peel and seed the tomatoes, then cut the flesh into long strips. Add the strips to the melon.

3 Make the dressing: in a small bowl, whisk together the sunflower oil and vinegar, then add the sugar, and salt and pepper to taste. Pour the dressing over the melon and tomato mixture. Cover and chill for at least 1 hour.

4 To serve, stir the chopped mint into the melon and tomato mixture, spoon the salad into chilled bowls, and garnish each serving with a mint sprig.

Cook's know-how

Choose two or three varieties of melon to make an attractive color combination. Honeydew has pale greenish yellow flesh, cantaloupe has either pale or dark orange flesh, ogen has pale yellow or green flesh, and Charentais has deep orange flesh.

ANTIPASTI

This is the Italian equivalent of hors d'oeuvres – a selection of hot and cold appetizers. In Italy, you are most likely to find lavish displays of antipasti in restaurants; at home, only one or two simple appetizers are served.

MOZZARELLA, TOMATO, & BASIL SALAD

 Serves 8

4 beefsteak tomatoes

1/2 lb (250 g) fresh mozzarella cheese

1/4 cup (30 g) shredded fresh basil

1/4 cup (60 ml) olive oil

1 tbsp balsamic or wine vinegar

salt and black pepper

basil sprig to garnish

1 Peel the tomatoes: cut out the cores and score an "X" on the base of each one, then immerse in boiling water until the skins start to split. Transfer immediately to cold water; when cool, peel off the skin. Thinly slice the tomatoes.

2 Slice the mozzarella cheese. Arrange the tomato and cheese slices alternately on a plate, overlapping one another. Sprinkle with the basil, olive oil, and vinegar, and add salt and pepper to taste. Garnish with a basil sprig and serve.

Mozzarella

This is an unripened white cheese. Traditionally made with buffalo milk, less expensive varieties made with cow's milk are now widely available and often used in the place of mozzarella di bufala.

SUN-DRIED TOMATO CROSTINI

 Serves 8

8-in (20-cm) baguette

2 garlic cloves, crushed

about 3 tbsp olive oil

4 sun-dried tomatoes in oil

2 tbsp butter

salt and black pepper

12 pitted black olives, chopped

1/4 tsp dried rosemary

1 Cut the baguette into 24 thin slices and arrange them on 2 baking sheets. In a small bowl, combine the garlic with the olive oil, then brush about half of the mixture on the slices of bread. Bake in a 350°F (180°C) oven for 10 minutes.

2 Remove the baking sheets from the oven, turn the slices of bread over, brush with a little more garlic oil, and bake for 10 minutes longer or until crisp and golden. Leave to cool.

3 Dry the sun-dried tomatoes with a paper towel and cut them into pieces. Put the tomato and butter in a food processor and process until finely chopped. Season with salt and pepper to taste.

4 Spread the sun-dried tomato purée over the crostini, arrange the chopped olives on top, and sprinkle with rosemary.

Cook's know-how

Italian delicatessens are a wonderful hunting ground for prepared antipasti. Make up a large platter of cured meats, such as prosciutto, mortadella *(a stewed pork sausage from Bologna),* pepperoni, capicola, *or some slices of salami. Among the many varieties are* salame milano, *traditionally made of pork, sometimes a combination of pork and beef;* salame genoa, *pork studded with white peppercorns; and* salame finocchiona, *made from pork flavored with fennel. Serve a selection of bowls containing green olives stuffed with anchovies or pimientos; green and black olives marinated in olive oil, herbs, and spices; roasted red peppers marinated in olive oil, garlic, and parsley; and store-bought mixtures of shrimp, mussels, squid, and other seafood in an herb dressing.*

CAPONATA

 **Serves 4–6**

1 large eggplant

salt and black pepper

about ¹/₄ cup (60 ml) olive oil

¹/₂ head celery, diced

2 onions, thinly sliced

¹/₂ cup (125 g) tomato paste

¹/₄ cup (60 g) sugar

¹/₂–³/₄ cup (125–175 ml) red wine vinegar

1 cup (125 g) pitted green olives

2 tbsp capers (optional)

1–2 garlic cloves, crushed

1 cup (30 g) parsley, chopped

1 Cut the eggplant into ¹/₂-in (1-cm) chunks and sprinkle generously with salt. Leave to stand for 30 minutes to draw out the bitter juices, then rinse well with cold water, and dry thoroughly with paper towels.

2 Heat three-quarters of the oil in a large saucepan, add the eggplant, and cook gently, stirring, for 8 minutes or until tender. Remove the eggplant from the pan with a slotted spoon.

3 Heat the remaining oil in the pan, add the celery, and cook gently, stirring occasionally, for 7 minutes or until browned.

4 Return the eggplant to the pan with the onions, tomato paste, sugar, and vinegar. Cook over medium heat for 10 minutes to reduce the harshness of the vinegar. Add a little water if the mixture becomes too thick and starts sticking to the pan.

5 Remove from the heat and add the green olives, capers, if using, garlic, and half of the parsley. Add pepper to taste. Cover and leave to cool. To serve, transfer to serving plates and sprinkle with the remaining parsley.

Capers

These are the flower buds of a Mediterranean shrub, preserved by pickling in vinegar and salt. They have a tangy, sour taste.

WARM SALAD WITH PEARS & BLUE CHEESE

 Serves 4

8 thin slices of white bread

2 garlic cloves, halved

¹/₂ lb (250 g) Stilton cheese, sliced, or other blue cheese

2 bunches of watercress, trimmed and chopped

2 pears, peeled and cut into thin wedges

¹/₄ cup (60 ml) sunflower oil

1 small red onion, finely chopped

2 tbsp balsamic vinegar

✯ 3-in (7-cm) pastry cutter

1 With the pastry cutter, cut out decorative shapes from the slices of bread.

2 Toast the bread shapes on both sides under the broiler. Rub both sides of the bread with the garlic cloves and arrange the slices of cheese on top of each piece. Set aside.

3 Arrange the chopped watercress and pear wedges on 4 individual serving plates, then set aside.

4 Heat the sunflower oil in a skillet, add the onion, and cook gently for 5 minutes or until soft but not browned.

5 Meanwhile, put the cheese-topped toasts under the broiler, close to the heat, for 1–2 minutes, until the cheese is melted and warmed through. Cut the toasts in half.

6 Add the vinegar to the onion in the skillet, and let it heat through, stirring occasionally. Pour the onion mixture over the watercress and pears. Arrange the toasts on the plates and serve at once.

WARM SALAD WITH PEARS & BRIE

For a milder flavor, substitute ¹/₂ lb (250 g) Brie, thickly sliced, for the Stilton.

3

EGGS & CHEESE

⏱ Under 30 minutes

Spinach & mushroom frittata

Chunky Italian omelet filled with bacon, mushrooms, and spinach, sprinkled with Parmesan and browned under the grill.

SERVES 2 673 calories per serving

Takes 25 minutes   **PAGE 80**

Potato omelet

Traditional Spanish dish: diced potatoes, onions, and eggs cooked slowly make a nourishing and simple meal.

SERVES 4 389 calories per serving

Takes 25 minutes   **PAGE 81**

Raclette

Boiled new potatoes topped with Swiss raclette cheese and heated in the oven until sizzling. Served with cornichons and onions.

SERVES 4 446 calories per serving

Takes 25 minutes   **PAGE 93**

Oeufs en cocotte

Warm creamy dish: whole eggs in ramekins, topped with heavy cream and parsley and steamed or baked.

SERVES 4 176 calories per serving

Takes 25 minutes   **PAGE 96**

Zucchini frittata

Light and easy to make: thinly sliced zucchini and diced prosciutto cooked with eggs make a colorful Italian omelet.

SERVES 4 270 calories per serving

Takes 25 minutes

Browned under the broiler, cut into wedges, and garnished with shredded fresh basil. Served hot or cold.

PAGE 81

Huevos rancheros

Classic Mexican dish of tomatoes simmered with onion, garlic, green pepper, fresh chili, and cumin, topped with a poached egg.

SERVES 4 196 calories per serving

Takes 25 minutes   **PAGE 96**

Mushroom omelet with country bread

Italian country bread, filled with an omelet brimming with sliced shiitake mushrooms.

SERVES 2 673 calories per serving

Takes 25 minutes   **PAGE 80**

Eggs benedict

Hearty breakfast: poached eggs and Canadian bacon on toasted English muffins, topped with hollandaise sauce.

SERVES 4 602 calories per serving

Takes 25 minutes   **PAGE 95**

30–60 MINUTES

CHEESE FONDUE

Gruyère and Swiss cheeses melted in a fondue pot with wine and garlic. Served with bread and apple for dipping.

SERVES 4–6 1219–813 calories per serving

Takes 30 minutes **PAGE 93**

SAVORY SOUFFLE OMELET

Light and summery: zucchini, red pepper, and tomatoes combined with soufflé mixture. Flavored with garlic, onion, and thyme.

MAKES 2 479 calories per serving

Takes 35 minutes **PAGE 79**

MEDITERRANEAN ZUCCHINI PIE

Wholesome and rich: zucchini mixed with Parmesan and mozzarella cheeses, eggs, pesto, garlic, and mint. Topped with puff pastry.

SERVES 4 545 calories per serving

Takes 50 minutes **PAGE 84**

CROQUE SENOR

Sandwich of Cheddar cheese and ham given a Mexican flavor with salsa of tomatoes, chili, and red pepper. Cooked until golden.

SERVES 4 413 calories per serving

Takes 30 minutes **PAGE 91**

MEXICAN OMELET

Classic omelet with a substantial filling of onion and garlic cooked with green pepper, tomatoes, mushrooms, and Tabasco.

MAKES 2 547 calories per serving

Takes 50 minutes **PAGE 79**

BROCCOLI SOUFFLES

Broccoli, shallots, and blue cheese combined with soufflé mixture and flavored with nutmeg and cayenne pepper.

SERVES 4 499 calories per serving

Takes 45 minutes **PAGE 91**

EGGS FLORENTINE

Nutritious and creamy: spinach mixed with scallions and heavy cream, topped with a poached egg and Parmesan cheese sauce.

SERVES 4 475 calories per serving

Takes 30 minutes **PAGE 95**

ITALIAN CHEESE & RED PESTO TARTLETS

Rich and tangy: tomatoes, black olives, and Fontina cheese complemented by the Mediterranean flavors of garlic and oregano,

MAKES 12 198 calories each

Takes 55 minutes

set in short crust pastry tartlet shells spread with pesto. Sprinkled with Parmesan cheese to give a tasty, crispy finish.

PAGE 85

30–60 MINUTES

OVER 60 MINUTES

SWISS TOMATO RAREBIT

Variation of Welsh rarebit: tomatoes and wine cooked with Gruyère cheese and mushrooms. Served on buttered toast.

SERVES 4 640 calories per serving

Takes 30 minutes   **PAGE 94**

SOUFFLE CREPES WITH BROCCOLI & CHEESE

Crêpes with a soufflé filling combining tiny broccoli florets, Cheddar cheese, and mustard.

MAKES 8 300 calories per serving

Takes 45 minutes, plus standing   **PAGE 90**

BROCCOLI & RICOTTA TART

Ricotta, Cheddar, and Parmesan cheeses mixed with broccoli, eggs, garlic, and thyme, baked in a buttered crumb crust.

SERVES 4–6 689–460 calories per serving

Takes 1 hour 5 minutes   **PAGE 86**

STRATA WITH CHEESE AND PESTO

Custard of eggs, light sour cream, and milk poured over slices of bread and pesto. Sprinkled with Italian cheeses.

SERVES 4 896 calories per serving

Takes 50 minutes   **PAGE 86**

GARLIC & GOAT CHEESE SOUFFLES

Tangy soufflés combining garlic-flavored milk with butter, flour, goat cheese, egg yolks, and beaten egg whites.

SERVES 6 267 calories per serving

Takes 55 minutes   **PAGE 92**

QUICHE LORRAINE

Classic French tart: short crust pastry shell spread with lightly cooked onion and crispy pieces of bacon. Sprinkled with grated

SERVES 4–6 756–504 calories per serving

Takes 60 minutes, plus chilling

Gruyère cheese, then filled with an egg and cream mixture and baked until golden brown. Served warm or cold.

PAGE 82

OVER 60 MINUTES

CREAMY SEAFOOD CREPES

Pieces of cod fillet cooked with onion, garlic, tomatoes, dill seeds, cream, and shrimp, and flavored with fresh basil. The creamy filling *is spread over crêpes, which are then folded into triangles and garnished with shrimp, sprigs of basil, and lemon coronets.*

SERVES 6 308 calories per serving

Takes 50 minutes, plus standing **PAGE 87**

CHICKEN CREPES FLORENTINE

Crêpes filled with chicken, mushrooms, and thyme served on a bed of spinach. Sprinkled with Gruyère cheese and baked.

SERVES 4 721 calories per serving

Takes 50 minutes, plus standing **PAGE 90**

SPINACH, LEEK, & GRUYERE TART

Nourishing and creamy: leek and spinach in a short crust pastry shell with a mixture of eggs, milk, cream, and Gruyère cheese.

SERVES 4–6 721–480 calories per serving

Takes 60 minutes, plus chilling **PAGE 84**

SMOKED SALMON & ASPARAGUS QUICHE

Salmon and asparagus set in a short crust pastry shell with a tangy custard of yogurt, eggs, and dill.

SERVES 6–8 321–241 calories per serving

Takes 1¼ hours, plus chilling **PAGE 83**

CLASSIC CHEESE SOUFFLE

Delicate and light: milk flavored with bay leaf and a clove-studded onion, combined with butter, flour, eggs, and Cheddar cheese.

SERVES 4 640 calories per serving

Takes 1¼ hours **PAGE 91**

SWISS DOUBLE-CHEESE SOUFFLES

Rich and very creamy: individual soufflés flavored with Gruyère cheese and chives. Baked until golden and firm, then unmolded *and topped with heavy cream and Parmesan cheese. Baked again until golden, and garnished with snipped fresh chives.*

SERVES 6 465 calories per serving

Takes 1 hour 5 minutes **PAGE 92**

ROQUEFORT QUICHE

Roquefort and low-fat cream cheese combined with eggs, light sour cream, and chives, set in a short crust pastry shell, and baked.

SERVES 4–6 504–336 calories per serving

Takes 1 hour 5 minutes **PAGE 83**

EGGS & CHEESE KNOW-HOW

EGGS AND CHEESE, alone or used together, are found in countless dishes. Eggs enrich pastries and doughs, give volume and moistness to cakes and many other desserts, thicken sauces and custards, bind mixtures ranging from burgers to pâtés, and provide a coating for foods to be fried. On their own, eggs can be cooked in many delicious ways, from simple boiling or poaching to frying in omelets and baking in soufflés, to be enjoyed at any meal.

Cheese has countless culinary uses; it is good as a sandwich filling, or in snacks, sauces, fondues, and pizza toppings. Cheese flavors savory pastries and doughs as well as quiche and tart fillings. It is essential in many pasta dishes. Soft fresh cheeses such as ricotta and cottage cheese are used to make cheesecake fillings. And, of course, a cheeseboard can begin or end a special dinner.

BUYING & STORING

When buying eggs, choose the freshest ones and check that none are damaged or cracked. Store the eggs in the refrigerator (in the carton or in a separate compartment so that they do not absorb flavors and odors of strong foods through their shells). They will keep in the refrigerator for up to 2 weeks — check the date stamp before using. If you place them pointed end down, the yolk will remain centered in the white.

When buying cheese, rely on appearance, and smell if possible. Hard and firm cheeses should be moist but not sweaty and should not have any mold unless they are blue-veined; soft ripened cheeses such as Brie and Camembert should feel springy and creamy throughout. Soft fresh cheese should be refrigerated, although other cheeses can be stored in a cool place such as a cellar; keep them well wrapped or covered.

SEPARATING EGGS

For best results, make sure eggs are chilled before you start.

1 Holding an egg over a bowl, break open the shell and carefully transfer the yolk from one half shell to the other. Repeat several times, letting the egg white run into the bowl.

2 Put the yolk in another bowl. Remove any yolk from the white with the tip of a spoon (the white can't be beaten if there is any trace of yolk).

COOKING WITH CHEESE

Cheese should be cooked with care. Hard and firm cheeses can withstand heat best, melting and blending smoothly. Parmesan, Gruyère, Swiss, and Cheddar are most commonly used in cooking. Other cheeses have their own particular applications; mozzarella, for example, is usually used on top of pizzas.

MICROWAVING

Never microwave an egg that is still in its shell, or it will burst. Even out of its shell, a whole egg may burst, so always pierce the membrane on the yolk before cooking. The yolk cooks more quickly than the white, so standing time should be allowed to let the white continue cooking. Where yolks and whites are combined, as for scrambled eggs, the mixture will appear undercooked but will firm up during standing time.

Cheeses melt quickly in the microwave oven, so care must be taken not to overcook or burn them. Hard or firm mature cheeses and processed cheeses are the best to use. Frozen soft ripened cheeses can be softened and brought to room temperature in the microwave oven before serving.

FREEZING

Shelled raw eggs freeze very successfully and can be stored for up to 6 months. If whole, beat gently to mix the yolk and white. Add a little salt to whole eggs and egg yolks for use in savory foods and sugar for use in sweet dishes (nothing needs to be added to whites). Thaw at room temperature. Cooked egg in dishes such as quiches, custard, and mousses can also be frozen.

Hard and firm cheeses freeze well, as do soft ripened cheeses such as Brie. Store them for 1 month. Thaw in the refrigerator before use. Note that the texture may change after freezing, making the cheeses suitable only for cooking. Soft fresh cheeses and blue-veined cheeses do not freeze well.

BAKING WITH EGGS

Eggs are used in a variety of dishes to set, thicken, aerate, or emulsify. For most preparations, eggs should be warmed to room temperature before using. This helps maximize the volume if the eggs are beaten, and it will discourage the eggs from curdling, which can occur as a result of any abrupt temperature changes.

BOILING

Put the eggs into a pan of boiling salted water (if you use eggs at room temperature, the shells are less likely to crack). Bring back to a boil, then simmer gently. Cooking times are calculated from the time the water comes back to a boil, and can vary according to individual taste and on the freshness of the eggs. For soft-boiled eggs, simmer gently for 3½–5 minutes. For hard-boiled eggs, allow 10–12 minutes, crack to allow steam to escape, then plunge the eggs into ice water and leave to cool. Peel and keep in a bowl of cold water or store, unpeeled, in the refrigerator.

Salmonella & listeria

There is a slight risk of salmonella poisoning from eggs. Listeria bacteria has been found in soft cheeses such as Brie and Camembert, in some blue-veined cheeses and in goat's and sheep's milk cheese. Pregnant women, young children, the elderly, and the immuno-compromised should avoid these cheeses and undercooked eggs, and no one should eat raw eggs.

SCRAMBLING

Scrambled eggs can be served plain, or made with herbs, cheese, ham, or smoked salmon. Allow 2 eggs per person.

1 Lightly beat the eggs with salt and pepper to taste and a little milk if you like. Melt a little butter in a pan. Add the eggs.

2 Cook over medium heat, stirring constantly with a wooden spatula or spoon until almost set – the eggs will continue to cook after they have been removed from the heat. Serve at once.

FRYING

Fresh eggs are essential for successful frying because they keep their shape during cooking. Fry fresh eggs in oil, drippings, or bacon fat, with a little butter added if you like.

1 Heat a thin layer of oil in a heavy skillet. When the oil is very hot and starting to sizzle, slip in an egg and cook over medium heat.

2 Spoon the oil over once or twice to give a white top. Remove and serve or turn over and cook for a few seconds to set the yolk a little more.

POACHING

The classic method for poaching eggs is in a pan of simmering water. Adding a small quantity of vinegar to the water prevents the egg white from breaking up.

1 Add 2 tbsp vinegar to a pan of boiling water. Lower the heat so that the water is simmering, and slide in an egg. Swirl the water around the egg to make a neat shape. Simmer for about 4 minutes until yolk is set.

2 Lift out the egg with a slotted spoon and drain briefly on paper towels. To keep poached eggs warm, or to reheat them if they have been prepared ahead of time, immerse them in a bowl of warm water.

MAKING AN OMELET

These are best made in a special omelet pan kept solely for the purpose. If you don't have one, use a small skillet, about 8 in (20 cm) in diameter.

Omelet know-how

Don't overbeat the eggs; beat them just enough to combine the yolks with the whites.

◆

Make sure the pan is hot and the butter foaming when you add the eggs.

◆

The omelet will continue to cook when you remove it from the heat, so the center should still be a little moist.

1 Beat *2–3 eggs* with *1 tbsp water, salt* and *pepper* to taste, and *chopped herbs, if you like.* Heat the pan, then add *a little butter.* When butter is foaming, pour in the eggs.

2 Cook over medium heat. As the eggs begin to set, lift and pull back the edge of the omelet, tilting the pan so that the liquid egg can run to the side of the pan.

3 Continue cooking until the omelet is just set and the underside is golden brown. Loosen the edge and flip over one half to fold it. Slide onto a plate and serve.

MAKING CREPES

These are easy and fun to make. The quantities given here will make enough batter for about 12 crêpes, using a 7- to 8-in (18- to 20-cm) pan. If you don't need 12 crêpes, use up all the batter and just freeze the crêpes that are not used. Don't worry if the first crêpe is a failure: it acts as a test for the consistency of the batter and the heat of the pan.

1 Sift *1 cup (125 g) all-purpose flour* into a bowl and make a well in the center. Beat together *1 egg, 1 egg yolk,* and *a little milk* taken from *1¼ cups (300 ml),* pour into the well, and beat.

2 Beat in half of the remaining milk, drawing in the flour, a little at a time, to make a smooth batter. Stir in the remaining milk. Cover and leave to stand for 30 minutes.

3 Heat the skillet and brush with *a little oil.* Ladle about 3 tbsp batter into the pan, tilting the pan so that the batter spreads out evenly over the base.

5 Cook the other side for about 30 seconds until golden. Slide the crêpe out of the pan. Heat and lightly grease the pan again before making the next crêpe. Serve the crêpes as they are made or stack them on a plate and reheat before serving.

4 Cook the crêpe over medium-high heat for 45–60 seconds, until small holes appear in the surface, the underside is lightly browned, and the edge has started to curl. Loosen the crêpe and turn it over to cook the other side by tossing or flipping it with a narrow spatula.

MEXICAN OMELET

An omelet is one of the most useful of all egg dishes, quick and easy to make and delicious either plain or with a filling. This recipe combines a classic French omelet with a piquant filling, but you can add whatever filling you like.

 Makes 2

6 eggs

2 tbsp water

2 tbsp butter

chopped parsley to garnish

FILLING

2 tbsp olive oil

1 onion, finely chopped

1 garlic clove, crushed

1 green pepper, cored, seeded, and finely chopped

2 ripe tomatoes, peeled (page 39), seeded, and finely chopped

1 1/2 cups (125 g) thinly sliced mushrooms

1/4 tsp Worcestershire sauce

few drops of Tabasco sauce

salt and black pepper

1 Make the filling: heat the oil in a skillet, add the onion and garlic, and cook for 5 minutes or until softened. Add the pepper and cook, stirring, for 5 minutes.

2 Add the tomatoes and mushrooms and cook, stirring, for 10 minutes. Add the Worcestershire and Tabasco sauces and salt and pepper to taste and simmer for 5 minutes. Keep warm.

3 Beat 3 of the eggs with 1 tbsp of the measured water. Heat an omelet pan or small skillet and add half of the butter.

4 When the butter is foaming, add the eggs and cook over medium heat, pulling back the edge as the eggs set and tilting the pan to allow the uncooked egg to run to the side of the pan. Continue until lightly set and golden.

5 Spoon half of the filling onto the half of the omelet farthest from the pan handle. With a narrow spatula, lift the uncovered half of the omelet and flip it over the filling.

6 Slide the omelet onto a warmed plate and garnish with chopped parsley. Make the second omelet in the same way, reheating the pan before adding the butter.

MUSHROOM OMELET

Substitute 2 1/2 cups (175 g) sliced mixed mushrooms for the filling. Cook in a little melted butter and season with salt and pepper to taste. Proceed as directed.

SMOKED CHICKEN OMELET

Substitute 1 scant cup (125 g) diced smoked chicken and 1 tbsp snipped fresh chives for the filling. Proceed as directed in the recipe.

TOMATO OMELET

Substitute 5 peeled (page 39), seeded, and chopped tomatoes for the filling. Cook the tomatoes in a little butter for 2–3 minutes. Season well and stir in a few snipped fresh chives. Proceed as directed.

SAVORY SOUFFLE OMELET

 Makes 2

4 eggs, separated

2 tbsp butter

FILLING

2 tbsp olive oil

1/2 onion, thinly sliced

1 garlic clove, crushed

1 zucchini, sliced

1 red pepper, cored, seeded, and sliced

8 oz (250 g) canned chopped tomatoes

1 tbsp chopped fresh thyme

salt and black pepper

1 Make the filling: heat the oil in a skillet, add the onion and garlic, and cook gently for 5 minutes or until softened. Add the zucchini and red pepper and cook for 2 minutes. Add the tomatoes, thyme, and salt and pepper to taste and simmer for 20 minutes.

2 Beat together the egg yolks and salt and pepper to taste. Beat the egg whites until stiff, then fold into the yolks.

3 Melt half of the butter in an omelet pan. When it foams, add half of the egg mixture and cook over gentle heat for 3 minutes. Add half of the filling, fold the omelet in half, and serve. Repeat with the remaining eggs and filling.

MUSHROOM OMELET WITH COUNTRY BREAD

 Serves 2

4 eggs

salt and black pepper

2 tbsp water

2 tbsp butter

3/4 cup (60 g) sliced shiitake mushrooms

1 tsp chopped fresh thyme

1 loaf of country bread, warmed and split lengthwise

1 Break the eggs into a small bowl, add salt and black pepper to taste, and beat in the measured water with a fork.

2 Melt half of the butter in a small skillet, add the mushrooms, and cook quickly, stirring, for 3–5 minutes, until tender. Add the thyme, and salt and pepper to taste. Keep the mushrooms warm while you make the omelet.

3 Heat an omelet pan or small skillet until very hot. Add the remaining butter and swirl the pan to coat the base and side evenly. When the butter is foaming, pour in the seasoned egg mixture.

4 Cook the omelet over medium heat, pulling back the edge as the eggs set and tilting the pan to allow the uncooked egg to run to the side of the pan. Continue until the omelet is lightly set and the underside is golden brown. Remove from the heat.

5 Put the mushrooms on the half of the omelet farthest from the pan handle and flip the uncovered half over the filling. Fill the warmed split bread with the omelet, cut the bread in half crosswise, and serve immediately.

SPINACH & MUSHROOM FRITTATA

 Serves 2

3 tbsp olive oil

2 thick slices of smoked bacon, diced

1/2 lb (250 g) cremini mushrooms, quartered

4 cups (125 g) spinach leaves, coarsely chopped

6 eggs

salt and black pepper

2 tbsp grated Parmesan cheese

1 Heat the oil in a large skillet. Add the bacon and mushrooms and cook over high heat, stirring constantly, for 7 minutes or until the bacon is crisp. Add the chopped spinach and turn in the oil for just 1–2 minutes. Do not allow the spinach to wilt. Lower the heat.

2 Break the eggs into a bowl, add salt and pepper to taste, and beat with a fork.

3 Pour the eggs over the mushroom and spinach mixture and cook over medium heat for about 10 minutes. As the eggs set, lift the frittata with a spatula and tilt the pan to allow the uncooked egg to run underneath.

4 When the eggs are set, sprinkle with grated Parmesan and place the pan under the broiler, 4 in (10 cm) from the heat, for 1–2 minutes until the top is golden brown and firm when pressed. Serve at once, cut in half.

Frittata

This is an Italian omelet. Unlike the classic French omelet, it is first cooked in a pan until set, then it is put under the broiler until firm. A frittata is always served flat rather than folded over.

ZUCCHINI FRITTATA

 Serves 4

2 tbsp olive oil

4 1/3 cups (625 g) thinly sliced zucchini

6 eggs

salt and black pepper

2 oz (60 g) prosciutto, diced

shredded fresh basil to garnish

1 Heat the olive oil in a large skillet. Add the zucchini and cook gently for 5 minutes or until just tender.

2 Break the eggs into a bowl, add salt and pepper to taste, and beat with a fork.

3 Add the prosciutto to the zucchini in the skillet, then pour over the eggs. Cook over medium heat for about 10 minutes. As the eggs set, lift the frittata with a spatula and tilt the pan to allow the uncooked egg to run underneath. Continue until almost set and the underside is golden brown.

4 Place the skillet under the broiler, 4 in (10 cm) from the heat, for 1–2 minutes, until the top is a light golden brown color and the egg is cooked through and quite firm when pressed.

5 Cut the zucchini frittata into wedges and lightly garnish with shredded fresh basil. Delicious served both hot or cold.

CORN & PEPPER FRITTATA

Substitute 1 red pepper, cut into strips, 7 oz (200 g) canned corn kernels, and 3 chopped scallions for the zucchini and prosciutto. Cook the pepper strips for 3 minutes, add the corn and scallions, and cook for 1 minute. Remove with a slotted spoon and proceed as directed.

POTATO OMELET

 Serves 4

3 tbsp olive oil

2 large potatoes, diced

2 large onions, chopped

6 eggs

salt and black pepper

1 tbsp chopped parsley

1 Heat the oil in a skillet, add the potatoes and onions, and stir until coated with the oil. Cook gently for about 10 minutes until golden brown. Pour the excess oil from the pan.

2 Break the eggs into a bowl, season with salt and pepper to taste, and beat with a fork.

3 Pour the eggs into the pan and mix with the vegetables. Cook for about 10 minutes, until the eggs are almost set, then brown the top of the omelet under the broiler for 1–2 minutes.

4 Slide the omelet onto a warmed plate and cut into quarters. Sprinkle with chopped parsley and serve warm or cold.

Tortilla

Omelets are a traditional part of the Spanish tapas – a selection of small, tasty dishes often served with sherry or other drinks. This substantial omelet, known in Spain as "tortilla," can be served warm or cold, but not chilled.

MIXED BEAN OMELET

Lightly cook 2/3 cup (60 g) thin green beans and 3/4 cup (125 g) shelled fava beans. Add to the pan after cooking the potatoes and onions and stir to coat in the oil. Add the eggs and proceed as directed.

QUICHE LORRAINE

A quiche is a flat, open tart filled with a savory egg custard. This most famous of all quiches is named after the area it comes from – Alsace Lorraine in northeastern France – where it was traditionally served on May Day, following a dish of roast suckling pig.

 Serves 4–6

2 tbsp butter

1 onion, chopped

6 thick slices of bacon, diced

1 cup (125 g) grated Gruyère cheese

1 cup (250 ml) light cream

2 eggs, beaten

salt and black pepper

SHORT CRUST PASTRY

1 cup (125 g) all-purpose flour

4 tbsp butter

about 1 tbsp cold water

✿ 8-in (20-cm) quiche dish or pan

✿ dried beans or pie weights

1 Make the pastry with the flour, butter, and water (see box, right). Cover with plastic wrap and chill for 30 minutes.

2 Roll out the pastry on a lightly floured work surface, and use to line the quiche dish or pan. Prick the bottom of the pastry shell with a fork.

3 Line the pastry shell with foil or waxed paper, and fill with dried beans or pie weights. Place the quiche dish on a heated baking sheet and bake the shell in a 425°F (220°C) oven for 15–20 minutes, removing the foil and dried beans for the final 10 minutes.

4 Meanwhile, make the filling: melt the butter in a skillet, add the onion and bacon, and cook gently, stirring occasionally, for 10 minutes or until the onion is golden brown and the bacon is crisp.

5 Spoon the onion and bacon into the shell and sprinkle with the cheese. Mix the cream and eggs in a large measuring cup, add salt and pepper to taste, and pour into the shell.

6 Reduce the oven temperature to 350°F (180°C) and bake the quiche for 25–30 minutes, until the filling is golden and set. Serve warm or cold.

Making short crust pastry

Sift the flour into a bowl. Add the butter and rub in lightly with your fingertips until the mixture looks like fine bread crumbs.

Add the water and mix with a round-bladed knife to form a soft but not sticky dough.

PANCETTA & SUN-DRIED TOMATO QUICHE

Make the short crust pastry shell and the filling as directed, using 1/4 lb (125 g) chopped pancetta instead of the bacon. Add 1 cup (60 g) drained and coarsely chopped sun-dried tomatoes in oil after cooking the pancetta and onion, and cook for 1 minute. Proceed as directed.

SMOKED SALMON & ASPARAGUS QUICHE

 Serves 6–8

1/4 lb (125 g) thin asparagus, cooked, drained, and cut into 1 1/2 in (3.5 cm) lengths

3 oz (90 g) smoked salmon, cut into strips

1 1/4 cups (300 g) plain yogurt

2 eggs

1 tbsp chopped fresh dill

black pepper

SHORT CRUST PASTRY

1 1/2 cups (175 g) all-purpose flour

6 tbsp (90 g) butter

about 2 tbsp cold water

✩ *9-in (23-cm) quiche dish or pan*

✩ *dried beans or pie weights*

1 Make the pastry: put the flour in a bowl, add the butter, and rub in. Add enough water to bind to a soft dough. Cover with plastic wrap and chill for 30 minutes.

2 Roll out the pastry and use to line the dish. Prick the pastry with a fork.

3 Line the pastry shell with foil or waxed paper and fill with dried beans or pie weights. Place the quiche dish on a heated baking sheet and bake in a 425°F (220°C) oven for 15–20 minutes, removing the foil and dried beans for the final 10 minutes.

4 Arrange the asparagus and half of the salmon in the pastry shell. Mix the yogurt, eggs, dill, and plenty of pepper and pour into the shell. Arrange the remaining salmon on top.

5 Reduce the oven temperature to 350°F (180°C) and bake for 35 minutes or until golden and set. Serve warm or cold.

ROQUEFORT QUICHE

 Serves 4–6

3/4 cup (90 g) crumbled Roquefort or other blue cheese

1 1/2 cups (175 g) low-fat cream cheese

2 eggs, beaten

2/3 cup (150 ml) light sour cream

1 tbsp snipped fresh chives

salt and black pepper

SHORT CRUST PASTRY

1 cup (125 g) all-purpose flour

4 tbsp butter

about 1 tbsp cold water

✩ *8-in (20-cm) quiche dish or pan*

✩ *dried beans or pie weights*

1 Make the pastry: put the flour in a bowl, add the butter and rub in with the fingertips. Add enough water to bind to a soft dough. Cover with plastic wrap and chill for 30 minutes.

2 Roll out the short crust pastry, and use to line the quiche dish. Prick the bottom of the pastry shell with a fork.

3 Line the pastry shell with foil or waxed paper and fill with dried beans or pie weights. Place the quiche dish on a heated baking sheet and bake in a 425°F (220°C) oven for 15–20 minutes, removing the foil and dried beans for the final 10 minutes.

4 Meanwhile, make the filling: mix the Roquefort and cream cheese in a bowl, then beat in the eggs, sour cream, chives, and salt and pepper to taste. Be careful not to add too much salt as blue cheese is already quite salty.

5 Pour the mixture into the pastry shell, reduce the oven temperature to 350°F (180°C), and bake the quiche for about 30 minutes until golden and set. Serve warm or cold.

SPINACH, LEEK, & GRUYERE TART

 Serves 4–6

2 tbsp butter

1 1/2 cups (175 g) trimmed and finely sliced leeks

8 cups (250 g) coarsely chopped spinach leaves

2 eggs, beaten

2/3 cup (150 ml) milk

2/3 cup (150 ml) heavy cream

3/4 cup (90 g) grated Gruyère cheese

salt and black pepper

SHORT CRUST PASTRY

1 1/2 cups (175 g) all-purpose flour

6 tbsp (90 g) butter

about 2 tbsp cold water

☆ 9-in (23-cm) quiche dish or pan

☆ dried beans or pie weights

1 Make the pastry: put the flour in a bowl, add the butter and rub in with the fingertips. Add enough water to bind to a soft dough. Cover with plastic wrap and chill for 30 minutes.

2 Roll out the pastry on a lightly floured surface, and line the dish. Prick the bottom of the pastry shell.

3 Line the pastry shell with foil or waxed paper and fill with dried beans or pie weights. Put the quiche dish on a heated baking sheet, and bake the shell in a 425°F (220°C) oven for 15–20 minutes, removing the foil and dried beans for the final 10 minutes.

4 Make the filling: melt the butter in a skillet, add the leeks and cook over a high heat for 5 minutes or until just beginning to turn golden brown. Add the spinach and cook for about 2 minutes, until it just begins to wilt. Arrange the filling in the shell.

5 Mix together the eggs, milk, cream, and Gruyère cheese, add salt and pepper to taste, and pour into the pastry shell.

6 Reduce the oven temperature to 350°F (180°C) and bake for 25 minutes or until the filling is golden and set. Serve warm or cold.

MEDITERRANEAN ZUCCHINI PIE

 Serves 4

1 lb (500 g) zucchini

1 cup (90 g) grated Parmesan cheese

3/4 cup (90 g) grated mozzarella or Fontina cheese

2 eggs, lightly beaten

2–3 tbsp store-bought pesto

2–3 garlic cloves, crushed

1 tsp dried mint

salt and black pepper

1/2 lb (250 g) puff pastry

beaten egg for glazing

☆ 9-in (23-cm) square baking dish or pan

Grating zucchini

Grate zucchini onto a plate, using the large holes of a grater and making firm, downward strokes.

1 Grate the zucchini (see box, right). Put them into a colander to drain for about 10 minutes. (If they seem bitter or very wet, toss them with a little salt and leave for 10 minutes longer, then rinse with cold water.) Squeeze dry, then blot with paper towels.

2 In a large bowl, combine the zucchini with the Parmesan and mozzarella cheeses, eggs, pesto, garlic, mint, and salt and pepper to taste. Spoon the mixture into the baking dish.

3 Roll out the pastry into a rough square, about 1 in (2.5 cm) larger than the dish and 1/8–1/4 in (3–5 mm) thick. Cover the dish with the pastry, trimming the edges. Cut slits in the top with a knife.

4 Using a pastry cutter, cut out shapes from the trimmings. Brush the top of the pie with beaten egg, arrange the pastry shapes on top, and glaze them with the beaten egg.

5 Bake the pie in a preheated oven at 400°F (200°C) for 15–20 minutes, until lightly browned on top and puffy.

ITALIAN CHEESE & RED PESTO TARTLETS

These tartlets, with their tangy Italian flavors, will serve 4 people as a light lunch or supper dish, accompanied by a crisp green salad. They also make a tasty appetizer to serve with predinner drinks. They taste just as good cold as hot, so they can be prepared well in advance.

 Makes 12

3-oz (90-g) jar store-bought red pesto or sun-dried tomato puree

1 large tomato, peeled (page 39), seeded, and chopped

9 black olives, pitted and quartered

1 cup (125 g) grated Fontina or mozzarella cheese

2–3 garlic cloves, crushed

2–3 tbsp grated Parmesan cheese

1 tsp dried oregano

SHORT CRUST PASTRY

1 1/2 cups (175 g) all-purpose flour

6 tbsp (90 g) butter

about 2 tbsp cold water

1 Make the pastry: put the flour in a bowl, add the butter and rub in with the fingertips. Add enough water to bind to a soft dough. Cover with plastic wrap and chill for 30 minutes.

2 Make the tartlet shells (see box, right).

3 Spread the red pesto in the tartlet shells, then fill the shells with the tomato, garlic, black olives, and Fontina cheese.

4 Sprinkle the grated Parmesan cheese over the tartlets, covering the pastry edges as well as the filling. Sprinkle the dried oregano on top.

5 Bake the tartlets in a 400°F (200°C) oven for 20–30 minutes, until the edges of the tartlets are golden brown in color and the Parmesan cheese topping has melted and become crispy.

6 Serve the tartlets warm or cold.

GOAT CHEESE TARTLETS

Substitute 3 oz (90 g) store-bought green pesto for the red pesto and 12 slices from a log of goat cheese for the grated Fontina. Proceed as directed.

Making tartlet shells

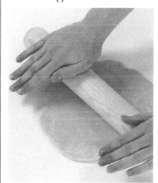

Sprinkle a work surface with flour, then roll out the short crust pastry to a 1/8–1/4 in (3–5 mm) thickness.

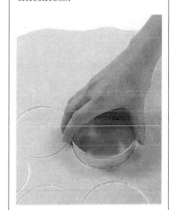

Cut out 12 rounds from the pastry, using a 4-in (10-cm) pastry cutter.

Fold up the edges of the rounds to form rims; put on a baking sheet.

STRATA WITH CHEESE & PESTO

 Serves 4

4–6 thick slices of stale bread

3-oz (90-g) jar store-bought green pesto

4 eggs, lightly beaten

1/2 cup (125 ml) light sour cream

1/2 cup (125 ml) milk

3 cups (375 g) grated Fontina, mozzarella, or aged Cheddar cheese

3 tbsp grated Parmesan cheese

1 Cut off and discard the crusts from the bread. Spread the slices with pesto, then arrange them in a single layer in a baking dish or roasting pan.

2 In a large bowl, combine the beaten eggs with the sour cream and milk, then pour the mixture over the bread. Sprinkle with the grated cheeses.

3 Bake the strata in a 400°F (200°C) oven for 35–40 minutes, until golden brown. The strata will puff up slightly as it bakes, but unlike a soufflé, it can be safely left to stand for about 5 minutes before serving.

Cook's know-how

This is an excellent way of using up stale bread. In fact, for this recipe, the staler the bread the better, although if it is very hard you will have to make the custard more liquid. If you do not have any leftover bread, dry slices of fresh bread in a low oven for 15 minutes or so.

BROCCOLI & RICOTTA TART

 Serves 4–6

1/2 lb (250 g) broccoli (about 1/3 bunch or 2 stalks)

salt and black pepper

11/2 cups (375 g) lightly mashed ricotta or cottage cheese

1 cup (125 g) grated aged Cheddar cheese

2/3 cup (60 g) grated Parmesan cheese

2 eggs, lightly beaten

2–3 garlic cloves, crushed

1 tsp chopped fresh thyme

5 tbsp (75 g) butter

3 cups (175 g) fresh bread crumbs

★ 9-in (23-cm) baking dish

1 Trim the broccoli and cut the stalks from the tops. Peel and dice the stalks and break the tops into small florets. Plunge the florets and stalks into a pan of boiling salted water for 1 minute. Drain, rinse under cold water, and drain again.

2 Put the ricotta cheese into a large bowl with the Cheddar and Parmesan, the eggs, garlic, thyme, and salt and pepper to taste. Mix until smooth, then add the broccoli stalks.

3 Melt the butter in a saucepan, remove it from the heat and stir in the bread crumbs.

4 Line the baking dish with about three-quarters of the buttered bread crumbs, pushing them up the side of the dish to form a loose crust. Spoon in the cheese mixture and then sprinkle with the remaining buttered bread crumbs. Arrange the broccoli florets on top.

5 Bake the tart in a 350°F (180°C) oven for about 40 minutes, until it is firm. Serve warm or cold.

SPINACH & RICOTTA TART

Substitute 1 packed cup (250 g) chopped cooked spinach for the broccoli or use a mixture of chopped cooked spinach and sautéed diced red pepper.

CREAMY SEAFOOD CREPES

A succulent filling of shrimp and whitefish in an herbed cream sauce makes these crêpes an excellent light lunch dish or dinner party first course. The unfilled crêpes can be made in advance and stored in the freezer for up to 1 month: leave them to cool after frying, layer them with waxed paper, and wrap in foil.

Serves 6

FILLING

1/2 lb (250 g) cod fillet, skinned
3/4 lb (375 g) shrimp, cooked
2 tbsp olive oil
1 small onion, finely chopped
1 garlic clove, crushed
4 tomatoes, peeled (page 39), seeded, and finely chopped
1 tbsp dill seeds, crushed
salt and black pepper
3 tbsp light cream
2 tbsp chopped fresh basil
basil sprigs and lemon coronets to garnish

CREPES

1 cup (125 g) all-purpose flour
1 egg, plus 1 egg yolk
1 1/4 cups (300 ml) milk
sunflower or corn oil for frying

1 Make the crêpe batter: sift the flour into a large bowl and make a well in the middle. Add the egg, extra egg yolk, and a little of the milk.

2 Gradually blend in the flour, beating until smooth. Add the remaining milk to give the batter the consistency of thin cream. Leave to stand for about 30 minutes.

3 Meanwhile, make the filling: cut the cod into 1/2-in (1-cm) pieces. Reserve 12 of the shrimp for garnish and peel the remainder.

4 Heat the oil in a medium saucepan, add the onion and garlic, and cook gently, stirring occasionally, for a few minutes, until soft but not browned.

5 Add the cod, tomatoes, dill seeds, and salt and pepper to taste. Cook over medium heat, stirring, for 10 minutes or until the mixture is thick and rich.

6 Stir in the cream and shrimp and heat gently. Remove from the heat and stir in the basil. Keep warm.

7 Heat a small skillet, and brush with a little oil. Ladle about 3 tbsp batter into the pan and cook for 1 minute, until the underside is golden. Turn and cook the second side. Keep warm. Repeat to make 12 crêpes.

8 Fill the crêpes with the seafood mixture and fold (see box, right). Garnish with the reserved shrimp, basil sprigs, and lemon coronets.

Filling and folding the crepes

Put a crêpe on a board or clean serving plate. Put 2–3 spoonfuls of the seafood filling on one half of the crêpe and spread it to within 1/4 in (5 mm) of the edge.

Fold the unfilled half of the crêpe over the seafood filling to enclose it.

Fold the crêpe in half again to form a triangle. Transfer to a serving plate and keep warm. Repeat with the remaining crêpes and filling.

BUFFET CREPES

With no more than a basic crêpe recipe, some simple fillings, and a little dexterity, you can create a stunning buffet display, whether you decide to make only one of these recipes or choose two or three. Each recipe makes enough for 6–8 guests when served as an appetizer with other small dishes.

BASIC CREPES

 Makes 16

2 cups (250 g) all-purpose flour

3 eggs, lightly beaten

1 cup (250 ml) milk

1 cup (250 ml) water

5 tbsp (75 ml) sunflower or corn oil, plus extra for frying

★ 8–9 in (20–23 cm) crêpe pan or small skillet

1 Sift the flour into a bowl and make a well in the middle. Add the eggs and a little of the milk and gradually blend in the flour. Whisk together the remaining milk, the measured water, and oil and stir into the flour mixture. Leave to stand for 30 minutes.

2 Heat the crêpe pan. Brush with a little oil and add 2–3 tbsp batter, tilting the pan to coat with batter. Cook for 1 minute, turn, and cook the second side until golden.

CHICKEN & DILL TRIANGLES

1 1/2 cups (175 g) finely diced cooked chicken

3 tbsp frozen baby peas, thawed

2 tbsp mayonnaise

1 tbsp chopped fresh dill

1 tsp Dijon mustard

3 scallions, thinly sliced

salt and black pepper

4 crêpes (see above), cooled

1 Combine the chicken, baby peas, mayonnaise, chopped fresh dill, mustard, scallions, and salt and pepper to taste.

2 Cut each crêpe into quarters. Place a little of the chicken mixture in the middle of each quarter. Fold 1 long edge of each quarter toward the middle and overlap with the other long edge to enclose the filling.

BLUE CHEESE CORNUCOPIA

4 crêpes (see left), cooled

1 cup (125 g) crumbled blue cheese

4 tbsp butter

fresh basil and walnut halves to garnish

1 Cut each crêpe into 8 pieces. Blend together the blue cheese and butter. Place a little blue cheese mixture in the middle of each piece of crêpe.

2 Fold the point up over the filling, then fold the 2 sides over. Tuck in a basil leaf and top with a walnut half.

MULTI-COLORED PINWHEELS

2/3 cup (125 g) frozen corn kernels, thawed

1/4 lb (125 g) garlic-and-herb soft cheese

3/4 cup (90 g) grated aged Cheddar cheese

1 scallion, chopped

1 garlic clove, crushed

1/4 tsp ground cumin

dash of Tabasco sauce

pinch of salt

4 crêpes (see left), cooled

3–4 tbsp chopped fresh cilantro

1 tomato, finely diced

1 Mix the corn with 1–2 tbsp of the soft cheese to bind together. Mix in the Cheddar cheese, scallion, garlic, cumin, Tabasco, and salt and stir to combine.

2 Spread a little soft cheese over each crêpe. Arrange a quarter of the corn mixture in a strip across the middle of the crêpe. To one side of this, arrange a strip of cilantro, then a strip of diced tomato, leaving a little space between strips.

3 Beginning at the side with the tomato, tightly roll each crêpe. Chill, then slice crosswise into rounds.

MUSHROOM TRIANGLES

6–8 mushrooms, finely chopped

1 cup (125 g) grated aged Cheddar cheese

2 tsp chopped fresh tarragon

salt and black pepper

4 crêpes (see left), cooled

1 Mix together the mushrooms, cheese, tarragon, and salt and pepper to taste. Cut each crêpe into quarters. Place a little of the filling in the middle of each quarter. Fold 1 long edge over the other and enclose the filling to form a triangle.

2 Heat a nonstick skillet, add the triangles, and cook on both sides.

BASIL CREPES WITH GOAT CHEESE

1 1/2 cups (175 g) all-purpose flour

3 eggs, lightly beaten

1/2 cup (125 ml) milk

1/2 cup (125 ml) water

3 tbsp olive oil, plus extra for frying

1 cup (30 g) fresh basil, finely chopped

5 oz (150 g) goat cheese, cut into 20 wedges

1 tbsp chopped parsley

1 tsp paprika

1 Make a crêpe batter (see left) with the flour, eggs, milk, measured water, oil, and basil.

2 Heat a skillet and brush with oil. Add 1 tbsp batter to form a crêpe about 3 in (7 cm) in diameter. Cook over low heat for 2 minutes on each side. Repeat with the remaining batter to make 20 crêpes.

3 Top each crêpe with a wedge of goat cheese, and sprinkle with parsley and paprika.

Clockwise from top; *Blue Cheese Cornucopia, Chicken & Dill Triangles, Mushroom Triangles, Multi-colored Pinwheels, Basil Crêpes with Goat Cheese.*

SOUFFLE CREPES WITH BROCCOLI & CHEESE

 Makes 8

8 crêpes (page 78)

butter for greasing

2 tbsp grated Parmesan cheese

FILLING

1 1/3 cups (125 g) tiny broccoli florets

salt and black pepper

3 tbsp butter

1/3 cup (45 g) all-purpose flour

1 1/4 cups (300 ml) milk

1/2 tsp Dijon mustard

1 cup (125 g) grated aged Cheddar cheese

4 eggs, separated

1 Make the filling: blanch the broccoli florets in boiling salted water for about 1 minute. Drain, rinse under cold running water and drain again.

2 Melt the butter in a small saucepan, add the flour, and cook, stirring occasionally, for about 1 minute.

3 Remove the pan from the heat and gradually blend in the milk. Bring to a boil, stirring until thickened. Remove from the heat and add the mustard, cheese, and salt and pepper to taste. Leave to cool slightly.

4 Beat the egg yolks into the sauce. In a large bowl, whisk the egg whites until soft peaks form, then fold into the cheese sauce with the broccoli florets.

5 Put the crêpes on 2 lightly buttered baking sheets. Divide the soufflé mixture among the crêpes, arranging it down the middle of each one. Fold the sides of each crêpe loosely over the top of the filling, and sprinkle with grated Parmesan cheese.

6 Bake in a 400°F (200°C) oven for 15–20 minutes, until the soufflé mixture has risen and the crêpes are crisp.

CHICKEN CREPES FLORENTINE

 Serves 4

1 lb (500 g) spinach leaves, coarsely chopped

2 tbsp butter

pinch of grated nutmeg

8 crêpes (page 78)

1 cup (125 g) grated Gruyère cheese

FILLING

4 tbsp butter

3/4 lb (375 g) cremini mushrooms, quartered

1/3 cup (45 g) all-purpose flour

1 1/4 cups (300 ml) chicken stock

2 2/3 cups (375 g) diced cooked chicken

1 tbsp chopped fresh thyme

salt and black pepper

1 Make the filling: melt the butter in a heavy pan, add the mushrooms, and cook, stirring occasionally, for 2–3 minutes.

2 Add the flour and cook, stirring, for 1 minute. Remove the pan from the heat and gradually blend in the stock. Bring to a boil, stirring, and simmer for 2–3 minutes. Add the chicken, thyme, and salt and pepper to taste.

3 Rinse the spinach and put into a saucepan with only the water that clings to the leaves. Cook for about 2 minutes until tender. Drain well, squeezing to extract any excess water, then stir in the butter and nutmeg. Spoon into a shallow ovenproof dish.

4 Divide the chicken and mushroom mixture among the 8 crêpes. Roll up the crêpes and place them in a single layer on top of the spinach.

5 Sprinkle with cheese and bake in a 375°F (190°C) oven for about 25 minutes, until golden. Serve hot.

Cook's know-how

Ready-made crêpes, available in packages at supermarkets and delicatessens, are a convenient alternative to homemade crêpes. They work particularly well in recipes such as this one, in which they are rolled around a filling and baked in the oven.

CLASSIC CHEESE SOUFFLE

 Serves 4

1 cup (250 ml) milk

1 bay leaf

1/2 onion, studded with several cloves

salt and black pepper

2 tbsp butter, plus extra for greasing

2 tbsp all-purpose flour

6 eggs, separated

2 tbsp Dijon mustard

3 cups (375 g) grated aged Cheddar cheese

☆ *6-cup (1.4-liter) soufflé dish*

1 Pour the milk into a small saucepan, add the bay leaf and clove-studded onion half, and bring to a boil. Remove from the heat, cover, and leave to steep for 20 minutes. Strain the milk and season to taste.

2 Melt the butter in a large pan, add the flour, and cook, stirring, for 1 minute. Remove the pan from the heat, gradually blend in the milk, then bring to a boil, stirring until thickened. Simmer for 2–3 minutes. Leave to cool for 10 minutes.

3 Beat the egg yolks in a bowl. Stir them into the cooled white sauce, then stir in the mustard and all but 1/4 cup (30 g) of the Cheddar.

4 Whisk the egg whites until they form stiff but not dry peaks. Stir 1–2 tbsp of the egg whites into the cheese mixture until evenly combined, then fold in the remaining egg whites.

5 Lightly butter the soufflé dish and then pour in the egg and cheese mixture. Sprinkle with the remaining cheese and bake in the top half of a 350°F (180°C) oven for 30 minutes. Serve the soufflé immediately.

CORN & CUMIN SOUFFLE

Substitute 2 cups (375 g) cooked fresh or frozen corn kernels, coarsely pureed, for the Cheddar cheese and add 2 tsp cumin seeds.

BROCCOLI SOUFFLES

 Serves 4

3 tbsp butter, plus extra for greasing

3 tbsp all-purpose flour

1 cup (250 ml) milk

pinch of grated nutmeg

salt and cayenne pepper

4 cups (375 g) broccoli florets

3–4 shallots, finely chopped

2 tbsp grated Parmesan cheese

4 egg yolks

1 1/2 cups (175 g) crumbled blue cheese

6 egg whites

☆ *4 1-cup (250-ml) soufflé dishes*

1 Melt 2 tbsp butter in a large pan, add the flour, and cook, stirring, for 1 minute. Remove from the heat, gradually blend in the milk, then bring to a boil, stirring, until thickened. Add the nutmeg and salt and cayenne pepper to taste. Leave to cool for 10 minutes.

2 Steam the broccoli for 2–3 minutes, until just tender. Rinse in cold water, then chop coarsely.

3 Heat the remaining butter in a pan, add the shallots, and cook gently for 3 minutes or until soft.

4 Prepare the soufflé dishes (see box, below).

5 Beat the egg yolks and add to the cooled sauce with the broccoli, shallots, and blue cheese.

6 Whisk the egg whites until they form stiff but not dry peaks. Stir 1–2 tbsp of the egg whites into the broccoli mixture, then fold in the remaining egg whites.

7 Pour the mixture into the soufflé dishes. Bake the soufflés in the top half of a 350°F (180°C) oven for 30 minutes. Serve the soufflés immediately.

Preparing the soufflé dishes

Butter the bottoms and sides of the soufflé dishes. Sprinkle with a thin layer of grated Parmesan cheese.

GARLIC & GOAT CHEESE SOUFFLES

 Serves 6

1 head of garlic

1 cup (250 ml) milk

1/2 cup (125 ml) water

2 tbsp butter, plus extra
for greasing

2 tbsp all-purpose flour

5 oz (150 g) goat cheese, diced

6 eggs, separated

salt and black pepper to taste

fresh chives to garnish

★ 6 2/3-cup (150-ml) soufflé
dishes

1 Separate and peel the
garlic cloves. Put the milk,
measured water, and all but
one of the garlic cloves into
a saucepan. Bring to a boil,
then simmer for 15–20
minutes, until the garlic is
tender and the liquid has
reduced to 1 cup (250 ml).
Leave to cool. Lightly mash
the garlic in the milk.

2 Melt the butter in a
saucepan, add the flour,
and cook, stirring, for
1 minute. Remove from the
heat and gradually blend
in the garlic milk.

3 Return to the heat and
bring to a boil, stirring
constantly, until the mixture
thickens. Simmer for
2–3 minutes. Transfer to a
large bowl and leave to cool
for 10 minutes. Chop the
remaining garlic clove.

4 Add the chopped garlic,
diced goat cheese, egg
yolks, and salt and pepper
to taste to the cooled sauce.

5 In a large bowl, whisk the
egg whites until stiff but
not dry. Stir 1 tbsp of the egg
whites into the garlic and
cheese mixture, then fold in
the remaining egg whites.

6 Lightly butter the
soufflé dishes, pour in
the soufflé mixture, and
bake in a 350°F (180°C)
oven for 15–20 minutes.
Serve immediately,
garnished with chives.

SWISS DOUBLE-CHEESE SOUFFLES

 Serves 6

3 tbsp butter, plus extra for
greasing

1/3 cup (45 g) all-purpose flour

1 1/4 cups (300 ml) milk

1/2 cup (60 g) grated Gruyère
cheese

2 tbsp snipped fresh chives

salt and black pepper

3 eggs, separated

2/3 cup (60 g) grated Parmesan
cheese

1 1/4 cups (300 ml) heavy cream

snipped fresh chives to garnish

1 Melt the butter in a large
saucepan, add the flour,
and cook, stirring, for
1 minute. Remove from the
heat and gradually blend in
the milk. Return to the heat
and bring to a boil, stirring
until the mixture thickens.

2 Remove the pan from
the heat and beat in the
Gruyère cheese and chives.
Add salt and pepper to taste
and stir in the egg yolks.

3 Whisk the egg whites
until stiff but not dry. Stir
1 tbsp into the mixture, then
fold in the rest.

4 Generously butter
6 small ramekins and
divide the mixture equally
among them. Place the
ramekins in a small roasting
pan, and pour boiling water
into the pan to come halfway
up the sides of the ramekins.

5 Bake the soufflés in a
425°F (220°C) oven for
15–20 minutes, until golden
and springy to the touch.
Leave the soufflés to stand
for 5–10 minutes; they will
shrink by about one-third.

6 Butter a large shallow
gratin dish. Sprinkle half
of the Parmesan cheese over
the bottom. Run a narrow
spatula around the edge of
each soufflé, unmold
carefully, and arrange on
top of the Parmesan in the
gratin dish.

7 Season the cream with
salt and pepper and
pour over the soufflés.
Sprinkle the remaining
Parmesan over the top and
return to the oven for
15–20 minutes, until golden.
Garnish with snipped chives.

RACLETTE

 Serves 4

2 lb (1 kg) new potatoes, halved

salt

1/2 lb (250 g) Swiss raclette cheese, cut into 16 thin slices

1 red onion, thinly sliced

12 cornichons

12 pickled cocktail onions

1 Cook the potatoes in boiling salted water for 12–15 minutes, until just tender. Drain and keep the potatoes warm.

2 Put 4 heavy ovenproof serving plates into a 475°F (240°C) oven to warm for 3–5 minutes.

3 Divide the potatoes among the plates and arrange 4 slices of raclette cheese on top of each serving. Return the plates to the oven for 1–2 minutes, until the cheese is melted and sizzling.

4 Divide the red onion slices, cornichons, and pickled onions among the plates and serve immediately.

Raclette

This is a Swiss specialty where raclette cheese is melted over potatoes and served with cornichons and onions. The name means "scraper," because raclette was traditionally eaten by holding half a cheese in front of an open fire and scraping off the cheese as it melted. Gruyère or Swiss can be used instead of raclette.

CHEESE FONDUE

 Serves 4–6

1 large loaf of crusty bread, crusts left on, cut into 1-in (2.5-cm) triangles

2 cups (250 g) coarsely grated Gruyère cheese

2 cups (250 g) coarsely grated Swiss cheese

1/4 cup (30 g) all-purpose flour

2 cups (500 ml) dry white wine

1 garlic clove, lightly crushed

2 tbsp kirsch (optional)

pinch of grated nutmeg

salt and black pepper

2 tart apples, quartered and sliced

1/4 cup (60 g) sesame seeds, lightly toasted

1/4 cup (30 g) cumin seeds, lightly toasted

☆ 1 fondue set

1 Place the pieces of bread on a large baking sheet and put into a 325°F (160°C) oven for 3–5 minutes, until dried out slightly.

2 Put the Gruyère and Swiss cheeses into a medium bowl and toss with the flour.

3 Put the wine and garlic into a fondue pot and boil for 2 minutes, then lower the heat so that the mixture is barely simmering. Add the cheese mixture, a spoonful at a time, stirring constantly with a fork and letting each spoonful melt before adding the next.

4 When the fondue is creamy and smooth, stir in the kirsch if using, nutmeg, and season to taste.

5 To serve, put the fondue pot onto a small burner and set the heat on low so that the mixture barely simmers. Arrange the bread, apple slices, and sesame and cumin seeds in dishes for your guests to dip into as desired.

CROQUE SENOR

 Serves 4

8 slices of white bread

4 slices (250 g) Cheddar cheese

4 slices of ham

2 tbsp butter, softened

lemon wedges and cilantro
   sprigs to serve

SPICY TOMATO SALSA

3 tomatoes, peeled (page 39),
   seeded, and finely chopped

1 red pepper, cored, seeded,
   roasted, and peeled (page
   354), finely chopped

1 garlic clove, crushed

2 scallions, thinly sliced

1 fresh green chili, cored,
   seeded, and chopped

1 tbsp red wine vinegar

salt

1 Make the salsa: combine
the tomatoes, red pepper,
garlic, scallions, chili, and
vinegar in a bowl. Add salt
to taste and set aside.

2 Put 4 slices of bread on
a board and arrange the
cheese slices, then the ham
slices, on top. Spoon the
salsa over the ham.

3 Lightly spread the butter
over one side of the
remaining slices of bread
and put them, butter side
up, on top of the salsa.

4 Heat a heavy skillet and
cook each sandwich,
butter side down, over
medium-high heat, until the
cheese begins to melt and
the bread becomes golden.
Lightly spread the second
side of each sandwich with
butter. Turn over and cook
the other side until golden.

5 Garnish with lemon
wedges, cilantro sprigs,
and any remaining spicy
tomato salsa. Serve at once.

Croque señor
*This is an unusual variation
of* croque monsieur, *the
classic French grilled cheese and
ham sandwich. The spicy tomato
salsa adds a tangy Mexican
flavor to the filling.*

SWISS CHEESE &
TOMATO RAREBIT

 Serves 4

3 garlic cloves

1 tbsp butter, plus extra for
   spreading

2 tbsp all-purpose flour

1 large ripe tomato, peeled
   (page 39), seeded, and chopped

1/2 cup (125 ml) dry white wine

3 cups (375 g) grated Gruyère
   cheese

1/4 lb (125 g) mushrooms,
   chopped

1 tbsp chopped fresh tarragon

salt and black pepper

4 slices of bread, crusts
   removed

chopped parsley to garnish

1 Crush 2 of the garlic
cloves. Melt the butter in
a saucepan, add the crushed
garlic, and cook gently,
   stirring, for 1–2 minutes.
   Add the flour and cook,
stirring, for 1 minute. Add
the chopped tomato and
cook for 2 minutes.

2 Pour in the wine and
cook, stirring, for
5 minutes or until the
mixture thickens. Add the
Gruyère cheese, a little at a
time, and stir until it has
melted. Add the chopped
mushrooms, tarragon, and
salt and pepper to taste and
cook for 3 minutes or until
the mushrooms are tender.

3 Cut the remaining garlic
clove in half. Toast the
bread on both sides under
the broiler. Rub one side of
the toast with the cut garlic.

4 Spread the garlic side of
the toast with butter,
place on warmed plates, and
top with the cheese mixture.
Serve at once, sprinkled with
chopped parsley.

EGGS BENEDICT

Serves 4

8 slices of lean Canadian bacon

2 English muffins, halved

2 tbsp vinegar

4 eggs

butter for spreading

flat-leaf parsley to garnish

HOLLANDAISE SAUCE

2 tsp lemon juice

2 tsp white vinegar

3 egg yolks, at room temperature

8 tbsp (125 g) unsalted butter, melted

salt and black pepper

1 Cook the bacon under the broiler, 3 in (7 cm) from the heat, for 5–7 minutes, until crisp. Keep the bacon warm.

2 Toast the cut sides of the muffin halves under the broiler. Keep the muffin halves warm.

3 Make the hollandaise sauce: put the lemon juice and white vinegar into a small bowl, add the egg yolks, and whisk with a balloon whisk until light and frothy.

4 Place the bowl over a pan of simmering water and whisk until the mixture thickens. Gradually add the melted butter, whisking constantly until thick. Season. Keep warm.

5 Poach the eggs: add the vinegar to a large pan of boiling water. Lower the heat so that the water is simmering and slide in the eggs. Swirl the water around the eggs to make neat shapes. Simmer for about 4 minutes. Lift out with a slotted spoon.

6 Butter the muffins and put onto warmed plates. Put 2 bacon slices and an egg on each one, and top with the sauce. Serve immediately, garnished with parsley.

SPICY LIME HOLLANDAISE

Substitute 2 tsp lime juice for the lemon juice in the hollandaise sauce and add 1/2 tsp each of paprika and mild chili powder.

EGGS FLORENTINE

Serves 4

8 cups (250 g) spinach leaves

3 scallions, thinly sliced

2 tbsp heavy cream

4 eggs

2 tbsp vinegar

3 tbsp grated Parmesan cheese

CHEESE SAUCE

2 tbsp butter

1 tbsp all-purpose flour

1 cup (250 ml) milk

1 1/2 cups (175 g) grated aged Cheddar cheese

pinch each of cayenne pepper and grated nutmeg

salt and black pepper

1 Rinse the spinach and put into a saucepan with only the water that clings to the leaves. Cook for about 2 minutes until tender. Drain and set aside.

2 Make the cheese sauce: melt the butter in a saucepan, add the flour and cook, stirring, for 1 minute. Remove from the heat and gradually blend in the milk. Bring to a boil, stirring constantly until the mixture thickens. Simmer for 2–3 minutes.

3 Stir in the Cheddar cheese, cayenne pepper, nutmeg, and salt and pepper to taste. Keep warm.

4 In a bowl, combine the spinach with the scallions, cream, and salt and pepper to taste. Set aside.

5 Poach the eggs: add the vinegar to a large pan of boiling water. Lower the heat so that the water is simmering and slide in the eggs, one at a time. Swirl the water around the eggs to make neat shapes. Lift out with a slotted spoon.

6 Divide the spinach and spring onion mixture among 4 warmed flameproof dishes. Arrange the poached eggs on the spinach and spoon the cheese sauce over the eggs.

7 Sprinkle the grated Parmesan cheese over the sauce, then place the dishes under the broiler, 3 in (7 cm) from the heat, until the cheese has melted and is lightly browned and the whole dish is heated through. Serve hot.

OEUFS EN COCOTTE

 Serves 4

1 tbsp butter

4 eggs

salt and black pepper

4 tbsp heavy cream

1 tbsp chopped parsley

★ 4 small ramekins

1 Melt the butter and pour a little into each ramekin.

2 Break each egg into a saucer, then slide into a prepared ramekin. Add salt and pepper to taste and top each egg with 1 tbsp cream.

3 Place the ramekins in a roasting pan and pour in boiling water to come halfway up the sides of the ramekins. Cover with foil.

4 Bake in a 400°F (200°C) oven for 10 minutes or until the whites are opaque and firm but the yolks still soft. Alternatively, put the ramekins into a large skillet, add boiling water to come halfway up the sides, cover, and cook over medium heat for 10 minutes, letting the water boil and gently steam the eggs.

5 Sprinkle a little parsley over each baked egg 1–2 minutes before the end of cooking time.

FETA CHEESE COCOTTES

After pouring the butter into the ramekins, divide 1/4 lb (125 g) diced feta cheese, marinated in chopped fresh herbs and diced fresh red chili, among the ramekins. Proceed as directed, substituting 2–3 thinly sliced scallions for the parsley.

HUEVOS RANCHEROS

 Serves 4

2 tbsp sunflower or corn oil

1 onion, finely chopped

3 garlic cloves, crushed

1 green pepper, cored, seeded, and chopped

1–2 fresh green chilies, cored, seeded, and chopped

2 large tomatoes, peeled (page 39), seeded, and diced

1 tsp ground cumin

1/4 tsp sugar

salt

2 tbsp vinegar

4 eggs

cilantro sprigs to garnish

1 Heat the oil in a skillet, add the onion, garlic, green pepper, and chilies, and cook gently, stirring occasionally, for about 5 minutes until the onion is soft.

2 Add the tomatoes, cumin, sugar, and salt to taste and simmer, stirring occasionally, for 10 minutes or until the mixture is thick.

3 Meanwhile, poach the eggs: add the vinegar to a large pan of boiling water. Lower the heat so that the water is simmering and slide in the eggs, one at a time. Swirl the water around the eggs to make neat shapes. Simmer for 4 minutes. Lift out with a slotted spoon.

4 Taste the tomato sauce for seasoning, and ladle onto serving plates. Top each of the servings with a poached egg and garnish with a cilantro sprig.

HUEVOS RANCHEROS WITH CHEESE

Fry the eggs instead of poaching them. Transfer the eggs to serving plates, top with the sauce, and sprinkle with 1/2 cup (60 g) grated aged Cheddar cheese. Serve immediately.

4

FISH & SHELLFISH

UNDER 30 MINUTES

THAI SHRIMP STIR-FRY

Spicy Asian dish: shrimp, red pepper, ginger, chili, and lemongrass, stir-fried with rice noodles, soy sauce, and lime juice.

SERVES 4 522 calories per serving
Takes 15 minutes **PAGE 109**

SCALLOPS WITH ASPARAGUS & LEMON

Fresh and aromatic: scallops cooked with asparagus and garlic with a parsley, lemon, and tarragon sauce.

SERVES 4 342 calories per serving
Takes 20 minutes **PAGE 112**

DEVILED CRAB

Crabmeat in a sauce flavored with nutmeg, sherry, scallion, and Tabasco sauce. Topped with bread crumbs and baked.

SERVES 4 502 calories per serving
Takes 25 minutes **PAGE 110**

SHRIMP WITH TARRAGON SAUCE

Shrimp simmered with wine, garlic, and parsley, served with a tarragon sauce spiked with mustard.

SERVES 4 252 calories per serving
Takes 20 minutes **PAGE 108**

HERRING WITH AN OAT CRUST

Crispy and wholesome: herring coated in oatmeal and mustard, then broiled. Served with deep-fried parsley.

SERVES 4 461 calories per serving
Takes 15 minutes **PAGE 117**

OYSTER STEW WITH SAFFRON

An unusual Mediterranean-style dish: fresh oysters simmered with Pernod, light cream, white wine, fish stock, leek, carrot, watercress,

saffron, and lemon juice. Lightly seasoned with cayenne pepper and garnished with fresh chervil.

SERVES 4 251 calories per serving
Takes 25 minutes **PAGE 115**

WATERCRESS SALMON

Baked salmon flavored with pepper, in a pool of sauce made from cream, watercress, lemon juice, butter, and egg yolk.

SERVES 6 414 calories per serving

Takes 25 minutes   PAGE 122

LOW FAT

BROILED TROUT WITH CUCUMBER & DILL

Trout with a stuffing of lightly cooked cucumber, dill, and lemon juice.

SERVES 4 435 calories per serving

Takes 25 minutes   PAGE 118

HIGH PROTEIN

SCALLOPS WITH SPICY CASHEW SAUCE

Scallops stir-fried with mustard seeds and garlic, served in a cashew and chili sauce.

SERVES 4 414 calories per serving

Takes 25 minutes   PAGE 112

DINNER PARTY

CHINESE-STYLE OYSTERS

Oysters wrapped in bacon and stir-fried with green pepper, garlic, and water chestnuts, then sprinkled with scallion slices.

SERVES 4 248 calories per serving

Takes 25 minutes   PAGE 115

LOW CALORIE

SALMON WITH SPINACH

Broiled salmon served with a salsa of lightly cooked scallions mixed with spinach, lemon juice, and mustard.

SERVES 4 454 calories per serving

Takes 25 minutes   PAGE 122

FAMILY FARE

BEST-EVER FRIED FISH

Crispy and nourishing: whitefish fillets coated in flour, beaten egg, and fresh bread crumbs. Cooked until golden and served with lemon.

SERVES 4 298 calories per serving

Takes 25 minutes   PAGE 128

HERRING WITH MUSTARD SAUCE

Baked herring served with a classic sauce made from dry mustard, sugar, and white vinegar.

SERVES 4 479 calories per serving

Takes 25 minutes   PAGE 117

FILLETS OF SOLE MEUNIERE

Fresh and summery: lemon sole fillets lightly floured and cooked in butter, then served with parsley and lemon-flavored butter.

SERVES 4 274 calories per serving

Takes 20 minutes   PAGE 126

SHRIMP TACOS

Crispy and hot: taco shells with a spicy filling of shrimp, cilantro, tomatoes, onion, garlic, green pepper, and paprika.

SERVES 4 414 calories per serving

Takes 25 minutes   PAGE 108

CAJUN-SPICED RED SNAPPER

Red snapper fillets marinated in a piquant mixture of garlic, paprika, cumin, and chili powder. Topped with cilantro butter.

SERVES 4 258 calories per serving

Takes 15 minutes, plus marinating **PAGE 132**

HOT & SOUR MACKEREL

Red pepper, fresh chili, carrots, and scallions stir-fried, then broiled with mackerel fillets. Served with a hot and sour sauce.

SERVES 4 539 calories per serving

Takes 35 minutes **PAGE 116**

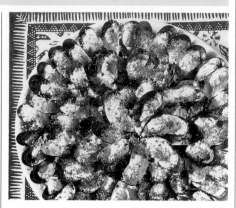

MUSSEL GRATIN

Mussels simmered with wine, shallot, and garlic, topped with cream and parsley sauce and bread crumbs, then broiled.

SERVES 4 448 calories per serving

Takes 35 minutes **PAGE 113**

FAMILY CHOICE

GOLDEN FISH CAKES

Cod or haddock simmered in milk flavored with bay leaf and peppercorns. Mixed with potato and coated in fresh bread crumbs.

SERVES 4 613 calories per serving

Takes 50 minutes **PAGE 136**

LOBSTER WITH BLACK BEAN SALSA

Lobster tails spread with garlic, and oregano-flavored butter and broiled. Served with black bean salsa.

SERVES 4 531 calories per serving

Takes 35 minutes **PAGE 111**

CHEESE-TOPPED PORGY

Bream fillets baked with finely grated lemon zest and juice. Covered in a white sauce and sprinkled with Cheddar cheese, then broiled.

SERVES 4 401 calories per serving

Takes 40 minutes **PAGE 133**

MACKEREL WITH GREEN GRAPES

Broiled mackerel served with a tangy sauce made from green grapes simmered with water and sugar and mixed with butter and ginger.

SERVES 4 489 calories per serving

Takes 35 minutes **PAGE 116**

SALMON WITH AVOCADO

Succulent salmon steaks baked with tarragon and served with a rich sauce of avocado, yogurt, and lime zest and juice.

SERVES 4 543 calories per serving

Takes 35 minutes **PAGE 123**

MUSHROOM-STUFFED SOLE FILLETS

Sole fillets rolled and stuffed with onion and mushrooms. Baked with tarragon and wine, which form the base for a cream sauce.

SERVES 4 568 calories per serving

Takes 35 minutes **PAGE 126**

CLAMS IN SALSA VERDE

Clams cooked in a delicious sauce made of fish stock, olive oil, sherry, garlic, onion, and chopped parsley.

SERVES 4 291 calories per serving

Takes 40 minutes   **PAGE 114**

SPICED FISH WITH COCONUT

Sweet and spicy: monkfish pieces lightly coated in flour, cooked with coconut milk, onion, cilantro, cumin, and turmeric.

SERVES 4 389 calories per serving

Takes 45 minutes   **PAGE 131**

SPICY CLAMS WITH CILANTRO PESTO

Clams cooked with tomatoes and stock, richly flavored with garlic, paprika, chili powder, and cumin. Served with cilantro pesto.

SERVES 4–6 349–233 calories per serving

Takes 45 minutes   **PAGE 114**

CITRUS MONKFISH

Light and tangy: monkfish fillets cooked with tangerines, ginger, scallions, and stock, served with a sauce spiked with lime.

SERVES 4 221 calories per serving

Takes 40 minutes   **PAGE 130**

DINNER PARTY

COD STEAKS WITH ANCHOVY & FENNEL

Cod steaks baked with a topping of anchovies, fennel, parsley, and bread crumbs.

SERVES 4 429 calories per serving

Takes 40 minutes   **PAGE 132**

SEA BASS WITH LEMON BUTTER SAUCE

Fresh and aromatic: sea bass baked in foil with tarragon, lemon, and wine. Served with a warm and creamy lemon sauce.

SERVES 4 363 calories per serving

Takes 40 minutes   **PAGE 135**

LOW FAT

FISH EN PAPILLOTE

An aromatic Asian dish: whitefish fillets sprinkled with ginger, scallion, soy sauce, and rice wine, baked in a package.

SERVES 4 312 calories per serving

Takes 35 minutes   **PAGE 135**

PORGY NIÇOISE

Baked black bream on a bed of fennel, onion, and garlic, sprinkled with lemon juice, olives, and chopped parsley.

SERVES 4 356 calories per serving

Takes 50 minutes   **PAGE 133**

CRISPY-TOPPED SEAFOOD PIE

Cod poached in milk, then baked with shrimp, leeks, and broccoli. Topped with white sauce, Gruyère, and crispy pastry.

SERVES 4 575 calories per serving

Takes 55 minutes   **PAGE 136**

30–60 MINUTES

 OVER 60 MINUTES

GINGERED WHITEFISH

Light and tangy: whitefish fillets marinated in sunflower and sesame oils, fresh ginger, garlic, sherry, and vinegar, then broiled.

SERVES 4 247 calories per serving

Takes 15 minutes, plus marinating   **PAGE 127**

LOBSTER TAILS WITH MANGO & LIME

Lobster tail meat coated in a sauce of wine, cream, mango, and grated lime zest and juice. Sprinkled with Parmesan cheese and baked.

SERVES 4 442 calories per serving

Takes 40 minutes   **PAGE 110**

SEAFOOD & AVOCADO SALAD

Poached monkfish with crabmeat and shrimp on a bed of salad greens, avocado, and tomatoes, dressed with sour cream.

SERVES 4 396 calories per serving

Takes 35 minutes, plus cooling   **PAGE 111**

STUFFED SQUID

Baked squid sacs filled with bread crumbs, onion, garlic, tomato juice, chopped squid, olives, parsley, rosemary, egg, and vinegar.

SERVES 4 410 calories per serving

Takes 40 minutes   **PAGE 109**

ROAST MONKFISH NIÇOISE

Richly flavored monkfish cooked with roasted garlic, lemon, wine, artichoke hearts, herbs, olives, and sun-dried tomatoes.

SERVES 4 448 calories per serving

Takes 50 minutes   **PAGE 130**

LEMON SOLE FLORENTINE

Lemon sole fillets baked on a bed of white sauce and spinach and topped with Parmesan. Served with hot lemon bread.

SERVES 4 422 calories per serving

Takes 1 hour 5 minutes   **PAGE 127**

MUSSELS WITH POTATOES & SAUSAGE

Mussels cooked with potatoes, spicy Spanish chorizo sausage, garlic, stock, sherry, and cumin seeds.

SERVES 4 784 calories per serving

Takes 40 minutes   **PAGE 113**

HADDOCK WITH MUSHROOMS & CREAM

Baked haddock topped with mushrooms, a creamy sauce, bread crumbs, and Parmesan.

SERVES 4–6 429–286 calories per serving

Takes 55 minutes   **PAGE 129**

HALIBUT IN PHYLLO PACKAGES

Delicate and moist: leek and carrot strips cooked with wine, stock, and saffron form a bed for halibut wrapped in phyllo pastry.

SERVES 4 564 calories per serving

Takes 1 hour 5 minutes   **PAGE 134**

OVER 60 MINUTES

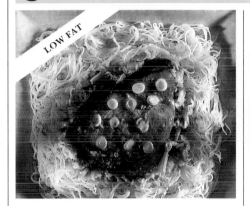

TUNA TERIYAKI

Light and simple: tuna steaks marinated in garlic, ginger, soy sauce, and sesame oil. Broiled and sprinkled with scallion.

SERVES 4 339 calories per serving

Takes 15 minutes, plus marinating **PAGE 119**

TUNA WITH FENNEL & TOMATO RELISH

Tuna marinated in oil, lemon juice, garlic, and herbs, broiled and topped with relish.

SERVES 4 467 calories per serving

Takes 25 minutes, plus marinating **PAGE 119**

MONKFISH KEBABS

Pieces of monkfish marinated in oil, lemon zest and juice, and dill, threaded with lightly cooked cucumber, lemon, and bay leaves.

SERVES 4 286 calories per serving

Takes 30 minutes, plus marinating **PAGE 131**

COULIBIAC

Russian classic: salmon, rice, onion, tomatoes, parsley, and lemon, all in a puff-pastry crust.

SERVES 8–10 518–414 calories per serving

Takes 1¼ hours **PAGE 121**

INDIAN SPICED HADDOCK

Pieces of haddock marinated in a mixture of coriander, cayenne, and turmeric. Simmered with ginger, chili, and potato.

SERVES 4 365 calories per serving

Takes 40 minutes, plus marinating **PAGE 129**

SALMON EN CROUTE

Salmon fillets marinated in dill and lemon zest and juice, baked in puff pastry with spinach, scallions, and soft cheese.

SERVES 6 993 calories per serving

Takes 1½ hours, plus marinating **PAGE 123**

SWORDFISH WITH ORANGE RELISH

Swordfish steaks marinated in orange and lemon juices, olive oil, and garlic. Broiled, then served with orange relish.

SERVES 4 429 calories per serving

Takes 20 minutes, plus marinating **PAGE 120**

SHARK WITH TROPICAL SALSA

Shark steaks marinated in cumin, garlic, lemon juice, and cilantro. Served with a salsa of pineapple, papaya, and chili.

SERVES 4 534 calories per serving

Takes 25 minutes, plus marinating **PAGE 120**

BAKED TROUT WITH ORANGE

Fresh and hearty dish: trout stuffed with mushrooms, shallots, orange zest and juice, white vinegar, thyme, and parsley.

SERVES 4 378 calories per serving

Takes 45 minutes, plus chilling **PAGE 118**

FISH & SHELLFISH KNOW-HOW

Seafood is one of the most delicious, versatile, and nutritious foods we can eat. Compared with other protein foods it is an excellent value – usually there is very little waste – and it is easy to prepare and quick to cook. Fish and shellfish are good sources of essential nutrients, but oily fish are particularly rich in vitamins A and D and should be a regular part of a healthy diet.

Seafood is divided into two broad categories: fish and shellfish. Fish can be subdivided into "round whitefish," such as cod or snapper; "flat whitefish," like flounder and turbot; and "oily fish," which includes herring and mackerel. All of these are vertebrates with fins and gills. Among shellfish, crab, shrimp, and mussels have shells on the outside, while squid have reduced internal shells.

BUYING & STORING

When choosing fish and shellfish, smell and appearance are your guides. Fresh saltwater fish should smell like the sea. If the fish smells at all unpleasant or ammonialike, it is not fresh. Whole fresh fish should have clean red gills, shiny scales, and should feel firm and elastic. The flesh of fillets and steaks should look moist and lustrous. If buying prepackaged fish, check the color of any liquid that has accumulated in the pack: it should not be cloudy or off-white.

Shellfish is sold both in the shell and shelled, raw and cooked. The shells of crabs, lobsters, and shrimp become pink or red when cooked. Live shellfish, such as mussels, clams, and oysters should have tightly closed shells. Open shells should close if tapped lightly; if they do not, the shellfish is dead and should be discarded. Shelled oysters, scallops, and clams should be plump; scallops should smell slightly sweet. Shrimp should also smell faintly sweet and feel firm.

Keep the fish or shellfish cool until you get home, then unwrap it, cover with a wet cloth or wet paper towels, and store in the coldest part of the refrigerator. Use the same day or within 1 day at the most.

FISH STOCK

Ask at the fish store for heads, bones, and trimmings from lean whitefish (oily fish make a bitter-tasting stock).

1 Rinse *1¹/₂ lb (750 g) trimmings* and put them into a large pan. Add *1 quart (1 liter) water* and *1 cup (250 ml) dry white wine*. Bring to a boil, skimming the surface.

2 Add *1 sliced onion, 1 sliced carrot, 1 chopped celery stalk, 1 bay leaf, a few parsley sprigs,* and *a few black peppercorns*. Simmer for 20–25 minutes. Strain. Use immediately or cool, cover, and refrigerate. Use within 2 days or freeze for up to 3 months.

MICROWAVING

Fish and shellfish cook well in a microwave, retaining their texture, flavor, and juices. But care must be taken not to overcook the delicate flesh. Whether cooking or thawing, arrange pieces of fish so that the thicker areas are at the outside of the dish; overlap thin areas or fold them under. With whole fish, shield delicate areas, such as the tail and head, with smooth strips of foil. If thawing seafood, again protect thin, delicate areas by shielding them with smooth strips of foil.

FREEZING

It's best to buy fish already frozen, since it is frozen very soon after catching – often while still at sea – and won't have begun to deteriorate. Some fresh seafood, particularly shrimp, may already have been frozen, then thawed, so it should not be refrozen.

Clean fish before freezing, wrap tightly, and, for the best flavor, store for no longer than 2 months. Fish can be cooked very successfully from frozen but if you need to thaw it, do so slowly in the refrigerator or quickly in the microwave.

SCALING

Unless the fish is to be skinned, remove the scales before cooking. Dip your fingers in salt to ensure a firm grip and grasp the fish tail. Using the blunt side of a knife, with firm strokes scrape off the scales from the tail to the head. Rinse the fish well under cold running water.

CLEANING & FILLETING ROUND FISH

Fish stores will clean and fillet fish for you, but if you have to do it yourself, here's how. Round fish such as trout, mackerel, herring, or even salmon, are often cooked whole, and boning makes them easier to serve and eat.

1 Snip off the fins. Cut along the belly, from the vent end to just below the head. Remove the innards, scraping away any dark blood. Lift the gill covering and remove the accordion-shaped gills. Rinse well.

2 Extend the belly opening so that it goes all the way to the tail. Hold the belly open and carefully run the knife between the flesh and the bones along one side, from tail to head, to cut the flesh from the rib cage.

3 Turn the fish around and cut the flesh from the rib cage on the other side. Snip through the backbone at each end and gently pull it away from the flesh, removing it with the rib cage in one piece.

4 If the head and tail have been cut off, open out the fish and lay it skin side up. Press along the backbone to loosen the bones. Turn over and lift out the rib cage and backbone, freeing it with a knife if necessary.

SKINNING A FLATFISH

A flatfish may be skinned before filleting.

1 With the dark side up, make a shallow cut between the tail and the body. Gently cut a little of the skin from the flesh.

2 Holding the tail with one hand, grip the skin with salted fingers and pull it away. Repeat on the other side.

FILLETING FLATFISH

Either 2 or 4 fillets may be cut from a small flatfish, depending on whether you would like 2 wide or 4 narrow fillets. Larger flatfish yield 4 fillets.

1 Make a shallow cut around the edge of the fish, where the fin bones meet the body. Cut across the tail and make a curved cut around the head. Cut along the center of the fish, cutting through to the bone.

2 Insert the knife between the flesh and the bones at the head end, keeping it almost parallel to the fish. Cut, close to the bones, to remove the flesh.

3 Continue cutting, to detach the flesh in one piece. Repeat to remove the second fillet. Turn the fish over and remove the fillets on the other side in the same way. Check the flesh for any stray bones.

4 To skin, lay each fillet skin side down, hold the tail with salted fingers to ensure a firm grip, and pull away. Cut through the flesh at the tail end, then hold the knife at an angle and cut the flesh from the skin.

PREPARING SHRIMP

Both cooked and uncooked shrimp can be used successfully in a variety of tasty dishes. One lb (500 g) of shrimp with shells but no heads will give you about ³/4 lb (375 g) peeled and cooked shrimp.

1 Gently pull off the head and then the legs. Peel the shell from the body, starting at the head end. When you reach the tail, pull it out of the shell.

2 Make a shallow cut along the center of the back of the shrimp. Lift out the black intestinal vein and rinse the shrimp under cold running water.

PREPARING MUSSELS & CLAMS

Most mussels and clams are sold live and are cooked by steaming in their shells. They must be scrubbed before cooking. The anchoring threads found on mussels, known as beards, must also be removed.

1 To clean the shells of mussels and clams, hold under cold running water and scrub with a small stiff brush. Use a small knife to scrape off any barnacles.

2 To remove the beard from a mussel, hold the beard firmly between your thumb and the blade of a small knife and pull the beard away from the shell.

PREPARING A COOKED CRAB

The lump crabmeat from inside the crab's body is highly prized, but the meat from the legs and claws is also flavorful.

1 Put the crab on its back and twist off the legs and claws, close to the body.

2 Using nutcrackers, a small hammer, or a rolling pin, crack the shells of the claws without crushing them. Break open the shells and carefully remove the meat, using a small fork or skewer.

3 Press your thumbs along the "perforation" to crack the central section of the shell and pry it apart. Remove and discard the "apron" flap from the underside of the body.

4 Pull the central body section up and away from the shell. Scoop the creamy-textured brown meat out of the shell and put it into a bowl (keeping it entirely separate from the white claw and leg meat). Scoop out any roe. Discard the stomach sac, which is located between the eyes.

5 Pull the spongy gills (known as "dead man's fingers") from the body and discard them.

6 Cut the body in half with a large knife and pick out all the meat from the crevices. Add to the meat in the bowl.

PREPARING A COOKED LOBSTER

Cooked lobster can be added to cooked dishes or served cold with mayonnaise, in which case the shell is simply cut into 2 halves and the flesh loosened and returned to the shell.

Removing the meat

1 Twist off the large claws. Using a strong nutcracker, small hammer, or rolling pin, crack the shells of the claws without crushing them. Pick out the meat in 1 or 2 large pieces. If the shell is not to be used for serving, pull apart the body and tail. Twist off the small legs and remove the meat with a skewer or lobster pick.

2 Lift off the top of the body shell, scoop out the gray-green liver (tomalley) and any coral-colored roe, both of which are edible, and reserve. Discard the stomach and spongy gills ("dead man's fingers").

To serve in the shell

1 Use a knife to cut the lobster in half lengthwise, cutting from the head to the tail. Keep the shell for serving.

4 Bend back the flaps and carefully remove the tail meat, keeping it in 1 piece. Remove and discard the intestine that runs through the center of the tail meat. Slice the tail meat or prepare as required and serve with the claw and leg meat.

3 With scissors or a sharp knife, cut along the soft underside of the tail.

2 Scoop out the liver and roe and discard the intestine. Twist off the legs and claws and remove the meat. Loosen the tail meat.

PREPARING OYSTERS

To shuck oysters, use an oyster knife or a small, strong knife.

Hold oyster round side down and insert the knife near the hinge. Lever the shells apart. Slide in the knife to sever the top muscle. Lift off the shell. Run the knife under the oyster to loosen.

PREPARING A SQUID

Once cleaned, fresh squid yields an empty, tubelike body and separate tentacles. The body may be stuffed before cooking, or sliced and cooked with the tentacles.

1 Pull the body of the squid away from the head and tentacles. The innards will come away with the head. Cut off the tentacles just in front of the eyes.

2 Squeeze the tentacles near the cut end to remove the hard beak and then discard it. Rinse the tentacles well and set aside. Discard the head and innards.

3 Peel the skin from the body. Pull the quill out of the body and discard. Rinse the body thoroughly, dislodging any remaining innards with your fingers.

SHRIMP TACOS

 Serves 4

2 tbsp sunflower or corn oil

2 onions, chopped

3 garlic cloves, crushed

1 green pepper, cored, seeded, and diced

1 tbsp paprika

2 tsp mild chili powder

1/2 tsp ground cumin

4 tomatoes, peeled (page 39), seeded, and chopped

1 lb (500 g) cooked peeled shrimp

2 tbsp chopped fresh cilantro

salt and black pepper

12 taco shells

1 head of iceberg lettuce, shredded

sliced pickled chilies, large cooked peeled shrimp, and cilantro leaves to garnish

1 Heat the oil in a large skillet, add the onions, and cook gently, stirring occasionally, for 3–5 minutes, until softened but not browned. Add the garlic and diced green pepper and cook, stirring occasionally, for 3 minutes or until the pepper is soft.

2 Stir in the paprika, chili powder, and cumin and cook, stirring, for 1 minute. Add the tomatoes and cook for 3–5 minutes, until soft.

3 Lower the heat and stir in the shrimp, chopped cilantro, and salt and pepper to taste.

4 Meanwhile, heat the taco shells in a 350°F (180°C) oven for 3 minutes or according to package instructions.

5 Spoon the shrimp mixture into the taco shells, top with the shredded lettuce, and garnish with chilies, shrimp, and cilantro. Serve immediately.

SEAFOOD TACOS

Substitute 1 diced snapper fillet and shellfish, such as mussels or thinly sliced rings of squid, for 10 oz (300 g) of the shrimp.

SHRIMP WITH TARRAGON SAUCE

 Serves 4

12 uncooked jumbo or tiger shrimp in their shells

olive oil for brushing

1 1/4 cups (300 ml) dry white wine

1 garlic clove, crushed

1/4 cup (30 g) chopped parsley

lemon and tarragon to garnish

TARRAGON SAUCE

2/3 cup (150 ml) sour cream

1/4 cup (30 g) chopped fresh tarragon

1 tsp Dijon mustard

squeeze of lemon juice

salt and black pepper

1 Make the tarragon sauce: combine the sour cream, tarragon, mustard, and lemon juice, and season to taste.

2 Heat a heavy skillet. Brush the shrimp with oil, add to the pan, and cook the shrimp over high heat for 2 minutes or until pink.

3 Keeping the heat high, add half of the wine and the garlic. Boil rapidly for 2–3 minutes, then stir in 2 tbsp of the parsley.

4 When the wine has reduced slightly, lower the heat, and add the remaining wine with salt and pepper to taste. Simmer for 5 minutes or until the shrimp have released their juices into the wine.

5 Spoon the cooking juices over the shrimp, sprinkle with the remaining parsley, and garnish with lemon and tarragon. Serve hot, with the tarragon sauce.

Tiger shrimp

Tiger shrimp are large with distinctive "tiger stripes." Jumbo shrimp are a fine alternative; the flavor is the same

STUFFED SQUID

Serves 4

3 tbsp olive oil

1 onion, chopped

3–4 garlic cloves, crushed

8 small squid, cleaned (page 107)

1 cup (60 g) fresh bread crumbs

1/4 cup (90 ml) tomato juice

2 tsp chopped fresh rosemary

10 pitted black olives, sliced

2 tbsp chopped parsley

1 egg, lightly beaten

2 tsp balsamic or red wine vinegar

salt and black pepper

cayenne pepper

lemon slices and chopped parsley to garnish

1 Make the stuffing: heat 2 tbsp of the oil in a saucepan, add the onion and garlic, and cook gently, stirring occasionally, for 3–5 minutes, until the onion is soft but not browned.

2 Chop the squid tentacles very finely. Add them to the pan and cook, stirring, for 2 minutes, then add the bread crumbs, tomato juice, and chopped rosemary and stir well.

3 Remove the pan from the heat and stir in the olives, parsley, beaten egg, and vinegar. Add salt, pepper, and cayenne pepper to taste. Mix well to combine. Fill the squid with the stuffing and seal the tops (see box, below).

4 Arrange the squid in an ovenproof dish, sprinkle them with the remaining oil, and season with salt and pepper. Bake in a 425°F (220°C) oven for about 20 minutes, until the squid and filling are quite firm to the touch. Garnish the squid with the lemon slices and parsley, and serve immediately.

Scaling the squid

Thread a toothpick carefully through the top of each stuffed squid to seal the opening.

THAI SHRIMP STIR-FRY

Serves 4

1/2 lb (250 g) rice noodles

salt

3 tbsp sunflower or corn oil

1 red pepper, cored, seeded, and cut into thin strips

1 carrot, cut into thin strips

1 fresh green chili, cored, seeded, and cut into thin strips

1 in (2.5-cm) piece of fresh ginger, peeled and cut into thin strips

1 garlic clove, crushed

8 scallions, sliced

2 lemongrass stalks, trimmed, peeled, and sliced

1 lb (500 g) cooked peeled jumbo shrimp

2 tbsp white vinegar

2 tbsp soy sauce

juice of 1/2 lime

1 tbsp sesame oil

3 tbsp chopped fresh cilantro to garnish

1 Put the rice noodles into a large saucepan of boiling salted water, stir to separate the noodles, then turn off the heat, cover, and leave to stand for 4 minutes. Drain well and set aside.

2 Heat 1 tbsp of the sunflower oil in a wok or large skillet. Add the red pepper, carrot, chili, ginger, garlic, scallions, and lemongrass, and then stir-fry over high heat for 2 minutes.

3 Add the shrimp and stir-fry for 1 minute, then stir in the noodles. Add the remaining sunflower oil, the vinegar, soy sauce, lime juice, and sesame oil and stir-fry for 1 minute.

4 Sprinkle with the chopped cilantro, and serve immediately.

SCALLOP STIR-FRY

Substitute 1 1/2 lb (750 g) scallops for the jumbo shrimp. Stir-fry for about 5 minutes, then add the red pepper, carrot, chili, fresh ginger, garlic, scallions, and lemongrass, and stir-fry for 2 minutes longer. Add the drained noodles and proceed as directed in the recipe.

DEVILED CRAB

 Serves 4

5 tbsp (75 g) butter

1¹/₂ tbsp all-purpose flour

³/₄ cup (175 ml) milk

¹/₄ tsp dry mustard

¹/₄ tsp grated nutmeg

1 egg yolk

1¹/₂ tbsp dry sherry

1 tsp Worcestershire sauce

2–3 dashes of Tabasco sauce

4 small cooked crabs, meat removed (page 106) and shells and claws reserved

1 scallion, thinly sliced

salt and black pepper

2 cups (125 g) fresh bread crumbs

paprika and lemon wedges to garnish

1 Melt 3 tbsp (45 g) of the butter in a saucepan, add the flour, and cook, stirring, for 1 minute. Remove from the heat and gradually blend in the milk. Bring to a boil, stirring constantly until the mixture thickens. Simmer for 2–3 minutes. Remove from the heat and stir in the mustard and nutmeg.

2 Put the egg yolk into a small bowl and whisk in a little of the sauce. Stir this mixture back into the sauce.

3 Add the dry sherry, Worcestershire sauce, Tabasco sauce, crabmeat, scallion, and salt and pepper to taste and stir to mix. Spoon the mixture into the reserved crab shells.

4 Melt the remaining butter in a saucepan, add the bread crumbs, and cook, stirring, for 5 minutes or until golden brown.

5 Spoon the bread crumbs over the crabmeat mixture, replace the claws, and bake in a 400°F (200°C) oven for 10 minutes or until the top of the crab is brown and bubbling. Sprinkle with paprika, garnish with the lemon wedges, and serve the crab immediately.

Cook's know-how

If you cannot find fresh crabs, 1¹/₂ lb (750 g) frozen or canned crabmeat can be used instead, or even diced crab sticks. Serve the deviled crab in individual ovenproof ramekins instead of the crab shells if you prefer.

LOBSTER TAILS WITH MANGO & LIME

 Serves 4

4 cooked lobster tails

¹/₃ cup (90 ml) dry white wine

1 cup (250 ml) heavy cream

1 small mango, peeled, pitted, and cut into cubes (page 430)

grated zest and juice of 1 lime

¹/₃ cup (30 g) grated Parmesan cheese

1 Remove the meat from the lobster tails (see box, below). With a large, sharp knife, cut the lobster meat in half lengthwise. Arrange the lobster tail halves cut side up in a large shallow ovenproof dish.

2 Pour the wine into a small saucepan and boil rapidly until it has reduced to about 2 tbsp.

3 Add the heavy cream to the saucepan and boil until the mixture has reduced to a coating consistency. Stir in the mango cubes and grated lime zest and juice.

4 Spoon the mango mixture over the grated lobster tail halves. Lightly sprinkle them with the Parmesan cheese and bake in a 425°F (220°C) oven for about 20 minutes. Serve the lobster immediately.

Removing the meat from a lobster tail

Hold the tail in 1 hand. With a pair of scissors, cut along both sides of the underside of the shell, toward the end, without damaging the meat.

Pull back the underside of the shell and lift out the lobster meat, making sure it is all in 1 piece.

LOBSTER WITH BLACK BEAN SALSA

 Serves 4

4 cooked lobster tails

lime twists and cilantro sprigs to garnish

BLACK BEAN SALSA

4 tomatoes, peeled (page 39), seeded, and diced

1/2 onion, chopped

1 garlic clove, crushed

2 tbsp chopped fresh cilantro

1 mild fresh green chili, cored, seeded, and chopped

1/4 tsp ground cumin

1 1/4 cups (375 g) drained canned black beans

salt and black pepper

GARLIC BUTTER

10 tbsp (150 g) butter

5 garlic cloves, crushed

2 tsp finely chopped fresh oregano

1 Make the black bean salsa: in a bowl, combine the tomatoes, onion, garlic, cilantro, chili, and cumin. Add the beans and salt and pepper to taste.

2 With a sharp knife, cut each lobster tail in half lengthwise and loosen the meat, keeping it in the shell.

3 Make the garlic butter: cream the butter in a bowl, add the garlic, oregano, and salt and pepper to taste, and mix well. Spread half of the butter mixture over the lobster meat.

4 Place the lobster under the broiler, 4 in (10 cm) from the heat, and broil for 5 minutes or until slightly browned in patches and heated through.

5 Spread the lobster with the remaining garlic butter and then garnish with lime twists and cilantro sprigs. Serve the lobster immediately with the black bean salsa.

LOBSTER WITH REFRIED BEANS

Substitute refried beans for the black bean salsa. Heat 1 1/4 cups (375 g) canned refried beans with a little water, and 1/4 tsp each ground cumin and chili powder, then lightly sprinkle with grated Cheddar cheese. Proceed as directed.

SEAFOOD & AVOCADO SALAD

 **Serves 4**

1 lb (500 g) monkfish, trimmed and skinned

2/3 cup (150 ml) fish stock

1 slice of onion

6 black peppercorns

squeeze of lemon juice

1 bay leaf

mixed salad greens, such as curly endive, radicchio, and arugula

2 avocados

lemon juice for brushing

2 large tomatoes, peeled (page 39), seeded, and cut into strips

1/4 lb (125 g) cooked peeled shrimp

3oz (90 g) canned white crabmeat

flat-leaf parsley to garnish

SOUR CREAM DRESSING

1/2 cup (125 ml) light sour cream

3 tbsp lemon juice

salt and black pepper

1 Put the monkfish into a saucepan with the stock, onion, peppercorns, lemon juice, and bay leaf. Bring to a boil, cover, and poach very gently, turning once, for 10–15 minutes, until opaque throughout and firm.

2 Lift the monkfish out of the liquid, leave to cool slightly, then cut the flesh into bite-sized pieces. Leave to cool completely.

3 Make the sour cream dressing: put the sour cream and lemon juice into a bowl, add salt and pepper to taste, and stir to mix.

4 To serve, arrange the salad greens on individual plates. Halve, pit (page 68), and peel the avocados, and brush with lemon juice. Slice lengthwise and arrange in a fan shape on the greens. Add the strips of tomato, the monkfish, shrimp, and crabmeat. Spoon the sour cream dressing over the salad, garnish with parsley, and serve immediately.

Cook's know-how

The liquid in which the monkfish is poached can be reused as a good fish stock. When cool, strain the liquid and freeze it in a small container.

SCALLOPS WITH ASPARAGUS & LEMON

Serves 4

1 lb (500 g) baby asparagus

3 tbsp butter

3–4 garlic cloves, crushed

1 1/2 lb (750 g) scallops, sliced if large

juice of 1 lemon

1 1/2 tbsp finely chopped parsley

1 1/2 tbsp chopped fresh tarragon

salt and black pepper

1 Steam the asparagus for 3 minutes or until just tender. Chop and set aside.

2 Melt half of the butter in a pan, add the garlic, and cook for 1 minute. Add the scallops and cook, stirring, for 1 minute or until opaque and firm to the touch. Add the asparagus and cook for 3 minutes. Remove with a slotted spoon and keep warm.

3 Add the remaining butter to the pan with the lemon juice, parsley, and tarragon, and season to taste. Cook, stirring, until the butter melts. Pour the sauce over the scallops and asparagus and serve immediately.

SCALLOPS WITH LIME

Substitute lime juice for the lemon juice and equal quantities of chopped fresh cilantro and mint for the parsley and tarragon. To serve as an appetizer, simply omit the asparagus, and proceed as directed in the recipe.

SOFT-SHELL CRABS WITH LEMON

Omit the asparagus and substitute 4 soft-shell crabs for the scallops. Dip into seasoned flour. Melt 4 tbsp butter in a large skillet, then cook the crabs for 4 minutes on each side. Remove from the pan with a slotted spoon and make the sauce as directed.

SCALLOPS WITH SPICY CASHEW SAUCE

Serves 4

1 cup (100 g) toasted, salted cashew nuts

3 tbsp sunflower or corn oil

1 tsp black mustard seeds

3 garlic cloves, crushed

1 lb (500 g) scallops

1 onion, chopped

1 green pepper, cored, seeded, and cut into thin strips

1 fresh red chili, cored, seeded, and finely chopped

1/2 tsp turmeric

1 cup (250 ml) fish stock

salt and black pepper

1 Work the cashew nuts in a food processor until smooth.

2 Heat the oil in a large skillet, add the mustard seeds, and cook until they just begin to pop. Add the garlic and scallops and stir-fry for 2 minutes or just until the scallops turn opaque. Remove with a slotted spoon and reserve.

3 Add the onion, green pepper, and chili to the skillet, and cook gently, stirring occasionally, for 3–5 minutes, until the onion is soft but not browned. Add the turmeric and cook, stirring, for 1 minute.

4 Add the ground cashew nuts and stock to the mixture in the skillet, bring to a boil, and simmer for 5–10 minutes, until the sauce thickens.

5 Stir the scallops into the sauce, add salt and pepper to taste, and heat gently to warm through. Serve immediately.

Cook's know-how

Black mustard seeds, known for their distinctive pungent flavor, are often used in Indian dishes. Yellow mustard seeds are more common, however, and may be substituted if black ones are not available.

MUSSEL GRATIN

²/3 cup (150 ml) dry white wine

1 shallot, finely chopped

1 garlic clove, crushed

6 lb (3 kg) large mussels, cleaned (page 106)

1¼ cups (300 ml) light cream

3 tbsp chopped parsley

salt and black pepper

½ cup (30 g) fresh white bread crumbs

2 tbsp butter, melted

1 Put the wine, chopped shallot, and crushed garlic into a large saucepan, and bring to a boil. Simmer for 2 minutes.

2 Add the mussels, cover tightly, and return to a boil. Cook, shaking the pan frequently, for 5–6 minutes until the mussels open.

3 Using a slotted spoon, transfer the mussels to a large bowl. Discard any that have not opened; do not try to force them open.

4 Strain the cooking liquid into a saucepan, bring to a boil, and simmer until reduced to about 3 tbsp. Add the cream and heat through. Stir in half of the parsley and season with salt and pepper.

5 Remove the top shell of each mussel and discard. Arrange the mussels, in their bottom shells, on a large flameproof serving dish.

6 Spoon the sauce over the mussels and sprinkle with the bread crumbs and melted butter. Cook under the broiler, 4 in (10 cm) from the heat, for 3–5 minutes, until golden. Garnish with the remaining parsley and serve immediately.

Cook's know-how

Mussels are often sold by volume; size varies, depending on the type and whether they have been farm-raised or ocean-harvested.

MUSSELS WITH POTATOES & SAUSAGE

 Serves 4

2 tbsp olive oil

2 large potatoes, diced

¾ lb (375 g) chorizo sausage, diced

3 garlic cloves, crushed

½ cup (125 ml) fish stock

4 tbsp dry sherry

about 2 dozen large mussels, cleaned (page 106)

½ tsp cumin seeds

salt and black pepper

chopped fresh cilantro to garnish

1 Heat the olive oil in a large saucepan, add the potatoes, and cook gently, stirring from time to time, for 12–15 minutes, until golden and softened. Add the chorizo sausage and garlic and cook, stirring constantly, for about 2 minutes.

2 Add the fish stock, sherry, mussels, cumin seeds, and salt and pepper to taste, cover the saucepan tightly, and bring to a boil. Cook, shaking the saucepan frequently, for 8–10 minutes, until the mussels have opened.

3 Discard any mussels that have not opened; do not try to force them open.

4 Transfer the mussel, potato, and chorizo mixture to a large serving dish and pour the cooking juices over the top. Garnish with cilantro and serve hot.

MUSSELS WITH FAVA BEANS

Substitute 1¼ cups (375 g) fresh young fava beans for the potatoes and proceed as directed.

Cook's know-how

Chorizo, the Spanish sausage flavored with paprika and garlic, adds a russet color to this simple peasant dish of sautéed mussels and potatoes. If chorizo is not available, use another spicy sausage, such as the North African merguez or Polish kielbasa.

 SPICY CLAMS WITH CILANTRO PESTO

Serves 4–6

1/4 cup (60 ml) olive oil

6 tomatoes, peeled (page 39), seeded, and diced

4 garlic cloves, crushed

2 tbsp paprika

1 tbsp mild red chili powder

1 tsp ground cumin

about 4 dozen baby clams, cleaned (page 106)

2 1/3 cups (600 ml) fish stock

juice of 1/2 lime

CILANTRO PESTO

12 cilantro sprigs

2 tbsp olive oil

1 large garlic clove, coarsely chopped

1 mild fresh green chili, cored, seeded, and chopped

salt and black pepper

1 Make the cilantro pesto: strip the cilantro leaves from the stalks. Puree the cilantro leaves, olive oil, garlic, and green chili in a food processor or blender until smooth. Add salt and pepper to taste; set aside.

2 Heat the oil in a large saucepan, add the tomatoes and garlic, and cook gently, stirring occasionally, for 8 minutes, or until slightly thickened. Stir in the paprika, chili powder, and ground cumin.

3 Add the clams and stir them in the hot spices for 1 minute, then pour in the stock. Cover the pan tightly and cook the clams over medium heat, shaking the pan frequently, for about 12 minutes until the clams open. Discard any that have not opened; do not try to force them open.

4 Using a slotted spoon, transfer the clams to a warmed bowl.

5 Pour the cooking juices into a small pan and boil until reduced by about half. Add the lime juice, and season to taste, then pour the sauce over the clams.

6 Serve the clams immediately, topped with the cilantro pesto.

CLAMS IN SALSA VERDE

 Serves 4

about 3 dozen clams, cleaned (page 106)

salt and black pepper

chopped parsley to garnish

SALSA VERDE

1 1/2 cups (350 ml) fish stock

1/4 cup (60 ml) olive oil

3 tbsp dry sherry

5 garlic cloves, chopped

1/2 onion, chopped

1/2 cup (60 g) all-purpose flour

1/4 cup (30 g) chopped parsley

1 Make the salsa verde: puree the stock, oil, sherry, garlic, onion, flour, and parsley in a food processor until smooth.

2 Transfer to a pan, bring to a boil, then simmer for 8 minutes or until thickened.

3 Add the clams, cover the pan, and bring to a boil. Cook, shaking the pan, for about 12 minutes, until the clams open. Discard any that have not opened.

4 Using a slotted spoon, transfer the clams to a warmed tureen. Stir the salsa thoroughly, adding more liquid if it is too thick, or boiling to reduce it if it is not thick enough.

5 Taste the salsa for seasoning. Pour the salsa over the clams, garnish with the chopped parsley, and serve immediately.

Cook's know-how

Salsa verde, *meaning "green sauce" in Spanish, also goes very well with broiled fish such as swordfish or tuna. To give it a slightly different flavor, add 3 tbsp pastis or another anise-flavored apéritif instead of the dry sherry.*

CHINESE-STYLE OYSTERS

 Serves 4

8 slices of bacon, cut in half

3 1/2 oz (100 g) canned smoked oysters, drained

1 small green pepper, cored, seeded, and cut into bite-sized pieces

1 garlic clove, crushed

8 oz (250 g) canned water chestnuts, drained

1 scallion, thinly sliced

lemon wedges, scallion brushes (see box, right), and Tabasco sauce to serve

1 Wrap half a bacon slice around each oyster and fasten securely with wooden toothpicks.

2 Heat a skillet, add the bacon-wrapped oysters, and cook gently for 6–8 minutes, until they are browned and lightly crisp. Add the green pepper, garlic, and water chestnuts and stir-fry over high heat for 2 minutes.

3 Sprinkle with the scallion slices, and serve with lemon wedges, scallion brushes, and Tabasco.

Making scallion brushes

Trim the root end of each scallion and cut it into 2-in (5-cm) lengths. Make several lengthwise cuts at both ends of each piece of scallion.

Put into ice water and chill for 30 minutes or until the ends curl. If you prefer, swirl the brushes in the water to make them open out and curl more.

OYSTER STEW WITH SAFFRON

 Serves 4

12 oysters in their shells

1 1/2 cups (350 ml) light cream

1 cup (250 ml) dry white wine

1 cup (250 ml) fish stock

1 leek, trimmed and chopped

1/2 carrot, diced

3/4 cup (30 g) watercress, tough stalks removed, coarsely chopped

pinch of saffron threads

1 tbsp Pernod

1 tbsp lemon juice

salt

pinch of cayenne pepper (optional)

chervil sprigs to garnish

1 Remove the oysters from their shells (page 107), and strain their liquid into a pitcher. Set aside.

2 Put the cream, wine, stock, leek, and carrot into a saucepan and bring to a boil. Simmer for 7–10 minutes, until the vegetables are just tender.

3 Add the reserved oyster liquid, watercress, saffron, Pernod, lemon juice, salt, and cayenne pepper, if using, to the pan. Bring to a boil, add the oysters, and simmer until the oysters heat through and curl slightly at the edges.

4 Serve the oyster stew immediately, garnished with chervil sprigs.

Saffron

Made from the dried stigmas of the saffron crocus, this is the most expensive spice in the world. Over 250,000 flowers must be picked, by hand, to produce 1 lb (500 g) of saffron. Saffron is cultivated in many Mediterranean countries; Spain is the major producer.

HOT & SOUR MACKEREL

 Serves 4

2 carrots

1 red pepper, cored and seeded

1 fresh green chili, cored and seeded

6 garlic cloves

8 scallions

1 lemongrass stalk, trimmed and peeled

2 tbsp sunflower oil

4 6-oz (175-g) mackerel fillets

cilantro sprigs to garnish

HOT AND SOUR SAUCE

¼ cup (60 ml) Thai fish sauce or light soy sauce

¼ cup (60 ml) cider vinegar

2 tbsp lime juice

2 tbsp sugar

1 Make the hot and sour sauce: in a small bowl, combine the fish sauce, vinegar, lime juice, and sugar. Cover and set aside.

2 Cut the carrots, red pepper, green chili, and garlic into matchsticks. Slice the scallions, and finely slice the lemongrass.

3 Line a broiler pan with foil. Arrange the mackerel on the foil, and cook under the broiler, 4 in (10 cm) from the heat, for 3 minutes on each side. Continue to broil until the fish is opaque and the flesh flakes easily. Meanwhile, stir-fry the vegetables.

4 Heat the sunflower oil in a wok or large skillet. Add the carrots, red pepper, chili, garlic, scallions, and lemongrass, and stir-fry over high heat for 3 minutes or until the vegetables are just tender.

5 Arrange the vegetable mixture on top of the fish, pour the sauce over, garnish with the cilantro sprigs, and serve immediately.

MACKEREL WITH GREEN GRAPES

 Serves 4

4 8-oz (250-g) mackerel, cleaned, with heads removed (page 105)

salt and black pepper

GREEN GRAPE SAUCE

2 cups (375 g) tart green grapes

2 tbsp water

2 tbsp superfine sugar, more if needed

2 tbsp butter

½ tsp ground ginger

1 Cut the fins off the mackerel and make 3–4 diagonal cuts on both sides of each fish. Season the mackerel inside and out with salt and pepper.

2 Make the green grape sauce: clean and trim the grapes and put them into a pan with the water and sugar. Cover tightly and simmer very gently, shaking the pan occasionally, for 5 minutes or until tender.

3 Reserve 12 of the cooked green grapes for garnish, then work the remainder through a nylon strainer. Beat in the butter and ginger and add more sugar if necessary. Return the sauce to the pan and keep warm.

4 Cook the mackerel under the broiler, 4 in (10 cm) from the heat, for 7–8 minutes on each side, until the fish is opaque and the flesh flakes easily.

5 Serve the mackerel hot, garnished with the reserved green grapes. Pass the sauce separately.

MACKEREL WITH CRANBERRY SAUCE

Substitute 2 cups (375 g) fresh or frozen cranberries for the green grapes and proceed as directed.

HERRING WITH AN OAT CRUST

 Serves 4

1 cup (125 g) oatmeal

2 tsp dry mustard

salt and black pepper

4 6- to 8-oz (175- to 250-g) herring, cleaned (page 105), heads removed, and filleted

8 parsley sprigs

sunflower or corn oil for deep-frying

chopped parsley and lemon wedges to garnish

1 In a shallow dish, combine the oatmeal, dry mustard, and salt and pepper to taste. Open out the herring and press them into the oatmeal mixture to coat well on both sides.

2 Grill the herring under the broiler, 4 in (10 cm) from the heat, for about 4 minutes on each side or until the fish is opaque and the flesh flakes easily.

3 Make sure the parsley sprigs are dry. Then deep-fry them (see box, below). Arrange the broiled herring and deep-fried parsley sprigs on a warmed serving platter, and garnish with the chopped parsley and lemon wedges. Serve the herring immediately.

Deep-frying parsley

Heat 2 in (5 cm) oil in a large saucepan. Add the parsley sprigs and deep-fry for 30 seconds or until crisp. Lift out with a slotted spoon and drain on paper towels.

HERRING WITH MUSTARD SAUCE

 Serves 4

4 6- to 8-oz (175- to 250 g) herring, cleaned (page 105), heads removed, and filleted

salt and black pepper

butter for greasing

lemon wedges and parsley sprigs to garnish

MUSTARD SAUCE

2 tbsp butter

1/4 cup (30 g) all-purpose flour

1 1/4 cups (300 ml) milk

2 tsp dry mustard

1 tsp sugar

2 tsp white vinegar

1 Season the herring inside and out with salt and black pepper, fold the fish over, and place in a single layer in a buttered ovenproof dish.

2 Cover the herring and bake in a 400°F (200°C) oven for 12 minutes or until the fish is opaque and the flesh flakes easily.

3 Meanwhile, make the mustard sauce: melt the butter in a saucepan, add the flour and cook, stirring, for 1 minute. Remove from the heat and gradually blend in the milk. Bring to a boil, stirring constantly until the mixture thickens. Simmer for 2–3 minutes. Add the dry mustard, sugar, vinegar, and salt and pepper to taste and cook 1 minute longer.

4 To serve, garnish the herring with lemon wedges and parsley sprigs, and pass the mustard sauce separately.

Cook's know-how

For a milder-tasting sauce, substitute 2 tsp Dijon mustard for the dry mustard.

117

BAKED TROUT WITH ORANGE

 Serves 4

4 12- to 14-oz (375- to 425-g) trout, cleaned (page 105)

4 large thyme sprigs

4 large parsley sprigs

1/4 lb (125 g) mushrooms, sliced

2 shallots, chopped

1/4 cup (60 ml) white vinegar

grated zest and juice of 1 orange

salt and black pepper

orange slices and thyme sprigs to garnish

1 With a knife, make 2 diagonal cuts in the flesh on both sides of each trout.

2 Strip the thyme and parsley leaves from their stalks. In a bowl, combine the mushrooms, shallots, white vinegar, orange zest and juice, thyme and parsley leaves, and salt and pepper to taste.

3 Reserve one-quarter of the mushroom and herb mixture to spoon over the stuffed trout.

4 Stuff the trout with the remaining mushroom and herb mixture (see box, below).

5 Arrange the trout in a nonmetallic ovenproof dish and spoon over the reserved mushroom mixture. Cover and chill for 4 hours.

6 Bake in a 350°F (180°C) oven for 20–25 minutes until the fish is opaque and flakes easily. Garnish the trout with the orange slices and thyme sprigs and serve immediately.

Stuffing the trout

Hold open the cavity of each trout with 1 hand, and spoon in one-quarter of the mushroom and herb mixture.

BROILED TROUT WITH CUCUMBER & DILL

 Serves 4

1 cucumber, peeled

2 tbsp butter

small bunch of fresh dill, chopped

salt and black pepper

juice of 1 lemon

4 12- to 14-oz (375- to 425-g) trout, cleaned (page 105)

dill sprigs and fresh chives to garnish

dill cream sauce (page 128) to serve

1 Cut the cucumber in half lengthwise, scoop out the seeds, and cut the flesh into 1/4-in (5-mm) slices. Melt the butter in a saucepan, add the cucumber, and cook gently for 2 minutes.

2 In a bowl, combine two-thirds of the cooked cucumber with the chopped dill, add salt and pepper to taste, and sprinkle with the lemon juice. Stuff the trout with the mixture.

3 Line a broiler pan with foil. Arrange the trout on the foil and put the remaining cucumber around them.

4 Broil the trout 4 in (10 cm) from the heat, for 4–7 minutes on each side, until the flesh flakes easily.

5 Garnish the trout with dill sprigs and fresh chives, and serve them immediately. Pass the dill cream sauce separately.

TROUT WITH ALMONDS

Dip the trout in seasoned flour. Melt 4 tbsp butter in a large skillet, and cook the trout, in batches if necessary, for 6–8 minutes on each side, until the fish is opaque and the flesh flakes easily. Drain on paper towels and keep warm. Wipe the pan, melt 1 tbsp butter, and fry 1/2 cup (60 g) slivered almonds until lightly browned. Add a squeeze of lemon juice, then pour the lemon and almond mixture over the trout. Serve immediately.

TUNA WITH FENNEL & TOMATO RELISH

 Serves 4

1/4 cup (60 ml) olive oil

juice of 1/2 lemon

3 garlic cloves, crushed

1/2 tsp herbes de Provence

4 6-oz (175-g) tuna steaks, about 1 in (2.5 cm) thick

salt and black pepper

lime wedges and dill sprigs to garnish

FENNEL AND TOMATO RELISH

1 small fennel bulb, chopped

2 tomatoes, peeled (page 39), seeded, and diced

2 tbsp olive oil

1 tbsp lemon juice

1 tbsp black olive paste

1 garlic clove, chopped

1 Combine the olive oil, lemon juice, garlic, and herbes de Provence in a large nonmetallic dish. Add the tuna steaks and turn to coat. Cover and leave to marinate in the refrigerator, turning occasionally, for about 1 hour.

2 Meanwhile, make the relish: put the fennel, tomatoes, olive oil, lemon juice, black olive paste, and garlic into a bowl and stir well to combine.

3 Remove the tuna steaks from the marinade, reserving the marinade. Cook the steaks under the broiler, 3 in (7 cm) from the heat, basting once or twice with the reserved marinade, for 3–4 minutes on each side.

4 Season the steaks with salt and pepper to taste and top with the fennel and tomato relish. Garnish with lime wedges and dill sprigs, and serve immediately.

Black olive paste

This originally comes from Provence, where it is commonly known as tapenade. It is a deliciously tangy blend of olives, anchovies, and capers pureed with olive oil.

TUNA TERIYAKI

 Serves 4

4 6-oz (175-g) tuna steaks, about 1 in (2.5 cm) thick

2 scallions, thinly sliced, to garnish

MARINADE

3 tbsp dark soy sauce

2 tbsp sesame oil

1 tbsp Japanese rice wine or sweet sherry

3 garlic cloves, chopped

1 tbsp sugar

1/2-in (1-cm) piece of fresh ginger, peeled and chopped

1 Make the marinade: put the soy sauce, sesame oil, rice wine, garlic, sugar, and ginger into a nonmetallic dish. Add the tuna steaks to the marinade and turn to coat. Cover and marinate in the refrigerator for 8 hours.

2 Reserve the marinade. Cook the steaks under the broiler, 3 in (7 cm) from the heat, brushing with the marinade, for 3–4 minutes on each side. Serve immediately, garnished with scallions.

BARBECUED SALMON TERIYAKI

Make the marinade as directed. Cut 1 1/2 lb (750 g) salmon fillet into 1-in (2.5-cm) cubes. Cover and leave to marinate in the refrigerator for 8 hours. Thread on metal skewers. Cook over a hot barbecue, turning and brushing frequently with the marinade, for 6–8 minutes.

Teriyaki

This is a traditional Japanese marinade, used to flavor meat, poultry, or fish that is to be grilled, barbecued, or fried. When heated, the sugar in the marinade makes a thick and glossy glaze.

SWORDFISH WITH ORANGE RELISH

 Serves 4

4 6-oz (175-g) swordfish steaks

MARINADE

3 tbsp olive oil

juice of 1 orange

juice of 1 lemon

3 garlic cloves, crushed

salt and black pepper

ORANGE RELISH

2 oranges, peeled, separated into sections, and diced

3 tbsp olive oil

2 tbsp chopped fresh basil

1 Make the marinade: in a shallow nonmetallic dish, combine the olive oil, orange and lemon juices, garlic, and salt and pepper to taste. Turn the swordfish steaks in the marinade, cover, and leave to marinate in the refrigerator for at least 1 hour.

2 Make the orange relish: in a bowl, combine the oranges, olive oil, basil, and season with salt and pepper to taste.

3 Remove the swordfish from the marinade, reserving the marinade. Place the steaks under the broiler, 3 in (7 cm) from the heat, and broil, basting once or twice with the marinade, for 5 minutes on each side or until the fish is opaque and the flesh flakes easily. Serve immediately, with the relish.

TUNA WITH ORANGE RELISH

Substitute tuna steaks for the swordfish steaks and fresh cilantro for the basil and proceed as directed.

Cook's know-how

Swordfish has a meaty texture and a mild flavor. Its firmness makes it ideal for broiling, baking, or poaching.

SHARK WITH TROPICAL SALSA

 Serves 4

4 6-oz (175-g) shark steaks

MARINADE

1/2 cup (125 ml) olive oil

juice of 1/2 lemon

3 garlic cloves, crushed

1 tbsp shredded fresh cilantro

1 tsp ground cumin

pinch of cayenne pepper

salt and black pepper

TROPICAL SALSA

9 oz (275 g) canned pineapple pieces in natural juices, drained

1 small ripe papaya, peeled, seeded, and diced

1 small red pepper, cored, seeded, and diced

1 mild fresh red or green chili, cored, seeded, and diced

2 tbsp chopped fresh cilantro

1 tbsp white vinegar

sugar (optional)

1 Make the marinade: in a shallow nonmetallic dish, combine the oil, lemon juice, garlic, cilantro, cumin, cayenne pepper, and salt and black pepper to taste.

2 Turn the shark steaks in the marinade, cover, and marinate in the refrigerator for at least 1 hour.

3 Make the tropical salsa: in a large bowl, combine the pineapple, papaya, red pepper, chili, cilantro, vinegar, and salt and pepper to taste. If the fruit is tart, add a little sugar.

4 Remove the steaks from the marinade, reserving the marinade. Place the steaks under the broiler, 3 in (7 cm) from the heat, basting once or twice with the marinade, for 3–4 minutes on each side until the fish is opaque and the flesh flakes easily. Serve with the salsa.

SHARK WITH FRUITY SALSA

Peel, section, and finely chop 1 orange. Mix with 2 cups (250 g) chopped cranberries and 1/2 cup (125 g) sugar. Chill for a few hours. Cook the shark as directed above and serve with the fruity salsa.

COULIBIAC

This is a salmon, rice, and tomato mixture enclosed in crisp puff pastry that makes an impressive dish for a dinner party or other special occasion. In Russia, its country of origin, there is a saying: "Houses make a fine street; pies make a fine table."

 Serves 8–10

¹/₃ cup (75 g) long-grain rice

salt and black pepper

4 tbsp butter, plus extra for greasing

1 large onion, chopped

13 oz (400 g) canned chopped tomatoes, drained

1 lb (500 g) salmon, cooked and flaked

2 tbsp chopped parsley

grated zest and juice of 1 lemon

1 lb (500 g) puff pastry

1 egg, beaten

4 tbsp butter, melted, and juice of ¹/₂ lemon to serve

lemon twists and watercress sprigs to garnish

1 Simmer the rice in salted water, covered tightly, for 12 minutes or until just tender.

2 Meanwhile, melt the butter in a saucepan, add the onion, and cook gently for a few minutes, until soft but not browned. Add the tomatoes and cook for 15 minutes. Leave to cool.

3 Drain the rice if needed, and combine with the onion and tomato mixture, the flaked salmon, parsley, lemon zest and juice, and salt and pepper to taste.

4 Roll out seven-eighths of the puff pastry into a 11- x 16-in (28- x 40-cm) rectangle.

5 Arrange the salmon mixture down the middle of the rectangle, leaving a 3-in (7-cm) border on each side. Brush the border with a little of the beaten egg and wrap and decorate the coulibiac (see box, right).

6 Bake the coulibiac in a 425°F (220°C) oven for 30–45 minutes until golden.

7 Transfer the coulibiac to a warmed serving dish and pour the melted butter and lemon juice into the cuts. Serve in thick slices, garnished with lemon twists and watercress sprigs.

Coulibiac

This became popular in western Europe in the mid-19th century. Described as "a salmon pie in the Russian manner," authentic versions contain layers of fish, buckwheat, hard boiled eggs, and vesiga, *the dried spinal cord of the sturgeon. In Russia, other fish, such as sturgeon and pike, were sometimes used instead of salmon.*

Wrapping and decorating the coulibiac

Fold the shortest ends of pastry over the salmon filling and brush the top of the folded pastry with beaten egg.

Fold the longest sides over the filling to make a long package. Turn the package over and place on a lightly buttered baking sheet. Brush all over with beaten egg.

Make 2 decorative cuts in the top of the pastry. Roll the remaining pastry into a 2- x 12-in (5- x 30-cm) piece, trim, then cut into 3 equal strips. Press the ends together and braid the strips. Lay the braid down the middle of the package, and glaze with beaten egg.

SALMON WITH SPINACH

 Serves 4

4 6-oz (175-g) salmon steaks

salt and black pepper

1 tbsp butter

lemon twists to garnish

SPINACH SALSA

2 tbsp olive oil

8 scallions, finely sliced

1 garlic clove, crushed

1/4 cup (60 ml) lemon juice

1 tsp coarse mustard

1 lb (500 g) spinach, finely chopped

1 Season the salmon steaks with black pepper and dot with the butter.

2 Cook the salmon steaks under the broiler, 3 in (7 cm) from the heat, for 5–6 minutes on each side, until the fish is opaque and the flesh flakes easily.

3 Meanwhile, make the spinach salsa: heat the oil in a skillet, add the scallions and garlic, and cook, stirring, for about 1 minute. Stir in the lemon juice, mustard, and spinach, and cook, stirring, for about 2 minutes. Transfer to a bowl and season with salt and pepper to taste.

4 Garnish the salmon with lemon twists and serve immediately, with the salsa.

WATERCRESS SALMON

Salmon served with a creamy watercress sauce makes an excellent dish for a summer dinner simple to prepare, elegant to look at, and delicious to eat. The salmon is baked in the oven with a foil covering to keep it moist.

 Serves 6

1 1/2 lb (750 g) salmon steak, skinned

butter for greasing

salt and black pepper

watercress sprigs to garnish

WATERCRESS CREAM SAUCE

1 1/4 cups (300 ml) light cream

1 1/2 cups (60 g) watercress, tough stalks removed

6 tbsp (90 g) butter, melted

1 tsp all-purpose flour

juice of l lemon

1 egg yolk

1 Divide the salmon into 6 pieces (see box, right).

2 Butter a roasting pan. Arrange the salmon pieces in a single layer and sprinkle with black pepper.

3 Cover tightly with foil, and bake in a 350°F (180°C) oven for 15–20 minutes, until the fish is opaque and flakes easily.

4 Meanwhile, make the watercress cream sauce: puree the cream, watercress, butter, flour, lemon juice, egg yolk, and salt and pepper to taste in a food processor until smooth.

5 Transfer the cream and watercress mixture to a small saucepan and cook over gentle heat, stirring, until the sauce thickens. Taste for seasoning.

6 Serve the salmon immediately on a bed of watercress cream sauce and garnish with watercress sprigs.

Dividing salmon into 6 pieces

Put the salmon on a cutting board and slice it crosswise in half.

Cut the thinner end crosswise in half. Cut the thicker section crosswise in half, then lengthwise in half, making 4 pieces.

SALMON EN CROUTE

 Serves 6

3½–4 lb (1.7–2 kg) salmon, cleaned and filleted (page 105), skinned

1 tbsp chopped fresh dill

grated zest and juice of 1 lemon

salt and black pepper

2 tbsp butter

8 scallions, sliced

8 cups (250 g) spinach leaves, coarsely shredded

½ lb (250 g) low-fat cream cheese

all-purpose flour for dusting

1½ lb (750 g) puff pastry

1 egg, beaten

lemon slices, cherry tomatoes, and parsley sprigs to garnish

1 Put the salmon fillets into a shallow nonmetallic dish and sprinkle with the dill, lemon zest and juice, and salt and pepper to taste. Cover and leave to marinate in the refrigerator for at least 1 hour.

2 Melt the butter in a small saucepan, add the scallions, and cook gently for 2–3 minutes until soft but not browned.

3 Add the spinach, toss in the butter, and remove from the heat. Leave to cool, then stir in the cheese. Add salt and pepper to taste.

4 Lightly dust a work surface with flour and roll out half of the pastry to a 8- x 15-in (20- x 38-cm) rectangle. Put the pastry on a baking sheet, and place 1 salmon fillet on top. Spread with the spinach and cheese mixture, then put the second fillet on top. Brush the pastry border with a little of the egg.

5 Roll out the remaining pastry to a slightly larger rectangle, cover the salmon completely, then seal the edges.

6 Decorate and trim the pastry (see box, right). Brush the pastry with the beaten egg and bake in a 400°F (200°C) oven for 40–45 minutes, until the pastry is well risen and golden brown.

7 Garnish with lemon slices, cherry tomatoes, and parsley sprigs and serve immediately.

Decorating and trimming the pastry

Mark "scales" all over the pastry, using the rounded edge of a soup spoon. Make 2 small holes in the top of the pastry to allow the steam to escape.

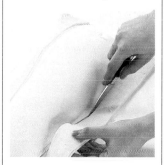

Trim the edges of the pastry to form a fish shape. If you prefer, make fins from the trimmings and attach with beaten egg.

SALMON WITH AVOCADO

 **Serves 4**

2 tbsp butter, melted

4 6-oz (175-g) salmon steaks

salt and black pepper

4 tarragon sprigs

4 slices of lime

AVOCADO SAUCE

2 avocados, halved, pitted (page 68), and peeled

⅔ cup (150 ml) plain yogurt

grated zest and juice of 1 lime

1 Brush 4 large squares of foil with melted butter. Put a salmon steak on each square, season, and top with a tarragon sprig and a slice of lime. Wrap the foil around the salmon. Put on a baking sheet, and bake in a 300°F (150°C) oven for 25 minutes or until the fish is opaque and the flesh flakes easily.

2 Meanwhile, make the avocado sauce: put the flesh of 1 avocado into a food processor with the yogurt, lime zest and juice, and salt and pepper to taste and puree until smooth. Transfer to a serving bowl. Dice the remaining avocado and stir into the sauce.

3 Unwrap the salmon, transfer to warmed serving plates, and serve immediately with the avocado sauce.

POACHED SALMON WITH DILL MAYONNAISE

This is the perfect centerpiece for a buffet party. The salmon is gently poached, with the skin and head for added flavor, and left to cool in the cooking liquid to keep it moist. A poacher is useful, but you can improvise with a large pot and a wire rack that fits inside.

 Serves 10

1 5¹/₂-lb (2.75-kg) salmon, cleaned (page 105)
salt and black peppercorns
4 bay leaves
1 onion, sliced
¹/₄ cup (60 ml) white vinegar
mayonnaise (page 338)
3 tbsp chopped fresh dill
TO GARNISH
¹/₄-oz (7-g) envelope unflavored gelatin
1 cucumber, thinly sliced
2 lemons
¹/₂ lb (250 g) shrimp, cooked and peeled
dill sprigs
small pieces of red pepper

1 Lift out the rack from a poacher and set aside. Half fill the poacher with cold water and add 2 tbsp salt, 12 black peppercorns, the bay leaves, onion, and vinegar.

2 Put the salmon on the rack and lower into the poacher. Bring to a boil, then simmer for 1 minute only. Remove from the heat, cover, and leave to stand for about 2 hours, until the fish is just warm.

3 Lift the rack and salmon out of the poacher. Strain the cooking liquid and reserve. Cover the salmon with a large piece of plastic wrap and flip the fish over onto the plastic wrap. Bone and skin the salmon (see box, below). Cover and chill in the refrigerator for at least 1 hour.

4 Reserve 2 tbsp of the mayonnaise. Add the dill to the remaining mayonnaise, put into a serving bowl, and chill until ready to serve.

5 Make an aspic by following the gelatin package instructions, using 2 cups (600 ml) of the cooking liquid. Arrange the cucumber slices over the fish to represent scales. When the aspic has just started to thicken, brush a thin glaze over the fish and cucumber. Leave to set, then brush another layer of aspic over the fish and cucumber.

6 Cut lengthwise grooves in the lemons with a small knife, cut in half lengthwise, and slice. Garnish the salmon with the lemon slices, shrimp, reserved mayonnaise, dill sprigs, and red pepper. Serve with mayonnaise.

Boning and skinning a salmon

1 Using a chef's knife, neatly remove the head from the salmon.

2 Run the knife along the backbone of the fish to loosen the top fillet.

3 Flip the top fillet over and remove the bones from the fish.

4 Use the plastic wrap to flip the bottom fillet back onto the top and remove the skin and any dark flesh.

5 Use the plastic wrap to flip the fish onto a large serving plate and remove the remaining skin.

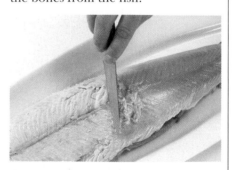

6 With a small knife, gently scrape away the brownish flesh, leaving behind only the pink flesh.

FILLETS OF SOLE MEUNIERE

 Serves 4

1/2 cup (60 g) all-purpose flour

salt and black pepper

4 small lemon sole, skinned and each cut into 4 fillets (page 105)

2 tbsp butter

1 tbsp chopped parsley

juice of 1/2 lemon

lemon twists and parsley sprigs to garnish

1 Sprinkle the flour onto a plate and season with salt and pepper. Dip the fillets into the seasoned flour and shake off any excess.

2 Melt half of the butter in a large skillet. When it is foaming, add the fillets and cook for 2 minutes on each side or until the fish is opaque and the flesh flakes easily. Transfer to warmed serving plates and keep warm.

3 Wipe the skillet with paper towels. Melt the remaining butter and heat quickly until golden. Stir in the parsley and lemon juice, then quickly pour over the fillets. Serve, garnished with lemon twists (see box, below) and parsley sprigs.

Making a lemon twist

Slice a lemon thinly, then cut from the center to the edge of each slice. Gently twist the lemon to form a curved shape.

MUSHROOM-STUFFED SOLE FILLETS

 Serves 4

4 tbsp butter

1 onion, finely chopped

5 cups (375 g) mushrooms, finely chopped

2 large sole, skinned and each cut into 4 fillets (page 105)

1 cup (250 ml) dry white wine

2 tsp chopped fresh tarragon

salt and black pepper

1 cup (250 ml) heavy cream

squeeze of lemon juice

1 Melt half of the butter in a saucepan, add the onion and mushrooms, and cook gently for 5 minutes.

2 Roll the fillets (see box, right). Stand the rolls in a shallow ovenproof dish and fill them with the mushroom mixture.

3 Add the wine, tarragon, and salt and pepper to taste. Cover with foil and bake in a 350°F (180°C) oven for 15 minutes or until the fish is opaque and the flesh flakes easily.

4 Remove the fish from the dish and keep warm. Pour the juices into a pan and boil for 3 minutes or until reduced by half. Stir in the cream and lemon juice, taste for seasoning, and serve immediately.

Rolling the fillets

Bring around the 2 ends of each fillet to form a circle, with the smaller tail end on the outside.

Thread a wooden toothpick through both ends of each fillet to seal.

GINGERED WHITEFISH

 Serves 4

4 large whitefish fillets

sliced scallions and scallion brushes (page 115) to garnish

GINGER MARINADE

1-in (2.5-cm) piece of fresh ginger, peeled and finely sliced

1 large garlic clove, sliced

2 tbsp sunflower or corn oil

1 tbsp sesame oil

1 tbsp dry sherry

1 tbsp sherry vinegar

2 tsp light soy sauce

1 Put the fillets into a shallow nonmetallic dish.

2 Make the marinade: combine the ginger, garlic, sunflower and sesame oils, sherry, sherry vinegar, and soy sauce and pour over the fish.

3 Cover the fish and leave to marinate in the refrigerator, turning once, for 30 minutes.

4 Grill the fillets, skin side down, under the broiler, 3 in (7 cm) from the heat, for 4–5 minutes, until the fish is opaque and the flesh flakes easily.

5 Serve hot, garnished with sliced scallions and scallion brushes.

LEMON SOLE FLORENTINE

Fillets of lemon sole are topped with a cheese sauce and baked on a bed of spinach so they stay moist while cooking. Slices of hot lemon bread – an interesting variation on garlic bread – make an unusual accompaniment.

 Serves 4

4 large lemon sole fillets, skinned (page 105)

juice of 1/2 lemon

salt and black pepper

3 tbsp butter

1/3 cup (45 g) all-purpose flour

1 3/4 cups (450 ml) milk

1 1/2 lb (750 g) spinach

1/3 cup (30 g) grated Parmesan cheese

hot lemon bread to serve (see box, below)

1 Sprinkle the lemon sole fillets with the lemon juice and salt and pepper. Fold the fillets in half crosswise and set aside.

2 Melt the butter in a saucepan, add the flour, and cook, stirring, for 1 minute. Remove from the heat and gradually blend in the milk. Bring to a boil, stirring constantly until the white sauce mixture thickens. Simmer for 2–3 minutes, then add salt and pepper to taste.

3 Wash the spinach and put into a pan with only the water remaining on the leaves. Cook for 2 minutes or until wilted. Drain well.

4 Stir half of the white sauce into the spinach and spoon into a shallow ovenproof dish. Arrange the sole on top. Pour the remaining sauce over the top and sprinkle with the cheese. Bake the lemon sole in a 400°F (200°C) oven for 30–40 minutes. Serve hot, with hot lemon bread.

Hot lemon bread

Beat the *grated zest of 1/2 lemon* into *1/1 lb (125 g) softened butter*, using a fork. Slowly add the *juice of 1/2 lemon*, beating between additions. Add *salt and pepper to taste*.

Cut *1 baguette* into *1/2-in (1-cm) slices*, leaving the slices attached at the bottom.

Spread the butter over the slices and a little over the top. Wrap in foil and bake in a 400°F (200°C) oven for 20 minutes, opening the foil for the last 5 minutes to crisp the top.

BEST-EVER FRIED FISH

These whitefish fillets are shallow-fried in a crisp coating of fresh bread crumbs. This is far superior to a batter coating in both flavor and texture, and it protects the fish from the heat of the fat, keeping it moist in the same way as batter.

 Serves 4

3 tbsp all-purpose flour

salt and black pepper

1 large egg, beaten

1/2 cup (30 g) fresh white bread crumbs

4 large whitefish fillets, skinned

2 tbsp sunflower or corn oil

lemon wedges to garnish

1 Sprinkle the flour into a shallow dish and season with salt and pepper. Pour the beaten egg into another dish and sprinkle the bread crumbs into a third.

2 Lightly coat the fish fillets with breadcrumbs (see box, below).

3 Heat the oil in a large skillet, add the coated fillets, in 2 batches if necessary, and fry over high heat for 2–3 minutes on each side, until they are crisp, golden, and juicy inside.

4 Lift the fillets out of the skillet with a spatula and put on paper towels to drain. Serve the fish immediately, garnished with the lemon wedges.

Fried fish

Catfish, long a regional favorite for fish fries, is now available across the country thanks to farming. The farmed fish have a less pronounced "muddy" flavor. Choose scrod for "the kind of fish that doesn't taste fishy."

DILL CREAM SAUCE

Puree *1 1/4 cups (300 ml) light cream, 6 tbsp (90 g) butter, 1 egg yolk, the juice of 1 lemon,* and *1 tsp all-purpose flour* in a food processor until smooth. Transfer the mixture to a small saucepan and heat very gently, stirring constantly, until the sauce has thickened and will coat the back of a spoon. Add *salt and pepper to taste,* then stir in *2 tbsp chopped fresh dill* and *1 tbsp snipped fresh chives.*

TARTAR SAUCE

Puree *1 egg, 1 1/2 tsp sugar, 1/2 tsp dry mustard,* and *salt and pepper to taste* in a food processor or blender until smooth. Add *1 1/4 cups (300 ml) sunflower or corn oil,* pouring in a steady stream, and puree until the mixture is very thick and all of the oil has been incorporated. Add *the juice of 1 lemon* and puree. Transfer to a bowl and stir in *1 tbsp each chopped pickles, capers,* and *parsley* and *2 tbsp chopped fresh tarragon.* Cover and leave to stand for at least 1 hour to allow the flavors to blend.

Coating a fish fillet

Dip the fillet into the seasoned flour to coat. Shake off any excess.

Dip the floured fillet into the beaten egg, letting any excess drain off.

Dip the fillet into the bread crumbs, making sure it is evenly coated.

INDIAN SPICED HADDOCK

 Serves 4

1 1/2 lb (750 g) thick pieces of haddock fillet, skinned

1 tsp cumin seeds

1 tsp coriander seeds

pinch of cayenne pepper

1/4 tsp turmeric

1 tsp salt

2 tbsp sunflower or corn oil

1 small onion, sliced

1-in (2.5-cm) piece of fresh ginger, peeled and finely chopped

1 fresh green chili, cored, seeded, and finely chopped

1 small cauliflower, cut into small florets

2 potatoes, diced

1 large green pepper, cored, seeded, and cut into strips

2/3 cup (150 ml) water

black pepper

plain yogurt to serve

Crushing the spices

Crush the cumin and coriander seeds, cayenne pepper, turmeric, and salt until finely ground, using a mortar and pestle.

1 Cut the haddock into 2-in (5-cm) squares and put them into a bowl.

2 Crush the spices and salt (see box, right). Sprinkle the mixture over the haddock, stir to coat evenly, cover, and leave to marinate in the refrigerator for 1 hour.

3 Heat half of the oil in a skillet, add the onion, and cook over high heat for 5 minutes. Stir in the ginger and chili and cook for 2 minutes. Add the cauliflower, potatoes, and green pepper and cook for 5–7 minutes. Remove the vegetables with a slotted spoon and set aside.

4 Heat the remaining oil, add the haddock and brown lightly all over. Add the cooked vegetables and measured water and simmer for 10 minutes or until the fish is cooked and the vegetables are tender. Taste for seasoning. Serve at once, with the yogurt.

HADDOCK WITH MUSHROOMS & CREAM

 Serves 4–6

1 1/4 cups (300 ml) milk

1 slice of onion

6 black peppercorns

1 bay leaf

4 tbsp butter, plus extra for greasing

1 1/2 lb (750 g) haddock fillet, skinned

salt and black pepper

squeeze of lemon juice

1/2 lb (250 g) mushrooms, sliced

1/4 cup (30 g) all-purpose flour

3 tbsp light cream

1/2 cup (30 g) fresh white bread crumbs

1/3 cup (30 g) grated Parmesan cheese

chopped parsley to garnish

1 Put the milk into a small saucepan with the onion, peppercorns, and bay leaf and bring just to a boil. Remove from the heat, cover, and leave to steep for 10 minutes. Lightly butter a shallow ovenproof dish.

2 Cut the haddock into 3-in (7-cm) pieces and place in a single layer in the dish. Sprinkle with salt and pepper to taste.

3 Melt half of the butter in a saucepan, add the lemon juice, mushrooms, and salt and pepper to taste, and cook gently, stirring occasionally, for 3 minutes or until just tender. Remove the mushrooms with a slotted spoon and put them on top of the fish.

4 Strain the milk and set aside. Melt the remaining butter in a saucepan, add the flour, and cook, stirring, for 1 minute. Remove from the heat and gradually blend in the infused milk. Bring to a boil, stirring constantly until the mixture thickens. Simmer for 2–3 minutes. Stir in the cream and add salt and pepper to taste.

5 Pour the sauce over the fish and mushrooms, then sprinkle with the bread crumbs and Parmesan. Bake in a 375°F (190°C) oven for 25–30 minutes, until the fish is cooked and the top is golden and bubbling. Garnish with parsley, and serve immediately.

ROAST MONKFISH NIÇOISE

 Serves 4

3 tbsp olive oil

1 head of garlic, separated

1 lemon, thickly sliced

4 6-oz (175-g) monkfish fillets, skinned

1 tsp herbes de Provence

1 cup (250 ml) dry white wine

1/2 cup (125 ml) fish stock

13 oz (400 g) canned artichoke hearts, drained and rinsed

15 pitted black olives

10 sun-dried tomatoes in oil, drained

squeeze of lemon juice

salt and black pepper

lemon wedges and thyme sprigs to garnish

1 Put 1 tbsp of the oil into an ovenproof dish, add the garlic cloves, and roast in a 375°F (190°C) oven for about 10 minutes, until soft.

2 Arrange the lemon slices in the dish and put the garlic and monkfish on top. Sprinkle with the remaining oil and the herbs and pour in the wine and stock. Return to the oven for 15 minutes.

3 Add the artichoke hearts, olives, and sun-dried tomatoes and cook for 5 minutes to heat through.

4 Transfer the fish and vegetables to a serving dish, discarding the lemon slices. Keep warm.

5 Pour the cooking juices into a small saucepan and boil for about 8 minutes, until reduced to about 1/2 cup (125 ml). Add the lemon juice and salt and pepper to taste and pour over the fish. Garnish with lemon and thyme and serve immediately.

ROAST MONKFISH BASQUAISE

Substitute 1 yellow and 1 red pepper for the artichoke hearts. Core, seed, and cut into strips and roast with the garlic cloves. Proceed as directed.

CITRUS MONKFISH

 Serves 4

2 unpeeled tangerines, washed and thinly sliced

1 onion, chopped

1/2-in (1-cm) piece of fresh ginger, peeled and finely chopped

1 lb (500 g) monkfish fillets, skinned

3 scallions, thinly sliced

1 cup (250 ml) fish stock

grated zest of 1/2 lime

5 tbsp (75 ml) lime juice

salt and cayenne pepper

4 tbsp unsalted butter, chilled and cubed

tangerine slices to garnish

1 Put the tangerines, onion, and ginger into a pan. Add the monkfish, scallions, and stock. Bring to a boil and simmer, without stirring, for 10 minutes or until the fish is firm. With a slotted spoon, transfer to a serving dish. Keep warm.

2 Put a strainer over a bowl and work through the remaining contents of the pan, pressing hard with the back of a spoon to extract all the juices.

3 Pour the juices into a small saucepan and boil rapidly, uncovered, for about 12 minutes, until the liquid has reduced to about 2 tbsp.

4 Add the lime zest and juice, salt and cayenne pepper to taste and heat gently, stirring, to warm through. Remove the pan from the heat and finish the sauce (see box, below).

5 Pour the citrus sauce over the monkfish and serve immediately, garnished with tangerine slices.

Finishing the sauce

Add the cubes of butter, one at a time, to the citrus sauce, whisking constantly between additions, until the butter melts and the sauce thickens slightly and becomes glossy.

MONKFISH KEBABS

 Serves 4

1 lb (500 g) monkfish fillets, skinned

1/4 cup (60 ml) olive oil

grated zest and juice of 1 large lemon

1 tbsp chopped fresh dill

salt and black pepper

1/2 cucumber

2 tbsp butter

12 fresh bay leaves

2 lemons, thinly sliced

dill sprigs to garnish

1 Cut the monkfish fillets into 1-in (2.5-cm) pieces and put them into a bowl. Whisk together the olive oil, lemon zest and juice, dill, and salt and pepper to taste and pour over the fish. Cover and leave to marinate in the refrigerator for about 4 hours.

2 Peel the cucumber and cut it in half lengthwise. Scoop out the seeds from each half and cut the flesh across into 3/4-in (2-cm) slices. Melt the butter in a small saucepan, add the cucumber slices, and cook gently for 2 minutes or until they begin to soften.

3 Lift the monkfish out of the marinade with a slotted spoon, reserving the marinade. Thread the kebabs (see box, below).

4 Brush the kebabs with marinade and put under the broiler, 3 in (7 cm) from the heat. Cook the kebabs, brushing them occasionally with the marinade, for 5–6 minutes on each side, until the fish is cooked through. Serve at once, garnished with dill sprigs.

Threading the kebabs

Push a piece of fish and a bay leaf onto a skewer. Fold a lemon slice around a cucumber slice and push onto the skewer. Keep threading the fish, bay leaves, and lemon and cucumber until 4 skewers are filled.

SPICED FISH WITH COCONUT

 Serves 4

1 1/2 lb (750 g) monkfish fillets, skinned

salt and black pepper

1 tbsp all-purpose flour

2 tbsp sunflower or corn oil

1 onion, finely sliced

1 garlic clove, crushed

1/2 tsp ground coriander

1/2 tsp ground cumin

1/4 tsp turmeric

2/3 cup (150 ml) coconut milk

2 large tomatoes, peeled (page 39), seeded, and cut into strips

3 tbsp chopped fresh cilantro

cilantro sprigs to garnish

1 Cut the monkfish into 5-cm (2-in) squares. Season the flour and lightly coat the monkfish.

2 Heat the oil in a large skillet, add the onion, garlic, coriander, cumin, and turmeric, and cook gently, stirring occasionally, for 3 minutes or until the onions begin to soften.

3 Stir the coconut milk into the onion and spice mixture and cook for 1 minute.

4 Add the monkfish and tomatoes, cover, and cook gently, stirring occasionally, for 15 minutes or until the fish is opaque and the flesh flakes easily. Add the chopped cilantro and taste for seasoning. Serve hot, garnished with cilantro sprigs.

Cook's know-how

Coconut milk is available in cans in many stores. To make it, bring grated fresh coconut along with its liquid or some water just to a boil, cool, then drain through 2 layers of cheesecloth, squeezing the meat to extract all the liquid.

CAJUN-SPICED RED SNAPPER

Serves 4

4 5- to 6-oz (150- to 175-g) red snapper fillets

2 tbsp butter

cilantro butter (page 221) and watercress sprigs to serve

CAJUN SPICE MIXTURE

2–3 tbsp all-purpose flour

1 tsp garlic powder

1 tsp paprika

1 tsp onion salt

1 tsp ground cumin

1 tsp mild chili powder

1/2 tsp dried oregano

1/4 tsp each black and cayenne pepper

1 Make the Cajun spice mixture: combine the flour, garlic powder, paprika, onion salt, cumin, chili powder, oregano, and black and cayenne peppers. Rub over the red snapper fillets, cover, and marinate in the refrigerator for at least 30 minutes.

2 Melt the butter in a large skillet, add the snapper fillets, and cook gently for 2–3 minutes on each side, until the fish is opaque and the flesh flakes easily.

3 Top the fillets with pats of cilantro butter, garnish with watercress sprigs, and serve immediately.

Snapper and spice

Cajun spices bring out the best in snapper, a pinkish red fish found in tropical waters. The fish has a large head, plump body, and firm, moist flesh. Cajun spice mixes often feature garlic powder – its pungent flavor adds a distinctive note.

COD STEAKS WITH ANCHOVY & FENNEL

Serves 4

2 oz (60 g) canned anchovy fillets

2 tbsp butter, plus extra for greasing

1 small onion, finely chopped

1 small fennel bulb, finely chopped

1 cup (30 g) chopped parsley

2 cups (125 g) fresh white bread crumbs

salt and black pepper

4 8-oz (250-g) cod steaks

dill sprigs, lemon wedges, and watercress sprigs to garnish

1 Drain the anchovy fillets, reserving the oil. Cut the anchovies into small pieces and set aside.

2 Melt the butter in a pan, add the onion and fennel, and cook over medium heat, stirring, for 5 minutes or until soft but not browned. Remove from the heat, stir in the anchovies, parsley, and bread crumbs, and season to taste with salt and pepper.

3 Put the cod steaks into a buttered ovenproof dish and top each one with the anchovy and fennel mixture, pressing it down firmly with your hand.

4 Drizzle a little of the reserved anchovy oil over each steak. Bake the cod steaks in a 400°F (200°C) oven for 15–20 minutes, until the fish is opaque and the flesh flakes easily from the bone.

5 Transfer to a warmed serving plate. Garnish the cod steaks with dill sprigs, lemon wedges, and watercress sprigs, and serve immediately.

COD STEAKS WITH SUN-DRIED TOMATOES

Omit the anchovies, fennel, parsley, and bread crumbs. Peel (page 39), seed, and chop 4 tomatoes. Drain 2 tbsp sun-dried tomatoes in oil and snip them into small pieces. Add the tomatoes to the softened onion in step 2, with 12 pitted and chopped black olives, and salt and pepper to taste. Drizzle the cod steaks with 1 tbsp olive oil, then top with the tomato mixture and bake as directed.

CHEESE-TOPPED BAKED PORGY

 Serves 4

2 18-oz (560-g) porgy, filleted and skinned

grated zest and juice of 1/2 lemon

salt and black pepper

2/3 cup (150 ml) water

butter for greasing

1/4 cup (30 g) grated aged Cheddar cheese

lemon zest and parsley sprigs to garnish

WHITE SAUCE

2 tbsp butter

1 tbsp all purpose flour

2/3 cup (150 ml) milk

1 Cut the porgy fillets in half lengthwise and arrange them in a single layer in a large ovenproof dish.

2 Sprinkle the fish fillets evenly with the grated lemon zest and salt and pepper to taste. Pour the lemon juice and measured water over the fish fillets. Cover the dish with buttered waxed paper.

3 Bake in a 325°F (160°C) oven for about 20 minutes until the flesh flakes easily.

4 Transfer the fish to a warmed flameproof platter, cover, and keep warm. Strain the cooking liquid and reserve.

5 Make the white sauce. melt the butter in a small saucepan, add the flour, and cook, stirring, for 1 minute. Remove from the heat and gradually blend in the milk and the reserved cooking liquid. Bring to a boil, stirring constantly until the mixture thickens. Simmer for 2–3 minutes. Taste for seasoning.

6 Pour the white sauce over the porgy fillets, sprinkle with the cheese, and place under the broiler 4 in (10 cm) from the heat, for 3–5 minutes until heated through and golden.

7 Serve the porgy fillets immediately, garnished with lemon zest and parsley sprigs.

PORGY NIÇOISE

 Serves 4

2 18-oz (560-g) porgy, cleaned (page 105), with heads removed

salt and black pepper

3 tbsp olive oil

1 large onion, sliced

1 small fennel bulb, sliced

1 garlic clove, crushed

12 pitted black olives

2 tbsp chopped parsley

juice of 1 lemon

lemon sections and parsley sprigs to garnish

1 Prepare the porgy (see box, below).

2 Heat 2 tbsp of the oil in a skillet, add the onion, fennel, and garlic, and cook gently, stirring occasionally, for 5–8 minutes, until the vegetables are soft but not browned.

3 Spoon the vegetables into an ovenproof dish and place the bream on top. Scatter the olives and chopped parsley over the fish, sprinkle with the lemon juice, and drizzle with the remaining olive oil.

4 Cover the fish loosely with foil and bake in a 400°F (200°C) oven for about 20 minutes.

5 Remove the foil and bake for 10 minutes or until the fish is cooked. Garnish with lemon sections and parsley sprigs before serving.

Porgy
A relatively inexpensive saltwater fish with silver skin and a flattish body. The firm flesh has a sweet flavor.

Preparing the porgy

Make 2 deep diagonal cuts in the flesh on both sides of each porgy, using a sharp knife.

Put salt and pepper into a bowl and combine. Sprinkle on the inside and outside of the fish.

HALIBUT IN PHYLLO PACKAGES

Halibut is a very fine fish with a delicate flavor and firm texture. Enclosing the halibut steaks in phyllo packages with matchstick-thin vegetables keeps the fish moist and seals in all the flavors, while the pastry trimmings on top provide an attractive, crunchy finish.

 Serves 4

3/4-lb (375-g) halibut steaks, skinned and boned

1 carrot

1 leek, trimmed

2/3 cup (150 ml) fish stock

2 tbsp dry white wine

2 tsp lemon juice

3 saffron threads or 1/4 tsp turmeric

salt and black pepper

8 large sheets of phyllo pastry

4 tbsp (60 g) butter, melted

lemon slices and dill sprigs to garnish

1 Halve the halibut steaks crosswise and set aside. Cut the carrot and leek into matchsticks.

2 Put the vegetables into a pan with the stock, wine, lemon juice, and saffron.

3 Bring to a boil and cook, uncovered, for 5 minutes or until the vegetables are just tender. Drain and add salt and pepper to taste.

4 Cut the phyllo pastry into eight 10-in (25-cm) squares and reserve the trimmings. Brush 1 square with a little melted butter, put a second square on top, and brush with more melted butter. Make a phyllo package (see box, right). Repeat to make 4 phyllo packages.

5 Place the phyllo packages on a baking sheet, and bake in a 400°F oven for 20 minutes or until golden and crispy. Garnish with lemon slices and dill sprigs and serve immediately.

Cook's know-how

Sheets of phyllo pastry are usually sold in a roll, fresh or frozen. The size of the sheets may vary with different brands, so don't worry if they are slightly smaller than 10 in (25 cm) wide – just be sure there is enough pastry to cover the filling.

HADDOCK IN PHYLLO PACKAGES

Substitute skinned haddock fillets for the halibut and 1 zucchini and 4 scallions, cut into matchsticks, for the carrot and leek. Proceed as directed.

Making a package

Spoon one-quarter of the vegetable mixture into the middle of the pastry square. Put 1 piece of halibut on top of the vegetable mixture.

Fold 2 sides of the phyllo pastry over the halibut and vegetables and tuck the remaining 2 ends underneath to form a neat package. Brush the top of the package with a little melted butter.

Crumple some of the reserved phyllo trimmings, and arrange them on top of the phyllo package. Brush with melted butter.

SEA BASS WITH LEMON BUTTER SAUCE

 Serves 4

sunflower or corn oil for greasing

2¼ lb (1.1 kg) sea bass, cleaned and filleted (page 105)

4 tarragon sprigs

1 lemon, sliced

salt and black pepper

2 tbsp dry white wine

LEMON BUTTER SAUCE

⅔ cup (150 ml) light cream

juice of ½ lemon

3 tbsp butter, melted

1 egg yolk

1 tsp all-purpose flour

white pepper

1 tsp chopped fresh tarragon

1 Put a large piece of foil on a baking sheet and brush lightly with oil. Put the sea bass on the foil, tuck 3 of the tarragon sprigs and all but 1–2 of the lemon slices inside the stomach cavity, and sprinkle with salt and black pepper to taste.

2 Season the outside of the fish, and lift up the sides of the foil. Pour the wine over the fish, then seal the foil into a loose package. Bake in a 400°F (200°C) oven for 30 minutes or until the fish is opaque and the flesh flakes easily.

3 Meanwhile, make the sauce: whisk the cream in a pan with the lemon juice, butter, egg yolk, and flour until mixed. Heat very gently, stirring constantly, until the mixture is thick enough to coat the back of a spoon. Add salt and white pepper to taste and stir in the tarragon. Keep warm.

4 Remove the sea bass from the foil and arrange on a warmed serving dish. Pour on the cooking juices. Garnish with the remaining lemon slices and tarragon sprig and serve immediately. Pass the warm lemon butter sauce separately.

FISH EN PAPILLOTE

 Serves 4

3 tbsp butter

4 8-oz (250-g) whitefish fillets, such as sole or grouper, skinned

¾-in (2-cm) piece of fresh ginger, peeled and thinly sliced

3 scallions, thinly sliced

2–3 garlic cloves, crushed

2 tbsp light soy sauce

1 tbsp rice wine or dry sherry

½ tsp sugar

★ 4 sheets of baking parchment

1 Cut the sheets of baking parchment into four 12- x 15-in (30- x 37-cm) rectangles, and cut out 4 hearts (see box, right).

2 Melt 2 tbsp of the butter in a small saucepan. Brush the paper hearts and 2 large baking sheets with the butter.

3 Place a fish fillet on one half of each heart. Top each one with ginger, scallions, and garlic and dot with the remaining butter. Whisk together the soy sauce, rice wine, and sugar and drizzle over the fish. Fold the paper over the fish, pleat the edges, and twist the pointed ends to seal.

4 Put the paper cases onto the prepared baking sheets and bake the fish in a 450°F (230°C) oven for 8–10 minutes, until the paper has turned brown and the cases have puffed up.

5 With a spatula, transfer the paper cases to warmed individual plates and serve immediately.

Cutting a paper heart

Fold a baking parchment rectangle in half and draw a curve to make a heart when unfolded.

Cut out the heart shape just inside the penciled line, and unfold.

135

GOLDEN FISH CAKES

 Serves 4

2 large potatoes, roughly chopped

salt and black pepper

1 lb (500 g) cod or haddock fillets

1¼ cups (300 ml) milk

1 bay leaf

9 black peppercorns

4 tbsp butter

4 tbsp chopped parsley

3 cups (175 g) fresh bread crumbs

1 egg, beaten

sunflower or corn oil for frying

tartar sauce (page 128) to serve

1 Cook the potatoes in boiling salted water for 15–20 minutes, until tender.

2 Meanwhile, put the fish into a pan with the milk, bay leaf, and peppercorns. Bring slowly to a boil and simmer for 10 minutes or until the fish is just opaque.

3 Drain the fish, reserving the liquid. Leave the fish to cool, then remove and discard the skin and bones and flake the fish.

4 Drain the potatoes. Turn into a large bowl, add the butter and 3 tbsp of the reserved fish-cooking liquid, and mash until smooth and creamy. Add the flaked fish, parsley, and salt and pepper to taste and mix well.

5 Spread the bread crumbs on a plate. With your hands, shape the fish and potato mixture into 8 flat cakes, 3 in (7 cm) in diameter. Dip each fish cake into the beaten egg, then coat with bread crumbs.

6 Heat a little oil in a skillet and fry the fish cakes, a few at a time, for about 5 minutes on each side, until golden brown. Serve immediately with the tartar sauce.

CRISPY-TOPPED SEAFOOD PIE

 Serves 4

1 lb (500 g) cod fillet

1¼ cups (300 ml) milk

1 bay leaf

2 leeks, trimmed and sliced

2 cups (175 g) broccoli florets

6 oz (175 g) cooked peeled shrimp

1 tbsp butter

2 tbsp all-purpose flour

salt and black pepper

½ lb (250 g) store-bought pie pastry, chilled

¼ cup (30 g) grated Gruyère cheese

1 Put the cod into a saucepan with the milk and bay leaf, bring slowly to a boil, and poach gently for about 10 minutes until the fish flakes easily.

2 Meanwhile, blanch the leeks and broccoli for 3 minutes in a saucepan of boiling salted water. Drain.

3 Lift out the fish, remove and discard the skin and bones, and flake the fish. Strain and reserve the milk.

4 Put the leeks and broccoli into a pie plate, and add the cod and shrimp.

5 Melt the butter in a small saucepan, add the flour, and cook, stirring, for 1 minute. Remove from the heat and gradually blend in the reserved milk. Bring to a boil, stirring constantly until thickened. Simmer for 2–3 minutes. Season to taste and pour over the pie filling.

6 Grate the pastry (see box, below) and sprinkle over the sauce. Sprinkle with the grated Gruyère cheese. Bake in a 400°F (200°C) oven for 25–30 minutes. Serve immediately.

Grating the pastry

Grate the pastry onto a plate, using the coarse holes of a grater. Be sure the pastry is well chilled.

5

POULTRY & GAME

UNDER 30 MINUTES

HERB-GRILLED CHICKEN

Fresh and summery: chicken quarters brushed with parsley, chives, and garlic in melted butter, then barbecued or broiled.
SERVES 8 297 calories per serving
Takes 25 minutes   **PAGE 160**

CHICKEN KEBABS

Pieces of chicken marinated in soy sauce, vinegar, oil, and thyme. Broiled with green pepper, mushrooms, and cherry tomatoes.
SERVES 4 662 calories per serving
Takes 25 minutes   **PAGE 166**

WARM CHICKEN SALAD WITH MANGO & AVOCADO

Marinated chicken with mango and avocado and rum-flavored cooking juices.
SERVES 4 411 calories per serving
Takes 25 minutes   **PAGE 176**

MUSTARD CHICKEN

Hot and creamy: strips of chicken coated with garlic in a cream sauce piquantly flavored with mustard.
SERVES 4 380 calories per serving
Takes 25 minutes   **PAGE 165**

TURKEY WITH SOUR CREAM & CHIVES

Strips of turkey breast in a bacon, mushroom, and sour cream sauce.
SERVES 4 542 calories per serving
Takes 25 minutes   **PAGE 180**

STIR-FRIED CHICKEN WITH VEGETABLES

Strips of chicken dry-marinated in ginger, mustard, sugar, turmeric, and curry powder. Stir-fried with mixed vegetables.
SERVES 4 405 calories per serving
Takes 25 minutes   **PAGE 164**

GREEK SPICED CHICKEN

Creamy and intensely flavored with herbs: pieces of cooked chicken coated in yogurt, sour cream, scallions, and herbs.
SERVES 6 264 calories per serving
Takes 15 minutes   **PAGE 176**

CHICKEN STIR-FRY

Light Asian dish: strips of chicken stir-fried with scallions, ginger, carrots, and peppers. Flavored with soy sauce and sherry.
SERVES 4 381 calories per serving
Takes 15 minutes   **PAGE 167**

HOT & SPICY STIR-FRIED DUCK

Strips of duck marinated in soy sauce, vinegar, ginger, chili, and orange. Stir-fried with vegetables and water chestnuts.
SERVES 4 453 calories per serving
Takes 25 minutes   **PAGE 189**

CURRIED CHICKEN SALAD

Bite sized pieces of chicken in a sauce made from scallions, curry powder, wine, lemon, apricot jam, mayonnaise, and yogurt.

SERVES 6 580 calories per serving

Takes 15 minutes, plus cooling **PAGE 175**

HERB-MARINATED CHICKEN BREASTS

Chicken breasts marinated in lemon juice, herbs, and garlic. Cooked until crispy and served with a hot stock sauce.

SERVES 4 641 calories per serving

Takes 30 minutes, plus marinating **PAGE 170**

ASIAN CLASSIC

THAI CHICKEN WITH WATER CHESTNUTS

Aromatic stir-fry: chicken with water chestnuts, lemongrass, garlic, ginger, cilantro, chili, and tofu.

SERVES 4 272 calories per serving

Takes 30 minutes **PAGE 164**

DINNER PARTY

DUCK BREASTS WITH RASPBERRY SAUCE

Rich and fruity: slices of broiled duck breast served with a sauce of raspberries mixed with port, sugar, and orange juice.

SERVES 4 975 calories per serving

Takes 45 minutes **PAGE 188**

STIR-FRIED TURKEY MEATBALLS

Mixture of ground turkey, garlic, soy sauce, and ginger, stir-fried with onion, pepper, zucchini, mushrooms, and bean sprouts.

SERVES 4 232 calories per serving

Takes 30 minutes **PAGE 183**

TARRAGON CHICKEN WITH LIME

Chicken breasts coated with lime butter and sprinkled with lime juice and tarragon. Baked and served with a sour cream sauce.

SERVES 4 128 calories per serving

Takes 45 minutes **PAGE 168**

TURKEY CUTLETS

Golden and tender: turkey breast cutlets coated in seasoned flour, beaten egg, and fresh bread crumbs and decorated with a crisscross pattern. Chilled in the refrigerator, then cooked until golden. Garnished with lemon slices and chopped parsley.

SERVES 4 394 calories per serving

Takes 25 minutes, plus chilling **PAGE 181**

CHEESE & GARLIC STUFFED CHICKEN

Chicken breasts stuffed with cream cheese, onion, garlic, fresh tarragon, egg yolk, and nutmeg, then baked. Served cut into slices.

SERVES 6 628 calories per serving

Takes 45 minutes **PAGE 168**

DEVILED CHICKEN DRUMSTICKS

Crispy and piquant: chicken drumsticks covered with a mixture of wine vinegar, ketchup, mustard, and sugar, then baked.

MAKES 12 138 calories each

Takes 45 minutes **PAGE 174**

TURKEY WITH CHEESE & PINEAPPLE

Bite-sized pieces of turkey with a cheese and pineapple sauce, sprinkled with fresh pumpernickel crumbs, then baked.

SERVES 6 450 calories per serving

Takes 40 minutes **PAGE 184**

CHICKEN SATAY

Pieces of chicken marinated in soy sauce, lemon juice, garlic, and scallions. Served with a peanut and coconut sauce.

SERVES 4 815 calories per serving

Takes 25 minutes, plus marinating **PAGE 166**

CHICKEN THIGHS NORMANDY

Chicken thighs baked with leeks, bacon, hard cider, and thyme, richly flavored with garlic. Served with a sour cream sauce.

SERVES 4 599 calories per serving

Takes 55 minutes **PAGE 171**

BACON-WRAPPED CHICKEN BREASTS

Tender and tangy: boneless chicken breasts spread with coarse mustard and wrapped in bacon strips.

SERVES 6 528 calories per serving

Takes 50 minutes **PAGE 169**

TURKEY & LEMON STIR-FRY

Turkey breast strips marinated in white wine and lemon zest and juice, stir-fried with zucchini, green pepper, and baby corn.

SERVES 4 342 calories per serving

Takes 20 minutes, plus marinating **PAGE 181**

CHICKEN PINWHEELS

Pounded chicken breasts spread with a cheese and basil mixture, rolled up, simmered, then sliced. Served with a tomato and herb sauce.

SERVES 4 423 calories per serving

Takes 50 minutes **PAGE 167**

FRAGRANT CHICKEN CURRY WITH ALMONDS

Chicken breasts cooked in an authentic blend of Indian spices, including cinnamon, cardamom seeds, cloves, cumin seeds, ginger, and garam masala, with a creamy yogurt sauce. Served with a sprinkling of golden raisins and toasted almonds.

SERVES 4 527 calories per serving

Takes 45 minutes **PAGE 162**

ASIAN GAME HENS

Tangy and succulent: game hens brushed with soy and hoisin sauces, sherry, garlic, and ginger, and baked.

SERVES 4 395 calories per serving

Takes 50 minutes **PAGE 157**

CHICKEN THIGHS WITH CHESTNUT STUFFING

Delicious and filling: boneless chicken thighs stuffed with a mixture of diced bacon, chestnuts, onion, fresh pumpernickel crumbs, chopped parsley, and egg yolk and then roasted until a golden brown. Served with a fruity cranberry jelly sauce.

SERVES 4 598 calories per serving

Takes 55 minutes **PAGE 171**

FAMILY CHOICE

TURKEY BURGERS HOLSTEIN

Golden and tasty: ground turkey combined with chopped ham, parsley, and onion, then shaped into burgers. Served with a fried egg.

SERVES 4 429 calories per serving

Takes 30 minutes, plus chilling **PAGE 183**

BARBECUE

JERK CHICKEN

Crispy and spicy: chicken pieces spread with blended lime juice, rum, scallions, chili, garlic, and spices, then barbecued.

SERVES 4 304 calories per serving

Takes 30 minutes, plus marinating **PAGE 161**

PICNIC FARE

LEMON & HERB DRUMSTICKS

Fresh and easy to make: chicken drumsticks marinated in olive oil, lemon juice and zest, onion, garlic, and parsley, then broiled.

MAKES 12 200 calories each

Takes 25 minutes, plus marinating **PAGE 174**

TEX-MEX CHICKEN

Chicken breasts marinated in oil, orange juice, and cumin, then broiled. Served with sliced avocado and a tomato and lime salsa.

SERVES 4 659 calories per serving

Takes 30 minutes, plus marinating **PAGE 161**

ASIAN CLASSIC

ASIAN DUCK WITH GINGER

Duck marinated in orange, soy sauce, sesame oil, rice wine, honey, and ginger. Served with baby corn and toasted sesame seeds.

SERVES 4 445 calories per serving

Takes 30 minutes, plus marinating **PAGE 189**

TURKEY MOLE

Hot and spicy: turkey pieces cooked with a blended sauce of tomatoes, almonds, chocolate, chili, cinnamon, and cloves.

SERVES 4 501 calories per serving

Takes 55 minutes **PAGE 182**

30–60 MINUTES

OVER 60 MINUTES

SWEET & SOUR CHINESE CHICKEN

Pieces of chicken marinated in soy sauce and rice wine. Stir-fried with peppers, celery, onion, ketchup, pineapple, and litchis.

SERVES 4–6 458–305 calories per serving

Takes 30 minutes, plus marinating **PAGE 165**

DUCK BREASTS WITH RED WINE SAUCE

Duck marinated in garlic, balsamic vinegar, and rosemary, then cooked, sliced, and served with a wine sauce.

SERVES 4 906 calories per serving

Takes 40 minutes, plus chilling **PAGE 188**

PERFECT FRIED CHICKEN

Pieces of buttermilk-soaked chicken, coated in flour seasoned with paprika. Cooked until golden and served with bacon.

SERVES 4 683 calories per serving

Takes 40 minutes, plus standing **PAGE 160**

SAFFRON CHICKEN

Chicken breasts marinated in saffron, ginger, lemon, cardamom, coriander, and cinnamon, then roasted. Served with a sour cream sauce.

SERVES 6 527 calories per serving

Takes 40 minutes, plus marinating **PAGE 163**

CORNISH HENS WITH ROMESCO SAUCE

Rock Cornish game hens and scallions marinated in oil, vinegar, and cinnamon. Served with a tomato-almond sauce.

SERVES 2 845 calories per serving

Takes 60 minutes, plus marinating **PAGE 157**

CHICKEN TIKKA

Chicken marinated in yogurt, tomato puree, garlic, tamarind paste, paprika, and ginger. Served with cucumber raita.

SERVES 4 266 calories per serving

Takes 20 minutes, plus marinating **PAGE 163**

CHICKEN WITH SAGE & ORANGE

Fresh and tangy: chicken breasts marinated in orange juice, soy sauce, sage, and ginger. Served with a sage and orange sauce.

SERVES 6 435 calories per serving

Takes 40 minutes, plus marinating **PAGE 169**

MOROCCAN GAME HENS

Rock Cornish game hens marinated in lime, garlic, cilantro, paprika, curry powder, cumin, and saffron, then broiled.

SERVES 2 467 calories per serving

Takes 45 minutes, plus marinating **PAGE 156**

CHICKEN CORDON BLEU

Golden and tender: pounded chicken breasts filled with ham and Gruyère cheese, and folded. Coated with egg and bread crumbs.

SERVES 4 602 calories per serving

Takes 45 minutes, plus chilling **PAGE 170**

⏲ OVER 60 MINUTES

LEMON GAME HENS WITH MARINATED ARTICHOKE HEARTS

Roasted Rock Cornish game hens served with artichokes marinated in lemon and garlic.

SERVES 4   555 calories per serving

Takes 1¼ hours   **PAGE 156**

TURKEY CASSEROLE WITH PEPPERS

Turkey pieces cooked in a delicious sauce of hard cider or white wine, red and yellow peppers, onion, and garlic.

SERVES 4   351 calories per serving

Takes 1½ hours   **PAGE 182**

PROVENÇAL BRAISED CHICKEN

Chicken stuffed with garlic and parsley, cooked with red pepper, carrot, and stock, which form the basis of a sauce.

SERVES 4   298 calories per serving

Takes 1½ hours   **PAGE 154**

COQ AU VIN

Rich and nourishing: chicken pieces cooked with bacon, shallots, mushrooms, red wine, stock, and a medley of fresh herbs.

SERVES 4   531 calories per serving

Takes 1½ hours   **PAGE 159**

ROAST PHEASANT

Two pheasants, buttered and covered with bacon strips, then roasted and served with red-currant-flavored gravy and   *accompaniments of cottage fries, fried bread crumbs, and bread sauce. Garnished with watercress sprigs.*

SERVES 4   660 calories per serving

Takes 1½ hours   **PAGE 191**

MUSHROOM-STUFFED QUAIL

Whole boned quail stuffed with shallots, mushrooms, and bread crumbs and served with a lime and sour cream sauce.

SERVES 6   651 calories per serving

Takes 1¼ hours   **PAGE 190**

TURKEY SALAD WITH MANGO & GRAPES

Turkey breast poached with parsley and peppercorns, coated in lemon mayonnaise. Served with mango, grapes, and walnuts.

SERVES 4   734 calories per serving

Takes 1½ hours, plus cooling   **PAGE 184**

CHICKEN MARENGO

Chicken pieces cooked with shallots, wine, stock, tomatoes, mushrooms, garlic, parsley, thyme, bay leaf, and shrimp.

SERVES 4   479 calories per serving

Takes 1¾ hours   **PAGE 159**

OVER 60 MINUTES

NORMANDY PHEASANT

Rich and tangy: pheasant cooked with apples, celery, onion, stock, and wine. Served with a creamy sauce and apple rings.

SERVES 6–8 751–563 calories per serving

Takes 1³⁄4 hours   **PAGE 192**

BRAISED RABBIT WITH MUSHROOMS

Rabbit cooked with shallots, mushrooms, hard cider or white wine, herbs, and enriched with cream.

SERVES 4 506 calories per serving

Takes 2 hours   **PAGE 194**

FRENCH ROAST CHICKEN

Tender and succulent: a whole chicken spread with softened butter, seasoned with black pepper, and roasted with chicken stock and a sprig of tarragon. Served with gravy made from the cooking juices, and garlic flowers, drizzled with olive oil, then roasted.

SERVES 4 433 calories per serving

Takes 2 hours   **PAGE 153**

FAMILY CHICKEN CASSEROLE

Popular wholesome meal: chicken quarters cooked with bacon, carrots, celery, onion, stock, bay leaf, thyme, and parsley.

SERVES 4 659 calories per serving

Takes 1³⁄4 hours   **PAGE 158**

ROAST CHICKEN WITH ORANGE & PEPPERS

Chicken with red pepper and garlic, flambéed with brandy and served with orange sauce.

SERVES 4 411 calories per serving

Takes 1³⁄4 hours   **PAGE 154**

SUNDAY ROAST CHICKEN

Perfect for Sunday dinner: chicken flavored with parsley and thyme, and roasted with an apple, lemon, and herb stuffing.

SERVES 4 534 calories per serving

Takes 2 hours, plus cooling   **PAGE 152**

⏱ OVER 60 MINUTES

ROAST TURKEY WITH GARLIC & TARRAGON

Turkey breast marinated in lemon, tarragon, thyme, and garlic, roasted with the marinade.

SERVES 4 296 calories per serving

Takes 1³/4 hours, plus marinating **PAGE 180**

PHEASANT STEW

Pieces of pheasant simmered with red wine, game stock, bacon, celery, mushrooms, shallots, and garlic.

SERVES 6–8 633–475 calories per serving

Takes 2 hours **PAGE 192**

CHICKEN POT PIE

Hearty meal: chicken simmered with stock, garlic, carrots, and potatoes. Flavored with nutmeg and parsley and baked with pastry.

SERVES 6 508 calories per serving

Takes 2 hours, plus cooling **PAGE 155**

MARINATED CHICKEN WITH PEPPERS

Chicken roasted with strips of red and yellow peppers, cooled, then tossed with a honey and herb marinade. Served with black olives.

SERVES 4–6 563–376 calories per serving

Takes 1³/4 hours, plus cooling **PAGE 175**

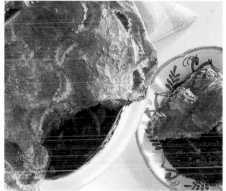

SQUAB PIE WITH FENNEL & CARROTS

Strips of squab breast cooked with fennel, carrots, onion, stock, and wine, and baked with a puff pastry lid.

SERVES 6 672 calories per serving

Takes 2 hours **PAGE 193**

GUINEA FOWL MADEIRA

Pieces of guinea fowl cooked with shallots, stock, wine, and Madeira, enriched with heavy cream and green grapes.

SERVES 6 613 calories per serving

Takes 1³/4 hours **PAGE 190**

RABBIT WITH MUSTARD & MARJORAM

Pieces of rabbit marinated in mustard and marjoram and cooked with garlic, bacon, and stock. Served with a mustard sauce.

SERVES 4 548 calories per serving

Takes 2 hours, plus marinating **PAGE 194**

CHICKEN CACCIATORE

Pieces of chicken sprinkled with thyme, and cooked with bacon, onion, green pepper, garlic, mushrooms, wine, tomatoes, and sage.

SERVES 4 540 calories per serving

Takes 1³/4 hours **PAGE 158**

RABBIT CASSEROLE

Rich and full of flavor: rabbit marinated in port, and cooked with shallots, bacon, cremini mushrooms, and herbs.

SERVES 6 712 calories per serving

Takes 2¹/2 hours, plus marinating **PAGE 193**

OVER 60 MINUTES

PEKING DUCK

Asian specialty: whole duck brushed before cooking with sherry, honey, and soy sauce. Served with Chinese pancakes.

SERVES 6 848 calories per serving

Takes 2¹/₂ hours, plus drying **PAGE 186**

BRAISED VENISON

Rolled shoulder of venison marinated in red wine, orange and lemon zests, and juniper berries and slowly braised in the marinade with chopped carrots, celery, and onions. Red currant jelly is added to the sauce just before serving.

SERVES 4–6 681–454 calories per serving

Takes 3¹/₂ hours, plus marinating **PAGE 195**

ROAST DUCK WITH CRANBERRIES

Duck stuffed with onion, fresh pumpernickel crumbs, and cranberries, roasted until crisp-skinned. Served with cranberry sauce.

SERVES 4 580 calories per serving

Takes 2¹/₂ hours, plus cooling **PAGE 187**

HEARTY VENISON CASSEROLE

Rich stew: cubes of venison marinated in wine, parsley, and allspice and cooked with celery, mushrooms, and carrots.

SERVES 4 699 calories per serving

Takes 2¹/₄ hours, plus marinating **PAGE 195**

TRADITIONAL GAME PIE

A selection of game, chicken, and pork marinated in port. Baked in a pastry case filled with jellied stock, then chilled.

SERVES 18 563 calories per serving

Takes 6 hours, plus marinating **PAGE 196**

BALLOTINE OF CHICKEN

Boned chicken pounded and stuffed with pork, liver, bacon, brandy, ham, and pistachio nuts. Rolled, cooked, chilled, and sliced.

SERVES 8–10 617–494 calories per serving

Takes 2³/₄ hours, plus chilling **PAGE 177**

CHRISTMAS ROAST GOOSE

Succulent and fruity: goose stuffed with pork sausage, sage, and apple and roasted. Served with wine-flavored gravy, enriched with goose stock and baked apples with a stuffing of Calvados, ground cinnamon, ground allspice, and prunes.

SERVES 8 921 calories per serving

Takes 5¹/₄ hours, plus cooling **PAGE 185**

POULTRY & GAME KNOW-HOW

POULTRY IS THE TERM applied to all domesticated farmyard birds and includes chicken, turkey, geese, and duck. Chicken is sold whole, in pieces, or cut into boneless pieces, and lends itself to an infinite variety of recipes. Turkey is equally versatile and you can now enjoy whole birds, breasts, and boneless breasts or cutlets at any time of year. Though eaten less frequently, the richer, fattier meat of duck and goose has a truly wonderful flavor, as does the leaner meat of game and game birds.

BUYING & STORING

Poultry and game birds should have a plump breast and moist skin. Poultry should smell fresh and sweet. Game birds, which are aged to tenderize their flesh and to enhance their "gamy" flavor, should nevertheless have an appealing odor. They should be hung in a cool, well-ventilated place for 2 days during warm weather and for up to 2 weeks during cold weather.

There is a great variety of poultry available. With chicken, for instance, the cook can choose free-range birds that have been allowed to roam in the open air and have been fed a diet of grain. They are more expensive but are thought to have a superior flavor. Corn-fed chickens are another option; their diet gives their flesh a yellow color and a delicious flavor. Chickens range in size from Rock Cornish game hens, which serve 1–2, to oven-ready birds weighing from 3 lb (1.5 kg) up to 6 lb (3 kg) or more. Turkeys can weigh as much as 30 lb (15 kg).

Poultry and game are very perishable, so they must be kept cool. Remove any tight plastic wrapping and giblets and refrigerate the bird, loosely wrapped, immediately. It's a very good idea to set the bird on a plate to collect any drips. Cook smaller birds within 2 days of purchase and store goose and turkey for up to 4 days.

MICROWAVING

Casseroles and stews made from poultry and game can be cooked quite easily in the microwave oven. They are quick to prepare and when cooked properly, the meat stays tender and juicy. You may choose to brown the poultry or game and any vegetables on top of the stove first, then transfer the dish to finish cooking in the microwave oven. If you use two different pans, be sure to transfer the flavorful pan drippings to the casserole in the microwave as well.

Roasted game and poultry are best cooked in a conventional oven; however, the microwave oven can speed up the process by quickly thawing meat that has been frozen.

FREEZING

To freeze poultry and plucked, oven-ready game at home, wrap it well and freeze without delay. When buying frozen poultry and game, check that it is completely frozen and transport it home as quickly as possible. Chicken, turkey, game birds, and small game animals can be stored in the freezer for 6 months; duck, goose, and guinea fowl can be kept for 4 months; and large game animals for 8 months.

Poultry and game must be thoroughly thawed before cooking. Pierce the wrapping and set the bird on a plate in the refrigerator (or use the microwave). Remove the giblets as soon as possible. Never refreeze raw poultry or game.

Poultry safety

Raw poultry can carry bacteria such as salmonella. To reduce the risk of food poisoning, it is vital to store and handle poultry properly and to cook it thoroughly. Wash your hands and all utensils in hot soapy water. Keep a cutting board just for raw poultry (preferably one that can be scalded, or washed in a dishwasher). Never let raw poultry (or its preparation utensils) come into contact with cooked poultry or meat. Don't stuff a bird until just before cooking and make sure the stuffing is cold. It's best to ensure that the stuffing is cooked thoroughly before being placed in the bird.

THOROUGH COOKING

Cook poultry thoroughly to kill any bacteria.

If you are roasting a whole bird, lift it on a long fork – the juices that run out should be clear. Insert a skewer into the thickest part of the meat and check the color of the juices. Large birds are best tested with a meat thermometer – the internal temperature should be 190°F (90°C) when properly cooked.

POULTRY OR GAME STOCK

To make 10 cups (2.5 liters) stock, use 3 lb (1.5 kg) poultry or game pieces, the carcasses and trimmings from 3–4 chickens, or a turkey or a whole chicken.

1 Put the cooked or uncooked bones into a stockpot or large pan with *2 or 3 halved unpeeled onions.* Cook until browned. If using a whole chicken, brown just the onions, not the bird.

2 Add *4 quarts (4 liters) water.* Bring to a boil, skimming off any scum from the surface. Add *3 chopped carrots, 3 chopped celery stalks, 1 large bouquet garni,* and *a few black peppercorns.*

3 Half cover the pan and simmer for 2½–3 hours. Strain the stock into a bowl. Leave to cool, then remove the solidified fat from the surface of the stock and discard. Cover and keep in the refrigerator for up to 3 days or freeze for up to 3 months.

GIBLET STOCK

Use the giblets from 1 or 2 birds (poultry or game), excluding the liver.

1 In a stockpot or large saucepan, cook the giblets until lightly browned. Stir in *1 quart (1 liter) water* (or previously made stock). Bring to a boil, skimming off any scum that forms on the surface.

2 Add *1–2 quartered unpeeled onions, 1 chopped carrot, 1 chopped celery stalk, 1 bouquet garni,* and *a few black peppercorns.* Simmer for about 1 hour. Cool, cover, and keep in the refrigerator for 3 days or freeze for 3 months. Strain before use.

JELLIED STOCK

This stock is used in cold dishes such as raised pies, where it forms a jelly around the meat. Make it in the same way as other stocks, but use bones only, rather than a whole chicken or other meats, since bones contain a high level of gelatin. Crack the bones before adding them to the pot. The stock will set when cool.

Stock know-how

Do not add salt when making stock because it may be reduced in recipes to concentrate the flavor.

◆

Peppercorns, instead of ground black pepper, are used in stock. Prolonged cooking can turn ground black pepper bitter.

◆

Skim fat with a large spoon, soak it up with paper towels, or allow to cool and lift it off.

CUTTING UP A CHICKEN

Chicken pieces are widely available, but cutting a bird into serving pieces is not at all difficult to do yourself, and it can be done before or after cooking. A pair of special poultry shears makes the job particularly easy; otherwise, use good, strong scissors or a sharp chef's knife.

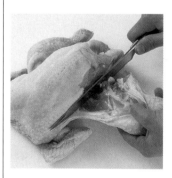

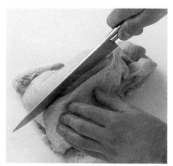

Drumstick   Thigh

Breast   Wing

1 Cut through to the joint between one of the legs and the body. Twist the leg out and away from the body to pop the ball-and-socket joint, then cut through the joint to remove the leg. Remove the second leg.

2 To remove the breasts, cut through the skin and flesh along both sides of the breastbone. Cut through the bones of the rib cage where it joins the sides of the breastbone, then remove the breastbone.

3 Open up the bird and cut along the backbone to give 2 breasts with wings attached. For 8 pieces, cut each breast diagonally in two: the wing half should be slightly smaller. Cut each leg through the joint.

BONING A WHOLE CHICKEN

Although boning a chicken requires a little time and effort, the result is impressive. Stuffed and rolled into a ballotine, it is ideal for entertaining because it is so easy to carve. Other birds can be boned in the same way.

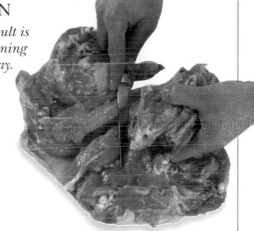

1 Set the bird breast side down and slit the skin along the backbone. Remove the wishbone (page 150). Slide the knife into the cut and gently pull and scrape the flesh away from the rib cage. Continue cutting away the flesh until you reach the leg and wing joints.

2 Scrape away the flesh from the other side of the rib cage. Be careful not to make any holes in the skin as you bone the bird. Cut through the ball-and-socket joints connecting the thighs to the bird.

3 Keep cutting until you reach the breastbone in the middle. Cut the breastbone free without cutting through the skin. Press each leg out and away from the body to pop the ball-and-socket joint.

4 Cut through the tendons that join the legs to the body. Cut and scrape back the flesh until the bones of each leg have been freed, then pull out the bones.

5 Bone the wings in the same way as the legs. The chicken is now ready for stuffing and rolling. Keep the carcass and bones of the bird for making chicken stock.

BONING A QUAIL

For a special occasion, tiny quail can be boned but left whole. Then it's simple to fill them with a savory stuffing and secure with a toothpick, ready for roasting. Make sure you use a very small knife and be careful not to pierce the skin.

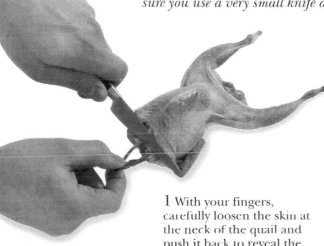

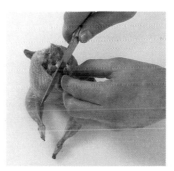

1 With your fingers, carefully loosen the skin at the neck of the quail and push it back to reveal the wishbone. With a small, sharp knife, cut the flesh from around the wishbone to remove it.

2 Loosen 1 wing by carefully cutting through the tendon at the base. Repeat with the other wing.

3 Insert the knife between the rib cage and the flesh and, working all around the bird, scrape the flesh from the bones, pushing it back as you go. Remove the rib cage. The bird is now ready to stuff.

SPLITTING POULTRY FOR GRILLING

This method of splitting and flattening a bird makes it quicker to cook and suitable for grilling or cooking over a barbecue. Rock Cornish game hens, chickens, and game birds can all be split for grilling.

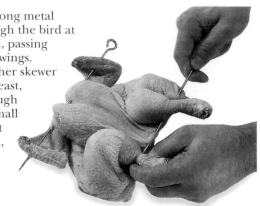

1 With poultry shears or a knife, cut along both sides of the backbone and discard. Cut off the wing tips and the ends of the legs. Remove the wishbone.

2 Turn the bird over. Put your hands on top of the breast and press down firmly with the heels of your hands to break the breastbone and flatten the bird.

3 Thread a long metal skewer through the bird at the neck end, passing through the wings. Thread another skewer below the breast, passing through the legs. If small birds are split and flattened, 2 or 3 can be threaded on the same skewers.

PREPARING POULTRY FOR ROASTING

Tying or skewering a bird before roasting holds it together so that it keeps a neat shape during cooking. It will also prevent any stuffing from falling out. Be sure the stuffing has cooled completely before it's placed into the bird.

Trussing with string
1 Thread a trussing needle with string. Put the bird breast side up. Push the legs back and down. Insert the needle into a knee joint, through the bird, and then out through the other knee.

2 Pull the neck skin over the cavity and tuck the wing tips over it. Push the needle through both sections of each wing, through the neck skin, and beneath the backbone.

3 With the bird on its side, pull the string tightly, tie the ends together, and trim. Tuck the tail into the cavity and fold the top skin over it.

4 Push the needle through the top skin. Loop the string around one of the drumsticks, under the breastbone, and around the other drumstick. Pull the string tight and tie the ends.

Simple trussing
1 Put the bird breast side up and push the legs back and down. Hold the legs with one hand, insert a skewer below the knee joint, and push it through the bird.

2 Turn the bird over. Pull the neck skin over the cavity and tuck the wing tips over it. Push a skewer through 1 wing, the neck skin and out through the other wing.

REMOVING THE WISHBONE

A bird is easier to carve if the wishbone is removed before cooking.

With your fingers, loosen the skin from the flesh at the neck end. Fold back the skin to expose the breastbone. Use a small, sharp knife to cut the wishbone free, taking any fat with it.

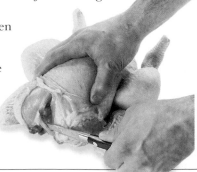

CARVING DUCKS & GEESE

Once cooked, small ducks need simply to be cut into quarters or even halves for serving. Larger ducks and geese can be carved as for other poultry (below).

3 Carve the breast meat in diagonal slices. For a larger bird, carve the breast meat without removing it first, as for a chicken (below).

1 Remove trussing. Cut through the joints between legs and body to remove the legs. (Cook them longer if necessary.) Cut the wings in the same way.

2 Slit the skin along both sides of the breastbone. Slide the knife blade into the cut on one side to free the breast meat in a single piece. Repeat on the other side.

CARVING POULTRY

Leave a bird to rest for about 15 minutes before carving. First remove any trussing string or skewers, then spoon stuffing into a serving dish.

1 Put the bird breast side up on a carving board (ideally one with a well to catch all the juices). Insert a carving fork into one breast to keep the bird steady, then cut into the joint between the far leg and body.

2 Turn the bird on its side and cut away the meat close to the backbone, cutting around the "oyster" meat on the back so that it remains attached to the thigh. Turn the bird over.

3 Twist the leg outward to break the joint, then cut it to remove the leg and the thigh. If preferred, divide into thigh and drumstick, cutting through the ball-and-socket joint. Remove the other leg.

4 Make a horizontal cut into the breast above the wing joint on one side, cutting all the way to the bone. Carve neat slices from the breast, holding the knife blade parallel to the rib cage. Repeat on the other side.

ROASTING TIMES

These times are only a guide; always test a bird to make sure it is thoroughly cooked (page 147).

BIRD	OVEN TEMPERATURE	TIME
Rock Cornish game hen	375°F (190°C)	40–45 minutes total cooking, depending on size
Chicken	375°F (190°C)	20 minutes per 1 lb (500 g) plus 20 minutes
Duck	400°F (200°C)	25 minutes per 1 lb (500 g) for "just cooked"
Goose	350°F (180°C)	20 minutes per 1 lb (500 g) plus 20 minutes
Pheasant	400°F (200°C)	50 minutes total cooking
Turkey 7–9 lb (3.5–4.5 kg)	375°F (190°C)	2½– 3 hours total cooking
10–12 lb (5–6 kg)	375°F (190°C)	3½–4 hours total cooking
13–17 lb (6.5–8.5 kg)	375°F (190°C)	4½–5 hours total cooking

Roasting know-how

To calculate roasting time, weigh the bird after you have added any stuffing. Do not stuff duck or goose.

♦

Cover large birds loosely with foil to prevent the skin from becoming too browned.

♦

Place fatty birds, such as duck and goose, on a rack to allow the fat to drain away and keep the skin crisp.

SUNDAY ROAST CHICKEN

Amid the many exotic recipes available today, a simple stuffed roast chicken sometimes gets overlooked. However, with its crisp skin, light, juicy stuffing of onion, apple, herbs, and lemon zest, and accompaniment of rich gravy, it is hard to beat.

 Serves 4

a few parsley and thyme sprigs

3 1/2–4 lb (1.7–2 kg) chicken, with giblets reserved for stock

1/2 lemon, sliced (optional)

1/2 onion, sliced (optional)

4 tbsp butter, softened

APPLE & HERB STUFFING

2 tbsp butter

1 small onion, finely chopped

1 cooking apple, peeled, cored, and grated

1 cup (60 g) fresh white bread crumbs

1 small egg, beaten

1 tbsp chopped parsley

1 tbsp chopped fresh thyme

grated zest of 1 lemon

salt and black pepper

GRAVY

2 tsp all-purpose flour

1 1/4 cups (300 ml) chicken giblet stock (page 148)

1 Make the apple and herb stuffing: melt the butter in a saucepan, add the onion, and cook gently for a few minutes, until softened. Remove from the heat, leave to cool slightly, then stir in the apple, bread crumbs, egg, parsley, thyme, lemon zest, and salt and pepper to taste. Leave to cool completely.

2 Put the parsley and thyme sprigs into the cavity of the chicken, add the lemon and onion, if using, and season well with black pepper. Truss the chicken if desired (page 150).

3 Spoon the stuffing into the neck end of the chicken, secure the skin flap over the stuffing with a small skewer, and pat into a rounded shape. Put any leftover stuffing into a small ovenproof dish.

4 Rub the softened butter over the chicken breast and season with salt and pepper.

5 Place the chicken, breast side down, in a roasting pan. Cook in a 375°F (190°C) oven for about 1 1/2–1 3/4 hours. Turn the chicken over when lightly browned. Continue cooking, basting every 20 minutes. Cook any leftover stuffing with the chicken for the last 40 minutes of cooking time.

6 Test the chicken: insert a skewer into the thigh – the juices will run clear when the chicken is cooked.

7 Transfer to a warmed serving platter and keep warm while you make the gravy (see box, right).

8 Remove the stuffing from the neck cavity and transfer to a serving dish with any leftover stuffing. Carve the chicken and serve with the gravy.

Making gravy

Tilt the roasting pan, and spoon off all but 1 tbsp of the fat that rises to the surface, leaving behind the cooking juices. Put the roasting pan on top of the stove.

Add the flour and cook over medium heat for 1–2 minutes, stirring constantly with a whisk or metal spoon to dissolve any browned bits on the bottom of the pan.

Pour in the stock and bring to a boil, stirring constantly until the gravy thickens. Simmer for 2 minutes, then taste for seasoning. Strain into a warmed gravy boat and serve immediately.

FRENCH ROAST CHICKEN

The flesh of a chicken roasted in the traditional French style remains particularly moist and succulent because of the stock added to the roasting pan. In France, the chicken liver is cooked in a little butter, then sliced and added to the gravy, but this is optional.

 Serves 4

1 tarragon or rosemary sprig

6 tbsp (90 g) butter, softened, plus extra for greasing

3¹/₂– 4 lb (1.7–2 kg) chicken, with giblets reserved for stock

black pepper

1¹/₄ cups (300 ml) chicken giblet stock (page 148)

2 tsp all-purpose flour

4 roast garlic flowers (see box, right) to serve

1 Put the tarragon sprig and 2 tbsp of the butter into the cavity of the chicken and season well with black pepper. Truss the chicken if desired (page 150). Rub the remaining butter over the breast.

2 Put the chicken, breast side down, into a small roasting pan. Pour on the stock and cover with buttered waxed paper.

3 Cook in a 375°F (190°C) oven for about 1¹/₂–1³/₄ hours, turning the chicken onto its sides and finally onto its back, basting occasionally, to brown all over.

4 Test the chicken by inserting a thin skewer into the thickest part of a thigh: the juices will run clear when the chicken is cooked through.

5 Transfer the chicken to a warmed serving platter and keep warm. Reserve the cooking juices.

6 Spoon off all but 1 tbsp fat from the pan. Make the gravy (steps 2 and 3, page 152), using the flour and reserved stock.

ITALIAN ROAST CHICKEN

Omit the roast garlic flowers. Put the chicken into a large roasting pan and add 2 trimmed and sliced fennel bulbs 30 minutes before the end of the cooking time. Remove with a slotted spoon before making the gravy and keep warm.

Roast garlic flowers

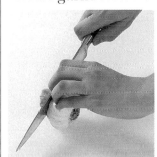

Cut the stalk ends off *4 heads of garlic*, arrange in an oiled baking dish, and drizzle a little olive oil over the tops. Cook in a 375°F (190°C) oven for 45–60 minutes. To eat, squeeze the soft cloves of garlic from the papery skins.

ROAST CHICKEN WITH ORANGE & PEPPERS

 Serves 4

3 oranges

3 lb (1.5 kg) chicken, with giblets removed

a few parsley sprigs

1 head of garlic, separated into cloves

salt and black pepper

1 tsp paprika

pinch of cayenne pepper

1 tbsp butter, softened

1 red pepper, cored, seeded, and diced

5 tbsp (75 ml) brandy

6 tbsp (90 ml) orange juice

chopped fresh basil to garnish

1 Cut 2 of the oranges lengthwise into quarters, leaving them unpeeled. Peel the remaining orange and separate it into sections.

2 Fill the chicken cavity with the parsley, orange quarters, and half the garlic.

3 Rub the chicken with salt, pepper, paprika, cayenne, and butter. Place the chicken, breast side down, in a roasting pan. Add the red pepper and the remaining garlic.

4 Roast the chicken in a 375°F (190°C) oven for 1¼–1½ hours, turning it breast side up halfway through cooking.

5 Heat the brandy in a small saucepan, pour it over the chicken, and light it with a match.

6 When the flames have died down, remove the chicken, red pepper, and garlic from the pan. Carve the chicken, discarding the parsley, orange, and garlic from the cavity. Arrange the sliced chicken, red pepper, and garlic cloves on a warmed serving platter and keep warm.

7 Spoon off all but 1 tbsp fat from the roasting pan, leaving behind the cooking juices. Add the orange juice and boil until reduced. Add the orange sections and heat through.

8 Spoon the orange sections and sauce over the chicken pieces, sprinkle with the chopped basil, and serve immediately.

PROVENÇAL BRAISED CHICKEN

 Serves 4

1 large head of garlic, separated into cloves

3–3 ½ lb (1.5–1.7 kg) chicken, with giblets removed

salt and cayenne pepper

6 parsley sprigs

1 red pepper, cored, seeded, and diced

1 carrot, diced

1½ cups (350 ml) chicken stock

1 cup (250 ml) red wine vinegar

1 tbsp tomato paste

¼ tsp herbes de Provence

chopped parsley to garnish

1 Peel half of the garlic cloves. Season the chicken inside and out with salt and cayenne pepper. Put the unpeeled garlic cloves and the parsley sprigs inside the chicken.

2 Place the chicken in a casserole, arrange the red pepper, carrot, and peeled garlic cloves around it, then pour in the stock. Cover the casserole and roast in a 375°F (190°C) oven for 1½ hours.

3 Remove the chicken from the casserole. Pour the pan juices, carrot, red pepper, and garlic into a food processor and puree until smooth. Return the sauce to the casserole and, if very liquid, boil it until thickened. In another saucepan, boil the vinegar until it has reduced to 3 tbsp.

4 Stir the vinegar, tomato puree, and herbes de Provence into the sauce and taste for seasoning. Return the chicken to the casserole, spoon the sauce over the chicken, and heat through.

5 Garnish with chopped parsley and serve at once.

WINTER BRAISED CHICKEN

Substitute 2 sliced celery stalks, 1 diced parsnip, and ¼ tsp celery salt for the red pepper and herbes de Provence and proceed as directed.

CHICKEN POT PIE

*This recipe makes a great family dish, packed with tender chicken and a variety of colorful vegetables.
You can vary the vegetables according to season and availability. The pie will be a great
success any time of the year.*

 Serves 6

2 lb (1 kg) chicken, with giblets removed

5 cups (1.25 liters) chicken stock

1 onion, quartered

1 celery stalk, thickly sliced

2 garlic cloves, crushed

2 small carrots

2 small waxy potatoes

3 tbsp butter

3 tbsp all-purpose flour, plus extra for dusting

pinch of grated nutmeg

salt and black pepper

1 cup (125 g) frozen peas

1 tbsp chopped parsley

store-bought pastry for a short crust pie

beaten egg yolk for glazing

★ 8-cup (2 liter) deep pie dish

1 In a large pan, bring the chicken, stock, onion, celery, and garlic to a boil. Simmer for 30 minutes.

2 Add the carrots and potatoes and simmer for 20 minutes or until all the vegetables are cooked and the chicken is just tender. Leave to cool.

3 Remove the meat from the chicken and cut it into bite sized pieces, discarding the skin and bones. Dice the vegetables and set aside.

4 Skim the fat from the stock, then bring 2 1/3 cups (600 ml) of the stock to a boil. Melt the butter in a large pan, add the flour, and cook, stirring occasionally, for 1 minute. Stir in the hot stock, whisking until it comes to a boil and thickens. Add the nutmeg and salt and pepper to taste.

5 Stir the chicken, diced vegetables, peas, and parsley into the sauce, then set aside until cold.

6 On a lightly floured work surface, roll out the short crust pastry, then cut out the lid and fill, cover, and decorate the pie (see box, right).

7 Bake in a 375°F (190°C) oven for 30 minutes or until the top of the pie is crisp and golden brown. Serve hot.

CHICKEN, LEEK, & MUSHROOM PIE

Omit the celery and carrots. Trim and slice 1 leek and cook in a little butter for 5 minutes or until soft. Add 3/4 cup (60 g) sliced mushrooms and cook for 2 minutes. Remove with a slotted spoon; add to the sauce with the chicken and vegetables.

Filling, covering, and decorating the pie

Invert the pie dish onto the pastry and use a small knife to cut around the edge, keeping the blade close to the dish. Reserve all trimmings. Transfer the filling to the pie dish and top with the pastry.

Press the pastry with your fingertips onto the rim of the pie dish. Crimp the edge of the pastry with a fork. Brush the pastry with the beaten egg yolk, making a lattice pattern.

Cut decorative shapes from the reserved pastry trimmings with a pastry cutter. Arrange on top of the pie and glaze the shapes with the beaten egg yolk.

MOROCCAN GAME HENS

 Serves 2

2 3/4-lb (375-g) Rock Cornish game hens, split for grilling (page 150)

MARINADE

3 tbsp olive oil

grated zest of 1/4 lime and juice of 2 limes

1 small onion, finely chopped

5 garlic cloves, crushed

2 tbsp chopped fresh cilantro

2 tsp paprika

1 tsp curry powder

1 tsp ground cumin

large pinch of saffron threads

salt and cayenne pepper

1 Make the marinade: in a nonmetallic dish, mix the olive oil, lime zest and juice, onion, garlic, cilantro, paprika, curry powder, cumin, saffron, and salt and cayenne pepper to taste.

2 Turn the game hens in the marinade, cover, and leave to marinate in the refrigerator, turning occasionally, for 3 hours.

3 Place the hens under the broiler, 6 in (15 cm) from the heat, and broil, brushing occasionally with the marinade, for 15–20 minutes on each side. Serve immediately.

LEMON GAME HENS WITH MARINATED ARTICHOKE HEARTS

Roasting game hens with lemon, rosemary, and whole cloves of garlic in the cavity makes them fragrant and juicy. The marinated artichokes also give an interesting twist to this classic Italian dish – add some sun-dried tomatoes as well if you like.

 Serves 4

4 3/4-lb (375-g) Rock Cornish game hens

salt and black pepper

4 garlic cloves

1 lemon, cut into quarters lengthwise

4 rosemary sprigs

4 tbsp butter, softened

26 oz (800 g) canned artichoke hearts, drained and halved

3/4 cup (175 ml) dry white wine

fresh rosemary and lemon wedges to garnish

MARINADE

1/4 cup (60 ml) olive oil

2 tbsp lemon juice

3 garlic cloves, crushed

1 tbsp chopped parsley

2 tsp chopped fresh thyme

1 Season the game hens inside and out with salt and pepper and put a garlic clove, lemon quarter, and rosemary sprig into each one. Truss (page 150). Rub with butter (see box, right).

2 Put the hens on a rack in a roasting pan. Roast in a 375°F oven, basting occasionally, for 40–45 minutes, until they are golden brown.

3 Meanwhile, combine the marinade ingredients, adding salt and pepper to taste. Turn the artichokes in the marinade and leave to stand for at least 30 minutes.

4 Boil the wine for about 15 minutes until it has reduced to 6 tbsp (90 ml). Set aside.

5 Remove the hens from the pan, and keep warm. Spoon off all but 1 tbsp fat from the pan, leaving the cooking juices.

6 Add the reduced wine to the pan, and mix with the juices. Stir in the artichokes, add 2–3 tbsp marinade and bring to a boil. Serve the hens with the artichokes and sauce, garnished with rosemary and lemon wedges.

Rubbing game hens with butter

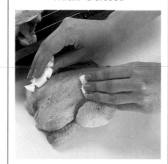

Cut the butter into pieces, and use your fingertips to rub it generously onto the skin of the game hens.

GAME HENS WITH MUSHROOMS

Substitute 3/4 lb (375 g) halved cremini mushrooms for the artichoke hearts and proceed as directed.

CORNISH HENS WITH ROMESCO SAUCE

 Serves 2

2 3/4-lb (375-g) Rock Cornish game hens, split for grilling (page 150)

8 scallions, trimmed

cilantro sprigs to garnish

MARINADE

2 tbsp olive oil

1 tbsp balsamic vinegar

4 garlic cloves, crushed

1/2 tsp ground cinnamon

salt and black pepper

ROMESCO SAUCE

3 tomatoes, peeled (page 39), seeded, and chopped

3/4 cup (90 g) slivered almonds

1 slice of stale bread, crusts removed, coarsely chopped

2 tbsp olive oil

1 tbsp balsamic vinegar

1 garlic clove

1 small dried red chili, cored, seeded, and chopped

1 tbsp chopped parsley

1/2 tsp ground cinnamon

1 Make the marinade: combine the oil, vinegar, garlic, and cinnamon and season. Brush over the game hens and scallions, cover, and leave to marinate in the refrigerator for 1 hour.

2 Place the hens under the broiler, 6 in (15 cm) from the heat, and broil for 15–20 minutes on each side until lightly browned. Broil the scallions close to the heat for 5–8 minutes on each side, until the scallions are slightly charred.

3 Meanwhile, make the romesco sauce: purée the tomatoes, almonds, bread, olive oil, balsamic vinegar, garlic, chili, parsley, and cinnamon in a food processor until smooth. Add salt and pepper to taste.

4 Serve the hens immediately, with the scallions and the romesco sauce. Garnish each serving with a cilantro sprig.

GAME HENS WITH NIÇOISE SAUCE

Make the romesco sauce as directed, but omit the cinnamon and add 2 tbsp store-bought black olive paste (tapenade). Garnish with black olives before serving.

ASIAN GAME HENS

 Serves 4

2 1 1/4-lb (625-g) Rock Cornish game hens

1/2 cup (125 ml) dark soy sauce

3 tbsp dry sherry

3 tbsp hoisin sauce

3 tbsp sunflower or corn oil

6 garlic cloves, crushed

2 tbsp brown sugar

1 tsp five spice powder

1/2-in (1-cm) piece of fresh ginger, peeled and chopped

scallions to garnish

blanched snow pea and red pepper strips to serve

1 Halve the game hens and remove the backbones (see box, right).

2 Combine the soy sauce, sherry, hoisin sauce, oil, garlic, sugar, five-spice powder, and ginger. Brush this mixture on both sides of the hen halves.

3 Put the hens, skin side up, into a roasting pan, and roast in a 375°F (190°C) oven, basting occasionally with any remaining soy sauce mixture, for 30 minutes or until cooked through.

4 With a sharp knife, thinly slice just the green tops of the scallions. Garnish the hen halves with the scallion slices, and serve with the snow pea and red pepper strips.

Halving a game hen

Cut along the middle of the hen breast with a pair of poultry shears. Take the 2 sides and open out slightly.

Turn the hen over and cut in half, along one side of the backbone. Remove and discard the backbone.

FAMILY CHICKEN CASSEROLE

 Serves 4

2 tbsp sunflower or corn oil

4 chicken quarters

4 thick slices of bacon, cut into strips

1/2 lb (250 g) carrots, thickly sliced

2 celery stalks, thickly sliced

1 large onion, sliced

1/4 cup (30 g) all-purpose flour

2 1/3 cups (600 ml) chicken stock

1 bay leaf

1 thyme sprig

1 parsley sprig

salt and black pepper

4 potatoes, cut into large chunks

chopped parsley to garnish

1 Heat the oil in a large flameproof casserole. Add the chicken, skin side down, and cook for 10–12 minutes, until browned all over. Lift out and drain on paper towels. Add the bacon, carrots, celery, and onion, and cook over high heat, stirring, until golden. Lift out with a slotted spoon and drain on paper towels.

2 Spoon off all but 1 tbsp fat from the casserole. Add the flour and cook, stirring constantly, for 3–5 minutes, until lightly browned. Gradually pour in the chicken stock, stirring until smooth. Add the bay leaf, thyme, parsley, and salt and pepper to taste.

3 Return the chicken, bacon, carrots, celery, and onion to the casserole, add the potatoes, and bring to a boil. Cover the casserole and cook in a 325°F (160°C) oven for 1 1/4 hours or until the chicken is cooked through. Garnish with chopped parsley.

ITALIAN CHICKEN CASSEROLE

Substitute 1 3/4 cups (250 g) sliced zucchini for the carrots and 13 oz (400 g) canned chopped tomatoes and 1 tbsp tomato paste for the chicken stock. Proceed as directed in the recipe, adding water if the mixture is too thick.

CHICKEN CACCIATORE

 **Serves 4**

3 lb (1.5 kg) chicken, cut into 8 serving pieces (page 148)

salt and black pepper

1 tbsp chopped fresh thyme

all-purpose flour for dusting

3–4 tbsp olive oil

3 thick slices of bacon, cut into strips

1 large onion, chopped

1 small green pepper, cored, seeded, and diced

4 garlic cloves, crushed

1/2 lb (250 g) mushrooms, quartered

1/2 cup (125 ml) red wine

13 oz (400 g) canned chopped tomatoes

5 tbsp (75 ml) tomato paste

2 tsp chopped fresh sage

1/4 cup (30 g) chopped parsley

grated zest of 1 lemon

2 tbsp capers

fresh sage to garnish

1 Sprinkle the chicken pieces with salt, pepper, and thyme, then lightly dust them with flour, shaking off any excess.

2 Heat half of the oil in a large skillet, add the bacon and chicken, and cook for 10–12 minutes, until browned all over. Transfer to a casserole.

3 Pour the fat from the skillet and wipe clean with a paper towel. Heat the remaining oil, add the onion, green pepper, and half of the garlic, and cook gently, stirring, for 5 minutes until soft but not browned. Transfer to the casserole with a slotted spoon. Add the mushrooms and cook for 2 minutes. Add to the casserole.

4 Pour the red wine into the skillet and boil for 10 minutes, until reduced to about 1/4 cup (60 ml). Add to the casserole with the tomatoes, tomato paste, and sage. Cover the casserole and cook in a 350°F (180°C) oven for 1 hour or until the chicken is cooked.

5 Combine the remaining garlic with the chopped parsley, lemon zest, and capers. Stir into the casserole and heat through. Taste for seasoning. Serve at once, garnished with sage.

Cacciatore

Meaning "hunter" in English, cacciatore is the Italian word used to describe dishes containing mushrooms, tomatoes, herbs, and wine.

CHICKEN MARENGO

2 tbsp butter

1 tbsp sunflower or corn oil

3 lb (1.5 kg) chicken, cut into
   8 serving pieces (page 148)

6 shallots

¼ cup (30 g) all-purpose flour

1¼ cups (300 ml) dry white wine

⅔ cup (150 ml) chicken stock

13 oz (400 g) canned chopped
   tomatoes

½ lb (250 g) mushrooms

1 tbsp tomato paste

2 garlic cloves, crushed

1 parsley sprig

1 thyme sprig

1 bay leaf

salt and black pepper

½ lb (250 g) cooked peeled
   shrimp

chopped parsley to garnish

1 Melt the butter with the oil in a large flameproof casserole. When the butter is foaming, add the chicken pieces and cook for 10–12 minutes, until browned all over. Lift out and drain.

2 Add the shallots and cook over high heat for about 8 minutes, until browned all over. Lift out and drain on paper towels.

3 Spoon off all but 1 tbsp of the fat from the casserole. Add the flour and cook, stirring, for 3–5 minutes, until lightly browned. Lower the heat and blend in the wine and stock, stirring until well combined. Add the tomatoes, mushrooms, tomato paste, garlic, parsley, thyme, bay leaf, and salt and pepper to taste.

4 Return the shallots and chicken to the casserole and bring to a boil. Cover and cook in a 350°F (180°C) oven for 1 hour or until the chicken is almost tender. Stir in the shrimp and return the casserole to the oven for 10 minutes. Garnish each serving with chopped parsley and serve immediately.

Chicken Marengo

This dish takes its name from the battle of Marengo in 1800, when Napoleon defeated the Austrians. The original version, improvised on the battlefield by Napoleon's chef, was made with a chicken, tomatoes, eggs, crayfish, garlic, and a splash of brandy from the general's flask.

COQ AU VIN

2 tbsp butter

1 tbsp sunflower or corn oil

3 lb (1.5 kg) chicken, cut into
   8 serving pieces (page 148)

4 thick slices of bacon, cut into
   strips

8 shallots

½ lb (250 g) mushrooms

¼ cup (30 g) all-purpose flour

1¼ cups (300 ml) chicken stock

1¼ cups (300 ml) red wine

1 bay leaf

1 thyme sprig

1 parsley sprig

1 large garlic clove, crushed

salt and black pepper

4 slices of white bread, crusts
   removed, to serve

2 tbsp chopped parsley
   to garnish

1 Melt the butter with the oil in a large flameproof casserole. When the butter is foaming, add the chicken pieces and cook for 10–12 minutes, until browned all over. Lift out and drain on paper towels.

2 Spoon off any excess fat, then add the bacon, shallots, and mushrooms and cook over high heat, stirring, until golden brown. Lift out with a slotted spoon and drain thoroughly on paper towels.

3 Add the flour and cook for 3–5 minutes, stirring constantly until lightly browned. Gradually pour in the stock, then the wine, stirring until smooth.

4 Return the chicken, bacon, shallots, and mushrooms to the casserole and add the bay leaf, thyme, parsley, garlic, and salt and pepper to taste. Bring to a boil, cover, and cook in a 350°F (180°C) oven for 45–60 minutes, until the chicken is cooked through.

5 Toward the end of the cooking time, toast the bread slices on both sides under the broiler. Cut each slice into 4 triangles.

6 Garnish the chicken with the chopped parsley and serve immediately with the toasted bread triangles.

PERFECT FRIED CHICKEN

 Serves 4

1 1/2 cups (350 ml) buttermilk

2 1/2–3 lb (1.25–1.5 kg) chicken, cut into 8 serving pieces (page 148)

1 cup (125 g) all-purpose flour

1 1/2 tsp salt

1 tsp paprika

1/2 tsp black pepper

1/2 tsp garlic powder

large pinch of grated nutmeg

oil for deep-frying

4 slices of bacon to serve

parsley sprigs to garnish

1 Pour the buttermilk into a large nonmetallic bowl. Add the chicken pieces and turn to coat. Cover and chill in the refrigerator, turning occasionally, for 2–3 hours.

2 In a large bowl, combine the flour with the salt, paprika, pepper, garlic powder, and nutmeg.

3 Lift the chicken pieces out of the buttermilk and shake off any excess liquid. Coat with the seasoned flour (see box, right).

4 Pour 3/4 in (2 cm) of oil into a deep skillet and heat to 350°F or until a cube of white bread browns in 1 minute.

5 Fry the chicken pieces in the hot oil, in 2–3 batches if necessary, turning them several times so they cook evenly, for 10–15 minutes, until golden brown. Drain the chicken on paper towels.

6 Put the bacon under the broiler, 4 in (10 cm) from the heat, and cook for 3–4 minutes on each side until crisp. Serve the chicken immediately, garnished with the bacon and parsley.

Coating chicken

Dip the chicken pieces, one at a time, into the seasoned flour, turning to coat evenly.

HERB-GRILLED CHICKEN

 Serves 8

8 chicken quarters

HERB BUTTER

6 tbsp (90 g) butter

3 tbsp chopped parsley

3 tbsp snipped fresh chives

2 garlic cloves, crushed (optional)

salt and black pepper

1 Melt the butter in a small saucepan. Add the parsley, chives, and garlic, if using, and add salt and pepper to taste.

2 Brush the chicken with the herb butter and put, skin side down, on a hot barbecue, or skin side up under the broiler, 4 in (10 cm) from the heat. Cook, brushing with the butter, for 10 minutes on each side, until cooked through.

Cook's know-how

To prepare this dish in advance, don't melt the butter, just soften it, and blend with the herbs and garlic. Chill until needed. Melt the butter and brush over the chicken before cooking.

JAMAICAN CHICKEN

Substitute 1/2 tsp crushed mixed peppercorns, 1/2 tsp chopped fresh thyme, and 3 chopped scallions for the parsley, chives, and garlic. Melt the butter, add the flavorings, and proceed as directed.

ROSY PAPRIKA CHICKEN

Substitute 2 tsp paprika and 2 tsp dry mustard for the parsley, chives, and garlic. Melt the butter, add the flavorings, and proceed as directed.

ASIAN CILANTRO CHICKEN

Substitute 1–2 tbsp chopped fresh cilantro, 1–2 cored, seeded, and chopped fresh green chilies, and 1/4 tsp cumin seeds for the parsley and chives.

JERK CHICKEN

Serves 4

2 lb (1 kg) chicken, cut into
  4 serving pieces (page 148)

chopped fresh thyme to garnish

broiled pineapple rings to serve

JERK PASTE

3 tbsp lime juice

2 tbsp dark rum

2 tbsp sunflower or corn oil

1 tsp soy sauce

4 scallions, thinly sliced

1–2 fresh green chilies, cored,
  seeded, and coarsely chopped

2 garlic cloves, coarsely chopped

2 tbsp ground allspice

1/2 tsp ground cinnamon

pinch of grated nutmeg

2 tsp chopped fresh thyme

salt and black pepper

1 Make the jerk paste:
puree the lime juice, rum,
oil, soy sauce, scallions,
chilies, garlic, spices, thyme,
and salt and pepper in a
food processor until smooth.

2 Brush the chicken pieces
with the jerk paste (see
box, right). Leave to
marinate in the refrigerator
for 30 minutes.

3 Put the chicken on a
hot barbecue, or under
the broiler, 4 in (10 cm)
from the heat. Cook for
about 10 minutes on each
side, until the juices run
clear. Serve the chicken
immediately, garnished with
thyme and accompanied by
broiled pineapple rings.

Jerk

*Jerk is a spicy paste from the
West Indies. It is spread over
chicken or meat, which is left to
marinate, then barbecued or
grilled. The rum and lime juice
tenderize the meat.*

Jerking the chicken

Brush a layer of jerk paste
over both sides of each
piece of chicken with a
pastry brush.

TEX-MEX CHICKEN

Serves 4

4 skinless, boneless chicken
  breast halves

2 avocados

2 tbsp lime juice

1 red onion, finely chopped

MARINADE

1/4 cup (60 ml) olive oil

1/4 cup (60 ml) orange juice

1/2 tsp ground cumin

SALSA

2 large tomatoes, peeled (page
  39), seeded, and diced

1 small onion, diced

3 tbsp olive oil

2 tbsp lime juice

3 tbsp chopped fresh cilantro

2 garlic cloves, crushed

1 fresh green chili, cored,
  seeded, and chopped

salt

1 Make several diagonal
slashes in each chicken
breast and put in a shallow
dish. Make the marinade:
combine the oil, orange
juice, and cumin and pour
over the chicken. Cover and
leave to marinate in the
refrigerator for 30 minutes.

2 Make the salsa: combine
the tomatoes, onion, oil,
lime juice, cilantro, garlic,
chili, and salt to taste. Cover
the salsa and chill until
ready to serve.

3 Remove the chicken
from the marinade, put
under the broiler, 4 in
(10 cm) from the heat, and
broil for 6 minutes on each
side, until golden and
cooked through.

4 Meanwhile, halve, pit
(page 68), and peel the
avocados. Slice lengthwise
and brush with lime juice.

5 Thinly slice the chicken
breasts (see box, below).
Arrange the avocado and
chicken on individual plates
and sprinkle the chopped
red onion around the edges.
Spoon a little of the salsa
into the middle of each
serving and pass the
remainder separately.
Serve immediately.

Slicing the chicken

Cut the chicken breasts
into 1/8-in (3-mm) slices
with a sharp chef's knife,
carefully following the
diagonal slashes.

Blanching, slivering, and toasting almonds

Blanch the almonds and loosen the skins: immerse in a bowl of boiling water. When cool enough to handle, squeeze the almonds between your fingers to slide and pull off the skin.

Slice the almonds in half lengthwise. Cut the halves into slivers.

Scatter the slivered almonds on a baking sheet, and toast in a 350°F (180°C) oven, stirring the almonds occasionally with a wooden spatula to ensure that they color evenly, for 8–10 minutes until lightly browned.

FRAGRANT CHICKEN CURRY WITH ALMONDS

The spices in this recipe are among those used in store-bought curry powders, but using your own individual blend of spices gives a truly authentic flavor to a curry. This is a creamy, mild dish – not too hot and spicy.

 Serves 4

2 tbsp sunflower or corn oil

4 skinless, boneless chicken breast halves

1-in (2.5-cm) piece of cinnamon stick

seeds of 4 cardamom pods, crushed

4 cloves

2 tsp cumin seeds, ground

1 bay leaf

1 large onion, finely chopped

2 garlic cloves, crushed

1-in (2.5-cm) piece of fresh ginger, peeled and grated

1/4 tsp garam masala

pinch of cayenne pepper

salt and black pepper

2/3 cup (150 ml) light cream

3 tbsp water

2/3 cup (150 g) plain yogurt

1/3 cup (60 g) golden raisins and 1/2 cup (60 g) whole almonds, blanched, slivered, and toasted (see box, right), to garnish

1 Heat the oil in a small flameproof casserole. Add the chicken breasts and cook for 5 minutes on each side, until golden. Lift out and drain on paper towels.

2 Add the cinnamon, cardamom seeds, cloves, cumin seeds, and bay leaf to the hot oil and stir over high heat for 1 minute.

3 Add the onion, garlic, and ginger and cook gently, stirring occasionally, for a few minutes, until just beginning to soften. Stir in the garam masala and cayenne pepper.

4 Return the chicken to the casserole and season to taste. Pour in the cream and measured water and bring to a boil. Cover and simmer very gently for 20 minutes or until the chicken is tender. Remove and discard the cinnamon stick, cloves, and bay leaf.

5 Stir in the yogurt, taste for seasoning, then heat through very gently. Spoon into a serving dish and sprinkle with the raisins and toasted slivered almonds. Serve immediately.

Cook's know-how

Cardamom comes in 3 forms: as pods, whole seeds, or ground seeds. Since the seeds lose their flavor quickly, it is best to buy whole cardamom pods and remove the seeds when you need them. As with the other spices in this recipe, frying cardamom seeds over high heat releases their full flavor.

SAFFRON CHICKEN

 Serves 6

6 boneless chicken breast halves,
  with the skin left on

1 tbsp olive oil

3/4 cup plus 1 tbsp (200 ml)
  light sour cream

salt and black pepper

chopped parsley to garnish

MARINADE

2 pinches of saffron threads

1-in (2.5-cm) piece of fresh
  ginger, peeled and chopped

juice of 1 lemon

1 tsp ground cardamom

1 tsp ground coriander

1 tsp ground cinnamon

1 Make the marinade: put
the saffron and the ginger
into a mortar and grind with
a pestle until smooth. Add
the lemon juice, cardamom,
coriander, and cinnamon,
and mix well.

2 Put the chicken breast
halves into a shallow
nonmetallic dish. Pour on
the marinade and turn to
coat evenly. Cover and
leave to marinate in the
refrigerator for about
20 minutes.

3 Pour the oil into a small
roasting pan. Turn the
chicken breasts in the oil and
place them, skin side up, in
the roasting pan. Cook in a
375°F (190°C) oven for
20–25 minutes. Remove the
chicken from the pan, cover,
and keep warm.

4 Put the roasting pan on
top of the stove, pour in
the sour cream, and stir to
combine with the juices. Add
salt and pepper to taste and
heat through.

5 Divide the sauce among
6 warmed plates. Place
the chicken breasts on top,
sprinkle them lightly with
chopped parsley, and serve
immediately.

TURMERIC CHICKEN

Substitute 1 tsp ground
turmeric for the saffron threads.
Mix with the ginger, lemon
juice, cardamom, coriander,
and cinnamon and proceed
as directed.

CHICKEN TIKKA

 Serves 4

1 1/2 lb (750 g) skinless, boneless
  chicken breast halves, cut into
  1-in (2.5-cm) cubes

cucumber raita (see box, right)
  to serve

MARINADE

2 tbsp plain yogurt

2 tbsp tomato paste

1 small onion, finely chopped

3 garlic cloves, crushed

1 tbsp tamarind paste

1 tbsp paprika

1 tsp ground ginger

1/2 tsp salt

1/2 tsp ground cumin

large pinch of cayenne pepper

large pinch of grated nutmeg

☆ 4 metal skewers

1 Make the marinade: in a
bowl, combine the yogurt,
tomato paste, onion, garlic,
tamarind paste, paprika,
ginger, salt, cumin, cayenne
pepper, and nutmeg.

2 Toss the chicken in the
marinade. Cover and
marinate in the refrigerator
for at least 2 hours.

3 Thread the chicken on
skewers, put under the
broiler, 4 in (10 cm) from
the heat, and cook for 3–5
minutes on each side. Serve
immediately, with the raita.

Cucumber raita

Cut half a cucumber in half
lengthwise. Scoop out the
seeds and coarsely grate
the cucumber. Put the
cucumber in a strainer over
a bowl and leave to drain
for 10 minutes. Press the
cucumber into the strainer
to extract the juices.

Combine the cucumber
with 3 thinly sliced scallions,
reserving some green
slices for garnish, 1 cup
(250 g) plain yogurt, and
salt and pepper to taste.
Garnish with the scallion
slices and serve.

STIR-FRIED CHICKEN WITH VEGETABLES

 Serves 4

4 skinless, boneless chicken
 breast halves, cut diagonally
 into 1/4-in (5-mm) strips

8 scallions

3 tbsp sunflower or corn oil

4 carrots, cut into matchsticks

1 1/2 cups (175 g) baby corn

1 1/2 cups (175 g) sugar snap
 peas

2–3 tbsp lemon juice

2 tbsp honey

1-in (2.5-cm) piece of fresh
 ginger, peeled and grated

1 cup (125 g) fresh bean
 sprouts, soaked in cold water
 for 10 minutes, then drained

DRY MARINADE

1 tsp superfine sugar

1/2 tsp ground ginger

1/2 tsp dry mustard

1/4 tsp turmeric

1/4 tsp mild curry powder

salt and black pepper

1 Make the dry marinade:
in a large bowl, mix
together the sugar, ginger,
mustard, turmeric, mild
curry powder and add salt
and pepper to taste. Toss the
chicken strips in the dry
marinade, cover, and leave
to stand for a few minutes.

2 Finely slice the scallions,
reserving the green tops
to make scallion brushes
(page 115) to garnish the
finished dish.

3 Heat 2 tbsp of the oil in a
wok or large skillet. Add
the carrots and baby corn
and stir-fry over high heat
for 2–3 minutes, until they
just begin to brown. Lift out
with a slotted spoon and
drain on paper towels.

4 Add the sugar snap
peas and scallions and
stir-fry over high heat for
1–2 minutes. Remove with a
slotted spoon and drain on
paper towels.

5 Heat the remaining oil,
add the chicken strips,
and stir-fry for 5 minutes or
until golden. Add the
lemon juice, honey, and
ginger and cook for 3–4
minutes, until the chicken
strips are tender.

6 Return all the cooked
vegetables to the wok,
add the bean sprouts and
stir-fry over high heat for
1–2 minutes, until all the
vegetables are heated
through. Serve immediately,
garnished with the
scallion brushes.

THAI CHICKEN WITH WATER CHESTNUTS

 Serves 4

3/4 lb (375 g) skinless, boneless
 chicken breasts, cut into
 1-in (2.5-cm) pieces

3 tbsp sunflower or corn oil

5 garlic cloves, chopped

1-in (2.5-cm) piece of fresh
 ginger, peeled and grated

salt and black pepper

7 oz (200 g) canned sliced water
 chestnuts, drained and rinsed

2 1/3 cups (600 ml) chicken
 stock

1 tsp sliced fresh lemongrass

1 small bunch of fresh cilantro,
 coarsely chopped

4 large lettuce leaves,
 coarsely chopped

1/2 –1 fresh green chili, cored,
 seeded, and chopped

1 tsp light soy sauce

1/2 tsp sugar

1/2 tsp fennel seeds

6 oz (175 g) firm tofu, cut into
 bite-sized pieces

lime wedges, sliced scallions,
 and skinned natural peanuts
 to garnish

1 Put the chicken into a
dish, sprinkle with the oil,
half of the garlic and ginger,
and salt and pepper to taste;
leave to stand for 3 minutes.

2 Heat a wok or skillet, add
the chicken mixture and
sliced water chestnuts and
stir-fry for 8–10 minutes.
Remove the wok from the
heat and set aside.

3 Pour half of the stock
into a pan, add the
lemongrass, bring to a boil,
and simmer for 5 minutes.

4 Meanwhile, puree the
remaining stock, garlic,
and ginger with the cilantro,
lettuce, chili, light soy sauce,
sugar, and fennel seeds in a
food processor until smooth.

5 Add the simmering
stock, the pureed
cilantro mixture, and
the tofu pieces to the
chicken and water chestnuts
in the wok. Stir well and
heat through.

6 Serve the chicken
immediately, garnished
with lime wedges, scallion
slices, and peanuts.

SWEET & SOUR CHINESE CHICKEN

 Serves 4–6

1 lb (500 g) skinless, boneless chicken breasts, cut into 1-in (2.5-cm) pieces

8 oz (250 g) canned pineapple chunks in natural juice, drained and juice reserved

2 tbsp cornstarch

3 tbsp sunflower or corn oil

1 green pepper, cored, seeded, and cut into bite-sized pieces

1 red pepper, cored, seeded, and cut into bite-sized pieces

1 celery stalk, thickly sliced

1 onion, cut into bite-sized chunks

1/4 cup (60 ml) ketchup

8 oz (250 g) canned litchis, drained and juice reserved

salt and black pepper

chopped fresh cilantro to garnish

MARINADE

2 tbsp dark soy sauce

1 tbsp Chinese rice wine or dry sherry

1 tbsp water

1 Make the marinade: in a large bowl, combine the soy sauce, rice wine, and measured water.

2 Toss the chicken pieces in the marinade, cover, and leave to marinate in the refrigerator for 30 minutes.

3 Add water to the reserved pineapple juice to make 1 cup (250 ml) and blend with the cornstarch. Set aside.

4 Heat the oil in a wok or large skillet, add the chicken and stir-fry for 8–10 minutes, until golden all over. Lift out with a slotted spoon and drain on paper towels.

5 Add the green and red peppers, celery, and onion to the wok and stir-fry for 5 minutes.

6 Add the cornstarch and pineapple juice mixture, ketchup, and reserved litchi juice to the wok and cook for 3–5 minutes, until thickened.

7 Return the chicken to the wok with the litchis and pineapple chunks and heat through. Add salt and pepper to taste, and serve immediately, garnished with chopped fresh cilantro.

MUSTARD CHICKEN

 Serves 4

1 tbsp olive oil

1 garlic clove, crushed

4 skinless, boneless chicken breast halves, cut diagonally into 1-in (2.5-cm) strips

1 cup (250 ml) light cream

1 tbsp all-purpose flour

1 tbsp coarse mustard

salt and black pepper

flat-leaf parsley sprigs to garnish

1 Heat the oil in a skillet, add the garlic, and cook, stirring, for 1–2 minutes. Add the chicken strips, then lower the heat and cook, stirring frequently, for 10 minutes.

2 With a slotted spoon, lift the chicken strips out of the skillet and keep them warm.

3 In a small bowl, mix a little of the cream with the flour to make a smooth paste and set aside.

4 Pour the remaining cream into the pan and stir to mix with the cooking juices. Bring to a boil, stir in the cream and flour mixture, then lower the heat and cook for 2 minutes, stirring constantly until the sauce has thickened. Stir in the mustard and heat through gently, then add salt and pepper to taste.

5 Return the chicken to the pan, coat with the sauce, and reheat gently. Serve immediately, garnished with parsley sprigs.

Cook's know-how

Do not let the sauce boil once you have added the mustard or it will taste bitter. Coarse mustard gives an interesting texture to this dish, but if you prefer a smooth sauce, use Dijon mustard.

CHICKEN SATAY

This is a traditional Indonesian specialty that is becoming popular around the world. The rich satay sauce, made from peanuts and coconut, complements the pieces of chicken tenderized by a tangy marinade. Serve as an appetizer or a buffet party dish.

 Serves 4

4 skinless, boneless chicken breast halves, cut into 3/4-in (2-cm) pieces

flat-leaf parsley sprigs and coarsely chopped skinned natural peanuts to garnish

MARINADE

6 tbsp (90 ml) dark soy sauce

juice of 1 lemon

3 tbsp sunflower or corn oil

2 tbsp dark brown sugar

3 garlic cloves, crushed

3 scallions, thinly sliced

☆ 12 bamboo skewers

1 Make the marinade: in a bowl, combine the soy sauce, lemon juice, oil, sugar, garlic, and scallions.

2 Toss the chicken with the marinade. Cover and leave to marinate in the refrigerator for 30 minutes.

SATAY SAUCE

1 cup (250 g) peanut butter

2 garlic cloves, crushed

3/4 cup (175 ml) coconut milk

1 tbsp dark soy sauce

1 tbsp dark brown sugar

1/2-in (1-cm) piece of fresh ginger, peeled and finely chopped

1 tbsp lemon juice

cayenne pepper

salt and black pepper

3 Soak the skewers in warm water for 30 minutes.

4 Make the satay sauce: in a saucepan, heat the peanut butter with half of the garlic for 2 minutes. Add the coconut milk, soy sauce, sugar, and ginger and cook, stirring constantly, for 2 minutes or until the sauce is smooth.

5 Add the lemon juice and remaining garlic and season to taste with cayenne pepper, salt, and black pepper. Keep warm.

6 Thread the chicken pieces on the skewers. Place under the broiler, 4 in (10 cm) from the heat, and broil for 2–3 minutes on each side until cooked through.

7 Serve the chicken satay immediately, garnishing the sauce with parsley sprigs and peanuts.

Cook's know-how
Soaking the bamboo skewers in warm water before threading with the chicken prevents the skewers from burning when under the broiler.

CHICKEN KEBABS

 Serves 4

4 skinless, boneless chicken breasts, cut into 1-in (2.5-cm) pieces

2 green peppers, cored, seeded, and cut into 1-in (2.5-cm) pieces

1 pint (500 g) cherry tomatoes

3/4 lb (375 g) mushrooms

MARINADE

3/4 cup (175 ml) olive oil

1/2 cup (125 ml) light soy sauce

1/4 cup (60 ml) red wine vinegar

1 tsp dried thyme

freshly ground black pepper

☆ 12 bamboo skewers

1 Soak the skewers in warm water for 30 minutes.

2 Make the marinade: in a large bowl, combine the oil, soy sauce, wine vinegar, thyme, and pepper to taste. Add the chicken and stir to mix well. Cover and leave to marinate in the refrigerator for at least 10 minutes.

3 Lift the chicken out of the marinade, reserving the marinade. Thread the skewers, alternating green pepper, tomatoes, chicken, and mushrooms.

4 Place the kebabs under the broiler, 4 in (10 cm) from the heat, and broil, basting with the marinade, for 3–5 minutes on each side, until cooked through.

CHICKEN PINWHEELS

An elegant dinner party dish that's simple and economical to make yet looks stunning. An accompaniment of fresh tagliatelle pasta goes well with the tomato and herb sauce and makes a light meal that will appeal to everyone.

 Serves 4

4 skinless, boneless chicken breast halves

melted butter for greasing

basil sprigs to garnish

FILLING

1/4 lb (125 g) garlic and herb cheese spread such as Boursin

2 tbsp sun-dried tomatoes in oil, drained and chopped

1/4 cup (30 g) shredded fresh basil

salt and black pepper

TOMATO & HERB SAUCE

1 tbsp olive oil

1 small onion, chopped

13 oz (400 g) canned chopped tomatoes

1 tbsp chopped fresh herbs, such as parsley, chives, and thyme

1 Make the filling: combine the cheese, sun-dried tomatoes, basil, and salt and pepper to taste. Mix well.

2 Put the chicken breasts between sheets of waxed paper, and pound with a rolling pin until 1/4 in (5 mm) thick. Spread one-quarter of the filling over each breast and tightly roll up each one.

3 Brush 4 squares of waxed paper with melted butter and wrap each chicken roll in a square. Wrap each roll in foil, twisting the ends to seal them tightly. Put the rolls into a shallow pan of gently simmering water, cover, and simmer for 15 minutes.

4 Meanwhile, make the tomato and herb sauce: heat the oil in a pan, add the onion, and cook, stirring often, for a few minutes, until soft. Stir in the tomatoes with half of their juice, bring to a boil, and simmer for 3 minutes.

5 Puree the tomato mixture in a food processor until smooth. Work the puree through a strainer, stir in the chopped fresh herbs, and add salt and pepper to taste.

6 Unwrap the chicken and cut into pinwheels (see box, below). Serve with the tomato and herb sauce and garnish with basil.

Making the pinwheels

Cut each chicken roll on the diagonal into 1/2-in (1-cm) slices, using a sharp knife.

CHICKEN STIR-FRY

Serves 4

3 tbsp sunflower or corn oil

4 scallions, sliced

1-in (2.5-cm) piece of fresh ginger, peeled and chopped

3 carrots, thinly sliced

1 red pepper, cored, seeded, and cut into thin strips

1 yellow pepper, cored, seeded, and cut into thin strips

1/4 cup (60 ml) dark soy sauce

2 tbsp dry sherry mixed with 2 tsp cornstarch

4 skinless, boneless chicken breast halves, cut into 1/2-in (1-cm) strips

1/2 cup (125 ml) water

1 Heat 1 tbsp of the oil in a wok or large skillet, add the scallions and ginger and stir-fry for 1 minute.

2 Heat the remaining oil, add the carrots and peppers, and stir-fry over high heat for 2–3 minutes. Add the soy sauce, sherry mixture, and chicken strips and stir-fry for 3–4 minutes.

3 Add the measured water and continue stir-frying for 1–2 minutes, until the liquid boils and thickens slightly. Serve immediately.

TARRAGON CHICKEN WITH LIME

 Serves 4

4 tbsp butter, softened

grated zest of 1 lime and juice of 2 limes

4 skinless, boneless chicken breast halves

1 tbsp chopped fresh tarragon

salt and black pepper

1 tbsp water

²/₃ cup (150 ml) light sour cream

lime sections and fresh tarragon to garnish

1 Put the butter into a bowl and beat in the lime zest. Prepare the chicken breasts (see box, right).

2 Put the chicken breasts into a roasting pan. Sprinkle with the lime juice, tarragon, and salt and pepper to taste and bake in a 400°F (200°C) oven for 20 minutes or until the juices run clear and the chicken is cooked through.

3 Transfer the chicken breasts to warmed serving plates and keep warm.

4 Put the pan on top of the stove, add the measured water to the cooking juices, stirring to dissolve any browned bits, and bring to a boil, stirring. Cook, stirring, for 1–2 minutes. Stir in the sour cream and heat gently until warmed through.

5 Serve the chicken with the sauce, and garnish each serving with the lime sections and fresh tarragon.

Preparing the chicken

Make 3–4 deep diagonal cuts in each chicken breast with a sharp knife. Spread the top of each breast with one-quarter of the lime butter.

CHEESE & GARLIC STUFFED CHICKEN

 Serves 6

6 boneless chicken breast halves, with the skin left on

melted butter for brushing

STUFFING

2 tbsp butter

1 onion, finely chopped

2 large garlic cloves, crushed

¹/₂ lb (250 g) cream cheese

1 tbsp chopped fresh tarragon

1 egg yolk

pinch of grated nutmeg

salt and black pepper

1 Make the stuffing: melt the butter in a small saucepan, add the onion and garlic, and cook gently, stirring occasionally, for a few minutes, until soft but not browned. Turn the onion mixture into a bowl and leave to cool slightly.

2 Add the cream cheese to the onion mixture with the tarragon, egg yolk, nutmeg, and salt and pepper to taste and mix well.

3 Stuff the chicken breasts (see box, right). Put the chicken breasts into an ovenproof dish and brush with the melted butter.

4 Bake the chicken in a 375°F (190°C) oven for 25–30 minutes, until the juices run clear and the chicken is cooked through. Cut each breast into diagonal slices, remove the toothpicks and serve hot.

Stuffing a chicken breast

Loosen the skin from one end of the chicken breast. Push a finger between the skin and the flesh, leaving the skin attached at the sides, to form a pocket.

Fill the pocket with the stuffing. Seal the open end of the breast with a wooden toothpick.

BACON-WRAPPED CHICKEN BREASTS

 Serves 6

6 skinless, boneless chicken
  breast halves

1/4 cup (60 ml) coarse mustard

black pepper

18 slices of bacon

snipped fresh chives to garnish

1 Spread both sides of the
chicken breasts with the
mustard and season with
black pepper.

2 Take 3 slices of bacon,
stretch them with the
back of a knife, and arrange
them on a plate side by side
and slightly overlapping.
Wrap a chicken breast
with the bacon (see box,
right). Repeat with the
remaining slices of bacon
and chicken breasts.

3 Place the chicken breasts
in a roasting pan, and
bake in a 375°F (190°C)
oven for 25–30 minutes,
until the slices of bacon are
crisp and brown and the
chicken cooked through.
Serve immediately, garnished
with snipped fresh chives.

Wrapping a chicken breast in bacon

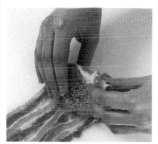

Place a chicken breast at
one end of the bacon
slices, and then wrap the
slices diagonally around
the breast.

Secure the bacon slices
around the chicken by
threading a wooden
toothpick or small skewer
through the loose ends of
the slices.

CHICKEN WITH SAGE & ORANGE

 Serves 6

6 boneless chicken breast halves,
  with the skin left on

1 tbsp all-purpose flour

orange sections and fresh sage
  leaves to garnish

MARINADE

11/4 cups (300 ml) orange juice

1 tbsp light soy sauce

2 garlic cloves, crushed

2 tbsp chopped fresh sage

1/2-in (1-cm) piece of fresh
  ginger, peeled and
  finely chopped

salt and black pepper

1 Make the marinade:
combine the orange juice,
soy sauce, garlic, sage, ginger,
and season to taste. Toss the
chicken in the marinade,
cover, and leave to marinate
in the refrigerator for
20–30 minutes.

2 Reserve the marinade
and arrange the chicken
breasts, skin side up, in a
large roasting pan.

3 Bake the chicken in a
375°F (190°C) oven for
about 20 minutes. Pour the
reserved marinade over the
chicken and return to the
oven for 5–10 minutes, until
cooked through.

4 Remove the chicken with
a slotted spoon, and
arrange on a warmed platter.
Cover and keep warm.

5 Pour all but 2 tbsp of the
marinade into a pitcher
and reserve. Add the flour to
the marinade remaining in
the roasting pan and mix to
a smooth paste.

6 Put the roasting pan on
top of the stove, and
cook, stirring, for 1 minute.
Gradually stir in the
reserved marinade. Bring to
a boil, simmer for 2 minutes,
and taste for seasoning.
Strain, pour a little of the
sauce around the chicken
breasts, and garnish with the
orange sections and fresh
sage. Serve the remaining
sauce separately.

CHICKEN CORDON BLEU

 Serves 4

4 skinless, boneless chicken
  breast halves

4 thin slices of Gruyère cheese

4 thin slices of cooked ham

salt and black pepper

1 egg, beaten

2 cups (125 g) fresh white
  bread crumbs

2 tbsp butter

3 tbsp sunflower or corn oil

1 With a sharp knife, cut each chicken breast horizontally, leaving it attached at one side.

2 Open out each chicken breast, place between 2 sheets of waxed paper, and pound to a ⅛-in (3-mm) thickness with a rolling pin. Fill and fold the chicken breasts (see box, right).

3 Dip each folded chicken breast into the beaten egg, then dip each breast into the bread crumbs, making sure each one is evenly coated. Cover and chill for 15 minutes.

4 Melt the butter with the sunflower oil in a large skillet. When the butter is foaming, add the chicken breasts and cook for 10 minutes on each side or until the bread crumb coating is crisp and golden and the chicken is cooked through. Remove the chicken breasts with a slotted spoon and drain thoroughly on paper towels. Cut into ½-in (1-cm) slices and serve immediately.

Folding the chicken

Place 1 slice of cheese and 1 slice of ham on half of each chicken breast, season to taste, and fold the breast to cover the filling. Seal with a wooden toothpick.

HERB-MARINATED CHICKEN BREASTS

Serves 4

4 boneless chicken breast halves,
  with the skin left on

¼ cup (30 g) all-purpose flour

2 tbsp butter

2 tbsp sunflower or corn oil

⅔ cup (150 ml) chicken stock

1 bunch of watercress, tough
  stalks removed, to serve

chopped parsley to garnish

MARINADE

2 tbsp olive oil

1 tbsp lemon juice

3 garlic cloves, crushed

3 tbsp chopped parsley

½ tsp herbes de Provence

salt and black pepper

1 Make the marinade: combine the oil, lemon juice, garlic, parsley, herbes de Provence, and seasoning to taste. Turn the chicken in the marinade, cover, and leave to marinate in the refrigerator for 30 minutes.

2 Remove the chicken from the marinade and dry on paper towels. Lightly coat the chicken breasts with the flour, shaking off the excess.

3 Melt the butter with the oil in a large skillet. When the butter is foaming, add the chicken breasts, skin side down, and cook for 10 minutes. Turn the chicken and cook for 10 minutes longer or until golden and cooked through.

4 Using a slotted spoon, remove the chicken breasts and keep warm. Pour off the fat and discard any dark brown sediment.

5 Pour the chicken stock into the pan and boil for 8 minutes or until reduced to about 2–3 tbsp.

6 Arrange the chicken breasts on beds of watercress, and then pour over the hot sauce. Serve immediately, garnished with chopped parsley.

SPICY CHICKEN BREASTS

Substitute ¼ tsp crushed red peppers for the herbes de Provence in the marinade. Add 1 tsp paprika to the flour for coating and proceed as directed.

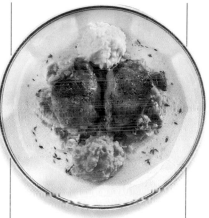

CHICKEN THIGHS WITH CHESTNUT STUFFING

You don't need to roast a whole bird to enjoy the classic combination of chicken with stuffing. This dish features chicken thighs wrapped around a nutty filling of chestnuts and bacon and served with cranberry sauce.

 Serves 4

8 boneless chicken thighs, with the skin left on

²/₃ cup (150 ml) chicken stock

1 tbsp jellied cranberry sauce

STUFFING

1 tbsp butter

2 slices of bacon, diced

1 small onion, finely chopped

¹/₄ lb (125 g) chestnuts, peeled and finely chopped

¹/₂ cup (30 g) fresh pumpernickel crumbs

1 tbsp chopped parsley

salt and black pepper

1 egg yolk

1 Make the stuffing: melt the butter in a skillet, add the bacon and onion, and cook over medium heat for 3–5 minutes, until the bacon is crisp and the onion soft but not browned.

2 Add the chestnuts and cook, stirring occasionally, for 5 minutes. Remove the skillet from the heat, add the bread crumbs, parsley, and salt and pepper to taste, then bind together with the egg yolk.

3 Place the chicken thighs, skin side down, on a cutting board and divide the stuffing among them. Roll up each thigh to enclose the stuffing and fasten with a wooden toothpick or tie with string.

4 Arrange the chicken thighs in a single layer in a roasting pan, and cook in a 375°F (190°C) oven for 20–25 minutes until the chicken is lightly browned and cooked through.

5 Lift the chicken thighs out of the roasting pan, remove the toothpicks or string, and keep warm.

6 Spoon off any excess fat, put the pan on top of the stove, and pour in the stock. Bring to a boil and boil for 3–5 minutes until syrupy, stirring to dissolve any sediment and cooking juices. Stir in the cranberry sauce and cook for 1 minute to melt it. Taste for seasoning. Strain the sauce and serve immediately with the chicken thighs.

CHICKEN THIGHS WITH PINE NUTS

Substitute 1 cup (100 g) chopped pine nuts for the chestnuts in the stuffing and proceed as directed.

CHICKEN THIGHS NORMANDY

 Serves 4

3 leeks, trimmed and thinly sliced

4 lean slices Canadian bacon, diced

5 garlic cloves, crushed

1¹/₃ cups (350 ml) hard cider or white wine

8 chicken thighs, with the bone in and skin left on

¹/₂ tsp chopped fresh thyme

salt and black pepper

¹/₂ cup (125 ml) light sour cream

1 Put the leeks, bacon, and garlic into a roasting pan. Pour in the cider and put the chicken on top. Sprinkle with the thyme and season.

2 Bake in a 375°F (190°C) oven for 20–25 minutes, until the chicken is tender and cooked through. Remove the chicken thighs, bacon, and vegetables and keep warm.

3 Spoon off any fat from the pan. Put the pan on top of the stove and boil the cooking juices until reduced by half. Stir in the sour cream and heat gently. Pour the sauce onto warmed serving plates, arrange the bacon, vegetables, and chicken on top, and serve immediately.

MARINATED BARBECUED CHICKEN

Smoke-scented, crisp-skinned, and with juicy tender flesh, marinated chickens and game hens are delicious when cooked over a barbecue. Use chicken pieces (see page 148) or whole birds split for grilling (see page 150) so that they can be cooked quickly and easily.

ORANGE & BASIL

 Serves 4

3 lb (1.5 kg) chicken, quartered

MARINADE

5 tbsp (75 ml) olive oil

5 tbsp (75 ml) dry white wine

1 orange, sliced

5–8 garlic cloves, crushed

2 tbsp shredded fresh basil

salt and black pepper

PINEAPPLE SALSA

4 oz (125 g) canned pineapple chunks, drained

1 orange, peeled, segmented, and diced

1/4 red pepper, cored, seeded, and diced

1/4 tsp hot red pepper flakes

1/4 tsp sugar

juice of 1/4 lime or lemon

1 Combine the marinade ingredients in a shallow nonmetallic dish. Add the chicken, turn to coat, and leave to marinate in the refrigerator for 12 hours.

2 Cook the chicken over a barbecue, turning and basting, for 20 minutes or until the juices run clear. Remove the orange slices from the marinade and broil until lightly browned.

3 Mix together the ingredients for the salsa. Serve the chicken hot with the orange slices and the salsa.

FRUITY CILANTRO

 Serves 4

2 3/4-lb (375-g) Rock Cornish game hens, split for grilling

MARINADE

5 tbsp (75 ml) olive oil

juice of 1 orange

1 lime and 1 lemon, sliced

1-in (2.5-cm) piece of fresh ginger, peeled and grated

leaves from 1/2 large bunch cilantro, chopped

salt and black pepper

NECTARINE SALSA

1 ripe nectarine, peeled and diced

1/2-in (1-cm) piece of fresh ginger, peeled and grated

1/2 banana, diced

1 scallion, thinly sliced

1 tsp lime juice

1/4 tsp hot red pepper flakes

1 Combine the marinade ingredients in a nonmetallic dish. Add the game hens and marinate for 12 hours.

2 Cook the game hens, turning and basting, for 15 minutes or until the juices run clear. Remove the fruit slices from the marinade and barbecue.

3 Mix together the ingredients for the salsa. Serve the game hens hot with the lime and lemon slices and the salsa.

LEMON & MARJORAM

 Serves 4

3 lb (1.5 kg) chicken, split for grilling

MARINADE

5 tbsp (75 ml) olive oil

juice of 2 lemons

3 garlic cloves, crushed

1 cup (30 g) chopped fresh marjoram

salt and black pepper

CURRY SAUCE

1/4 cup (60 g) plain yogurt

1 tbsp mayonnaise

1 tbsp chopped fresh marjaram

1 garlic clove, crushed

1/2 tsp mild curry powder

1/4 tsp lemon juice

1/4 tsp each ground cumin and turmeric

1 Combine the marinade ingredients in a nonmetallic dish. Add the chicken, turn to coat, and marinate in the refrigerator for at least 12 hours.

2 Cook the chicken over a barbecue, turning and basting, for 20 minutes or until the juices run clear.

3 Combine the sauce ingredients. Cut up the chicken; serve with the sauce.

Clockwise from top: *Fruity Cilantro Game Hens, Lemon & Marjoram Chicken, Orange & Basil Chicken.*

Successful marinating

A marinade will give poultry or meat extra flavor before it is cooked on a barbecue. Here are some useful points to remember:

• A marinade is a mixture of liquids and seasonings. There is always an acid such as lemon juice, wine, or vinegar, which makes poultry or meat more tender.

• An oil, such as olive, sesame, or sunflower, keeps the meat or poultry moist and carries the flavors of the seasonings into the food.

• Seasonings usually include salt and pepper, but all kinds of spices and herbs can be used as well. Marinades often include garlic, onions, and celery, which also add flavor.

• Allow enough time for large pieces of poultry or meat to pick up the flavor of the marinade. Smaller pieces will pick up the flavor more quickly.

• Turn the food in the marinade occasionally to ensure an even coating and baste with the marinade when barbecuing.

LEMON & HERB DRUMSTICKS

 Makes 12

12 chicken drumsticks

MARINADE

2/3 cup (150 ml) olive oil

grated zest and juice of 1 lemon

6 large parsley sprigs, chopped

1 onion, thinly sliced

2 large garlic cloves, crushed

salt and black pepper

1 Make the marinade: in a large bowl, combine the olive oil, lemon zest and juice, parsley sprigs, onion, garlic, and salt and pepper to taste.

2 Turn the drumsticks in the marinade. Cover and leave to marinate in the refrigerator for at least 30 minutes.

3 Place the drumsticks under the broiler, 4 in (10 cm) from the heat, and broil, turning frequently and basting with the marinade, for 20 minutes, until crisp, brown, and cooked through. Serve the drumsticks hot or cold.

Cook's know-how

It is a good idea to wrap the bone ends of the drumsticks in a little foil to make them easier to eat with the fingers, especially if you are serving them hot.

HONEYED DRUMSTICKS

Omit the lemon and parsley marinade. In a large bowl, combine 1 cup (250 g) plain yogurt, 2 tbsp honey, 1 tsp ground coriander, and salt and pepper to taste. Add the drumsticks, turn to coat, and leave to marinate in the refrigerator for 30 minutes. Remove the drumsticks from the marinade and proceed as directed, brushing frequently with the marinade.

DEVILED CHICKEN DRUMSTICKS

Makes 12

12 chicken drumsticks

2 tbsp sesame seeds

SPICY COATING

2 tbsp olive oil

2 tbsp white vinegar

2 tbsp ketchup

1 tbsp Dijon mustard

1 small onion, quartered

2 tbsp packed dark brown sugar

1 large garlic clove, coarsely crushed

1/4 tsp chili powder

salt and black pepper

tortilla chips to serve

1 Make the spicy coating: puree the oil, vinegar, ketchup, mustard, onion, sugar, garlic, chili powder, and salt and pepper to taste in a food processor until fairly smooth.

2 Make 3 deep cuts in each chicken drumstick, arrange in a single layer in a shallow ovenproof dish, and spoon the spicy coating over them. Sprinkle with half of the sesame seeds.

3 Bake in a 375°F (190°C) oven, basting, for 30 minutes, until the drumsticks are cooked. Turn halfway through cooking and sprinkle with the remaining sesame seeds. Serve the drumsticks hot or cold with tortilla chips.

RED CHILI ROASTED DRUMSTICKS

Omit the spicy coating. Combine 3 tbsp lemon juice, 4 crushed garlic cloves, 1 1/2 tbsp paprika, 1 tbsp mild chili powder, 1 tsp ground cumin, and 1/4 tsp oregano. Coat the drumsticks with the mixture, then wrap each one in a slice of bacon. Cover and leave to marinate in the refrigerator for at least 1 hour. Bake in a 375°F (190°C) oven for 30 minutes or until the drumsticks are cooked through.

CURRIED CHICKEN SALAD

 Serves 6

1 tbsp sunflower or corn oil

4 large scallions, chopped

1 tbsp mild curry powder

²/₃ cup (150 ml) red wine

pared zest and juice of 1 lemon

1 tbsp tomato paste

2 tbsp apricot jam

1¹/₄ cups (300 ml) mayonnaise

²/₃ cup (150 g) plain yogurt

salt and pepper

3¹/₂ cups (500 g) cut-up cooked chicken, in bite-sized pieces

watercress sprigs to garnish

1 Heat the oil in a small saucepan, add the scallions, and cook for about 2 minutes, until beginning to soften but not brown. Stir in the curry powder and cook, stirring, for 1 minute.

2 Add the red wine, lemon zest and juice, and tomato paste. Simmer, uncovered, stirring, for 5 minutes or until reduced to ¹/₄ cup (60 ml). Strain into a bowl, cover, and leave to cool.

3 Work the apricot jam through a strainer, then stir it into the curry paste and wine mixture. Add the mayonnaise, yogurt, and salt and pepper to taste, stirring well to blend evenly. The mixture should be of a coating consistency and the color of pale straw.

4 Add the chicken pieces to the mayonnaise mixture and stir to coat evenly. Garnish with watercress sprigs before serving.

CHICKEN VERONIQUE

Substitute white wine for the red wine. Add 1 scant cup (175 g) halved seedless green grapes to the mayonnaise mixture when you add the chicken.

MARINATED CHICKEN WITH PEPPERS

 Serves 4–6

3¹/₂ lb (1.7 kg) chicken, with giblets removed

2 tbsp olive oil

1 large red pepper, cored, seeded, and cut into thin strips

1 large yellow pepper, cored, seeded, and cut into thin strips

1 cup (125 g) pitted black olives

MARINADE

4 tbsp olive oil

2 tbsp honey

juice of ¹/₂ lemon

1 tbsp chopped mixed fresh herbs, such as parsley, thyme, and basil

salt and black pepper

1 Put the chicken into a roasting pan, rub the breast with oil, and cook in a 375°F (190°C) oven for 20 minutes per 1 lb (500 g). Spoon off the fat and juices, and then add the peppers. Return to the oven for 20 minutes.

2 Remove the chicken and peppers from the roasting pan, and leave to stand until cool enough to handle.

3 Meanwhile, make the marinade: in a large bowl, combine the olive oil, honey, lemon juice, herbs, and salt and pepper to taste.

4 Strip the chicken meat from the bones, and cut it into small bite-sized strips. Toss the strips in the marinade, stirring gently to coat them evenly. Cover the chicken and leave to cool completely.

5 Spoon the chicken onto a serving platter, arrange the peppers and the olives around the edge, and serve at room temperature.

CHICKEN WITH SHALLOTS

Substitute ¹/₂ lb (250 g) peeled shallots for the red and yellow peppers and proceed as directed.

GREEK SPICED CHICKEN

 Serves 6

3 1/2 cups (500 g) cut-up cooked chicken, in bite-sized pieces

pita bread to serve

1 scallion, cut into strips, to garnish

MARINADE

2/3 cup (150 g) plain yogurt

2/3 cup (150 ml) light sour cream

8 scallions, thinly sliced

2 tbsp chopped fresh cilantro

1 tbsp chopped parsley

1 1/2 tsp ground coriander

1 1/2 tsp ground cumin

salt and black pepper

1 Make the marinade: in a large bowl, combine the yogurt, light sour cream, scallions, cilantro, parsley, ground coriander, cumin, and salt and black pepper to taste.

2 Toss the chicken pieces in the marinade.

3 Sprinkle the pita bread with a little water and cook under the broiler for 1 minute on each side. Garnish the chicken with the scallion strips and serve with the pita bread.

WARM CHICKEN SALAD WITH MANGO & AVOCADO

This unusual salad combines refreshing slices of mango and avocado with spicy chicken breast and a warm, rum-flavored dressing. The combination of flavors makes a truly tropical dish.

 Serves 4

3 skinless, boneless chicken breast halves, cut into 1-in (2.5-cm) strips

1 head of Boston or Bibb lettuce, leaves separated

1 bunch of watercress, trimmed

1 avocado, peeled, pitted (page 68), and sliced lengthwise

1 mango, peeled, pitted (page 430), and sliced lengthwise

1/4 cup (60 ml) dark rum

paprika to garnish

MARINADE

2 tbsp olive oil

2 tbsp lemon juice

2 tsp balsamic vinegar

2 garlic cloves, crushed

1 tbsp paprika

2 tsp chopped red chili

1/2 tsp ground cumin

salt

1 Make the marinade: combine the oil, lemon juice, vinegar, garlic, paprika, chili, cumin, and salt to taste. Toss the chicken strips in the marinade, cover, and leave to marinate for a few minutes.

2 Arrange beds of lettuce and watercress on 4 serving plates. Arrange the avocado and mango slices on top.

3 Heat a large skillet and add the chicken strips with the marinade. Cook over high heat, stirring, for 5–6 minutes, until golden on all sides and cooked through.

4 Using a slotted spoon, remove the chicken strips from the pan and arrange on top of the avocado and mango.

5 Return the skillet to the heat and pour in the rum. Let it simmer, stirring constantly to dissolve any browned bits in the skillet and incorporate the cooking juices, for about 1 minute. Pour the hot rum mixture over the salads, sprinkle with a little paprika, and serve immediately.

Balsamic vinegar

Made in Italy from grape juice aged in wooden casks, balsamic vinegar is a high-quality, expensive vinegar with a smooth, mellow taste. Less expensive, mass-produced versions are available. If you prefer, use wine vinegar instead.

BALLOTINE OF CHICKEN

A ballotine is a bird or cut of meat that has been boned, stuffed, and rolled. It is cooked slowly in the oven, allowed to cool, then chilled for several hours or overnight until firm. With its colorful, pistachio-studded filling, this attractive, flavorful dish makes an excellent centerpiece for a buffet and is easy to slice and serve.

 Serves 8–10

4 lb (2 kg) chicken, boned (page 149)

4 thin slices of cooked ham

1 cup (125 g) pistachio nuts, shelled

4 tbsp butter, softened

2 1/3 cups (600 ml) chicken stock

STUFFING

1 lb (500 g) pancetta, thickly sliced

3/4 lb (375 g) chicken livers, trimmed

1/2 lb (250 g) bacon, coarsely chopped

2 shallots, quartered

2 garlic cloves

1/4 cup (60 ml) brandy

2 tsp chopped fresh thyme

1 tsp chopped fresh sage

1/2 tsp ground ginger

1/2 tsp ground cinnamon

salt and black pepper

1 Make the stuffing: chop the pancetta into 1/4-in (5 mm) pieces, and place in a bowl.

2 Puree the chicken livers, bacon, shallots, garlic, and brandy in a food processor until smooth. Add to the pancetta in the bowl with the thyme, sage, ginger, and cinnamon and season generously with salt and pepper. Stir well to combine.

3 Place the boned chicken, skin side down, between 2 sheets of waxed paper and pound to an even thickness with a rolling pin.

4 Remove the waxed paper from the chicken, and assemble the ballotine (see box, right). Tie several pieces of string around the chicken to hold its shape.

5 Spread the softened butter over the chicken skin and season generously with salt and pepper.

6 Roll the chicken tightly in a piece of cheesecloth and tie the ends. Place the chicken roll on a wire rack in a roasting pan.

7 Bring the stock to a boil and pour over the chicken in the roasting pan. Cook in a 325°F (160°C) oven, basting occasionally and adding more stock if necessary, for 2 hours or until the juices run clear when the chicken is pierced with a thin skewer.

8 Remove the cheesecloth, put the ballotine onto a plate, and leave to cool. Cover and chill overnight. Cut into thin slices to serve.

Assembling the ballotine

Spread half of the stuffing over the chicken, to within 1 in (2.5 cm) of the edges. Arrange the ham slices on top. Scatter the pistachio nuts on top of the ham.

Spoon on and spread the remaining stuffing over the pistachio nuts.

Fold the chicken over the stuffing to form a sausage shape and sew the edges together with thin string or fasten them with small metal skewers.

HOLIDAY ROAST TURKEY

If you've got a large group to feed, be sure to order a fresh turkey from your butcher or grocery store; you can pick it up the day before you plan to roast it or store it for up to 3 days in the refrigerator. If you buy a frozen turkey, make sure that it is thoroughly thawed before cooking.

 Serves 12

pared zest of 1 lemon

a few parsley sprigs

a few thyme sprigs

2 celery stalks, roughly sliced

10 lb (5 kg) oven-ready turkey, with giblets

1/4 lb (125 g) butter, softened

salt and black pepper

1/2 lb (250 g) bacon slices

CHESTNUT STUFFING

2 tbsp butter

1 onion, finely chopped

6 oz (175 g) bulk pork sausage

6 oz (175 g) dried chestnuts, soaked, finely chopped

3 tbsp chopped parsley

1 tbsp chopped fresh thyme

salt and black pepper

1 small egg, beaten

GRAVY

1/4 cup (30 g) all-purpose flour

2 1/3 cups (600 ml) giblet stock (page 148)

salt and black pepper

TO SERVE

bread sauce

cranberry sauce

bacon rolls

chipolatas

1 Prepare the stuffing: melt the butter in a skillet, add the onion and cook gently for a few minutes until softened. Add the pork sausage and cook for 3–5 minutes, stirring, until browned all over.

2 Place the lemon zest, parsley sprigs, thyme, and celery into the cavity of the turkey. Fill the crop with cooled stuffing. Put any leftover stuffing into an ovenproof dish and set aside.

3 Shape the stuffed end of the turkey into a neat round and secure the loose skin with thin skewers. Tie the legs with string to give a neat shape.

4 Calculate the cooking time based on the weight of the turkey, allowing 20 minutes per 1 lb (500 g). Arrange 2 large sheets of foil across a large roasting pan. Place the turkey on top and spread the butter thickly over the bird, concentrating on the breast in particular.

5 Season with a little salt and plenty of pepper, then overlap the bacon slices across the turkey, again concentrating on the breast.

6 Fold the sheets of foil loosely over the turkey, leaving a large air gap between the turkey and the foil. Roast the turkey in a 425°F (220°C) oven for 30 minutes.

7 Reduce the oven temperature to 325°F (160°C) and cook for the remaining calculated cooking time. The turkey's internal temperature, measured with a meat thermometer in the inner thigh, should be 180°F (80°C).

8 Thirty minutes before the end of the cooking time, fold back the foil and remove the bacon to allow the breast to brown. Baste occasionally with cooking juices. Pierce the thickest part of the thigh with a thin skewer: the juices will run clear when the turkey is cooked. Lift onto a warmed serving platter and leave to stand for 30 minutes before carving.

9 Meanwhile, put the reserved stuffing in the oven and cook for 25–30 minutes.

10 Make the gravy: spoon all but 2 tbsp of fat from the roasting pan, leaving behind the cooking juices. Place the roasting pan over low heat and add the flour. Cook, stirring, for 1 minute. Add the stock and cook, stirring, until thickened. Season to taste.

11 Carve the turkey and serve with the extra stuffing, gravy, bread sauce, cranberry sauce, bacon rolls, and chipolatas.

BREAD SAUCE

Insert *8 cloves* into *1 onion*. Put it into a pan with *3 2/3 cups (900 ml) milk, 1 bay leaf*, and *6 black peppercorns*. Bring to a boil, remove from the heat, cover, and leave to steep for 1 hour. Strain the milk and return to the pan. Gradually add about *3 cups (175 g) fresh white bread crumbs*, then bring to a boil, stirring. Simmer for 2–3 minutes. Add *salt and black pepper to taste* and stir in *4 tbsp butter*. If desired, stir in *1/4 cup (60 ml) heavy cream* before serving. Serve hot.

CRANBERRY SAUCE

Put *1 lb (500 g) fresh cranberries* into a saucepan with *1/2 cup (125 ml) water*. Bring to a boil and simmer for about 5 minutes, until the cranberries have begun to break down. Stir in *1/2 cup (125 g) sugar* and simmer until it dissolves. Stir in *2 tbsp port (optional)* before serving. Serve hot or cold.

BACON ROLLS

With the back of a knife, stretch *6 slices of bacon* until twice their original size. Cut in half and roll up loosely. Thread onto skewers and cook under the broiler, turning, for 6 minutes or until browned.

CHIPOLATAS

Twist *6 chipolata sausages* in the center and cut in half to make 12 small sausages. Cook under the broiler for 10–15 minutes, until cooked through and browned all over.

TURKEY WITH SOUR CREAM & CHIVES

Serves 4

2 tbsp butter

2 tbsp sunflower or corn oil

4 turkey breast tenderloins, cut diagonally into ¹/2-in (1-cm) strips

4 slices of bacon, diced

1 large onion, sliced

¹/2 lb (250 g) mushrooms, halved

¹/4 cup (30 g) all-purpose flour

²/3 cup (150 ml) turkey or chicken stock

salt and black pepper

²/3 cup (150 ml) sour cream

2 tbsp snipped fresh chives

1 Melt the butter with the oil in a large skillet. When the butter is foaming, add the turkey strips and cook over high heat, stirring constantly, for 8 minutes. Remove the turkey strips from the pan with a slotted spoon and keep warm.

2 Lower the heat and add the bacon, onion, and mushrooms. Cook gently, stirring occasionally, for 3–5 minutes, until the onion is soft but not browned. Add the flour and cook, stirring, for 1 minute.

3 Pour in the stock and bring to a boil, stirring until thickened. Return the turkey to the pan and season to taste. Cover and simmer for 5 minutes or until the turkey is tender.

4 Stir the sour cream into the turkey and mushroom mixture and gently heat the mixture without boiling. Serve immediately, sprinkled with the snipped chives.

ROAST TURKEY WITH GARLIC & TARRAGON

Serves 4

2¹/2-lb (1.25-kg) turkey breast

1 tsp all-purpose flour

1¹/4 cups (300 ml) chicken stock

salt and black pepper

watercress sprigs to garnish

MARINADE

3 tbsp sunflower or corn oil

grated zest and juice of 1 lemon

1 small onion, sliced

1 garlic clove, crushed

1 large tarragon sprig

1 large lemon thyme sprig

1 Make the marinade: in a bowl, combine the sunflower oil, lemon zest and juice, onion, garlic, tarragon, and lemon thyme. Spoon the marinade over the turkey, cover, and leave to marinate in the refrigerator, turning occasionally, for 8 hours.

2 Put the turkey into a roasting pan. Strain the marinade, and pour around the turkey. Cover with a sheet of foil and cook in a 375°F (190°C) oven for 20 minutes per 1 lb (500 g). Remove the foil after 20 minutes of cooking to brown the turkey.

3 Test whether the turkey is done by inserting a thin skewer into the thickest part: the juices will run clear when it is cooked. Remove the turkey from the roasting pan and keep warm while you make the gravy.

4 Put the pan on top of the stove, add the flour to the juices in the pan, and cook, stirring, for 1 minute until lightly browned. Add the stock and bring to a boil, stirring constantly until lightly thickened. Simmer for 2–3 minutes. Add salt and pepper to taste. Strain into a warmed gravy boat.

5 Garnish the turkey with watercress and serve the gravy separately.

Cook's know-how

Turkey pieces are now available from supermarkets; they are excellent if you like roast turkey but don't want to buy a whole bird. Turkey breasts come with the breastbone or boneless. Often both whole and half breasts are available.

TURKEY & LEMON STIR-FRY

 Serves 4

4 turkey breast tenderloins,
cut diagonally into 1-in
(2.5-cm) strips

2 medium zucchini

1 large green pepper, cored
and seeded

1 tbsp olive oil

13 oz (400 g) canned baby corn,
drained

chopped parsley and lemon
twists to garnish

MARINADE

1/2 cup (125 ml) dry white wine

grated zest and juice of
1 large lemon

2 tbsp olive oil

salt and black pepper

1 Make the marinade:
combine the wine, lemon
zest and juice, oil, and salt
and pepper to taste. Toss the
turkey in the marinade, cover,
and leave to marinate in the
refrigerator for 30 minutes.

2 Slice the zucchini thickly
on the diagonal and cut
the green pepper into long
thin strips.

3 Heat the oil in a wok,
add the zucchini,
corn, and green pepper,
and stir-fry over high heat
for 2 minutes. Remove
with a slotted spoon and
keep warm.

4 Remove the turkey strips
from the marinade,
reserving the marinade. Add
the turkey to the wok and
stir-fry over high heat for
5 minutes or until golden.

5 Pour the reserved
marinade over the turkey
and cook for 3 minutes or
until tender. Return the
vegetables to the wok and
heat through. Taste for
seasoning. Serve the turkey
immediately, garnished with
parsley and lemon twists.

Baby corn

*This is corn on the cob, picked
when not fully grown. Often
used in Asian dishes, it should
be cooked only briefly to preserve
its sweetness.*

TURKEY CUTLETS

 Serves 4

3 tbsp all-purpose flour

salt and black pepper

1 large egg, beaten

1 cup (60 g) fresh white
bread crumbs

4 6-oz (175-g) turkey breast
cutlets

2 tbsp sunflower or corn oil

1 tbsp butter

lemon slices and chopped parsley
to garnish

1 Sprinkle the flour on
a plate and season
generously with salt and
pepper. Pour the beaten egg
onto another plate and
sprinkle the bread crumbs
onto a third plate.

2 Coat each cutlet with the
seasoned flour, shaking
off any excess. Dip each
floured cutlet into the
beaten egg, then dip into
the bread crumbs.

3 With a sharp knife, score
the cutlets in a crisscross
pattern. Cover and chill in
the refrigerator for about
30 minutes.

4 Heat the oil with the
butter in a large skillet.
When the butter is foaming,
add the cutlets, and cook
over high heat until golden
on both sides.

5 Lower the heat and cook
for 10 minutes or until
the turkey is tender. Test
the cutlets by piercing with
a thin skewer: the juices
should run clear.

6 Lift the cutlets out of the
pan with a slotted spoon
and drain on paper towels.
Garnish with lemon slices
and chopped parsley and
serve immediately.

Cook's know-how

*If you can't find turkey breast
cutlets, buy breast tenderloins:
put them between 2 sheets
of waxed paper and pound
with a rolling pin until
1/4 in (5 mm) thick.*

TURKEY MOLE

 Serves 4

2 tbsp sunflower or corn oil

1¹/₂ lb (750 g) turkey pieces

1¹/₄ cups (300 ml) turkey or chicken stock

salt and black pepper

MOLE SAUCE

13 oz (400 g) canned chopped tomatoes

1 small onion, coarsely chopped

¹/₂ cup (90 g) blanched almonds

2¹/₂ tbsp (30 g) raisins (optional)

1 oz (30 g) baker's semisweet chocolate, coarsely chopped

1 garlic clove

1 tbsp sesame seeds

1 tbsp hot chili powder

1 tsp ground cinnamon

¹/₂ tsp ground cloves

¹/₂ tsp ground coriander

¹/₂ tsp ground cumin

¹/₄ tsp ground aniseed

¹/₄ cup (60 ml) water

1 Make the mole sauce: put the tomatoes, onion, almonds, raisins (if using), chocolate, garlic, sesame seeds, chili powder, cinnamon, cloves, coriander, cumin, aniseed, and the measured water into a food processor or blender and process briefly.

2 Heat the sunflower oil in a large saucepan, add the turkey pieces, and cook over high heat for about 5 minutes, until golden on all sides.

3 Add the mole sauce mixture and cook, stirring, for 2 minutes. Pour in the stock and bring to a boil. Cover and simmer very gently for 40 minutes or until the turkey is tender. Add salt and pepper to taste. Serve immediately.

Turkey mole

Pronounced "molay," this is an ancient Mexican dish. The hot spicy sauce, often served with turkey, is given depth of flavor by a little dark chocolate, which often features in Mexican dishes. For an authentic touch, serve with tortillas, black beans, avocado, and red onion rings.

TURKEY CASSEROLE WITH PEPPERS

 Serves 4

2 tbsp butter

1 tbsp sunflower or corn oil

1¹/₂ lb (750 g) turkey pieces

1 onion, sliced

1 garlic clove, crushed

1 red pepper, cored, seeded, and thinly sliced

1 yellow pepper, cored, seeded, and thinly sliced

1¹/₄ cups (300 ml) hard cider or white wine

salt and black pepper

chopped parsley to garnish

1 Melt the butter with the oil in a flameproof casserole. When the butter is foaming, add the turkey pieces and cook over high heat for 5 minutes or until golden on all sides. Lift out with a slotted spoon and drain on paper towels.

2 Lower the heat, add the onion, garlic, and red and yellow pepper slices to the casserole, and cook for 5 minutes or until just beginning to soften.

3 Return the turkey to the casserole, pour in the cider, and bring to a boil. Add salt and pepper to taste, cover, and cook in a 325°F (160°C) oven for 1 hour or until the turkey is tender.

4 Using a slotted spoon, transfer the turkey and vegetables to a warmed platter. Put the casserole on top of the stove and boil, stirring, until the cooking juices are thickened. Taste for seasoning.

5 Spoon the sauce over the turkey and vegetables, garnish with the chopped parsley, and serve immediately.

TURKEY & APPLE CASSEROLE

Substitute 2 cored, halved, and sliced cooking apples for the red and yellow peppers and add to the casserole 20 minutes before the end of cooking time.

STIR-FRIED TURKEY MEATBALLS

 Serves 4

3 tsp sunflower or corn oil

1 onion, thinly sliced

1 green pepper, cored, seeded, and cut into bite-sized pieces

1 zucchini, sliced

4–6 mushrooms, thinly sliced

1 cup (125 g) bean sprouts

MEATBALLS

³/4 lb (375 g) ground turkey

³/4 cup (45 g) stuffing mix

2 tbsp minced parsley

1 onion, finely chopped

4 garlic cloves, crushed

3 tbsp soy sauce

¹/2-in (1-cm) piece of fresh ginger, peeled and chopped

salt and black pepper

1 Make the meatballs: in a bowl, combine the turkey, stuffing mix, parsley, onion, garlic, 1 tbsp of the soy sauce, the ginger, and salt and pepper to taste. Shape into meatballs (see box, right).

2 Heat 1 tsp of the oil in a wok, add the onion, green pepper, and zucchini and stir-fry for 2–3 minutes. Remove with a slotted spoon and keep warm.

3 Heat another tsp of the oil, add the mushrooms, and stir-fry for 2–3 minutes. Remove with a slotted spoon and keep warm.

4 Heat the remaining oil in the wok, add the turkey meatballs, and cook gently, turning, for 6–7 minutes, until cooked through. Return the vegetables to the wok, add the bean sprouts, sprinkle with the remaining soy sauce, and cook for 1 minute to heat through. Serve immediately.

Shaping meatballs

Break off pieces of the turkey mixture and, with moistened hands to keep the mixture from sticking, roll into 2-in (5-cm) meatballs.

TURKEY BURGERS HOLSTEIN

 Serves 4

4 tbsp butter

1 small onion, very finely chopped

1 lb (500 g) ground turkey

¹/2 cup (90 g) finely chopped cooked ham

1 tbsp chopped parsley

salt and black pepper

2 tbsp sunflower or corn oil

4 eggs to serve

1 Melt half of the butter in a small saucepan, add the onion, and cook gently, stirring occasionally, for 3–5 minutes, until soft but not browned. Leave to cool.

2 Put the onion into a large bowl, add the turkey, ham, parsley, and salt and pepper to taste, and mix thoroughly. Shape into 4 burgers. Cover and chill for 30 minutes.

3 Melt the remaining butter with the oil in a skillet. When the butter is foaming, add the burgers, and cook over high heat for 2–3 minutes on each side.

4 Lower the heat and cook, turning once, for about 10 minutes, until the burgers are cooked through.

5 Lift the turkey burgers out of the skillet with a slotted spoon and drain on paper towels.

6 Break the eggs into the skillet and fry over medium heat until the whites are firm and the yolks are still soft. Divide the turkey burgers among 4 serving plates, top each burger with an egg, and serve immediately.

BLUE CHEESE TURKEY BURGERS

Omit the eggs. Make the burgers as directed. Arrange 1 cup (125 g) crumbled blue cheese, such as Roquefort, Stilton, or Danish blue, on top of the burgers 5 minutes before the end of the cooking time.

TURKEY WITH CHEESE & PINEAPPLE

 Serves 6

4 tbsp butter

1 onion, sliced

1/2 cup (60 g) all-purpose flour

1 3/4 cups (450 ml) turkey or chicken stock

8 oz (250 g) canned pineapple chunks in natural juice, drained and juice reserved

2 cups (250 g) grated aged Cheddar cheese

salt and black pepper

3 1/2 cups (500 g) cut-up cooked turkey, in bite-sized pieces

3 tbsp fresh pumpernickel crumbs

chopped parsley to garnish

1 Melt the butter in a saucepan, add the onion, and cook gently, stirring occasionally, for 3–5 minutes, until soft but not browned. Add the flour, and cook, stirring, for 1 minute.

2 Gradually blend in the stock and the pineapple juice and bring to a boil, stirring until thickened.

3 Add the pineapple chunks, reserving 6 for garnish. Stir in three-quarters of the cheese and salt and pepper to taste.

4 Divide the turkey pieces among 6 individual gratin dishes or put into 1 large ovenproof dish. Pour the sauce over the turkey, and sprinkle with the remaining cheese and then the bread crumbs.

5 Bake in a 400°F (200°C) oven for 15–20 minutes, until the turkey has heated through and the topping is golden. Garnish with chopped parsley and the reserved pineapple pieces and serve immediately.

TURKEY SALAD WITH MANGO & GRAPES

 Serves 4

2 1/2-lb (1.25-kg) turkey breast

1 onion, quartered

1 carrot, sliced

a few parsley sprigs

pared zest of 1 lemon

6 black peppercorns

1 bay leaf

3/4 cup plus 1 tbsp (200 ml) mayonnaise

1 bunch of watercress, tough stalks removed

1 ripe mango, peeled, pitted, and cut into cubes (page 430)

1/2 cup (125 g) seedless green grapes

1/2 cup (90 g) walnut pieces

1 Put the turkey into a large saucepan and cover with cold water. Add the onion, carrot, parsley, lemon zest, peppercorns, and bay leaf and bring to a boil. Cover and simmer very gently for 1 hour or until the turkey is tender. Remove from the heat and leave the turkey to cool completely in the poaching liquid.

2 Lift the turkey out of the poaching liquid and remove the meat from the bones. Discard the skin and bones, then cut the meat into bite-sized pieces.

3 Put the turkey pieces into a large bowl and add the mayonnaise. Stir well to coat the turkey pieces thoroughly and evenly.

4 Arrange the watercress on individual serving plates and pile the turkey mixture on top. Arrange the mango cubes and grapes around the edge, sprinkle with the walnut pieces, and serve at room temperature.

Cook's know-how

Cooling the turkey in the poaching liquid helps keep the meat moist. Reserve the poaching liquid and use it as stock for soups and sauces.

WALDORF TURKEY SALAD

Substitute 2 large cored and cubed red apples and 2 sliced celery stalks for the mango and green grapes and then add them to the turkey and mayonnaise mixture. Proceed as directed in the recipe.

CHRISTMAS ROAST GOOSE

Goose was once the traditional Christmas bird, although today turkey is more popular. It is simple to cook and tastes delicious with a fruit stuffing and spicy accompaniments. Try it for an extra-special Christmas lunch or dinner.

 Serves 8

10–12 lb (5–6 kg) goose, with giblets reserved for stock

1 onion, quartered

1 cooking apple, quartered

a few sage sprigs

salt and black pepper

2 tbsp all-purpose flour

1 ³/4 cups (450 ml) goose giblet stock (page 148)

²/3 cup (150 ml) dry white wine

spiced stuffed apples (see box, right) to serve

watercress sprigs to garnish

PORK & APPLE STUFFING

10 oz (300 g) bulk pork sausage

1 cup (60 g) fresh bread crumbs

2 tsp dried sage

2 tbsp (30 g) butter

1 onion, finely chopped

1 large cooking apple, peeled, cored, and finely chopped

1 Make the pork and apple stuffing: in a bowl, combine the sausage, bread crumbs, and sage.

2 Melt the butter in a pan, add the onion, and cook gently, stirring occasionally, for 3–5 minutes, until soft but not browned.

3 Add the cooking apple and cook for 5 minutes, stirring occasionally. Stir the onion and apple into the pork sausage mixture, add salt and pepper to taste, and leave to cool.

4 Remove the fatty deposits from the cavity of the goose. Put the onion and apple quarters into the cavity along with the sage. Spoon the stuffing into the neck end of the goose, pat it into a rounded shape, and seal the skin flap with a small skewer.

5 Prick the skin of the goose all over with a fork and rub with salt and pepper. Place the goose, breast side down, on a wire rack in a large roasting pan, and cook in a 425°F (220°C) oven for 30 minutes.

6 Turn the goose breast side up and cook for 20 minutes. Reduce the oven temperature to 350°F (180°C) and cook for 20 minutes per 1 lb (500 g).

7 Test the goose by inserting a thin skewer into the thickest part of a thigh: the juices should run clear when the meat is thoroughly cooked.

8 Lift the goose onto a warmed serving platter and then leave to stand, covered with foil, for about 20 minutes.

9 Make the gravy while the goose is standing: pour off all but 2 tbsp of the fat from the roasting pan. Put the pan on top of the stove, add the flour, and cook, stirring, for 1 minute. Add the stock and wine and bring to a boil, stirring constantly. Simmer for 2–3 minutes, then taste for seasoning. Strain into a warmed gravy boat.

10 To serve, arrange the spiced stuffed apples around the goose and garnish with watercress. Pass the gravy separately.

Cook's know-how

Goose is even richer and fattier than duck. Putting it on a wire rack set in a roasting pan prevents it from sitting in the fat during cooking and gives it a good, crisp skin.

Spiced stuffed apples

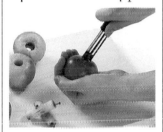

Core *8 apples*, keeping them whole. In a small bowl, mix together *2 tbsp Calvados, 1 tsp ground cinnamon, ¹/2 tsp ground allspice,* and *8 finely chopped pitted prunes* for the stuffing.

Place the apples in a buttered ovenproof dish and spoon a little of the stuffing into the center of each one. Melt *4 tbsp butter,* pour over the apples, and cover with a sheet of foil. Bake in a 350°F (180°C) oven for 1 hour or until tender.

PEKING DUCK

This traditional Chinese dish is great fun to eat and ideal for serving at an informal dinner party. Let guests help themselves to some crispy-skinned duck, scallions, cucumber, and hoisin sauce, so they can assemble their own pancakes.

 Serves 6

5 lb (2.5 kg) duck, with
   giblets removed

3 tbsp dry sherry

3 tbsp honey

3 tbsp soy sauce

CHINESE PANCAKES

2¼ cups (275 g) all-purpose
   flour

¾ cup plus 1 tbsp (200 ml)
   boiling water

2 tbsp sesame oil

TO SERVE

6 scallions, cut into matchsticks

½ cucumber, peeled and cut
   into matchsticks

6 tbsp (90 ml) hoisin sauce,
   sprinkled with sesame seeds

6 scallion brushes (page 115)
   to garnish

1 Remove fat from inside the duck. Put in a bowl and pour boiling water over. Dry in and out. Brush with sherry and hang (see box, right).

2 Mix together the honey and soy sauce and brush over the duck. Leave to hang for 4 hours longer or until the skin is dry again.

3 Put the duck, breast side down, on a wire rack in a roasting pan, and cook in a 400°F (200°C) oven for 25 minutes or until browned. Turn the duck breast side up and cook for 1–1¼ hours, until tender.

4 Meanwhile, make the pancake dough: sift the flour into a large bowl, add the boiling water, and mix to form a soft dough. Knead until smooth. Cover and leave to stand for about 30 minutes.

5 Knead the dough for 5 minutes. Shape into a roll about 1 in (2.5 cm) in diameter. Cut into 18 pieces then roll into balls. Shape and cook the pancakes (see box, far right).

6 Leave the duck to stand for about 15 minutes. Meanwhile, arrange the pancakes on a plate in a steamer, cover, and steam for 10 minutes. Cut the duck into small pieces. Serve with the pancakes, scallions, cucumber, and hoisin sauce. Garnish with scallion brushes.

Hanging the duck

Tie a long piece of string around the skin at the neck opening. Hang the duck in a cool, drafty place for 4 hours, until the skin is dry.

Shaping and cooking Chinese pancakes

Pour the sesame oil into a bowl. Take 2 balls of dough, dip half of 1 ball into the oil, then press the oiled half onto the second ball.

Flatten the dough balls with the palms of your hands and roll out to a pancake about 6 in (15 cm) in diameter. Heat a skillet. Put the double pancake into the pan and cook for 1 minute. Flip over and cook the other side for 1 minute.

Remove from the pan and peel the 2 pancakes apart. Repeat with the remaining dough to make 18 pancakes in all. Cover the pancakes with a damp dish towel to keep them from drying out.

ROAST DUCK WITH CRANBERRIES

Many people like the meat of roast duck breast a little pink. However, the legs need to be well cooked, or they may be tough. To accommodate the difference, serve the breast meat first, and return the duck to the oven for 15 minutes to finish cooking the legs.

 Serves 4

5 lb (2.5 kg) duck, with giblets reserved for stock

cranberry sauce to serve (page 178)

watercress sprigs to garnish

CRANBERRY STUFFING

2 tbsp butter

1 small onion, finely chopped

3 cups (175 g) fresh pumpernickel crumbs

1 cup (125 g) cranberries

1 tbsp chopped parsley

1/4 tsp ground mixed spice

salt and black pepper

1 egg, beaten

GRAVY

1 tsp all-purpose flour

2/3 cup (300 ml) duck giblet stock (page 148)

1 Make the cranberry stuffing: melt the butter in a pan, add the onion, and cook gently for 3–5 minutes, until softened.

2 Stir in the bread crumbs, cranberries, parsley, mixed spice, and salt and pepper to taste. Bind with the egg and leave to cool.

3 Remove any fat from the cavity of the duck. Spoon the stuffing into the neck end of the duck, seal the skin flap over the stuffing with a small skewer, and pat into a rounded shape. Put any leftover stuffing into an ovenproof dish and set aside.

4 Prick the skin of the duck all over with a fork and rub salt and pepper into the skin. Place the duck, breast side down, on a wire rack in a deep roasting pan, and cook in a 400°F (200°C) oven for 25 minutes or until golden brown.

5 Pour off some of the fat from the pan to reduce spattering. Turn the duck breast side up and cook for 20 minutes or until brown.

6 Reduce the oven temperature to 350°F (180°C) and cook the duck, without basting, for 1–1¼ hours. Cook any leftover stuffing with the duck for the last 10 minutes.

7 Test the duck by inserting a thin skewer into the thickest part of a thigh: the juices will run clear when it is cooked. Keep warm, uncovered, while you make the gravy.

8 Pour off all but 1 tbsp of the fat from the roasting pan. Set the pan on top of the stove, add the flour, and cook, stirring constantly, for 2 minutes. Pour in the stock and bring to a boil, stirring until lightly thickened. Taste for seasoning and strain into a warmed gravy boat.

9 Put the stuffing into a serving dish, carve the duck (page 151), and garnish with watercress. Serve with the gravy and cranberry sauce.

SAUCES FOR DUCK

ORANGE SAUCE

Put *2 finely chopped shallots, 1¼ cups (300 ml) chicken stock,* and the *juice of 2 oranges* into a pan and bring to a boil. Simmer until reduced by half. Add *salt and pepper to taste.* Push through a strainer, add the *pared zest of 1 large orange, cut into fine strips,* and reheat gently. Serve hot.

HONEY SAUCE

Cook *2 finely chopped shallots* in *2 tbsp butter* until soft. Add *1 tbsp all-purpose flour,* and cook, stirring, for 1 minute. Blend in *1¼ cups (300 ml) chicken stock* and *5 tbsp (75 ml) dry white wine.* Boil, stirring, until thick. Add *3 tbsp honey, 1 tbsp white vinegar,* and *salt and pepper to taste* and cook for 1 minute. Push through a strainer and add *3 tbsp finely chopped parsley.* Serve hot.

BLUEBERRY SAUCE

Put *2 cups (250 g) blueberries or blackcurrants* and *1¼ cups (300 ml) water* into a pan and bring slowly to a boil. Simmer for 10 minutes, until tender. Add *1 cup (250 g) sugar* and *1 tbsp port (optional)* and cook gently until the sugar has dissolved. Serve hot or cold.

DUCK BREASTS WITH RASPBERRY SAUCE

 Serves 4

4 8- to 10-oz (250- to 300-g) duck breasts, with the skin left on

salt and black pepper

RASPBERRY SAUCE

2/3 cup (150 ml) port

5 tbsp (75 ml) water

3 tbsp sugar

1 cup (250 g) raspberries

1 tsp cornstarch

juice of 2 oranges

salt and black pepper

1 Make the raspberry sauce: pour the port, measured water, and sugar into a small saucepan and bring to a boil, stirring until the sugar has dissolved. Add the raspberries and bring back to a boil. Cover and simmer very gently for 5 minutes.

2 With a wooden spoon, push the raspberry mixture through a nylon strainer to extract the seeds. Return the raspberry puree to the saucepan, and bring back to a boil.

3 Mix the cornstarch with the orange juice. Add a little of the raspberry puree to the cornstarch mixture and blend together. Return to the saucepan and bring back to a boil, stirring constantly until thickened. Add salt and pepper to taste and set aside.

4 Score each duck breast (see box, below right) and rub with a little salt and pepper.

5 Place the duck breasts under the broiler, 4 in (10 cm) from the heat, and cook for 8 minutes on each side or until the skin is crisp and the duck is tender but still slightly pink inside.

6 Slice the duck breasts, skin side up, and arrange in a fan shape on warmed serving plates. Spoon a little raspberry sauce around each of the servings and pass the remainder separately.

DUCK BREASTS WITH RED WINE SAUCE

 Serves 4

4 8- to 10-oz (250- to 300-g) duck breasts, with the skin left on

1/2 cup (125 ml) beef stock

1/2 cup (125 ml) red wine

1 tsp tomato paste

1 tsp lemon juice

1 tbsp butter

salt and black pepper

1 tbsp chopped fresh rosemary to garnish

MARINADE

5 garlic cloves, sliced

2 tbsp balsamic vinegar

1 tbsp chopped fresh rosemary

1 Make the marinade: in a bowl, combine the garlic, vinegar, and rosemary. Score the duck breasts and spread with the marinade (see box, below). Chill for 30 minutes.

2 Put the duck breasts, skin side down, with the marinade, in a skillet and cook for 5–7 minutes. Turn and cook for 5 minutes longer. Remove from the pan and keep warm.

3 Spoon any excess fat from the skillet. Add the stock and wine and bring to a boil. Cook over high heat until reduced to a dark glaze, then add the tomato paste and lemon juice.

4 Remove from heat and whisk in the butter, letting it thicken the sauce as it melts. Taste for seasoning.

5 Slice the duck breasts and arrange on warmed serving plates. Spoon the sauce around the duck, sprinkle with the rosemary, and serve immediately.

Scoring and marinating the duck breasts

Score the skin of each duck breast with crisscross lines. Season both sides with salt and pepper.

Put the duck breasts in a shallow dish, skin side down, and spoon the marinade over the top.

HOT & SPICY STIR-FRIED DUCK

 Serves 4

4 8- to 10-oz (250- to 300-g) skinless duck breasts, cut diagonally into 1/2-in (1-cm) strips

2 tbsp sunflower or corn oil

8 scallions, cut into 1-in (2.5-cm) lengths

2 carrots, cut into matchsticks

1/2 lb (250 g) snow peas

7 oz (200 g) canned water chestnuts, drained, rinsed, and sliced

MARINADE

2 tsp dark soy sauce

2 tsp red wine vinegar

1-in (2.5-cm) piece of fresh ginger, peeled and grated

2 fresh red chilies, cored, seeded, and coarsely chopped

grated zest and juice of 1 orange

1 tsp sesame oil

1 tsp cornstarch

1 tsp sugar

salt and black pepper

1 Make the marinade: in a large bowl, combine the soy sauce, vinegar, ginger, chilies, orange zest and juice, sesame oil, cornstarch, sugar, and salt and pepper to taste.

2 Toss the duck strips in the marinade, cover, and leave to stand for 10 minutes.

3 Lift the duck strips out of the marinade, reserve the marinade, and drain the duck on paper towels.

4 Heat the oil in a wok or large skillet, add the duck, and stir-fry over high heat for 5 minutes or until browned all over. Add the scallions and carrots and stir-fry for 2–3 minutes. Add the snow peas and stir-fry for 1 minute.

5 Pour the marinade into the wok and stir-fry for 2 minutes longer or until the duck is just tender. Stir in the water chestnuts, heat through, and season to taste.

ASIAN DUCK WITH GINGER

 Serves 4

4 8- to 10-oz (250- to 300-g) skinless duck breasts

1 tbsp sunflower or corn oil

8 baby corn

bean sprouts and 1 tbsp toasted sesame seeds to garnish

MARINADE

1 cup (200 ml) orange juice

3 tbsp soy sauce

1 tbsp sesame oil

1 tbsp Chinese rice wine or dry sherry

1 tbsp honey

1 1/2-in (3.5-cm) fresh ginger, peeled and chopped

1 garlic clove, crushed

1 tsp ground ginger

salt and black pepper

1 Make the marinade: in a large bowl, combine the orange juice, soy sauce, sesame oil, rice wine, honey, fresh ginger, garlic, ground ginger, and salt and pepper to taste.

2 With a sharp knife, make several diagonal slashes in each duck breast. Pour the marinade over the duck breasts, turn, then cover and marinate in the refrigerator for 30 minutes.

3 Lift the duck breasts out of the marinade, reserving the marinade. Heat the oil in a skillet, add the duck breasts, and cook over high heat, turning frequently, for 10–12 minutes, until tender. Add the marinade and simmer for 2–3 minutes, until slightly reduced.

4 Meanwhile, blanch the baby corn in salted water for 1 minute. Drain, then make several lengthwise cuts in each one, leaving them attached at the stem.

5 To serve, slice each duck breast and arrange on 4 individual serving plates. Spoon the hot sauce over the duck, add the corn, then garnish with bean sprouts and the toasted sesame seeds. Serve immediately.

ASIAN DUCK WITH PLUMS

Substitute 2 large finely sliced dark red plums for the baby corn and bean sprouts. Add to the wok with the marinade. Simmer for 3–4 minutes and serve as above.

GUINEA FOWL MADEIRA

 Serves 6

2 tbsp sunflower or corn oil

2 2¹/₂ lb (1.25 kg) guinea fowl
or small chickens, cut into
serving pieces (page 148)

4 shallots, halved

1 tbsp all-purpose flour

2 ¹/₃ cups (600 ml) chicken stock

²/₃ cup (150 ml) dry white wine

¹/₄ cup (60 ml) Madeira

salt and black pepper

1³/₄ cups (375 g) seedless green
grapes

²/₃ cup (150 ml) heavy cream

chopped parsley to garnish

1 Heat the oil in a
flameproof casserole
and cook the guinea fowl
pieces, in batches, for a few
minutes, until browned all
over. Lift out and drain.

2 Lower the heat, add
the shallots, and cook,
stirring, for 5 minutes or until
softened. Lift out and drain.

3 Add the flour and cook,
stirring, for 1 minute.
Pour in the stock and bring to
a boil, stirring. Add the wine
and Madeira and season to
taste. Add the guinea fowl and
shallots and bring to a boil.
Cook in a 325°F (160°C) oven
for about 1 hour until tender.

4 Add the grapes and cook
for 15 minutes. Add the
cream and heat gently.
Garnish with parsley and
serve immediately.

MUSHROOM-STUFFED QUAIL

*Whole quail make a very impressive dinner party dish. They can be tricky to eat, so
boning and stuffing them makes it much easier for your guests. Ask your butcher
if he can bone the birds for you – or do it yourself at home (see page 149).*

 Serves 6

12 quail, boned (page 149)

2 tbsp butter, plus extra
for greasing

1 tbsp lime marmalade

MUSHROOM STUFFING

4 tbsp butter

3 shallots, finely chopped

³/₄ lb (375 g) mushrooms,
coarsely chopped

1 cup (60 g) fresh white
bread crumbs

salt and black pepper

1 egg, beaten

LIME SAUCE

²/₃ cup (150 ml) chicken stock

juice of 1 lime

1 cup (200 ml) light sour cream

¹/₄ cup (30 g) chopped parsley

1 Make the mushroom
stuffing: melt the butter
in a saucepan, add the
shallots, and cook gently,
stirring occasionally, for
3–5 minutes, until soft but
not browned.

2 Add the mushrooms and
cook for 2 minutes, then
remove from the heat. Stir in
the bread crumbs, salt and
pepper to taste, and the egg,
then leave to cool. Stuff the
quail (see box, right).

3 Put the quail into a
buttered roasting pan.
Melt the butter gently in a
saucepan, add the lime
marmalade, and heat gently,
stirring, until combined.
Brush the lime butter over
the quail and cook in a 400°F
(200°C) oven for 15–20
minutes, until golden brown
and tender. Remove the quail
from the pan and keep warm.

4 Make the lime sauce:
put the roasting pan on
top of the stove. Add the
stock, and bring to a boil,
then stir for 5 minutes or
until reduced a little.

5 Stir in the lime juice and
sour cream and heat
gently, stirring constantly,
until the sauce has a smooth,
creamy consistency.

6 Add half of the parsley
and salt and pepper to
taste. Serve the quail with
the lime sauce, and garnish
with the remaining parsley.

Stuffing the quail

Spoon some of the stuffing
into the cavity of each
quail; secure the skin with
a wooden toothpick.

STUFFED PHEASANT BREASTS

*Substitute 6 pheasant breasts
with skin for the quail, put
the stuffing beneath the skin,
and proceed as directed,
cooking for 35 minutes.*

190

ROAST PHEASANT

Pheasants are often sold in a brace – a cock and a hen. Make sure you get young pheasants for this recipe; old ones are not suitable for roasting and can be very tough unless cooked slowly in a casserole.

 Serves 4

2 oven-ready pheasants, with giblets reserved for stock

6 tbsp (90 g) butter, softened

salt and black pepper

4 slices of bacon

1 tsp all purpose flour

1¼ cups (300 ml) pheasant giblet stock (page 148)

1 tsp red currant jelly

watercress sprigs to garnish

TO SERVE

fried bread crumbs (far right)

cottage fries (far right)

bread sauce (page 178)

1 Prepare the oven-ready pheasants for roasting (see box, right).

2 Put the pheasants into a roasting pan, and cook in a 400°F (200°C) oven, basting once, for 1 hour or until the birds are tender.

3 Test the pheasants by inserting a thin skewer in the thickest part of a thigh: the juices should run clear when they are cooked.

4 Lift the pheasants onto a warmed serving platter, cover with foil, and keep warm. Pour off all but 1 tbsp of the fat from the roasting pan, reserving any juices. Put the pan on top of the stove, add the flour, and cook, stirring, for 1 minute.

5 Add the stock and red currant jelly and bring to a boil, stirring until lightly thickened. Simmer for 2–3 minutes, then taste for seasoning. Strain into a warmed gravy boat.

6 To serve, garnish the pheasants with the watercress sprigs and serve with fried bread crumbs, cottage fries, bread sauce, and the gravy.

Preparing pheasants for roasting

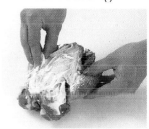

Rub the pheasants all over with the softened butter and season with salt and black pepper

Lay the bacon slices crosswise over the breast of each pheasant.

EXTRAS FOR GAME

These traditional British accompaniments can be served with roast pheasant and many other game dishes, including grouse and partridge.

FRIED BREAD CRUMBS

Melt *2 tbsp butter* with *1 tbsp sunflower or corn oil*. When the butter foams, add *1½ cups (90 g) fresh white bread crumbs* and cook, stirring, for 3–5 minutes, until golden.

COTTAGE FRIES

Using a mandoline or the finest blade on a food processor, slice *2 large baking potatoes* finely, then dry them. Heat some *sunflower or corn oil* in a deep-fryer, add the potato slices, and deep-fry for 3 minutes or until crisp and golden. Drain, then sprinkle with *salt*.

STUFFING BALLS

Combine *2 cups (125 g) fresh white bread crumbs, 4 tbsp grated cold butter, 1 beaten egg, 2 tbsp chopped parsley, the grated zest of 1 lemon,* and *salt and pepper to taste.* Stir to mix, then roll into 12 small balls. *Melt 2 tbsp butter* with *1 tbsp olive oil* in a skillet. When the butter foams, add the stuffing balls and cook for 5 minutes or until golden all over. Drain thoroughly.

PHEASANT STEW

 Serves 6–8

2 tbsp sunflower or corn oil

2 pheasants, cut into serving pieces (page 148)

³/4 lb (375 g) shallots, chopped

4 thick slices of bacon, cut into strips

3 garlic cloves, crushed

1 tbsp all-purpose flour

2 1/3 cups (600 ml) game stock (page 148)

1 1/4 cups (300 ml) red wine

1 head of celery, separated into stalks, sliced

1/2 lb (250 g) mushrooms

1 tbsp tomato paste

salt and black pepper

chopped parsley to garnish

1 Heat the oil in a large flameproof casserole. Add the pheasant pieces and cook over high heat until browned. Lift out and drain.

2 Add the shallots and bacon and cook for 5 minutes. Add the garlic and flour and cook, stirring, for 1 minute. Add the stock and wine and bring to a boil. Add the celery, mushrooms, tomato paste, and season to taste. Simmer for 5 minutes.

3 Add the pheasant, bring back to a boil, cover, and cook in a 325°F (160°C) oven for 2 hours. Garnish with parsley.

NORMANDY PHEASANT

Apples and cream are traditional ingredients in the cuisine of Normandy. Here, apples and a rich sauce perfectly complement the pheasant, which is cooked slowly and gently in wine and stock to keep it moist and tender.

 Serves 6–8

2 tbsp butter

1 tbsp sunflower or corn oil

2 pheasants, cut into serving pieces (page 148)

2 cooking apples, quartered, cored, and sliced

4 celery stalks, sliced

1 onion, sliced

1 tbsp all-purpose flour

1 1/4 cups (300 ml) chicken or game stock (page 148)

2/3 cup (150 ml) dry white wine

salt and black pepper

2/3 cup (150 ml) heavy cream

apple rings to serve (see box, right)

chopped parsley to garnish

1 Melt the butter with the oil in a flameproof casserole. When the butter is foaming, add the pheasant pieces and cook for about 5 minutes, until browned. Lift out and drain.

2 Lower the heat, add the apples, celery, and onion and cook for 5–6 minutes, until soft.

3 Add the flour and cook, stirring, for 1 minute. Pour in the stock and wine, add salt and pepper to taste, and bring to a boil, stirring until lightly thickened.

4 Return the pheasant to the casserole and spoon the sauce over the top. Bring back to a boil, cover with parchment paper and the casserole lid and cook in a 350°F (180°C) oven for 1–1 1/2 hours, until tender. Remove the pheasant from the casserole with a slotted spoon and keep warm.

5 Strain the sauce into a pan. Whisk in the cream, taste for seasoning, then reheat gently. Arrange the pheasant on serving plates with the apple rings. Spoon the sauce over the pheasant and serve immediately, garnished with parsley.

Apple rings

Core *2 cooking apples,* leaving them whole, and slice crosswise into 1/4-in (5-mm) rings.

Melt *2 tbsp butter* in a skillet, add the apple rings, and sprinkle with *a little sugar.* Cook over high heat, turning once, for 3 minutes or until the sugar has caramelized and the apple rings are golden brown. Lift out and keep warm.

SQUAB PIE WITH FENNEL & CARROTS

 Serves 6

2 tbsp sunflower or corn oil

4 squabs, breasts removed and cut into strips, and carcasses used for stock

2 large carrots, sliced

1 fennel bulb, sliced

1 large onion, chopped

2 tsp all-purpose flour

1 1/4 cups (300 ml) game stock (page 148)

2/3 cup (150 ml) red wine

1 tbsp red currant jelly

salt and black pepper

all-purpose flour for dusting

1/2 lb (250 g) store-bought puff pastry

beaten egg for glazing

chopped parsley to garnish

★ 8-cup (2-liter) pie plate

1 Heat the oil in a large flameproof casserole. Add the squab in batches and cook over high heat until browned all over. Lift out and drain on paper towels.

2 Lower the heat, add the carrots, fennel, and onion, and cook, stirring occasionally, for 5 minutes or until softened. Add the flour and cook, stirring, for about 1 minute.

3 Gradually pour in the stock and bring to a boil, stirring constantly until lightly thickened. Add the squab, wine, red currant jelly, and salt and pepper to taste. Cover tightly and simmer very gently for 1 hour. Leave to cool.

4 Lightly flour a work surface. Roll out the puff pastry until 1 in (2.5 cm) larger than the pie plate. Invert the pie plate onto the dough and cut around the edge. Cut a long strip of pastry from the trimmings and press onto the rim of the pie plate. Reserve the remaining trimmings. Spoon in the squab and vegetable mixture. Brush the pastry strip with water, top with the pastry lid, and crimp the edge with a fork.

5 Make a hole in the top of the pie to let the steam escape. Roll out the reserved pastry and cut decorative shapes with a pastry cutter. Brush the bottoms of the shapes with beaten egg and arrange on the pie. Glaze the top with beaten egg.

6 Bake the pie in a 400°F (200°C) oven for 25–30 minutes until the pastry is well risen and golden. Garnish with the parsley.

RABBIT CASSEROLE

 Serves 6

1 rabbit, cut into serving pieces

2 tbsp butter

2 tbsp olive oil

4 thick slices of bacon, cut into strips

16 small shallots

1/2 lb (250 g) cremini mushrooms, halved

1/4 cup (30 g) all-purpose flour

3 2/3 cups (900 ml) game stock (page 148)

2 large thyme sprigs

2 large parsley sprigs

salt and black pepper

stuffing balls (page 191)

fresh thyme to garnish

MARINADE

1 1/4 cups (300 ml) ruby port

1/4 cup (60 ml) olive oil

1 large onion, sliced

2 bay leaves

1 Make the marinade: in a large bowl, combine the port, oil, onion, and bay leaves. Add the rabbit pieces, turn in the marinade, cover, and leave to marinate in the refrigerator for 8 hours.

2 Remove the rabbit from the marinade, reserving the marinade. Melt the butter with the oil in a large flameproof casserole. When the butter is foaming, add the rabbit pieces and cook over high heat until browned all over. Lift out and drain on paper towels.

3 Lower the heat, add the bacon and shallots, and cook for 5 minutes or until lightly browned. Add the mushrooms and cook for 2–3 minutes. Remove and drain on paper towels. Add the flour and cook, stirring, for 1 minute. Gradually add the stock and bring to a boil, stirring until thickened.

4 Return the rabbit, bacon, shallots, and mushrooms to the casserole with the strained marinade. Add the thyme and parsley, season to taste, and bring to a boil. Cover and cook in a 325°F (160°C) oven for 2 hours.

5 Taste for seasoning. Place the stuffing balls on top of the casserole, garnish with fresh thyme, and serve immediately.

RABBIT WITH MUSTARD & MARJORAM

 Serves 4

1/4 cup (60 ml) Dijon mustard

1 tsp chopped fresh marjoram

1 rabbit, cut into serving pieces

2 tbsp butter

2 tbsp olive oil

1 large onion, chopped

2 garlic cloves, crushed

3 thick slices of bacon, cut into pieces

1 tsp all-purpose flour

1 3/4 cups (450 ml) chicken stock

salt and black pepper

2/3 cup (150 ml) light cream

2 tbsp chopped parsley to garnish

1 Mix the mustard and marjoram and spread over the rabbit pieces. Place in a shallow dish, cover, and leave to marinate in the refrigerator for 8 hours.

2 Melt the butter with the oil in a large flameproof casserole. When the butter is foaming, add the rabbit pieces and cook for about 5 minutes, until browned all over. Lift out and drain on paper towels.

3 Add the onion, garlic, and bacon to the casserole and cook for 3–5 minutes, until the onion is soft and the bacon golden. Add the flour and cook, stirring, for 1 minute. Gradually blend in the stock and bring to a boil, stirring until thickened.

4 Return the rabbit to the casserole, add salt and pepper to taste, and bring back to a boil. Cover the casserole and cook in a 325°F (160°C) oven for 1 1/2 hours or until the rabbit is tender and cooked through.

5 Transfer the rabbit to a warmed platter and keep warm. Boil the sauce for 2 minutes or until reduced to a coating consistency. Stir in the cream. Taste for seasoning, reheat gently, and spoon the sauce over the rabbit. Serve immediately, garnished with parsley.

BRAISED RABBIT WITH MUSHROOMS

 Serves 4

2 tbsp butter

1 tbsp sunflower or corn oil

1 rabbit, cut into serving pieces

8 small shallots

3/4 lb (375 g) mushrooms, quartered

1 1/4 cups (300 ml) hard cider or white wine

a few parsley sprigs

3–4 tarragon sprigs

salt and black pepper

1 1/4 cups (300 ml) light cream

2 tbsp chopped parsley to garnish

1 Melt the butter with the oil in a flameproof casserole. When the butter is foaming, add the rabbit pieces and cook for about 5 minutes, until browned all over. Lift out the rabbit with a slotted spoon and drain on paper towels.

2 Add the shallots to the casserole and cook over high heat, stirring, for about 3 minutes, until golden. Add the mushrooms and cook, stirring occasionally, for 3–4 minutes, until softened.

3 Return the rabbit pieces to the casserole, add the cider, parsley sprigs, tarragon, and salt and pepper to taste, and bring to a boil. Cover the casserole and cook in a 325°F (160°C) oven for 1 1/2 hours or until the rabbit is tender.

4 Transfer the rabbit to a warmed platter and keep warm. Remove and discard the parsley and tarragon. Bring the sauce in the casserole to a boil, then boil until slightly reduced. Stir in the cream. Taste for seasoning and reheat gently.

5 Pour the sauce over the rabbit and garnish with parsley. Serve immediately.

BRAISED RABBIT WITH PRUNES

Substitute 1/4 lb (125 g) prunes for the mushrooms and add to the casserole 30 minutes before the end of cooking time.

BRAISED VENISON

 Serves 4–6

2¹/₂–3 lb (1.25–1.5 kg) shoulder of venison, rolled and tied

2 tbsp butter

2 tbsp sunflower oil

1 large onion, chopped

2 large carrots, sliced

2 celery stalks, sliced

1¹/₄ cups (300 ml) beef stock

salt and black pepper

1 tbsp red currant jelly

MARINADE

1¹/₄ cups (300 ml) red wine

2 tbsp olive oil

pared zest of 1 orange

pared zest of 1 lemon

2 tsp crushed juniper berries

6 black peppercorns

1 garlic clove, crushed

1 large thyme sprig

1 large parsley sprig

1 Make the marinade: in a large bowl, combine the wine, oil, orange and lemon zests, juniper berries, black peppercorns, garlic, thyme, and parsley. Turn the venison in the marinade, cover, and leave to marinate in the refrigerator, turning occasionally, for 2–3 days.

2 Lift the venison out of the marinade, straining and reserving the marinade, and pat dry. Melt the butter with the oil in a large flameproof casserole. When the butter is foaming, add the venison and cook over high heat for 5 minutes or until well browned all over. Remove the venison from the casserole.

3 Lower the heat and add the onion, carrots, and celery to the casserole. Cover and cook very gently for 10 minutes. Place the venison on top of the vegetables, add the stock, the strained marinade, and salt and pepper to taste, and bring to a boil. Cover with baking parchment and the casserole lid and cook in a 325°F (160°C) oven for 2¹/₂–3 hours, until tender.

4 Lift out the venison and keep warm. Strain the liquid in the casserole, spoon off the fat, then return to the casserole. Add the red currant jelly and boil for a few minutes, until syrupy. Slice the venison and arrange on a warmed serving platter. Pour the sauce over the venison and serve immediately.

HEARTY VENISON CASSEROLE

 Serves 4

2 lb (1 kg) stewing venison, cut into 1-in (2.5-cm) cubes

2 tbsp olive oil

6 celery stalks, thickly sliced on the diagonal

2 cups (150 g) cremini mushrooms, quartered

¹/₄ cup (30 g) all-purpose flour

salt and black pepper

2 carrots, cut into 3-in (7.5-cm) sticks

chopped parsley to garnish

MARINADE

1³/₄ cups (450 ml) red wine

3 tbsp sunflower or corn oil

1 onion, sliced

1 tsp ground allspice

a few parsley sprigs

1 bay leaf

1 Make the marinade: in a bowl, combine the red wine, oil, onion, allspice, parsley sprigs, and bay leaf. Toss the venison cubes in the marinade to coat thoroughly, cover, and leave to marinate in the refrigerator, turning occasionally, for 2 days.

2 Lift the venison and onion out of the marinade and pat dry. Strain and reserve the marinade.

3 Heat the oil in a large flameproof casserole, add the venison and onion, and cook for 3–5 minutes, until well browned. Lift out and drain on paper towels.

4 Lower the heat, add the celery and mushrooms, and cook for 2–3 minutes, until softened. Remove with a slotted spoon. Add the flour and cook, stirring, for 1 minute. Gradually blend in the marinade and bring to a boil, stirring until thickened.

5 Return the venison, onion, celery, and mushrooms to the casserole, and add salt and pepper to taste. Bring to a boil, cover, and cook in a 325°F (160°C) oven for 1¹/₂ hours.

6 Add the carrots and return to the oven for 30 minutes or until the venison is tender. Garnish and serve immediately.

TRADITIONAL GAME PIE

This game pie follows a classic recipe that takes about 6 hours to make, over 3 days, but it's well worth the effort. Game meats such as pheasant, rabbit, and venison are available in specialty food markets. There is chicken in the pie, too, which goes very well with game, but you could use turkey.

 Serves 18

4 lb (2 kg) chicken, boned and skinned (page 149)

2 lb (1 kg) boneless mixed game meats, cut into ½-in (1-cm) pieces

¾ lb (375 g) pancetta, coarsely chopped

1 lb (500 g) bacon, cut into small pieces

butter for greasing

hot-water crust pastry (see box, right)

about 2 tsp salt

black pepper

1 egg, beaten

1¾ cups (450 ml) jellied stock (page 148)

MARINADE

⅔ cup (150 ml) port

1 small onion, finely chopped

3 garlic cloves, crushed

leaves of 4 thyme sprigs, chopped

1 tsp grated nutmeg

★ 11½-in (29-cm) springform pan or tart pan with a removable bottom

1 Make the marinade: in a bowl, combine the port, onion, garlic, thyme, and grated nutmeg.

2 Cut the chicken breast into long strips, about ½ in (1 cm) wide, and set aside. Cut the rest of the chicken into ½-in (1-cm) chunks. Add the chunks to the marinade with the game meats, pancetta, and bacon. Cover and leave to marinate in the refrigerator for 8 hours.

3 Lightly butter the pan. Take two-thirds of the hot-water crust pastry, pat it out over the bottom of the pan, and push it up the side, until it stands ½ in (1 cm) above the rim.

4 Season the meat mixture with plenty of salt and pepper and spoon half into the pastry shell. Smooth the surface evenly.

5 Arrange the reserved chicken breast strips on top of the meat, radiating from the middle. Season with salt and pepper.

6 Top with the remaining meat mixture. Brush the top edge of the pastry with beaten egg. Roll out the remaining pastry and cover the pie, reserving the trimmings. Pinch around the edge to seal, then crimp.

7 Decorate the pie with the pastry trimmings, attaching them with beaten egg. Make 3 steam holes in the pastry lid and glaze the pie with beaten egg.

8 Bake the pie in a 425°F (220°C) oven for 1 hour. If the pastry starts to brown too quickly, cover it with a sheet of foil. Reduce the heat to 325°F (160°C) and continue to cook for 2–2¼ hours.

9 Test the pie by piercing the center with a skewer: the juices will run clear and the meat will feel tender when it is done. Leave the pie to cool in the pan for 8 hours.

10 Put the jellied stock into a saucepan and heat until melted. Using a funnel, slowly pour the stock through the steam holes in the pie. Cover and chill for 6 hours or until the stock has set. Unmold the pie and cut into wedges to serve.

Making the pastry

Sift *6 cups (750 g) all-purpose flour* and *1 tsp salt* into a bowl. Put *1¾ cups (400 ml) water* and *1⅔ cups (300 g) vegetable shortening* into a saucepan and heat until the water is boiling and the fat has melted.

Pour onto the flour and mix quickly with a wooden spoon until the mixture holds together.

Turn the dough onto a floured surface, invert the bowl over the top to keep the dough moist, and leave to cool until lukewarm.

6

MEAT
DISHES

🕐 UNDER 30 MINUTES

BEEF STROGANOFF

Classic Russian dish: strips of steak cooked with shallots and mushrooms, and mixed with sour cream.

SERVES 4 493 calories per serving

Takes 20 minutes   **PAGE 223**

LAMB CHOPS WITH MINTED HOLLANDAISE SAUCE

Broiled chops served with hollandaise sauce, flavored with lemon juice and fresh mint.

SERVES 4 611 calories per serving

Takes 20 minutes   **PAGE 252**

STEAK DIANE

Flambéed steaks served with a light sauce combining onion, beef stock, lemon juice, Worcestershire sauce, and parsley.

SERVES 4 373 calories per serving

Takes 25 minutes   **PAGE 222**

STEAKS WITH SMOKED OYSTER RELISH

Steaks rubbed with garlic and sprinkled with smoked oyster relish flavored with parsley.

SERVES 4 278 calories per serving

Takes 15–20 minutes   **PAGE 221**

HERBED BUTTERFLY CHOPS

Lamb chops brushed with olive oil, sprinkled with pepper, and flavored with rosemary, mint, and thyme sprigs, then broiled.

SERVES 4 320 calories per serving

Takes 15 minutes   **PAGE 252**

LIVER & BACON WITH ONION SAUCE

Strips of liver cooked with onion and bacon. Simmered with beef stock, ketchup, tarragon, and Worcestershire sauce.

SERVES 4 441 calories per serving

Takes 15 minutes   **PAGE 243**

TOURNEDOS ROQUEFORT

Crunchy and substantial: grilled tenderloin steaks topped with a mixture of melted Roquefort cheese, butter, and chopped walnuts.

SERVES 4 430 calories per serving

Takes 20 minutes   **PAGE 222**

STEAK AU POIVRE

Piquant and creamy: filet mignon encrusted with black peppercorns. Served in a pool of cream and brandy sauce.

SERVES 4 489 calories per serving

Takes 25 minutes   **PAGE 220**

CALF'S LIVER WITH SAGE

Slices of calf's liver coated with seasoned flour and cooked quickly. Served with pan juices flavored with sage and lemon juice.

SERVES 4 364 calories per serving

Takes 10 minutes   **PAGE 244**

UNDER 30 MINUTES

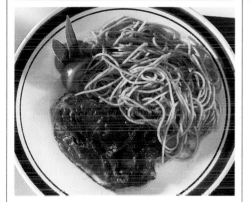

SALTIMBOCCA

Veal scallops topped with sage leaves and prosciutto and cooked with garlic. Served with a wine and cream sauce.

SERVES 4   342 calories per serving

Takes 25 minutes   **PAGE 241**

BEEF TACOS

Ground beef and tomatoes richly seasoned with garlic, chili, and cilantro. Served in taco shells with lettuce and sour cream.

SERVES 4   407 calories per serving

Takes 25 minutes   **PAGE 237**

CHATEAUBRIAND WITH BEARNAISE SAUCE

Broiled steak basted with butter, served with a béarnaise sauce flavored with tarragon.

SERVES 2   761 calories per serving

Takes 25 minutes   **PAGE 220**

30–60 MINUTES

VEAL MARSALA

Veal scallops lightly coated in seasoned flour and cooked until golden. Served in a Marsala sauce and garnished with parsley.

SERVES 4   239 calories per serving

Takes 30 minutes   **PAGE 242**

CORNED BEEF HASH

Quick and nourishing: chunks of corned beef cooked with onion, pieces of potato, and stock and broiled until crispy and brown.

SERVES 2–3   887–591 calories per serving

Takes 30 minutes   **PAGE 232**

BEEF & BEAN BURRITOS

Popular and piquant: strips of steak cooked with garlic, chili, tomatoes, and pinto beans. Wrapped in tortillas.

SERVES 4   471 calories per serving

Takes 35 minutes   **PAGE 223**

BROILED PORK CHOPS WITH MANGO SAUCE

Sweet and tender: chops served with a sauce combining fresh mango and mango chutney.

SERVES 4   347 calories per serving

Takes 35 minutes   **PAGE 262**

PORK CHOPS WITH ORANGES

Fresh and tangy: pork chops spread with coarse mustard, topped with orange slices and sugar, and baked.

SERVES 6   361 calories per serving

Takes 55 minutes   **PAGE 263**

PORK STEAKS WITH MIXED PEPPERCORNS

Lean pork steaks encrusted with mixed peppercorns, served with a sauce of white wine, beef stock, and heavy cream.

SERVES 4   567 calories per serving

Takes 30 minutes, plus standing   **PAGE 264**

🕐 **30–60 MINUTES**

LAMB WITH MINT GLAZE

Lamb chops glazed with white wine, vinegar, mint sprigs, honey, and Dijon mustard, then barbecued or broiled.

SERVES 4 304 calories per serving

Takes 15 minutes, plus marinating **PAGE 251**

MADEIRA PORK WITH PAPRIKA

Rich and creamy: pork tenderloin simmered with Madeira, stock, onion, mushrooms, red pepper, and paprika, then mixed with cream.

SERVES 4 560 calories per serving

Takes 50 minutes **PAGE 261**

VEAL CHOPS WITH MUSHROOMS & CREAM

Veal chops cooked with mushrooms, cream, shallots, garlic, wine, and tarragon.

SERVES 4 604 calories per serving

Takes 30 minutes, plus soaking **PAGE 240**

BRAISED MEATBALLS

Balls of ground beef and pork in a sauce of cider or beer and tomato paste, with onion, garlic, celery, red pepper, and mushrooms.

SERVES 4 416 calories per serving

Takes 40 minutes **PAGE 233**

KIDNEYS TURBIGO

Lamb kidneys cooked with chipolata sausages, then simmered with stock, sherry, onions, mushrooms, and a bay leaf.

SERVES 4 455 calories per serving

Takes 50 minutes **PAGE 258**

WIENER SCHNITZEL

A classic Viennese dish: veal scallops coated in beaten egg and fresh white bread crumbs, chilled, then cooked until light golden brown.

SERVES 4 373 calories per serving

Takes 20 minutes, plus chilling

Traditionally served with piquant anchovy fillets, chopped capers, lemon wedges, and a few parsley sprigs.

PAGE 241

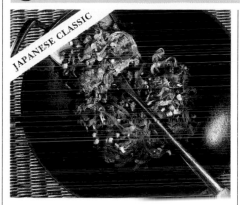

BEEF TERIYAKI

Strips of tender steak marinated in soy sauce, Japanese rice wine, and sugar. Stir-fried with onion and red pepper.

SERVES 4   329 calories per serving

Takes 15 minutes, plus marinating   **PAGE 226**

LAMB NOISETTES WITH ORANGE & HONEY

Noisettes marinated in honey, orange, olive oil, garlic, and herbs and broiled. Served with a sauce made from the marinade.

SERVES 4   457 calories per serving

Takes 20 minutes, plus marinating   **PAGE 253**

LEMON BROILED LAMB

Butterflied leg of lamb marinated in a tangy mixture of lemon juice, honey, garlic, and mustard and broiled.

SERVES 6–8   425–318 calories per serving

Takes 45 minutes, plus marinating   **PAGE 247**

BACON-WRAPPED PORK IN VERMOUTH SAUCE

Pork tenderloin wrapped in bacon and served with a vermouth and mushroom sauce.

SERVES 6   547 calories per serving

Takes 1¼ hours   **PAGE 261**

FAJITAS

Steak marinated in orange and lime juices, tequila, garlic, cilantro, and chili, and broiled. Served with salsa and tortillas.

SERVES 4   543 calories per serving

Takes 40 minutes, plus marinating   **PAGE 226**

MEAT LOAF

Ground beef mixed with tomatoes, stuffing, onion, carrot, parsley, and garlic, wrapped in bacon and baked.

SERVES 4–6   717–478 calories per serving

Takes 1½ hours   **PAGE 236**

PORK WITH CHILI & COCONUT

Strips of pork in a dry marinade of ginger, chili, and curry powder. Cooked with coconut, scallions, and red pepper.

SERVES 4   498 calories per serving

Takes 40 minutes, plus marinating   **PAGE 262**

CREAMED SWEETBREADS

Veal sweetbreads simmered with onion, parsley, and bay leaf. Served with a lemon-flavored sauce.

SERVES 4   345 calories per serving

Takes 40 minutes, plus soaking   **PAGE 244**

SPINACH-STUFFED PORK CHOPS

Loin chops stuffed with spinach, bacon, Parmesan cheese, and herbs, cooked in wine, and topped with Gruyère cheese.

SERVES 4   737 calories per serving

Takes 1¼ hours   **PAGE 263**

⏱ Over 60 minutes

EXOTIC BEEF

South African classic: ground beef baked with garlic, apricots, almonds, chutney, lemon, and bread. Topped with eggs and almonds.

SERVES 6–8 656–492 calories per serving

Takes 1 hour 5 minutes **PAGE 237**

DANISH MEATBALLS

Minced pork seasoned with onion, thyme, and paprika and shaped into ovals. Cooked in a tomato sauce and topped with plain yogurt.

SERVES 4 586 calories per serving

Takes 1¹/₂ hours **PAGE 266**

SHEPHERD'S PIE

Ground lamb baked with mushrooms, carrot, onion, garlic, stock, and Worcestershire sauce. Topped with mashed potato.

SERVES 4 574 calories per serving

Takes 1¹/₂ hours **PAGE 257**

SPICED LAMB WITH COCONUT

Cubes of lamb dry-marinated in ginger and spices are cooked with tomato, lime, mango chutney, and coconut, then mixed with yogurt.

SERVES 4–6 745–496 calories per serving

Takes 1¹/₄ hours **PAGE 256**

PASTICCIO

Greek favorite: ground pork with red wine, tomatoes, garlic, and herbs. Baked with macaroni and cheese custard.

SERVES 4–6 1019–679 calories per serving

Takes 1¹/₄ hours **PAGE 266**

BEEF WITH ROAST VEGETABLE SALAD

Roast beef served with a salad of roasted eggplant, zucchini, fennel, and peppers.

SERVES 4–6 522–348 calories per serving

Takes 1³/₄ hours, plus cooling **PAGE 218**

SAUSAGES WITH POTATOES & PEPPERS

Bite-sized pieces of spicy merguez sausage in a casserole with potatoes, red and green peppers, and garlic.

SERVES 4 381 calories per serving

Takes 1¹/₄ hours, plus cooling **PAGE 258**

MARINATED LOIN OF PORK WITH PINEAPPLE

Pork marinated in pineapple juice, maple syrup, soy sauce, and herbs, then roasted.

SERVES 6–8 426–320 calories per serving

Takes 2¹/₂ hours, plus marinating **PAGE 260**

BEEF FLORENTINE

Layer of ground beef, tomato, and garlic, topped with spinach and three types of cheese. Covered with phyllo pastry.

SERVES 8 576 calories per serving

Takes 1¹/₂ hours **PAGE 233**

⏱ OVER 60 MINUTES

SAUSAGE & LENTIL CASSEROLE

Herby pork sausages baked with lentils, stock, and vegetables. Flavored with bay leaves, parsley, and sage.

SERVES 4 783 calories per serving

Takes 1¾ hours   **PAGE 270**

RACK OF LAMB WITH A WALNUT & HERB CRUST

Rack of lamb coated with a walnut and parsley crust and roasted.

SERVES 6 626–417 calories per serving

Takes 1¾ hours, plus chilling   **PAGE 251**

BLANQUETTE OF LAMB

Chunks of lamb simmered with onion, carrot, bay leaves, lemon juice, and mushrooms. Served with a cream and egg sauce.

SERVES 4–6 658–439 calories per serving

Takes 2 hours   **PAGE 255**

MOUSSAKA

Ground lamb flavored with garlic, onion, strained tomatoes, and red wine, layered with eggplant, and topped with cheese sauce.

SERVES 6–8 653–490 calories per serving

Takes 1¾ hours, plus standing   **PAGE 257**

TOAD IN THE HOLE

An English favorite: bulk pork sausage combined with leek, sage, and parsley and baked in a batter.

SERVES 4 802 calories per serving

Takes 45 minutes, plus standing   **PAGE 270**

MEAT PIES WITH CHEESY POTATO TOPPING

Ground beef cooked with vegetables and stock. Topped with mashed potato and cheese.

SERVES 4 850 calories per serving

Takes 1½ hours   **PAGE 236**

LEMON ROAST VEAL WITH SPINACH STUFFING

Veal marinated in lemon and thyme, with a stuffing of spinach, shallot, and bacon.

SERVES 4–6 666–444 calories per serving

Takes 1¾ hours, plus marinating   **PAGE 239**

ROAST LEG OF LAMB WITH RED WINE GRAVY

Lamb flavored with herbs, roasted and served with red wine gravy and mint sauce.

SERVES 4–6 517–344 calories per serving

Takes 2 hours   **PAGE 245**

LAMB TAGINE

North African classic: cubes of lamb cooked with apricots, fennel, and green peppers. Flavored with saffron, ginger, and orange.

SERVES 6–8 550–412 calories per serving

Takes 1¾ hours   **PAGE 256**

⏱ OVER 60 MINUTES

CHILI CON CARNE

Tex-Mex specialty: cubes of chuck cooked with red kidney beans, chili, onion, garlic, stock, tomato puree, and red pepper.

SERVES 4 543 calories per serving

Takes 3¼ hours, plus soaking   **PAGE 231**

SPINACH-STUFFED LAMB

Succulent and nutritious: boned leg of lamb stuffed with spinach and garlic, and roasted with wine and anchovies.

SERVES 6–8 459–344 calories per serving

Takes 2½ hours, plus cooling   **PAGE 246**

SHOULDER OF LAMB WITH GARLIC & HERBS

Lamb flavored with garlic, rosemary, mint, and thyme. Served with great northern beans.

SERVES 6 464 calories per serving

Takes 1¾ hours   **PAGE 250**

FARMER'S BACON

Lean bacon simmered with vegetables, parsley, and peppercorns, cut into pieces, and baked with a cheese sauce.

SERVES 4 765 calories per serving

Takes 2¼ hours   **PAGE 268**

PORK IN RED WINE

From Cyprus: cubes of pork marinated in red wine, coriander seeds, and cinnamon, cooked with wine and cumin seeds.

SERVES 4 582 calories per serving

Takes 2 hours, plus marinating   **PAGE 265**

WINTER BEEF CASSEROLE

Cubes of chuck and strips of bacon cooked with stock, celery, and carrots and flavored with wine and tomatoes.

SERVES 4–6 680–454 calories per serving

Takes 2¾ hours   **PAGE 227**

SWEET & SOUR CHINESE SPARERIBS

Spareribs baked until tender and coated in a sauce combining ginger, garlic, soy and hoisin sauces, tomato paste, and sherry.

SERVES 4 491 calories per serving

Takes 2 hours   **PAGE 264**

CURRIED LAMB WITH ALMONDS

Rich and creamy: chunks of lamb marinated in yogurt and garam masala and cooked with ginger, garlic, almonds, and spices.

SERVES 6–8 855–642 calories per serving

Takes 2½ hours, plus marinating   **PAGE 254**

BEEF ROLLS WITH VEGETABLE JULIENNE

Slices of round wrapped around stir-fried vegetables and cooked with beef stock.

SERVES 4 386 calories per serving

Takes 2¼ hours   **PAGE 231**

BONED LOIN OF PORK WITH APRICOT STUFFING

Pork filled with an apricot and herb stuffing, then rolled and roasted.

SERVES 6–8 571–428 calories per serving

Takes 2¼ hours, plus cooling   **PAGE 259**

BEEF WITH HORSERADISH

Chuck steak cooked with stock, shallots, curry powder, sugar, ginger, and horseradish cream and garnished with parsley.

SERVES 4–6 448–298 calories per serving

Takes 3 hours   **PAGE 229**

AROMATIC LAMB WITH LENTILS

Chunks of lamb marinated in orange juice, garlic, ginger, and coriander. Cooked with apricots, stock, onion, and lentils.

SERVES 6–8 633–475 calories per serving

Takes 2½ hours, plus marinating   **PAGE 255**

CORNED BEEF WITH MUSTARD SAUCE

Corned beef cooked with carrots, celery, potatoes, turnips, and leeks. Served with a mustard sauce flavored with wine vinegar.

SERVES 4–6 863–575 calories per serving

Takes 2¼ hours, plus soaking   **PAGE 217**

HUNGARIAN GOULASH

Cubes of chuck cooked with stock, onion, tomatoes, red pepper, potatoes, paprika, and sour cream.

SERVES 4–6 711–474 calories per serving

Takes 2½ hours   **PAGE 228**

CHIANTI BEEF CASSEROLE

Cubes of chuck marinated in Chianti, garlic, and thyme and cooked with sun-dried tomatoes, artichoke hearts, and olives.

SERVES 4–6 815–543 calories per serving

Takes 2½ hours, plus marinating   **PAGE 229**

THAI RED BEEF CURRY

Cubes of chuck cooked with cardamom, cinnamon, bay leaves, cloves, ginger, garlic, paprika, tomatoes, yogurt, and red pepper.

SERVES 4–6 490–327 calories per serving

Takes 2½ hours   **PAGE 230**

BEEF WELLINGTON

Roasted beef tenderloin coated with mushrooms, onion, and liver pâté and encased in puff pastry. Served with a mushroom gravy.

SERVES 8 580 calories per serving

Takes 2¼ hours, plus cooling   **PAGE 219**

FRENCH-STYLE BRAISED BEEF

Beef marinated in wine, vinegar, garlic, orange, and herbs and cooked with bacon, carrots, mushrooms, tomatoes, and olives.

SERVES 4–6 604–402 calories per serving

Takes 2½ hours, plus marinating   **PAGE 217**

FRENCH CLASSIC

BOEUF BOURGUIGNON

Rich casserole: cubes of chuck cooked with shallots, bacon, red Burgundy, beef stock, mushrooms, and herbs.

SERVES 4–6   735–490 calories per serving

Takes 2¾ hours   **PAGE 227**

OSSO BUCO

Slices of veal shank cooked with onion, tomato, carrots, celery, garlic, white wine, and stock. Sprinkled with gremolata.

SERVES 6   354 calories per serving

Takes 2¾ hours   **PAGE 242**

FAMILY CHOICE

COUNTRY BEEF CASSEROLE

Chunky and nourishing: cubes of chuck cooked in a casserole with stock and vegetables. Served with herb dumplings.

SERVES 6–8   540–405 calories per serving

Takes 3 hours   **PAGE 230**

DINNER PARTY

VEAL STEW WITH OLIVES & PEPPERS

Cubes of veal cooked in a casserole of peppers, wine, tomatoes, and olives and flavored with garlic and rosemary.

SERVES 6–8   473–355 calories per serving

Takes 2 hours   **PAGE 243**

SHOULDER OF LAMB WITH LEMON & OLIVE STUFFING

Lamb rolled with an olive, lemon, and herb stuffing and roasted in wine and stock.

SERVES 6–8   460–345 calories per serving

Takes 2¾ hours   **PAGE 247**

TRADITIONAL

TRADITIONAL ROAST BEEF

Succulent roast, a family favorite: rolled beef sirloin basted and cooked until deliciously tender. Served with a variety of vegetables, traditional Yorkshire puddings, a rich red wine gravy, and creamy horseradish sauce.

SERVES 8   394 calories per serving

Takes 3¼ hours   **PAGE 215**

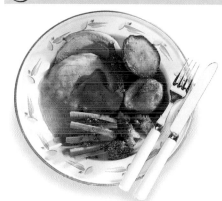

ROAST FRESH HAM

Tender and nourishing: fresh ham roasted with carrot and onion until crisp. Served with gravy and apple sauce.

SERVES 6   338 calories per serving

Takes 2 1/4 hours   **PAGE 260**

IRISH STEW

Traditional Irish family meal: lamb chops cooked in layers of potato and onion and flavored with bay leaf, thyme, and parsley.

SERVES 4   539 calories per serving

Takes 3 1/4 hours   **PAGE 254**

HEARTY PORK CASSEROLE

Shoulder of pork cut into cubes, cooked in a casserole with stock, white wine vinegar, honey, soy sauce, mushrooms, and prunes.

SERVES 6–8   536–402 calories per serving

Takes 3 1/4 hours   **PAGE 265**

MEAT HOT POT

Lamb chops and kidneys cooked with potatoes, carrots, and onions and flavored with thyme, parsley, and bay leaf.

SERVES 4   689 calories per serving

Takes 3 hours   **PAGE 253**

TEXAS BARBECUE BEEF BRISKET

Spicy and rich: beef baked in a marinade of barbecue sauce, pale ale, lemon juice, onions, garlic, and Worcestershire sauce.

SERVES 6   693 calories per serving

Takes 3 1/2 hours, plus marinating   **PAGE 216**

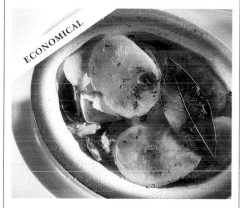

BAKED SAUSAGE

Slices of pork sausage with layers of vegetables, lentils, and potatoes, cooked in a casserole with stock, bay leaves, and cloves.

SERVES 6   712 calories per serving

Takes 3 1/4 hours   **PAGE 269**

STEAK & KIDNEY PIE

Rich and satisfying: cubes of beef and kidney cooked with stock, Worcestershire sauce, and mushrooms. Topped with short crust pastry.

SERVES 4–6   865–577 calories per serving

Takes 3 1/4 hours, plus cooling   **PAGE 232**

SAUSAGE CASSOULET

Garlic sausage, pork sausages, and bacon baked with beans, tomatoes, wine, onion, and herbs. Topped with bread crumbs.

SERVES 8   619 calories per serving

Takes 3 hours, plus soaking   **PAGE 269**

TRINIDAD PEPPERPOT BEEF

Boneless beef simmered with stock, vinegar, Worcestershire sauce, chilies, sugar, parsley, peppercorns, cinnamon, and thyme.

SERVES 4–6   697–465 calories per serving

Takes 3 3/4 hours   **PAGE 218**

OVER 60 MINUTES

BEEF POT ROAST WITH WINTER VEGETABLES

Round of beef in a casserole with onions, rutabaga, celery, carrot, wine, and herbs.

SERVES 6 360 calories per serving

Takes 3¹/₂ hours   **PAGE 216**

GREEK ROAST LAMB

Traditional Greek dish: leg of lamb richly flavored with garlic, rosemary, and lemon juice, cooked until tender.

SERVES 6 328 calories per serving

Takes 4¹/₄ hours   **PAGE 246**

OXTAIL STEW

Tender thick stew: slices of oxtail simmered slowly with beef stock, onions, tomato puree, celery, and herbs.

SERVES 4 505 calories per serving

Takes 4¹/₂ hours   **PAGE 238**

CARBONNADE OF BEEF

Cubes of chuck cooked with onion, garlic, fresh herbs, dark beer, and stock and topped with mustard croutes.

SERVES 4–6 698–465 calories per serving

Takes 3¹/₂ hours   **PAGE 228**

INDIAN SPICED LAMB

Lamb coated in a mixture of spices, honey, yogurt, and saffron, roasted, and garnished with cashew nuts and chopped coriander.

SERVES 4–6 569–379 calories per serving

Takes 4¹/₄ hours, plus marinating   **PAGE 250**

BOSTON BAKED BEANS

Great northern beans, bacon, and onions cooked with dark brown sugar, tomato paste, molasses, and dry mustard.

SERVES 4 650 calories per serving

Takes 5³/₄ hours, plus soaking   **PAGE 268**

VITELLO TONNATO

Italian classic: veal flavored with garlic and rosemary and roasted in white wine. Served cold with a tuna mayonnaise.

SERVES 6–8 848–636 calories per serving

Takes 3¹/₂ hours, plus cooling   **PAGE 240**

MUSTARD-GLAZED HAM

Smoked ham cooked with cider, glazed with sugar and mustard, roasted, and served with a lemon mustard sauce.

SERVES 16–20 477–382 calories per serving

Takes 4 hours, plus soaking   **PAGE 267**

PRESSED TONGUE

Salted ox tongue simmered with bay leaf and onion, then covered with gelatin, pressed, and chilled until set.

SERVES 10 392 calories per serving

Takes 4¹/₄ hours, plus chilling   **PAGE 238**

MEAT KNOW-HOW

FOR CENTURIES, MEAT HAS BEEN the protein food around which the majority of meals have been planned. And even though more and more people are changing their diets to include more vegetables, pasta, rice, and beans, meat is still enjoyed by most families several times a week, and it still forms the traditional centerpiece for many celebration meals. Make sure the cooking method suits the cut of meat you are preparing. Lean meats are best cooked quickly, while tougher cuts of meat are made more tender with long, slow cooking.

BUYING & STORING

If possible, buy your meat from a butcher because he's most likely to have just the cut you want (or will be prepared to cut it for you), and he will also advise you how to cook it. Wherever you shop, choose meat that looks fresh and moist (not wet), with a good color and no grayish tinge. If possible, smell the meat: it should smell fresh. Check that pieces are neatly trimmed, without excess fat and splinters of bone. Appetites vary, but as a general guide, allow 4–7 oz (125–200 g) of lean boneless meat per person and about 8 oz (250 g) per person if the meat has a reasonable amount of bone.

Store meat, both raw and cooked, in the refrigerator. Ground meat and organ meats are more perishable than other kinds of meat, so cook them within 1–2 days of purchase. Chops, steaks, and roasts can be kept for 2–4 days; remove the wrapping and replace with a loose covering. Eat cooked meat within 2–3 days.

PREPARING MEAT FOR COOKING

Trim off excess fat before cooking. If grilling or frying steaks, chops, or bacon strips, slash or snip the fat at intervals to prevent the meat from curling up during cooking. If necessary, trim away sinew and tough connective tissue.

Lean meats that are to be roasted sometimes require barding. This means protecting them with a thin layer of fat such as bacon or pork fat, tied in place with string. Alternatively, lean cuts can be larded with fat: use a long larding needle to insert strips of fat evenly through the meat.

MICROWAVING

Because microwave cooking is so fast, meat does not have time to brown and become crisp. This can be overcome by using a special browning dish that sears meat in the way a skillet does.

The microwave oven is very useful for defrosting frozen meat. This must be done evenly at the manufacturer's recommended setting to prevent some parts of the meat beginning to cook before others are totally defrosted. All wrapping should be removed from the meat before defrosting to ensure that the meat does not start cooking.

FREEZING

Meat to be frozen must be very fresh. Wrap it tightly so that all the air is excluded. Pad any sharp bones so that they don't pierce the wrapping. If packing chops, cutlets, steaks, or hamburgers, separate them with freezerproof plastic wrap or freezer paper. The larger the piece of meat the longer it will keep. Ground meat and sausages can be stored in the freezer for 3 months; organ meats, chops, and cutlets for 4 months; roasts and steaks for 6 months. Thaw frozen meat, in its wrapping and on a plate to catch any juices, in the refrigerator.

MEAT STOCK

Ask your butcher to saw 4 lb (2 kg) bones into 2 1/2-in (6-cm) pieces. Beef and veal bones are best.

1 Roast the bones in a 450°F (230°C) oven for about 30 minutes until well browned. Add *2–3 roughly chopped onions, carrots, and celery stalks.* Roast for 30 minutes.

2 Transfer the browned bones and vegetables to a large stockpot. Add *4 quarts (4 liters) water, a bouquet garni made of 1–2 bay leaves, a few parsley stalks, and 1–2 sprigs of thyme, tied together with fine string, and a few black peppercorns.*

3 Bring to a boil, skim off scum, then simmer for 4–6 hours. Using a ladle, strain the meat stock. Skim off fat, or let cool and lift off solidified fat.

BASIC COOKING TECHNIQUES

Tougher pieces of meat should be cooked slowly by stewing or braising. More tender pieces can be cooked quickly by frying or broiling. Beef and lamb when roasted, broiled, or fried can be served pink in the middle, but pork should be thoroughly cooked.

Stewing

Cut the meat into cubes. Put into a flameproof casserole with any vegetables and liquid to cover. Bring to a boil, cover, and simmer on top of the stove or in the oven.

Alternatively, to seal in juices, heat some oil in the casserole and brown the cubes. Brown the vegetables, add liquid and flavorings, bring to a boil, cover, and simmer as above.

Braising

1 Brown the meat in the casserole to add flavor and to seal in the cooking juices. Remove the meat from the casserole.

2 Add chopped vegetables and cook until beginning to brown. Return the meat and add liquid and flavorings. Bring to a boil, cover, and cook gently according to the recipe.

Frying and sautéing

1 Dry the meat with paper towels (if too moist, it will not brown quickly and evenly). Heat oil or a mixture of oil and butter in a heavy skillet until it is very hot and add the meat, being careful not to crowd the pan.

2 Cook until well browned all over. Reduce the heat and continue until the meat is done to your taste. When turning meat, use tongs rather than a fork since a fork pierces the meat and allows the juices to run out.

Roasting

1 Take the meat from the refrigerator and allow it to come to room temperature.

2 Preheat the oven. Rub the meat with fat or oil and seasonings or make incisions all over and insert herbs or slivers of garlic. Insert a meat thermometer, if using.

3 Put the meat and any vegetables in a roasting pan. Roast in the preheated oven, basting with the juices, until

cooked to your taste (page 214). If not using a meat thermometer, test whether the meat is cooked by inserting a skewer into the center. If the juices that run out are bloody, the meat is rare; if pink, medium; if clear, well-done.

4 Transfer the roast to a carving board and leave to rest for 10–15 minutes while making gravy. Carve the roast (page 213) and serve.

Broiling and barbecuing

1 Preheat the broiler to hot, or light the barbecue (it will take 20–30 minutes to reach cooking temperature unless it is a gas barbecue, which will heat up immediately).

2 Arrange the meat on the broiler pan and put under the broiler, or arrange on the grid over the charcoal fire. Brush with oil or melted butter and cook the meat until it is browned all over.

3 For sausage or thicker pieces of meat that need to be cooked thoroughly, reduce the heat or move the meat farther away from the heat and complete cooking.

Stir-frying

1 Cut the meat into uniform pieces for even cooking. Heat a wok or heavy skillet, then add a little oil.

2 When the oil is hot, start adding the meat, a little at a time – adding too much at once will lower the temperature of the oil. Using a slotted spoon or a spatula, stir and toss the meat constantly until it is evenly browned.

3 If some pieces of meat are cooked before others, they can be pushed up the side of the wok or to the side of the pan, where they will stay warm but not overcook.

BONING & BUTTERFLYING A LEG OF LAMB

A boned leg of lamb is much easier to carve than meat still on the bone. Tunnel boning leaves a pocket that can be filled with stuffing. Cutting the leg open to lie flat is known as butterflying.

1 To tunnel bone, trim the skin and most or all of the fat from the lamb. Cut around the pelvic bone, at the wide end of the leg, to separate it from the meat. Sever the tendons that connect it to the leg bone. Remove the pelvic bone.

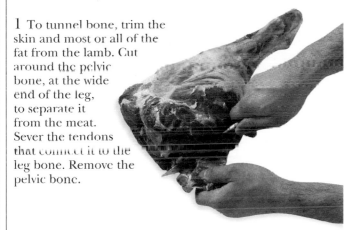

2 At the narrow end of the leg, cut around the shank bone and then scrape the meat away from the whole length of the bone using short strokes.

3 Cut away the meat to expose the joint that joins the shank bone to the leg bone. Sever the tendons and then remove the shank bone.

6 Open out the boned leg into a "butterfly" shape. Cut through any thick portions of meat so that the whole leg can be opened out flat and is roughly even in thickness. Trim off excess fat and any remaining tendons

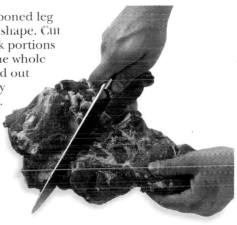

4 Cut around each end of the leg bone. Ease the leg bone out, cutting and scraping away the meat as you twist and pull it out. Trim off the tendons.

5 If you want to butterfly the boned leg, carefully insert a large chef's knife into the cavity left by the leg bone and cut to one side to slit open the meat.

BONING A SHOULDER OF LAMB

A special boning knife, with a narrow, pointed blade, is useful for preparing shoulders of lamb, pork, and veal. If you don't have one, a small, sharp chef's knife can be used instead.

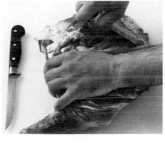

1 Remove the skin and fat. Set the shoulder meat side up. Cut through the meat to the blade bone, and then cut away the meat on either side, keeping the knife as close to the bone as possible, until the bone is revealed.

2 Cut through the ball-and-socket joint between the blade bone and the central shoulder bone to separate the 2 bones.

3 Cut beneath the ball-and-socket joint to free the end. Hold it firmly in one hand and pull the blade bone away from the meat.

4 Cut around the central shoulder bone, severing the tendons and cutting and scraping away the meat. Pull out the bone. If necessary, enlarge the pocket left by the bone so that it will accommodate a stuffing.

Preparing rack of lamb

Rack of lamb is a tender cut for roasting or broiling. A single rack, which is one side of the upper rib cage, comprises 6–9 cutlets and serves 2–3 people. Two racks can be used to make impressive cuts such as a guard of honor or a crown roast.

Rack of lamb
1 Set the rack on a board and cut away the cartilage at one end. Pull off the skin. Score the fat and meat 2 in (5 cm) from the ends of the rib bones.

2 Turn the rack over and set it at the edge of the cutting board so the ends of the rib bones are suspended. Score the meat along the rack, about 2 in (5 cm) from the ends of the rib bones, cutting through to the bones.

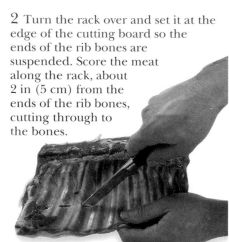

3 Cut out the meat from between the bones, cutting from the crosswise cuts to the ends. Turn the rack over and scrape the ends of the bones clean.

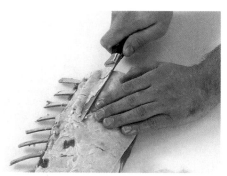

4 Trim away most of the fat from the meat. Repeat the preparation process with the second rack, if using.

Guard of honor
Hold 1 rack in each hand, fat side outward, and push them together, interlocking the rib bones. Cook as directed, covering the rib bones with foil if desired, to prevent them from charring during cooking.

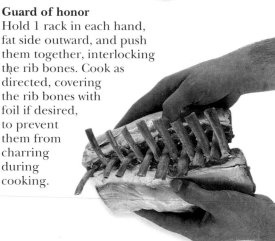

Crown roast

Two racks of lamb are tied together in the shape of a crown.

1 Prepare 2 racks as above. Slit the membrane between the rib bones at the meaty end so that the racks can be bent.

2 Stand the racks, meat side innermost, on a work surface and curve to form a crown shape. Bend the bones so that the crown will stand upright.

3 Tie string around the middle of the 2 racks to hold them in place.

4 Fill the center of the roast with a stuffing or add a filling just before serving. Carve the roast by cutting down between the rib bones.

Stuffing, rolling, & tying a roast

Cuts that have been boned and opened out can be rolled around a stuffing, which gives both moisture and flavor to the meat during cooking.

1 Open out the meat and spread with an even layer of stuffing, leaving a small margin around the edge of the meat.

2 Roll up or fold the meat around the stuffing to make a compact bolster shape. Turn it so that the seam is underneath.

3 Tie string around the meat at regular intervals, to hold it in shape during cooking. Remove the string before carving.

CARVING A ROAST

Once a roast has finished cooking, transfer it to a carving board and let it rest in a warm place for 10–15 minutes. During this time, the temperature of the meat will even out, and the flesh will reabsorb most of the juices. To carve, use a 2-pronged carving fork and a long carving knife.

Shoulder of lamb
1 Insert the fork into the shank end. Cut a narrow, wedge-shaped piece from the center, in the meatiest part between the angle formed by the blade bone and the shoulder bone.

2 Carve neat slices from either side of this wedge-shaped cut until the blade and central shoulder bones are reached. Turn the shoulder over and cut horizontal slices lengthwise.

Beef rib roast
1 Set the roast upright on a carving board, insert the carving fork into the meaty side to steady the joint, and cut close to the large rib bones at the base of the meat to remove them.

2 With the meat on its side, hold the knife at a slight angle and carve the meat into slices, 3/4 in (2 cm) thick.

Leg of lamb
1 Set the roast with the meaty side upward, and insert the carving fork firmly into the knuckle end. Cut a narrow, wedge-shaped piece from the center of the meaty portion, cutting all the way to the bone.

2 Carve neat slices from either side of this wedge-shaped cut, gradually changing the angle of the knife to make the slices larger. Turn the leg over. Trim off the fat, then carve off horizontal slices.

Whole ham
1 Cut a few horizontal slices from one side of the ham to make a flat surface. Turn the ham over onto this surface. Insert the carving fork in the shank end. Make 3 or 4 cuts through to the bone at the shank end.

2 Insert the knife into the last cut and slide it along the bone to detach the slices. Make a few more cuts in the ham and continue to remove the slices in the same way. Turn over and carve off horizontal slices.

MAKING GRAVY

A delicious gravy can be made from a good stock and the richly flavored drippings left after roasting meat. Be sure to remove most of the fat before you begin.

3 Gradually add *1 quart (1 liter) stock or other liquid*, whisking constantly to combine with the flour paste. Whisk until smooth. Simmer, stirring frequently, until the gravy reaches the desired consistency. Season to taste, strain into a warmed gravy boat and serve.

1 Pour all but *1 tbsp fat* from the roasting pan, leaving the juices. Set the pan on top of the stove and heat until sizzling. Stir in *1 tbsp all-purpose flour*.

2 Stir briskly to mix the flour with the juices and scrape the bottom and sides of the pan to dissolve any browned bits. Keep stirring to form a well-browned paste.

ROASTING MEATS

As all ovens are different, these times are only a guide – a meat thermometer is the best way to ensure properly cooked roasts. Cooking times vary, particularly for beef and pork, according to the thickness of the meat.

MEAT		OVEN TEMPERATURE	TIME	INTERNAL TEMPERATURE
Beef	Rare	350°F (180°C)	15 mins per 1 lb (500 g)	140°F (60°C)
	Medium	350°F (180°C)	20 mins per 1 lb (500 g)	160°F (70°C)
	Well-done	350°F (180°C)	25 mins per 1 lb (500 g)	170°F (75°C)
Veal	Well-done	350°F (180°C)	25 mins per 1 lb (500 g)	170°F (75°C)
Lamb	Medium	350°F (180°C)	20 mins per 1 lb (500 g)	170°F (75°C)
	Well-done	350°F (180°C)	25 mins per 1 lb (500 g)	175°F (80°C)
Pork	Well-done	350°F (180°C)	25 mins per 1 lb (500 g)	190°F (90°C)

USING A MEAT THERMOMETER

The most accurate way to test if a large piece of meat is cooked is to use a meat thermometer, which registers the internal temperature of the meat. Before cooking, insert the spike of the thermometer into the middle or thickest part of the meat. Make sure that the thermometer does not touch a bone because bones become hotter than meat and will therefore give a false reading. Start checking the temperature reading toward the end of the suggested cooking time. A roast will continue to cook by retained heat for 5–10 minutes after it is removed from the oven, so take it out as soon as the thermometer reaches the desired temperature.

PREPARING ORGAN MEATS

Sweetbreads are glands from the throat and heart of calves or lambs. They have a delicate flavor and a rich, creamy texture. Lamb, beef, and veal kidneys are sometimes sold surrounded by a layer of hard, white fat – this is suet.

Sweetbreads
1 Soak the sweetbreads in cold water with 1 tbsp lemon juice for 2–3 hours to clean them. Drain and rinse well. Cut away any discolored parts. Use your fingers to carefully peel off the thin membrane surrounding the sweetbreads.

2 Cut away the ducts and any fat and discard. Don't remove too much, or the sweetbreads will break up. Put into a saucepan of cold water and bring to a boil. Blanch calf's sweetbreads for 5 minutes, lamb's sweetbreads for 3 minutes.

Kidneys
1 If the kidneys are surrounded by suet, pull it away. Separate the kidneys (if using beef or veal). Carefully cut through the fine membrane around each kidney and use your fingers to peel it off (cut the ducts from beef or veal kidneys).

2 Set each kidney rounded side up and slice lengthwise in half (or leave attached at the base, according to recipe directions). With a sharp pair of scissors, snip out the small fatty white core and the tubes.

TRADITIONAL ROAST BEEF

 Serves 8

6 1/2 lb (3.25 kg) rolled beef
rib roast

4 tbsp butter, melted

2 tbsp all-purpose flour

salt and black pepper

1 onion, quartered

horseradish sauce and Yorkshire
puddings to serve (see boxes,
below and right)

GRAVY

2/3 cup (150 ml) red wine

2/3 cup (150 ml) beef stock

1 Insert a meat thermometer, if using, into the middle of the meat. Put the beef into a roasting pan and brush with the butter. Sprinkle with the flour and season to taste. Add the onion and roast with the beef in a 400°F (200°C) oven for 20 minutes. Make the Yorkshire pudding batter and set aside.

2 Baste the beef with the juices from the pan and lower the oven temperature to 350°F (180°C).

3 Roast, basting frequently, for 1 1/2 hours longer for rare beef, 1 3/4 hours for medium, and 2 hours for well done or until the meat thermometer registers 140°F, 160°F, or 170°F (60°C, 70°C, or 75°C).

4 Transfer the beef to a carving board, cover with foil, and leave to stand in a warm place. Increase the oven temperature and bake the Yorkshire puddings.

5 Meanwhile, make the gravy: spoon the excess fat from the roasting pan. Put the pan on top of the stove, add the wine and stock, and bring to a boil, stirring constantly to dissolve the cooking juices. Simmer for 5 minutes or until the gravy has a syrupy consistency.

6 Season to taste and strain into a gravy boat. Transfer the beef to a platter and serve with the gravy, horseradish sauce, and Yorkshire puddings.

Horseradish sauce

Mix 2–3 tbsp grated fresh horseradish with 1 tbsp white vinegar in a bowl. In another bowl, whisk 2/3 cup (150 ml) heavy cream until thick.

Fold the cream into the horseradish mixture and add salt, black pepper, and sugar to taste. Cover the sauce and leave to chill until ready to serve.

Yorkshire puddings

Sift 1 cup (125 g) all-purpose flour and a pinch of salt into a bowl. Make a well in the middle and add 2 beaten eggs and a little milk.

Whisk the milk and egg, then whisk in 1/2 cup (125 ml) milk, drawing in the flour to make a smooth batter. Stir in another 1/2 cup (125 ml) milk. Cover and leave to stand for at least 30 minutes.

Put some vegetable shortening into each cup of a 12-hole muffin pan and heat in a 425°F (220°C) oven until very hot. Remove the pan from the oven. Whisk the batter and pour into the cups in the pan. Bake the Yorkshire puddings in the oven for 15 minutes or until well risen, golden, and crisp. Serve immediately.

BEEF POT ROAST WITH WINTER VEGETABLES

 Serves 6

2 tbsp sunflower or corn oil

2 1/2 lb (1.15 kg) beef bottom round or rump

4 onions, quartered

1 large rutabaga, cut into thick chunks

2 celery stalks, thickly sliced

2 large carrots, thickly sliced

2/3 cup (150 ml) dry white wine

2/3 cup (150 ml) hot water

a few parsley sprigs

2 fresh thyme sprigs

1 bay leaf

salt and black pepper

chopped parsley to garnish

1 Heat the sunflower oil in a large flameproof casserole. Add the beef and cook, turning, for about 10 minutes, until browned all over.

2 Lift the beef out of the casserole and put in the onions, rutabaga, celery, and carrots. Stir well to coat the vegetables in the oil, then cook, stirring occasionally, for about 5 minutes.

3 Insert a meat thermometer, if using, into the middle of the beef. Push the vegetables to the side of the casserole and place the meat in the middle, arranging the vegetables around it.

4 Add the wine, measured water, parsley, thyme, bay leaf, and salt and pepper to taste. Bring to a boil, then cover tightly, and cook in a 300°F (150°C) oven for 2 1/2–3 hours, until the meat is tender. The meat thermometer should register well-done: 170°F (75°C).

5 Transfer the meat and vegetables to a warmed platter, cover, and keep warm.

6 Spoon the fat from the surface of the cooking liquid, then boil over high heat until the liquid is reduced by half. Add salt and pepper to taste and strain into a warmed gravy boat. Carve the meat into thin slices, garnish with the chopped parsley and serve with the gravy.

TEXAS BARBECUE BEEF BRISKET

 Serves 6

2 1/2–3 lb (1.15–1.5 kg) beef brisket

2 tbsp sunflower or corn oil

cayenne pepper

MARINADE

3 cups (750 ml) spicy barbecue sauce

1 cup (250 ml) beer

juice of 1 lemon

2 tbsp Worcestershire sauce

3 onions, chopped

5 garlic cloves, crushed

3 tbsp brown sugar

2 tsp ground cumin

1/2 tsp ground ginger

1 Make the marinade: in a large bowl, combine the barbecue sauce, beer, lemon juice, Worcestershire sauce, onions, garlic, brown sugar, cumin, and ginger. Turn the brisket in the marinade, cover loosely, and leave to marinate in the refrigerator, turning occasionally, for 1–2 days.

2 Remove the beef from the marinade, reserving the marinade, and pat dry with paper towels.

3 Heat the vegetable oil in a flameproof casserole, add the brisket, and brown.

4 Insert a meat thermometer, if using, into the middle of the brisket. Pour over the marinade, cover, and cook in a 325°F (160°C) oven for 2 1/2–3 hours until tender, adding a little water if the sauce becomes too thick. The meat thermometer should register well-done: 170°F (75°C).

5 Remove the casserole from the oven and leave to stand for 15–20 minutes. Remove the meat and slice. Season the sauce with cayenne pepper to taste, then heat through. Arrange the meat on a serving platter, and pour the sauce over.

Cook's know-how

This dish can be cooked a day ahead. As it cools, the fat will rise to the surface and solidify. It can then be lifted off, producing a less fatty dish.

FRENCH-STYLE BRAISED BEEF

 Serves 4–6

2-lb (1-kg) piece of boneless chuck

2 tbsp olive oil

4 thick slices of lean bacon, cut into strips

1 onion, sliced

4 carrots, thickly sliced

1/2 lb (250 g) mushrooms, quartered

2 large tomatoes, peeled (page 39), seeded, and chopped

1 cup (125 g) pitted black olives

2 1/3 cups (600 ml) beef stock

salt and black pepper

chopped parsley to garnish

MARINADE

2 cups (500 ml) red wine

3 tbsp red wine vinegar

2 large garlic cloves

1 strip of orange zest

2 bay leaves

1 thyme sprig

1 parsley sprig

1 Make the marinade: in a large bowl combine the wine, vinegar, garlic, orange zest, and herbs. Add the beef, cover, and leave to marinate in the refrigerator overnight.

2 Remove the beef from the marinade and pat dry with paper towels. Strain the marinade and reserve. Heat the oil in a large flameproof casserole, add the beef and bacon, and brown all over. Lift out and drain on paper towels.

3 Add the onion, carrots, and mushrooms and cook, stirring, for 5 minutes or until lightly browned.

4 Add the beef, bacon, tomatoes, olives, and reserved marinade. Insert a meat thermometer, if using, into the middle of the beef. Pour in enough stock to cover the meat and add salt and pepper to taste.

5 Bring to a boil, cover the casserole tightly, and cook in a 350°F (180°C) oven for 1 1/2–2 hours or until the meat is very tender.

6 Slice the meat and arrange on a warmed platter with the vegetables. Skim the sauce and pour over the meat. Garnish with parsley before serving.

CORNED BEEF WITH MUSTARD SAUCE

 Serves 6–8

2 lb (1 kg) boned and rolled corned beef

1 lb (500 g) baby carrots

8 potatoes, halved

8 celery stalks, cut into chunks

3 2-in (5 cm) turnips, cut into chunks

chopped parsley to garnish

MUSTARD SAUCE

2 tbsp butter

1/4 cup (30 g) all-purpose flour

2/3 cup (150 ml) milk

4 tsp white vinegar

2 tsp dry mustard

2 tsp sugar

salt and black pepper

1 If very salty, put the beef into a large bowl. Cover with cold water and leave to soak overnight to remove any excess salt.

2 Rinse the beef under cold running water, place in a large saucepan, and cover with cold water. Cover the pan with its lid, bring to a boil, and simmer very gently, replenishing the water in the pan when necessary, for about 1 hour.

3 Add the carrots, potatoes, celery, and turnips and cook for 40 minutes or until the beef and vegetables are tender.

4 Transfer the meat to a warmed platter. Lift out the vegetables with a slotted spoon, reserving the liquid, and arrange around the meat. Cover and keep warm.

5 Make the sauce: melt the butter in a saucepan, add the flour, and cook, stirring, for 1 minute. Remove from the heat and gradually blend in the milk and 2/3 cup (150 ml) of the cooking liquid from the beef. Bring to a boil, stirring constantly, until the sauce thickens. Simmer for 2 minutes.

6 In a bowl, combine the vinegar, dry mustard, and sugar and stir into the sauce. Cook for 1 minute, then add salt and pepper to taste. (Be careful not to add too much salt because the liquid from the beef is salty.)

7 Slice the beef and arrange on warmed serving plates with the vegetables. Pour the mustard sauce over the beef, and sprinkle with parsley.

217

TRINIDAD PEPPERPOT BEEF

 Serves 4–6

2 lb (1 kg) boneless beef, such as brisket, trimmed

2–3 quarts (2–3 liters) beef stock

2 large onions, coarsely chopped

2–4 fresh red chilies, cored, seeded, and chopped

2 tbsp chopped parsley

1/4 cup (60 ml) vinegar, plus extra if necessary

2 tbsp dark brown sugar

1 tbsp Worcestershire sauce

1 tbsp mixed peppercorns, coarsely crushed, plus extra if necessary

1 tsp ground cinnamon

1 tsp dried thyme

large pinch of ground allspice

salt

1 Put the beef into a large pan, add enough stock to cover, and bring to a boil, skimming off any scum that rises to the surface. Lower the heat, cover, and simmer for 1 1/2 hours or until the meat feels just tender when pierced with a skewer.

2 Add the onions, chilies, and half of the parsley, vinegar, sugar, Worcestershire sauce, mixed peppercorns, cinnamon, thyme, allspice, and salt to taste. Cover and simmer for 2 hours or until the beef is very tender.

3 Transfer the beef to a carving board, cover, and keep warm.

4 Skim any fat from the cooking liquid, and boil for about 10 minutes until reduced to 1 1/4 cups (300 ml). Season, adding more vinegar and crushed peppercorns if needed. Slice the beef thickly, discarding any fat. Pour the sauce over the beef and sprinkle with the remaining parsley.

Mixed peppercorns

Also known as tropical peppercorns, mixed peppercorns are a mixture of black, white, green, and pink peppercorns.

BEEF WITH ROAST VEGETABLE SALAD

 Serves 4–6

2 lb (1 kg) beef tenderloin cut from the center, trimmed

2 tbsp store-bought tapenade

1 tbsp black peppercorns, coarsely crushed

2 tbsp olive oil

chopped parsley to garnish

ROAST VEGETABLE SALAD

1–2 tbsp olive oil

1 eggplant, cut into 1/4-in (5-mm) slices

3 zucchini, cut into 1/4-in (5-mm) slices

1 fennel bulb, cut lengthwise into 1/4-in (5-mm) pieces

1 red pepper, cored, seeded, and cut into 1/4-in (5-mm) strips

1 yellow pepper, cored, seeded, and cut into 1/4-in (5-mm) strips

salt and black pepper

2 tsp balsamic vinegar

1 Tie the beef to retain its shape if necessary. Spread the tapenade all over the beef, then press on the black peppercorns.

2 Pour the oil into a roasting pan and heat in a 450°F (230°C) oven.

3 Insert a meat thermometer, if using, into the middle of the beef, put the meat into the hot oil, and roast for 20 minutes.

4 Lower the heat to 425°F (220°C) and roast for 15 minutes longer for rare beef, 20 minutes for medium, or 25 minutes for well-done or until the meat thermometer registers 140°F, 160°F, or 170°F (60°C, 70°C, or 75°C). Leave to cool.

5 Make the roast vegetable salad: put the olive oil into a large bowl. Add the eggplant, zucchini, fennel, and red and yellow peppers and toss in the oil.

6 Transfer the vegetables into the roasting pan and add salt and pepper to taste. Cook in the oven at 400°F (200°C), turning the vegetables once, for 30 minutes or until tender. Leave the vegetables to cool, then toss with the vinegar.

7 When the beef is cold, slice very thinly and serve with the roast vegetable salad. Garnish with parsley.

Roll out three-quarters of the pastry to a 12- by 16-in (30- by 40-cm) rectangle. Spread half of the pâté mixture down the middle, leaving a 4-in (10-cm) border on each side.

Remove the string from the beef and place on the pâté mixture. Cover with remaining pâté mixture.

Brush the pastry border with beaten egg. Fold the short sides of the pastry over the beef.

Fold over the long ends and turn the parcel over. Brush with beaten egg. Roll out the remaining pastry and cut into strips 1/4 in (5 mm) wide. Arrange in a lattice pattern on top of the pastry, then glaze the strips with beaten egg.

BEEF WELLINGTON

Inside a puff pastry case is a succulent piece of prime beef and a rich stuffing of liver pâté and mushrooms. The pastry locks in all the juices and ensures that none of the wonderful flavors are lost. Serve with a mushroom and red wine gravy.

 Serves 8

3 lb (1.5 kg) beef tenderloin, trimmed and tied

salt and black pepper

2 tbsp sunflower or corn oil

3 tbsp butter

1 small onion, finely chopped

1/2 lb (250 g) mushrooms, diced

7 oz (200 g) canned smooth liver pâté

3/4 lb (375 g) store-bought puff pastry

1 egg, beaten

thin mushroom gravy to serve (page 239)

1 Season the beef with black pepper. Heat the oil in a large skillet, add the beef, and cook over high heat until browned all over.

2 Put the beef fillet in a roasting pan and cook in a 425°F (220°C) oven for 25 minutes for rare beef, 30 minutes for medium, or 40 minutes for well-done. Leave to cool completely.

3 Meanwhile, melt the butter in the skillet, add the chopped onion and mushrooms, and cook, stirring constantly, for 3 minutes or until softened. Increase the heat to high and cook until the excess moisture has evaporated. Transfer to a bowl and leave to cool completely.

4 Add the liver pâté to the mushroom and onion mixture and stir well to combine. Add salt and pepper to taste.

5 Wrap the beef in the pastry (see box, right).

6 Bake at 425°F (220°C) for 45 minutes or until the pastry is crisp and golden. Cover with foil after 30 minutes to prevent the pastry from becoming too brown. Leave to stand for about 10 minutes, then slice and serve with the gravy.

INDIVIDUAL BEEF WELLINGTONS

Cut the raw beef into 8 slices. Brown the slices in a skillet, then wrap each one in pastry with a little of the pâté mixture. Bake for 25–30 minutes.

STEAK AU POIVRE

Serves 4

4 5- to 6-oz (150- to 175-g) filet mignons, about 1 in (2.5 cm) thick, trimmed

salt and black pepper

2 tbsp black peppercorns

2 tbsp butter

1 tbsp sunflower or corn oil

2 tbsp brandy

2/3 cup (150 ml) heavy cream

chopped parsley to garnish

1 Season the steaks on both sides with salt. Crush the peppercorns and spread them on a plate. Coat the steaks with the peppercorns (see box, right).

2 Melt the butter with the oil in a skillet. When the butter is foaming, add the steaks and cook over high heat for 2 minutes on each side.

3 Lower the heat and continue cooking until the steaks are to your liking: rare steaks need 1–2 minutes on each side, medium steaks 3 minutes on each side, and well-done steaks 4–5 minutes on each side. Lift out of the skillet and keep warm.

4 Pour the brandy into the skillet, remove from the heat, and light the brandy. When the flames have died down, stir in the cream and add salt and pepper to taste. Gently reheat the sauce, pour it over the steaks, and garnish with parsley. Serve immediately.

Coating steaks

Press each steak firmly onto the peppercorns until both sides are well coated.

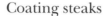

Cook's know-how

It is easiest to crush peppercorns using a mortar and pestle. Alternatively, put the peppercorns on a board and crush them with a rolling pin.

CHATEAUBRIAND WITH BEARNAISE SAUCE

Serves 2

3/4 lb (375 g) Chateaubriand steak

2 tbsp butter, melted

black pepper

béarnaise sauce (see box, right)

1 Cut the steak crosswise in half. Brush one side of each half with melted butter and season with pepper.

2 Put the steaks, buttered side up, under the broiler, 3 in (7 cm) from the heat, and cook for 2 minutes or until browned. Turn the steaks over, brush with melted butter, and season with pepper. Broil for about 2 minutes, until browned.

3 Move the broiler pan and cook, 6 in (15 cm) from the heat, turning once and brushing with the butter, for 4–5 minutes. Cover and leave to stand for 5 minutes. Slice the steaks and serve with the béarnaise sauce.

Chateaubriand

A thick piece of beef from the center of the tenderloin, ideal for serving 2 people.

Béarnaise sauce

Put 1/4 cup (60 ml) tarragon vinegar, 1 finely chopped shallot, and 1 tbsp chopped tarragon into a pan and boil until reduced by one-third. Leave to cool.

Pour 2 egg yolks into a bowl over a saucepan of simmering water, add the vinegar mixture, and whisk over low heat until thick and fluffy.

Melt 6 tbsp (90 g) butter and gradually add to the sauce, whisking constantly until thick. Add *salt and white pepper to taste.*

STEAKS WITH SMOKED OYSTER RELISH

 Serves 4

4 6-oz (175-g) boneless steaks

salt and black pepper

2 garlic cloves, crushed

1 tbsp olive oil

smoked oyster relish (see box, below) and lemon wedges to serve

1 Season the steaks with salt and pepper, rub with the garlic, and brush with the oil.

2 Heat a skillet over high heat, add the steaks, and cook for 3–4 minutes on each side for rare steaks, 4–5 minutes for medium steaks, or 7–8 minutes for well-done steaks. Transfer the steaks to warmed serving plates

3 Generously spoon the smoked oyster relish over the steaks and serve immediately, accompanied by lemon wedges.

OYSTER-STUFFED STEAKS

Melt 1 tbsp butter and cook 2 chopped shallots until softened. Remove from the heat and add 6 chopped fresh oysters, 2 cups (125 g) fresh bread crumbs, 1 tbsp chopped parsley, and salt and pepper. Cut a pocket in each steak and fill with the stuffing. Cook as directed.

Smoked oyster relish

Drain 3½ oz (100 g) canned smoked oysters. Finely chop a small onion and a handful of parsley sprigs.

Chop the drained smoked oysters with a large, sharp chef's knife.

Put the oysters, onion, and parsley into a small bowl and mix well. Chill until needed.

FLAVORED BUTTERS

These simple butters are ideal for livening up plain broiled meats such as steaks, chops, and noisettes.

CILANTRO BUTTER

Soften ¼ lb (125 g) butter and blend in 2 tbsp chopped fresh cilantro, 1 tbsp lemon juice, 1 tsp ground coriander, and salt and black pepper to taste. Chill. Garnish with a cilantro sprig and a sprinkling of ground coriander.

ANCHOVY BUTTER

Soften ¼ lb (125 g) butter and blend in 2 tbsp finely chopped anchovies, 1 tbsp lemon juice, 1 tsp ground coriander, and black pepper to taste. Chill. Garnish with anchovy fillets.

PARSLEY BUTTER

Soften ¼ lb (125 g) butter and blend in 2 tbsp chopped parsley, 1 tbsp lemon juice, and salt and black pepper to taste. Chill. Garnish with a lemon twist and a parsley sprig.

MUSTARD BUTTER

Soften ¼ lb (125 g) butter and blend in 2 tbsp Dijon mustard, 2 tbsp chopped fresh tarragon, and salt and black pepper to taste. Chill. Garnish with a tarragon sprig.

STEAK DIANE

 Serves 4

4 5- to 6-oz (150- to 175-g)
  boneless steaks, trimmed

2 tbsp butter

2 tbsp sunflower or corn oil

1 small onion, finely chopped

1¼ cups (300 ml) beef stock

2 tbsp Worcestershire sauce

1 tbsp lemon juice

1 tbsp chopped parsley

salt and black pepper

3 tbsp brandy

1 Place the steaks between 2 sheets of waxed paper and pound with a rolling pin until ¼ in (5 mm) thick.

2 Melt the butter with the sunflower oil in a large skillet. When the butter is foaming, add the pounded steaks and cook over high heat for about 3 minutes on each side, until browned. Lift the steaks out of the skillet and cover with foil to keep warm.

3 Add the onion and cook gently, stirring, for a few minutes, until softened. Stir in the stock, Worcestershire sauce, lemon juice, parsley, and salt and pepper to taste and cook for 2 minutes.

4 Return the steaks to the pan and remove from the heat. Flambé the steaks (see box, below). Let the flames die down and serve.

Flambéing steaks

Warm the brandy gently in a small saucepan. Light it with a taper and pour over the steaks.

TOURNEDOS ROQUEFORT

 Serves 4

1 cup (125 g) crumbled
  Roquefort cheese

½ cup (60 g) roughly chopped
  walnut pieces

2 tbsp butter, softened

salt and black pepper

4 ¼-lb (125-g) tournedos
  steaks, 1 in (2.5 cm) thick

chopped parsley to garnish

1 In a small bowl, combine the Roquefort, walnuts, butter, and pepper to taste.

2 Season the tournedos on both sides with salt and pepper and place them under the broiler, 3–4 in (7–10 cm) from the heat. Broil for 3–4 minutes on each side for rare steaks, 4–5 minutes for medium steaks, or 7–8 minutes for well-done steaks.

3 Two minutes before the steaks are ready, sprinkle with the Roquefort mixture, and return to the broiler until the cheese has melted. Serve hot, garnished with chopped parsley.

TOURNEDOS WITH MUSHROOMS

Substitute a mushroom topping for the cheese and walnut topping. Coarsely chop 1 garlic clove, 1 shallot, and 2 thick slices of bacon, put into a food processor, and process to a paste. Transfer to a skillet and cook for 3 minutes or until browned. Process ½ lb (250 g) cremini mushrooms in a food processor until finely chopped. Add to the mixture in the skillet and cook for 15 minutes. Stir in 2 tbsp chopped parsley, 1 tsp grated lemon zest, and salt and pepper to taste. Arrange the mushroom mixture on top of the steaks just before serving.

BEEF & BEAN BURRITOS

 Serves 4

³/₁ lb (375 g) boneless round or sirloin steak, trimmed and cut into thin strips

salt and black pepper

2 tbsp olive oil

1 garlic clove, crushed

¹/₂–1 fresh red chili, cored, seeded, and chopped

¹/₂ tsp cumin seeds

13 oz (400 g) canned tomatoes, drained, juice reserved

13 oz (400 g) canned pinto or black beans, drained

8 flour tortillas

¹/₄ cup (60 ml) sour cream or crème fraîche

chopped fresh cilantro to garnish

1 Season the steak strips with salt and pepper. Heat the olive oil in a large skillet, add the steak, crushed garlic, chopped chili, and cumin seeds and cook, stirring, for 5 minutes or until lightly browned.

2 Add the tomatoes to the pan and cook for about 3 minutes. Pour in the reserved tomato juice and boil for 8–10 minutes, until the liquid is reduced.

3 Add the beans and cook until heated through. Taste for seasoning, cover, and keep warm.

4 Warm the tortillas (page 226).

5 Divide the steak and tomato mixture among the tortillas and roll them up. Serve topped with sour cream and garnished with cilantro.

Burritos

These take their name from the Spanish word burro, *meaning donkey – like a donkey, a burrito is heavily laden. Buy the smaller 6- to 8-in (15- to 20-cm) tortillas for these burritos, not the 12-in (30-cm) size.*

PORK & BEAN BURRITOS

Substitute ³/₁ lb (375 g) pork fillet for the steak and proceed as directed.

BEEF STROGANOFF

 Serves 4

2 tbsp butter

1 tbsp sunflower or corn oil

1¹/₂ lb (750 g) beef tenderloin or boneless sirloin steak, trimmed and cut into strips (see box, right)

8 shallots, quartered

10 oz (300 g) mushrooms, halved

salt and black pepper

1¹/₄ cups (300 ml) sour cream

chopped parsley to garnish

1 Melt the butter with the oil in a large skillet. When the butter is foaming, add the steak strips, in batches if necessary, and cook over high heat for 5 minutes or until browned all over. Remove from the pan with a slotted spoon.

2 Add the shallots and mushrooms and cook for about 5 minutes, until soft and browned.

3 Return the steak strips to the pan and add salt and pepper to taste. Stir in the sour cream and heat gently. Garnish with parsley and serve immediately.

Cutting the beef

Slice the beef into thin strips, ¹/₄ in (5 mm) wide and 2 in (5 cm) long, using a sharp chef's knife.

Beef Stroganoff

This classic Russian dish has been known in Western Europe since the 18th century. It takes its name from the Stroganoffs, a family of wealthy merchants from Novgorod. A family member had a French cook, and it is thought that he gave his employer's name to the dish.

MEXICAN STEAK PLATTER

A traditional Mexican meal usually includes a number of separate dishes to be eaten together, with the classic accompaniments of refried beans and guacamole. Prepare this selection of dishes for a special family meal or, if you prefer, try just one or two of them — each dish tastes just as good on its own.

STEAKS WITH ROASTED PEPPER SAUCE

 Serves 4

4 6-oz (175-g) boneless sirloin steaks

MARINADE

1/4 cup (60 ml) sunflower or corn oil

1/4 tsp ground allspice

1/4 tsp black pepper

2 tbsp lime juice

ROASTED PEPPER SAUCE

1 tbsp sunflower or corn oil

1/2 onion, thinly sliced

1 garlic clove, crushed

1 green and 1 red pepper, roasted, peeled (page 354), and cut into strips

6 tbsp (90 ml) light sour cream

1/4 tsp dried mixed herbs

salt and black pepper

chopped parsley to garnish

1 Make the marinade: heat the oil in a small saucepan and add the allspice and pepper. Remove from the heat and leave to cool, then add the lime juice. Put the boneless steaks into a shallow nonmetallic dish and brush with the marinade. Cover and chill, turning occasionally, for 8 hours.

2 Make the roasted pepper sauce: heat the oil in a skillet, add the onion, and cook gently, stirring, for 5 minutes or until golden.

3 Add the garlic and pepper strips and cook for 2 minutes. Stir in the sour cream and herbs and season with salt. Simmer for 3–5 minutes, until the sauce is reduced and just coats the vegetables. Set aside.

4 Remove the steaks from the marinade, drain, but do not dry completely. Season with salt and pepper to taste. Heat another skillet, add the steaks, and cook for 3–6 minutes on each side. Top the steaks with the roasted pepper sauce and sprinkle with chopped parsley.

ENCHILADAS

 Serves 4

1/4 cup (60 ml) sunflower or corn oil

4 corn tortillas

1/2 cup (60 g) crumbled queso fresco or feta cheese

1 onion, finely chopped

chopped parsley to garnish

MEXICAN TOMATO SAUCE

4 medium ripe tomatoes, peeled (page 39), cored, and chopped

1 fresh green chili, cored, seeded, and chopped

1/2 small onion, chopped

1 garlic clove, chopped

1 tbsp sunflower or corn oil

salt

1 Make the sauce: put the tomatoes, chili, onion, and garlic into a food processor. Process briefly until combined but still retaining a little texture. Heat the oil in a skillet and add the tomato mixture. Cook, stirring, for 5 minutes or until the sauce thickens. Season with salt and keep warm.

2 Put the oil in another skillet and heat over medium-high heat. Add the tortillas, one at a time, and fry for about 3 seconds on each side, until golden. Drain on paper towels.

3 Fill each tortilla with a little tomato sauce and 1 tbsp cheese, roll up, and arrange on a plate. Top with the remaining sauce, and sprinkle with the rest of the cheese, onion, and parsley.

GUACAMOLE

Put the flesh of *1 large ripe avocado* into a bowl and roughly mash with a fork. Add *1/2 finely chopped onion, 1 tbsp chopped fresh cilantro,* and *the juice of 1 lime* and mix well. Chill for no more than 30 minutes before serving.

MEXICAN RICE

 Serves 4

1 tbsp sunflower or corn oil

1 onion, finely chopped

1 cup (200 g) long-grain rice

1 garlic clove, crushed

8 oz (200 g) canned chopped tomatoes

1 1/2 cups (375 ml) hot chicken stock

salt and black pepper

1 cup (125 g) frozen peas, thawed and drained

1 cup (30 g) fresh cilantro, chopped

1 Heat the oil in a large saucepan, add the onion and rice, and cook for 8–10 minutes, until lightly browned. Add the garlic and cook for 2 minutes.

2 Add the tomatoes and stock and season with salt and pepper. Bring to a boil, cover tightly, and simmer over very low heat for 15 minutes.

3 Remove from the heat and leave to stand, still covered, for 10 minutes, until all the liquid has been absorbed.

4 Stir in the peas and sprinkle with the cilantro.

REFRIED BEANS

Heat *1–2 tbsp sunflower or corn oil* in a skillet. Add *1/2 finely chopped onion,* and cook for 8 minutes, until lightly browned. Add *1 crushed garlic clove,* and cook for 2 minutes. Drain *13 oz (400 g) canned red kidney beans* and add to the pan. Cook over low heat until warmed through, mashing the beans with a potato masher or fork and adding *1–2 tbsp water* if necessary, to prevent sticking.

Clockwise from top: *Refried Beans, Enchiladas, Steaks with Roasted Pepper Sauce, Guacamole, Mexican Rice.*

BEEF TERIYAKI

 Serves 4

1 lb (500 g) boneless sirloin or round steak, trimmed and cut into thin strips

2 tbsp sunflower or corn oil

1 large onion, thinly sliced

1 red pepper, cored, seeded, and cut into strips

2 scallions, sliced, to garnish

MARINADE

1/2 cup (125 ml) dark soy sauce

6 tbsp (90 ml) Japanese rice wine or dry sherry

2 tbsp superfine sugar

1 Make the marinade: in a bowl, combine the soy sauce, rice wine, and sugar. Toss the steak strips in the marinade, cover, and leave in the refrigerator overnight.

2 Remove the steak strips from the marinade, reserving the marinade. Heat 1 tbsp of the oil in a wok, add the onion and red pepper, and stir-fry for about 2 minutes. Remove from the wok with a slotted spoon and set aside. Heat the remaining oil and stir-fry the steak strips for 5 minutes or until just cooked through.

3 Return the onion and red pepper to the wok with the marinade and cook for 2 minutes or until heated through. Garnish with the scallions before serving.

FAJITAS

This Mexican specialty features slices of steak marinated in spices and laced with tequila. Serve with tortillas, avocado, sour cream, and salsa fresca.

 Serves 4

1 lb (500 g) boneless sirloin steak

8 corn tortillas

chopped fresh cilantro to garnish

1 avocado, pitted, peeled (page 336), and diced

sour cream

MARINADE

juices of 1 orange and 1 lime

2 tbsp tequila or brandy

3 garlic cloves, crushed

2 tbsp chopped fresh cilantro

1 tbsp chili powder

1 tbsp paprika

1 tsp cumin

salt and black pepper

SALSA FRESCA

6 tomatoes, peeled (page 39), seeded, and diced

10 radishes, coarsely chopped

5 scallions, thinly sliced

1–2 green chilies, cored, seeded, and chopped

1/4 cup (30 g) chopped fresh cilantro

juice of 1/2 lime

1 Make the marinade: in a large bowl, combine the orange and lime juices, tequila, garlic, cilantro, chili powder, paprika, cumin, and salt and pepper to taste. Turn the steak in the marinade, cover, and leave to marinate in the refrigerator overnight.

2 Make the salsa fresca: in a bowl, combine the tomatoes, radishes, scallions, chilies, cilantro, lime juice, and salt to taste. Cover and leave in the refrigerator until ready to serve.

3 Remove the steak from the marinade and pat dry. Put the steak under the broiler, 3–4 in (7–10 cm) from the heat, and broil for 3 minutes on each side for rare steak, 4 minutes for medium steak, or 5–6 minutes for well-done steak. Cover with foil and leave to stand for 5 minutes.

4 Meanwhile, warm the tortillas (see box, right).

5 Slice the steak, arrange on serving plates, and sprinkle with cilantro. Serve with the tortillas, salsa fresca, diced avocado, and sour cream.

Warming tortillas

Sprinkle each tortilla with a little water and stack the tortillas in a pile.

Wrap the tortillas in a sheet of foil and warm through in a 275°F (140°C) oven for 10 minutes.

WINTER BEEF CASSEROLE

 Serves 4–6

2 tbsp sunflower or corn oil

2-lb (1-kg) boneless chuck, trimmed and cut into 1-in (2.5-cm) cubes

3 slices of bacon, cut into thin strips

1 large onion, chopped

1/3 cup (45 g) all-purpose flour

2 cups (500 g) strained tomatoes

1 3/4 cups (450 ml) beef stock

2/3 cup (150 ml) red wine

6 celery stalks, sliced

4 carrots, cut into thin strips

1 garlic clove, crushed

1 tsp chopped fresh marjoram

salt and black pepper

chopped parsley to garnish

1 Heat the oil in a large flameproof casserole, add the beef and bacon, and cook over moderate to high heat for 2–3 minutes, until browned all over. Using a slotted spoon, lift out and drain on paper towels.

2 Add the onion and cook, stirring occasionally, for a few minutes, until soft but not browned.

3 Add the flour and cook, stirring, for 1 minute. Add the strained tomatoes, stock, and red wine and bring to a boil, stirring until smooth and thickened. Return the meat to the casserole, add the celery, carrots, garlic, marjoram, and salt and pepper to taste, and bring back to a boil.

4 Cover the casserole and cook in a 325°F (160°C) oven for 2 hours or until the beef is tender. Taste for seasoning and garnish with the parsley before serving.

Passata

This is made from pureed, strained tomatoes and makes an ideal base for all kinds of casseroles, sauces, and soups. It is available from most supermarkets and Italian delicatessens.

BOEUF BOURGUIGNON

 **Serves 4–6**

2 tbsp sunflower or corn oil

2 lb (1 kg) boneless chuck, trimmed and cut into 2-in (5-cm) cubes

1/2 lb (250 g) bacon, cut into thin strips

12 shallots

1/4 cup (30 g) all purpose flour

1 1/4 cups (300 ml) red Burgundy

2/3 cup (150 ml) beef stock

a few parsley sprigs

1 thyme sprig

1 bay leaf

1 garlic clove, crushed

salt and black pepper

1/2 lb (250 g) mushrooms

1 Heat the oil in a large flameproof casserole, add the beef in batches, and cook over high heat until browned all over. Remove with a slotted spoon and drain on paper towels.

2 Add the bacon and shallots and cook gently, stirring occasionally, for 3 minutes or until the bacon is crisp and the shallots are softened. Lift out and drain on paper towels.

3 Add the flour and cook, stirring, for 1 minute. Gradually blend in the wine and stock and bring to a boil, stirring until thickened.

4 Return the beef and bacon to the casserole and add the parsley, thyme, bay leaf, garlic, and salt and pepper to taste. Cover and cook in a 325°F (160°C) oven for 1 1/2 hours.

5 Return the shallots to the casserole, add the mushrooms, and cook for 1 hour or until the beef is very tender.

6 Remove the parsley and thyme sprigs and the bay leaf and discard. Taste the sauce for seasoning before serving.

Boeuf Bourguignon

Bourguignon describes dishes that come from the Burgundy region of central France, an area renowned for its fine red wines.

CARBONNADE OF BEEF

 Serves 4–6

2 tbsp sunflower or corn oil

2 lb (1 kg) boneless chuck, trimmed and cut into 2-in (5-cm) cubes

2 large onions, sliced

1 garlic clove, crushed

2 tsp packed light brown sugar

1 tbsp all-purpose flour

1³/4 cups (450 ml) dark beer

²/3 cup (150 ml) beef stock

1 tbsp red wine vinegar

a few parsley sprigs

1 thyme sprig

1 bay leaf

salt and black pepper

thyme sprigs to garnish

MUSTARD CROUTES

¹/2 baguette, cut into ¹/2-in (1.25-cm) slices

Dijon mustard for spreading

1 Heat the oil in a large flameproof casserole, add the beef and cook over high heat for a few minutes, until browned. Lift out with a slotted spoon. Lower the heat and add the onions, garlic, and sugar. Cook, stirring, for 4 minutes or until browned.

2 Add the flour and cook, stirring, for 1 minute. Add the dark beer and stock and bring to a boil, stirring until thickened.

3 Return the meat to the casserole and add the red wine vinegar, parsley sprigs, thyme sprig, bay leaf, and salt and pepper to taste. Bring back to a boil, cover the casserole with the lid, and cook in a 300°F (150°C) oven for 2¹/2 hours or until the meat is very tender. Remove the herbs and discard. Taste for seasoning.

4 Increase the oven temperature to 375°F (190°C). Make the mustard croutes (see box, below).

5 Return the casserole to the oven, uncovered, for 10 minutes or until the croutes are just crisp. Garnish with thyme sprigs before serving.

Making croutes

Toast the slices of baguette on both sides and spread one side with mustard. Put the croutes, mustard side up, on top of the casserole and baste with the sauce.

HUNGARIAN GOULASH

 Serves 4–6

2 tbsp sunflower or corn oil

2 lb (1 kg) boneless chuck, trimmed and cut into 2-in (5-cm) cubes

2 large onions, sliced

1 garlic clove, crushed

1 tbsp all-purpose flour

1 tbsp paprika

2 ¹/3 cups (600 ml) beef stock

13 oz (400 g) canned tomatoes

2 tbsp tomato paste

salt and black pepper

2 large red peppers, cored, seeded, and cut into 1-in (2.5-cm) pieces

4 potatoes, peeled and quartered

²/3 cup (150 ml) sour cream

paprika to garnish

1 Heat the oil in a large flameproof casserole, add the beef and cook over high heat until browned.

2 Lift out the beef with a slotted spoon. Lower the heat slightly, add the onions and garlic, and cook gently, stirring occasionally, for a few minutes, until soft but not browned.

3 Add the flour and paprika and cook, stirring, for 1 minute. Pour in the stock and bring to a boil, stirring until thickened.

4 Return the meat to the casserole and add the tomatoes, tomato paste, and salt and pepper to taste. Bring back to a boil, cover, and cook in a 325°F (160°C) oven for 1 hour.

5 Add the red peppers and potatoes and return the casserole to the oven for 1 hour or until the potatoes and meat are tender and cooked through.

6 Taste for seasoning and stir in the sour cream. Sprinkle with a little paprika before serving.

CHIANTI BEEF CASSEROLE

 Serves 4–6

2 lb (1 kg) boneless chuck, trimmed and cut into 2-in (5-cm) cubes

3 tbsp olive oil

$^1/_4$ cup (30 g) all-purpose flour

$1^1/_4$ cups (300 ml) beef stock

1 cup (60 g) sun-dried tomatoes, roughly chopped

13 oz (400 g) canned artichoke hearts, drained and halved

$6^1/_2$ oz (185 g) canned pitted black olives, drained

thyme sprigs to garnish

MARINADE

1 bottle of Chianti

3 tbsp olive oil

2 tbsp tomato paste

1 large onion, chopped

2 garlic cloves, crushed

a few thyme sprigs

salt and black pepper

1 Make the marinade: in a large bowl, combine the Chianti, oil, tomato paste, onion, garlic, thyme, and salt and pepper to taste. Toss the beef in the marinade, cover, and leave to marinate in the refrigerator overnight.

2 Remove the beef from the marinade, reserving the marinade. Heat the oil in a large flameproof casserole, add the beef in batches, and cook over high heat until browned. Remove the beef.

3 Add the flour and cook, stirring, for 1 minute. Pour in the marinade and stock and bring to a boil, stirring until thickened. Return the beef to the casserole and add the sun-dried tomatoes. Bring back to a boil, cover with the lid, and cook in a 325°F (160°C) oven for 2 hours.

4 Add the artichokes and olives and return to the oven for 15 minutes. Taste for seasoning and garnish with thyme before serving.

Chianti

This is a fruity Italian red wine, well known for the raffia covered bottles in which it is often sold.

BEEF WITH HORSERADISH

 Serves 4–6

2 tbsp sunflower or corn oil

2 lb (1 kg) boneless chuck, trimmed and cut into strips

12 shallots or pearl onions

$^1/_4$ cup (30 g) all-purpose flour

2 tsp mild curry powder

2 tsp packed light brown sugar

1 tsp ground ginger

$2^1/_3$ cups (600 ml) beef stock

2 tbsp Worcestershire sauce

salt and black pepper

3 tbsp chopped parsley

2 tbsp horseradish cream

extra chopped parsley to garnish

1 Heat the sunflower oil in a large flameproof casserole and cook the beef strips over high heat until browned all over. Lift out with a slotted spoon and drain on paper towels.

2 Lower the heat, add the shallots, and cook gently, stirring occasionally, for a few minutes, until softened. Lift out with a slotted spoon and drain on paper towels.

3 Add the flour, curry powder, sugar, and ginger to the casserole and cook, stirring, for 1 minute. Pour in the stock and bring to a boil, stirring until smooth and thickened. Add the Worcestershire sauce and salt and pepper to taste and return to a boil.

4 Return the beef and shallots to the casserole and stir in the chopped parsley. Bring back to a boil, cover, and cook in a 325°F (160°C) oven for 2–$2^1/_2$ hours, until the meat is tender and cooked through.

5 To serve, stir in the horseradish cream, taste for seasoning, and garnish with parsley.

Cook's know-how

Horseradish cream is a simple blend of grated horseradish, cream, vinegar, and seasoning. It is widely available in jars at large supermarkets and delicatessens.

THAI RED BEEF CURRY

 Serves 4–6

3 tbsp sunflower or corn oil

2 lb (1 kg) boneless chuck, trimmed and cut into 1-in (2.5-cm) cubes

8 cardamom pods, split

1-in (2.5-cm) piece of cinnamon stick

2 bay leaves

6 cloves

8 black peppercorns

1 large onion, chopped

2-in (5-cm) piece of fresh ginger, peeled and grated

4 garlic cloves, crushed

4 tsp paprika

2 tsp cumin seeds, coarsely ground

1 tsp coriander seeds, coarsely ground

1 tsp salt

1/2 tsp cayenne pepper

2 1/3 cups (600 ml) water

6 tbsp (90 g) plain yogurt

13 oz (400 g) canned chopped tomatoes

1 large red pepper, cored, seeded, and cut into chunks

1 Heat the oil in a large flameproof casserole, add the beef in batches, and cook over high heat until browned all over. Lift out with a slotted spoon and drain on paper towels.

2 Add the cardamom pods, cinnamon stick, bay leaves, cloves, and peppercorns and cook over high heat, stirring constantly, for 1 minute. Remove from the pan and tie in a cheesecloth bag.

3 Add the onion to the pan and cook over high heat, stirring, for about 3 minutes, until beginning to brown. Add the ginger, garlic, paprika, cumin and coriander seeds, salt, cayenne pepper, and 1/4 cup (60 ml) of the water. Cook, stirring, for about 1 minute.

4 Return the beef and spices to the casserole, then gradually add the yogurt, stirring. Stir in the remaining water. Add the tomatoes and red pepper, and bring to a boil. Cover and cook in a 325°F (160°C) oven for 2 hours or until tender. Remove the bag of spices before serving.

Cook's know-how

Many curries benefit from being made a day in advance and left overnight. This brings out the flavors, allowing them to permeate the meat. Ensure the dish is well heated before serving.

COUNTRY BEEF CASSEROLE

 Serves 6–8

3 tbsp sunflower or corn oil

2 lb (1 kg) boneless chuck, trimmed and cut into 2-in (5-cm) cubes

1 lb (500 g) carrots, thickly sliced

3 2-in (5-cm) turnips, cut into large chunks

3 small to medium parsnips, thickly sliced

2 onions, sliced

1 large leek, sliced

1 tbsp all-purpose flour

2 1/3 cups (600 ml) beef stock

13 oz (400 g) canned chopped tomatoes

2 tbsp chopped fresh herbs, such as parsley and thyme

1 large bay leaf

salt and black pepper

herb dumplings (see box, right)

1 Heat the oil in a large flameproof casserole, add the beef in batches, and cook over high heat until browned. Lift out the beef with a slotted spoon.

2 Add the carrots, turnips, parsnips, onions, and leek and cook over high heat, stirring occasionally, for 5 minutes or until the vegetables are softened.

3 Add the flour and cook, stirring, for 1 minute. Add the stock, tomatoes, half of the herbs, and salt and pepper to taste and bring to a boil. Return the meat to the casserole and bring to a boil. Cover with the lid and cook in a 325°F (160°C) oven for 2 hours.

4 Place the dumplings on the meat. Increase the oven temperature to 375°F (190°C) and cook for 20–25 minutes, until the dumplings are firm. Sprinkle the casserole with the remaining herbs before serving.

Herb dumplings

Sift *1 cup (125 g) self-rising flour* into a bowl and add *1/3 cup (60 g) shredded vegetable shortening, 1 tbsp chopped fresh thyme or parsley,* and *pepper.* Add *enough water* to make a soft dough. Shape into 12–16 balls.

CHILI CON CARNE

 Serves 4

1¹/4 cups (250 g) dried red kidney beans

2 tbsp sunflower or corn oil

1¹/2 lb (750 g) boneless chuck, trimmed and cut into 1¹/2-in (3.5-cm) cubes

2 onions, chopped

2 fresh red chilies, cored, seeded, and finely chopped

1 garlic clove, crushed

1 tbsp all-purpose flour

3²/3 cups (900 ml) beef stock

2 tbsp tomato paste

1 square of baker's semisweet chocolate, grated (optional)

salt and black pepper

1 large red pepper, cored, seeded, and cut into chunks

chopped fresh cilantro to garnish

1 Put the red kidney beans into a large bowl, cover generously with cold water, and leave to soak overnight.

2 Drain the beans, rinse under cold running water, and drain again. Put the beans into a large saucepan. Cover with cold water, bring to a boil, and boil rapidly for 10 minutes. Lower the heat and simmer, partially covered, for 50 minutes or until the beans are just tender. Drain.

3 Heat the oil in a large flameproof casserole. Add the beef and cook in batches over high heat for 5–7 minutes, until browned. Lift out with a slotted spoon and set aside.

4 Lower the heat, add the onions, chilies, and garlic, and cook, stirring occasionally, for a few minutes, until softened.

5 Add the flour and cook, stirring, for 1 minute. Add the stock, tomato paste, chocolate, and salt and pepper to taste. Return the beef to the casserole, add the beans, and bring to a boil. Cover and cook in a 300°F (150°C) oven for 1¹/2 hours.

6 Add the red pepper and cook for 30 minutes. Taste for seasoning, and garnish with cilantro.

QUICK CHILI CON CARNE

Substitute 13 oz (400 g) canned red kidney beans for the dried beans and ground beef for the boneless chuck. Simmer gently on top of the stove for 45 minutes.

BEEF ROLLS WITH VEGETABLE JULIENNE

 Serves 4

8 thin slices of beef round, total weight about 1¹/2 lb (750 g)

2 tbsp sunflower or corn oil

¹/2 4-in (10-cm) celeriac, peeled and cut into matchsticks

4 carrots, cut into matchsticks

2 small leeks, cut into matchsticks

salt and black pepper

¹/4 cup (30 g) all-purpose flour

1 onion, sliced

1 garlic clove, sliced

1³/4 cups (450 ml) beef stock

1 Put each slice of beef between 2 sheets of waxed paper and pound to a ¹/8-in (3-mm) thickness with a rolling pin.

2 Heat 1 tbsp of the oil in a large skillet, add the celeriac, carrots, and leeks, and stir-fry over high heat for 1 minute. Add salt and pepper to taste, then lift out with a slotted spoon and drain. Leave to cool.

3 Divide the vegetables among the beef slices. Roll up and secure with wooden toothpicks.

4 Lightly coat the beef rolls in half of the flour, shaking off any excess. Heat the remaining oil in a flameproof casserole, add the beef rolls, and cook over high heat for 5–7 minutes, until browned. Lift out with a slotted spoon.

5 Add the onion and garlic and cook gently until softened. Add the remaining flour and cook, stirring constantly, for 1 minute. Gradually blend in the stock, add salt and pepper to taste, and bring to a boil, stirring until thick.

6 Return the beef rolls to the casserole, bring back to a boil, cover, and cook in a 350°F (180°C) oven for 1¹/2 hours. Lift out the beef rolls and remove the toothpicks. Slice and arrange on serving plates. Work the sauce through a strainer, and serve with the beef rolls.

Beef rolls

This refers to a dish of beef slices wrapped around a stuffing.

CORNED BEEF HASH

 Serves 2–3

4 tbsp butter

1 large onion, chopped

3 large potatoes, cut into small chunks

1 1/4 cups (300 ml) beef stock

salt and black pepper

12 oz (325 g) canned corned beef, cut into chunks

chopped parsley to garnish

1 Melt the butter in a large skillet, add the onion, and cook gently, stirring occasionally, for a few minutes, until softened.

2 Add the potatoes and stir to coat in the butter. Pour in the stock and add salt and pepper to taste. Simmer for 10–15 minutes until the potatoes are tender and the stock is absorbed.

3 Gently stir in the corned beef and heat to warm through. Put the pan under the broiler, 3 in (7.5 cm) from the heat, to brown the top. Garnish with chopped parsley before serving.

Cook's know-how

Corned beef hash can be made ahead and then refried to warm through. You can add other vegetables or a splash of Worcestershire sauce or Tabasco sauce or top each serving with a fried egg if you like.

TRADITIONAL STEAK & KIDNEY PIE

This pie is a family favorite, with its tender steak and kidney filling and short crust pastry topping. For convenience, the meat can be cooked a day in advance; then all you have to do on the day of serving is make the pastry and pop the pie in the oven.

 Serves 4–6

2 tbsp sunflower or corn oil

1 large onion, chopped

1 1/2 lb (750 g) skirt steak, cut into 1-in (2.5-cm) cubes

1/2 lb (250 g) beef kidney, trimmed (page 214) and cut into 1-in (2.5-cm) cubes

1/4 cup (30 g) all-purpose flour

1 1/4 cups (300 ml) beef stock

1/2 tsp Worcestershire sauce

salt and black pepper

1/2 lb (250 g) mushrooms

beaten egg for glazing

SHORT CRUST PASTRY

2 cups (250 g) all-purpose flour

1/4 lb (125 g) butter

about 3 tbsp cold water

1 Heat the oil in a large pan, add the onion, and cook, stirring occasionally, for a few minutes, until soft but not browned.

2 Add the beef and kidney and cook until browned. Add the flour and cook, stirring, for 1 minute. Add the stock, Worcestershire sauce, and salt and pepper to taste and bring to a boil, stirring. Partially cover and simmer gently for 1 1/2 hours.

3 Add the mushrooms and cook for 30 minutes or until the meat is tender. Taste for seasoning, then leave to cool completely.

4 Make the pastry: sift the flour into a bowl. Add the butter and rub in lightly with your fingertips until the mixture looks like fine bread crumbs. Add the water and mix with a flat-bladed knife until the dough comes together to form a ball.

5 Roll out the pastry on a floured work surface until 2.5 cm (1 in) larger than the pie dish. Invert the dish over the pastry and cut around the dish. Brush the rim of the dish with water and press on a strip of pastry cut from the trimmings.

6 Put a pie funnel into the middle of the dish, then spoon in the meat mixture.

7 Lightly brush the pastry strip with water and top with the pastry lid. Seal the edges and crimp them all around with a fork. Make a hole in the pastry lid above the pie funnel to let the steam escape. Decorate the pie lid with the pastry trimmings, attaching them with beaten egg.

8 Brush the pastry all over with beaten egg and bake in a 400°F (200°C) oven for 25–30 minutes, until the pastry is crisp and golden. Serve immediately.

STEAK & KIDNEY PUDDING

Mix 2 1/2 cups (300 g) self-rising flour, 1 cup (150 g) shredded suet, salt and pepper, and 1 scant cup (200 ml) water. Use 3/4 pastry to line a 2 quart (1.7 liter) baking mold. Add the uncooked filling, top with pastry, and steam for 5 hours.

 BRAISED MEATBALLS

Serves 4

1/2 lb (250 g) ground beef

1/4 lb (125 g) ground pork

salt and black pepper

all-purpose flour for dusting

2 tbsp sunflower or corn oil

2 large onions, sliced

1 garlic clove, crushed

1 1/4 cups (300 ml) hard cider or beer

3 tbsp tomato paste

4 celery stalks, thickly sliced

1 large red pepper, cored, seeded, and cut into strips

1/4 lb (125 g) mushrooms, sliced

2 tsp sugar

1 Mix together the beef and pork and add salt and pepper to taste. On a floured work surface, shape into 16 even-sized balls.

2 Heat the oil in a flameproof casserole, add the meatballs, and cook over high heat until browned. Remove and drain on paper towels. Lower the heat, add the onions and garlic, and cook gently, stirring occasionally, until softened.

3 Return the meatballs to the casserole. Add the cider, tomato paste, celery, red pepper, mushrooms, sugar, and salt and pepper to taste and bring to a boil. Cover and simmer for 20 minutes or until the meatballs are cooked through. Serve immediately.

BEEF FLORENTINE

Store-bought phyllo pastry provides a quick and easy way to cover a pie, and it gives a crisp, golden topping. In this dish, it is cooked with a delicious combination of ground beef in tomato sauce and fresh spinach mixed with three types of cheese.

 Serves 8

11 sheets of phyllo pastry

4 tbsp butter, melted

BEEF LAYER

2 tbsp butter

2 lb (1 kg) lean ground beef

1 tbsp all-purpose flour

13 oz (400 g) canned chopped tomatoes

2 tbsp tomato paste

2 garlic cloves, crushed

1 tsp sugar

salt and black pepper

SPINACH & CHEESE LAYER

1 1/4 lb (625 g) spinach, tough stalks removed, roughly chopped

3/4 cup (90 g) grated aged Cheddar cheese

3/4 cup (90 g) grated Gruyère or Swiss cheese

1/4 lb (125 g) cream cheese

2 eggs, lightly beaten

1 Prepare the beef layer: melt the butter in a large saucepan, add the ground beef, and cook, stirring constantly, for 10–15 minutes or until the meat is browned all over.

2 Add the flour and cook, stirring, for 1 minute. Add the tomatoes, tomato paste, garlic, sugar, and salt and pepper to taste and bring to a boil. Cover and simmer, stirring occasionally, for 35 minutes. Taste for seasoning.

3 Meanwhile, prepare the spinach and cheese layer: wash the spinach and put it into a large saucepan with only the water that clings to the leaves. Cook over low heat until the spinach has just wilted. Drain thoroughly, squeezing to remove excess water. Mix the spinach with the Cheddar, Gruyère, cream cheese, eggs, and salt and pepper to taste.

4 Spoon the beef mixture into a shallow ovenproof dish, then spoon the spinach mixture over the top.

5 Prepare the phyllo topping (see box, right).

6 Bake the pie in a 400°F (200°C) oven for 20–25 minutes until the phyllo pastry is crisp and golden. Serve immediately.

Preparing the phyllo topping

Brush 3 of the phyllo pastry sheets with a little of the melted butter and layer them on top of the spinach mixture, trimming to fit the dish if necessary.

Arrange the remaining 8 phyllo pastry sheets over the dish, lightly brushing with a little butter and scrunching each one up, in order to completely cover the lower layer of phyllo pastry.

HAMBURGERS

Hamburgers, especially homemade ones, are hard to resist, but there's no need to stick to the basic ground beef on a burger bun every time. All kinds of meat can be used, and adding different flavorings, serving burgers on a variety of breads and rolls, and topping them with tasty sauces make the possibilities limitless.

ROQUEFORT BEEF BURGERS

 Serves 4

1 lb (500 g) lean ground beef

5 shallots, finely chopped

salt and black pepper

6 oz (175 g) Roquefort or other blue cheese, cut into 4 slices

country bread and green salad to serve

1 Put the ground beef and shallots into a bowl, season, and mix well.

2 Divide the mixture into 8 balls, then flatten each ball to form a thin patty. Place a slice of cheese on top of half of the patties, then top with the remaining patties. Press the edges together to enclose the filling.

3 Cook the burgers over medium heat for 3–4 minutes on each side, until the burgers are brown and feel firm when pressed.

4 Serve the burgers on toasted sliced country bread, accompanied by a tossed green salad.

PROVENÇAL PORK BURGERS

 Serves 4

1 lb (500 g) ground pork

juice of 1/2 lemon

2–3 tbsp olive oil

1/4 tsp herbes de Provence

1/2 onion, finely chopped

3 oz (90 g) garlic-and-herb cream cheese

1/2 tsp each fennel seeds and dried oregano

salt and black pepper

baguette, sliced tomatoes, and pitted black olives to serve

1 Put the ground pork into a bowl with the lemon juice, oil, herbes de Provence, onion, cream cheese, fennel seeds, oregano, and salt and pepper to taste and mix well. Divide the mixture into 4 balls and flatten to form patties.

2 Cook the burgers over medium heat for 3–4 minutes on each side, until browned and firm when pressed. Serve between slices of baguette with tomatoes and olives.

TURKISH LAMB BURGERS

 Serves 4

1 lb (500 g) ground lamb

4 garlic cloves, crushed

1 cup (60 g) fresh bread crumbs

1 tbsp each chopped fresh cilantro and plain yogurt

1 tsp each ground cumin, paprika, curry powder, and tomato paste

1/4 tsp each ground cinnamon, turmeric, and salt

pita bread, plain yogurt, mint, and cucumber slices to serve

1 Put the ground lamb into a bowl with the remaining ingredients and mix well. Shape into 4 patties.

2 Put under the broiler, 4 in (10 cm) from the heat, and cook for 3–4 minutes on each side, until browned and firm. Serve in pita bread with yogurt, mint, and cucumber slices.

Clockwise from top: *Turkish Lamb Burgers, Roquefort Beef Burgers, Provençal Pork Burgers.*

TOPPINGS FOR HAMBURGERS

EGGPLANT & FENNEL

Slice *1/2 eggplant* and *1 fennel bulb* and brush with *olive oil.* Cook under the broiler, 4 in (10 cm) from the heat, for 3–5 minutes on each side, until lightly browned and tender. Cut into strips and put into a bowl. Mix together *2 tbsp olive oil, the juice of 1/2 lemon, 1/4 tsp herbes de Provence,* and *salt and pepper to taste.* Pour the topping over the eggplant and fennel strips and stir to coat. Serve hot or cold.

CHILI AIOLI

In a small bowl, combine *2 egg yolks, 1 tbsp lemon juice, 1 tsp Dijon mustard,* and *salt and pepper to taste* and whisk until thick. Gradually add *1 cup (250 ml) olive oil,* whisking constantly until the mixture is very thick. Stir in *1 crushed garlic clove, 1/2 tsp chili powder,* and *1/4 tsp ground cumin.* Taste for seasoning. Cover and leave to chill in the refrigerator until ready to serve.

BARBECUE SAUCE

Heat *1 tbsp sunflower or corn oil* in a saucepan and cook *1 finely chopped onion* and *1 crushed garlic clove* until soft but not browned. Add *13 oz (400 g) canned chopped tomatoes, 2 tbsp water, 2 tbsp lemon juice, 1 tbsp brown sugar, 1 tbsp Worcestershire sauce, 2 tsp Dijon mustard, 1/2 tsp paprika, 1/2 tsp chili powder,* and *salt and pepper to taste.* Bring to a boil and simmer for 20 minutes. Serve warm.

MEAT LOAF

 Serves 4–6

1¹/₂ lb (750 g) ground beef

13 oz (400 g) canned chopped
    tomatoes

1¹/₄ cups (90 g) herbed stuffing
    mix

1 onion, chopped

1 carrot, coarsely shredded

3 garlic cloves, crushed

2 tbsp chopped parsley

1 egg, beaten

1 tbsp Worcestershire sauce

salt and black pepper

4–5 slices of bacon

★ 8¹/₂- x 4¹/₂- x 2¹/₂-in (21.5-
    x 11.5- x 6-cm) loaf pan

1 Combine the ground
beef, tomatoes, stuffing
mix, onion, carrot, garlic,
parsley, beaten egg,
Worcestershire sauce, and
salt and pepper to taste.

2 Arrange bacon slices
crosswise in the loaf pan,
letting them hang over the
sides. Put the beef mixture
into the pan and fold over
the bacon. Turn the meat
loaf out into a roasting pan
and bake in a 375°F (190°C)
oven, basting once or twice,
for 1 hour.

3 Increase the heat to
450°F (230°C) and bake
for 15 minutes or until the
meat loaf is firm. Spoon off
any fat, slice the meat loaf,
and serve hot.

MEAT PIES WITH CHEESY POTATO TOPPING

*A hearty mixture of ground beef and vegetables lies beneath a lightly browned
topping of cheesy mashed potato. Cook it in 4 small dishes if you have them
so everyone can have an individual pie.*

 **Serves 4**

2 tbsp sunflower or corn oil

1 large onion, finely chopped

1 celery stalk, finely chopped

1 large carrot, finely chopped

1¹/₂ lb (750 g) ground beef

2 tsp all-purpose flour

1¹/₄ cups (300 ml) beef stock

1 tbsp tomato paste

2 tbsp Worcestershire sauce

salt and black pepper

TOPPING

3 large potatoes, cut into chunks

2 tbsp butter

2–3 tbsp hot milk

1 cup (125 g) grated aged
    Cheddar cheese

1 Heat the oil in a large
saucepan, add the onion,
celery, and carrot, and cook
for 3 minutes. Add the
ground beef and cook,
stirring occasionally, for
5 minutes or until browned.

2 Add the flour and cook,
stirring, for 1 minute.
Add the stock, tomato paste,
Worcestershire sauce, and
salt and pepper to taste and
bring to a boil. Cover and
simmer, stirring occasionally,
for 45 minutes.

3 Meanwhile, prepare the
potato topping: cook the
potatoes in boiling salted
water for 20 minutes or until
tender. Drain. Add the
butter and milk to the
potatoes and mash until soft.
Add salt and pepper to taste
and stir in the cheese.

4 Spoon the ground beef
mixture into 4 individual
ovenproof dishes, or 1 large
dish, and cover with the
mashed potato mixture
(see box, right). Cook the
individual pies in a 400°F
(200°C) oven for 20–25
minutes until the potato
topping is golden brown
and the meat mixture is
bubbling. Serve the pies hot.

Covering the pies

Spoon the mashed potato
onto the beef mixture
and spread over the top
to cover completely

Score the surface of the
mashed potato, using a
fork, to make a decorative
design.

EXOTIC BEEF

 Serves 6–8

1 slice of white bread, crust
removed

1¼ cups (300 ml) milk

2 tbsp butter

1 large onion, chopped

2 garlic cloves, crushed

2 lb (1 kg) ground beef

1 tbsp medium-hot curry powder

½ cup (90 g) ready-to-eat dried
apricots, coarsely chopped

¾ cup (90 g) blanched
almonds, coarsely chopped

2 tbsp fruit chutney

1 tbsp lemon juice

salt and black pepper

2 eggs

¼ cup (30 g) slivered almonds

1 Put the bread into a
shallow dish. Sprinkle on
2 tbsp of the milk and leave
to soak for 5 minutes.

2 Meanwhile, melt the
butter in a large skillet,
add the onion and garlic,
and cook gently, stirring
occasionally, for a few
minutes, until soft.

3 Increase the heat, add
the ground beef, and
cook, stirring, for 5 minutes
or until browned. Spoon any
excess fat from the pan.

4 Add the curry powder
and cook, stirring, for
2 minutes. Add the chopped
apricots and almonds, the
chutney, lemon juice, and
salt and pepper to taste.

5 Mash the bread with the
milk in the dish, then
stir into the ground beef
mixture. Turn the mixture
into an ovenproof dish and
bake in a 350°F (180°C)
oven for 35 minutes.

6 Break the eggs into a
bowl and whisk in the
remaining milk and salt and
pepper to taste. Pour the egg
mixture over the ground
beef mixture, sprinkle with
the almonds, and bake for
25–30 minutes, until the
topping is set.

BEEF TACOS

 Serves 4

1 tbsp sunflower or corn oil

¾ lb (375 g) ground beef

1 onion, chopped

3 garlic cloves, crushed

1 tsp mild chili powder

1 tsp paprika

½ tsp ground cumin

3 ripe tomatoes, peeled (page
39), seeded, and diced

salt and black pepper

1 fresh green chili, cored, seeded,
and thinly sliced

2 tbsp chopped fresh cilantro

8 taco shells

8 lettuce leaves, finely shredded

¼ cup (60 ml) sour cream

chopped cilantro to garnish

1 Heat the oil in a large
skillet, add the ground
beef, onion, and garlic, and
cook, stirring, for 5 minutes
or until the beef is browned
and the onion and garlic are
softened.

2 Add the chili powder,
paprika, and cumin and
cook, stirring, for 2 minutes.
Stir in the tomatoes, cover,
and cook over medium heat
for 5 minutes. Add salt and
pepper to taste, remove
from the heat, and stir in the
chili and cilantro.

3 Place the taco shells on
a baking sheet and heat
through in a 350°F (180°C)
oven for 2–3 minutes or
according to the package
instructions.

4 Fill the taco shells
(see box, below) and
serve immediately.

Filling taco shells

Holding the shell in
one hand, put a layer of
shredded lettuce into the
bottom. Add a generous
spoonful of the ground
meat mixture and top
with a dollop of sour
cream and a sprinkling
of chopped cilantro.

PRESSED TONGUE

 Serves 10

4–5 lb (2–2.5 kg) salted
 ox tongue, trimmed

1 onion, quartered

1 bay leaf

1 tbsp unflavored gelatin

3 tbsp cold water

* 8-in (20-cm) round cake pan

1 Put the ox tongue, onion, and bay leaf into a large saucepan, cover with cold water, and bring to a boil. Simmer very gently for 3–4 hours, until tender. Test the water after 2 hours; if it is very salty, replace it with fresh water.

2 Lift the tongue out of the saucepan, reserving the cooking liquid, and leave to cool slightly. Remove and discard the skin, then cut the tongue in half lengthwise.

3 Sprinkle the gelatin over the measured water in a small bowl. Leave to stand for 3 minutes or until the gelatin has softened. Put the bowl into a saucepan of simmering water and leave for 3 minutes or until the gelatin has dissolved.

4 Add ²/₃ cup (150 ml) of the cooking liquid to the gelatin and mix well.

5 Arrange one half of the tongue, cut side down, in the cake pan, and put in the other half, cut side up. Cover with the gelatin mixture (see box, below). Cover with a small plate and weigh down with weights or heavy cans. Chill in the refrigerator overnight.

6 Dip the base of the cake pan into a bowl of hot water, just long enough to melt the gelatin slightly and free it from the edges of the pan. Serve the tongue very thinly sliced.

Covering with gelatin

Pour the gelatin mixture over the tongue until well covered.

OXTAIL STEW

 Serves 4

1 tbsp sunflower or corn oil

2¹/₂ lb (1.25 kg) oxtail, cut into
 2-in (5-cm) slices and trimmed

¹/₄ cup (30 g) all-purpose flour

3 ²/₃ cups (900 ml) beef stock

2 large onions, sliced

1 tbsp tomato paste

1 tbsp chopped parsley

1 tbsp chopped fresh thyme

1 bay leaf

salt and black pepper

8 celery stalks, thickly sliced

chopped parsley to garnish

1 Heat the oil in a large flameproof casserole, add the oxtail, and cook over high heat for 10 minutes or until browned all over. Remove the oxtail and drain on paper towels.

2 Add the flour and cook, stirring occasionally, for about 1 minute. Blend in the beef stock and bring to a boil, stirring until the sauce has thickened.

3 Return the oxtail to the casserole, add the onions, tomato paste, parsley, thyme, bay leaf, and salt and pepper to taste, and bring to a boil. Cover and simmer gently for 2 hours.

4 Add the celery and cook for 1¹/₂–2 hours longer, until the meat can easily be removed from the bones. Skim any fat from the top of the casserole, then taste for seasoning. Sprinkle with parsley before serving.

Cook's know-how

Oxtail stew needs long, slow cooking to develop its rich brown gravy and to make the meat so soft that it falls off the bone. If possible, make the stew the day before serving; the excess fat can then easily be lifted from the surface of the cooled stew. If you make the stew with lots of sauce, this can be used, thinned down and with added vegetables, for a tasty soup.

LEMON ROAST VEAL WITH SPINACH STUFFING

Veal can be dry because it is so lean. Marinating the meat for 2 days before roasting makes it more juicy and succulent.

 Serves 4–6

2 1/2 lb (1.25 kg) boneless veal roast, such as loin

2/3 cup (150 ml) dry white wine

2/3 cup (150 ml) chicken stock

MARINADE

3 tbsp olive oil

grated zest and juice of 1 lemon

4 thyme sprigs

black pepper

STUFFING

2 tbsp butter

1 shallot, finely chopped

2 thick slices of bacon, finely chopped

6 cups (175 g) spinach leaves, coarsely shredded

grated zest of 1 lemon

1 cup (60 g) fresh pumpernickel bread crumbs

salt and black pepper

1 small egg, lightly beaten

1 Combine the marinade ingredients. Turn the veal in the marinade, cover, and leave to marinate in the refrigerator for 2 days.

2 Make the stuffing: melt the butter in a saucepan, add the shallot and bacon, and cook for 5 minutes or until the shallot is softened. Stir in the spinach and cook for 1 minute. Remove from the heat and add the lemon zest, pumpernickel bread crumbs, and salt and pepper to taste. Mix well, then bind with the beaten egg. Leave to cool completely.

3 Remove the veal from the marinade, reserving the marinade. Spread the stuffing over the veal and roll up (see box, right).

4 Insert a meat thermometer, if using, into the middle of the meat and place in a roasting pan. Pour the marinade around the meat. Roast in a 350°F (180°C) oven for about 1 1/4 hours, until the juices run clear or until the thermometer registers 170°F (75°C). Transfer to a platter, cover loosely with a sheet of foil, and leave to stand in a warm place for 10 minutes.

5 Meanwhile, spoon the fat from the pan, and remove the thyme sprigs. Add the wine and stock and bring to a boil, stirring to dissolve the drippings from the bottom of the pan. Boil for 5 minutes or until thickened and reduced by about half.

6 Season the gravy to taste and pour into a warmed gravy boat. Carve the veal and serve immediately.

Rolling up the veal

Bring the 2 sides of the veal together, enclosing the stuffing completely. Tie kitchen string around the veal to secure.

GRAVIES FOR MEAT

MUSHROOM GRAVY

Melt *2 tbsp butter* in a saucepan. Add *1 finely chopped shallot* and cook for 2 minutes until softened. Add *1/2 lb (250 g) sliced mushrooms* and cook gently for 5 minutes. Pour in *1 1/4 cups (300 ml) beef stock* and simmer for about 5 minutes. Add *1 tbsp chopped parsley*, *1 tsp chopped fresh thyme*, and *salt and pepper to taste*.

ONION GRAVY

Heat *1 tbsp sunflower oil* and *2 tbsp butter* in a saucepan. Add *1 sliced onion* and cook for 5–7 minutes, until golden. Add *1 tbsp all-purpose flour* and cook, stirring, for 1 minute. Add *1 1/4 cups (300 ml) chicken stock*. Simmer for about 5 minutes. Add *salt and pepper to taste*.

RED WINE GRAVY

Melt *2 tbsp butter* in a saucepan. Add *1 sliced small onion* and cook for 5 minutes or until beginning to brown. Add *1 tbsp all-purpose flour* and cook, stirring, for 1 minute. Add *7 tbsp (100 ml) red wine* and *1 1/4 cups (300 ml) beef stock*. Simmer for about 5 minutes. Pour in any juices from the meat and add *salt and pepper to taste*.

VEAL CHOPS WITH MUSHROOMS & CREAM

 Serves 4

1/4 cup (15 g) dried porcini mushrooms

2 tbsp all-purpose flour

salt and black pepper

4 1/2-lb (250-g) veal loin chops

3 tbsp butter

8 shallots, chopped

3 garlic cloves, crushed

1/2 lb (250 g) mushrooms, thinly sliced

1 cup (250 ml) dry white wine

1 1/4 cups (300 ml) light cream

1 tbsp chopped fresh tarragon

pinch of grated nutmeg

chopped fresh tarragon to garnish

1 Put the dried mushrooms into a bowl, cover them with warm water, and soak for 30 minutes or until soft.

2 Sprinkle the flour onto a plate and season with salt and pepper. Lightly coat the chops with the flour.

3 Melt half of the butter in a skillet, add the veal chops, and cook for about 4 minutes on each side.

4 Remove the chops and keep warm. Melt the remaining butter in the pan, add the shallots and garlic, and cook gently, stirring occasionally, for a few minutes, until softened.

5 Drain the dried mushrooms, reserving the soaking liquid. Rinse under cold running water and drain on paper towels. Add the dried and fresh mushrooms to the pan and cook for 3 minutes or until tender. Remove the shallots and mushrooms from the pan and keep warm.

6 Pour in the wine and boil until reduced to about 3 tbsp. Add the mushroom liquid and boil until reduced to about 1/2 cup (125 ml).

7 Stir in the cream and heat gently. Add the tarragon, nutmeg, and salt and pepper to taste. Return the chops, shallots, and mushrooms to the pan and heat through gently. Transfer to serving plates, sprinkle with chopped tarragon, and serve immediately.

VITELLO TONNATO

 **Serves 6–8**

3 lb (1.5 kg) veal roast

2 large rosemary sprigs

2 garlic cloves, cut into slivers

salt and black pepper

1 cup (250 ml) dry white wine

TUNA MAYONNAISE

7 oz (200 g) canned tuna in oil, drained

2 tbsp lemon juice

1 garlic clove, coarsely chopped

2 tbsp capers

1 tsp chopped fresh thyme

dash of Tabasco sauce

1/2 cup (125 ml) olive oil

1 cup (250 ml) mayonnaise

1 tbsp mustard seeds

TO GARNISH

black olives

1 red pepper, cored, seeded, and cut into strips

fresh basil

1 Make slits in the veal and push 1 or 2 rosemary leaves and a sliver of garlic into each slit. Season, and rub with any remaining rosemary and garlic.

2 Place the veal in a large roasting pan and pour the wine around it. Cover with a sheet of foil and roast in a 325°F (160°C) oven for 2–2 1/2 hours or until the veal is tender and cooked through.

3 Remove the veal from the oven and leave to cool completely in the cooking liquid. Remove any fat that solidifies on the surface. Slice the veal thinly and arrange the slices on a serving platter.

4 Make the tuna mayonnaise: puree the tuna, reserving a little for the garnish, with the lemon juice, garlic, capers, thyme, and Tabasco sauce in a food processor until smooth. Gradually blend in the oil, then add the mayonnaise, mustard seeds, and salt and pepper to taste.

5 Pour the tuna mayonnaise over the veal and garnish with the reserved tuna, black olives, red pepper, and basil. Serve at room temperature.

WIENER SCHNITZEL

 Serves 4

4 2- to 3-oz (60- to 90-g) veal scallops

salt and black pepper

1 egg, beaten

2 cups (125 g) fresh white bread crumbs

4 tbsp butter

1 tbsp sunflower or corn oil

TO SERVE

8 anchovy fillets, drained and halved lengthwise

2 tbsp coarsely chopped capers

lemon wedges

parsley

1 Put each veal scallop between 2 sheets of waxed paper and pound to an 1/8-in (3-mm) thickness with a rolling pin. Season with salt and pepper.

2 Pour the egg onto a plate and sprinkle the bread crumbs on another plate. Dip each scallop into the beaten egg, then into the bread crumbs to coat evenly. Cover and chill.

3 Melt the butter with the oil in a large skillet. When the butter is foaming, add 2 of the scallops and cook for 2 minutes on each side until golden. Drain on paper towels and keep warm while cooking the remaining 2 scallops.

4 Serve the scallops with anchovy fillets, capers, lemon wedges, and parsley.

Wiener schnitzel

Wiener schnitzel is the name given to a veal scallop cooked the Viennese way. Traditionally served garnished with anchovies and capers, Wiener schnitzel is known as Holsteiner schnitzel when topped with a fried egg.

SALTIMBOCCA

 Serves 4

4 2- to 3-oz (60- to 90-g) veal scallops

8–12 fresh sage leaves

4 thin slices of prosciutto

2 tbsp all-purpose flour

salt and black pepper

2 tbsp butter

1 garlic clove, crushed

1/2 cup (125 ml) dry white wine

1/4 cup (60 ml) heavy cream

1 Put each veal scallop between 2 sheets of waxed paper and pound to an 1/8-in (3-mm) thickness with a rolling pin.

2 Lay 2 or 3 sage leaves on each scallop and press a slice of prosciutto firmly on top. Sprinkle the flour onto a plate and season with salt and pepper. Lightly coat both sides of the scallops with the flour, shaking off any excess.

3 Melt half of the butter in a large skillet. When the butter is foaming, add the scallops and cook in batches, sprinkling them with the garlic as they cook and adding more butter when needed, for 2 minutes on each side. Lift out and keep warm.

4 Pour the white wine into the pan and boil for a few minutes, until it is reduced to about 2 tbsp. Stir in the cream and heat gently, then taste for seasoning. Arrange the scallops on warmed plates and pour the sauce over them. Serve immediately.

Saltimbocca

Translated literally, saltimbocca means "jump in the mouth," presumably because this classic Italian dish is so delicious that it almost leaps into one's mouth. If veal is not available, saltimbocca can also be made with either pork, turkey, or chicken scallops.

VEAL WITH LEMON & BASIL

Omit the sage leaves and prosciutto. Coat the veal with seasoned flour and cook as directed. While still in the pan, sprinkle on the juice of 1 lemon, 2 tbsp shredded fresh basil, and season to taste.

VEAL MARSALA

 Serves 4

4 2- to 3-oz (60- to 90-g) veal
  scallops

1 tbsp all-purpose flour

salt and black pepper

3 tbsp butter

1 large onion, finely chopped

1/2 cup (125 ml) Marsala

1/2 cup (125 ml) veal or
  chicken stock

chopped parsley to garnish

1 Put each veal scallop
between 2 sheets of waxed
paper and pound to an
1/8-in (3-mm) thickness with
a rolling pin.

2 Season the flour with salt
and pepper and use to
lightly coat the scallops.

3 Melt 2 tbsp of the butter
in a skillet, and cook the
scallops, in batches if
necessary, for 2 minutes on
each side or until golden.
Remove from the pan and
keep warm.

4 Melt the remaining
butter, add the onion,
and cook gently for about
5 minutes, until soft and
lightly browned. Pour in
the Marsala and boil,
stirring, until reduced to
2 tbsp. Add the stock and
boil until reduced to about
1/3 cup (90 ml).

5 Return the scallops to
the pan, spoon the sauce
over, and warm the scallops
through. Sprinkle with
chopped parsley.

OSSO BUCO

*The name of this Italian classic, originally from Milan, means "bone with a hole" since
it is made from thick slices of veal shank that have the central bone containing marrow
left in. For authenticity, serve with gremolata and a creamy risotto Milanese (page 322).*

 Serves 6

1/4 cup (30 g) all-purpose flour

salt and black pepper

6 slices of veal shank with bones,
  1 1/2–2 in (3.5–5 cm) thick

2 tbsp butter

2 tbsp olive oil

2 onions, finely chopped

3 carrots, finely chopped

2 celery stalks, finely chopped

2 garlic cloves, crushed

1 1/4 cups (300 ml) dry white
  wine

1 1/4 cups (300 ml) veal or
  chicken stock

13 oz (400 g) canned chopped
  tomatoes

2 tsp chopped fresh oregano

1 bay leaf

gremolata (see box, right)
  to serve

1 Put the flour into a large
plastic bag and season
with salt and pepper. Put the
veal shanks into the bag and
shake until all the meat is
evenly coated with flour.

2 Melt the butter with the
oil in a large flameproof
casserole. When the butter is
foaming, add the veal shanks
and cook, in batches, for
10 minutes or until golden
all over. Lift out and drain
on paper towels. Lower the
heat, add the onions,
carrots, celery, and garlic
and cook, stirring
occasionally, for 5 minutes.

3 Pour in the wine and boil
until reduced by half.
Add the stock, tomatoes,
oregano, and bay leaf and
bring to a boil. Return the
veal to the casserole, bring
back to a boil, cover, and
cook in a 325°F (160°C)
oven for 1 1/2–2 hours, until
very tender.

4 If the sauce in the
casserole is too liquid, lift
out the veal shanks, keep
warm, and boil the sauce
until reduced to a thick
consistency. Taste for
seasoning. Sprinkle the
gremolata over the veal just
before serving.

Gremolata

Put 2 tbsp chopped parsley,
the grated zest of 1 lemon,
and 1 finely chopped garlic
clove into a small bowl and
stir to mix thoroughly.
Chill until needed.

Cook's know-how

*Make sure the slices of veal you
buy have the bone in, because the
marrow is the most important
part of this traditional Italian
dish. Scoop it out of the bone
and eat it with the meat.*

VEAL STEW WITH OLIVES & PEPPERS

 **Serves 6–8**

2 tbsp all-purpose flour

salt and black pepper

3 lb (1.5 kg) stewing veal, cut into 1½-in (3.5 cm) cubes

2–3 tbsp olive oil

2 garlic cloves, crushed

1 red, 1 green, and 1 yellow pepper, cored, seeded, and cut into strips

1 cup (250 ml) dry white wine

2 large tomatoes, peeled (page 39), seeded, and chopped

¼ cup (60 g) tomato paste

4 rosemary sprigs, chopped

2 cups (250 g) pitted black olives

1 tbsp chopped fresh rosemary to garnish

1 tbsp chopped parsley to garnish

1 Put the flour into a plastic bag and season with salt and pepper. Toss the veal in the seasoned flour to coat lightly.

2 Heat the oil in a large flameproof casserole, add the veal, sprinkle with half of the garlic, and cook for 5–7 minutes, until browned all over. Lift out the veal and set aside.

3 Add the peppers and cook, stirring, for 3 minutes, until almost soft. Remove from the casserole and set aside.

4 Return the veal to the casserole and add the wine, tomatoes, tomato paste, remaining garlic, and rosemary. Cover and simmer for 1 hour.

5 Return the peppers to the casserole and cook for 30 minutes longer or until the meat is very tender.

6 Stir the olives into the casserole and heat through. Serve hot, lightly sprinkled with rosemary and parsley.

LIVER & BACON WITH ONION SAUCE

 Serves 4

2 tbsp sunflower or corn oil

1 large onion, thinly sliced

4 thick slices of bacon, cut into thin strips

1 lb (500 g) calf's liver, trimmed and cut into ½-in (1-cm) strips

2 tbsp all-purpose flour

2⅓ cups (600 ml) beef stock

3 tbsp ketchup

dash of Worcestershire sauce

salt and black pepper

chopped fresh tarragon to garnish

1 Heat the oil in a large skillet, add the onion and bacon, and cook gently, stirring occasionally, for a few minutes, until the onion is soft and the bacon crisp. Add the liver and cook, stirring, for 2 minutes. Remove with a slotted spoon and keep warm.

2 Add the flour to the pan and cook, stirring, for 1 minute. Pour in the stock and bring to a boil, stirring until thickened.

3 Add the ketchup and Worcestershire sauce, and season. Return the onion, bacon, and liver to the pan, cover, and simmer for 5 minutes. Sprinkle with tarragon before serving.

Cook's know-how

Lamb's liver can also be used in this recipe. Pig's liver is a less expensive alternative to calf's or lamb's liver, but it has a stronger flavor. To reduce its pronounced taste, soak it in milk for about 30 minutes.

LIVER STROGANOFF

Use ⅔ cup (150 ml) chicken stock instead of the beef stock and omit the ketchup and Worcestershire sauce. Stir in ⅔ cup (150 ml) sour cream.

CALF'S LIVER WITH SAGE

 Serves 4

2 tbsp all-purpose flour

salt and black pepper

1 lb (500 g) calf's liver

4 tbsp butter

1 tbsp sunflower or corn oil

juice of 1 lemon

3 tbsp chopped fresh sage

sage leaves and lemon slices
  to garnish

1 Sprinkle the flour onto a large plate and season with salt and pepper. Use to coat both sides of the liver, shaking off any excess.

2 Melt half of the butter with the oil in a large skillet. When the butter is foaming, add half of the liver and cook over high heat for 2–3 minutes on each side, until browned all over. Lift out with a slotted spoon and keep warm. Repeat with the remaining liver.

3 Melt the remaining butter in the pan and add the lemon juice and sage, stirring to dissolve any browned bits from the bottom of the pan. Pour the pan juices over the liver, garnish with sage leaves and lemon slices, and serve.

Cook's know-how

Overcooking liver will toughen it, so make sure that the butter and oil are really hot. Then the liver will cook quickly.

CALF'S LIVER WITH APPLE

Halve and slice 1 sweet cooking apple and add to the pan with the lemon juice and sage. Cook, stirring, for 3 minutes and serve with the liver.

CREAMED SWEETBREADS

 Serves 4

1 lb (500 g) veal sweetbreads

2 tbsp lemon juice

1 small onion, chopped

a few parsley sprigs

1 bay leaf

salt and black pepper

3 tbsp butter

1/3 cup (45 g) all-purpose flour

1 1/4 cups (300 ml) milk

chopped parsley to garnish

1 Put the sweetbreads into a bowl, cover with cold water, add 1 tbsp of the lemon juice, and leave to soak for 2–3 hours.

2 Drain, rinse, and trim the sweetbreads (page 214).

3 Put the sweetbreads into a large saucepan with the onion, parsley, bay leaf, and salt and pepper to taste. Cover with cold water and bring slowly to a boil. Simmer gently for 15 minutes or until just tender, skimming off any foam as it rises to the surface.

4 Drain the sweetbreads, reserving 1 1/4 cups (300 ml) of the cooking liquid. Rinse again and shape (see box, right).

5 Melt the butter in a saucepan, add the flour, and cook, stirring, for 1 minute. Remove the pan from the heat and gradually blend in the milk and reserved cooking liquid. Bring to a boil, stirring constantly, and boil for 2–3 minutes, until the mixture thickens. Add the remaining lemon juice and salt and pepper to taste.

6 Unwrap the sweetbreads and slice into thin rounds. Add to the sauce and simmer gently for about 5 minutes to warm through. Transfer to warmed plates and garnish with chopped parsley before serving.

Shaping sweetbreads

Place the sweetbreads on a large sheet of foil and roll it up very tightly, twisting the ends to make a sausage shape. Chill for 2 hours or until firm.

ROAST LEG OF LAMB WITH RED WINE GRAVY

Roast leg of lamb, a traditional dish, is served here with a rich gravy that incorporates all the flavorful juices from the meat as well as a dash of red wine. A bowl of freshly made mint sauce completes the scene for a perfect Sunday dinner.

 Serves 4–6

4 lb (2 kg) leg of lamb

salt and black pepper

1 tbsp chopped fresh rosemary

1 tbsp chopped fresh thyme

1 tbsp all-purpose flour

1 1/4 cups (300 ml) lamb stock

6 tbsp (90 ml) red wine

rosemary and thyme to garnish

mint sauce (see far right) to serve

1 Trim the skin and excess fat from the lamb. Score the fat (see box, right).

2 Insert a meat thermometer, if using, into the middle of the meat. Put the lamb, fat side up, on a rack in a roasting pan, and sprinkle with pepper and the chopped rosemary and thyme. Roast in a 400°F (200°C) oven for 20 minutes.

3 Lower the oven temperature to 350°F (180°C) and cook for about 1 hour and 20 minutes for well-done meat or until the meat thermometer registers 175°F (80°C) and the fat is crisp and golden.

4 Remove the lamb, cover loosely with a sheet of foil, and leave to stand for 10 minutes.

5 Meanwhile, make the gravy: spoon all but 1 tbsp fat from the pan. Put the roasting pan on top of the stove, add the flour, and cook, stirring, for 1 minute. Pour in the stock or water and wine and bring to a boil, stirring to dissolve any drippings from the bottom and sides of the pan. Simmer for about 3 minutes, taste for seasoning, and strain into a warmed gravy boat.

6 Transfer the leg of lamb to a warmed serving platter and garnish with rosemary and thyme sprigs. Pass the red wine gravy and mint sauce separately.

Scoring the fat

Score the fat in a crisscross pattern using a small, sharp knife, making sure that only the fat is cut and that the meat underneath remains completely untouched.

SAUCES FOR LAMB

MINT SAUCE

In a small bowl, combine *3 tbsp chopped fresh mint* and *1–2 tsp superfine sugar*. Pour on *2 tbsp boiling water* and stir until the sugar has completely dissolved. Add *2 tbsp wine vinegar* and leave to cool before serving.

CITRUS SAUCE

Put *2 tbsp red currant jelly* into a small saucepan and heat gently until melted. Add *1 1/4 cups (300 ml) red wine* and the *grated zest of 1 orange*. Bring to a simmer and cook, whisking constantly, for 5 minutes. Add *the juices of 1 orange and 1/2 lemon* and simmer for 5 minutes longer. Strain, then add *salt and pepper to taste*. Serve hot.

YOGURT & LIME SAUCE

Put *2/3 cup (150 g) plain yogurt*, the *grated zest and juice of 1 lime*, *1 crushed garlic clove*, *1 tbsp chopped fresh mint*, and *salt and pepper to taste* into a small bowl. Mix well to combine. Cover and chill until needed.

GREEK ROAST LAMB

 Serves 6

4 lb (2 kg) leg of lamb

4 garlic cloves, cut into slivers

2 large rosemary sprigs, chopped

juice of ¹/₂ lemon

salt and black pepper

chopped fresh rosemary to garnish

1 With a sharp chef's knife, carefully make small slits all over the leg of lamb and insert a sliver of garlic into each slit.

2 Put the lamb into a casserole with the rosemary sprigs, sprinkle with the lemon juice, and add salt and pepper to taste.

3 Roast in a 425°F (220°C) oven for 30 minutes or until the lamb is browned. Lower the oven temperature to 275°F (140°C), cover the casserole, and cook for 3¹/₂ hours longer or until the lamb is very tender. Leave to stand for 10 minutes.

4 Remove the lamb from the casserole and spoon off any fat from the cooking juices. Taste for seasoning and strain into a gravy boat. Carve the lamb, garnish with the chopped rosemary, and serve immediately.

SPINACH-STUFFED LAMB

The lamb in this recipe is distinctively flavored with spinach, wine, and anchovies. Stuffed mushrooms are a perfect accompaniment.

 Serves 6–8

4 lb (2 kg) leg of lamb, boned but left whole (page 211)

²/₃ cup (150 ml) dry white wine

4 anchovy fillets, chopped

²/₃ cup (150 ml) lamb stock or water

salt and black pepper

stuffed mushrooms (page 349)

SPINACH STUFFING

2 tbsp butter

3–4 garlic cloves, crushed

8 cups (250 g) spinach leaves, coarsely shredded

1 cup (60 g) fresh pumpernickel bread crumbs

1 egg, beaten

1 Make the stuffing: melt butter in a saucepan. Add the garlic and cook, stirring, for 2–3 minutes, until softened. Stir in the spinach, add salt and pepper to taste, and cook for 1 minute. Add the bread crumbs and leave to cool. Bind with the egg.

2 Stuff the lamb (see box, right). Seal with thin skewers or kitchen string.

3 Put the lamb on a rack in a roasting pan and roast in a 400°F (200°Cß) oven for 15 minutes. Turn the lamb, insert a meat thermometer, if using, and cook for 15 minutes.

4 Drain the fat from the pan. Add the wine and anchovy fillets. Cover the lamb with a sheet of foil, lower the oven temperature to 350°F (180°C) and cook for 1¹/₂ hours or until the juices run slightly pink. The meat thermometer should register 170–175°F (75–80°C).

5 Remove the lamb, cover loosely with foil, and leave to stand for 10 minutes.

6 Pour the cooking liquid into a measuring cup and add enough stock or water to make 1¹/₄ cups (300 ml).

7 Return the cooking liquid to the pan. Bring to a boil, stirring to dissolve the sediment. Season and strain into a warmed gravy boat. Serve the lamb with the stuffed mushrooms and pass the gravy separately.

Stuffing the lamb

Season the cavity of the lamb with salt and pepper, then spoon in the spinach stuffing, packing it in tightly.

SHOULDER OF LAMB WITH LEMON & OLIVE STUFFING

The flavors of lemon zest, black olives, and fresh herbs combine together to make a glorious stuffing, which is especially good with succulent lamb. Boning the lamb before cooking makes it easier to carve into neat slices.

 Serves 6–8

4 lb (2 kg) shoulder of lamb, boned

2 garlic cloves, cut into slivers

2/3 cup (150 ml) dry white wine

2/3 cup (150 ml) lamb stock or water

LEMON & OLIVE STUFFING

1 tbsp olive oil

1 shallot, finely chopped

2 cups (125 g) fresh bread crumbs

1/4 cup (30 g) pitted black olives, roughly chopped

grated zest of 1 lemon

1 tbsp chopped fresh thyme

1 tbsp chopped fresh rosemary

1 small egg, beaten

salt and black pepper

1 Make the stuffing: heat the olive oil in a small pan, add the shallot, and cook for about 5 minutes. Remove from the heat and add the bread crumbs, olives, lemon zest, herbs, egg, and salt and pepper to taste. Leave to cool.

2 Stuff and roll the lamb (see box, right).

3 Put the lamb into a roasting pan and insert a meat thermometer, if using, into the middle of the meat. Pour the wine and stock over the lamb and cook in a 400°F (200°C) oven for 20–25 minutes. Lower the oven temperature to 350°F (180°C) and cook for 1 hour and 40 minutes or until the juices run clear. The meat thermometer should register 170–175°F (75–80°C).

4 Remove the lamb, cover loosely with a sheet of foil, and leave to stand for 10 minutes.

5 Make the gravy: spoon any fat from the cooking juices. Put the pan on top of the stove. Bring to a boil and boil for 5 minutes, stirring to dissolve any drippings from the bottom of the pan. Taste for seasoning, strain into a warmed gravy boat, and serve with the lamb.

Stuffing and rolling the lamb

Make slits in the meat side of the lamb using a small knife and push a sliver of garlic into each slit. Season the lamb with salt and pepper.

Spread the lemon and olive stuffing over the lamb. Roll up the lamb and tie with string.

LEMON BROILED LAMB

 Serves 6–8

4–5 lb (2–2.5 kg) leg of lamb, butterflied (page 211)

MARINADE

juice of 3 lemons

1/4 cup (60 g) honey

3 large garlic cloves, quartered

1 tbsp dry mustard

1 tbsp coarse mustard

1 Make the marinade: in a nonmetallic dish, mix together the lemon juice, honey, garlic, and mustards. Turn the lamb in the marinade, cover loosely, and leave to marinate in the refrigerator, turning the lamb occasionally, for 1–2 days.

2 Remove the lamb from the marinade. Strain and reserve the marinade. Cook the lamb under the broiler, 6 in (15 cm) from the heat, basting occasionally with the marinade, for 20–25 minutes on each side.

3 Test the lamb: insert a skewer into the thickest part – the juices will run clear when it is cooked.

4 Leave the lamb to stand, covered loosely with foil, in a warm place for 5–10 minutes. Spoon the fat from the broiler pan, strain the juices into a gravy boat, and serve with the lamb.

KEBABS

Cooking food over a barbecue is a sociable, enjoyable way to cook, but if you're tired of the usual barbecue fare, here's a selection of kebabs to choose from, with mouthwatering marinades or flavored butter to enhance each one. There's bound to be a kebab to suit everyone's taste.

BEEF & ONION

 Serves 4

1 lb (500 g) boneless beef sirloin, cut into chunks

2 onions, cut into chunks

salt and black pepper

fresh tarragon to garnish

MARINADE

1/2 cup (125 ml) olive oil

6 tbsp (90 ml) port

6–8 shallots, finely chopped

2 tbsp Dijon mustard

1 tbsp chopped fresh tarragon

1 Combine the marinade ingredients, add the beef, and stir well. Cover and chill for at least 2 hours.

2 Thread the beef and onions onto skewers. Season and cook for 2–3 minutes on each side for rare beef, 3–4 for medium, and 4–5 for well-done.

CURRIED LAMB

 Serves 4

1 lb (500 g) boneless leg of lamb, trimmed and cut into chunks

lime wedges to serve

MARINADE

3 tbsp plain yogurt

juice of 1/2 lime

4 garlic cloves, crushed

3 tbsp chopped fresh cilantro

1 tbsp chopped fresh mint

1 tsp each curry powder and cumin

pinch each of salt and cayenne pepper

1 Combine the marinade ingredients in a large bowl. Add the lamb and stir. Cover and chill for at least 2 hours.

2 Thread the lamb onto skewers, then cook for 4 minutes on each side for medium lamb or 5 minutes for well-done lamb. Serve with lime wedges.

ASIAN PORK

 Serves 4

1 lb (500 g) pork tenderloin, cut into chunks

1 red pepper, cored, seeded, and cut into chunks

1 green pepper, cored, seeded, and cut into chunks

1 onion, cut into chunks

1/4 fresh pineapple, peeled and cut into chunks

MARINADE

6 tbsp (90 ml) sunflower or corn oil

6 tbsp (90 ml) soy sauce

juice of 1 lime

3 garlic cloves, crushed

3 tbsp sugar

1/4 tsp ground ginger

1/4 tsp fennel seeds

1 Combine the marinade ingredients in a bowl. Add the pork, peppers, onion, and pineapple, and stir well. Cover and chill for at least 2 hours.

2 Thread the meat onto skewers, alternating with the peppers, onions, and pineapple. Baste the kebabs with any remaining marinade. Cook for 4–5 minutes on each side, basting occasionally, until the pork is cooked through.

LIVER & SAUSAGE

 Serves 4

8 slices of bacon, cut into 1 1/2-in (3.5-cm) pieces

1/4 lb (125 g) chicken livers, trimmed and cut into bite-sized pieces

2 mild Italian or other pork sausages, cut into bite-sized pieces

salt and black pepper

chopped parsley to garnish

lemon wedges to serve

MUSTARD BUTTER

3 tbsp butter

2 garlic cloves, crushed

1 tbsp chopped fresh rosemary

1 tbsp coarse mustard

1 Wrap the bacon pieces around the chicken livers and thread onto skewers, alternating with the sausages. Soften the butter slightly, then mix in the garlic, rosemary, and mustard.

2 Spread half of the butter over the kebabs. Cook for 4–5 minutes on each side, until cooked through. Season, garnish, and serve with the remaining butter and the lemon wedges.

Clockwise from top: *Curried Lamb Kebabs, Asian Pork Kebabs, Beef & Onion Kebabs, Mustard Butter, Liver & Sausage Kebabs.*

Successful barbecues

It's not very difficult to get successful results when cooking over charcoal. Just remember a few simple points.

• It is usually best to marinate meat to be cooked over a barbecue. The basis of a marinade should be an oil, to keep the food moist; an acid such as lemon or lime juice, which tenderizes the meat; and herbs, spices, or other seasonings to add flavor. Baste with the marinade while the meat is cooking if stated in the recipe.

• Start to cook when the coals have stopped glowing, which takes about 30 minutes.

• Some metal skewers have wooden handles, but if not, handle with care since they become very hot. Soak bamboo skewers in water for 30 minutes before use so that they don't burn.

SHOULDER OF LAMB WITH GARLIC & HERBS

 Serves 6

4 lb (2 kg) shoulder of lamb, trimmed of excess fat

creamed great northern beans (page 347) to serve

HERB BUTTER

6 tbsp (90 g) butter, softened

2 garlic cloves, crushed

1 tbsp chopped fresh thyme

1 tbsp chopped fresh rosemary

1 tbsp chopped fresh mint

2 tbsp chopped parsley

salt and black pepper

GRAVY

1 tbsp all-purpose flour

2/3 cup (150 ml) red wine

2/3 cup (150 ml) lamb stock or water

1 Make the herb butter: mix the butter, garlic, thyme, rosemary, mint, parsley, and salt and pepper to taste.

2 Using a knife, slash the lamb at regular intervals and push a little of the herb butter into each slit. Rub any remaining butter over the lamb.

3 Put the lamb on a rack in a roasting pan and insert a meat thermometer, if using, into the middle of the meat. Cook in a 400°F (200°C) oven for 30 minutes.

4 Lower the temperature to 350°F (180°C) and cook for about 1 hour for medium meat or 1 hour and 20 minutes for well-done meat. The thermometer should register 170–175°F (75–80°C).

5 Remove the lamb. Cover loosely with foil and leave to stand for 10 minutes.

6 Make the gravy: drain all but 1 tbsp of the fat from the pan. Set the pan on top of the stove, add the flour, and cook, stirring, for 1 minute. Pour in the wine and stock, bring to a boil, and simmer for 2–3 minutes. Add salt and pepper to taste and strain into a warmed gravy boat. Serve with the lamb and creamed great northern beans.

INDIAN SPICED LAMB

 Serves 4–6

3 lb (1.5 kg) shoulder or leg of lamb

1/2 tsp lemon juice

salt and black pepper

cashew nuts and chopped fresh cilantro to garnish

SPICED YOGURT MARINADE

8 garlic cloves, coarsely chopped

3-in (7-cm) piece of fresh ginger, chopped

2 tbsp honey

1 tbsp lemon juice

seeds of 5 cardamom pods

1 tsp cumin seeds

1 tsp turmeric

1 tsp cayenne pepper

1 tsp salt

1/2 tsp ground cinnamon

1/4 tsp ground cloves

2/3 cup (150 g) plain yogurt

large pinch of saffron threads, crumbled

1 Make the spiced yogurt marinade: puree the garlic, ginger, honey, lemon juice, cardamom and cumin seeds, turmeric, cayenne, salt, cinnamon, cloves, yogurt, and saffron in a food processor until smooth.

2 Spread the mixture over the lamb (see box, right).

3 Cover the lamb and leave to marinate in the refrigerator for 2 hours.

4 Put the lamb on a rack in a roasting pan and cook in a 325°F (160°C) oven for 3 1/2 hours or until tender.

5 Remove the lamb and keep warm. Spoon the fat from the pan. Set the pan on top of the stove and add the lemon juice. Boil until thickened and season with salt and pepper to taste.

6 Cut the lamb from the bone, then cut the meat into chunks. Mix the meat chunks with the sauce, and serve immediately, garnished with cashew nuts and chopped fresh cilantro.

Coating the lamb

Make slits in the lamb and, using a spatula, spread the spiced yogurt marinade over the lamb to cover it completely.

RACK OF LAMB WITH A WALNUT & HERB CRUST

A favorite for parties, a rack of lamb consists of 8 chops. The walnut and herb crust and light wine and grape sauce make this cut of lamb the perfect main course.

 Serves 4–6

2 prepared racks of lamb (page 212)

1 egg, beaten

WALNUT & HERB CRUST

1/2 cup (30 g) fresh whole-wheat bread crumbs

1 cup (30 g) chopped parsley

2 tbsp coarsely chopped walnut pieces

2 large garlic cloves, crushed

finely grated zest of 1 lemon

1 tbsp walnut oil

salt and black pepper

WINE & GRAPE SAUCE

2/3 cup (150 ml) dry white wine

2/3 cup (150 ml) lamb stock or water

1/2 cup (125 g) seedless green grapes, halved

1 Brush the outsides of the racks of lamb with some of the beaten egg.

2 Prepare the walnut and herb crust: combine the bread crumbs, parsley, walnuts, garlic, lemon zest, oil, and salt and pepper to taste and bind with the remaining beaten egg. Chill for 30 minutes.

3 Coat the lamb with the walnut and parsley crust (see box, right). Put the racks crust side up into a roasting pan. Cook in a 400°F (200°C) oven for 20 minutes per 1 lb (500 g) plus 20 minutes for medium meat or plus 30 minutes for well-done.

4 Remove the lamb from the oven, cover loosely with a sheet of foil, and leave to stand in a warm place for 10 minutes.

5 Meanwhile, make the sauce: spoon all but 1 tbsp of the fat from the roasting pan. Set the pan on top of the stove, pour in the wine, and bring to a boil, stirring to dissolve any browned bits from the bottom of the pan.

6 Add the stock and boil, stirring occasionally, for 2–3 minutes. Taste the sauce for seasoning, strain into a warmed gravy boat, and stir in the grapes. Serve with the lamb.

CROWN ROAST WITH RED WINE

Shape 2 prepared racks of lamb into a crown roast (page 212). Place in a roasting pan with 2 tbsp oil and cook as for Rack of Lamb. Make the gravy from the juices and 1 tbsp fat in the roasting pan, stirring in 1 tbsp all-purpose flour, and adding 1 1/4 cups (300 ml) lamb stock or water and 6 tbsp (90 ml) red wine. To serve, put a bunch of watercress inside the crown.

Coating the lamb

Press half of the walnut and herb crust mixture onto the skin side of each rack of lamb, using a metal spatula.

LAMB WITH MINT GLAZE

 Serves 4

8 rib or loin lamb chops, trimmed

MINT GLAZE

3 tbsp dry white wine

1 tbsp white wine vinegar

4 mint sprigs, leaves stripped and chopped

1 tbsp honey

1 tsp Dijon mustard

salt and black pepper

1 Make the mint glaze: combine the wine, vinegar, mint, honey, mustard, and salt and pepper to taste. Brush the glaze over the chops and leave to marinate for about 30 minutes.

2 Place the chops over a barbecue or under the broiler, 3 in (7 cm) from the heat, and cook, brushing often with the glaze, for 4–6 minutes on each side, until done to your liking.

LAMB WITH ORANGE GLAZE

In a small bowl, combine 3 tbsp orange juice with 1 tbsp each white vinegar, orange marmalade, and chopped fresh thyme, 1 tsp Dijon mustard, and salt and pepper to taste. Glaze the lamb chops with the mixture.

HERBED BUTTERFLY CHOPS

 Serves 4

4 butterfly lamb chops

1 tbsp olive oil

black pepper

4 rosemary sprigs

4 mint sprigs

4 thyme sprigs

1 Place the lamb chops on a broiler pan. Brush each chop with half of the oil and sprinkle with black pepper. Arrange 1 rosemary sprig, 1 mint sprig, and 1 thyme sprig on each chop.

2 Place the chops under the broiler, 4 in (10 cm) from the heat, and cook for 4–6 minutes. Remove from the heat, lift off the herbs, and turn the chops over. Brush the chops with the remaining oil, replace the herbs, and broil for 4–6 minutes until done to your liking.

Butterfly chops

These are double-sided chops, cut from a double loin. The oil and herb mixture used here adds flavor to any cut.

LAMB CHOPS WITH MINTED HOLLANDAISE SAUCE

Instead of the traditional mint sauce, lamb chops are served here with a creamy hollandaise sauce flavored with fresh mint. The sauce is not difficult to make, as long as it is cooked over gentle heat.

 Serves 4

4 shoulder lamb chops

a little olive oil

salt and black pepper

minted hollandaise sauce to serve (see box, below)

1 Brush the chops on both sides with a little oil and season with black pepper.

2 Put the chops under the broiler, 4 in (10 cm) from the heat, and cook for 3–4 minutes on each side for medium-rare chops, slightly longer for well-done.

3 Arrange the lamb chops on warmed serving plates and serve immediately with the warm minted hollandaise sauce.

LAMB CHOPS WITH LEMON & THYME HOLLANDAISE

Make the sauce as directed, substituting 1 tsp grated lemon zest and 1 tbsp chopped fresh thyme for the chopped mint. Serve with the lamb chops.

Minted hollandaise sauce

Whisk together *2 tsp lemon juice, 2 tsp white vinegar, and 3 egg yolks at room temperature.* Put over a saucepan of simmering water and whisk until thick.

Melt *1/4 lb (125 g) unsalted butter,* and add, a little at a time, to the egg-yolk mixture, whisking constantly until the sauce thickens.

Stir in *2 tbsp chopped fresh mint* and season with *salt and pepper to taste.* Transfer to a gravy boat and serve immediately.

MEAT HOT POT

 Serves 4

2 tbsp sunflower or corn oil

2 lb (1 kg) shoulder lamb chops, trimmed

3 lamb kidneys, trimmed (page 214) and halved

4 large potatoes, cut into ¼-in (5-mm) slices

1 lb (500 g) carrots, sliced

2 large onions, chopped

1 tsp sugar

salt and black pepper

1 bay leaf

1 rosemary sprig

a few parsley sprigs

2 ⅓–3 cups (600–750 ml) lamb stock or water

chopped parsley to garnish

1 Heat the oil in a flameproof casserole, add the lamb in batches, and brown over medium heat for 5 minutes. Remove and set aside. Add the kidneys and cook for 3–5 minutes. Remove and set aside.

2 Add the potatoes, carrots, and onions and cook for 5 minutes. Remove from the casserole.

3 Make layers of lamb chops, kidneys, and vegetables in the casserole, adding sugar and salt and pepper to taste and putting the herbs in the middle. Top with a neat layer of potatoes. Pour on enough stock to come up to the potato layer. Cover tightly with the lid and cook the hot pot in a 325°F (160°C) oven for 2 hours or until the meat and vegetables are tender.

4 Remove the casserole lid, increase the oven temperature to 425°F (220°C), and cook for 20–30 minutes to brown the potato. Sprinkle with the chopped parsley before serving.

COUNTRY HOT POT

Omit the kidneys and substitute ½ large peeled rutabaga for half of the carrots. Layer the meat and vegetables and add ⅓ cup (60 g) pearl barley. Proceed as directed.

LAMB NOISETTES WITH ORANGE & HONEY

 Serves 4

8 lamb noisettes

2 lamb kidneys, trimmed (page 214) and quartered (optional)

chopped fresh thyme and rosemary to garnish

MARINADE

grated zest and juice of 1 orange

¼ cup (60 g) honey

3 tbsp olive oil

2 garlic cloves, crushed

1 tbsp chopped fresh thyme

1 tbsp chopped fresh rosemary

salt and black pepper

1 Make the marinade: in a shallow, nonmetallic dish, combine the orange zest and juice, honey, oil, garlic, thyme, rosemary, and salt and pepper to taste. Add the lamb noisettes to the marinade, turn them, then cover and leave to marinate in the refrigerator overnight.

2 Lift the lamb noisettes out of the marinade, reserving the marinade. Place a piece of kidney, if using, in the middle of each lamb noisette.

3 Put under the broiler, 4 in (10 cm) from the heat, and cook for 7 minutes on each side, until the lamb is tender.

4 Meanwhile, strain the marinade into a small saucepan, bring to a boil, and simmer for a few minutes, until it reaches a syrupy consistency. Taste for seasoning, spoon over the lamb noisettes, and garnish with thyme and rosemary.

Lamb noisettes

These are taken from the loin. The eye of meat is cut away, then rolled, tied, and cut into thick slices. It is an expensive cut but gives neat portions of tender, lean meat.

IRISH STEW

 Serves 4

4 large baking potatoes, cut into 1/4-in (5-mm) slices

2 large onions, sliced

2 lb (1 kg) shoulder lamb chops, trimmed

a few parsley stalks

1 thyme sprig

1 bay leaf

salt and black pepper

1 1/4–2 cups (300–500 ml) water

chopped parsley to garnish

1 Put half of the potatoes into a flameproof casserole, cover with half of the onions, then add the chops, parsley, thyme, bay leaf, and salt and pepper to taste. Add the remaining onions, then the remaining potatoes, seasoning each layer with salt and pepper.

2 Pour in enough water to half-fill the casserole and then bring to a boil. Cover the casserole tightly with the lid and cook in a 325°F (160°C) oven for 2–2 1/2 hours until the lamb and potatoes are just tender.

3 Remove the lid, increase the oven temperature to 425°F (220°C) and cook for 20–30 minutes to brown the topping. Sprinkle with parsley before serving.

CURRIED LAMB WITH ALMONDS

In this rich and aromatic lamb dish, the lamb is marinated in creamy yogurt and spicy garam masala, flavored with ground almonds, and garnished with mint and paprika. For an authentic accompaniment, serve with spiced red lentils.

 Serves 6–8

1/2 cup (125 g) plain yogurt

1 tsp garam masala

3 lb (1.5 kg) lamb stew meat, trimmed and cut into chunks

6 tbsp (90 ml) sunflower oil

4 onions, sliced

2-in (5-cm) piece of fresh ginger, peeled and chopped

4–5 garlic cloves, crushed

1/2 tsp sugar

salt and black pepper

1 1/4 cups (300 ml) lamb stock or water

1/4 cup (30 g) ground almonds

4 bay leaves

1 cardamom pod, crushed

1 cup (250 ml) heavy cream

juice of 1/4 lemon

1/2 tsp ground coriander

1/4 tsp ground cinnamon

1/4 tsp cayenne pepper

chopped fresh mint and paprika to garnish

1 In a large bowl, combine the yogurt and garam masala. Add the meat, and turn to coat in the yogurt. Cover and leave to marinate in the refrigerator for 3–4 hours.

2 Heat the oil in a large flameproof casserole, add the onions, ginger, garlic, sugar, and 1/2 tsp salt, and cook very gently, stirring occasionally, for about 10 minutes, until the onions are soft and golden brown.

3 Add the stock, almonds, bay leaves, and cardamom and bring to a boil, stirring constantly.

4 Remove the meat from the marinade. Add to the casserole and stir to coat evenly with the sauce. Cover the casserole tightly with the lid and cook in a 325°F (160°C) oven for 2 hours or until the meat is tender.

5 Lift the meat out of the casserole and keep warm. Skim any fat from the juices in the casserole. If the cooking juices are too liquid, boil until reduced to a thick consistency. Stir in the cream, lemon juice, coriander, cinnamon, cayenne pepper, and salt and pepper to taste, and heat through.

6 Return the meat to the casserole and heat through. Garnish with mint and paprika before serving.

Garam masala

Garam masala is an Indian blend of spices usually sold already mixed. The spices vary according to individual brands, but usually include cumin, coriander, cardamom, cinnamon, cloves, mace, bay leaves, and pepper.

BLANQUETTE OF LAMB

 **Serves 4–6**

2 lb (1 kg) boneless shoulder
of lamb, trimmed and cut
into chunks

5 cups (1.25 liters) water

8 pearl onions

2 large carrots, thickly sliced

2 bay leaves

juice of 1/2 lemon

salt and black pepper

1/2 lb (250 g) small mushrooms

3 tbsp butter

1/3 cup (45 g) all-purpose flour

2/3 cup (150 ml) light cream

1 egg yolk

chopped parsley to garnish

1 Put the chunks of lamb
into a large saucepan,
cover with cold water, and
bring to a boil. Strain and
rinse the meat thoroughly
to remove the foam.

2 Return the meat to the
saucepan and pour in
the measured water. Add the
pearl onions, carrots, bay
leaves, lemon juice, and salt
and pepper to taste. Bring to
a boil, cover, and simmer
gently for 1 hour.

3 Add the mushrooms and
simmer for 30 minutes.
Lift out the lamb and
vegetables, reserving the
liquid, and keep warm.

4 Melt the butter in a small
pan. Add the flour and
cook, stirring occasionally,
for 1 minute. Gradually
blend in the reserved
cooking liquid, stirring
constantly. Bring to a boil,
stirring, then simmer until
the sauce thickens.

5 In a bowl, whisk together
the cream and egg yolk.
Blend in 2 tbsp of the hot
sauce. Take the saucepan
off the heat, stir the cream
mixture into the sauce, then
reheat very gently. Taste for
seasoning. Pour the sauce
over the lamb and garnish
with parsley before serving.

LAMB & TOMATO CASSEROLE

*Substitute 13 oz (400 g) canned
chopped tomatoes and 1 1/4 cups
(300 ml) dry white wine for the
water. Cook the lamb as directed,
but do not make the white sauce.*

AROMATIC LAMB WITH LENTILS

 Serves 6–8

3 lb (1.5 kg) boneless shoulder
of lamb, trimmed and cut into
chunks

2 tbsp olive oil

2 onions, chopped

2/3 cup (125 g) brown lentils,
rinsed

2/3 cup (175 g) dried apricots

salt and black pepper

2 1/3 cups (600 ml) lamb or
chicken stock

MARINADE

3/4 cup (175 ml) orange juice

2 tbsp olive oil

3 garlic cloves, crushed

1 tsp ground ginger

1 tsp ground coriander

1/2 tsp ground cinnamon

1 Make the marinade: in
a large bowl, combine
the orange juice, olive oil,
garlic, ginger, coriander,
and cinnamon.

2 Turn the chunks of lamb
in the marinade, cover
loosely, and then leave to
marinate in the refrigerator
overnight.

3 Remove the lamb from
the marinade, reserving
the marinade. Heat the olive
oil in a large flameproof
casserole, add the lamb in
batches, and cook over high
heat for 5 minutes or until
browned all over. Lift out
the lamb chunks with a
slotted spoon.

4 Lower the heat slightly,
add the onions, and cook
gently, stirring occasionally,
for a few minutes, until just
soft but not browned. Lift
out of the casserole.

5 Make layers of lamb,
onions, lentils, and
apricots in the casserole,
seasoning each layer with
salt and pepper to taste.
Pour in the stock and
reserved marinade and bring
to a boil. Cover and cook in
a 325°F (160°C) oven for
2 hours or until the meat is
tender. Taste for seasoning
and serve immediately.

LAMB TAGINE

 Serves 6–8

1/4 tsp saffron threads

2/3 cup (150 ml) hot water

3 tbsp olive oil

3 lb (1.5 kg) boneless shoulder of lamb, trimmed and cut into 1-in (2.5-cm) cubes

1 fennel bulb, trimmed and sliced crosswise

2 green peppers, cored, seeded, and cut into strips

1 large onion, sliced

1/4 cup (30 g) all-purpose flour

1/2 tsp ground ginger

1 3/4 cups (450 ml) lamb stock or water

grated zest and juice of 1 orange

1/2 cup (125 g) dried apricots

salt and black pepper

mint sprigs to garnish

1 Prepare the saffron (see box, right). Heat the oil in a flameproof casserole, add the lamb in batches and cook over high heat for 5 minutes or until browned. Lift out and drain on paper towels.

2 Lower the heat, add the fennel, peppers, and onion, and cook gently, stirring, for 5 minutes.

3 Add the flour and ground ginger to the vegetables and cook, stirring occasionally, for about 1 minute. Add the saffron liquid to the casserole, return the cubes of lamb, then add the stock, orange zest, and salt and black pepper to taste. Bring to a boil, cover with the lid, and cook the casserole in a 325°F (160°C) oven for 1 hour.

4 Add the orange juice and apricots and cook for about 30 minutes, until the lamb is very tender. Taste for seasoning and garnish with mint sprigs before serving.

Preparing saffron

Put the saffron threads into a small bowl, add the measured hot water, and soak for 10 minutes.

SPICED LAMB WITH COCONUT

 Serves 4–6

2 lb (1 kg) boneless shoulder of lamb, trimmed and cut into 1-in (2.5-cm) cubes

2 tbsp butter

1 tbsp sunflower or corn oil

1 large Spanish onion, sliced

2 large garlic cloves, crushed

1 tbsp all-purpose flour

13 oz (400 g) canned chopped tomatoes

2/3 cup (150 ml) lamb stock or water

grated zest and juice of 1 lime

2 tbsp mango chutney

1/4 cup (60 ml) coconut milk

1 cup (250 g) plain yogurt

cilantro sprigs to garnish

DRY MARINADE

1-in (2.5-cm) piece of fresh ginger, peeled and grated

1 tbsp ground cumin

1 tbsp ground coriander

1 tbsp mild curry powder

1 tsp turmeric

salt and black pepper

1 Make the dry marinade: combine the ginger, cumin, coriander, curry powder, turmeric, and salt and pepper to taste.

2 Toss the lamb in the marinade, cover, and leave to marinate in the refrigerator overnight.

3 Melt the butter with the oil in a large flameproof casserole. When the butter is foaming, add the lamb in batches and cook over high heat for about 5 minutes, until browned all over.

4 Lift out with a slotted spoon and set aside. Lower the heat, add the onion and garlic, and cook gently, stirring occasionally, for a few minutes, until soft but not browned.

5 Add the flour and cook, stirring, for 1 minute. Add the tomatoes, stock, lime zest and juice, chutney, and salt and pepper to taste. Bring to a boil, stirring.

6 Return the lamb to the casserole, add the coconut milk, and bring back to a boil. Cover and cook in a 325°F (160°C) oven for 1 hour or until tender and cooked through.

7 Stir in the yogurt and taste for seasoning. Garnish with cilantro sprigs before serving.

SHEPHERD'S PIE

 Serves 4

1½ lb (750 g) ground lamb

1½ cups (125 g) sliced mushrooms

2 carrots, diced

1 large onion, chopped

1 garlic clove, crushed

¼ cup (30 g) all-purpose flour

1¼ cups (300 ml) lamb stock or water

1 tbsp Worcestershire sauce

salt and black pepper

3 large potatoes

about ¼ cup (60 ml) hot milk

2 tbsp butter

1 Put the ground lamb into a large skillet and heat gently until the fat runs. Increase the heat and cook, turning and mashing the lamb, until it browns. Using a slotted spoon, lift the lamb out of the pan and spoon off the excess fat.

2 Add the mushrooms, carrots, onion, and garlic to the pan and cook gently, stirring occasionally, for a few minutes, until just beginning to soften.

3 Return the lamb to the skillet. Add the flour and cook, stirring, for 1 minute.

4 Add the stock, Worcestershire sauce, and salt and pepper to taste and bring to a boil. Cover and simmer very gently for 30 minutes.

5 Meanwhile, cook the potatoes in boiling salted water for 15–20 minutes, until tender. Drain. Add the milk and butter to the potatoes and mash until soft, adding salt and pepper to taste.

6 Taste the lamb mixture for seasoning. Transfer the mixture to an ovenproof dish, then spread the mashed potato on top. With a fork, score the potato in a decorative pattern. Cook in a 400°F (200°C) oven for about 20 minutes until the potato topping is golden and the lamb mixture bubbling.

MONDAY LAMB PIE

Substitute 1½ lb (750 g) cooked leftover lamb, finely chopped, for the ground lamb. Cook the mushrooms, carrots, onions, and garlic as directed and add the cooked lamb after 15 minutes. Proceed as directed.

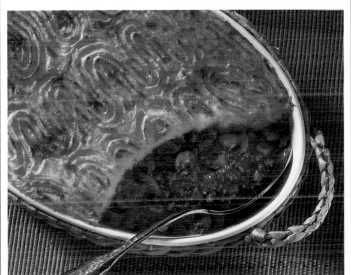

MOUSSAKA

 Serves 6–8

2 large eggplant, sliced

1½ lb (750 g) ground lamb

3 medium-large onions, chopped

3 garlic cloves, crushed

⅓ cup (45 g) all-purpose flour

2 cups (500 ml) strained tomatoes

⅔ cup (150 ml) red wine

2 tbsp tomato paste

2 tsp dried oregano

olive oil for brushing

salt and black pepper

chopped parsley to garnish

CHEESE SAUCE

3 tbsp butter

⅓ cup (45 g) all-purpose flour

1¾ cups (450 ml) milk

1 cup (125 g) grated Gruyère cheese

1½ tsp Dijon mustard

pinch of grated nutmeg

1 large egg, beaten

1 Put the eggplant slices into a colander, sprinkle generously with salt, and leave to stand for 30 minutes.

2 Put the ground lamb into a skillet and heat gently to render the fat. Increase the heat and cook, stirring, until browned. Spoon off the excess fat.

3 Add the onions and garlic and cook until softened. Add the flour and cook, stirring, for 1 minute. Add the tomatoes, wine, tomato paste, oregano, and salt and pepper to taste and bring to a boil. Cover and simmer for 20 minutes.

4 Rinse the eggplant slices and pat dry. Place on a broiler rack and brush with oil. Cook under the broiler, 4 in (10 cm) from the heat, for 5–6 minutes, until golden on both sides.

5 Make the cheese sauce: melt the butter in a pan, add the flour, and cook, stirring, for 1 minute. Remove from the heat and gradually blend in the milk. Bring to a boil, stirring constantly until thick. Simmer for 2–3 minutes. Add the cheese, mustard, nutmeg, and salt and pepper to taste. Leave to cool slightly, then stir in the egg.

6 Spoon half of the lamb mixture into a shallow ovenproof dish and top with half of the eggplant slices. Repeat with the remaining lamb and eggplant, then pour the cheese sauce over. Cook in a 350°F (180°C) oven for 45 minutes or until golden brown and bubbling.

KIDNEYS TURBIGO

 Serves 4

6 lamb kidneys

4 tbsp butter

1/2 lb (250 g) chipolata sausage

12 pearl onions, peeled, with a little of the roots attached to hold the onions together

1/2 lb (250 g) mushrooms

1 tbsp all-purpose flour

1 1/4 cups (300 ml) lamb stock

1 tbsp medium sherry

2 tsp tomato paste

1 bay leaf

salt and black pepper

2 tbsp chopped parsley to garnish

croutes (page 31) to serve

1 Prepare the kidneys (page 214).

2 Melt the butter in a large skillet, add the kidneys, and cook, stirring, over high heat for about 3 minutes, until browned. Lift out and drain on paper towels. Add the sausage and cook for 3 minutes or until browned. Lift out and drain on paper towels.

3 Add the onions and mushrooms to the pan and cook for 3–5 minutes, until browned.

4 Add the flour and cook, stirring, for 1 minute. Add the stock, sherry, and tomato paste, and bring to a boil, stirring constantly. Add the bay leaf and salt and pepper to taste.

5 Slice the sausage thickly and return to the pan with the kidneys. Cover and simmer gently for 20–25 minutes, until tender.

6 Spoon the kidney mixture onto a warmed platter, garnish with the chopped parsley, and serve with croutes.

Kidneys Turbigo

This classic French dish is named after the town of Turbigo in Lombardy, the site of two French victories over the Austrians in the 19th century.

SAUSAGES WITH POTATOES & PEPPERS

 Serves 4

3 large potatoes, unpeeled

salt and black pepper

1 red pepper

1 green pepper

1/2 lb (250 g) merguez sausage, cut into bite-sized pieces, or other sausage

3 garlic cloves, crushed

1/2 tsp ground cumin

1–2 tbsp olive oil, more if needed

chopped fresh cilantro to garnish

1 Put the potatoes into a large saucepan of boiling salted water and cook for 10 minutes. Drain the potatoes and leave to cool.

2 Put the peppers under the broiler, 4 in (10 cm) from the heat, and broil, turning as needed, for 10–12 minutes until charred and blistered. Put the peppers into a plastic bag, seal, and leave to cool.

3 Peel the peppers, rinse under running water, and pat dry. Core and seed the peppers and slice the flesh lengthwise into strips.

4 Cut the potatoes into wedges and put into a casserole with the peppers and merguez. Stir in the garlic, cumin, salt and pepper to taste, and the oil. Cook in a 375°F (190°C) ßoven, turning occasionally, for 45 minutes or until the potatoes are tender and the sausage is cooked through, adding a little more oil to the casserole if the potatoes look dry.

5 Remove the casserole from the oven and spoon off any excess fat. Garnish with cilantro before serving.

FRANKFURTERS WITH POTATOES & PEPPERS

Substitute 1/2 lb (250 g) frankfurters, cut into bite-sized pieces, for the merguez sausage and proceed as directed.

BONED LOIN OF PORK WITH APRICOT STUFFING

Succulent boned loin of pork, with an apricot stuffing flavored with lemon juice and lemon thyme, is served here with a white wine gravy. The crackling (the skin, if available) is cooked separately, in the top half of the oven, to ensure that it is deliciously crisp.

 Serves 6–8

3 lb (1.5 kg) boned loin of pork

sunflower oil for brushing

APRICOT STUFFING

2 tbsp butter

1 small onion, finely chopped

1¹/₂ cups (90 g) fresh pumpernickel bread crumbs

¹/₃ cup (90 g) coarsely chopped dried apricots

1 tbsp chopped parsley

1 tbsp lemon juice

? tsp chopped fresh lemon thyme

1 egg, beaten

salt and black pepper

GRAVY

1 tbsp all-purpose flour

²/₃ cup (150 ml) chicken stock

²/₃ cup (150 ml) dry white wine

1 Make the apricot stuffing: melt the butter in a small saucepan, add the onion, and cook gently, stirring occasionally, for a few minutes, until just soft but not browned.

2 Remove the pan from the heat and stir in the bread crumbs, apricots, parsley, lemon juice, lemon thyme, egg, and salt and black pepper to taste. Leave the stuffing to cool completely.

3 With the point of a small knife, score the pork skin in long strokes, about ¹/₂ in (1 cm) apart. Cut the skin off the meat, brush with a little oil, and sprinkle generously with salt and pepper. Place the skin on a rack in a small roasting pan.

4 Stuff and roll the pork (see box, right).

5 Place the pork skin in the top of a 350°F (180°C) oven. Put the pork loin into another roasting pan. Brush with oil and season generously. Insert a meat thermometer, if using, into the middle of the loin, and cook the pork in the oven for about 2 hours or until the meat thermometer registers 190°F (90°C).

6 Transfer the pork to a carving board, cover loosely with a sheet of foil, and leave to stand for 10 minutes. If the crackling is not really crisp, increase the oven temperature to 400°F (200°C) and let it continue to cook while making the gravy.

7 Put the roasting pan on top of the stove and spoon off all but 1 tbsp of the fat. Add the flour, and cook, stirring to dissolve any drippings from the bottom of the pan, for 1 minute. Pour in the stock and wine and bring to a boil, stirring constantly. Simmer for 3 minutes. Season to taste and strain into a warmed gravy boat. Serve with the pork.

Stuffing and rolling a loin of pork

Open out the loin of pork and spread the stuffing over the meat.

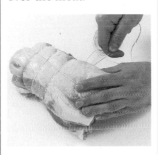

Roll the pork around the stuffing and tie at intervals with fine string.

SAUCES FOR PORK

APRICOT SAUCE

Melt *2 tbsp butter* and cook *1 thinly sliced small onion* until soft. Add *¹/₂ cup (125 g) halved dried apricots*, *²/₃ cup (150 ml) chicken stock*, *²/₃ cup (150 ml) dry white wine*, *¹/₄ tsp ground cinnamon*, and *salt and black pepper to taste*. Simmer for about 20 minutes.

APPLE SAUCE

Peel, core, and slice *2 large cooking apples* and put into a saucepan with the *grated zest of 1 lemon* and *2–3 tbsp water*. Cover the pan tightly and cook gently for about 10 minutes, until soft. Stir in *2 tbsp sugar*. Beat the sauce until smooth or push through a nylon strainer. Stir in *1 tbsp butter*.

SWEET & SOUR SAUCE

Finely slice *1 onion, 1 leek, and 2 celery stalks*. Cut *2 carrots* into matchsticks. Heat *2 tbsp oil* in a pan and cook the vegetables for 3 minutes or until softened. Blend *2 tbsp ketchup, 1 tbsp soy sauce, 1 tbsp white vinegar, 4 tsp cornstarch, and 2 tsp superfine sugar*, then blend in *1¹/₄ cups (300 ml) water*. Add this mixture to the pan and bring to a boil, stirring until thickened.

MARINATED LOIN OF PORK WITH PINEAPPLE

 Serves 6–8

3 lb (1.5 kg) boneless loin of pork

broiled pineapple rings to serve

MARINADE

1 cup (250 ml) pineapple juice

2 tbsp maple syrup

2 tbsp soy sauce

2 garlic cloves, crushed

2 tbsp chopped fresh thyme

1 tsp ground coriander

1 Make the marinade: in a large nonmetallic bowl, combine the pineapple juice, maple syrup, soy sauce, garlic, thyme, and coriander. Add the pork, cover, and leave to marinate in the refrigerator, turning occasionally, for 8 hours.

2 Remove the pork from the marinade, reserving the marinade. Put the pork flat, fat side up, in a small roasting pan. Insert a meat thermometer, if using, into the middle of the pork. Cover loosely with a sheet of foil and cook in a 425°F (220°C) oven for 1 hour.

3 Remove the foil and pour the marinade over the pork. Return to the oven and cook for 20–30 minutes or until the marinade has darkened and the meat juices run clear when tested with a thin skewer. The meat thermometer should register 190°F (90°C).

4 Transfer the pork to a carving board, cover loosely with foil, and leave to stand for 10 minutes. Strain the marinade and remove the fat (see box, below). Gently heat the marinade to warm through. Serve the pork with the marinade and broiled pineapple rings.

Removing the fat

Skim the layer of fat from the surface of the marinade, using a spoon.

ROAST LEG OF PORK

 Serves 6

4 lb (2 kg) fresh ham (leg of pork)

sunflower or corn oil for brushing

salt and black pepper

1 carrot, thickly sliced

1 onion, thickly sliced

1 tbsp all-purpose flour

1 1/4 cups (300 ml) chicken stock

apple sauce to serve (page 259)

1 With the point of a small knife, score the pork skin in long strokes, about 1/2 in (1 cm) apart. Cut the skin off the meat, brush with a little oil, and sprinkle generously with salt and black pepper. Place on a rack in a small roasting pan.

2 Place the pork skin in the top of a 350°F (180°C) oven.

3 Put the pork into a large roasting pan and add the carrot and onion. Brush the meat with oil and season. Insert a meat thermometer, if using, into the middle of the pork and cook in the oven for 2 1/2 hours or until the thermometer registers 190°F (90°C).

4 Transfer the pork to a carving board, cover loosely with a sheet of foil, and leave to stand for 10 minutes. If the skin is not really crisp, increase the oven temperature to 400°F (200°C) and let the skin continue to cook while making the gravy.

5 Put the roasting pan on top of the stove. Remove and discard the carrot and onion and spoon off all but 1 tbsp of the fat from the pan.

6 Add the flour and cook, stirring to dissolve any drippings from the bottom of the pan, for 1 minute. Add the stock and bring to a boil. Simmer for 3 minutes, then season, and strain into a gravy boat. Serve the pork with the gravy and apple sauce.

Cook's know-how

The high oven temperature needed for crisp crackling can make meat tough and dry. Removing the skin and cooking it separately, above the pork, avoids this problem.

MADEIRA PORK WITH PAPRIKA

 Serves 4

2 tbsp butter

3 tbsp sunflower or corn oil

1½ lb (750 g) pork tenderloin, trimmed and cut diagonally into ½-in (1-cm) slices

1 onion, chopped

1 large red pepper, cored, seeded, and cut into strips

1 tbsp paprika

1 tbsp all purpose flour

1¼ cups (300 ml) chicken stock

5 tbsp (75 ml) Madeira

2½ cups (175 g) mushrooms

1 tsp tomato paste

⅔ cup (150 ml) light cream

salt and black pepper

1 Melt the butter with the oil in a large skillet. When the butter is foaming, add the pork tenderloin slices, in batches if necessary, and cook over high heat for about 3 minutes, until just beginning to brown. Lift out with a slotted spoon and drain on paper towels.

2 Add the onion and red pepper and cook, stirring, for 2 minutes. Add the paprika and flour and cook, stirring, for 1 minute. Remove the pan from the heat and blend in the stock. Return to the heat and add the Madeira, mushrooms, and tomato paste. Simmer for 2–3 minutes.

3 Return the pork to the pan and season to taste. Cover and simmer very gently for 20 minutes or until the pork is tender and cooked through.

4 Stir the cream into the pork mixture, taste for seasoning, and heat through gently. Serve hot.

Cook's know-how

Madeira is a fortified wine from the Portuguese island of the same name. Ruby port can be used as a substitute if preferred.

BACON-WRAPPED PORK IN VERMOUTH SAUCE

 Serves 6

2 pork tenderloins, about ¾ lb (375 g) each, trimmed

2 tbsp Dijon mustard

salt and black pepper

12 thick slices of bacon

VERMOUTH SAUCE

2 tbsp butter

1 tbsp olive oil

1 shallot, finely chopped

1 tbsp all-purpose flour

¾ cup plus 1 tbsp (200 ml) chicken stock

6 tbsp (90 ml) dry vermouth

1½ cups (125 g) sliced mushrooms

1 Spread the pork tenderloins with the mustard and season with salt and pepper. Stretch the bacon slices with the back of a knife and wrap around the tenderloins (see box, right).

2 Place the fillets in a roasting pan and cook in a 425°F (220°C) oven, turning the tenderloins halfway through cooking, for 30–35 minutes, until the pork juices run clear when tested with a thin skewer and the bacon slices are crisp.

3 Meanwhile, make the sauce: melt the butter with the oil in a small pan. When the butter is foaming, add the shallot, and cook gently, until softened.

4 Add the flour and cook, stirring, for 1 minute. Gradually blend in the stock and vermouth. Bring to a boil, add the mushrooms, and simmer for 15 minutes.

5 Transfer the pork to a warmed platter. Spoon off the fat from the roasting pan and strain the juices into the sauce. Heat through and taste for seasoning. Serve with the pork.

Wrapping tenderloins

Overlap half of the bacon slices on a work surface. Lay 1 tenderloin across the bacon and braid the slices around the meat. Secure with a thin skewer. Repeat with the second tenderloin.

PORK WITH CHILI & COCONUT

 Serves 4

1½ lb (750 g) pork tenderloin, trimmed and cut into ¼-in (5-mm) strips

2 tbsp sunflower or corn oil

8 scallions, cut into 1-in (2.5-cm) pieces

1 large red pepper, cored, seeded, and cut into thin strips

13 oz (400 g) canned chopped tomatoes

¼ cup coconut milk

2 tbsp chopped fresh cilantro

1 tbsp lemon juice

salt and black pepper

cilantro sprigs to garnish

DRY MARINADE

1-in (2.5-cm) piece of fresh ginger, peeled and grated

2 fresh red chilies, cored, seeded, and finely chopped

1 garlic clove, crushed

1 tbsp mild curry powder

¼ tsp ground turmeric

¼ tsp garam masala

1 Make the dry marinade: in a bowl, combine the ginger, chilies, garlic, curry powder, turmeric, garam masala, and salt and pepper to taste. Turn the pork in the marinade, cover, and leave to marinate in the refrigerator for 2 hours.

2 Heat a wok or large skillet, add the oil, and heat until hot. Add the strips of pork in batches and stir-fry over high heat for 5 minutes or until browned all over.

3 Add the scallions and stir-fry for 1 minute. Add the red pepper and stir-fry for 1 minute, then add the tomatoes and coconut milk. Bring to a boil, cover, and simmer very gently for 15 minutes or until the pork is tender.

4 Add the chopped cilantro, lemon juice, and salt and pepper to taste. Garnish with the cilantro sprigs before serving.

BROILED PORK CHOPS WITH MANGO SAUCE

 Serves 4

4 pork loin chops, on the bone

sunflower or corn oil for brushing

salt and black pepper

1 ripe mango

flat-leaf parsley to garnish

MANGO SAUCE

1 ripe mango

⅔ cup (150 ml) chicken stock

1 tbsp mango chutney

1 Prepare the pork chops (see box, right). Brush the chops on each side with oil and sprinkle with black pepper. Put under the broiler, 4 in (10 cm) from the heat, and broil for 8–10 minutes on each side, until cooked through.

2 Meanwhile, make the mango sauce: peel, pit, and cube the mango (page 430). Puree in a food processor until smooth. Put into a small saucepan with the stock, mango chutney, and salt and pepper to taste. Bring to a boil and simmer for about 3 minutes, until heated through. Taste for seasoning.

Preparing a pork chop

Cut the fat along the outside of the chop at regular intervals. This will prevent it from curling up while under the broiler.

3 Peel the remaining mango and cut it into 2 pieces lengthwise, slightly off-center to miss the pit. Cut the flesh from around the pit. Slice the flesh into thin strips.

4 Arrange the mango strips on the chops, garnish with the flat-leaf parsley, and serve with the mango sauce.

SPINACH-STUFFED PORK CHOPS

Tender pork loin chops, with a stuffing of finely chopped spinach, Parmesan cheese, cream, bacon, and herbs, are cooked in dry white wine and topped with melted Gruyère cheese. A hearty main course for a cold winter's day.

 Serves 4

4 pork loin chops

1½ cups (350 ml) dry white wine

6 oz (175 g) Gruyère cheese, thinly sliced

salt and black pepper

SPINACH STUFFING

1 lb (500 g) spinach

⅞ cup (60 g) herbed stuffing mix

2 thick slices of bacon, finely chopped

⅔ cup (60 g) Parmesan cheese, freshly grated

1 egg, beaten

2 garlic cloves, crushed

2 tbsp heavy cream

1 tbsp chopped parsley

2 tsp chopped fresh rosemary

1 Make the stuffing: wash and trim the spinach, put it into a pan with only the water that clings to the leaves, and cook over low heat until it has just wilted.

2 Drain the spinach, reserving the cooking liquid, then chop finely. In a bowl, mix the spinach with the cooking liquid, stuffing mix, bacon, Parmesan cheese, egg, garlic, cream, parsley, and rosemary. Add a little of the wine, if needed, to make the stuffing moist.

3 Cut and stuff the chops (see box, right). Put into an ovenproof casserole just large enough to hold the chops, and pour in the wine. Cover the casserole and cook in a 325°F (160°C) oven for 50 minutes or until the pork is cooked through.

4 Remove the casserole from the oven and increase the temperature to 425°F (220°C).

5 If the sauce is too liquid, pour it into a small pan and boil it until it has thickened and reduced to a saucelike consistency.

6 Put the cheese slices on top of the chops, pour the sauce around them, and return to the oven. Cook for 10–15 minutes, until the cheese has melted. Serve hot.

Cutting and stuffing the pork chops

Cut into each chop horizontally with a sharp knife, cutting through to the bone to make a pocket. Sprinkle each chop inside and out with salt and pepper.

Spoon the spinach stuffing into the pockets in the chops. If there is any extra stuffing, put it into a small dish and cook it in the oven at the same time as the chops.

PORK CHOPS WITH ORANGES

 Serves 6

6 boneless pork loin chops

3 tbsp coarse mustard

⅔ cup (125 g) light brown sugar

3 small oranges

6 tbsp (90 ml) orange juice

salt and black pepper

1 Spread both sides of each pork chop with the mustard, and sprinkle one side with half of the brown sugar. Arrange the chops, sugared side down, in a single layer in a shallow ovenproof dish.

2 With a sharp knife, carefully peel the oranges, removing all the pith. Cut the oranges into thin slices.

3 Cover the chops with the orange slices. Pour the orange juice over the top, add salt and pepper to taste, and sprinkle with the remaining sugar.

4 Cook, uncovered, in a 400°F (200°C) oven for about 35 minutes, basting the chops occasionally, until tender and cooked through.

PORK STEAKS WITH MIXED PEPPERCORNS

 Serves 4

4 lean boneless pork steaks

salt

3–4 tbsp mixed peppercorns

2 tbsp butter

1 1/2 cups (350 ml) dry white wine

1 1/2 cups (350 ml) beef stock

3/4 cup (175 ml) heavy cream

1 Season the steaks on each side with salt. Coarsely crush the peppercorns and spread them on a plate. Press the steaks onto the peppercorns to encrust the surface of the meat on both sides. Cover and set aside for 30 minutes.

2 Melt the butter in a large skillet, add the steaks, and cook for 5–7 minutes on each side, until the meat is just cooked through but still juicy. Lift the steaks out of the pan and keep warm.

3 Pour the wine into the pan and boil until it has reduced by half, stirring to mix in the peppercorns and the drippings from the bottom of the pan.

4 Pour in the stock and cook for 5 minutes. Strain the sauce to remove the peppercorns, then return to the pan and boil for 3 minutes or until the sauce is reduced but not too thick.

5 Add the cream and cook, stirring, over high heat until the sauce is reduced and thickened. Return the pork steaks to the pan, heat through, and serve immediately.

CRISPY PORK STEAKS WITH APPLE

Dip the pork steaks into beaten egg and then into bread crumbs. Proceed as directed. Meanwhile, peel, core, and slice 2 sweet apples. Wipe the pan and add 1 tbsp butter. Add the apple slices and cook until golden. Serve with the chops.

SWEET & SOUR CHINESE SPARERIBS

 Serves 4

2 1/2 lb (1.25 kg) pork spareribs

salt and black pepper

scallion tassels to garnish

SWEET & SOUR SAUCE

1-in (2.5-cm) piece of fresh ginger, peeled and grated

2 garlic cloves, crushed

2 tbsp soy sauce

2 tbsp dry sherry

2 tbsp hoisin sauce

2 tbsp tomato paste

1 tbsp sesame oil

1 tbsp sugar

1 Arrange the spareribs in 1 layer in a roasting pan, season with salt and pepper, and cook in a 275°F (140°C) oven for 1 1/2 hours.

2 Make the sauce: combine the ginger, garlic, soy sauce, sherry, hoisin sauce, tomato paste, sesame oil, and sugar.

3 Spoon the sweet and sour sauce over the spareribs, turning them to coat evenly. Increase the oven temperature to 350°F (180°C) and cook for 25–30 minutes. Garnish with the scallion tassels before serving.

Cook's know-how

Sweet and sour spareribs are excellent for a barbecue. Cook them in the oven and coat with the sweet and sour sauce, then cook over hot charcoal for 15 minutes on each side.

SPICY SPARERIBS

Mix together the ginger, garlic, soy sauce, dry sherry, and sesame oil as directed. Add 1 tbsp brown sugar, 1/2 tsp grated nutmeg, 1/4 tsp ground cloves, and 1/4 tsp ground cinnamon. Cook the spareribs as directed.

PORK IN RED WINE

Serves 4

1¹/₂ lb (750 g) pork blade, cut into 1¹/₂-in (3.5 cm) cubes

6 tbsp (90 ml) olive oil

1 large onion, chopped

3 garlic cloves, crushed

1 cup (250 ml) beef stock

1 cup (250 ml) red wine

¹/₂ tsp cumin seeds

MARINADE

1 cup (250 ml) red wine

2 tbsp crushed coriander

¹/₂ tsp ground cinnamon

salt and black pepper

1 Make the marinade: in a large bowl, combine the red wine, crushed coriander, ground cinnamon, and salt and pepper to taste. Toss the pork cubes in the marinade, cover, and leave to marinate in the refrigerator overnight.

2 Remove the pork from the marinade, reserving the marinade. Pat the pork dry with paper towels.

3 Heat the oil in a large skillet, add the onion and garlic, and cook gently, stirring occasionally, for a few minutes until soft but not browned.

4 Add the pork and cook over medium to high heat for 5 minutes or until golden brown all over. Discard any excess fat. Pour in the reserved marinade, the stock, and wine and bring to a boil. Simmer for 1 hour or until the meat is tender.

5 Remove the meat with a slotted spoon and transfer to a shallow ovenproof dish into which it just fits in 1 layer. Skim any fat from the sauce, then strain into a small pitcher to remove the crushed coriander. Pour the sauce over the meat, sprinkle with cumin seeds and salt, and cook in a 400°F (200°C) oven for 40 minutes or until the top is crisp and browned.

Cook's know-how

This stew, in which the pork is marinated and then cooked in red wine, is a specialty of Cyprus, where it is called afelia. Crushed coriander is the classic seasoning, and in this recipe the cumin seeds add interest. Afelia can be marinated and cooked ahead of time, frozen, then thawed and reheated.

HEARTY PORK CASSEROLE

 Serves 6–8

2 tbsp sunflower or corn oil

3 lb (1.5 kg) shoulder of pork, trimmed and cut into 1¹/₂-in (3.5-cm) cubes

¹/₂ cup (60 g) all-purpose flour

1³/₄ cups (450 ml) chicken stock

4 tbsp white vinegar

3 tbsp honey

2 tbsp soy sauce

¹/₂ lb (250 g) large mushrooms, quartered

¹/₂ lb (250 g) pitted prunes

salt and black pepper

chopped parsley to garnish

1 Heat the oil in a large flameproof casserole. Add the pork in batches and cook over medium to high heat for 5 minutes or until golden brown all over.

2 Return all of the meat to the casserole, sprinkle in the flour, and cook, stirring, for 1 minute.

3 Stir in the chicken stock, white vinegar, honey, soy sauce, and salt and pepper to taste and bring to a boil. Cover the casserole with the lid and cook in a 325°F (160°C) oven for 2 hours.

4 Stir the mushrooms and prunes into the casserole and cook for 1 hour or until the pork is tender and cooked through. Taste for seasoning and garnish with the chopped parsley before serving.

BOSTON PORK & BEAN CASSEROLE

Add 2 tbsp tomato paste with the stock and substitute 13 oz (400 g) canned great northern beans for the mushrooms and prunes. Proceed as directed.

DANISH MEATBALLS

 Serves 4

1 lb (500 g) ground pork

1 small onion, very finely chopped

¼ cup (30 g) all-purpose flour, plus extra for coating

1 tsp chopped fresh thyme

¼ tsp paprika

salt and black pepper

1 egg, beaten

a little milk

2 tbsp butter

1 tbsp sunflower or corn oil

plain yogurt to serve

chopped fresh thyme to garnish

TOMATO SAUCE

2 tbsp butter

¼ cup (30 g) all-purpose flour

1¾ cups (450 ml) chicken stock

13 oz (400 g) canned chopped tomatoes

1 tbsp tomato paste

1 garlic clove, crushed

1 bay leaf

1 Mix the pork and onion in a large bowl, then stir in the flour, thyme, paprika, and salt and pepper to taste. Bind with the egg, adding enough milk to give a soft but not sticky texture.

2 Using 2 soup spoons, shape the mixture into 20 ovals. Roll the meatballs lightly in flour and chill in the refrigerator.

3 Make the tomato sauce: melt the butter in a pan, add the flour, and cook, stirring, for 1 minute. Blend in the stock, then add the tomatoes, tomato paste, garlic, bay leaf, and salt and pepper to taste. Bring to a boil, stirring until thickened. Cover and simmer for 20–25 minutes.

4 Work the sauce through a nylon strainer, then taste for seasoning. Set aside.

5 Melt the butter with the oil in a flameproof casserole. Cook the meatballs in batches for 5 minutes or until browned all over. Lift out the meatballs and drain on paper towels.

6 Pour the fat out of the casserole. Return the meatballs, add the sauce, and bring to a boil. Cover and cook in a 350°F (180°C) oven for 30 minutes. Spoon on a little yogurt and garnish with thyme before serving.

PASTICCIO

 Serves 4

1 tbsp sunflower or corn oil

1 lb (500 g) ground pork or beef

2 onions, chopped

3–5 garlic cloves, crushed

13 oz (400 g) canned chopped tomatoes

⅔ cup (150 g) tomato paste

6 tbsp (90 ml) red wine

2 bay leaves

1 tsp sugar

½ tsp chopped fresh oregano

½ tsp ground cinnamon

2 cups (250 g) elbow macaroni

salt and black pepper

CHEESE CUSTARD

4 tsp butter

3 tbsp all-purpose flour

1¼ cups (300 ml) milk

2 cups (250 g) grated aged Cheddar cheese

2 eggs, lightly beaten

large pinch of grated nutmeg

1 Heat the sunflower oil in a large skillet, add the meat, onions, and garlic, and cook over medium heat for 5 minutes or until lightly browned.

2 Add the tomatoes, tomato paste, and wine. Bring to a boil and simmer for 15 minutes.

3 Add the bay leaves, sugar, oregano, cinnamon, and salt and pepper to taste. Simmer gently for 10 minutes or until the sauce is thickened.

4 Meanwhile, cook the macaroni in boiling salted water for 8–10 minutes, until just tender. Drain and set aside.

5 Spoon half of the meat mixture into an ovenproof dish and add half of the macaroni. Cover with the remaining meat mixture, then top with the remaining macaroni. Bake in 350°F (180°C) oven for 20 minutes.

6 Make the cheese custard: melt the butter in a saucepan, add the flour, and cook, stirring, for 1 minute. Remove from the heat and gradually blend in the milk. Bring to a boil, stirring constantly, and simmer for 2–3 minutes, until the mixture thickens. Remove from the heat and stir in the cheese, eggs, nutmeg, and salt and pepper to taste.

7 Remove the dish from the oven, pour on the cheese custard, and bake for 20 minutes longer or until the custard topping is golden and cooked through.

MUSTARD-GLAZED HAM

Ham tastes best when it is cooked on the bone, especially if it is home-baked and coated with a tangy glaze as in this recipe. Here, the ham slowly steam-roasts in its own juices, spiked with cider or sweetened with apple juice. Watercress and orange slices are the perfect finishing touch.

 Serves 16–20

8–10 lb (4–5 kg) country ham

1¼ cups (400 ml) hard cider or apple juice

3 tbsp dry mustard

3 tbsp cold water

½ cup (90 g) light brown sugar

LEMON MUSTARD SAUCE

¼ cup (60 ml) olive oil

juice of 1 lemon

1 tbsp superfine sugar

2 tsp coarse mustard

salt and black pepper

⅔ cup (150 ml) light sour cream

1 Put the ham into a large container, cover with cold water, and leave to soak for at least 12 hours.

2 Drain the ham and rinse under cold running water. Arrange 2 pieces of foil, long enough to cover the ham, across a large roasting pan.

3 Pour the cider into the foil. Stand a wire rack on the foil and stand the ham on the rack. Insert a meat thermometer, if using, into the thickest part of the meat.

4 Wrap the foil loosely over the ham, leaving plenty of space for the air to circulate. Place the ham just below the center of a 325°F (160°C) oven and cook for 20 minutes per 1 lb (500 g). The meat thermometer should register 170°F (75°C). Remove the ham from the oven and leave to cool for a few minutes.

5 Increase the oven temperature to 450°F (230°C). Transfer the ham to a board, drain the cooking juices from the foil, and discard. Mix the dry mustard with the measured water. Glaze the ham with the mustard and brown sugar (see box, right).

6 Return the ham to the rack in the roasting pan. Cover any lean parts of the ham with foil, return to the oven, and cook, turning the roasting pan if necessary, for 15–20 minutes longer, until the glaze is golden brown all over.

7 Meanwhile, make the lemon mustard sauce: put the olive oil, lemon juice, superfine sugar, mustard, and salt and pepper to taste into a screw-top jar and shake vigorously to mix the ingredients together.

8 Put the light sour cream into a bowl and stir in the lemon and mustard mixture. Taste for seasoning and leave to chill in the refrigerator until needed.

9 Carve the ham into slices and serve either warm or cold, with the lemon mustard sauce.

Glazing ham

Cut away the skin with a sharp knife, leaving behind a thin layer of fat. Discard the skin.

Score the fat all over in a diamond pattern, so that the glaze penetrates the fat.

Spread a generous layer of mustard over the fat, using a narrow spatula or your hands.

Press the light brown sugar onto the layer of mustard, making sure it is evenly coated all over.

BOSTON BAKED BEANS

 Serves 4

scant 2 cups (375 g) dried great
  northern beans

1/4 cup packed (60 g) dark
  brown sugar

2 tbsp tomato paste

2 tsp molasses

2 tsp maple syrup

2 tsp dry mustard

2 tsp salt

black pepper

1/2 lb (250 g) slab of bacon, cut
  into 1-in (2.5-cm) cubes

3 onions, quartered

2 1/3 cups (600 ml) water

1 Put the great northern
beans into a large bowl,
cover with plenty of cold
water, and leave to soak
overnight.

2 Drain the beans and
rinse under cold running
water. Put the beans into a
saucepan, cover with cold
water, and bring to a boil.
Boil rapidly for 10 minutes,
then partially cover the pan
and simmer for 30 minutes.
Drain and set aside.

3 Put the sugar, tomato
paste, molasses, maple
syrup, mustard, and salt and
pepper to taste into a large
flameproof casserole and
heat gently, stirring
constantly.

4 Add the bacon and
onions to the casserole
with the drained beans and
measured water. Bring to a
boil, cover tightly with a
piece of foil and the lid,
and cook in a 275°F (140°C)
oven, stirring occasionally,
for 4 1/2–5 hours. Taste for
seasoning before serving.

Boston baked beans

*This classic dish needs long,
slow cooking to let the flavors
mingle and mellow. It dates
back to the early days of the
Puritan settlers in New
England. Because no cooking
was allowed on the Sabbath, the
dish was cooked on Saturday
and then served for Saturday
dinner, Sunday breakfast, and
Sunday lunch.*

FARMER'S BACON

 Serves 4

1 1/2 lb (750 g) slab of lean bacon

a few parsley stalks

6 black peppercorns

1 bay leaf

4 potatoes, cut into large chunks

4 carrots, thickly sliced

4 celery stalks, thickly sliced

chopped parsley to garnish

CHEESE SAUCE

3 tbsp butter

1/3 cup (45 g) all-purpose flour

1 scant cup (200 ml) milk

3/4 cup (90 g) grated aged
  Cheddar cheese

salt and black pepper

1 Put the bacon into a large
pan, cover with cold
water, and bring to a boil.
Drain, rinse, and cover with
fresh cold water. Add the
parsley stalks, peppercorns,
and bay leaf and bring to a
boil. Cover and simmer very
gently for 45 minutes.

2 Add the potatoes,
carrots, and celery and
bring back to a boil. Cover
and simmer very gently for
20 minutes or until the meat
and vegetables are tender.
Drain, reserving the cooking
liquid, and allow the bacon
to cool slightly.

3 Remove all of the rind
and fat from the bacon,
cut the meat into bite-sized
pieces, and arrange in a
shallow ovenproof dish with
the vegetables. Keep warm.

4 Make the cheese sauce:
melt the butter in a
saucepan, add the flour, and
cook, stirring, for 1 minute.
Remove from the heat and
gradually blend in the milk
and 1 cup (250 ml) of the
reserved cooking liquid.
Bring to a boil, stirring
constantly until the mixture
thickens. Simmer for
2–3 minutes. Add three-
quarters of the cheese and
salt and pepper to taste.

5 Pour the sauce over the
meat and vegetables and
sprinkle with the remaining
cheese. Bake in a 350°F
(180°C) oven for 30 minutes
or until the cheese is heated
through and bubbling.
Garnish with the chopped
parsley before serving.

SAUSAGE CASSOULET

Cassoulet is a hearty dish from Languedoc in the southwest of France. This is a simple and satisfying version. The types of meat used in more traditional recipes may include duck, goose, or lamb.

 Serves 8

scant 2 cups (375 g) dried great northern beans

2 tbsp olive oil

1 lb (500 g) coarse pork sausages

1/2 lb (250 g) slab of bacon, cut into strips

2 large onions, sliced

1/2 lb (250 g) piece of garlic sausage, cut into 1-in (2.5-cm) chunks

26 oz (800 g) canned chopped tomatoes

1 1/4 cups (300 ml) chicken stock

2/3 cup (150 ml) dry white wine

2 tbsp tomato paste

2 garlic cloves, crushed

3 thyme sprigs

a few parsley stalks

salt and black pepper

2–3 cups (125–175 g) fresh white bread crumbs

chopped parsley to garnish

1 Put the beans into a large bowl, cover with plenty of cold water, and leave to soak overnight.

2 Drain the beans and rinse under cold running water. Put the beans into a saucepan, cover with fresh cold water, and bring to a boil. Boil rapidly for 10 minutes, then simmer for 30 minutes or until just tender. Drain.

3 Heat the olive oil in a large flameproof casserole, add the sausage and bacon, and cook for 5 minutes or until browned all over. Lift out and drain on paper towels. Thickly slice the sausage.

4 Pour off all but 1 tbsp of the fat from the casserole. Add the onions and cook gently, stirring occasionally, for a few minutes, until soft but not browned.

5 Return the bacon and sausage to the casserole, add the beans, the garlic sausage, tomatoes, stock, wine, tomato paste, garlic, thyme, parsley stalks, and salt and pepper to taste and bring back to a boil.

Adding the topping to the cassoulet

Remove the cassoulet from the oven and sprinkle with a thick, even layer of bread crumbs.

6 Cover and cook in a 325°F (160°C) oven for 1 hour. Add the bread crumb topping (see box, above). Return the casserole to the oven and cook, uncovered, for 30 minutes or until the topping is golden brown. Taste for seasoning. Garnish with chopped parsley before serving.

BAKED SAUSAGE

 Serves 6

1 tbsp sunflower or corn oil

2 lb (1 kg) coarse pork sausage

4 trimmed medium leeks, thickly sliced

3 large potatoes, cut into 1/4-in (5-mm) slices

1/2 cup (90 g) red lentils

salt and black pepper

2 bay leaves

2 cloves

1 garlic clove, crushed

3 2/3 cups (900 ml) chicken stock

chopped parsley to garnish

1 Heat the oil in a large flameproof casserole and brown the sausage. Lift out, then cut into thick slices.

2 Layer the leeks, potatoes, sausage, and lentils in the casserole, adding seasoning to taste and placing the bay leaves, cloves, and garlic among the layers. Top with a layer of potatoes.

3 Pour in the stock and bring to a boil. Cover the casserole tightly and cook in a 325°F (160°C) oven, checking the liquid level occasionally, for 2 1/2 hours.

4 Remove the lid, increase the oven temperature to 400°F (200°C) and cook for 20–25 minutes, until the potatoes are browned. Garnish with the chopped parsley and serve.

TOAD IN THE HOLE

 Serves 4

3/4 lb (400 g) bulk pork sausage

1 leek, finely chopped

2 tbsp chopped fresh sage

1 tbsp chopped parsley

3 tbsp sunflower or corn oil

3 onions, chopped

2 tbsp all-purpose flour

1¼ cups (300 ml) milk

1 cup (250 ml) chicken stock

chopped parsley to garnish

BATTER

1 cup (125 g) self-rising flour

3 eggs, beaten

1¼ cups (300 ml) milk

1 tbsp chopped parsley

pinch of grated nutmeg

salt and black pepper

1 Make the batter: sift the self-rising flour into a bowl. Make a well in the middle of the flour and add the eggs and a little milk. Blend to a smooth paste, then gradually whisk in the remaining milk until the batter has the pouring consistency of heavy cream.

2 Whisk in the chopped parsley, nutmeg, and salt and pepper to taste. Cover the batter and leave to stand for 30 minutes.

3 Meanwhile, combine the sausage, leek, sage, parsley, and salt and pepper to taste. Shape the mixture into 12 balls and set aside.

4 Heat the oil in a saucepan, add the onions, and cook for a few minutes, until soft but not browned. Transfer one-third of the onions to 4 small ovenproof dishes or 1 large dish. Set aside the remainder.

5 Add the sausage balls to the dishes and bake in a 425°F (220°C) oven for about 10 minutes until golden brown.

6 Add the batter mixture and return immediately to the oven. Bake for 20–25 minutes, until the batter is well risen and golden.

7 Meanwhile, add the all-purpose flour to the onions in the pan and cook, stirring, for 1 minute. Remove from the heat and gradually blend in the milk and stock. Bring to a boil, stirring constantly, and simmer for 2–3 minutes, until the mixture thickens. Transfer the sauce to a bowl. Serve the toad in the hole sprinkled with parsley and pass the sauce separately.

SAUSAGE & LENTIL CASSEROLE

 Serves 4

1½ cups (300 g) brown lentils

2 bay leaves

2 tbsp sunflower or corn oil

2 large onions, chopped

1 large potato, chopped

1 celery stalk, diced

1 carrot, diced

2 tomatoes, peeled (page 39), seeded, and diced

2 tbsp all-purpose flour

1 cup (250 ml) chicken or vegetable stock

2–3 tbsp chopped parsley

1 tbsp chopped fresh sage

salt and black pepper

3/4 lb (375 g) herbed pork sausage

chopped parsley to garnish

1 Put the lentils and bay leaves into a saucepan, cover with cold water, and bring to a boil. Cover and simmer for 30 minutes or until the lentils are just tender. Drain and set aside.

2 Heat the oil in a large saucepan, add the onions, and cook gently, stirring occasionally, for a few minutes, until softened.

3 Add the potato, celery, carrot, and tomatoes and cook for 10 minutes or until the onions are browned and the other vegetables are softened. Using a slotted spoon, lift out the vegetables and set aside.

4 Add the flour to the pan and cook, stirring, for 1 minute. Remove the pan from the heat and gradually blend in the stock. Bring to a boil, stirring constantly, and simmer for 2–3 minutes, until the sauce thickens.

5 Add the lentils to the sauce with the vegetables, parsley, sage, and salt and pepper to taste. Mix well and transfer to a large ovenproof casserole.

6 Arrange the sausage on top and cook in a 375°F (190°C) oven for about 30 minutes, until the sausage is browned all over and cooked through. Garnish with parsley before serving.

7

VEGETARIAN DISHES

FETA & VEGETABLE KEBABS

Cubes of feta cheese, cherry tomatoes, baguette slices, and red pepper threaded onto skewers, then briefly marinated, and broiled.

SERVES 4 722 calories per serving

Takes 25 minutes **PAGE 293**

COUSCOUS WITH ROASTED PEPPERS

Tasty and simple to make: couscous with garbanzo beans, zucchini, carrots, and spices. Topped with peppers and almonds.

SERVES 4 418 calories per serving

Takes 45 minutes **PAGE 287**

MEXICAN CHILI WITH TOFU

Bite-sized pieces of tofu cooked with red kidney beans and tomato sauce seasoned with garlic, chili, paprika, cumin, and oregano.

SERVES 4–6 386–257 calories per serving

Takes 35 minutes **PAGE 294**

RED BEAN & TOMATO CURRY

Rich and spicy: red kidney beans cooked with tomatoes, garlic, chili, ginger, curry powder, turmeric, coriander, and cayenne.

SERVES 4 218 calories per serving

Takes 20 minutes **PAGE 292**

FALAFEL WITH SESAME YOGURT SAUCE

Blended garbanzo beans, scallions, herbs, and spices, shaped into patties and cooked until golden. Served with sesame yogurt sauce.

SERVES 4–6 489–326 calories per serving

Takes 20 minutes, plus standing **PAGE 293**

CARROT ROULADE

Fresh and creamy: carrot mixed with garlic, red pepper, tomatoes, and eggs, baked, then rolled around a cheese and cucumber filling.

SERVES 4 725 calories per serving

Takes 30 minutes, plus chilling **PAGE 297**

VEGETABLE STIR-FRY WITH TOFU

Tofu marinated in soy sauce and sherry, stir-fried with carrots, ginger, mushrooms, bean sprouts, endive, and scallions.

SERVES 4 335 calories per serving

Takes 15 minutes, plus marinating **PAGE 294**

SPINACH & RICOTTA TRIANGLES

Light and crispy: spinach combined with ricotta cheese, onion, and nutmeg and baked in cases of phyllo pastry until golden.

MAKES 4 307 calories per serving

Takes 40 minutes **PAGE 289**

VEGETARIAN BURGERS

Soybeans combined with tomato juice, TVP, sesame seeds, and herbs. Shaped into burgers, and served with lettuce dressing.

SERVES 6 380 calories per serving

Takes 30 minutes, plus chilling **PAGE 295**

30–60 MINUTES

MIXED BEANS

Adzuki and lima beans simmered with mushrooms, tomatoes, and parsley. Topped with leeks and a cheese sauce.

SERVES 4   564 calories per serving

Takes 60 minutes   **PAGE 279**

SPINACH ROULADE

Combined spinach, butter, and eggs, briefly baked, sprinkled with Parmesan, and rolled with a sour cream and mushroom filling.

SERVES 6–8   250–187 calories per serving

Takes 30 minutes, plus chilling   **PAGE 297**

OVER 60 MINUTES

EGGPLANT PARMIGIANA

Rich and tangy: eggplant slices layered with garlic- and basil-flavored tomato sauce and mozzarella and Parmesan cheeses.

SERVES 4–6   774–516 calories per serving

Takes 1¼ hours, plus standing   **PAGE 282**

ITALIAN STUFFED ZUCCHINI

Baked zucchini with a delicious tomato and basil stuffing. Topped with capers and Fontina cheese.

SERVES 4   437 calories per serving

Takes 50 minutes   **PAGE 284**

RED LENTIL & COCONUT CURRY

Lentils cooked with coconut and seasoned with ginger, chili, garlic, and turmeric. Topped with mustard-seed butter

SERVES 4–6   722–481 calories per serving

Takes 40 minutes   **PAGE 292**

POLENTA WITH GRILLED VEGETABLES

Barbecued strips of polenta served with marinated and barbecued zucchini, fennel, tomatoes, and red onion.

SERVES 4–6   479–319 calories per serving

Takes 45 minutes, plus marinating   **PAGE 286**

BAKED ZUCCHINI NIÇOISE

Rich and aromatic: black olives, zucchini, tomatoes, red onion, and garlic sprinkled with capers, herbes de Provence, and pepper

SERVES 4   237 calories per serving

Takes 60 minutes

and baked. Garnished with shredded fresh basil. It is delicious served hot or cold with croutons or toasted baguette.

PAGE 278

CHEESE SAUSAGES

Cheddar and goat cheeses combined with bread crumbs, leek, walnuts, sage, lemon zest, mustard, and eggs and fried until crisp.

SERVES 4   526 calories per serving

Takes 35 minutes, plus chilling   **PAGE 295**

MUSHROOM GOUGERE

Savory choux pastry with a filling of mixed mushrooms flavored with tarragon and baked until golden brown.

SERVES 4 558 calories per serving

Takes 1 1/2 hours, plus chilling   PAGE 288

SPINACH GNOCCHI WITH TOMATO SAUCE

Dumplings of spinach, ricotta and Parmesan cheeses, and eggs, served with tomato sauce.

SERVES 4 738 calories per serving

Takes 1 1/4 hours, plus chilling   PAGE 286

ECONOMICAL

COUNTRY VEGETABLE PIES

Carrots and parsnips baked with onion, garlic, and parsley sauce. Topped with mashed potato for a nourishing meal.

SERVES 4 642 calories per serving

Takes 1 1/4 hours   PAGE 279

HIGH FIBER

VEGETABLE & BARLEY CASSEROLE

Pearl barley, shallots, carrots, parsnips, zucchini, snow peas, and cauliflower cooked with stock. Topped with dumplings.

SERVES 4 509 calories per serving

Takes 1 1/4 hours   PAGE 287

POTATO, CELERIAC, & PARMESAN GRATIN

Potatoes and celeriac baked with cream and ricotta cheese, bread crumbs, and Parmesan.

SERVES 4 676 calories per serving

Takes 1 3/4 hours   PAGE 282

CHESTNUT LOAF

Chestnuts baked with potatoes and celery, flavored with garlic, parsley, soy sauce, and tomato paste. Served with spicy tomato salsa.

SERVES 6 226 calories per serving

Takes 1 1/4 hours   PAGE 296

PICNIC FARE

TOMATO & OLIVE TART

Poppy-seed pastry base baked with a topping of onions, tomatoes, tomato paste, basil, garlic, mozzarella cheese, and black olives.

SERVES 6 502 calories per serving

Takes 60 minutes, plus chilling   PAGE 288

STUFFED RED PEPPERS

Baked peppers with a nourishing stuffing of mushrooms, onion, long-grain rice, red lentils, pine nuts, and parsley.

SERVES 4 622 calories per serving

Takes 1 1/2 hours   PAGE 283

CHEESE-TOPPED BAKED EGGPLANT

Eggplant spiked with garlic slivers dipped in herbs and olive oil. Topped with Gorgonzola and Cheddar cheeses.

SERVES 4 447 calories per serving

Takes 1 1/4 hours   PAGE 283

MUSHROOM LASAGNE

Lasagne layered with mushroom and tomato sauce, spinach balls, béchamel sauce, and grated Cheddar cheese, then baked.

SERVES 6 684 calories per serving

Takes 1¼ hours **PAGE 285**

DAIRY-FREE LASAGNE

Tomato sauce layered with lasagne, lightly browned eggplant slices and spinach, topped with zucchini and baked.

SERVES 4–6 364–243 calories per serving

Takes 60 minutes, plus standing **PAGE 285**

DINNER PARTY

EGGPLANT & CHEESE PHYLLO PIE

Diced eggplant, onions, feta cheese, lentils, red peppers, spices, and oregano combined and baked in phyllo pastry.

SERVES 6 569 calories per serving

Takes 1¼ hours, plus standing **PAGE 289**

HIGH PROTEIN

FESTIVE NUT LOAF

Brown rice blended with porcini, mushrooms, carrots, parsley, and rosemary and baked in a loaf pan with walnuts, Brazil nuts, pine nuts, and Cheddar cheese. Garnished with rosemary sprigs, served in slices, and accompanied by cranberry sauce.

SERVES 6–8 600–450 calories per serving

Takes 2½ hours, plus soaking **PAGE 296**

FAMILY CHOICE

CHEESE & VEGETABLE PIE

A variety of vegetables mixed with parsley and marjoram in a Cheddar cheese and mustard sauce. Topped with cheese pastry.

SERVES 4–6 610–406 calories per serving

Takes 1½ hours, plus chilling **PAGE 278**

WINTER VEGETABLE TERRINE

Three colorful layers of pureed carrot, celeriac, and broccoli, baked and served in slices.

SERVES 4–6 142–95 calories per serving

Takes 1¾ hours, plus chilling **PAGE 298**

DINNER PARTY

MIDDLE EASTERN STUFFED SQUASH

Baked summer squash slices filled with a mixture of steamed couscous, mushrooms, lemon, scallions, yogurt, mint, and olives.

SERVES 4 247 calories per serving

Takes 1¼ hours **PAGE 284**

CREAM CHEESE TERRINE

Eggplant and red and yellow peppers layered with a cream cheese mixture, wrapped in spinach leaves, and baked.

SERVES 8 194 calories per serving

Takes 2¼ hours, plus chilling **PAGE 298**

VEGETARIAN KNOW-HOW

THERE ARE THREE BASIC types of vegetarian diet. A vegan diet is the strictest – vegans do not eat any meat, fish, eggs, or dairy products. A vegetarian diet excludes meat, poultry, and fish and may or may not include eggs and dairy products. A semi-vegetarian diet can include fish and poultry. With such a great variety of foods from which to choose, vegetarian diets, based largely on complex carbohydrates, legumes, vegetables, fruits, nuts, and seeds, can be both imaginative and nutritious.

MAINTAINING A BALANCED DIET

Fish, meat, poultry, dairy products, and eggs are "complete" protein foods, which means that they contain almost all the essential dietary amino acids that the body needs. Many vegetarians replace fish, meat, and poultry with eggs, cheese, and other dairy products, but this is not the ideal solution since dairy foods are high in saturated fats and calories. Instead, complete protein can be obtained by combining two or more vegetable protein sources, or adding nonanimal complete protein foods to the diet, such as tofu and TVP (textured vegetable protein).

Legumes, grains, nuts, and seeds, although rich in protein, are deficient in one or more of the essential amino acids, but combining vegetable protein sources makes the protein complete. Examples of complete vegetarian protein combinations drawn from cuisines around the world are beans and rice, hummus and pita bread, or a mixed nut, lentil, and vegetable salad.

Another dietary interaction that vegetarians should be aware of is that between iron and vitamin C. The form of iron found in meat is easily absorbed by the body, but the iron in vegetables, nuts, grains, legumes, and eggs needs a helping hand, and this is provided by vitamin C. Be sure to include a green vegetable, tomatoes, or citrus fruit when serving these foods.

ALTERNATIVE PROTEIN FOODS

Tofu and TVP are complete protein foods that are low in fat, calories, and cholesterol and so make a healthy basis for a great variety of dishes.

Tofu
Made from processed, pressed soybeans, tofu has no taste of its own (unless it is the smoked variety), but it quickly takes on the flavors of marinades and sauces. It contains no fat. Silken tofu has a soft, creamy texture: use it in sauces, dips, and desserts. Firm tofu can be stir-fried, broiled, or used in casseroles. Before use, drain and pat dry with paper towels.

TVP
Textured vegetable protein, or TVP, is made from soy flour and is virtually fat free. It is available as chunks or "ground" and has a rather chewy texture, like meat. It is often used in commercial vegetarian products such as sausages. It keeps well, so keep a pack in your cabinet and use it in homemade burgers or cook it in a stew or casserole.

A gelatin substitute

Gelatin is a natural protein found in the bones, skin, and connective tissues of animals. Commercial powdered gelatin is derived from pig skin and is thus unacceptable in a vegetarian diet. The most common substitute is agar-agar, a flavorless dried seaweed sold in stick or powder form.

Before use, stir the agar-agar into boiling water and simmer for 5 minutes, to dissolve. It has stronger setting properties than gelatin, so less needs to be used.

VEGETABLE STOCK

Add any vegetable trimmings you have (celery tops or tomato skins, for example) or vary the ingredients to emphasize the flavor of the dish in which you want to use the stock.

1 Coarsely chop *2 onions, 2–3 carrots, 3 celery stalks,* and *1 leek.* Put into a large saucepan or stockpot and add *1 large bouquet garni.* Add *1 crushed garlic clove* too, if desired.

2 Add *5 cups (1.25 liters) water* and bring to a boil. Skim off any foam that rises to the surface. Lower the heat and simmer for 30 minutes.

3 Pour the stock through a strainer. If not using immediately, leave to cool, cover, and store in the refrigerator for up to 5 days or in the freezer for up to 1 month.

COOKING LEGUMES

Legumes are the dried, edible seeds of beans, peas, and lentils. Stored in a cool, dark place, they will keep for up to 6 months. Many types are now available in cans and need no soaking or cooking, but if you want to prepare your own, it's very easy.

1 Put the beans into a large bowl and cover with plenty of cold water. Leave to soak (see below). Drain and rinse under cold running water.

2 Put into a saucepan with twice their volume of cold water. Bring to a boil. Lower the heat, cover, and simmer until tender (see below).

Better beans

When cooking legumes such as red kidney beans, soybeans, or black-eyed peas, it is a good idea to boil them rapidly for 10 minutes first. Drain the beans, add fresh water, and return to a boil. If preferred, you may treat all legumes (except split peas and lentils) in this way; it helps reduce their "gassy" effect.

Bean know-how

Beans can be left to soak for 8 hours, but if you prefer, you can speed up the process by boiling them for 3 minutes, then leaving them to soak, covered, for 1–2 hours before cooking as usual.

◆

Add salt toward the end of cooking time; if it is added at the beginning, it will toughen the skins of legumes.

◆

Legumes double in size and weight when cooked, so if a recipe calls for 1/2 lb (250 g) cooked legumes, you will need 1/4 lb (125 g) before cooking.

SOAKING & COOKING TIMES OF LEGUMES

Cooking times depend on the age of the legume: the older legumes are, the longer they will take to cook. The cooking times given below are therefore only a guide.

LEGUME	SOAKING	COOKING
Adzuki beans	8–12 hours	30–45 minutes
Black-eyed peas	8–12 hours	1 hour
Cannellini	8–12 hours	1 1/4 hours
Garbanzo beans	8–12 hours	1 1/2–2 hours
Great northern beans	8–12 hours	1–1 1/2 hours
Lentils		
Green and brown lentils	not required	30–45 minutes
Red lentils	not required	20–30 minutes
Lima beans	8–12 hours	1 hour
Mung beans	8–12 hours	45 minutes
Red kidney beans	8–12 hours	1 1/4–1 1/2 hours
Soybeans	8–12 hours	1 1/2 hours

GRAINS

Whole grains are first-class sources of carbohydrate, fiber, vitamins, and minerals.

Bulgur wheat
Also known as burghul wheat. Made from steamed, dried, and crushed wheat kernels, it cooks very quickly. It can also be soaked and used in salads.

Couscous
Grains of semolina. To prepare, soak the couscous first to allow the grains to swell and soften. For extra flavor, steam the couscous over vegetables in a colander set over a large pot.

Cornmeal
Made from ground corn, and sometimes known as polenta. Cook in simmering water, stirring constantly until the water is absorbed. Cook, stirring, for 10–20 minutes, until thick. Serve warm or leave to cool, then broil.

Pearl barley
Has a nutty flavor and chewy texture. Add sauce to vegetable soups and stews to thicken them.

Millet
Available as flakes or grains, millet can be cooked with water, stock, or milk. Add a small handful to soups to thicken them.

Oats
Available in various sizes and textures. Oat flakes are used in cooked cereal and granola; ground oatmeal can be used to make cookies or to thicken soups.

BAKED ZUCCHINI NIÇOISE

 Serves 4

1¹/₂ lb (750 g) zucchini, sliced

13 oz (400 g) canned tomatoes, drained and chopped

1 large red onion, thinly sliced

3 garlic cloves, crushed

¹/₄ cup (60 ml) olive oil, more if needed

1 cup (125 g) black olives, pitted

2 tsp herbes de Provence

1 tbsp capers

black pepper

1 tbsp shredded fresh basil

1 In an ovenproof dish, toss the zucchini, tomatoes, onion, and garlic, and drizzle the oil over the top.

2 Arrange the black olives on top of the vegetables, then sprinkle with the herbes de Provence, capers, and black pepper to taste.

3 Bake in a 375°F (190°C) oven for 45 minutes or until the zucchini and onion are tender, checking occasionally to see if the surface is getting too dry. If it is, drizzle a little more olive oil over the vegetables.

4 Sprinkle the dish with the shredded fresh basil. Serve hot or cold.

CHEESE & VEGETABLE PIE

 Serves 4–6

2 tbsp butter

1 onion, chopped

2 carrots, sliced

1 lb (500 g) zucchini, sliced

2 large tomatoes, peeled (page 39), seeded, and chopped

1¹/₂ cups (125 g) sliced mushrooms

2 tbsp chopped parsley

1 tsp chopped fresh marjoram

salt and black pepper

CHEESE SAUCE

2 tbsp butter

¹/₄ cup (30 g) all-purpose flour

1¹/₄ cups (300 ml) milk

¹/₂ cup (60 g) grated aged Cheddar cheese

1 tsp dry mustard

pinch of cayenne pepper

CHEESE PASTRY

1 cup (125 g) all-purpose flour

4 tbsp butter

¹/₂ cup (60 g) grated aged Cheddar cheese

1 small egg, beaten

1 Make the cheese pastry: sift the flour into a bowl. Add the butter and rub in lightly until the mixture resembles fine bread crumbs. Stir in the cheese, then bind to a soft but not sticky dough with 1 tbsp of the beaten egg and 1 tbsp cold water. Chill for 30 minutes.

2 Melt the butter in a large pan, add the onion, and cook gently for 3–5 minutes, until softened. Add the carrots and cook for about 5 minutes.

3 Add the zucchini, tomatoes, mushrooms, parsley, marjoram, and salt and pepper to taste and cook over gentle heat, stirring occasionally, for 10–15 minutes, until just softened. Set aside.

4 Make the cheese sauce: melt the butter in a saucepan, add the flour, and cook, stirring, for 1 minute. Remove from the heat and gradually blend in the milk.

5 Bring to a boil, stirring until the mixture thickens. Simmer for 2–3 minutes, then stir in the cheese, mustard, cayenne, and salt and pepper to taste. Stir the vegetables into the sauce, remove from the heat, and leave to cool.

6 Roll out the pastry on a floured work surface. Invert a pie dish onto the pastry and cut around the edge. Reserve the trimmings for decoration.

7 Transfer the vegetable and sauce mixture to the pie dish and top with the pastry. Crimp the edges with a fork and make a hole in the top of the pastry to allow steam to escape.

8 Decorate the pie with the pastry trimmings, attaching them with beaten egg. Brush the pastry all over with the remaining beaten egg. Bake in a 400°F (200°C) oven for 30 minutes or until the pastry is crisp and golden.

COUNTRY VEGETABLE PIES

 Serves 4

8 carrots, diced

8 parsnips, diced

1 1/4 cups (300 ml) vegetable stock

2 tbsp olive oil

1 onion, chopped

1 head of garlic, separated into cloves and peeled

3 large potatoes, diced

salt and black pepper

3 tbsp butter

1/4 cup (60 ml) hot milk

paprika to garnish (optional)

PARSLEY SAUCE

3 tbsp butter

1/3 cup (45 g) all-purpose flour

2/3 cup (150 ml) milk

1/4 cup (30 g) chopped parsley

1 Blanch the carrots and parsnips in the stock for 1 minute. Reserve the stock. Put the oil into an ovenproof dish, add the carrots, parsnips, onion, and half of the garlic. Bake in a 400°F (200°C) oven for 30 minutes.

2 Meanwhile, cook the potatoes and the remaining garlic in boiling salted water for 15–20 minutes, until tender. Drain. Add 2 tbsp of the butter and the hot milk. Mash, adding salt and pepper to taste.

3 Remove the vegetables with a slotted spoon and divide among 4 individual ovenproof dishes. Add salt and pepper to taste.

4 Make the parsley sauce: melt the butter in a small pan, add the flour, and cook, stirring, for 1 minute. Remove from the heat and blend in the milk and reserved stock. Bring to a boil, stirring, until thick. Simmer for 2–3 minutes, then stir in the parsley and salt and pepper to taste.

5 Pour the sauce over the vegetables. Top with the mashed potato, dot with the remaining butter, and bake for 20 minutes. Serve immediately, sprinkled with paprika, if desired.

MIXED BEANS

 Serves 4

2 tbsp olive oil

3 large leeks, trimmed and sliced

1 garlic clove, crushed

1/2 lb (250 g) mushrooms, sliced

13 oz (400 g) canned adzuki beans, drained

13 oz (400 g) canned lima beans, drained

13 oz (400 g) canned chopped tomatoes

3 tbsp tomato paste

1/4 cup (30 g) chopped parsley

salt and black pepper

CHEESE SAUCE

2 tbsp butter

1/4 cup (30 g) all purpose flour

2/3 cup (300 ml) milk

1 egg, beaten

1 cup (125 g) grated Cheddar cheese

1 Heat the olive oil in a large saucepan. Add the leeks and cook gently, stirring, for a few minutes, until softened but not browned. Lift out with a slotted spoon and set aside.

2 Add the garlic and mushrooms and cook, stirring occasionally, for 5 minutes. Add the adzuki and lima beans, tomatoes, tomato paste, 3 tbsp of the parsley, and salt and pepper to taste. Bring to a boil. Cover and simmer very gently for about 20 minutes.

3 Meanwhile, make the cheese sauce: melt the butter in a small saucepan, add the flour, and cook, stirring, for 1 minute. Remove the pan from the heat and gradually blend in the milk. Bring to a boil, stirring constantly until the mixture thickens. Simmer for 2–3 minutes, then leave to cool slightly. Stir in the egg and cheese and add salt and pepper to taste.

4 Transfer the bean mixture to an ovenproof dish and arrange the leek slices on top. Pour the cheese sauce over the leeks, and bake in a 375°F (190°C) oven for 30 minutes or until the topping is golden and bubbling. Garnish with the remaining chopped parsley, and serve immediately.

VEGETABLE CASSEROLES

Fresh vegetables make delicious, satisfying casseroles whatever the season, particularly when the herbs, spices, and flavorings are chosen carefully to bring out the best in the vegetables. For even more variety, add some simple toppings or a puff pastry lid to any of these casseroles to create a whole new dish.

BABY VEGETABLE MEDLEY

 Serves 4

6 tbsp (90 g) butter

3 fresh sage leaves, chopped

3 thyme sprigs, chopped

leaves from 1 small sprig of rosemary

salt and black pepper

4 very small new potatoes

8 baby carrots, scrubbed and trimmed

1/2 small head of cauliflower, cut into florets

8 pearl onions, peeled

2 garlic cloves, crushed

2/3 cup (150 ml) dry white wine

1 1/3 cups (125 g) thin green beans

1/4 pint (125 g) cherry tomatoes

1/2 cup (60 g) frozen lima beans, thawed

2 tbsp balsamic vinegar

2 tbsp coarse mustard

fresh rosemary to garnish

1 Melt the butter in a flameproof casserole with the herbs and salt and pepper. Add the potatoes, carrots, cauliflower, onions, and garlic and cook, stirring, for 3 minutes.

2 Add the white wine, bring to a boil, cover, and simmer for 10 minutes.

3 Add the remaining vegetables, cover and simmer for 3–4 minutes. Stir in the vinegar. Increase the heat and cook, stirring, for 1 minute until the sauce has reduced and thickened. Stir in the mustard, and garnish with rosemary.

BABY VEGETABLE GRATIN

Transfer the vegetables to an ovenproof dish. Sprinkle the vegetables with *3/4 cup (90 g) grated smoked Cheddar cheese* and *1 cup (60 g) fresh bread crumbs.* Cook under the broiler until golden.

MUSHROOM STROGANOFF

 Serves 4

3/4 oz (20 g) dried mushrooms

2/3 cup (150 ml) boiling water

4 tbsp butter

1 onion, chopped

1 garlic clove, crushed

salt and black pepper

1/2 lb (250 g) mixed mushrooms

1 red pepper, cored, seeded, and sliced

1/2 tsp paprika

7 oz (200 g) canned artichoke hearts, drained

1 1/4 cups (300 ml) vegetable stock

2 tbsp red wine

1 tbsp tomato paste

2/3 cup (150 ml) light cream

1 Soak the dried mushrooms in the boiling water for 20 minutes. Line a strainer with paper towels and drain the mushrooms, reserving the water.

2 Melt half of the butter in a large flameproof casserole, add the onion and garlic, and cook, stirring occasionally, for 3–5 minutes, until softened. Season well to taste.

3 Add the remaining butter, all of the mushrooms, and the red pepper. Cook, stirring, for 5 minutes. Add the paprika, artichokes, stock, red wine, reserved mushroom water, tomato paste, and cream and bring to a boil. Simmer gently for 10–15 minutes. Taste for seasoning. Serve hot.

MUSHROOM VOL-AU-VENT

When cooking the mushrooms, increase the heat to reduce and thicken the sauce. Warm a *store-bought large puff pastry shell.* Fill the shell with the Mushroom Stroganoff and serve.

SQUASH CASSEROLE

 Serves 4

2 tbsp olive oil

1 tbsp butter

1 onion, cut into 8 wedges

salt and black pepper

1 turnip, diced

1 potato, diced

1 lb (500 g) butternut squash, peeled and cut into 1-in (2.5-cm) cubes

1 parsnip, cut into 1-in (2.5-cm) cubes

1 tsp medium curry powder or paste

1 1/2 cups (375 ml) vegetable stock

1/3 cup (90 ml) light sour cream

chopped fresh cilantro to garnish

1 Heat the olive oil and butter in a flameproof casserole. Add the onion and cook gently for 3–5 minutes or until softened. Season well.

2 Add the vegetables, curry powder, and stock and bring to a boil. Cover and simmer, stirring, for 20 minutes.

3 Remove the vegetables with a slotted spoon and transfer to a warmed serving dish. Bring the sauce to a boil and stir in the cream. Cook gently, stirring, until thickened. Spoon the sauce over the vegetables, garnish with cilantro, and serve hot.

Clockwise from top: *Baby Vegetable Medley, Mushroom Stroganoff, Squash Casserole.*

HEARTY SQUASH PIE

Put the vegetables and sauce into a pie dish. Mix *2 cups (250 g) self-rising flour, 3/4 cup (150 g) vegetable shortening, 2 tbsp chopped parsley* and *water* to bind. Bake in a 375°F (190°C) oven for 15 minutes.

POTATO, CELERIAC, & PARMESAN GRATIN

 Serves 4

4 tbsp butter, plus extra
  for greasing

1 onion, sliced

2 garlic cloves, crushed

4 large potatoes, thinly sliced

3/4 lb (375 g) celeriac, peeled
  and thinly sliced

1 1/4 cups (300 ml) light cream

2/3 cup (150 ml) milk

1 cup (250 g) ricotta cheese

1 tsp chopped fresh rosemary

1/2 tsp paprika

salt and black pepper

2 tbsp fresh bread crumbs

3 tbsp grated Parmesan cheese,
  plus extra for serving

rosemary sprigs to garnish

1 Melt the butter in a skillet, add the onion and garlic, and cook gently, stirring occasionally, for 3–5 minutes, until softened but not browned. Lightly butter a large gratin dish.

2 Arrange the potatoes, celeriac, and the onion mixture in layers in the prepared gratin dish, finishing with a neat layer of potatoes.

3 In a large bowl, combine the cream, milk, ricotta cheese, rosemary, paprika, and salt and pepper to taste. Beat well together and pour over the vegetables.

4 In a small bowl, combine the bread crumbs and grated Parmesan cheese, and then sprinkle evenly over the potatoes.

5 Bake in a 350°F (180°C) oven for 1 1/2 hours or until the potatoes and celeriac are tender and the top of the gratin is a golden brown color.

6 Serve the gratin hot, sprinkled with grated Parmesan cheese and garnished with a few rosemary sprigs.

EGGPLANT PARMIGIANA

 Serves 4–6

3 lb (1.5 kg) eggplant

salt and black pepper

2 eggs, lightly beaten

1/4 cup (60 g) all-purpose flour

2–3 tbsp olive oil

2 onions, chopped

2 lbs 7 oz (1.2 kg) canned
  chopped tomatoes, drained

1/2 cup (140 g) tomato paste

2 garlic cloves, crushed

2 tbsp chopped fresh basil

1/4 tsp sugar

10–12 oz (300–375 g)
  mozzarella cheese, sliced

1 1/3 cups (125 g) grated
  Parmesan cheese

1 Cut the eggplant into 1/2-in (1-cm) slices. Place in a colander, sprinkle with salt, and leave to stand for 30 minutes. Rinse the slices and pat dry with paper towels.

2 Dip the eggplant into the beaten eggs, then into the flour, shaking off any excess.

3 Heat 1 tbsp of the oil in a large skillet, add the eggplant slices in batches, and cook for 3–4 minutes on each side, until golden, adding more oil between batches if necessary. Lift out with a slotted spoon and drain on paper towels.

4 Heat 1 tbsp oil in a saucepan, add the onions, and cook gently until soft but not browned. Stir in the tomatoes, tomato paste, garlic, and basil. Bring to a boil, then simmer for 10–15 minutes. Add sugar and salt and pepper to taste.

5 Spoon some of the tomato mixture into a shallow ovenproof dish and cover with a layer of eggplant slices, then a layer each of mozzarella and Parmesan. Continue layering, finishing with tomato mixture, mozzarella, and Parmesan.

6 Bake in a 375°F (190°C) oven for 15–20 minutes, until the cheese is lightly browned.

STUFFED RED PEPPERS

 Serves 4

8 small red peppers

1/4 cup (60 ml) water

STUFFING

1/4 cup (60 ml) olive oil

1 large onion, finely chopped

1 garlic clove, crushed

2 1/4 cups (175 g) chopped
  mushrooms

1 cup (250 g) long-grain rice

1/2 cup (90 g) red lentils

1 3/4 cups (450 ml) vegetable stock

salt and black pepper

1/2 cup (60 g) pine nuts, toasted

1/4 cup (30 g) chopped parsley

fresh cilantro to garnish

1 Slice off the tops from the peppers and reserve. Cut out and discard the cores, seeds, and white ribs and set the peppers aside.

2 Make the stuffing: heat the oil in a pan. Add the onion and garlic and cook gently, stirring occasionally, for 3–5 minutes, until soft but not browned. Add the chopped mushrooms and cook for 10 minutes.

3 Add the rice and lentils and stir to coat in the oil. Pour in the stock, season to taste, and bring to a boil. Cover and simmer very gently for 15–20 minutes, until the rice is tender and the liquid has been absorbed. Stir in the pine nuts and parsley, then taste for seasoning.

4 Divide the stuffing among the peppers and replace the tops.

5 Stand the peppers upright in an ovenproof casserole that just contains them. Pour the measured water into the casserole, cover with the lid, and bake in a 350°F (180°C) oven for about 40 minutes, until the peppers are tender. Serve immediately, garnished with cilantro sprigs.

Cook's know-how

If the peppers will not stand upright, slice a little off the bases before stuffing them to give a more even surface.

CHEESE-TOPPED BAKED EGGPLANT

 Serves 4

5 tbsp chopped fresh basil

2 tbsp chopped parsley

2 tbsp olive oil

1 tsp salt

4 medium eggplant

6 garlic cloves, cut into
  thin slivers

1 1/2 cups (175 g) crumbled
  Gorgonzola or Danish blue
  cheese

1 1/2 cups (175 g) grated
  Cheddar or mozzarella cheese

1 In a small bowl, combine 4 tbsp of the basil, the parsley, olive oil, and salt.

2 Prepare the eggplant (see box, right). Put the eggplant into an ovenproof dish and bake in a 350°F (180°C) oven for 40–50 minutes, until they are very tender and soft to the touch.

3 Remove the eggplant from the oven, sprinkle with the Gorgonzola and Cheddar cheeses, and bake for 5 minutes or until the cheese is melted. Serve immediately, sprinkled with the remaining basil.

Preparing the eggplant

Cut diagonal slits one-third of the way into 1 eggplant. Repeat.

Stuff the garlic slivers and chopped herb mixture into each slit.

ITALIAN STUFFED ZUCCHINI

 Serves 4

4 large zucchini

2 tbsp butter

2 tbsp olive oil, plus extra
  for greasing

1 small onion, finely chopped

4 ripe tomatoes, peeled
  (page 39), seeded, and chopped

1/4 cup (30 g) chopped fresh basil

salt and black pepper

2 tbsp capers, drained and
  coarsely chopped

2 cups (250 g) grated Fontina
  cheese

1 Cut the zucchini in half
lengthwise. Scoop out the
flesh and chop finely.

2 Melt the butter with
1 tbsp of the olive oil in
a saucepan.

3 When the butter is
foaming, add the onion
and cook gently, stirring
occasionally, for 3–5
minutes, until softened but
not browned. Add the
zucchini flesh, tomatoes,
basil, and salt and pepper to
taste and cook, stirring, for
5 minutes.

4 Brush the insides of the
zucchini shells with the
remaining oil and arrange in
a lightly oiled shallow
ovenproof dish. Bake the
shells in a 350°F (180°C)
oven for 5–10 minutes.

5 Divide half of the tomato
mixture among the
zucchini shells. Cover with
the chopped capers and a
thin layer of cheese. Spoon
on the remaining tomato
mixture and top with the
remaining cheese. Return
to the oven and bake for
10–15 minutes, until the
cheese topping is bubbling.
Serve immediately.

Fontina

*This Italian cheese is made in
the region of Val d'Aosta. It is
pale yellow, with a scattering of
small holes, a dark brown rind,
and a sweet, nutty flavor. It is
most frequently used in an
Italian dish similar to a fondue,
but because it melts so well, it
can be used in many other
cooked dishes. Parmesan cheese
may be used as a substitute.*

MIDDLE EASTERN STUFFED SQUASH

 Serves 4

1 1/3 cups (250 g) couscous

2/3 cup (150 ml) hot vegetable
  stock

2 lb (1 kg) summer squash

salt and black pepper

butter for greasing

1 tbsp olive oil

1 shallot, finely chopped

1 1/2 cups (125 g) sliced
  mushrooms

grated zest and juice of
  1/2 lemon

2 scallions, finely chopped

1/4 cup (60 g) plain yogurt

1 tbsp chopped fresh mint

12 pitted green olives, chopped

chopped parsley to garnish

tomato sauce (page 286) to serve

1 Put the couscous into a
bowl and add the stock.
Leave to stand for about
10 minutes. Put into a
strainer over a pan of boiling
water, cover, and steam for
10 minutes.

2 Prepare the squash (see
box, right). Blanch in
boiling salted water for
2 minutes. Arrange the
squash slices in a lightly
buttered ovenproof dish.

3 Heat the oil in a
saucepan, add the shallot,
and cook gently for a few
minutes, until softened. Add
the mushrooms, lemon zest
and juice, and salt and
pepper to taste and cook for
8 minutes or until tender.

4 Strain the mushroom
mixture and stir into the
couscous. Add the scallions,
yogurt, mint, olives, and salt
and pepper to taste.

5 Spoon the couscous
mixture into the squash
slices. Cover loosely with foil
and bake in a 375°F (180°C)
oven for 20–25 minutes.
Serve immediately, with the
tomato sauce, and garnished
with the chopped parsley.

Preparing the squash

Peel the squash, cut it
into 2-in (5-cm) slices,
and scoop out and discard
the seeds from the middle.

MUSHROOM LASAGNE

 Serves 6

2 tbsp olive oil

1 large onion, chopped

1 lb (500 g) mushrooms, sliced

2 large garlic cloves, crushed

1/4 cup (30 g) all purpose flour

26 oz (800 g) canned chopped tomatoes

1 tbsp chopped fresh basil

1 tsp sugar

salt and black pepper

1 lb (500 g) frozen leaf spinach, thawed and drained

2 1/2 cups (300 g) grated aged Cheddar cheese

6–8 no-precook lasagne noodles

WHITE SAUCE

6 tbsp (90 g) butter

2/3 cup (90 g) all purpose flour

3 2/3 cups (900 ml) milk

1 tsp Dijon mustard

1 Heat the oil in a large saucepan, add the onion, and cook gently for 3–5 minutes, until softened. Add the mushrooms and garlic and cook for 5 minutes. Add the flour and cook, stirring, for 1 minute.

2 Add the tomatoes, basil, sugar, and salt and pepper to taste. Cover and simmer for 20 minutes.

3 Make the white sauce: melt the butter in a saucepan, add the flour, and cook, stirring, for 1 minute. Remove from the heat and gradually blend in the milk. Bring to a boil, stirring, until thickened. Simmer for 2–3 minutes. Add the mustard and season. Set aside.

4 Season the spinach with salt and pepper. Taking 1 teaspoonful at a time, shape it loosely into 24 balls.

5 Spoon one-third of the mushroom mixture into a large ovenproof dish and place 8 of the spinach balls on top. Cover with one-third of the sauce and one-third of the cheese. Arrange half of the lasagne noodles on top. Repeat the layers, finishing with the cheese.

6 Bake in a 375°F (190°C) oven for 35 minutes or until the pasta is tender and the top is golden.

DAIRY-FREE LASAGNE

 Serves 4–6

1 eggplant, cut into 1/4-in (5-mm) slices

salt and black pepper

3 tbsp olive oil

2 zucchini, sliced

1/2 lb (250 g) frozen chopped spinach, thawed and drained

2 onions, chopped

1 red pepper, cored, seeded, and diced

2 garlic cloves, crushed

26 oz (800 g) canned chopped tomatoes

1/2 cup (140 g) tomato paste

1/4 tsp sugar

3 tbsp chopped fresh basil

6–8 no-precook lasagne noodles

1 Place the eggplant slices in a colander, sprinkle generously with salt, and leave to stand for about 30 minutes.

2 Heat 1 tbsp of the oil in a large skillet, add the zucchini and cook for 3 minutes. Transfer the zucchini to a bowl and add salt to taste. Season the spinach with salt and pepper and set aside.

3 Rinse the eggplant and pat dry with paper towels. Heat the remaining oil in the skillet, and cook the eggplant for 3–5 minutes on each side, until golden. Remove and set aside.

4 Add the onions, red pepper, and garlic to the pan, and cook gently, stirring, for 3–5 minutes, until softened. Add the tomatoes, tomato paste, and sugar and bring to a boil. Simmer for 10 minutes, until thickened, then stir in the basil, and season with salt and pepper.

5 Spoon one-third of the tomato sauce into a large ovenproof dish and cover with one-third of the lasagne noodles. Add the eggplant, then half of the remaining tomato sauce. Add half of the remaining lasagne noodles, then the spinach. Add the remaining lasagne and tomato sauce, and finish with an overlapping layer of zucchini.

6 Bake in a 375°F (190°C) oven for 35 minutes or until tender and golden.

SPINACH GNOCCHI WITH TOMATO SAUCE

 Serves 4

2 lb (1 kg) spinach

1¹/₂ cups (375 g) ricotta cheese

3 eggs

¹/₄ cup (30 g) grated Parmesan cheese

pinch of grated nutmeg

salt and black pepper

8–9 tbsp (60–75 g) all-purpose flour

TOMATO SAUCE

2 tbsp butter

1 small onion, chopped

1 small carrot, chopped

¹/₄ cup (30 g) all-purpose flour

13 oz (400 g) canned chopped tomatoes

1¹/₄ cups (300 ml) vegetable stock

1 bay leaf

1 tsp sugar

TO SERVE

¹/₄ lb (125 g) butter

grated Parmesan cheese and Parmesan shavings

1 Wash the spinach and put into a saucepan with only the water remaining on the leaves. Cook over gentle heat until just wilted. Drain throughly, squeezing to remove any excess water.

2 Put the spinach, ricotta, eggs, Parmesan, nutmeg, and salt and pepper to taste into a food processor and puree until smooth. Transfer to a bowl. Gradually add flour until the mixture just holds its shape.

3 Using 2 soup spoons, form the mixture into 20 oval shapes. Cover and chill in the refrigerator for 1 hour.

4 Make the tomato sauce: melt the butter in a pan, add the onion and carrot, and cook for 10 minutes or until softened. Add the flour and cook, stirring, for 1 minute. Add the tomatoes, stock, bay leaf, sugar, and salt and pepper to taste and bring to a boil. Cover and simmer for 30 minutes. Puree in a food processor until smooth. Keep warm.

5 Cook the gnocchi in batches in boiling salted water for 5 minutes or until they float to the surface. Lift out and keep warm.

6 Melt the butter and pour over the gnocchi. Serve with the tomato sauce, grated Parmesan, and Parmesan shavings.

POLENTA WITH GRILLED VEGETABLES

 Serves 4–6

1 cup (175 g) instant polenta

2/3 cup (150 ml) cold water

2¹/₃ cups (600 ml) boiling salted water

2 tbsp butter

2 zucchini, halved and thickly sliced lengthwise

1 fennel bulb, trimmed and quartered lengthwise

2 tomatoes, cored and sliced

1 red onion, thickly sliced

melted butter for brushing

MARINADE

¹/₄ cup (60 ml) olive oil

2 tbsp red wine vinegar

3 garlic cloves, chopped

2–3 tbsp chopped parsley

salt and black pepper

1 Put the polenta into a saucepan, cover with the measured cold water, and leave to stand for 5 minutes.

2 Add the boiling salted water to the pan, return to a boil, and simmer for 10–15 minutes, stirring, until smooth and thickened.

3 Sprinkle a baking sheet with water. Stir the butter into the polenta, then spread the mixture over the baking sheet in a 1-cm (¹/₂-in) layer. Leave to cool.

4 Make the marinade: combine the oil, vinegar, garlic, parsley, and salt and pepper to taste. Add the zucchini, fennel, tomatoes, and onion. Cover and leave to marinate in the refrigerator for 30 minutes.

5 Lift the vegetables out of the marinade and cook over a hot barbecue for 2–3 minutes on each side. Cut the polenta into strips and cook over a hot barbecue, brushing with melted butter, for 1–2 minutes on each side, until golden. Serve hot.

Cook's know-how

Outside the barbecue season, cook the polenta and vegetables under the broiler, 4 in (10 cm) from the heat.

COUSCOUS WITH ROASTED PEPPERS

 Serves 4

1 large red pepper

1 large yellow pepper

1 cup (175 g) couscous

2 1/3 cups (600 ml) hot vegetable stock

2 tbsp olive oil

1/2 cup (60 g) blanched almonds

2 medium zucchini, sliced

1 large red onion, chopped

1 large carrot, thinly sliced

1–2 garlic cloves, crushed

13 oz (400 g) canned garbanzo beans, drained

1/2 tsp ground cumin

1/2 tsp curry powder

1/4–1/2 tsp crushed red pepper

salt and black pepper

chopped fresh cilantro to garnish

1 Cook the peppers under the broiler, 4 in (10 cm) from the heat, for 10 minutes or until charred. Seal in a paper bag and leave to cool.

2 Put the couscous into a bowl and add the stock. Cover and leave to stand for 10 minutes or until absorbed.

3 Meanwhile, heat the oil in a large skillet, add the almonds, and cook gently, stirring, for 3 minutes or until lightly browned.

4 Lift out with a slotted spoon and drain on paper towels. Add the zucchini, onion, carrot, and garlic to the pan and cook, stirring, for 5 minutes.

5 Stir in the garbanzo beans, cumin, curry powder, and crushed red pepper, and cook, stirring occasionally, for 5 minutes longer. Stir in the couscous, and cook for 3–4 minutes, until heated through. Season to taste.

6 Peel, core, and seed the peppers and cut into thin strips.

7 Divide the couscous among warmed serving plates and arrange the pepper strips on top. Serve immediately, sprinkled with the almonds and the chopped cilantro.

VEGETABLE & BARLEY CASSEROLE

 Serves 4

1 tbsp butter

8 large shallots or small onions, halved

5 cups (1.25 liters) vegetable stock

1/2 lb (250 g) baby carrots

1/2 lb (250 g) baby parsnips

1/3 cup (60 g) pearl barley

1 bay leaf

2 zucchini, sliced

1 small cauliflower, separated into florets

1/4 lb (125 g) snow peas

1 tbsp chopped fresh mixed herbs

DUMPLINGS

1 cup (125 g) self-rising flour

1/3 cup (60 g) vegetable shortening, in pieces

1 tbsp chopped fresh mixed herbs

salt and black pepper

1 Make the dumplings: sift the flour into a bowl, and add the shortening, herbs, and salt and pepper to taste. Add enough water to make a soft but not sticky dough. Shape into 16 balls. Cover and set aside.

2 Melt the butter in a large flameproof casserole. When the butter is foaming, add the shallots and cook gently, stirring occasionally, for 3–5 minutes, until soft but not browned.

3 Add the stock, carrots, parsnips, barley, and bay leaf, and bring to a boil. Cover and bake in a 375°F (190°C) oven for about 30 minutes.

4 Remove the casserole from the oven and stir in the zucchini, cauliflower, snow peas, herbs, and salt and pepper to taste.

5 Arrange the dumplings on top of the casserole, cover, and return to the oven for 20 minutes or until the dumplings are cooked. Remove and discard the bay leaf and serve immediately.

TOMATO & OLIVE TART

 Serves 6

3 tbsp olive oil

2 large onions, coarsely chopped

3 garlic cloves, crushed

13 oz (400 g) canned chopped tomatoes

1/2 cup (140 g) tomato paste

2 tsp chopped fresh basil

1 tsp sugar

1 cup (125 g) grated mozzarella cheese

3/4 cup (90 g) pitted black olives

shredded fresh basil to garnish

POPPY-SEED BASE

2 cups (250 g) all-purpose flour

1/4 lb (125 g) butter

heaped 1/2 cup (90 g) poppy seeds

1 tbsp packed dark brown sugar

salt and black pepper

about 1/4 cup (60 ml) cold water

1 Make the poppy-seed base: work the flour, butter, poppy seeds, dark brown sugar, and salt and pepper to taste in a food processor until the mixture resembles fine bread crumbs. Add the measured water and work until the mixture forms a ball. Knead lightly. Shape the base (see box, right).

2 Heat the oil in a pan, add the onions and garlic, and cook gently for 3–5 minutes, until soft. Add the tomatoes, tomato paste, basil, and sugar. Season to taste and bring to a boil. Boil for 5–7 minutes, until thick. Leave to cool slightly.

3 Bake the poppy-seed tart base in a 425°F (220°C) oven for 15 minutes. Spread the tomato mixture over the tart base, sprinkle with the grated cheese and olives, and bake for 15–20 minutes. Serve hot or cold, sprinkled with basil.

Shaping the tart base

Roll out the pastry into a 12-in (30-cm) round on a baking sheet, then pinch the edge to form a small rim. Prick the pastry base all over with a fork. Chill for 30 minutes.

MUSHROOM GOUGERE

 Serves 4

4 tbsp butter

4 1/2 cups (375 g) sliced mixed mushrooms, such as oyster, shiitake, and white

1/2 cup (60 g) all-purpose flour

1 3/4 cups (450 ml) milk

1 tsp chopped fresh tarragon

tarragon leaves to garnish

CHOUX PASTRY

1 cup (125 g) all-purpose flour

salt and black pepper

1 1/4 cups (300 ml) water

4 tbsp butter, plus extra for greasing

4 eggs, beaten

1 Make the choux pastry: sift the flour with a pinch of salt. Put the measured water and butter into a saucepan and bring to a boil.

2 Remove from the heat and add the flour. Beat well until the mixture is smooth and glossy and leaves the side of the pan clean. Leave to cool slightly.

3 Beat the eggs into the flour mixture until smooth and glossy. Make the gougère (see box, right). Cover and chill while preparing the filling.

4 Melt the butter in a large saucepan, add the mushrooms, and cook gently for 3–4 minutes. Lift out with a slotted spoon and set aside. Add the flour and cook, stirring, for 1 minute. Remove from the heat and gradually blend in the milk. Bring to a boil, stirring until the mixture thickens. Simmer for 2–3 minutes.

5 Return the mushrooms to the pan add the tarragon, and salt and pepper to taste. Pour into the middle of the choux ring and bake in a 425°F (220°C) oven for 35–40 minutes, until well risen and golden. Garnish with tarragon, and serve hot.

Making the gougère

Butter a large shallow ovenproof dish and lightly press the choux pastry around the edge.

SPINACH & RICOTTA TRIANGLES

 Serves 4

4 sheets of phyllo pastry

4 tbsp melted butter, plus extra for greasing

FILLING

2 tbsp butter

1 small onion, finely chopped

10 oz (300 g) spinach, shredded

1/2 cup (125 g) ricotta cheese

pinch of grated nutmeg

salt and black pepper

tomato sauce (page 286) to serve

1 Make the filling: melt the butter in a saucepan, add the onion, and cook gently for 3–5 minutes, until softened.

2 Add the spinach to the onion and cook for 1–2 minutes. Leave to cool. Add the ricotta cheese, nutmeg, and salt and pepper to taste, and mix well. Divide into 8 portions.

3 Lightly butter a baking sheet. Cut each sheet of phyllo pastry lengthwise into 2 long strips. Brush 1 strip with melted butter, covering the remaining strips with a damp kitchen towel. Fill and fold the triangles (see box, right).

4 Bake the triangles in a 400°F (200°C) oven for 20 minutes or until the pastry is crisp and golden. Serve with the tomato sauce.

Filling and folding the triangles

Spoon 1 portion of filling onto a corner of the phyllo strip. Fold over opposite corner to form a triangle.

Fold the filled triangle until you reach the end of the strip. Brush with melted butter and put onto the baking sheet. Butter, fill, and fold the remaining phyllo strips.

EGGPLANT & CHEESE PHYLLO PIE

Serves 6

2 eggplant, cut into 1/2-in (1-cm) dice

salt and black pepper

2 tbsp olive oil

2 large onions, chopped

2 tsp ground cumin

2 tsp ground coriander

2 tsp mild curry powder or paste

2 red peppers, cored, seeded, and diced

1 cup (175 g) red lentils

1/2 lb (250 g) feta cheese, diced

1/4 cup (30 g) chopped fresh oregano

10-oz (300-g) package phyllo pastry

4 tbsp melted butter

* 101/2-in (26-cm) springform cake pan

1 Put the eggplant into a colander, sprinkle generously with salt, and leave to stand for 30 minutes.

2 Heat the oil in a large pan. Cook the onions for 3–5 minutes. Add the cumin, coriander, and curry paste and cook for 2 minutes.

3 Drain the eggplant and pat dry with paper towels. Add to the onion mixture with the red peppers and cook for 10–15 minutes, until soft. Add salt and pepper to taste and leave to cool.

4 Meanwhile, put the lentils into a pan, cover with water, and bring to a boil. Simmer for 15 minutes or until just soft. Drain and cool.

5 Stir the lentils, feta cheese, and chopped oregano into the eggplant mixture. Taste for seasoning.

6 Using two-thirds of the phyllo pastry, line the bottom and side of the cake pan, brushing each sheet with butter, and letting the sheets hang over the rim of the pan. Spoon in the eggplant mixture and fold the phyllo sheets over the top. Brush the remaining phyllo with butter, crumple up, and arrange on top of the pie.

7 Bake the pie in a 375°F (190°C) oven for 40 minutes or until the pastry is golden and crisp. Serve hot.

VEGETARIAN CURRIES

The cuisine of India, with its use of aromatic spices to enhance the flavor of vegetables and legumes, is one in which vegetarians can find a whole range of dishes to whet their appetites. The tradition of eating a selection of small dishes, accompanied by rice and breads, makes for well-balanced, nutritious meals.

MIXED VEGETABLE CURRY

 Serves 4

2 tbsp sunflower or corn oil

2 tsp ground coriander

1/4– 1/2 tsp chili powder

1/4 tsp turmeric

1-in (2.5-cm) piece of fresh ginger, peeled and grated

1 large onion, chopped

2 garlic cloves, crushed

1 small cauliflower, cut into florets

2 potatoes, cut into chunks

2 large carrots, sliced

1 green pepper, cored, seeded, and cut into chunks

1 fresh green chili, cored, seeded, and finely chopped

13 oz (400 g) canned chopped tomatoes

2/3 cup (150 ml) coconut milk

salt and black pepper

juice of 1/2 lemon

fresh cilantro leaves to garnish

1 Heat the oil in a large saucepan, add the coriander, chili powder, and turmeric, and cook, stirring constantly, for 1 minute.

2 Add the ginger, onion, and garlic to the pan, and cook, stirring, for 3–5 minutes, until the onion is softened but not browned.

3 Add the cauliflower, potatoes, and carrots to the pan, and stir well to coat in the spices. Cook, stirring occasionally, for 5 minutes.

4 Add the green pepper, chili, tomatoes, and coconut milk to the pan, with salt and pepper to taste. Stir well to combine.

5 Bring to a boil. Cover and simmer gently for 25–30 minutes, until the vegetables are just tender. Stir in the lemon juice. Serve immediately, garnished with cilantro leaves.

ALU SAGH

 Serves 4

1 lb (500 g) new potatoes

salt

1 lb (500 g) frozen spinach, thawed

1 cup (250 ml) water

2 tbsp butter

1 onion, chopped

3 garlic cloves, chopped

1-in (2.5-cm) piece of fresh ginger, peeled and grated

1 small fresh green chili, cored, seeded, and finely chopped

1 tsp ground coriander

1/2 tsp ground cumin

1/2 tsp turmeric

1/2 tsp garam masala

2 tbsp lime or lemon juice

2–3 tbsp chopped fresh cilantro leaves

1 Cook the potatoes in a saucepan of boiling salted water for 10 minutes. Drain and leave to cool. Cut into bite-sized pieces and set aside.

2 In a food processor or blender, puree the spinach with the measured water. Set aside.

3 Melt the butter in a large, heavy skillet. When the butter is foaming, add the onion, garlic, ginger, and chili and cook for about 5 minutes, until softened.

4 Add 1 tsp salt, the ground coriander and cumin, turmeric, and garam masala. Cook, stirring, for 1 minute. Add the potatoes and turn to coat in the spices. Cover and cook over gentle heat for 15 minutes or until the potatoes are tender.

5 Remove the lid and add the spinach puree. Increase the heat and cook for about 10 minutes, until the spinach thickens into a saucelike consistency. Stir in the lime juice and cilantro leaves, and serve immediately.

DAL

 Serves 4

1/4 cup (60 ml) olive oil

2 onions, thinly sliced

1 large garlic clove, crushed

2 tsp cumin seeds

2 tsp hot Madras curry powder

2 tsp ground coriander

1 cinnamon stick

8 cloves

1 1/4 cups (250 g) red lentils

3 2/3 cups (900 ml) vegetable stock

2 bay leaves

salt and black pepper

1 Heat the oil in a saucepan, add the onions, garlic, and cumin, and cook for 3–5 minutes, until the onions are soft. Add the curry powder and coriander, increase the heat, and cook, stirring, until the onions begin to brown.

2 Add the cinnamon, cloves, and lentils. Cook, stirring, for 1 minute. Add the stock and bring to a boil.

3 Add the bay leaves and salt and pepper to taste, cover, and simmer, stirring occasionally, for about 1 hour, until the lentils are tender and the liquid has reduced. Remove the cinnamon stick. Serve immediately.

Clockwise from top: *Mixed Vegetable Curry, Dal, Alu Sagh.*

Curry accompaniments

Serve some of these side dishes for an authentic Indian meal:

- tomato and cilantro relish
- plain yogurt and cucumber
- grated carrot salad
- mango chutney
- papadoms
- basmati rice
- naan bread

Red Lentil & Coconut Curry

 Serves 4–6

1¹/₂ cups (300 g) red lentils

3²/₃ cups (900 ml) water

1-in (2.5-cm) piece of fresh ginger, peeled and chopped

1¹/₂ fresh green chilies, cored, seeded, and finely chopped

4 garlic cloves

1 cup (250 ml) coconut milk

¹/₂ tsp turmeric

¹/₂ tsp ground ginger

1 tbsp lemon juice

salt

2 tbsp butter

4 tsp black mustard seeds

1 Put the red lentils into a saucepan and add the measured water. Bring to a boil and simmer for 20 minutes or until tender.

2 Using a mortar and pestle, crush the fresh ginger, two-thirds of the chilies, and 2 of the garlic cloves until smooth. Add to the red lentils.

3 Add the coconut milk, turmeric, ground ginger, lemon juice, and salt to taste. Cook gently, stirring, for 1 minute, then increase the heat and cook for 5 minutes or until any excess liquid has evaporated. Taste for seasoning.

4 Crush the remaining garlic and set aside. Melt the butter in a skillet and add the mustard seeds. As soon as they begin to pop, remove the skillet from the heat and stir in the crushed garlic and the remaining chopped chili.

5 Transfer the lentil mixture to a warmed serving dish and top with the garlic, chili, and mustard seed butter. Serve the curry immediately.

Red Bean & Tomato Curry

 Serves 4

2 tbsp sunflower or corn oil

1 large onion, sliced

5 garlic cloves, crushed

1–2 fresh green chilies, cored, seeded, and sliced

1-in (2.5-cm) piece of fresh ginger, peeled and chopped

1 tsp curry powder

1 tsp turmeric

¹/₂ tsp ground coriander

pinch of cayenne pepper

salt

13 oz (400 g) canned chopped tomatoes

20 oz (600 g) canned red kidney beans, drained

1 tbsp lemon juice

fresh cilantro leaves to garnish

1 Heat the sunflower oil in a large skillet, add the onion, garlic, chilies, and ginger, and cook, stirring occasionally, for a few minutes, until all the aromas are released and the onion is softened but not browned.

2 Add the curry powder, turmeric, ground coriander, cayenne pepper, and salt to taste and cook, stirring, for 2 minutes.

3 Add the tomatoes with most of their juice and cook for about 3 minutes. Add the beans and cook for 5 minutes longer or until the beans are warmed through and the sauce is thickened. Add the lemon juice and serve hot, garnished with cilantro leaves.

Garbanzo Bean, Red Bean, & Tomato Curry

Substitute 13 oz (400 g) canned garbanzo beans for 13 oz (400 g) of the red kidney beans and proceed as directed in the recipe.

FALAFEL WITH SESAME YOGURT SAUCE

 Serves 4–6

13 oz (400 g) canned garbanzo beans, drained

6 scallions, finely chopped

1/2 cup (30 g) fresh white bread crumbs

1 egg, lightly beaten

grated zest and juice of 1/2 lemon

1 garlic clove, crushed

2 tbsp chopped fresh cilantro

2 tbsp chopped parsley

1 tbsp tahini paste

1 tsp ground coriander

1 tsp ground cumin

1/2 tsp ground cinnamon

pinch of cayenne pepper

salt and black pepper

sunflower oil for deep-frying

warmed mini pita bread to serve

chopped fresh cilantro to garnish

SESAME YOGURT SAUCE

4 tbsp plain yogurt

2 tbsp olive oil

1 tbsp lemon juice

1 tbsp tahini paste

1 In a food processor, puree the garbanzo beans, scallions, bread crumbs, egg, lemon zest and juice, garlic, cilantro, parsley, tahini, ground coriander, cumin, cinnamon, cayenne pepper, and salt and pepper to taste until smooth.

2 Transfer to a bowl, cover, and leave to stand for at least 30 minutes.

3 Meanwhile, make the sesame yogurt sauce: in a bowl, combine the yogurt, oil, lemon juice, tahini, and salt and pepper to taste. Cover and set aside.

4 With dampened hands, shape the falafel mixture into balls about the size of a walnut, then flatten them into patties.

5 In a deep-fat fryer, heat the oil to 375°F (190°C). Lower the falafel into the fryer in batches and cook for 2–3 minutes, until golden. Lift out and drain on paper towels. Serve warm, with pita bread and sesame yogurt sauce, garnished with chopped cilantro.

Tahini

This is a paste made from ground sesame seeds that has a rich smoky aroma and flavor. It is available in most supermarkets and Middle Eastern delicatessens.

FETA & VEGETABLE KEBABS

 Serves 4

1 small baguette

1/2 lb (250 g) feta cheese

1 small red pepper, cored and seeded

2/3 cup (150 ml) olive oil, plus extra for greasing

16 large cherry tomatoes

grated zest and juice of 1 lemon

1 garlic clove, crushed

2 tbsp chopped fresh basil

1 tbsp snipped fresh chives

salt and black pepper

✻ 8 metal skewers

1 Cut the bread into 8 thick slices and cut each slice in half. Cut the feta cheese into 16 cubes and cut the red pepper into 8 pieces.

2 Oil the skewers and thread alternately with the tomatoes, bread, cheese, and pepper. Place in a shallow flameproof dish.

3 Mix the oil, lemon zest and juice, garlic, herbs, and salt and pepper to taste. Drizzle over the kebabs. Leave to stand for 10 minutes.

4 Cook the kebabs over a hot barbecue or under the broiler, 4 in (10 cm) from the heat, and cook, turning once and basting with the marinade, for 3–4 minutes, until the cheese is lightly browned.

Cook's know-how

Feta is a crumbly Greek cheese that is usually made from sheep's milk. It has a chewy texture and, once heated, must be eaten while still hot or it becomes slightly rubbery.

TOFU & VEGETABLE KEBABS

Substitute smoked tofu for the feta cheese and 8 small whole mushrooms for the red pepper and proceed as directed.

VEGETABLE STIR-FRY WITH TOFU

 Serves 4

¹/2 lb (250 g) firm tofu, cut into bite-sized pieces

2 tbsp sesame oil

1 tbsp sunflower or corn oil

1 head of endive, halved lengthwise

4 carrots, thinly sliced diagonally

2-in (5-cm) piece of fresh ginger, peeled and finely chopped

¹/2 lb (250 g) shiitake mushrooms, sliced

8 scallions, sliced into 1-in (2.5-cm) pieces

2 cups (250 g) bean sprouts

3 tbsp toasted sesame seeds

MARINADE

3 tbsp soy sauce

3 tbsp dry sherry

1 garlic clove, crushed

salt and black pepper

1 Make the marinade: in a bowl, combine the soy sauce, sherry, garlic, and salt and pepper to taste. Turn the tofu in the marinade, cover, and leave to marinate at room temperature for at least 15 minutes.

2 Drain the tofu, reserving the marinade. Heat the sesame and sunflower oils in a wok or large skillet, add the tofu, and carefully stir-fry over high heat for 2–3 minutes, being careful not to break up the tofu. Remove from the wok with a slotted spoon and drain on paper towels.

3 Separate the endive halves into leaves. Add the carrots and ginger to the wok and stir-fry for about 2 minutes. Add the mushrooms and scallions and stir-fry for 2 minutes longer, then add the bean sprouts and endive leaves and stir-fry for 1 minute.

4 Return the tofu to the wok, pour the reserved marinade over the top, and boil quickly until almost all of the marinade has evaporated and the tofu has warmed through. Generously sprinkle the stir-fry with the toasted sesame seeds, taste for seasoning, and serve immediately.

MEXICAN CHILI WITH TOFU

 Serves 4–6

3 onions, chopped

3 garlic cloves

1 fresh green chili, cored, seeded, and chopped

2 tsp paprika

2 tsp mild chili powder

1 tsp ground cumin

¹/2 tsp dried oregano

¹/4 cup (60 ml) sunflower oil

13 oz (400 g) canned chopped tomatoes, drained and juice reserved

2 cups (500 ml) hot vegetable stock

1¹/4 lb (625 g) firm tofu, cut into bite-sized pieces

13 oz (400 g) canned red kidney beans, drained

salt and black pepper

chopped fresh cilantro to garnish

1 Put the onions, garlic, green chili, spices, and oregano into a food processor and work until smooth.

2 Heat the oil in a large skillet. Add the onion mixture and cook until fragrant.

3 Add half of the tomatoes to the pan and cook until reduced and thickened. Add the remaining tomatoes, allowing them to reduce and thicken. Pour in the stock and cook for 5–10 minutes, until the mixture thickens.

4 Add the tofu, kidney beans, and the reserved tomato juice and cook, spooning the sauce over the tofu pieces, for 5–8 minutes, until heated through. Do not stir the tofu as it may break up. Season, and serve hot, sprinkled with cilantro.

Cook's know-how

Reducing a sauce involves cooking it over high heat to allow the moisture to evaporate and the flavors to become concentrated.

VEGETARIAN BURGERS

Serves 6

13 oz (400 g) canned soybeans, drained

1/2 cup (125 ml) tomato juice or water

1/2 cup (90 g) "ground" textured vegetable protein (TVP)

1 onion, chopped

1/2 cup (30 g) fresh white bread crumbs

1 egg

2 tbsp lightly crushed sesame seeds

1 tbsp chopped parsley

1 vegetable bouillon cube, crumbled

1/2 tsp dried oregano

salt and black pepper

1/3 cup (45 g) all-purpose flour

1/4 cup (60 ml) olive oil

LETTUCE DRESSING

1/4 cup (60 ml) mayonnaise

2 tbsp Dijon mustard

dash of lemon juice

1/2 small iceberg lettuce, shredded

1/4 onion, thinly sliced

1 Puree the soybeans in a food processor. Put into a bowl and add the tomato juice, TVP, onion, bread crumbs, egg, sesame seeds, parsley, bouillon cube, oregano, and salt and pepper to taste. Chill for 30 minutes.

2 Shape the mixture into 6 burgers. Sprinkle the flour onto a plate. Dip each burger into the flour, coating both sides.

3 Heat the oil in a skillet, add the burgers, and cook for 1–2 minutes on each side, until browned.

4 Arrange the burgers on a baking sheet and cook in a 350°F (180°C) oven for about 20 minutes, until cooked through.

5 Make the lettuce dressing: combine the mayonnaise, mustard, and lemon juice. Stir in the shredded iceberg lettuce and onion. Serve the burgers immediately, with the dressing.

SPICY RED BEAN BURGERS

Substitute 13 oz (400 g) canned red kidney beans for the soybeans. Proceed as directed adding 1 tbsp chopped parsley, 1 tsp paprika, 1 tsp mild chili powder, and 1/2 tsp ground cumin.

CHEESE SAUSAGES

Serves 4

2 1/2 cups (150 g) fresh white bread crumbs

1 cup (125 g) grated Cheddar cheese

1 small leek, finely chopped

1/4 cup (30 g) walnuts, finely ground

2 tbsp chopped fresh sage

1 tsp grated lemon zest

1 tsp dry mustard

1/2 cup (60 g) coarsely chopped goat cheese

2 eggs

1 tbsp milk

salt and black pepper

1/3 cup (45 g) all-purpose flour

2 tbsp sunflower or corn oil

shredded fresh sage to garnish

1 In a bowl, combine the bread crumbs, cheese, leek, walnuts, sage, lemon zest, and mustard powder. Gradually blend the goat cheese into the mixture.

2 Separate 1 egg, reserving the white and adding the yolk to the remaining egg. Beat the egg and yolk into the cheese mixture with the milk. Season to taste.

3 Divide the mixture into 8 pieces and roll into sausages about 3 in (7 cm) long. Cover and chill for about 1 hour to allow the flavors to develop.

4 Sprinkle the flour onto a plate. Brush the sausages with the reserved egg white, then dip into the flour until lightly coated all over. Shake off any excess flour.

5 Heat the oil in a skillet, add the sausages, and cook over medium heat, turning occasionally, for 8–10 minutes, until golden. Drain on paper towels, and serve immediately, garnished with sage.

GOAT CHEESE NUGGETS

Cut the goat cheese into 16 cubes. Combine the bread crumbs with the other ingredients as above. Mold the mixture around the goat cheese cubes, forming small balls. Chill, then proceed as directed.

CHESTNUT LOAF

 Serves 6

1/2 lb (250 g) frozen chestnuts, thawed, or canned chestnuts

1 tbsp olive oil, plus extra for greasing

1 onion, coarsely chopped

2 celery stalks, chopped

2 garlic cloves, crushed

1 large potato, boiled and mashed

2 cups (125 g) fresh whole-wheat bread crumbs

1 egg, beaten

2 tbsp chopped parsley

1 tbsp soy sauce

1 tbsp tomato paste

salt and black pepper

red pepper strips and watercress sprigs to garnish

spicy tomato salsa (see box, right) to serve

★ 8 1/2- x 4 1/2- x 2 1/2-in (21.5- x 11.5- x 6-cm) loaf pan

1 Coarsely chop half of the chestnuts and finely chop the remainder.

2 Heat the oil in a pan, add the onion, celery, and garlic, and cook, stirring, for 3–5 minutes, until soft.

3 Remove from the heat. Stir in all of the chestnuts, the potato, bread crumbs, egg, parsley, soy sauce, and tomato paste. Season to taste.

4 Lightly grease the loaf pan, spoon in the chestnut mixture, and level the top. Cover with foil and cook in a 350°F (180°C) oven for 1 hour or until firm.

5 Turn out, cut into slices, and garnish. Serve hot or cold, with the salsa.

Spicy tomato salsa

Peel (page 39) and seed 8 large tomatoes. Dice and put into a bowl.

Stir in 2 chopped scallions, 1 chopped fresh green chili, zest and juice of 2 limes, 3 tbsp chopped fresh cilantro, 1 tsp superfine sugar, and salt and pepper. Chill.

FESTIVE NUT LOAF

 Serves 6–8

1/3 cup (75 g) brown rice

salt and black pepper

1/2 oz (15 g) dried porcini

2 tbsp butter

2 carrots, grated

1 small onion, finely chopped

1 garlic clove, crushed

1/2 lb (250 g) mushrooms, chopped

2 tbsp chopped parsley

1 tbsp chopped fresh rosemary

1 cup (125 g) walnuts, toasted and chopped

1 cup (125 g) Brazil nuts, toasted and chopped

1/2 cup (60 g) pine nuts, toasted

1 1/2 cups (175 g) grated Cheddar cheese

1 egg, beaten

sunflower or corn oil for greasing

rosemary sprigs to garnish

cranberry sauce to serve

★ 8 1/2- x 4 1/2- x 2 1/2-in (21.5- x 11.5- x 6-cm) loaf pan

1 Cook the rice in boiling salted water for 30–35 minutes, until tender. Drain.

2 Cover the porcini with boiling water and leave to soak for 30 minutes.

3 Drain the porcini, rinse under cold water, and pat dry. Chop finely.

4 Melt the butter in a skillet, add the carrots, onion, and garlic, and cook gently, stirring occasionally, for 5 minutes. Stir in the mushrooms, rice, porcini, parsley, and rosemary and cook until softened.

5 Puree the mixture in a food processor. Stir in the walnuts, Brazil nuts, pine nuts, cheese, egg, and salt and pepper to taste.

6 Lightly grease the loaf pan, spoon in the mixture, and level the top. Cover with foil and bake in a 375°F (190°C) oven for 1 1/2 hours or until firm. Turn out, cut into slices, and garnish. Serve hot, with cranberry sauce.

Porcini

Known as cèpes in French, porcini are small, flavorful mushrooms, often sold dried.

SPINACH ROULADE

Serves 6–8

1 lb 2 oz (560 g) spinach

2 tbsp butter, plus extra for greasing

4 eggs, separated

pinch of grated nutmeg

1 tbsp finely grated Parmesan cheese

FILLING

1 tbsp butter

1/2 lb (250 g) mushrooms, sliced

juice of 1/2 lemon

salt and black pepper

1 scant cup (200 ml) light sour cream

2 tbsp chopped parsley

★ 13- x 9-in (33- x 23-cm) jelly roll pan

1 Make the filling: melt the butter in a pan, add the mushrooms, lemon juice, and salt and pepper to taste, and cook for 3 minutes, until just softened. Leave to cool.

2 Wash the spinach and put into a saucepan with only the water remaining on the leaves. Cook over gentle heat for 1–2 minutes, until the spinach has just wilted. Drain well, squeezing to remove excess water.

3 Butter the pan and line with baking parchment. Butter the parchment.

4 Coarsely chop the spinach, transfer to a large bowl, and beat in the butter, egg yolks, nutmeg, and salt and pepper to taste. In another bowl, whisk the egg whites until firm but not dry, then fold gently into the spinach mixture.

5 Pour the spinach mixture into the jelly roll pan and bake in a 425°F (220°C) oven for 10–12 minutes, until firm.

6 Sprinkle the Parmesan cheese onto a sheet of baking parchment. Turn the roulade out onto the grated cheese, leave to cool for 5–10 minutes, then peel off the lining paper. Trim.

7 Drain the mushrooms, reserving some of the cooking liquid. Put them into a bowl, and add the light sour cream and parsley and season to taste. Add a little of the reserved liquid if too thick. Spread the filling over the roulade, leaving a 1-in (2.5-cm) border. Roll up from the long side. Cover and chill for 30 minutes. Cut into slices to serve.

CARROT ROULADE

Serves 4

1/4 lb (125 g) butter, plus extra for greasing

1 large garlic clove, crushed

1/2 red pepper, cored, seeded, and finely chopped

7 oz (200 g) canned tomatoes

1 1/2 lb (750 g) carrots, grated

6 eggs, separated

FILLING

1 cucumber, diced

salt and black pepper

1/4 lb (125 g) goat cheese

1/4 lb (125 g) cream cheese

3 scallions, thinly sliced

1 large garlic clove, crushed

2–3 tbsp finely chopped parsley

1/4 tsp dried thyme

plain yogurt if needed

★ 13- x 9-in (33- x 23-cm) jelly roll pan

1 Put the cucumber into a colander, sprinkle with salt, and leave to stand for 20 minutes.

2 Butter the pan and line with baking parchment. Butter the parchment.

3 Melt the butter, add half of the garlic, the red pepper, and tomatoes, and cook gently for 5 minutes.

4 Add the carrots and cook gently for 2 minutes or until soft. Transfer the carrot mixture to a large bowl and beat in the egg yolks and salt and pepper to taste. In another bowl, whisk the egg whites until firm but not dry, then fold into the carrot mixture.

5 Pour the mixture into the jelly roll pan and bake in a 400°F (200°C) oven for 10 minutes or until golden. Cover and leave to cool.

6 Make the filling: rinse the cucumber and pat dry with paper towels. Transfer the cucumber to a bowl and combine with the goat cheese, cream cheese, scallions, the garlic, parsley, thyme, and black pepper to taste. If the mixture is very thick, stir in 1–2 tbsp plain yogurt.

7 Turn the roulade out onto a sheet of baking parchment and peel off the lining paper. Trim the edges. Spread the filling over the roulade, leaving a 1-in (2.5-cm) border on each side. Roll up the roulade from the long side, using the paper for support. Cover and chill for 30 minutes. Cut into slices to serve.

CREAM CHEESE TERRINE

 Serves 8

12–16 large spinach leaves

salt and black pepper

1 eggplant, sliced lengthwise

1 tbsp olive oil, plus extra for greasing

2 large red peppers, cored, seeded, and halved

1 large yellow pepper, cored, seeded, and halved

1 lb (500 g) low-fat cream cheese

2 eggs, lightly beaten

1/4 cup (60 ml) light cream

1/3 cup (30 g) grated Parmesan cheese

2 tbsp store-bought pesto

★ *81/2- x 41/2- x 21/2-in (21.5- x 11.5- x 6-cm) loaf pan*

1 Blanch the spinach in boiling salted water for 30 seconds. Drain, rinse in cold water, and pat dry. Line the loaf pan (see box, right).

2 Brush the eggplant with the oil and cook under the broiler for 6–8 minutes on each side. Roast and peel the peppers (page 354). Cut the pepper halves into strips.

3 Combine the cream cheese, eggs, cream, grated Parmesan, pesto, and salt and pepper to taste.

Lining the loaf pan

Oil the loaf pan and line with the spinach leaves, letting 2 in (5 cm) hang over the sides.

4 Cover the bottom of the pan with some of the cheese mixture. Layer half of the red pepper, half of the eggplant, the yellow pepper, then the remaining eggplant and red pepper, spreading cheese mixture between each layer. Finish with the remaining cheese. Fold over the spinach leaves.

5 Oil a piece of foil and tightly cover the pan. Put the pan into a roasting pan and pour boiling water into the roasting pan to come halfway up the side of the loaf pan. Cook in a 350°F (180°C) oven for 1 1/2 hours or until firm. Remove the loaf pan, leave to cool, then chill thoroughly. Slice and serve.

WINTER VEGETABLE TERRINE

 Serves 4–6

6 carrots, coarsely chopped

1-in (2.5-cm) piece of fresh ginger, peeled and chopped

salt and black pepper

3/4 lb (375 g) celeriac, peeled and coarsely chopped

3/4 lb (375 g) broccoli, chopped

sunflower or corn oil for greasing

3 eggs

★ *81/2- x 41/2- x 21/2-in (21.5- x 11.5- x 6-cm) loaf pan or terrine*

1 Cook the carrots and fresh ginger in boiling salted water for 10–15 minutes, until just tender. Cook the celeriac in boiling salted water for 8–10 minutes, until tender.

2 Cut the stalks off the broccoli and cook them in boiling salted water for 8–10 minutes, until almost tender, then add the broccoli florets and cook for 1 minute longer.

3 Drain all of the vegetables separately and rinse in cold running water. Lightly oil the loaf pan and line the bottom with greaseproof paper.

4 Puree the broccoli, 1 of the eggs, and salt and pepper to taste in a food processor until smooth. Turn the broccoli mixture into the loaf pan and level the surface with a narrow spatula.

5 Puree the celeriac, 1 of the eggs, and salt and pepper to taste in the food processor until smooth. Spread over the broccoli mixture and level the surface.

6 Puree the carrots, ginger, the remaining egg, and salt and pepper to taste in the food processor until smooth. Spread over the celeriac layer and level the surface.

7 Oil a piece of foil and tightly cover the pan. Put the pan into a roasting pan and pour in boiling water to come halfway up the side of the pan. Cook in a 350°F (180°C) oven for 1 hour or until the terrine is firmly set.

8 Remove from the water and leave to cool in the loaf pan. Chill thoroughly in the refrigerator. Turn out the terrine and cut into slices to serve.

8

PASTA & RICE

UNDER 30 MINUTES

PENNE WITH SPINACH & STILTON

Pasta quills with mushrooms, cream, and garlic, mixed with spinach, Stilton cheese, and lemon juice.

SERVES 4 976 calories per serving

Takes 15 minutes   **PAGE 309**

PASTA ALLA MARINARA

Pasta bows combined with squid, scallops, shrimp, mushrooms, white wine, onion, and parsley. Enriched with cream.

SERVES 4 797 calories per serving

Takes 15 minutes   **PAGE 307**

SPAGHETTI CARBONARA

Crisp-cooked strips of bacon mixed with garlic, eggs, and Parmesan cheese, then tossed with spaghetti and light cream.

SERVES 4 906 calories per serving

Takes 20 minutes   **PAGE 312**

PASTA SHELLS WITH SCALLOPS

Scallops simmered with lemon juice, onion, peppercorns, and bay leaf. Served with a creamy mushroom sauce and pasta shells.

SERVES 4 753 calories per serving

Takes 25 minutes   **PAGE 308**

TAGLIATELLE WITH VEGETABLE RIBBONS

Zucchini and carrot ribbons cooked with tagliatelle. Mixed with cilantro sauce.

SERVES 4 878 calories per serving

Takes 25 minutes   **PAGE 309**

EGG-FRIED RICE

Delicious and simple: long-grain rice boiled and then stir-fried with bacon, peas, eggs, and bean sprouts. Sprinkled with scallions.

SERVES 4 441 calories per serving

Takes 25 minutes   **PAGE 326**

PENNE WITH ASPARAGUS

Bite-sized pieces of asparagus and pasta quills in a light, aromatic mixture of olive oil, garlic, basil, and goat cheese.

SERVES 4 693 calories per serving

Takes 20 minutes   **PAGE 310**

TORTELLINI WITH PEAS & BACON

Rich and creamy: baby peas and diced bacon combined with heavy cream, salt, black pepper, and a pinch of grated nutmeg.

SERVES 4 965 calories per serving

Takes 25 minutes

This delicious sauce is tossed with tortellini, and servings are sprinkled generously with grated Parmesan cheese.

PAGE 311

STIR-FRIED CHINESE NOODLES

Egg noodles stir-fried with snow peas, bean sprouts, shiitake mushrooms, garlic, and ginger, sprinkled with scallions.

SERVES 4 476 calories per serving

Takes 20 minutes, plus soaking   **PAGE 311**

CARIBBEAN RICE & BEANS

Traditional West Indian dish: rice cooked with kidney beans, stock, scallions, bacon, garlic, tomatoes, herbs, and spices.

SERVES 4 435 calories per serving

Takes 35 minutes   **PAGE 319**

RISI E BISI

Arborio rice cooked with peas, stock, and prosciutto. Flavored with garlic, onion, Parmesan cheese, and parsley.

SERVES 4–6 585–390 calories per serving

Takes 40 minutes   **PAGE 320**

SUMMER RISOTTO AL VERDE

Arborio rice cooked with stock and garlic, mixed with cream, blue cheese, pesto, and pine nuts. Served sprinkled with basil.

SERVES 4 734 calories per serving

Takes 35 minutes   **PAGE 323**

KEDGEREE

Anglo-Indian breakfast dish: long-grain rice baked with smoked haddock, hard-boiled eggs, cream, and lemon juice. Mixed with parsley.

SERVES 4 470 calories per serving

Takes 45 minutes   **PAGE 323**

TAGLIATELLE WITH SHRIMP

Ribbon pasta served with a sauce of mushrooms, tomatoes, shrimp, and light sour cream, garnished with parsley.

SERVES 4 734 calories per serving

Takes 35 minutes   **PAGE 308**

CONFETTI RICE

Long-grain rice simmered with tomatoes, stock, corn, onion, carrot, and peas, and flavored with garlic.

SERVES 4 356 calories per serving

Takes 30 minutes   **PAGE 319**

PASTA SPIRALS WITH MEATBALLS

Meatballs of ground veal, Parmesan cheese, bread crumbs, and parsley in a tomato and basil sauce. Served with pasta spirals.

SERVES 4–6 1022–681 calories per serving

Takes 35 minutes   **PAGE 313**

PERSIAN PILAF

Rice cooked with cumin and cardamom seeds, cinnamon, cloves, and bay leaves. Combined with pistachio nuts and raisins.

SERVES 4 426 calories per serving

Takes 40 minutes   **PAGE 321**

30–60 MINUTES

SPAGHETTI ALLE VONGOLE

Fresh clams cooked in tomatoes and wine and seasoned with onion, garlic, pepper flakes, and parsley. Served with spaghetti.

SERVES 4 626 calories per serving

Takes 40 minutes **PAGE 307**

BAKED WILD RICE

Basmati and wild rice baked with broccoli, garlic, onions, sour cream, mozzarella and Parmesan cheeses, and rosemary.

SERVES 4 669 calories per serving

Takes 60 minutes **PAGE 320**

FETTUCCINE PRIMAVERA

Asparagus, broccoli, zucchini, pepper, garlic, tomatoes, baby peas, and cream mixed with fettuccine. Served with basil and Parmesan.

SERVES 4 831 calories per serving

Takes 35 minutes **PAGE 312**

RISOTTO MILANESE

Rice cooked with stock and onion, flavored with saffron, and mixed with Parmesan cheese. Served with Parmesan shavings.

SERVES 4 604 calories per serving

Takes 45 minutes **PAGE 322**

PORTUGUESE RICE WITH TUNA

Nourishing meal: brown rice simmered with stock, bacon, and onion. Combined with fresh tuna, red peppers, and olives.

SERVES 4 603 calories per serving

Takes 45 minutes **PAGE 321**

TUNA CASSEROLE WITH FENNEL

Fresh and aromatic: fennel and onion baked with white sauce, pasta shells, tuna, eggs, and Cheddar cheese.

SERVES 4 768 calories per serving

Takes 45 minutes **PAGE 316**

SPAGHETTI ALL' AMATRICIANA

Diced bacon cooked with tomatoes, garlic, red and green peppers, fresh chili, and herbs, then tossed with spaghetti.

SERVES 4 646 calories per serving

Takes 40 minutes **PAGE 310**

CHICKEN LIVER RISOTTO

Wild and Arborio rice cooked with stock and bacon. Combined with chicken livers, mushrooms, and sun-dried tomatoes.

SERVES 4 619 calories per serving

Takes 40 minutes **PAGE 322**

VEGETABLES NAPOLETANA

Broccoli, shiitake mushrooms, red pepper, zucchini, and mustard-flavored white sauce baked with pasta corkscrews.

SERVES 4 713 calories per serving

Takes 55 minutes **PAGE 316**

THREE-CHEESE MACARONI

Macaroni baked with a sauce flavored with Fontina, mozzarella, and Parmesan cheeses and topped with bread crumbs.

SERVES 4–6 1272–848 calories per serving

Takes 1 hour 5 minutes   **PAGE 317**

LASAGNE

Pasta layered with ground beef, simmered with stock, tomatoes, celery, white sauce, and Cheddar and Parmesan cheeses.

SERVES 6 854 calories per serving

Takes 1½ hours, plus simmering   **PAGE 318**

CANNELLONI WITH RICOTTA & SPINACH

Cannelloni tubes filled with spinach and ricotta cheese and topped with tomato sauce.

SERVES 4–6 694–462 calories per serving

Takes 40 minutes, plus simmering   **PAGE 318**

FISHERMAN'S LASAGNE

Pasta layered with haddock, shrimp, zucchini, and parsley sauce. Sprinkled with Cheddar and Parmesan cheeses.

SERVES 6 636 calories per serving

Takes 1¼ hours   **PAGE 317**

SPAGHETTI BOLOGNESE

Traditional Italian dish: spaghetti served with a sauce of ground beef simmered with onion, celery, garlic, and tomatoes.

SERVES 4 904 calories per serving

Takes 15 minutes, plus simmering   **PAGE 313**

PAELLA

Chicken and rice are cooked in the oven with bacon, stock, tomatoes, onion, peppers, peas, and saffron. Mussels and shrimp are stirred *in and cooked gently on top of the stove, then the dish is served garnished with jumbo shrimp, lemon wedges, olives, and parsley.*

SERVES 6 718 calories per serving

Takes 1¼ hours   **PAGE 326**

PASTA & RICE KNOW-HOW

BOTH PASTA AND RICE are natural convenience foods. They're endlessly versatile and are easily combined with almost any ingredient imaginable to make appetizers, soups, main dishes, side dishes, salads, snacks, and even desserts.

Pasta and rice are very quick to cook and don't need any elaborate preparation. They are healthy too, providing essential nutrients, fiber, and, most important of all, carbohydrates for energy. And as long you don't overdo the rich ingredients such as butter, cream, and cheese, pasta and rice dishes can be very low in fat and calories.

BUYING & STORING

Pasta is now available both fresh and dried, in a variety of shapes. Commercial dried pasta is made from semolina mixed with water. Egg is sometimes added to dried pasta, and the fresh pasta available in supermarkets is normally enriched with eggs. Fresh pasta is convenient because it cooks quickly, but its texture and absorbency are not necessarily as good as those of some dried pasta. A good Italian brand of dried pasta, made from 100% durum wheat semolina (*semola di grano duro*), is often of superior quality.

Dried pasta, in a tightly closed package, will keep almost indefinitely in a kitchen cabinet (up to 2 years); fresh pasta must be refrigerated and can be kept for only 2–3 days (check the use-by date).

Rice is another good pantry standby. As long as it is stored in an airtight container in a dry, dark place, it will keep indefinitely. But make sure that the container is closed tightly to prevent moisture or insects from getting in. Store any leftover cooked pasta in a tightly closed container in the refrigerator and use it within 2 days. Rice should be eaten on the day it is cooked as it is susceptible to food poisoning bacteria.

MICROWAVING

There is no advantage to cooking pasta in a microwave oven since it takes just as long as cooking in a pan of boiling water. Many pasta sauces, however, are quickly prepared in the microwave, and dishes containing layered or filled pasta can also be cooked in the microwave. Another use for the microwave is reheating cooked pasta; be careful not to overcook it. The microwave is ideal for cooking rice, whether it is steamed or turned into a pilaf or risotto. The liquid does not have to be brought to a boil before the rice is added. Also, a risotto can be left unattended in the microwave and will turn out as tender and creamy as one made by the classic method.

FREEZING

Fresh pasta can be frozen for up to 3 months and then cooked from frozen. Layered or filled pasta dishes such as cannelloni, lasagne, and macaroni and cheese freeze very well and can also be stored for up to 3 months. Put them in foil or other freezer-proof containers that can go straight from the freezer into the oven.

There is no advantage to freezing cooked rice since it takes a long time to thaw – longer than it would take to cook a fresh batch.

It's not advisable to freeze pasta and rice in soups and other dishes that contain a lot of liquid because the pasta and rice become mushy when thawed. Instead, add when reheating the soup or casserole.

ASIAN NOODLES

Asian noodles are made from wheat, potato, or rice flour, and from soy or mung bean starch. The most popular types are available in supermarkets and delicatessens; fresh varieties can be found in Chinese or Japanese shops.

Egg noodles
The most common of Asian noodles. Made from wheat flour and egg and used in dishes such as chow mein. They are sold in flat sheets, which separate when cooked.

Cellophane noodles
Sometimes referred to as transparent noodles or bean thread noodles. They are made from ground mung bean flour.

Rice noodles
Long, thin, white strands, also called rice vermicelli. They are sold dried or fresh in bundles and will cook very quickly if soaked in water first.

Rice sticks
Made from ground rice and water. Similar to rice noodles but sold dried, as broad ribbons. They need to be soaked before cooking.

Noodles know-how

Allow 3–4 oz (90–125 g) or one flat sheet of noodles per person.

◆

Store dried noodles in the same way as pasta.

◆

Fresh noodles will keep for 3 days in the refrigerator.

PASTA SHAPES

Of the many pasta shapes available, there are some that are traditionally served with certain sauces – spaghetti with bolognese sauce, for example. But you can mix and match as you wish.

 Long, thin varieties Capelli d'angelo or angel hair, vermicelli, spaghettini, spaghetti, and bucatini are best served with a thin oily sauce that clings without making the strands stick together.

 Other shapes These include fusilli (spirals), conchiglie (shells), farfalle (bows), and a variety of small pasta shapes such as pastina and orzo, which are added to soups.

 Long flat ribbons Pastas such as linguine, fettuccine, and tagliatelle are usually served with a creamy sauce such as *alfredo*.

 Filled pastas Ravioli and tortellini are stuffed with ground meats or mixtures such as spinach and ricotta and served with a simple sauce.

 Tubular pasta Macaroni, penne (quills), and rigatoni are best with rich sauces that will coat them all over.

 Sheet pasta Flat sheets of lasagne are layered with sauce and baked. They can be rolled to make cannelloni for filling.

NO-PRECOOK LASAGNE

Sheets of dried lasagne, known as no-precook lasagne, are a great boon to the cook because they can be taken straight from the package and layered with the other ingredients. However, this lasagne absorbs liquid during cooking, so if you are using no-precook lasagne in a recipe that calls for fresh pasta or for ordinary dried lasagne, increase the quantity of sauce and make it thinner. Or briefly soak the no-precook lasagne in a bowl of hot water to soften it before layering in the baking dish.

Colored & flavored pasta

Not only does pasta come in a vast range of shapes, but you can also choose from a variety of colors and flavors. Green is the most common color and is derived from spinach. Other colors include red, made with tomato paste; pink, dyed with beets; yellow, dyed with saffron; and even black pasta colored with squid ink. These colorings affect the taste very little. Flavored pasta usually has such ingredients as herbs, garlic, or black pepper added to the dough. Serve with a complementary sauce.

COOKING PASTA

Here's the golden rule when cooking pasta: use plenty of salted water – at least 2 quarts (2 liters) water and 2 tsp salt for every 1/2 lb (250 g) of pasta.

1 Bring the salted water to a boil. Add the pasta and stir to separate. If cooking spaghetti, let the ends soften before stirring. Return the water to a boil as quickly as possible. Reduce the heat so that the water is bubbling briskly and cook, uncovered.

2 Immediately remove the pan from the heat and drain in a large colander, shaking the colander to drain the pasta thoroughly.

3 Return the pasta to the pan or transfer to a warmed bowl. Toss with olive oil or butter, add plenty of ground black pepper and chopped fresh herbs, if desired, and serve immediately.

Pasta know-how

To test pasta, lift out a piece and bite it – it should be tender but still a little firm. The Italians call this al dente, literally "to the tooth."

♦

If you are going to use the pasta in a baked dish such as lasagne, undercook it slightly. This stops it from becoming overcooked as it cooks in its own heat.

COOKING TIMES & QUANTITIES

These times can be only a guide because they depend on the freshness of fresh pasta and the age of dried pasta, as well as shape and thickness. Start timing as soon as the water returns to a boil and, for fresh pasta, start testing three-quarters of the way through the suggested cooking time. If using dried pasta, start testing as soon as the minimum time given on the package is reached. Fresh store-bought pasta takes 2–4 minutes, 7–10 minutes if filled. Most dried pastas cook in 8–12 minutes (less for fine pasta such as capelli d'angelo and vermicelli).

In Italy, pasta is usually eaten as a first course. Use 1 lb (500 g) fresh or dried pasta (uncooked weight) to serve 6 people as a first course and 4 people as a main dish. If the dish has a rich sauce or filling, it will stretch even farther. As an accompaniment to another dish, this amount would serve 6–8 people.

COOKING WITH RICE

The length of the rice grain determines the cooking method and its use. Short-grain rice (for example, Arborio rice) is almost round in shape. It is very starchy and best cooked by absorption, so after cooking it remains moist and sticky. Use short-grain rice for puddings, risottos, molded rice dishes, stir-fried rice, and croquettes. The grains of long-grain rice are separate, dry, and fluffy after cooking. Use it in pilafs, for rice salads, or in other savory dishes.

White rice has been milled to remove the husk, bran, and germ, while for brown rice only the tough outer husk has been removed, leaving the nutritious bran layer that gives the rice its distinctive color and nutty flavor.

COOKING RICE BY ABSORPTION

Cook the rice very gently in simmering salted water. Use 2 parts water to 1 part rice.

1 Bring the salted water to a boil and add the rice. Return to a boil and stir once. Cover, reduce the heat, and cook gently until the water is absorbed.

2 Remove the pan from the heat and leave to stand, covered, for at least 5 minutes. Fluff it up with chopsticks or a fork just before serving.

BOILING RICE

Long-grain rice should be rinsed well before boiling to remove starch that would cause stickiness.

1 Put the rice into a large bowl of cold water. Swirl it around with your fingertips until the water becomes milky. Drain and repeat until the water runs clear. Drain again. Bring a large saucepan of salted water to a boil and add the rice.

2 Bring the water back to a boil. Reduce the heat so that the water is simmering quite vigorously. Cook until the rice is just tender. Drain well and rinse with boiling water to remove any excess starch.

COOKING RISOTTO RICE

An authentic risotto requires constant attention since the liquid (usually stock) should be stirred into the rice very gradually. The stock must be hot, so bring it to a boil and keep it at a gentle simmer.

1 Heat butter or oil in a large saucepan and soften the onion, garlic, or other flavorings as specified in the recipe.

2 Add the rice and stir to coat the grains with the oil (this will keep them separate during cooking). Cook, stirring, for 1–2 minutes or until the rice grains look translucent.

3 Add a ladleful, about 2/3 cup (150 ml), of the stock. Cook until absorbed. Add another ladleful and cook until absorbed.

4 Continue adding stock, stirring, for 25–30 minutes. When the rice is tender but still firm to the bite, you have added enough stock.

RICE VARIETIES

There are many varieties of rice, each with a distinct flavor and aroma. Here are the most common.

 Long-grain
Mild in flavor. The most widely used type of white rice. Cook for 12–20 minutes.

 Basmati
Available both brown and white. Used in Indian dishes. Cook for 10–20 minutes.

 Brown
Has a slightly chewy texture with a mild nutty flavor. Cook for 30–45 minutes.

 Minute
Processed so the grains separate after cooking. Cook for 10–12 minutes.

 Risotto
A short-grain Italian variety, also called Arborio rice. Cook for 25–30 minutes.

Wild
Not a true rice, but an aquatic grass with a nutty flavor. Cook for 35–60 minutes.

PASTA ALLA MARINARA

 Serves 4

1 lb (500 g) pasta bows

salt and black pepper

2 tbsp olive oil

1 large onion, finely chopped

1 large garlic clove, crushed

1/2 cup (125 ml) dry white wine

1/4 lb (125 g) squid, cut into strips or rings

1 scant cup (60 g) sliced mushrooms

1/4 lb (125 g) scallops, halved if large

1/4 lb (125 g) cooked peeled shrimp

2/3 cup (150 ml) heavy cream

1/4 cup (30 g) chopped parsley

1 Cook the pasta bows in a large saucepan of boiling salted water for 8–10 minutes, until just tender.

2 Meanwhile, heat the oil in a large pan, add the onion and garlic, and cook gently, stirring occasionally, for 3–5 minutes, until softened but not browned.

3 Pour in the white wine and boil to reduce the liquid in the saucepan to about 2 tbsp, stirring constantly. Add the squid and cook for 1 minute, then add the mushrooms and scallops and cook, stirring, for 2 minutes longer. Add the shrimp, heavy cream, and half of the parsley and heat through.

4 Drain the pasta bows thoroughly and add to the seafood mixture, stirring well to combine. Season with salt and black pepper to taste, and serve immediately, garnished with the remaining parsley.

Cook's know-how

If you prefer, replace the squid, scallops, and shrimp with 3/4 lb (375 g) mixed seafood. Your mixture may contain any combination of shrimp, scallops, crabmeat, clams, squid, and mussels.

SPAGHETTI ALLE VONGOLE

 Serves 4

about 32 fresh clams in their shells, cleaned (page 106)

2 tbsp olive oil, plus extra for tossing

1 onion, chopped

1 garlic clove, crushed

1/4 tsp chili powder

13 oz (400 g) canned chopped tomatoes

1/4 cup (60 ml) dry white wine

salt and black pepper

1 lb (500 g) spaghetti

2 tbsp chopped parsley

1 Holding each clam in a cloth, insert a thin knife blade between the shells and twist the knife to open the shells. Reserve 4 clams for garnish. Remove the remaining clams from their shells, cut them into bite-sized pieces, and set aside with any juices.

2 Heat the olive oil in a large pan, add the onion and garlic, and cook gently, stirring occasionally, for 3–5 minutes, until softened but not browned. Add the chili powder and cook gently, stirring, for 1 minute.

3 Add the tomatoes, wine, and salt and pepper to taste and bring to a boil. Simmer, uncovered, for 15 minutes or until the mixture has thickened.

4 Meanwhile, cook the spaghetti in a large saucepan of boiling salted water for 8–10 minutes, until just tender. Drain, then toss the spaghetti in a little olive oil to prevent it from sticking. Transfer to warmed serving plates.

5 Add the parsley and the clams and their juices to the tomato mixture and cook for 2 minutes. Do not cook any longer, or the clams will toughen.

6 Taste for seasoning, then spoon the sauce over the spaghetti. Serve immediately, garnished with the reserved clams in their shells.

Cook's know-how

Live clams should have tightly closed shells. Discard any that do not open during cooking.

TAGLIATELLE WITH SHRIMP

 Serves 4

2 tbsp olive oil

1 large onion, chopped

1 garlic clove, crushed

3/4 lb (375 g) mushrooms, halved

1 lb (500 g) tomatoes, peeled (page 39), seeded, and chopped

salt and black pepper

1 lb (500 g) tagliatelle

3/4 lb (375 g) cooked peeled shrimp

1/2 cup (125 ml) light sour cream

1/4 cup (30 g) chopped parsley to garnish

1 Heat the oil in a large pan, add the onion and garlic, and cook gently, stirring, for 3–5 minutes, until softened but not browned. Add the mushrooms and cook over high heat, stirring, for about 5 minutes.

2 Add the tomatoes, season to taste and simmer gently, uncovered, for about 20 minutes or until the mixture has thickened.

3 Meanwhile, cook the tagliatelle in a large saucepan of boiling salted water for 8–10 minutes, until just tender.

4 Add the shrimp and light sour cream to the tomato mixture and cook gently for about 2 minutes, until the shrimp are heated through. Season to taste.

5 Drain the tagliatelle thoroughly and transfer to warmed serving plates. Arrange the shrimp mixture on top, garnish with parsley, and serve immediately.

PASTA WITH SMOKED SALMON

Substitute 1/4 lb (125 g) smoked salmon for 1/4 lb (125 g) of the shrimp. Proceed as directed, adding the smoked salmon just before serving.

PASTA SHELLS WITH SCALLOPS

 Serves 4

8 large scallops, each cut into 3 slices

5 tbsp (75 ml) water

juice of 1 lemon

1 slice of onion

6 black peppercorns

1 small bay leaf

1 lb (500 g) pasta shells

1 tbsp butter

chopped parsley and lemon slices to garnish

SAUCE

3 tbsp butter

1 1/2 cups (125 g) sliced mushrooms

1/4 cup (30 g) all-purpose flour

1 cup (250 ml) light cream

1 tbsp tomato paste

salt and black pepper

1 Put the scallops into a pan with the water, half of the lemon juice, the onion, peppercorns, and bay leaf and bring to a boil.

2 Cover and simmer until the scallops are opaque. Remove the scallops, strain the liquid, and reserve.

3 Make the sauce: melt the butter in a saucepan, add the mushrooms, and cook gently, stirring occasionally, for 2 minutes. Add the flour and cook, stirring, for 1 minute. Remove from the heat and blend in the strained poaching liquid. Cook, stirring, for 1 minute, until thickened.

4 Add the cream and tomato paste and bring to a boil, stirring constantly until the mixture thickens. Simmer for 2 minutes, then add salt and pepper to taste.

5 Cook the pasta shells in a large saucepan of boiling salted water for 8–10 minutes or until tender.

6 Drain the pasta shells, then toss with the butter and the remaining lemon juice. Add the scallops to the sauce, and heat through. Transfer to serving plates.

7 Spoon the sauce over the pasta shells, and serve immediately, garnished with the parsley and lemon slices.

TAGLIATELLE WITH VEGETABLE RIBBONS

 Serves 4

2 medium zucchini

4 carrots

1 lb (500 g) tagliatelle

CILANTRO SAUCE

leaves from 1 large bunch of fresh cilantro

1/2 cup (125 ml) olive oil

2 tbsp pine nuts

2 garlic cloves

salt and black pepper

2/3 cup (60 g) grated Parmesan or Romano cheese

1 Make the cilantro sauce: put the cilantro, olive oil, pine nuts, garlic, and salt and pepper to taste into a food processor and work until smooth. Fold in the grated cheese.

2 Cut the zucchini and carrots into wide ribbons (page 335).

3 Cook the tagliatelle in a large saucepan of boiling salted water for 8 minutes.

4 Add the zucchini and carrots to the pan of tagliatelle and cook for 1–2 minutes, until the pasta and vegetables are just tender.

5 Drain the tagliatelle and vegetables thoroughly and return to the saucepan. Add the cilantro sauce and toss over high heat to warm through completely. Taste for seasoning and serve.

Cook's know-how

The cilantro sauce can be made in advance and kept in an airtight container in the refrigerator for up to 2 weeks.

PENNE WITH SPINACH & STILTON

 Serves 4

1 lb (500 g) penne

salt and black pepper

3 tbsp butter

2 large garlic cloves, crushed

1/2 lb (250 g) cremini mushrooms, sliced

1 1/4 cups (300 ml) heavy cream

1 egg, lightly beaten

3 cups (90 g) spinach, coarsely shredded

3/4 cup (90 g) crumbled Stilton cheese

juice of 1/2 lemon

pinch of grated nutmeg

1 Cook the penne in a large pan of boiling salted water for 8–10 minutes, until just tender.

2 Meanwhile, melt the butter in a large pan, add the garlic, and cook, stirring, for 1 minute. Add the mushrooms and cook, stirring occasionally, for 2 minutes. Stir in the cream and boil for 2–3 minutes, until the mixture reaches a coating consistency.

3 Drain the penne, add to the mushroom and cream mixture with the egg, stirring well, and heat through. Add the spinach, Stilton cheese, lemon juice, nutmeg, and pepper to taste and stir well to coat the pasta. Serve immediately.

Cook's know-how

For best results, use young spinach leaves. No extra salt is needed in the sauce since Stilton is a salty cheese.

PENNE WITH BROCCOLI & STILTON

Substitute 1 1/2 cups (125 g) small broccoli florets for the spinach. Cook in boiling salted water for 5 minutes or until just tender. Add to the pasta with the cheese, lemon juice, nutmeg, and pepper, omitting the egg. Stir well and serve immediately.

PENNE WITH ASPARAGUS

 Serves 4

1 cup (125 g) goat cheese, cut in small pieces

3 tbsp olive oil

3 garlic cloves, crushed

3 tbsp shredded fresh basil

1 lb (500 g) penne or spaghetti

salt and black pepper

1 lb (500 g) asparagus

1 In a small bowl, combine the goat cheese, olive oil, garlic, and shredded fresh basil. Set aside.

2 Cook the pasta in a large saucepan of boiling salted water for 8–10 minutes, until just tender.

3 Meanwhile, trim the woody ends from the asparagus. Cut the asparagus into bite-sized pieces and cook in boiling salted water for about 3 minutes, until just tender.

4 Drain the pasta thoroughly, add the goat cheese mixture, and toss together. Drain the asparagus and add to the pasta mixture. Toss lightly together, add salt and black pepper to taste, and serve immediately.

SPAGHETTI ALL' AMATRICIANA

A specialty of Amatrice, near Rome, this tomato-based sauce is spiced with chilies and garlic, and richly flavored with diced pancetta and roasted peppers.

 Serves 4

1 red pepper

1 green pepper

4 tbsp olive oil

1/4 lb (125 g) pancetta, diced

1/2 –1 fresh green chili, cored, seeded, and thinly sliced

5 garlic cloves, crushed

2 ripe tomatoes, peeled (page 39), seeded, and diced

2 tbsp chopped parsley

1/2 tsp dried oregano

salt and black pepper

1 lb (500 g) spaghetti

grated Parmesan cheese to serve

1 Remove and discard the cores and seeds from the red and green peppers and cut each pepper in half. Roast and peel the peppers (page 354). Cut the roasted flesh into thin strips.

2 Heat the oil in a skillet, add the pancetta and cook over high heat for 5 minutes or until crisp. Add the red and green peppers and the chili and cook for 2 minutes. Stir in the garlic and cook for about 1 minute.

3 Add the tomatoes and parsley and cook for 3 minutes or until thickened. Remove the skillet from the heat and add the oregano and salt and pepper to taste.

4 Cook the spaghetti in a large saucepan of boiling salted water for 8–10 minutes, until just tender.

5 Drain the spaghetti thoroughly. Add the sauce and toss with the spaghetti. Generously sprinkle with grated Parmesan cheese and serve immediately.

SPAGHETTI ALL' ARRABBIATA

Melt 2 tbsp butter with 2 tbsp oil in a skillet, add 3 crushed garlic cloves and 1/2 –1 tsp crushed red pepper, and cook gently. Drain and stir in 13 oz (400 g) canned chopped tomatoes and bring slowly to a boil. Simmer until reduced and thickened. Add 1/4 tsp dried oregano and season. Toss with the spaghetti and serve.

Spaghetti all' amatriciana

This recipe originates in the Abruzzo region of Italy. This is where peperoncino *or green chilies are grown and widely used to flavor pasta sauces.*

STIR-FRIED CHINESE NOODLES

 Serves 4

5 dried shiitake mushrooms

1 cup (250 ml) hot vegetable stock

3/4 lb (375 g) Chinese egg noodles

salt

about 2 tsp soy sauce

1 tbsp sunflower or corn oil

1/2 lb (250 g) snow peas

3 garlic cloves, crushed

1/4-in (5-mm) piece of fresh ginger, peeled and chopped

1/4 tsp sugar (optional)

1 cup (125 g) bean sprouts

about 1/2 tsp crushed red pepper

TO SERVE

3 scallions, sliced

2 tsp sesame oil

1 tbsp chopped fresh cilantro

1 Put the mushrooms into a bowl, cover with the hot vegetable stock, and leave to soak for about 30 minutes.

2 Drain the mushrooms, reserving the liquid.

3 Pour the soaking liquid through a strainer lined with a paper towel to remove any grit. Reserve the liquid. Squeeze the shiitake mushrooms dry, then cut into thin strips.

4 Cook the noodles in a large saucepan of boiling salted water for 3 minutes or according to package instructions. Drain the noodles, toss with soy sauce to taste, and set aside.

5 Heat the sunflower oil in a wok or large skillet, add the mushrooms, snow peas, garlic, and ginger, and stir-fry for 2 minutes. Add the sugar, if using, bean sprouts, crushed red pepper to taste, and 3 tbsp of the reserved mushroom-soaking liquid, and stir-fry for 2 minutes.

6 Add the egg noodles and stir-fry for 2 minutes or until heated through. Serve immediately, sprinkled with the scallions, sesame oil, and cilantro.

TORTELLINI WITH PEAS & BACON

 Serves 4

1 lb (500 g) tortellini

salt and black pepper

1 tbsp sunflower or corn oil

1/2 lb (250 g) bacon, diced

1 1/4 cups (175 g) frozen baby peas

1 1/4 cups (300 ml) heavy cream

pinch of grated nutmeg

grated Parmesan or Romano cheese to serve

1 Cook the tortellini in boiling salted water for about 10–12 minutes, or according to package instructions, until tender.

2 Meanwhile, heat the oil in a skillet, add the bacon, and cook over high heat, stirring, for 3 minutes or until crisp.

3 Cook the baby peas in boiling salted water for about 2 minutes, until just tender. Drain.

4 Drain the tortellini thoroughly and return to the saucepan. Add the bacon, baby peas, cream, nutmeg, and salt and pepper to taste and heat gently for 1–2 minutes to warm through. Serve immediately, sprinkled with the grated cheese.

Tortellini

These are small, circular pieces of pasta enclosing a stuffing such as spinach and ricotta, or ground meats. In Bologna, northern Italy, their place of origin, tortellini are traditionally served in a broth or with a cream sauce.

FETTUCCINE PRIMAVERA

 Serves 4

4 medium asparagus spears, trimmed and cut into bite-sized pieces

1¹/₂ cups (125 g) broccoli florets

1 zucchini, sliced

salt and black pepper

3 tbsp olive oil

¹/₂ red and ¹/₂ yellow pepper, cored, seeded, and diced

3 garlic cloves, crushed

7 oz (200 g) canned plum tomatoes, drained and juice reserved, diced

²/₃ cup (90 g) frozen baby peas, thawed

¹/₂ cup (125 ml) heavy cream

1 lb (500 g) fettuccine

¹/₄ cup (30 g) chopped fresh basil

1 cup (90 g) grated Parmesan cheese to serve

1 Cook the asparagus, broccoli, and zucchini in boiling salted water for 3 minutes or until just tender. Drain, rinse, and set aside.

2 Heat the oil in a skillet, add the peppers and garlic, and cook, stirring, for 4 minutes or until the peppers are softened.

3 Add the tomatoes, 3 tbsp of their juice, and the baby peas, and cook for 5 minutes or until the liquid in the pan is reduced by half.

4 Add the asparagus, broccoli, and zucchini, stir in the cream, and boil for 1–2 minutes to reduce the liquid and concentrate the flavor. Add salt and pepper to taste.

5 Cook the fettuccine in a large saucepan of boiling salted water for 8–10 minutes, until just tender.

6 Drain the fettuccine thoroughly and toss with the vegetables and sauce. Stir in the basil and serve immediately, sprinkled with Parmesan cheese.

Fettuccine
The Roman equivalent of tagliatelle, these egg noodles are cut into flat, narrow strips, about ³/₈ in (1 cm) wide.

SPAGHETTI CARBONARA

 Serves 4

1 lb (500 g) spaghetti

salt and black pepper

6 thick slices of bacon, cut into strips

1 garlic clove, crushed

4 eggs

1¹/₃ cups (125 g) grated Parmesan or Romano cheese

²/₃ cup (150 ml) light cream

chopped parsley to garnish

1 Cook the spaghetti in a large saucepan of boiling salted water for 8–10 minutes, until just tender.

2 Meanwhile, put the bacon into a skillet and heat gently for 7 minutes, until the fat begins to run, then increase the heat. Add the garlic and cook quickly for 2–3 minutes, until the bacon is crisp.

3 Break the eggs into a bowl. Add the bacon and garlic mixture, using a slotted spoon. Add the Parmesan cheese, season generously with salt and pepper, and whisk until well blended.

4 Drain and return the spaghetti to the hot pan. Stir in the bacon and egg mixture and cook gently until the egg just begins to set. Stir in the cream and heat gently. Serve, garnished with parsley.

Cook's know-how
It's best to buy a whole piece of Parmesan cheese and grate the quantity you need for a given dish. Pregrated Parmesan in packages is less economical and lacks the flavor of freshly grated Parmesan.

SPAGHETTI ALFREDO

Heat ²/₃ cup (150 ml) light cream with 2 tbsp butter until the mixture has thickened. Set aside. Cook the pasta, drain, then add to the cream mixture. Add 6 tbsp (90 ml) more cream, 1 cup (90 g) grated Parmesan cheese, and a pinch of grated nutmeg and season to taste. Heat gently until thickened and serve.

PASTA SPIRALS WITH MEATBALLS

 Serves 4

2 tbsp olive oil

1 lb (500 g) pasta spirals

shredded basil to garnish

TOMATO BASIL SAUCE

1 tbsp olive oil

1 small onion, chopped

13 oz (400 g) canned chopped tomatoes, drained and juice reserved

1 tbsp chopped fresh basil

salt and black pepper

MEATBALLS

1 lb (500 g) ground veal

2 1/2 cups (150 g) fresh white bread crumbs

1 2/3 cups (150 g) grated Parmesan cheese

1 large egg, beaten

1/4 cup (30 g) chopped parsley

6 tbsp (90 ml) water

1 Make the tomato basil sauce: heat the oil in a saucepan, add the onion, and cook gently, stirring occasionally, for 3–5 minutes, until soft but not browned. Stir in the tomatoes with half of their juice, bring to a boil, and simmer for 3 minutes. Stir in the basil and season to taste. Set aside.

2 Make the meatballs: in a large bowl, combine the ground veal, bread crumbs, Parmesan cheese, egg, parsley, and salt and pepper to taste. Gradually add the measured water, mixing it in well. With dampened hands, shape the veal mixture into balls about the size of large walnuts.

3 Heat the oil in a large nonstick skillet, add the meatballs, and cook for 10–15 minutes, until browned and cooked through. Lift out with a slotted spoon and drain on paper towels. Add to the tomato basil sauce and heat gently for about 5 minutes.

4 Meanwhile, cook the pasta spirals in a large saucepan of boiling salted water for 8–10 minutes, until just tender. Drain the pasta spirals thoroughly, top with the meatballs and sauce, and serve, garnished with shredded basil.

SPAGHETTI BOLOGNESE

 Serves 4

3 tbsp olive oil

1 lb (500 g) ground beef

1 large onion, finely chopped

2 celery stalks, sliced

1 tbsp all-purpose flour

2 garlic cloves, crushed

1/3 cup (90 g) tomato paste

2/3 cup (150 ml) beef stock

2/3 cup (150 ml) red wine

13 oz (400 g) canned chopped tomatoes

salt and black pepper

1 lb (500 g) spaghetti

grated Parmesan or Romano cheese to serve

1 Heat 2 tbsp of the oil in a saucepan. Add the ground beef, onion, and celery and cook, stirring, for 5 minutes or until the beef is browned. Add the flour, garlic, and tomato paste and cook, stirring, for about 1 minute.

2 Pour in the stock and wine. Add the tomatoes and salt and pepper to taste and bring to a boil. Cook, stirring, until the mixture has thickened.

3 Lower the heat, partially cover the pan, and simmer very gently, stirring occasionally, for about 1 hour.

4 Meanwhile, cook the spaghetti in boiling salted water for 8–10 minutes, until just tender. Drain thoroughly.

5 Return the spaghetti to the saucepan, add the remaining oil, and toss gently to coat.

6 Divide the spaghetti among warmed serving plates and ladle some of the sauce on top of each serving. Sprinkle with a little Parmesan cheese and pass the remainder separately.

RAVIOLI

Ravioli is one of the easiest homemade pastas to prepare; roll out the dough, then fill with a savory stuffing. It is so delicious that it needs only a simple accompaniment of melted butter and freshly grated Parmesan cheese.

BASIC PASTA DOUGH

 Serves 3

2 1/2 cups (300 g) semolina flour or unbleached white flour

3 eggs

1 tsp salt

1 tbsp olive oil

1 Sift the flour into a mound on a work surface. Make a well in the middle of the flour and add the eggs, salt, and oil. Using your fingertips, gradually draw the flour into the egg mixture until a sticky ball of dough is formed.

2 Knead the dough on a floured work surface for 10 minutes or until the pasta dough is smooth and no longer sticks to the work surface.

3 Shape the dough into a ball, put into an oiled plastic bag, and leave to rest at room temperature for about 30 minutes.

4 On a lightly floured work surface, roll out the dough very thinly into a 15-in (37-cm) square. Leave the pasta uncovered for about 20 minutes to dry out slightly. Cut the pasta in half; fill and cook the ravioli (see box, right).

CRAB & SHRIMP

3 oz (90 g) cooked white crabmeat, flaked

2/3 cup (90 g) chopped cooked peeled shrimp

1/4 cup (60 g) cream cheese

1 scallion, very finely chopped

salt and black pepper

cilantro sauce (page 309) to serve

Parmesan shavings and cilantro sprigs to garnish

1 Combine the crabmeat and shrimp with the cream cheese, scallion, and salt and pepper.

2 Fill and cook the ravioli (see box, right). Toss in cilantro sauce and serve immediately, garnished with Parmesan shavings and cilantro sprigs.

VEAL & PROSCIUTTO

1 tbsp butter

1/2 cup (90 g) minced cooked veal or beef

1/3 cup (75 g) finely chopped prosciutto

1 tbsp fresh white bread crumbs

1 tbsp chopped parsley

2 tsp each water and tomato paste

salt and black pepper

1 egg

tomato basil sauce (page 313) to serve

basil sprigs to garnish

1 Melt the butter in a saucepan. Add the veal and fry for 5 minutes. Stir in the remaining ingredients.

2 Fill and cook the ravioli (see box, below). Toss in the tomato basil sauce, and serve immediately, garnished with basil sprigs.

CHEESE & SPINACH

1/2 cup (125 g) ricotta cheese

2/3 cup (60 g) grated Parmesan cheese

1 egg, beaten

pinch of grated nutmeg

1/2 lb (250 g) frozen chopped spinach, thawed and squeezed dry

salt and black pepper

2 tbsp butter to serve

1 Beat together the ricotta, half of the Parmesan, the egg, nutmeg, spinach, and salt and pepper to taste.

2 Fill and cook the ravioli (see box, below). Serve with butter, the remaining Parmesan, and black pepper.

Clockwise from top: *Cheese & Spinach Ravioli, Veal & Prosciutto Ravioli, Crab & Shrimp Ravioli.*

Filling and cooking the ravioli

1 Place 18 spoonfuls of filling at regular intervals onto one half of the pasta. Lightly brush the pasta between the filling with water.

2 Roll the remaining pasta around a rolling pin and unroll over the bottom sheet. Use your hand to press the pasta together between the filling.

3 With a sharp knife, pastry wheel, or pastry cutter, cut into round or square ravioli. Leave to stand, turning once, for about 30 minutes, until dried out.

4 Add a little oil to a large saucepan of boiling salted water, add the ravioli, and cook for 4–5 minutes, until just tender. Serve immediately.

TUNA CASSEROLE WITH FENNEL

 Serves 4

1/2 lb (250 g) pasta shells or spirals

salt and black pepper

1 tbsp sunflower or corn oil

1 fennel bulb, trimmed and finely sliced

1 onion, finely sliced

4 tbsp butter

1/2 cup (60 g) all-purpose flour

2 1/3 cups (600 ml) milk

7 oz (200 g) canned tuna in water, drained and flaked

3 hard-boiled eggs, coarsely chopped

1 cup (125 g) grated aged Cheddar cheese

2 tbsp chopped parsley to garnish

1 Cook the pasta shells in boiling salted water for 8–10 minutes, until just tender. Drain thoroughly and set aside.

2 Heat the sunflower oil in a large skillet, add the fennel and onion, and cook for 3–5 minutes, until softened but not browned. Set aside.

3 Melt the butter in a large saucepan, add the flour, and cook, stirring, for 1 minute. Remove from the heat and gradually blend in the milk. Bring to a boil, stirring constantly until the mixture thickens. Simmer for 2–3 minutes.

4 Stir in the pasta shells, the fennel and onion mixture, the flaked tuna, eggs, and grated Cheddar cheese. Add salt and pepper to taste, then transfer the mixture into a shallow ovenproof dish.

5 Bake in a 400°F (200°C) oven for about 30 minutes or until heated through and golden brown and bubbling on top. Serve immediately, lightly sprinkled with parsley.

TUNA CASSEROLE WITH CORN

Substitute 1 cup (200 g) cooked fresh or frozen corn kernels and 3/4 cup (90 g) frozen peas for the fennel bulb and cook as directed.

VEGETABLES NAPOLETANA

 Serves 4

1/2 lb (250 g) pasta twists

salt and black pepper

1/2 lb (250 g) broccoli

1 tbsp butter

1 tbsp olive oil

1 large onion, chopped

2 large garlic cloves, crushed

2 cups (150 g) coarsely chopped shiitake mushrooms

1 red pepper, cored, seeded, and sliced

1 3/4 cups (250 g) sliced zucchini

3/4 cup (75 g) grated aged Cheddar cheese

SAUCE

4 tbsp butter

1/2 cup (60 g) all-purpose flour

2 1/3 cups (600 ml) milk

1 tsp Dijon mustard

pinch of grated nutmeg

1 Cook the pasta twists in boiling salted water for 8–10 minutes, until just tender. Drain thoroughly.

2 Cut the stalks off the broccoli, trim, and chop. Cook them in boiling salted water for 3 minutes. Add the florets and cook for 2 minutes longer. Drain and rinse in cold water.

3 Melt the butter with the oil in a large skillet, add the onion and garlic, and cook gently for 3–5 minutes, until softened.

4 Add the mushrooms, red pepper, and zucchini slices, and cook, stirring occasionally, for 3 minutes. Remove from the heat and stir in the broccoli.

5 Make the sauce: melt the butter in a large saucepan, add the flour and cook, stirring, for 1 minute. Remove from the heat and gradually blend in the milk. Bring to a boil, stirring constantly until thickened. Simmer for 2–3 minutes. Add the mustard, nutmeg, and salt and pepper to taste.

6 Remove the sauce from the heat, add the vegetables and pasta, and stir well to coat.

7 Divide the mixture among 4 individual gratin dishes, sprinkle with the Cheddar cheese, and bake in a 400°F (200°C) oven for 20–25 minutes, until golden. Serve immediately.

FISHERMAN'S LASAGNE

 Serves 6

1¼ lb (625 g) haddock fillet

1 slice of onion

1 bay leaf

4 black peppercorns

1¼ cups (300 ml) dry white wine

½ lb (250 g) cooked peeled shrimp

2 tbsp butter

3½ cups (500 g) thickly sliced zucchini

1 garlic clove, crushed

6 no-precook lasagne noodles

½ cup (60 g) grated Cheddar cheese

2 tbsp grated Parmesan cheese

SAUCE

6 tbsp butter

⅔ cup (90 g) all-purpose flour

1¼ cups (300 ml) light cream

3 tbsp chopped parsley

1 tbsp chopped fresh dill

salt and black pepper

1 Put the haddock into a large pan with the onion, bay leaf, peppercorns, and wine. Add enough water to cover, bring to a boil, and simmer for 5 minutes or until the fish is just cooked. Lift out, remove the skin and bones, and flake the flesh. Mix with the shrimp.

2 Strain the liquid and add enough water to make 3⅔ cups (900 ml). Set aside.

3 Melt the butter in a saucepan, add the zucchini and garlic, and cook for 3 minutes, until beginning to soften.

4 Make the sauce: melt the butter in a saucepan, add the flour, and cook, stirring, for 1 minute. Remove the pan from the heat and gradually blend in the reserved cooking liquid. Bring to a boil, stirring until thickened. Simmer for 2–3 minutes. Stir in the cream, parsley, dill, and salt and pepper to taste.

5 Spoon one-third of the haddock and shrimp mixture into a shallow ovenproof dish, top with one-third of the zucchini, and pour on one-third of the sauce. Arrange half of the lasagne noodles in a single layer. Repeat the layers, finishing with the sauce.

6 Sprinkle with the Cheddar and Parmesan cheeses and bake the lasagne in a 400°F (200°C) oven for about 40 minutes until golden and bubbling.

THREE-CHEESE MACARONI

 Serves 4

2 cups (250 g) elbow macaroni

salt and black pepper

6 tbsp (90 g) butter, plus extra for greasing

⅓ cup (15 g) all-purpose flour

1 bay leaf

3⅔ cups (900 ml) milk

3 cups (375 g) grated Fontina cheese

1½ cups (175 g) chopped mozzarella cheese

1⅓ cups (125 g) grated Parmesan cheese

large pinch of grated nutmeg

1 cup (60 g) fresh white bread crumbs

1 Cook the macaroni in boiling salted water for 8–10 minutes, until just tender. Drain and set aside.

2 Melt the butter in a large pan. Add the flour and bay leaf and cook, stirring, for 1 minute. Remove from the heat and gradually blend in the milk. Bring to a boil, stirring constantly, until the mixture thickens. Simmer for 2–3 minutes.

3 Remove and discard the bay leaf, then stir in the Fontina and mozzarella cheeses, 1 cup (90 g) of the Parmesan cheese, and the cooked macaroni. Add the nutmeg and salt and pepper to taste.

4 Lightly butter a large shallow ovenproof dish and spoon in the macaroni mixture. Sprinkle with the white bread crumbs and top with the remaining grated Parmesan cheese and bake in a 350°F (180°C) oven for about 40 minutes, until golden and bubbling.

CHEESE & LEEK MACARONI

Omit the mozzarella cheese. Melt 2 tbsp butter in a saucepan, add 2–3 trimmed and finely sliced leeks, and cook gently for 3–5 minutes, until softened. Add to the sauce with the Fontina and Parmesan cheeses and macaroni and proceed as directed.

CANNELLONI WITH RICOTTA & SPINACH

 Serves 4–6

butter for greasing

18 no-precook cannelloni

1/3 cup (30 g) grated Parmesan cheese

TOMATO SAUCE

1 tbsp olive oil

2 celery stalks, chopped

1 small onion, chopped

1 carrot, chopped

1 garlic clove, crushed

1 1/4 cups (300 ml) chicken or vegetable stock

26 oz (800 g) canned chopped tomatoes

2 tbsp tomato paste

salt and black pepper

2 oz (60 g) sun-dried tomatoes in oil, drained and chopped

FILLING

2 tbsp olive oil

1 small onion, chopped

1 garlic clove, crushed

1 lb (500 g) spinach, chopped

2 cups (500 g) ricotta cheese

pinch of grated nutmeg

1 Make the tomato sauce: heat the oil in a saucepan, add the celery, onion, carrot, and garlic, and cook gently for 3–5 minutes, until softened. Stir in the stock, tomatoes, tomato paste, and salt and pepper to taste and bring to a boil. Cover and simmer, stirring occasionally, for 30 minutes.

2 Meanwhile, make the filling: heat the oil in a large pan, add the onion and garlic, and cook for 3–5 minutes, until softened. Add the spinach and cook over high heat for 1–2 minutes. Leave to cool slightly, then add the ricotta, nutmeg, and salt and pepper to taste.

3 Puree the tomato sauce in a food processor, then stir in the sun-dried tomatoes.

4 Grease an ovenproof dish. Spoon the spinach filling into the cannelloni. Arrange in the dish, spoon on the sauce, sprinkle with Parmesan, and bake in a 400°F (200°C) oven for 30 minutes.

LASAGNE

 Serves 6

1 cup (125 g) grated aged Cheddar cheese

1/3 cup (30 g) grated Parmesan cheese

6 no-precook lasagne noodles

chopped parsley to garnish

MEAT SAUCE

2 tbsp olive oil

2 lb (1 kg) ground beef

1/3 cup (45 g) all-purpose flour

1 1/4 cups (300 ml) beef stock

13 oz (400 g) canned chopped tomatoes

6 celery stalks, sliced

2 onions, chopped

2 large garlic cloves, crushed

1/4 cup (60 g) tomato paste

1 tsp sugar

salt and black pepper

WHITE SAUCE

4 tbsp butter

1/3 cup (45 g) all-purpose flour

2 1/3 cups (600 ml) milk

1 tsp Dijon mustard

pinch of grated nutmeg

1 Make the meat sauce: heat the oil, add the beef, and cook, stirring, until browned. Add the flour and cook, stirring, for 1 minute.

2 Add the stock, tomatoes, celery, onions, garlic, tomato paste, sugar, and salt and pepper to taste and bring to a boil. Cover and simmer for 1 hour.

3 Meanwhile, make the white sauce: melt the butter in a saucepan, add the flour, and cook, stirring, for 1 minute. Remove from the heat and gradually blend in the milk. Bring to a boil, stirring constantly until the mixture thickens. Simmer for 2–3 minutes. Stir in the mustard, nutmeg, and salt and pepper to taste.

4 Spoon one-third of the meat sauce into a large shallow ovenproof dish; cover with one-third of the white sauce and one-third of the Cheddar and Parmesan cheeses. Arrange half of the lasagne noodles in a single layer. Repeat the layers, finishing with the Cheddar and Parmesan cheeses.

5 Bake in a 375°F (190°C) oven for 45–60 minutes, until the pasta is tender and the topping is a golden brown color. Serve the lasagne immediately, garnished with the parsley.

318

CARIBBEAN RICE & BEANS

 Serves 4

2 tbsp olive oil

8 scallions, sliced

3 slices of bacon, diced

2 garlic cloves, crushed

1 1/4 cups (250 g) long-grain white rice

7 oz (200 g) canned tomatoes

3 tbsp chopped parsley

2 bay leaves

1 small green chili, cored, seeded, and thinly sliced

1/2 tsp turmeric

1/2 tsp cumin seeds

1/2 tsp dried thyme

13 oz (400 g) canned red kidney beans or black-eyed peas, drained

1 1/2 cups (375 ml) chicken stock

1 lime, cut into wedges, to serve

1 Heat the oil in a pan, add the scallions and bacon, and cook for about 5 minutes or until the bacon is crisp. Add the garlic and cook for 2 minutes.

 Add the rice and stir to coat the grains in the oil. Add the tomatoes with their juice, 2 tbsp of the parsley, the bay leaves, chili, turmeric, cumin, and thyme, and cook for 2 minutes.

3 Add the beans and stock and bring to a boil. Cover and cook over low heat for 15 minutes, until the rice is tender and the liquid has been absorbed.

4 Sprinkle with the remaining parsley and serve with lime wedges.

Rice and beans

Variations of this dish, both simple and elaborate, are found all over the West Indies. In the Caribbean the word peas means beans, and small round beans, known as pigeon peas, are traditionally used for this dish. Red kidney beans make a particularly colorful, and very good, substitute.

CONFETTI RICE

 Serves 4

2 tbsp olive oil

1 onion, chopped

1 carrot, diced

1 cup (200 g) long-grain white rice

1 large tomato, peeled (page 39), seeded, and diced

2 cups (500 ml) hot chicken or vegetable stock

1 cup (150 g) corn kernels

3/4 cup (90 g) frozen peas

2 tbsp tomato paste

salt and black pepper

1 garlic clove, crushed

chopped parsley to garnish

1 Heat the oil in a skillet, add the onion and carrot, and cook gently, stirring, for 3–5 minutes, until the onion is softened but not browned.

2 Add the rice and stir to coat the grains in the oil. Add the tomato and stock.

3 Add the corn, peas, and tomato paste and bring to a boil. Simmer, stirring occasionally, for 12–15 minutes or until the rice is tender and the liquid has been absorbed.

4 Add salt and pepper to taste and stir in the garlic. Serve immediately, garnished with parsley.

Cook's know-how

Confetti rice is a delicious accompaniment to simple broiled or roasted foods. Spoon any extra into hot homemade chicken or vegetable soup. Add a little chopped fresh cilantro, onion, or crushed chilies for extra flavor. Use the same day.

RISI E BISI

 Serves 4–6

4 tbsp butter

1 onion, finely chopped

1/3 cup (60 g) diced prosciutto or pancetta

2 garlic cloves, crushed

1 1/2 cups (300 g) Arborio rice

2 1/2 cups (300 g) frozen peas, thawed

salt and black pepper

4 cups (1 liter) hot chicken or vegetable stock

2/3 cup (60 g) grated Parmesan cheese

2 tbsp chopped parsley to garnish

1 Melt the butter in a large pan. When it is foaming, add the onion, prosciutto, and garlic, and cook gently, stirring occasionally, for 3–5 minutes, until the onion is soft but not browned.

2 Add the rice and stir to coat in the butter. Add the peas and salt and pepper to taste.

3 Pour in half of the stock and cook, stirring constantly, over low heat until it is absorbed. Add a little more stock and cook, stirring constantly until it has been absorbed.

4 Continue adding the stock in this way until the rice is just tender and the mixture is thick and creamy. It should take about 25 minutes.

5 Serve hot, sprinkled with chopped parsley and Parmesan cheese.

Risi e bisi

This is a classic Venetian dish meaning rice and peas. In the days when Venice was a republic, it was traditionally served at a dinner held by the doge, the city's chief magistrate, on April 25 in honor of St. Mark, the patron saint of Venice.

BAKED WILD RICE

 Serves 4

2 cups (375 g) mixed basmati and wild rice

salt and black pepper

1/2–3/4 lb (250–375 g) broccoli

1 tbsp butter

2 onions, chopped

3 garlic cloves, crushed

1/2 cup (125 ml) sour cream or crème fraîche

1 cup (125 g) grated mozzarella cheese

2/3 cup (60 g) grated Parmesan cheese

1 tbsp chopped fresh rosemary

1 Cook the rice in boiling salted water for about 35 minutes or according to package instructions. Drain thoroughly and rinse with cold water. Drain again.

2 Meanwhile, cut the stalks off the broccoli and cook them in boiling salted water for 8–10 minutes, until almost tender, then add the florets, and cook for 2 minutes longer. Drain and rinse in cold water. Drain again and set aside.

3 Melt the butter in a skillet, add the onions, and cook gently, stirring occasionally, for 3–5 minutes, until softened. Add the garlic, and cook, stirring occasionally, for 3–5 minutes, until the onion is lightly browned.

4 Coarsely chop the broccoli, then stir into the rice with the onion and garlic mixture, sour cream, three-quarters of the mozzarella and Parmesan cheeses, the rosemary, and salt and pepper to taste.

5 Transfer the mixture to an ovenproof dish and sprinkle with the remaining mozzarella and Parmesan cheeses. Bake in a 350°F (180°C) oven for about 20 minutes, until heated through and the cheese is melted. Serve immediately.

PERSIAN PILAF

 Serves 4

1 small cinnamon stick

2 tsp cumin seeds

6 black peppercorns

seeds of 4 cardamom pods, crushed

3 cloves

2 tbsp sunflower or corn oil

1 small onion, chopped

1 tsp turmeric

1¼ cups (250 g) long-grain rice

5 cups (1.25 liters) hot chicken stock

2 bay leaves, crumbled

salt and black pepper

½ cup (60 g) shelled pistachio nuts, coarsely chopped

2½ tbsp raisins

fresh cilantro to garnish

1 Heat a heavy pan and add the cinnamon stick, cumin seeds, peppercorns, cardamom seeds, and cloves.

2 Dry-fry the spices over a medium heat for 2–3 minutes, until they begin to release their distinctive flavors and aromas.

3 Add the oil to the pan and, when it is hot, add the onion and turmeric. Cook gently, stirring occasionally, for about 10 minutes, until the onion is softened.

4 Add the rice and stir to coat the grains in the oil. Slowly pour in the hot stock, add the bay leaves and salt and pepper to taste, and bring to a boil. Lower the heat, cover, and cook very gently for about 10 minutes without lifting the lid.

5 Remove the saucepan from the heat and leave to stand, still covered, for about 5 minutes.

6 Add the pistachio nuts and raisins to the pilaf and fork them in gently to fluff up the rice. Garnish with fresh cilantro and serve immediately.

PORTUGUESE RICE WITH TUNA

 Serves 4

3 slices of bacon, cut into strips

3 tbsp olive oil

1 small onion, thinly sliced

1¼ cups (250 g) long-grain brown rice

2⅓ cups (600 ml) hot chicken stock

salt and black pepper

¾ lb (375 g) fresh tuna, cut into chunks

2 7-oz (200-g) jars roasted red peppers, drained and cut into strips

16 pitted black olives

dill sprigs and lemon slices to garnish

1 Put the bacon into a large, heavy saucepan and heat until it begins to sizzle. Add the olive oil and onion, and cook gently, stirring occasionally, for 3–5 minutes, until soft but not browned. Add the rice and stir to coat the grains in the oil.

2 Pour the hot stock into the pan, add salt and pepper to taste, and bring to a boil. Cover and simmer for 25–30 minutes.

3 Add the tuna, red peppers, and olives and cook for 5 minutes or until all the liquid has been absorbed and the rice and tuna are tender. Season, garnish with dill sprigs and lemon slices.

PORTUGUESE RICE WITH CANNED TUNA

Substitute 13 oz (400 g) canned tuna in water for the fresh tuna. Flake the tuna roughly, and proceed as directed.

CHICKEN LIVER RISOTTO

 Serves 4

5 tbsp (75 g) butter

1 tbsp sunflower or corn oil

4 thick slices of bacon, diced

1 onion, chopped

1 garlic clove, crushed

1 cup (175 g) Arborio rice

1/4 cup (60 g) wild rice

2 1/3 cups (600 ml) hot chicken stock

1/2 lb (250 g) chicken livers, sliced

1 2/3 cups (125 g) sliced wild mushrooms, for example, oyster mushrooms or porcini

2 oz (60 g) sun-dried tomatoes in oil, drained and chopped

salt and black pepper

1/3 cup (30 g) grated Parmesan cheese

1 tbsp chopped fresh rosemary

1 Melt 4 tbsp (60 g) of the butter with the oil in a large skillet. When the butter is foaming, add the bacon, onion, and garlic and cook gently, stirring occasionally, for 3–5 minutes, until the onion is soft but not browned.

2 Add the Arborio rice and wild rice, stirring to coat the grains in the oil, then pour in the hot chicken stock. Cover and simmer for 25 minutes.

3 Meanwhile, melt the remaining butter in a saucepan. Add the chicken livers, and cook, stirring, for 2–3 minutes until a rich brown color. Add the mushrooms, and cook, stirring occasionally, for 5–7 minutes.

4 Stir the chicken liver mixture into the rice. Add the sun-dried tomatoes and salt and pepper to taste. Cook for 5 minutes or until all the liquid has been absorbed. Serve hot, garnished with Parmesan and rosemary.

Cook's know-how

Wild mushrooms add a special touch to this risotto. Chanterelles, porcini, morels, or oyster mushrooms would all be equally suitable.

RISOTTO MILANESE

 Serves 4

6 tbsp (90 g) butter

1 onion, chopped

2 cups (375 g) Arborio rice

5 cups (1.25 liters) hot chicken stock

a few pinches of saffron threads

salt and black pepper

2/3 cup (60 g) grated Parmesan cheese

Parmesan shavings to serve

1 Melt 2 tbsp (30 g) of the butter in a large saucepan, add the chopped onion, and cook gently, stirring occasionally, for 3–5 minutes, until softened but not browned.

2 Add the rice, stirring to coat the grains in the butter, and cook for 1 minute. Add a ladleful of hot chicken stock to the pan, and cook gently, stirring constantly, until all the stock has been absorbed.

3 Add the saffron and salt and pepper to taste. Continue to add the stock a ladleful at a time, stirring constantly, until the risotto is thick and creamy and the rice tender. This will take 20–25 minutes.

4 Stir in the remaining butter and the Parmesan cheese and season to taste. Top with Parmesan shavings, and serve immediately.

Cook's know-how

Risotto milanese is the traditional accompaniment to osso buco (page 242) but also complements many other meat and poultry dishes. In the past, it was always cooked with beef bone marrow. Many Italians now top the finished risotto with a few spoonfuls of the juices from a veal roast to give it a more traditional and authentic flavor.

KEDGEREE

Serves 4

1 cup (175 g) long-grain rice

1/4 tsp turmeric

3/4 lb (375 g) smoked haddock fillet

2 hard-boiled eggs

4 tbsp butter, plus extra for greasing

juice of 1/2 lemon

2/3 cup (150 ml) light cream

salt

cayenne pepper

2 tbsp finely chopped parsley

1 Simmer the rice and turmeric, covered, in boiling salted water for 12–15 minutes, until tender. Rinse with boiling water, drain, and keep warm.

2 Meanwhile, put the haddock, skin side down, in a skillet, cover with cold water, and poach for 8–10 minutes.

3 Cut 1 egg lengthwise into quarters and reserve for garnish. Coarsely chop the second egg.

4 Drain the haddock, remove the skin and bones, then flake the fish. Put into a large bowl, add the rice, chopped egg, butter, lemon juice, and cream, and season with salt and cayenne pepper. Stir gently to mix.

5 Butter an ovenproof dish, add the kedgeree, and bake in a 350°F (180°C) oven, stirring occasionally, for 10–15 minutes.

6 To serve, stir in the parsley and garnish with the reserved egg quarters.

Cook's know-how

Some smoked haddock is dyed bright yellow, so look for smoked haddock that is pale in color or is labeled "un-dyed" if you particularly want to avoid artificial colors.

SUMMER RISOTTO AL VERDE

Serves 4

1 tbsp butter

3 garlic cloves, crushed

1 1/4 cups (250 g) Arborio rice

4 cups (1 liter) hot vegetable stock

3/4 cup (175 ml) light cream

3/4 cup (90 g) crumbled blue cheese

1/4 cup (60 g) store-bought pesto

1 cup (90 g) grated Parmesan cheese

1/4 cup (30 g) pine nuts, lightly toasted

1/4 cup (30 g) shredded fresh basil

1 Melt the butter in a large saucepan. When it is foaming, add the garlic and cook gently for 1 minute.

2 Add the Arborio rice, stirring to coat the grains in the butter, and cook for 2 minutes. Add a ladleful of the hot vegetable stock, and cook gently, stirring, until the stock has been absorbed. Continue to add the stock a ladleful at a time and cook for 20–25 minutes or until the rice is just tender.

3 Add the cream and cook gently, stirring, until it has been absorbed. Stir in the blue cheese, then the pesto, Parmesan, and pine nuts. Garnish with shredded fresh basil and serve.

CHICKEN & MUSHROOM RISOTTO

Substitute chicken stock for the vegetable stock and omit the blue cheese and pesto. Add 1 3/4 cups (250 g) cooked diced chicken and 1 2/3 cups (125 g) sliced mushrooms to the pan with the garlic and proceed as directed.

ASPARAGUS RISOTTO

Omit the blue cheese and pesto. Add 1 finely chopped onion to the pan with the garlic and cook for 3–5 minutes, until soft. Add 3/4 lb (375 g) trimmed and chopped asparagus and proceed as directed.

NASI GORENG

The name of this Indonesian recipe simply means "fried rice." Prepared with a variety of ingredients, it is one of the best-known Indonesian dishes and one of the easiest to make. Traditional garnishes such as crushed peanuts and omelet strips give contrasting flavors and textures to the finished dish.

CHICKEN NASI GORENG

 Serves 6

2 cups (375 g) long-grain rice

6 tbsp (90 ml) olive oil

6 slices of bacon, chopped

2 large onions, chopped

3 garlic cloves, crushed

1/4 tsp chili powder

2 tsp mild curry powder

2 cooked chicken breasts, skinned and cubed

6 tbsp (90 ml) soy sauce

salt and pepper

6 scallions, chopped

1/2 cup (60 g) cooked peeled shrimp

1/2 cup (60 g) almonds, halved and toasted (page 162)

cilantro sprigs to garnish

shrimp crackers to serve

1 Cook the rice in boiling salted water for 12–15 minutes, until tender. Drain, rinse with boiling water, drain again, and set aside.

2 Heat 1 tbsp of the oil in a large skillet or wok, add the bacon, and cook for 3–5 minutes, until browned. Add the remaining oil, the onions, and garlic, and cook over low heat for 3–5 minutes, until the onions are soft but not browned.

3 Add the chili and curry powders and cook, stirring, for 1 minute or until fragrant. Add the chicken and cook for 5–6 minutes, until just beginning to brown.

4 Add the soy sauce and half of the rice and stir well. Add the remaining rice and salt and pepper to taste. Cook over low heat, stirring, for 7–8 minutes, until the rice is heated through.

5 Stir in the scallions, shrimp, and almonds and heat through. Garnish with cilantro sprigs and serve with shrimp crackers.

VEGETARIAN NASI GORENG

 Serves 6

2 cups (375 g) long-grain rice

salt

2 tbsp tamarind paste

2 tbsp vegetable oil

8 shallots, chopped

3 garlic cloves, crushed

1/2-in (1-cm) piece of fresh ginger, grated

2 tsp curry powder

1/4 tsp each hot red pepper flakes and turmeric

1/2 small cabbage, thinly sliced

2 medium tomatoes, peeled (page 39), seeded, and diced

3 tbsp soy sauce

1 tbsp packed dark brown sugar

TO GARNISH

3 tomatoes, coarsely chopped

1/2 red pepper, cored, seeded, and diced

1/2 cucumber, diced

1 celery stalk, diced

omelet strips (see right)

1 Cook the rice in boiling salted water for 12–15 minutes, until tender. Drain, rinse, and drain again. Stir in the tamarind paste and set aside.

2 Heat 1 tbsp of the oil in a large skillet or wok, add the shallots, and cook for 3–5 minutes, until softened. Add the garlic, ginger, curry powder, pepper flakes, and turmeric and cook gently, stirring, for 1 minute.

3 Add the cabbage and cook for 3–5 minutes. Add the tomatoes and cook for 2–3 minutes. Remove from pan.

4 Heat the remaining oil in the pan, add the rice, and cook gently until lightly browned. Return the vegetables to the pan. Add the soy sauce and sugar and heat gently to warm through.

5 Serve hot, garnished with tomatoes, red pepper, cucumber, celery, and omelet strips.

QUICK NASI GORENG

 Serves 6

2 cups (375 g) long-grain rice

2 tbsp vegetable oil

1 onion, chopped

1/2 tsp paprika

1 tsp ground ginger

1/4 lb (125 g) mushrooms, sliced

1/2 cup (60 g) bean sprouts

1 tsp soy sauce

1 cup (125 g) cooked peeled shrimp

2 scallions, finely sliced

chopped cilantro to garnish

1 Cook the rice in boiling salted water for 12–15 minutes, until tender. Drain, rinse with boiling water, drain again, and set aside.

2 Heat 1 tbsp of the oil in a skillet or wok, add the onion, and cook for 3–5 minutes, until soft. Add the paprika and ginger and cook over low heat for 1 minute. Add the mushrooms and bean sprouts and cook for 2–3 minutes, until softened. Remove from the pan.

3 Heat the remaining oil in the pan, add the rice, and cook over low heat, stirring, for 7–8 minutes to warm through. Stir in the soy sauce. Return the vegetables to the pan and add the shrimp and scallions. Garnish and serve.

OMELET GARNISH

Whisk *2 eggs* with plenty of *salt and pepper*. Melt *2 tbsp butter* in an omelet pan or small skillet. Add the eggs to the pan and cook until set. Leave to cool. Roll up the omelet and slice across into fine strips.

Clockwise from top: *Vegetarian Nasi Goreng, Shrimp Crackers, Quick Nasi Goreng, Chicken Nasi Goreng.*

EGG-FRIED RICE

 Serves 4

1¼ cups (250 g) long-grain rice

salt and black pepper

3 tbsp sunflower or corn oil

2 thick slices of bacon, diced

1 cup (125 g) frozen peas, thawed

2 eggs, beaten

1 cup (125 g) bean sprouts

6 scallions, sliced

1 Cook the rice in boiling salted water for 12–15 minutes, until tender. Drain.

2 Heat the oil in a wok or large skillet, add the bacon, and cook over high heat, stirring, for 2 minutes. Add the rice and peas and cook, stirring, for 5 minutes.

3 Add the eggs and bean sprouts, and stir-fry for 2 minutes, until the eggs have just set. Taste for seasoning, sprinkle with the sliced scallions, and serve immediately.

SPECIAL EGG-FRIED RICE

Add ¼ lb (125 g) cooked peeled shrimp with the rice and peas and cook as directed. Sprinkle with ½ cup (60 g) toasted cashew nuts just before serving.

 Serves 6

3 tbsp olive oil

6 chicken thighs

½ lb (250 g) bacon, cut into strips

1 large onion, chopped

4 cups (1 liter) chicken stock

1 large tomato, peeled (page 39), seeded, and chopped

2 garlic cloves, crushed

a few pinches of saffron threads, soaked in a little hot water

2½ cups (500 g) long-grain rice

1 red and 1 green pepper, cored, seeded, and sliced

1 cup (125 g) frozen peas, thawed

salt and black pepper

1 lb (500 g) mussels, cleaned (page 106)

¼ lb (125 g) cooked peeled shrimp

TO GARNISH

9 pitted black olives

6 large cooked shrimp

lemon wedges

2 tbsp chopped parsley

PAELLA

1 Heat the oil in a paella pan or a large flameproof casserole. Add the chicken and cook over medium heat for about 10 minutes, until browned all over. Add the bacon and onion and cook for 5 minutes.

2 Stir in the stock, tomato, garlic, and the saffron with its soaking liquid and bring to a boil. Add the rice, red and green peppers, and peas and season to taste with salt and pepper. Cover the pan with the lid and bake in a 350°F (180°C) oven for 35–40 minutes, until the rice is nearly tender and the stock has been absorbed.

3 Meanwhile, put the mussels into a large saucepan with about ½ in (1 cm) boiling water. Cover tightly and cook, shaking the pan occasionally, for 5 minutes or until the shells open. Drain the mussels and throw away any that have not opened; do not try to force them open.

4 Stir the mussels and peeled shrimp into the chicken and rice mixture, then cook gently on top of the stove for 5 minutes. Taste for seasoning. Arrange the olives, large shrimp, and lemon wedges on top, and sprinkle with parsley.

Paella

A traditional Spanish rice dish, paella is originally from Valencia. The basic ingredients are shellfish, chicken, peas, and saffron, which gives the rice its characteristic yellow color. Variations may include spicy sausage (chorizo), red and green peppers, or other types of poultry. It is best cooked in a traditional large, shallow two-handled paella pan.

9

VEGETABLES
& SALADS

UNDER 30 MINUTES

CUCUMBER & DILL SALAD

Light and summery: thin cucumber slices in a vinaigrette dressing of white vinegar and sunflower oil, sprinkled with dill.

SERVES 4–6 75–50 calories per serving

Takes 10 minutes   **PAGE 359**

CABBAGE WITH GARLIC AND OIL

Light and nutritious: cabbage leaves cut into thin strips, then blanched and stir-fried with olive oil and garlic.

SERVES 4 154 calories per serving

Takes 15 minutes   **PAGE 345**

WALDORF SALAD

Fruity salad: celery and apple flavored with lemon and coated with mayonnaise. Mixed with pieces of walnut.

SERVES 4 469 calories per serving

Takes 15 minutes, plus chilling   **PAGE 356**

GREEK SALAD

Tomato wedges with cucumber, green pepper, feta cheese, and olives. Flavored with olive oil, lemon, and oregano.

SERVES 4–6 503–335 calories per serving

Takes 10 minutes   **PAGE 359**

MIXED VEGETABLE STIR-FRY

Sliced zucchini stir-fried with yellow pepper and a variety of mushrooms. Flavored with lemon juice and sprinkled with almonds.

SERVES 4 155 calories per serving

Takes 10 minutes   **PAGE 350**

FRENCH CELERIAC SALAD

Matchstick-thin strips of celeriac tossed with yogurt and mayonnaise dressing flavored with capers and mustard.

SERVES 4–6 100–66 calories per serving

Takes 15 minutes   **PAGE 357**

MIXED GREEN SALAD

Crisp lettuce, mâche, watercress, and arugula leaves tossed with vinaigrette dressing and sprinkled with herbs.

SERVES 4–6 117–78 calories per serving

Takes 10 minutes   **PAGE 355**

RED SALAD BOWL

Bite-sized pieces of radicchio and oak leaf and lollo rosso lettuces mixed with onion, grapes, and balsamic vinegar dressing.

SERVES 4–6 387–258 calories per serving

Takes 15 minutes   **PAGE 355**

CARROT JULIENNE SALAD

Matchstick-thin strips of carrot briefly cooked, then coated in a dressing of olive oil, white vinegar, garlic, and parsley.

SERVES 4–6 79–53 calories per serving

Takes 20 minutes   **PAGE 357**

⏱ UNDER 30 MINUTES

CABBAGE & MIXED PEPPER STIR-FRY

Crunchy and nourishing: shredded green cabbage stir-fried with onion, celery, red and yellow peppers, and mushrooms.

SERVES 6–8 128–96 calories per serving

Takes 15 minutes　　　　　　　**PAGE 345**

THREE-COLOR SALAD

Thinly sliced beefsteak tomatoes arranged with slices of mozzarella cheese and avocado and drizzled with olive oil.

SERVES 4 509 calories per serving

Takes 20 minutes　　　　　　　**PAGE 358**

HOT SPICY OKRA

Hot and spicy: okra, onion, garlic, and fresh red chili, stir-fried until just tender but still slightly crisp.

SERVES 4 152 calories per serving

Takes 15 minutes　　　　　　　**PAGE 350**

SWEET & SOUR BEETS

Fresh and flavorful: diced beets cooked with onions, garlic, lemon juice, and mint. Served warm or cold.

SERVES 4 242 calories per serving

Takes 20 minutes　　　　　　　**PAGE 344**

FRENCH FRIES

Popular accompaniment or snack: potatoes, cut into sticks, then deep-fried until crispy and brown.

SERVES 4 422 calories per serving

Takes 20 minutes, plus soaking　**PAGE 340**

CRUNCHY SALAD

Iceberg lettuce, bean sprouts, scallions, and green pepper tossed with ginger dressing and sprinkled with sesame seeds.

SERVES 6 141 calories per serving

Takes 10 minutes, plus soaking　**PAGE 355**

CREAMED SPINACH

Creamy and nutritious: lightly cooked spinach mixed with sour cream, Parmesan cheese, chives, and nutmeg, then broiled.

SERVES 4 250 calories per serving

Takes 20 minutes　　　　　　　**PAGE 344**

SPROUTS WITH MUSTARD SEEDS

Tender and tangy: Brussels sprouts simmered, then tossed with mustard-seed butter and flavored with lemon juice.

SERVES 4 188 calories per serving

Takes 15 minutes　　　　　　　**PAGE 315**

CAESAR SALAD

Pieces of romaine lettuce tossed with olive oil, lemon juice, and hard-boiled egg quarters. Mixed with croutons and Parmesan cheese.

SERVES 4 421 calories per serving

Takes 20 minutes　　　　　　　**PAGE 356**

UNDER 30 MINUTES

AVOCADO SALAD

Fresh and tangy: avocado with orange, pine nuts, and mixed salad greens, tossed with orange and walnut oil dressing.

SERVES 6   240 calories per serving
Takes 20 minutes   **PAGE 358**

SAUTEED CELERY & LEEKS

Fresh and summery: sliced young leeks cooked with sliced celery, mixed with chives, and garnished with cashew nuts.

SERVES 6   235 calories per serving
Takes 20 minutes   **PAGE 348**

SUMMER PEAS & BEANS

Shelled peas cooked with green beans, then combined with cooked young fava beans, butter, and mint.

SERVES 6   107 calories per serving
Takes 20 minutes   **PAGE 347**

SALADE NIÇOISE

Lettuce, green beans, and cucumber topped with tomatoes, eggs, tuna, anchovies, olives, and a garlic and mustard dressing.

SERVES 4   530 calories per serving
Takes 25 minutes   **PAGE 360**

GLAZED CARROTS & TURNIPS

Strips of carrot and whole baby turnips glazed with chicken stock, butter, and sugar. Flavored with fresh mint and parsley.

SERVES 4   115 calories per serving
Takes 20 minutes   **PAGE 344**

HIGH PROTEIN

CREAMY SUCCOTASH

Hearty and tasty: corn kernels simmered with cream, borlotti beans, bacon, and onion. Flavored with chives.

SERVES 4   736 calories per serving
Takes 25 minutes   **PAGE 348**

SPINACH & BACON SALAD

Pieces of spinach and crispy bacon lightly tossed with vinaigrette or blue cheese dressing and topped with croutons.

SERVES 6   436 calories per serving
Takes 25 minutes   **PAGE 355**

HIGH FIBER

FRENCH-STYLE PEAS

Light and summery: sweetened shelled peas simmered with shredded lettuce, chopped scallions, butter, and parsley.

SERVES 4   237 calories per serving
Takes 25 minutes   **PAGE 347**

STUFFED MUSHROOMS

Tasty and healthy: mushrooms stuffed with chopped mushroom stalks, carrots, zucchini, and parsley, then baked.

SERVES 6   91 calories per serving
Takes 25 minutes   **PAGE 349**

30–60 MINUTES

WATERCRESS & ROAST VEGETABLE SALAD

Zucchini slices tossed with roasted peppers, watercress, and vinaigrette dressing.

SERVES 4–6 310–207 calories per serving

Takes 20 minutes, plus cooling **PAGE 354**

SAVORY PUMPKIN

Chunks of pumpkin sprinkled with a mixture of oil, balsamic vinegar, garlic, thyme, and paprika. Baked until tender.

SERVES 4 140 calories per serving

Takes 30 minutes **PAGE 350**

WILD RICE SALAD

Wild and long-grain rice in a dressing of oils, vinegar, and mustard. Mixed with green beans, mushrooms, parsley, and walnuts.

SERVES 4–6 554–369 calories per serving

Takes 30 minutes **PAGE 361**

TOMATOES WITH CILANTRO

Cherry tomatoes baked until lightly browned and tender. Dotted with butter combined with cilantro, garlic, and lemon juice.

SERVES 4 106 calories per serving

Takes 35 minutes **PAGE 350**

DINNER PARTY

GINGER PARSNIPS

Matchstick-thin strips of parsnip lightly cooked with ginger, covered with sour cream, then baked until tender.

SERVES 6 332 calories per serving

Takes 30 minutes **PAGE 344**

TOMATO & ZUCCHINI CASSEROLE

Light and delicious: layers of sliced zucchini and tomato baked in a white sauce flavored with nutmeg.

SERVES 4–6 238–159 calories per serving

Takes 40 minutes **PAGE 351**

SPICED YAMS

Chunky and spicy: cubed yams cooked with tomatoes, garlic, cumin, and cinnamon. Spiked with chili powder and paprika.

SERVES 4 381 calories per serving

Takes 30 minutes **PAGE 343**

ASPARAGUS WITH PARMESAN

Asparagus marinated in olive oil, wine, vinegar, and garlic. Rolled in Parmesan cheese and baked with the marinade.

SERVES 4 215 calories per serving

Takes 35 minutes, plus marinating **PAGE 349**

PASTA SALAD WITH PEPPERS

Cooked pasta bows combined with diced red and green peppers and scallions. Coated in mayonnaise.

SERVES 4–6 556–370 calories per serving

Takes 20 minutes, plus chilling **PAGE 362**

30–60 MINUTES

SWEET & SOUR RED CABBAGE

Shredded red cabbage cooked with bacon, apple, sugar, red wine, vinegar, golden raisins, and distinctive spices.

SERVES 4–6 450–300 calories per serving

Takes 55 minutes **PAGE 346**

POMMES ANNA

Thinly sliced potatoes, layered in a skillet, dotted with butter, and seasoned with salt and pepper, then cooked until tender.

SERVES 4 307 calories per serving

Takes 55 minutes **PAGE 341**

COUSCOUS SALAD

Couscous cooked with golden raisins·and ginger. Mixed with chili oil, vinegar, tomatoes, onion, scallions, and mint.

SERVES 4–6 420–280 calories per serving

Takes 20 minutes, plus cooling **PAGE 361**

GARLIC MASHED POTATOES

Hearty and satisfying: boiled potato, mashed, then mixed with roasted garlic, warm milk, and butter. Sprinkled with chives.

SERVES 4 282 calories per serving

Takes 45 minutes **PAGE 341**

CAULIFLOWER & BROCCOLI LAYERS

Florets of cauliflower and broccoli layered in rings and prepared in a mold. Topped with almonds and bread crumbs.

SERVES 4–6 341–227 calories per serving

Takes 35 minutes **PAGE 346**

RICE SALAD

Long-grain rice in a dressing flavored with mustard and garlic. Mixed with peas, red pepper, corn, and cilantro.

SERVES 4–6 517–345 calories per serving

Takes 25 minutes, plus cooling **PAGE 361**

ITALIAN FENNEL

Quartered fennel bulbs lightly cooked until tender, topped with mozzarella cheese, and baked until golden.

SERVES 6–8 145–108 calories per serving

Takes 30 minutes **PAGE 349**

GLAZED SHALLOTS

Whole shallots simmered gently in water, butter, sugar, and thyme until glazed and golden brown.

SERVES 4 225 calories per serving

Takes 30 minutes **PAGE 348**

TABBOULEH

Fresh and herby: bulgur wheat mixed with vinaigrette dressing, lemon juice, tomatoes, scallions, parsley, and mint.

SERVES 4 276 calories per serving

Takes 10 minutes, plus standing **PAGE 361**

OVER 60 MINUTES

TOMATO & BASIL SALAD

Assortment of tomatoes and chunks of yellow pepper dressed in oil and balsamic vinegar. Sprinkled with basil.

SERVES 4–6 146–97 calories per serving
Takes 10 minutes, plus standing **PAGE 359**

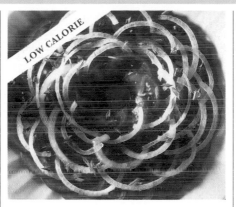

TOMATO & ONION SALAD

Thinly sliced tomatoes and mild onion dressed in olive oil, red wine vinegar, and sugar. Sprinkled with snipped chives.

SERVES 6 166 calories per serving
Takes 15 minutes, plus chilling **PAGE 359**

EGGPLANT WITH FRESH PESTO

Mediterranean flavors: slices of eggplant broiled until lightly browned, cooled, then spread with pesto and sprinkled with basil.

SERVES 4 499 calories per serving
Takes 20 minutes, plus standing **PAGE 354**

POTATO, APPLE, & CELERY SALAD

Hearty salad: pieces of boiled potato tossed with vinaigrette dressing, mixed with apple, celery, onion, and mayonnaise.

SERVES 6 332 calories per serving
Takes 30 minutes, plus chilling **PAGE 357**

THREE-BEAN SALAD

Green beans, garbanzo beans, and red kidney beans combined with olives in a yogurt dressing, flavored with vinegar and mustard.

SERVES 4 315 calories per serving
Takes 15 minutes, plus standing **PAGE 360**

COLESLAW

Shredded green cabbage tossed with onion, celery, carrot, golden raisins, vinaigrette dressing, mustard, and mayonnaise.

SERVES 8 245 calories per serving
Takes 15 minutes, plus chilling **PAGE 356**

PASTA & SMOKED FISH SALAD

Pasta shells tossed with zucchini, green beans, orange, smoked mackerel, walnuts, and a dressing of oils and orange juice.

SERVES 4–6 965–643 calories per serving
Takes 30 minutes, plus chilling **PAGE 362**

FRENCH POTATO SALAD

Tender new potatoes and onion coated in vinaigrette dressing, then mixed with chives and mayonnaise.

SERVES 4–6 714–476 calories per serving
Takes 30 minutes, plus chilling **PAGE 358**

MUSHROOM & YOGURT SALAD

Mushrooms cooked with coriander, then dressed in yogurt flavored with mustard and garlic. Chilled and mixed with celery.

SERVES 6 102 calories per serving
Takes 15 minutes, plus chilling **PAGE 358**

⏱ OVER 60 MINUTES

SWISS ROSTI

Potato pancakes from Switzerland: grated potatoes seasoned with pepper and shaped into a cake. Cooked in butter until golden.

SERVES 8 230 calories per serving

Takes 45 minutes, plus chilling **PAGE 339**

POTATOES LYONNAISE

Mouthwateringly delicious: thickly sliced potatoes layered with onion. Baked until the potatoes are tender.

SERVES 4 369 calories per serving

Takes 1³/4 hours **PAGE 340**

LOW FAT

RATATOUILLE

Slices of eggplant, zucchini, and red pepper cooked with tomatoes. Flavored with onion, garlic, and basil.

SERVES 4–6 236–157 calories per serving

Takes 1¹/2 hours, plus standing **PAGE 351**

TRADITIONAL

ROAST POTATOES

Classic accompaniment to roast meat or poultry: briefly simmered pieces of potato roasted in a little fat until crisp and golden.

SERVES 4 288 calories per serving

Takes 1¹/4 hours **PAGE 340**

SWEET POTATOES WITH GINGER BUTTER

Baked sweet potatoes flavored with soy sauce and served with ginger and garlic butter. Sprinkled with sesame seeds.

SERVES 4 381 calories per serving

Takes 1 hour 5 minutes **PAGE 343**

SPINACH & CHEESE BAKED POTATOES

Hearty and healthy: baked potatoes scooped out and mixed with spinach, onion, and ricotta cheese. Flavored with nutmeg.

SERVES 4 291 calories per serving

Takes 1³/4 hours **PAGE 342**

DINNER PARTY

CHEESY BAKED POTATOES

Simple to make: whole potatoes sliced almost through at intervals. Brushed with butter, sprinkled with Parmesan, and baked.

SERVES 4–6 366–244 calories per serving

Takes 1 hour 5 minutes **PAGE 342**

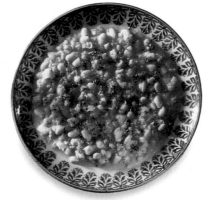

CREAMED WHITE BEANS

Hearty dish: great northern beans simmered with carrot, onion, parsley, thyme, and bay leaf. Thickened with some pureed beans.

SERVES 6 167 calories per serving

Takes 1¹/2 hours, plus soaking **PAGE 347**

FRENCH CLASSIC

POTATOES GRATIN

Rich and creamy: thinly sliced potato layered with cream, garlic, and grated Gruyère cheese, then baked until golden.

SERVES 6 372 calories per serving

Takes 1³/4 hours **PAGE 339**

VEGETABLES & SALADS KNOW-HOW

THE SELECTION OF VEGETABLES available from our farmers' markets and supermarkets seems to increase all the time. With every shopping trip there are new varieties of potatoes and tomatoes, pumpkins and other squashes, a wide variety of baby vegetables, and peppers of all colors. The choice is no longer limited by the season: vegetables once available only in spring and summer are now imported from sunnier climes during the winter. This wonderful bounty helps the cook to be innovative, trying new combinations and creating nutritious, appetizing dishes. Salad has never been more exciting – exotic salad greens such as arugula, radicchio, and curly endive are just a few of the leafy ingredients widely available to brighten up the salad bowl.

BUYING AND STORING

When choosing vegetables, look for the freshest available. Their color should be bright and their texture firm and crisp. Any vegetables that are bruised or show signs of age – those that are discolored, shriveled, or flabby – are past their prime. In general, small, young vegetables are more tender and have a better flavor than large, older ones, although very small baby vegetables can sometimes be bland.

Many vegetables, including onions, potatoes, garlic, rutabaga, and pumpkin, can be stored in a cool, dark, well-ventilated place. More perishable vegetables, such as peas, corn, celery, lettuces, and spinach, should be chilled. Keep them in the special salad drawer in the refrigerator, unwrapping them or piercing their bags to prevent moisture buildup. Rinse any leafy green vegetables, lettuces, or herbs, wrap in paper towels, and store in a plastic bag.

NUTRITION

A healthy, well-balanced diet should include plenty of vegetables, because they supply essential vitamins, minerals, fiber, and vegetable protein. Despite their reputation, starchy vegetables such as potatoes are not fattening in themselves – calories are increased by the oil they are fried in or the butter that is added to them. To get the maximum benefit from the vegetables you eat:

- choose the freshest produce
- keep all vegetables in a cool, dark place and use as quickly as possible
- avoid peeling vegetables unless absolutely necessary; most of the vitamins are in the skin
- rinse thoroughly but don't soak before cooking, particularly if peeled
- prepare as close to cooking time as possible.

CUTTING VEGETABLES

Keep pieces to a uniform size and shape to ensure they cook evenly.

Julienne
Cut into 1/4-in (5-mm) slices. Stack the slices, then cut into sticks 1/4 in (5 mm) thick.

Dice
Cut into 1/2-in (1-cm) strips, then cut across the strips to form neat dice.

Ribbons
Using a vegetable peeler, carefully shave off thin, wide ribbons.

MICROWAVING

The microwave oven is ideal for cooking vegetables: very little water is used, so they retain their nutrients as well as their colors and flavors. Cut vegetables into uniform pieces or pierce skins of those that are left whole. Arrange them so that the tender parts are in the center of the dish to prevent overcooking. Add salt when serving. Keep the dish tightly covered during cooking and turn or stir once or twice if necessary.

FREEZING

Most vegetables freeze very well, whether plain, in a sauce, or in a prepared dish. Potatoes, however, do not freeze successfully. Vegetables that are to be frozen plain should first be blanched in boiling water, then cooled quickly in iced water before freezing; this will set the color and prevent vitamin loss. Vegetables can be kept in the freezer for at least 6 months and can be cooked directly from frozen.

PREPARING VEGETABLES

Learning the correct way to prepare vegetables will save you time and effort in the kitchen. For most tasks, a cutting board and a sharp chef's knife, a small knife, or a vegetable peeler are all you'll need. Here's how the professionals deal with more unusual vegetables.

Fresh chili

1 Cut the chili in half lengthwise. Remove the stalk and core and scrape out the fleshy white ribs and seeds.

2 Set the chili cut side up and cut into thin strips. Hold the strips together and cut across to make dice.

Asparagus

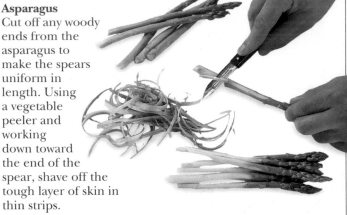

Cut off any woody ends from the asparagus to make the spears uniform in length. Using a vegetable peeler and working down toward the end of the spear, shave off the tough layer of skin in thin strips.

Pepper

1 Cut around the stalk and the core. Twist and pull them out in one piece.

2 Cut the pepper in half. Scrape out the fleshy white ribs and the seeds.

Garlic

1 Set the flat side of a knife on top of the clove and crush it lightly. Peel off the skin.

2 With a sharp chef's knife, chop the crushed garlic clove finely.

Avocado

Cut the avocado in half lengthwise and twist the 2 halves to separate them. Embed the blade of a chef's knife into the pit and pull it out. If the avocado is to be mashed, the flesh can simply be scooped out with a teaspoon. To serve in slices, lightly score the skin into 2 or 3 strips. Peel off the strips of skin and slice.

Fresh ginger

1 With a small knife, peel off the skin. Slice the ginger across the fibrous grain.

2 Set the flat of a knife on top and crush the slices. Chop the crushed slices.

Eggplant

Cut the eggplant as specified in the recipe. Put the pieces onto a plate or into a colander, sprinkle with salt (on all cut sides if possible), and leave for about 30 minutes. Rinse and dry with paper towels. This process, known as salting, removes any bitter juices from the eggplant.

Preparing vegetables know-how

The juices produced by fresh chilies can burn the skin, so it's best to wear rubber gloves when cutting them and to avoid any contact with the eyes.

◆

Large zucchini, which may be bitter, can be salted in the same way as eggplant.

◆

The more finely you chop garlic, the stronger the flavor.

◆

Avocados discolor quickly, so brush cut surfaces with lemon juice and use as soon as possible.

COOKING VEGETABLES

*Choose the right cooking method to bring out the best in vegetables and create
an exciting accompaniment to a main dish. If you are cooking a
variety of vegetables at the same time, remember that some take
longer to cook than others, so you may have to add them in*

Baking
Potatoes, sweet potatoes, eggplant, and pumpkin are all delicious baked. Prick the skins of whole vegetables or, if cut, moisten cut surfaces with oil or butter. Push a skewer through the centers of large vegetables to conduct heat and cut cooking time.

Broiling
Many types of quick-cooking vegetables can be broiled under a broiler or grilled over a barbecue. Halve the vegetables or cut into thick slices. Brush with oil and cook, turning at least once, until tender. For extra flavor, marinate vegetables first (page 452).

Braising
Carrots, celery, parsnips, and other root vegetables are ideal for braising. Put the vegetables into a heavy saucepan or casserole, add a small amount of water or stock, and bring to a boil. Cover tightly and cook over low heat until just tender.

Sautéing
Vegetables can be sautéed in oil or a mixture of oil and butter. Butter alone burns if it becomes too hot. Cook the vegetables over high heat, stirring and turning, until they start to brown. Reduce the heat and cook, stirring occasionally, until tender.

Roasting
Put olive oil or duck fat into a roasting pan and put in a preheated oven until hot. Cut any root vegetables into large chunks and parboil them. Add to the roasting pan, turning to coat with the fat. Roast at 350°F (180°C), turning occasionally, until well browned.

Boiling
Green vegetables should be dropped into a pan of boiling salted water; root vegetables should be put in a pan of cold water and brought to a boil. Cover and simmer until just tender, then drain. To stop further cooking and set the color, rinse in cold water.

Deep-frying
Apart from root vegetables, most vegetables need a protective coating such as batter before being deep-fried. Heat the oil in a deep-fat fryer to the required temperature. Add the vegetables in batches and fry until golden, bringing the oil to the required temperature between batches.

Stir-frying
Cut the vegetables into small, even-sized pieces. Heat a little oil in a wok or large skillet. When it is hot, add the vegetables, starting with those that need the longest cooking time. Keep the heat high for just a few minutes, until the vegetables are tender but still crisp.

Steaming
This method is ideal for flavorful vegetables such as cauliflower, broccoli, or asparagus. Bring water to a boil in a steamer. Put the vegetables in a single layer on the rack, cover, and steam until just tender. If you don't have a steamer, use a large saucepan with a steamer basket or a wok and a bamboo steamer.

VEGETABLE GARNISHES

Vegetables cut into attractive shapes or assembled decoratively can add a distinctive finishing touch to dishes and will make a meal more special.

Carrot flowers
With a canelle knife or other small sharp knife, cut lengthwise grooves at regular intervals all around the carrot, then slice thinly. Cucumber can also be prepared in this way.

Tomato roses
Peel a length of skin from a tomato. Hold the flat end of the strip and wind the rest of the strip around into a loose spiral, turning as you wind. Tuck in the other end of the strip.

Green bean bundles
1 Gather together small bundles of cooked green beans and cut the beans to the same length, about 3 in (7 cm).

2 With a vegetable peeler, shave a thin strip of skin from a zucchini. Cut the strip into very fine "strings." Tie each green bean bundle around the middle with a zucchini "string."

SALAD DRESSINGS

All of the following dressings can be made by hand, with a balloon whisk, but if you prefer, a screw-top jar is a handy alternative for mixing a vinaigrette, while a food processor or blender can produce mayonnaise or blue cheese dressing in a matter of seconds.

Mayonnaise
1 Put a bowl on a dish towel to steady it. Add *2 egg yolks, 1 tsp Dijon mustard,* and *salt and pepper to taste* and beat together with a balloon whisk until the egg yolks have thickened slightly.

2 Whisk in *2/3 cup (150 ml) olive or sunflower oil,* just a drop at a time at first, whisking until the mixture is thick. Stir in *2 tsp white vinegar* and serve at once or chill. Makes 3/4 cup (200 ml).

Vinaigrette dressing
Put *6 tbsp olive oil, 2 tbsp white vinegar, 1 tbsp lemon juice, 1 tbsp Dijon mustard, 1/4 tsp sugar,* and *salt and pepper* into a screw-top jar and shake until well combined. Makes 2/3 cup (150 ml).

Blue cheese dressing
Put *2/3 cup cup (150 ml) each of mayonnaise and sour cream, 3/4 cup (90 g) crumbled blue cheese, 1 tsp white vinegar, 1 crushed garlic clove,* and *black pepper to taste* into a bowl and whisk until smooth.

Food processor mayonnaise
1 Put *2 egg yolks, 1 tsp Dijon mustard,* and *salt and pepper to taste* in the bowl of a food processor or blender. Process briefly to combine.

2 With the blades turning, gradually add *2/3 cup (150 ml) olive or sunflower oil,* pouring it through the funnel in a slow, continuous stream.

Salad dressings know-how

If mayonnaise curdles, add 1 tbsp hot water and beat well or start again with fresh egg yolks and oil and slowly add the curdled mixture once the eggs and oil thicken.

◆

Be sure the eggs for mayonnaise are at room temperature.

◆

Keep mayonnaise, covered, in the refrigerator for up to 3 days. Bring to room temperature, stir, and serve.

◆

Keep vinaigrette dressings in the refrigerator for up to 1 week. Whisk before serving.

POTATOES GRATIN

 Serves 6

butter for greasing

²/₃ cup (150 ml) light cream

²/₃ cup (150 ml) heavy cream

1 large garlic clove, crushed

2 lb (1 kg) baking potatoes

salt and black pepper

1 cup (125 g) grated Gruyère cheese

1 Lightly butter a shallow gratin dish. Put the light and heavy creams into a bowl, add the garlic, and stir to mix.

2 Thinly slice the potatoes, preferably with the slicing disk of a food processor.

3 Prepare the potatoes gratin (see box, right).

4 Bake in a 325°F (160°C) oven for 1¹/₂ hours or until the potatoes are tender and the topping is golden brown. Serve immediately.

Preparing the potatoes gratin

Arrange a layer of potatoes in the bottom of the gratin dish and add salt and pepper to taste.

Pour a little of the cream mixture over the potatoes, then sprinkle with cheese. Continue layering the potatoes, cream, and cheese, adding salt and pepper and finishing with a layer of cheese.

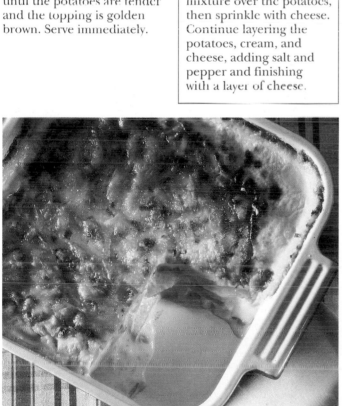

SWISS ROSTI

 Serves 8

3 lb (1.5 kg) large baking potatoes, scrubbed

black pepper

4 tbsp butter

2 tbsp sunflower or corn oil

fresh thyme to garnish

1 Cook the potatoes in boiling salted water for about 10 minutes, until just tender. Drain the potatoes thoroughly, leave to cool, then peel. Cover and chill for about 4 hours.

2 Coarsely grate the potatoes into a large bowl, add pepper to taste, and stir carefully to mix.

3 Melt 2 tbsp of the butter with 1 tbsp of the oil in a skillet, add the grated potato, and flatten into a cake with a spatula. Cook over low heat for about 15 minutes, until the base is crisp and golden brown. Transfer the potato cake to a large buttered plate.

4 Melt the remaining butter and oil in the skillet, slide in the potato cake, and cook for 5–10 minutes to brown the second side. Transfer to a warmed platter, garnish, and serve cut into wedges.

CELERIAC ROSTI

Substitute 1¹/₂ lb (750 g) celeriac for half of the potato. Toss in lemon juice to prevent discoloration, then proceed as directed.

ONION ROSTI

Heat 1 tbsp sunflower oil in a skillet, add 1 large chopped onion, and cook for 3–5 minutes until softened but not browned. Fork the onion into 2¹/₂ lb (1.15 kg) grated potato, add the pepper, and proceed as directed.

POTATOES LYONNAISE

 Serves 4

6 tbsp butter, plus extra
  for greasing

1 large onion, sliced

2 lb (1 kg) baking potatoes,
  thickly sliced

salt and black pepper

chopped parsley to garnish

1 Lightly butter a gratin dish. Melt the butter in a skillet, add the onion, and cook gently, stirring occasionally, for 3–5 minutes, until the onions are softened but not browned.

2 Layer the potatoes and onion in the gratin dish, seasoning each layer with salt and pepper and finishing with a neat layer of potatoes.

3 Pour any butter left in the skillet over the potatoes. Bake in a 375°F (190°C) oven for 1–1½ hours, until the potatoes are tender and cooked through. Garnish with parsley and serve hot.

FRENCH FRIES

 Serves 4

1½ lb (750 g) baking potatoes

sunflower oil for deep-frying

salt

★ deep-fat fryer

1 Cut the potatoes into 2- x ½-in (5- x 1-cm) sticks, put into a bowl of cold water, and leave to soak for 5–10 minutes.

2 Heat the oil in a deep-fat fryer to 325°F (160°C). Dry the fries thoroughly, then lower them into the deep-fat fryer, in batches if necessary, and deep-fry for 5–6 minutes, until soft.

3 Lift the basket out of the fryer. Increase the temperature of the oil to 375°F (190°C). Carefully return the basket of fries to the fryer and deep-fry for 3–4 minutes, until crisp and brown. Lift out the basket and drain the fries on paper towels. Sprinkle with salt and serve immediately.

Cook's know-how

Good French fries should be crisp and golden on the outside and soft and tender in the middle. The secret is to cook the potatoes first in medium-hot oil until tender, then lift them out, increase the temperature of the oil, and cook the fries quickly to brown and crisp the outsides. Drain on paper towels.

POMMES FRITES

Cut the potatoes into 2- x ¼-in (5-cm x 5-mm) sticks and leave to soak as directed. Heat the oil as directed and deep-fry the sticks for 4–5 minutes. Lift out of the fryer, increase the heat as directed, return and deep-fry the sticks for 1–2 minutes. Sprinkle with salt, and serve immediately.

ROAST POTATOES

 Serves 4

2 lb (1 kg) baking potatoes, cut
  into even-sized pieces

3 tbsp duck or goose fat,
  drippings, or sunflower oil

salt

1 Put the potatoes into a large saucepan, cover with cold water, and bring to a boil. Simmer for 1 minute, then drain.

2 Return the potatoes to the saucepan and shake over low heat to roughen the surfaces and dry the potatoes thoroughly.

3 Put the fat into a roasting pan, heat until very hot, then add the potatoes, turning to coat them in the fat. Roast the potatoes in a 425°F (220°C) oven, turning and basting them occasionally, for 45–60 minutes, until tender, crisp, and golden in color. Sprinkle with salt and serve immediately.

Cook's know-how

Roughening the surfaces of the potatoes before roasting gives them a particularly crisp texture. If you prefer, you can also score the surfaces with a fork.

POMMES ANNA

Serves 4

1¹/₂ lb (750 g) baking potatoes

6 tbsp (90 g) butter, plus extra for greasing

salt and black pepper

1 Slice the potatoes very thinly, preferably with the slicing disk of a food processor.

2 Generously butter the bottom and side of an ovenproof skillet. Layer the potatoes in the skillet, seasoning each layer with salt and pepper to taste and dotting with the butter.

3 Cover the skillet tightly with buttered foil and the lid and cook over medium heat for about 15 minutes or until the base of the potato cake is light golden brown.

4 Transfer the skillet to a 375°F (190°C) oven for 30 minutes or until the potato cake is tender and cooked through.

5 Invert a warmed serving platter over the skillet, and turn out the potato cake with the crisp layer on top. Serve immediately, cut into wedges.

Cook's know-how

Arrange the potatoes in the skillet as soon as they have been sliced; if you put them into water, the starch contained in them will be washed away and they won't hold together.

INDIVIDUAL POMMES ANNA

Layer the sliced potatoes in well-buttered individual ramekins. Cook them in the top half of a 425°F (220°C) oven for 30–35 minutes.

GARLIC MASHED POTATOES

Serves 4

1¹/₂ lb (750 g) baking potatoes, cut into large chunks

salt and black pepper

4 garlic cloves

about ²/₃ cup (150 ml) milk

4 tbsp butter

2 tbsp snipped fresh chives

1 Cook the potatoes in boiling salted water for 20–30 minutes, until tender. Drain thoroughly.

2 Meanwhile, roast the garlic cloves in a 350°F (180°C) oven for 10 minutes until softened. Remove the skins from the garlic cloves.

3 Return the potatoes to the saucepan and toss over low heat for a few seconds to dry thoroughly, shaking the saucepan so that the potatoes do not burn.

4 Mash the potatoes or work through a strainer, then push them to one side of the pan.

5 Pour the milk into the saucepan and heat until almost boiling. Beat the milk into the potatoes with the garlic, butter, and salt and pepper to taste. Sprinkle with chives and serve hot.

HERB & CHEESE MASHED POTATOES

Omit the garlic, and add 2 tbsp chopped parsley and ¹/₂ cup (60 g) finely grated Cheddar cheese when you beat in the milk, then proceed as directed.

MASHED POTATOES WITH RUTABAGA

Omit the garlic and fresh chives. Substitute ¹/₂ lb (250 g) peeled rutabaga, cut into small chunks, for ¹/₂ lb (250 g) of the potatoes and proceed as directed, adding a pinch of grated nutmeg just before serving.

CHEESY BAKED POTATOES

 Serves 4–6

2 lb (1 kg) baking potatoes

4 tbsp butter, melted, plus extra for greasing

salt and black pepper

1/4 cup (30 g) grated Parmesan cheese

parsley to garnish

1 Slice the potatoes (see box, right).

2 Put the potatoes into a buttered roasting pan and brush with the butter, separating the slices slightly so a little butter goes between them. Season.

3 Bake in a 425°F (220°C) oven for 45 minutes. Sprinkle the potatoes with 3 tbsp of the Parmesan cheese and return to the oven until tender.

4 Transfer to a serving platter and sprinkle with the remaining Parmesan. Garnish and serve.

Slicing the potatoes

Cut a thin slice off one side of each potato, if necessary, to steady it. Slice each potato, three-quarters of the way through, at 1/4-in (5-mm) intervals.

Cook's know-how

To make it easier to slice the potatoes, push a skewer lengthwise through the lower part of each potato and slice as far down as the skewer. Remove the skewer before cooking.

SPINACH & CHEESE BAKED POTATOES

 Serves 4

4 baking potatoes, scrubbed

8 cups loosely packed (250 g) spinach

1 tbsp olive oil

1 small onion, finely chopped

1/2 cup (125 g) ricotta cheese

pinch of grated nutmeg

salt and black pepper

1 Prick the potatoes all over with a fork. Bake in a 425°F (220°C) oven for 1–1 1/4 hours until tender.

2 Meanwhile, wash the spinach and put it into a saucepan with only the water remaining on the leaves. Cook over low heat for 1–2 minutes, until the spinach has just wilted. Drain thoroughly, squeezing to remove excess water. Chop the spinach finely.

3 Heat the olive oil in a small saucepan, add the onion, and cook gently, stirring occasionally, for 3–5 minutes, until softened but not browned.

4 Cut the potatoes in half lengthwise, scoop out the flesh, and transfer it to a bowl. Add the spinach, onion, any oil left in the pan, the ricotta cheese, nutmeg, and salt and pepper to taste and mix thoroughly. Fill the potato skins with the mixture, return to the oven, and cook for 20 minutes or until piping hot. Serve immediately.

SCALLION & HUMMUS BAKED POTATOES

Bake the potatoes, cut in half lengthwise, and scoop out the flesh as directed. Mix with 4 finely chopped scallions, 2/3 cup (150 g) hummus, and salt and pepper to taste. Fill the potato skins and proceed as directed in the recipe.

SWEET POTATOES WITH GINGER BUTTER

 Serves 4

4 sweet potatoes, scrubbed

1/2 cup (125 g) sesame seeds

soy sauce to taste

GINGER BUTTER

3 tbsp butter, softened

1 garlic clove, crushed

1/2-in (1-cm) piece of fresh ginger, peeled and chopped

1 Lightly prick the skins of the sweet potatoes with a fork. Bake in a 350°F (180°C) oven for 1 hour or until tender.

2 Meanwhile, make the ginger butter: put the butter into a small bowl and blend in the garlic and chopped ginger.

3 Put the sesame seeds into a skillet and toss over low heat for 2–3 minutes, until golden brown. Remove from the skillet. Lightly crush about half of the sesame seeds to release more of their fragrance. Set aside.

4 Cut the sweet potatoes into wedges and arrange on a serving plate with the ginger butter. Sprinkle the sweet potatoes with soy sauce and sesame seeds and serve immediately.

Sweet potatoes

Sweet potatoes are often served roasted as accompaniments to barbecued meats and chicken. The most popular varieties are a pale-skinned sweet potato with pale yellow flesh and a dark-skinned variety with orange, yellow, or white flesh. Both types have a deliciously sweet, rich flavor, and honey and sweet spices are often added to accentuate this. They are not from the same plant as yams but can be cooked in the same way.

SPICED YAMS

 Serves 4

3 tbsp butter

2 garlic cloves, crushed

2 yams, total weight about 2 lb (1 kg), trimmed but unpeeled, cubed

1/2 tsp mild chili powder

1/4 tsp paprika

1/4 tsp ground cumin

1/4 tsp ground cinnamon

7 oz (200 g) canned tomatoes, juice reserved, diced

salt

plain yogurt and chopped parsley to garnish

1 Melt the butter in a large pan. When it is foaming, add the garlic, and cook gently, stirring occasionally, for 1–2 minutes, until soft but not browned.

2 Add the yams to the pan and toss over medium to high heat for 1–2 minutes.

3 Stir in the chili powder, paprika, cumin, and cinnamon, then add the tomatoes and cook the mixture over medium heat for 1–2 minutes.

4 Add the juice from the tomatoes and salt to taste. Cover and simmer, gently turning the yams occasionally with a narrow spatula, for 15–20 minutes, until the yams are tender. Do not stir or they will break up. Serve immediately, garnished with yogurt and parsley.

GINGER PARSNIPS

 Serves 6

2 lb (1 kg) parsnips, cut into matchsticks

salt and black pepper

4 tbsp butter

1-in (2.5-cm) piece of fresh ginger, peeled and finely chopped

1¼ cups (300 ml) light sour cream

1 Blanch the parsnips in a large saucepan of boiling salted water for 2 minutes. Drain the parsnips.

2 Melt the butter in the saucepan. Add the ginger and cook gently, stirring, for 2–3 minutes. Add the parsnips, tossing to coat in the butter. Add salt and pepper to taste, then transfer the mixture to a large, shallow ovenproof dish.

3 Spread the light sour cream over the parsnip mixture and bake in a 375°F (190°C) oven for 10–15 minutes, until tender. Serve immediately.

GLAZED CARROTS & TURNIPS

 Serves 4

6 carrots, cut into 2-in (5-cm) strips

¾ lb (375 g) baby turnips

1¼ cups (300 ml) chicken stock

2 tbsp butter

1 tsp sugar

salt and black pepper

1 tbsp mixed chopped fresh mint and parsley

1 Put the vegetables into a pan with the stock, butter, sugar, and salt and pepper to taste and bring to a boil. Cover and cook for about 10 minutes, until the vegetables are almost tender.

2 Remove the lid and boil rapidly until the liquid in the pan has evaporated and formed a glaze on the vegetables. Stir in the herbs, and serve immediately.

CREAMED SPINACH

 Serves 4

1½ lb (750 g) frozen leaf spinach, thawed and drained

3 tbsp butter

½ cup (125 ml) light sour cream or crème fraîche

1–2 tbsp grated Parmesan cheese

1 tsp snipped fresh chives

large pinch of grated nutmeg

salt and black pepper

1 Coarsely chop the spinach leaves and set aside.

2 Melt the butter in a saucepan, add the spinach, and stir until it has absorbed the butter.

3 Add half of the sour cream or crème fraîche, the Parmesan cheese, chives, nutmeg. Season with salt and pepper to taste and heat through.

4 Transfer to a shallow flameproof dish, spread the remaining sour cream or crème fraîche over the spinach mixture, and put under the broiler for 4–5 minutes, until lightly browned. Taste for seasoning and serve hot.

SWEET & SOUR BEETS

 Serves 4

3 tbsp olive oil

2 onions, chopped

2 garlic cloves, crushed

4 cooked beets, diced

2 tbsp sugar

juice of 1 lemon

2 tsp chopped fresh mint

salt and black pepper

fresh mint to garnish

1 Heat the olive oil in a large saucepan, add the onions and garlic, and cook gently, stirring occasionally, for 3–5 minutes, until the onions are softened but not browned.

2 Stir in the beets, sugar, half of the lemon juice, the mint, and salt and pepper to taste and cook gently, stirring, for 10 minutes. Taste for seasoning, adding more lemon juice if needed.

3 Serve warm or cold, garnished with fresh mint.

CABBAGE & MIXED PEPPER STIR-FRY

 Serves 6–8

2–3 tbsp olive oil

1 large onion, finely sliced

6 celery stalks, sliced diagonally

1 small green cabbage, finely shredded

2 red peppers, cored, seeded, and cut into thin strips

1 yellow pepper, cored, seeded, and cut into thin strips

2 1/2 cups (175 g) mushrooms, quartered

salt and black pepper

1 Heat 1 tbsp of the olive oil in a wok or large skillet, add the sliced onion, and stir-fry over high heat for about 2 minutes, until beginning to brown.

2 Add the sliced celery and stir-fry for about 1 minute, then lower the heat and stir-fry for 2 minutes.

3 Add another 1 tbsp of olive oil to the wok, add the cabbage, and stir-fry for 2 minutes.

4 Add the peppers and mushrooms, with the remaining oil if needed, and stir-fry for 3 minutes. Add salt and pepper to taste, and serve immediately.

Cook's know-how

This is a good vegetable dish to serve when entertaining. Prepare and stir-fry the vegetables up to the end of step 2. The final cooking can be done in minutes, just before serving.

SAVOY CABBAGE STIR-FRY

Heat 1 tbsp sunflower oil in a wok and stir-fry 1 finely sliced large onion, and 2 crushed garlic cloves for 2 minutes. Add another tbsp sunflower oil, then 1 shredded small Savoy cabbage, and stir-fry for 2 minutes. Sprinkle with 2 tbsp soy sauce and 1 tsp sesame oil.

CABBAGE WITH GARLIC AND OIL

 Serves 4

2 lb (1 kg) cabbage leaves, tough stalks removed

salt

2 tbsp olive oil

3 garlic cloves, coarsely chopped

1 Roll up the cabbage leaves a few at a time and cut across into thin strips. Blanch in boiling salted water for 2 minutes.

2 Drain and rinse in iced water to cool. Drain thoroughly, squeezing to remove excess water.

3 Heat the olive oil in a large saucepan, add the garlic, and cook gently for 1 minute or until lightly browned. Add the cabbage strips, toss to coat thoroughly in the garlic and oil, and cook for 2–3 minutes, until the cabbage is heated through.

4 Season with salt to taste. Serve hot or cold.

SPROUTS WITH MUSTARD SEEDS

 Serves 4

2 lb (1 kg) Brussels sprouts

salt and black pepper

3 tbsp butter

2 tsp mustard seeds

1 tbsp lemon juice

1 Cut a cross in the base of each sprout and simmer the sprouts in boiling salted water for 5–10 minutes, until just tender. Drain.

2 Melt the butter in a large saucepan, add the mustard seeds, cover, and cook over low heat for 1–2 minutes, until the mustard seeds have stopped popping and the butter is lightly browned. Do not let the butter burn.

3 Add the sprouts to the pan, tossing to heat them through and coat them in the mustard-seed butter. Add the lemon juice and salt and black pepper to taste and serve immediately.

CAULIFLOWER & BROCCOLI LAYERS

Serves 4–6

1 lb (500 g) broccoli florets

1 lb (500 g) cauliflower florets

salt and black pepper

4 tbsp butter, plus extra for greasing

1/2 cup (60 g) slivered almonds

1/4 cup (30 g) fresh white bread crumbs

1 garlic clove, crushed

★ 4-cup (1-liter) mold

1 Cook the broccoli and cauliflower florets in a saucepan of boiling salted water for 10 minutes or until just tender. Drain.

2 Butter the mold and layer the cauliflower and broccoli (see box, right).

3 Cover the mold with a small plate and press down lightly to mold the vegetables. Leave in a warm place for 5 minutes.

4 Melt the remaining butter in a skillet. Add the almonds, bread crumbs, and garlic, and cook, stirring, for 3–5 minutes, until golden. Add salt and pepper to taste.

5 Invert the mold onto a warmed platter. Spoon the almond mixture over the top and serve.

Layering the vegetables

Arrange a layer of cauliflower florets, stalk sides up, in the bottom of the mold.

Place a ring of outward-facing broccoli florets, then of cauliflower florets on top. Continue layering alternately. Tightly pack the middle of the mold with the remaining florets.

SWEET & SOUR RED CABBAGE

Serves 4–6

1 tbsp sunflower or corn oil

4 slices of bacon, diced

1/2 cup (125 g) packed light brown sugar

2 onions, chopped

1 red cabbage, weighing about 2 lb (1 kg), shredded

1 tart apple, cored and diced

1 cup (250 ml) red wine

1/4 cup (60 ml) red wine vinegar

1/3 cup (60 g) golden raisins

2 tsp caraway seeds

1/4 tsp ground cinnamon

pinch of grated nutmeg

salt and black pepper

1 Heat the sunflower oil in a large saucepan, add the diced bacon, and cook for about 5 minutes, until crisp and browned.

2 Stir in 6 tbsp (90 g) of the sugar and cook gently, stirring constantly, for 1–2 minutes, taking care that it does not burn.

3 Add the onions, cabbage, and apple, and cook, stirring occasionally, for about 5 minutes.

4 Pour in the wine and half of the vinegar, then add the golden raisins, caraway seeds, cinnamon, nutmeg, and salt and pepper to taste. Cover and cook over low heat for 30 minutes or until the cabbage is tender but still firm. If there is too much liquid, uncover and boil rapidly until the liquid evaporates completely.

5 Stir in the remaining sugar and vinegar, heat through, and serve.

RED CABBAGE WITH CHESTNUTS

Omit the golden raisins. Add 1 cup (125 g) coarsely chopped chestnuts with the chopped onions, shredded cabbage, and diced apple and proceed as directed in the recipe.

CREAMED WHITE BEANS

 Serves 6

1¼ cups (250 g) great northern beans

2 tbsp butter

1 small carrot, finely chopped

1 small onion, finely chopped

a few parsley stalks

1 fresh thyme sprig

1 bay leaf

salt and black pepper

2 tbsp chopped parsley

1 Put the beans into a large bowl, cover with cold water, then leave to soak for at least 8 hours.

2 Drain the beans. Rinse under cold water and drain again. Put the beans into a saucepan and cover with cold water. Bring to a boil and boil rapidly for 10 minutes. Drain.

3 Melt the butter in a heavy saucepan, add the carrot and onion, and cook, stirring, for 3–4 minutes, until beginning to soften.

4 Add the beans, parsley, thyme, and bay leaf and pour in enough cold water to just cover the beans. Bring to a boil, cover, and simmer gently for 1 hour or until the beans are soft but not breaking up.

5 Strain the bean mixture, reserving the cooking liquid. Puree one-third of the mixture in a food processor.

6 Stir the puree back into the bean mixture, adding a little of the reserved cooking liquid to make a saucelike consistency. Add salt and pepper to taste. Reheat gently, sprinkle with chopped parsley, and serve immediately.

FRENCH-STYLE PEAS

 Serves 4

1 small round lettuce, shredded

6 scallions, chopped

4 tbsp butter

1 tbsp chopped parsley

1 tsp sugar

4 cups (500 g) shelled peas

¼ cup (60 ml) water

salt and black pepper

1 Line the bottom of a saucepan with the lettuce. Add the scallions, butter, parsley, and sugar and top with the peas. Add the measured water and salt and pepper to taste.

2 Simmer gently for 15–20 minutes, until the liquid has evaporated and the peas are tender. Taste for seasoning and serve immediately.

SUMMER PEAS & BEANS

 Serves 6

1½ cups (250 g) shelled young fava beans

salt and black pepper

2 cups (250 g) shelled peas

2 cups (250 g) green beans, halved

2 tbsp butter

2 tbsp chopped fresh mint

fresh mint to garnish

1 Cook the fava beans in a saucepan of boiling salted water for 10–15 minutes, until just tender. Cook the peas and green beans in a second pan of boiling salted water for 5–10 minutes, until tender.

2 Drain all the vegetables and return to one pan. Add the butter and mint and stir until the butter melts. Taste for seasoning, garnish with fresh mint, and serve hot.

GLAZED SHALLOTS

 Serves 4

1½ lb (750 g) shallots

6 tbsp (90 g) butter

1 tbsp sugar

1 tbsp chopped fresh thyme

salt and black pepper

chopped parsley to garnish

1 Place the shallots in a single layer in a large skillet and cover them with cold water.

2 Add the butter, sugar, thyme, and salt and pepper to taste, cover, and bring to a boil. Remove the lid and simmer gently, shaking the pan vigorously at intervals to prevent the shallots from sticking and burning, for 10–15 minutes, until the liquid has almost evaporated and the shallots are golden brown.

3 Garnish the shallots with parsley and serve hot.

SAUTEED CELERY & LEEKS

 Serves 6

2 tbsp butter

2 tbsp olive oil

1 lb (500 g) young leeks, trimmed and thinly sliced

12 celery stalks, thinly sliced diagonally

salt and black pepper

2 tbsp snipped fresh chives

1 cup (125 g) salted cashew nuts to garnish

1 Melt the butter with the olive oil in a wok or large skillet.

2 When the butter is foaming, add the leeks, and cook over high heat, stirring occasionally, for 7–10 minutes.

3 Add the celery and cook for 3–5 minutes. Add salt and pepper to taste, then stir in the snipped fresh chives.

4 Garnish with the salted cashew nuts and serve immediately.

CREAMY SUCCOTASH

 Serves 4

2 tbsp sunflower or corn oil

1 large onion, chopped

8 thick slices of bacon, diced

2⅔ cups (500 g) corn kernels

1 cup (250 ml) light cream

13 oz (400 g) canned beans, such as borlotti or fava beans, drained

salt

Tabasco sauce

3–4 tbsp snipped fresh chives

fresh chives to garnish

1 Heat the sunflower oil in a large skillet, add the onion and bacon, and cook gently, stirring occasionally, for 7 minutes or until they are lightly browned.

2 Stir in the corn and light cream and simmer for 2 minutes. Puree 3–4 tbsp of the corn mixture in a food processor until fairly smooth, then stir back into the skillet.

3 Add the beans and return to a boil. Simmer, stirring occasionally, for 5–10 minutes, until the mixture is thickened.

4 Add salt and Tabasco sauce to taste and stir in the snipped chives. Garnish and serve immediately.

Succotash

This is a native American dish. Any type of bean may be used in succotash, and dried, canned, and frozen beans are suitable for this recipe. Sometimes, for a summer succotash, large chunks of zucchini are simmered with the corn. It is a highly nutritious dish – the combination of corn and beans alone provides as much protein as steak.

STUFFED MUSHROOMS

 Serves 6

1/2 lb (250 g) mushrooms
4 tbsp butter
2 carrots, diced
1 small zucchini, diced
1 tbsp chopped parsley
salt and pepper

1 Remove the stems from the mushrooms and chop the stalks finely.

2 Melt the butter in a skillet. When it is foaming, add the mushroom stems, carrots, and zucchini, and cook, stirring, for 1 minute. Add the chopped parsley and season with salt and pepper to taste.

3 Put the mushroom cups in a single layer in a shallow ovenproof dish. Fill the mushrooms with the diced vegetable mixture.

4 Cook in a 350°F (180°C) oven for 15 minutes. Serve immediately.

GARLIC-STUFFED MUSHROOMS
Substitute 1 cup (60 g) fresh white bread crumbs and 4 crushed garlic cloves for the carrots and zucchini.

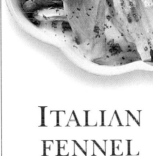

ITALIAN FENNEL

 Serves 6–8

4 fennel bulbs, trimmed and quartered lengthwise
salt and black pepper
butter for greasing
2 cups (250 g) grated mozzarella cheese
chopped parsley to garnish

1 Cook the fennel in boiling salted water for 3–5 minutes, until just tender. Drain thoroughly.

2 Butter a shallow ovenproof dish. Add the fennel and salt and pepper to taste. Arrange the mozzarella cheese on top.

3 Bake in a 400°F (200°C) oven for 15–20 minutes, until the cheese topping is golden and bubbling.

4 Sprinkle with chopped parsley, and serve hot.

ASPARAGUS WITH PARMESAN

 Serves 4

1 1/4 lb (625 g) asparagus
1 cup (90 g) grated Parmesan cheese
lemon wedges and flat-leaf parsley sprigs to garnish
MARINADE
2 tbsp olive oil
1 tbsp dry white wine
1 tsp white vinegar
3 garlic cloves, crushed
1/4 tsp herbes de Provence
salt and black pepper

1 Trim the woody ends from the asparagus.

2 Make the marinade: combine the oil, wine, vinegar, garlic, herbes de Provence, and salt and pepper to taste. Toss the asparagus in the marinade, cover, and leave to marinate for 15 minutes.

3 Sprinkle the Parmesan onto a plate. Roll the asparagus in the Parmesan to coat, then arrange in a single layer in a large ovenproof dish.

4 Pour any remaining marinade over the asparagus and bake in a 400°F (200°C) oven for 15–20 minutes, until lightly browned and sizzling hot. Garnish with the lemon wedges and parsley sprigs and serve immediately.

TOMATOES WITH CILANTRO

 Serves 4

1 pint (500 g) cherry tomatoes

fresh cilantro to garnish

CILANTRO BUTTER

3 tbsp butter, softened

2 tbsp chopped fresh cilantro

1 garlic clove, crushed

1/2 tsp lemon juice

salt

1 Arrange the cherry tomatoes in a single layer in an ovenproof dish. Cook in a 450°F (230°C) oven for 25–30 minutes, until the tomatoes are lightly browned and tender but still retain their shape.

2 Meanwhile, make the cilantro butter: put the butter into a small bowl and beat in the chopped fresh cilantro, garlic, lemon juice, and salt to taste.

3 Garnish the tomatoes with cilantro sprigs, and serve hot, dotted with cilantro butter.

SAVORY PUMPKIN

 Serves 4

2-lb (1-kg) piece of pumpkin

2–3 tbsp olive oil

1 tsp balsamic or red wine vinegar

3 garlic cloves, crushed

1/2 tsp chopped fresh thyme

1/2 tsp paprika

salt and black pepper

fresh thyme to garnish

1 Cut the flesh of the pumpkin into large chunks and arrange on a baking sheet.

2 Combine the olive oil, vinegar, garlic, thyme, and paprika in a measuring cup. Season with salt and pepper to taste and pour over the pumpkin.

3 Bake in a 375°F (190°C) oven for 15–20 minutes, until the pumpkin is just tender and lightly browned on top. Garnish with thyme and serve immediately. If preferred, leave to cool and serve with a vinaigrette dressing (page 338).

HOT SPICY OKRA

 Serves 4

3 tbsp sunflower or corn oil

1 small onion, sliced

1 garlic clove, crushed

1 lb (500 g) okra, trimmed

1 large fresh red chili, cored, seeded, and diced

salt and black pepper

1 Heat the oil in a wok or large skillet, add the onion, and stir-fry over high heat for 3 minutes or until golden. Add the garlic and stir-fry for 1 minute.

2 Add the okra and chili and stir-fry over high heat for 5–10 minutes, until the okra is tender but still retains some crispness. Add salt and pepper to taste. Serve immediately.

Cook's know-how

Because of its shape, okra is sometimes known as ladies' fingers. Trim the ends carefully so that the sticky juices and seeds are not exposed and released.

MIXED VEGETABLE STIR-FRY

 Serves 4

1 tbsp olive oil

1 zucchini, sliced diagonally

1 yellow pepper, cored, seeded, and thinly sliced

1/2 lb (250 g) mixed mushrooms, sliced

salt and black pepper

1 tbsp lemon juice

1/2 cup (60 g) slivered almonds, toasted

1 Heat the olive oil in a wok or large skillet, add the zucchini slices, and stir-fry for 3–4 minutes, until the zucchini is just beginning to brown.

2 Add the yellow pepper and mushrooms and stir-fry for 2 minutes. Add salt and pepper to taste, stir in the lemon juice, and leave the mixture to bubble for about 1 minute. Sprinkle the stir-fry with the toasted slivered almonds and serve immediately.

TOMATO & ZUCCHINI CASSEROLE

Serves 4–6

2 zucchini, sliced

salt and black pepper

3 large tomatoes, sliced

snipped fresh chives to garnish

WHITE SAUCE

4 tbsp butter

1/2 cup (60 g) all-purpose flour

1 1/4 cups (300 ml) milk

pinch of grated nutmeg

1 Arrange half of the zucchini slices in the bottom of a shallow ovenproof dish. Season with a little salt and pepper.

2 Arrange half of the tomato slices in a layer on top of the zucchini. Season to taste.

3 Layer the remaining zucchini and tomato slices in the dish, adding salt and pepper to taste.

4 Make the white sauce: melt the butter in a small saucepan. Add the flour and cook, stirring, for 1 minute. Remove from the heat and gradually blend in the milk. Bring to a boil, stirring, until the mixture thickens. Simmer for 2–3 minutes. Add the nutmeg, and salt and pepper to taste.

5 Pour the white sauce over the zucchini and tomatoes. Bake in a 375°F (190°C) oven for 15–20 minutes, until the vegetables are just cooked. Sprinkle with snipped chives, and serve immediately.

TOMATO & LEEK CASSEROLE

Substitute 2 sliced leeks for the zucchini. Stir-fry in 1 tbsp olive oil for 2–3 minutes, then layer with the tomatoes. Make the white sauce, substituting 1 tbsp Dijon mustard for the nutmeg, and proceed as directed.

RATATOUILLE

Serves 4–6

1 large eggplant

salt and black pepper

4 tbsp olive oil

1 large onion, sliced

1 large garlic clove, crushed

4 zucchini, sliced

6 tomatoes, peeled (page 39), quartered, and seeded

1 large red pepper, cored, seeded, and sliced

1/4 tsp sugar

1/4 tsp crushed coriander seeds (optional)

1 tbsp chopped fresh basil

1 Cut the eggplant into 1/2-in (1-cm) slices. Place in a colander, sprinkle generously with salt, and leave to stand for about 30 minutes. Rinse the eggplant slices and pat dry with paper towels.

2 Heat the olive oil in a large skillet, add the onion and garlic, and cook gently, stirring occasionally, for 3–5 minutes, until softened.

3 Add the eggplant slices, cover, and simmer gently for 20 minutes.

4 Add the zucchini, tomatoes, red pepper, sugar, and salt and pepper to taste and cook gently, covered, for 45–60 minutes, until the vegetables are soft but retain their shape. Do not stir vigorously or you may break them up.

5 Ten minutes before the end of cooking time, add the coriander seeds, if using, and taste for seasoning. Serve hot or cold, sprinkled with the chopped fresh basil.

Cook's know-how

A classic from the south of France, ratatouille may be served by itself as an appetizer or as an accompaniment to cold or broiled meats; it goes particularly well with lamb. It tastes just as good warm or cold

CHAR-GRILLED VEGETABLE PLATTER

Vegetables are delicious char-grilled – their flesh is tender and smoky in flavor. Serve them hot as a side dish with roast meat, poultry, or broiled fish or cold as an unusual salad with picnics and barbecues. Experiment with different vegetables, oils, and marinades to suit your taste.

 Serves 4

4 baby eggplant

salt and black pepper

4 baby zucchini

2 red peppers, cored and seeded

1 lb (500 g) asparagus

4 large mushrooms

6 oz (175 g) pattypan squash

6 oz (175 g) baby corn

olive oil for brushing

★ 8–10 wooden toothpicks

1 Prepare the vegetables. Trim the eggplant, cut in half lengthwise, and score a crisscross pattern on the cut surfaces. Sprinkle the cut surfaces with salt and set aside for 30 minutes.

2 Meanwhile, cut the zucchini in half lengthwise. Cut the red peppers in half lengthwise and cut out the fleshy ribs. Trim the woody ends from the asparagus and cut all the spears to an even length.

3 Gently wipe the mushrooms with damp paper towels and remove the stems. Trim the squash if necessary.

4 Rinse the eggplant under cold running water and pat dry with paper towels.

5 Place the asparagus spears side by side in groups of 3 or 4 (depending on thickness). Gently push a toothpick through the asparagus, about ¹/₂ in (1 cm) from the tips, until they are all skewered. Insert a second toothpick at the bases of the spears. Repeat for the remaining groups of asparagus spears.

6 Brush all of the vegetables generously with olive oil and season with salt and pepper to taste.

7 Cook on a hot grill or under the broiler a batch at a time, turning occasionally, for 15–20 minutes, until the outer skins are charred. Keep each batch warm while you cook the remaining vegetables.

VEGETABLE MARINADES

For extra flavor, soak the vegetables in a marinade for 1 hour before cooking.

HERB & GARLIC

Put *1 cup (250 ml) olive oil, 2 finely chopped garlic cloves, 1 tbsp chopped fresh rosemary, oregano, or thyme,* and *salt and pepper to taste* into a bowl and whisk to mix thoroughly.

HONEY & MUSTARD

Put *1 cup (250 ml) sunflower oil, 2 tbsp soy sauce, 1 tbsp honey, 2 tsp Dijon mustard,* and *salt and pepper to taste* into a small bowl and whisk to mix.

FLAVORED OILS

Flavored oils are easy to make and add an individual touch. One of these flavored oils can be used to baste the vegetables during char-grilling instead of the olive oil in the recipe above.

THAI PERFUMED OIL

Lightly bruise *2–3 sprigs cilantro* and *3 2-in (5-cm) pieces fresh lemongrass.* Put the cilantro, lemongrass, and *2 chili peppers* into a clean jar or bottle. Pour in *2 cups (500 ml) canola or corn oil* and seal the bottle. Leave in a cool, dark place for 2 weeks, remove the cilantro and lemongrass, and use to baste as directed.

PAPRIKA OIL

Spoon *2 tbsp paprika* into a clean jar or bottle. Pour in *2 cups (500 ml) extra-virgin olive oil* and seal the bottle. Leave in a cool, dark place, shaking the bottle occasionally, for 1 week. Line a funnel with a double layer of cheesecloth and then strain the oil into another bottle. Use the oil to baste as directed.

MIXED-HERB OIL

Lightly bruise *1 rosemary sprig* and *1 thyme sprig.* Peel and finely slice *1 pearl onion.* Put the herbs, onion, *1 bay leaf,* and *6 black peppercorns* into a clean jar or bottle. Pour in *2 cups (500 ml) extra-virgin olive oil* and seal the bottle. Leave in a cool, dark place for about 2 weeks. Use to baste as directed.

WATERCRESS & ROAST VEGETABLE SALAD

 Serves 4–6

2 zucchini, sliced lengthwise

1 tbsp olive oil

2 red peppers

2 yellow peppers

3 3/4 cups (150 g) watercress

vinaigrette dressing (page 338)

1 Brush the zucchini slices on both sides with the olive oil, and cook under the broiler, 4 in (10 cm) from the heat, for 1–2 minutes on each side until golden. Leave to cool.

2 Core, seed, and halve the peppers. Roast and peel the peppers (see box, right). Cut the flesh into chunks. Cut the zucchini slices crosswise.

3 Put the watercress into a large serving bowl. Add the peppers and zucchini and mix together. Pour on the vinaigrette dressing and toss to coat. Serve immediately.

Roasting and peeling peppers

Cook the pepper halves under the broiler, 4 in (10 cm) from the heat, until the skin is black and blistered. Put into a paper bag, seal, and leave to cool.

Peel away the skin, using a small knife.

EGGPLANT WITH FRESH PESTO

 Serves 4

1 large eggplant

salt

5 tbsp (75 ml) olive oil, plus extra for greasing

2–3 tsp balsamic or wine vinegar

fresh pesto (see box, below)

shredded fresh basil to garnish

1 Cut the eggplant crosswise into thin slices. Put the slices into a colander, sprinkle generously with salt, and leave to stand for about 30 minutes. Rinse and pat dry with paper towels.

2 Lightly grease a baking sheet with a little olive oil and arrange the eggplant slices in a single layer. Brush with one-quarter of the oil, place under the broiler, 3 in (7 cm) from the heat, and broil for 5 minutes or until lightly browned. Turn, brush with one-third of the remaining oil, and broil for 5 minutes longer.

3 Sprinkle the remaining oil and the vinegar over the eggplant slices. Leave to cool. Spread pesto over one side of each slice, garnish with fresh basil, and serve at room temperature.

Fresh pesto

Puree *2/3 cup (60 g) grated Parmesan cheese, 1 garlic clove, 1/2 cup (60 g) pine nuts, 2 cups (60 g) fresh basil leaves,* and *salt and pepper to taste* in a food processor until almost smooth.

Add *1/4 cup (60 ml) olive oil* gradually, with the blades turning, scraping the side of the bowl occasionally with a rubber spatula to ensure that all of the mixture is incorporated.

MIXED GREEN SALAD

 Serves 4–6

1 crisp lettuce, such as iceberg

1 bunch of watercress, tough stalks removed

1¹/2 cups (60 g) mâche

1 bunch arugula

about ¹/4 cup (60 ml) vinaigrette dressing (page 338)

1 tbsp snipped fresh chives to garnish

1 Tear the lettuce leaves into bite-sized pieces. Put the lettuce into a large salad bowl. Add the watercress, mâche, and arugula and mix together.

2 Pour the dressing over the salad and toss gently. Sprinkle with the chives and serve immediately.

Cook's know-how

The important thing to remember about making a mixed green salad is not to drown the leaves in the vinaigrette dressing; there should be just enough to cling to the leaves. Adding the dressing just before serving ensures that the greens will stay crisp.

RED SALAD BOWL

 Serves 4–6

1 small head of radicchio

1 small oak leaf lettuce

1 small lollo rosso lettuce

1 small red onion, thinly sliced

¹/2 cup (125 g) seedless red grapes

DRESSING

²/3 cup (150 ml) olive oil

3 tbsp balsamic vinegar

1 garlic clove, crushed (optional)

¹/2 tsp sugar

salt and black pepper

1 Tear the radicchio leaves and the oak leaf and lollo rosso lettuce leaves into bite-sized pieces. Put them into a large salad bowl and mix together, then add the onion and grapes.

2 Make the dressing: combine the oil, vinegar, garlic, if using, sugar, and salt and pepper to taste.

3 Pour just enough dressing over the salad to cling to the leaves, toss gently, and serve immediately.

CRUNCHY SALAD

 Serves 6

1¹/2 cups (175 g) bean sprouts

1 iceberg lettuce

6 scallions, thinly sliced diagonally

1 green pepper, cored, seeded, and thinly sliced

2 tbsp toasted sesame seeds

DRESSING

3 tbsp sunflower or corn oil

1 tbsp white vinegar

1 tsp sesame oil

1 garlic clove, crushed

¹/2-in (1-cm) piece of fresh ginger, peeled and grated

¹/2 tsp sugar

salt and black pepper

1 Soak the bean sprouts in cold water for 10 minutes. Drain. Tear the lettuce leaves into bite-sized pieces. Put the lettuce, bean sprouts, scallions, and pepper into a salad bowl and mix together.

2 Make the dressing: combine the sunflower oil, vinegar, sesame oil, garlic, ginger, sugar, and salt and pepper to taste.

3 Toss the salad with the dressing, sprinkle with the sesame seeds, and serve.

SPINACH & BACON SALAD

 Serves 6

1 lb (500 g) spinach

3 slices of thick-cut white bread, crusts removed

4 tbsp sunflower or corn oil

1 garlic clove, crushed

12 slices of bacon, cut into strips

4–5 tbsp vinaigrette or blue cheese dressing (page 338)

salt and black pepper

1 Tear the spinach leaves into large pieces and put them into a salad bowl.

2 Make the croutons: cut the bread into small cubes. Heat the sunflower oil in a skillet, add the garlic, and cook for 1 minute. Add the bread cubes and cook, stirring, for 1–2 minutes, until golden and crisp. Lift out the croutons and drain on paper towels.

3 Add the bacon to the pan and fry for 5 minutes or until crisp. Lift out and drain on paper towels.

4 Sprinkle the bacon over the spinach leaves. Spoon the dressing over the salad, add salt and pepper to taste, and toss gently. Scatter the croutons over the salad, and serve immediately.

CAESAR SALAD

 Serves 4

1 romaine lettuce

1/4 cup (60 ml) olive oil

2 tbsp lemon juice

salt and black pepper

2 hard-boiled eggs

1/3 cup (30 g) coarsely grated
Parmesan cheese

CROUTONS

3 slices of thick-cut white bread,
crusts removed

1/4 cup (60 ml) olive oil

1 garlic clove, crushed

1 Make the croutons: cut
the bread into small
cubes. Heat the olive oil in a
skillet, add the garlic, and
cook for 1 minute. Add the
bread cubes and cook,
stirring, for 1–2 minutes,
until crisp. Lift out and
drain on paper towels.

2 Tear the lettuce leaves
into bite-sized pieces and
put them into a salad bowl.
Add the oil, lemon juice,
and seasoning to taste, and
toss to coat.

3 Cut the hard-boiled eggs
into quarters and add to
the salad. Add the croutons
and Parmesan cheese, toss
gently, and serve immediately.

Caesar salad

*This recipe, said to have been
created by restaurateur Caesar
Cardini in Tijuana, Mexico,
in the 1920s, has deservedly
become a classic. Only crisp
salad leaves, preferably romaine
lettuce leaves, should be used.
Some versions replace the hard-
boiled eggs with soft-boiled ones,
while others break a raw egg
into the salad and toss it in
with the dressing.*

CAESAR SALAD
WITH ANCHOVIES

*Coarsely chop 6 anchovy fillets
and add to the salad with the
hard-boiled eggs. Proceed as
directed in the recipe.*

WALDORF
SALAD

 Serves 4

3 crisp red-skinned apples, cored
and diced

juice of 1/2 lemon

4 celery stalks, thickly sliced

3/4 cup (150 ml) mayonnaise
(page 338)

salt and black pepper

3/4 cup (90 g) walnut pieces,
coarsely chopped

chopped parsley to garnish

1 Put the diced apples into
a bowl, pour the lemon
juice over the top, and stir
to coat thoroughly to
prevent discoloration.
Transfer to a salad bowl and
add the celery.

2 Spoon the mayonnaise
over the salad, add salt
and pepper to taste, and toss
gently to mix. Cover and
chill until needed. Stir
in the walnut pieces and
garnish with chopped
parsley just before serving.

Waldorf salad

*This classic salad recipe was
created at the turn of the 20th
century by Oscar, the maître
d'hôtel at the Waldorf-Astoria
Hotel in New York.*

COLESLAW

 Serves 8

1 cabbage, about 1 1/2 lb (750 g)

2/3 cup (150 ml) vinaigrette
dressing (page 338)

1 small onion, finely chopped

1 tsp Dijon mustard

salt and black pepper

3 celery stalks, thinly sliced

2 carrots, grated

1/3 cup (60 g) golden raisins
(optional)

5–6 tbsp (75–90 ml)
mayonnaise (page 338)

1 Cut the cabbage into
quarters lengthwise and
cut out the core. Shred
the cabbage finely,
using either a sharp
knife or the slicing
blade of a food
processor.

2 Put the cabbage
into a large bowl,
add the vinaigrette
dressing, onion, Dijon
mustard, and salt and black
pepper to taste, and toss to
mix thoroughly. Cover the
bowl tightly and leave to
chill for about 8 hours.

3 Add the celery, carrots,
and golden raisins, if
using, and toss to mix well.
Stir in the mayonnaise.
Cover and leave to chill for
1 hour. Taste the coleslaw
for seasoning and serve.

POTATO, APPLE, & CELERY SALAD

 Serves 6

1¹/₂ lb (750 g) new potatoes, scrubbed

salt and black pepper

1/3 cup (75 ml) vinaigrette dressing (page 338)

6 celery stalks, sliced

1 small red onion, very finely sliced

2 red-skinned apples, such as Red Delicious or Spartan, cored and diced

1/2 cup (125 ml) mayonnaise (page 338)

2 tbsp snipped fresh chives to garnish

1 Put the potatoes into a large saucepan of boiling salted water and simmer gently for 10–15 minutes, until just tender. Drain, leave to cool, then cut the potatoes in half.

2 Put the potatoes into a large salad bowl, add the vinaigrette dressing, and toss gently while the potatoes are still warm.

3 Add the celery, onion, and apples to the potatoes. Mix together gently so that all the ingredients are thoroughly coated with the dressing, then add salt and pepper to taste. Cover and chill for at least 1 hour.

4 Gently stir in the mayonnaise, taste for seasoning, sprinkle with the chives, and serve immediately.

POTATO & TOMATO SALAD

Substitute 1 large peeled and chopped tomato for the apples and proceed as directed.

FRENCH CELERIAC SALAD

 Serves 4–6

1 lb (500 g) celeriac

juice of 1 lemon

1 tsp sliced dill pickle and 2 tbsp chopped parsley to garnish

DRESSING

2/3 cup (150 ml) plain yogurt

2 tbsp mayonnaise (page 338)

1 tsp finely chopped capers

1/2 tsp Dijon mustard

salt and black pepper

1 Peel the celeriac, cut into matchsticks, and place in a bowl of cold water. Add the lemon juice and toss to prevent discoloration.

2 Make the dressing: combine the yogurt, mayonnaise, capers, Dijon mustard, and salt and pepper to taste.

3 Drain the celeriac and transfer to a salad bowl. Pour on the dressing and toss gently to mix. Garnish with the dill pickle and chopped parsley, and serve immediately.

CARROT JULIENNE SALAD

 Serves 4–6

5 carrots

salt and black pepper

DRESSING

1 tbsp olive oil

1 tsp white vinegar

1 garlic clove, crushed

1 tsp chopped parsley

lemon twists and snipped fresh chives to garnish

1 Cut the carrots into matchsticks. Simmer in a saucepan of boiling salted water until just tender. Drain.

2 Make the dressing: combine the oil, white vinegar, garlic, parsley, and salt and pepper to taste.

3 Put the carrots into a salad bowl, pour on the dressing, and toss to coat evenly. Leave to cool. Garnish with lemon twists and chives and serve.

FRENCH POTATO SALAD

 Serves 4–6

2 lb (1 kg) new potatoes, scrubbed

salt and black pepper

1 small mild onion, very finely chopped

1/4 cup (60 ml) vinaigrette dressing (page 338)

1 cup (250 ml) mayonnaise (page 338)

2 tbsp snipped fresh chives

fresh chives to garnish

1 Put the potatoes into a large saucepan of boiling salted water and simmer for 10–15 minutes, until tender. Drain the potatoes thoroughly. Cut them into even-sized pieces.

2 Put the potatoes into a large salad bowl and add the chopped onion.

3 While the potatoes are still quite warm, spoon the vinaigrette dressing over them and then toss to mix thoroughly.

4 Add the mayonnaise and chives and mix together gently. Add salt and pepper to taste, cover, and chill for about 30 minutes. Garnish with chives, and serve immediately.

MUSHROOM & YOGURT SALAD

 Serves 6

3 tbsp sunflower or corn oil

1/2 tsp ground coriander

1 1/2 lb (750 g) small mushrooms

salt and black pepper

4 celery stalks, thinly sliced

shredded fresh basil to garnish

DRESSING

2/3 cup (150 ml) plain yogurt

1 tbsp lemon juice

1 tbsp white vinegar

1 tsp Dijon mustard

1 garlic clove, crushed

1 Heat the oil in a skillet, add the coriander, and cook gently, stirring, for 1 minute. Add the mushrooms and salt and pepper to taste, and cook over high heat, stirring, for 5 minutes. Lift out with a slotted spoon and leave to cool.

2 Make the dressing: combine the yogurt, lemon juice, vinegar, Dijon mustard, garlic, and salt and pepper to taste. Pour the dressing on the mushrooms and toss to mix. Cover and leave to chill for 8 hours. Stir in the celery, garnish with basil, and serve immediately.

AVOCADO SALAD

 Serves 6

1/2 cup (60 g) pine nuts

6 cups (250 g) mixed salad greens

2 oranges

2 avocados

DRESSING

finely grated zest of 1 orange

3 tbsp orange juice

1 tbsp walnut oil

1–2 tsp sugar

salt and pepper

1 Spread the pine nuts on a baking sheet and broil for 2 minutes.

2 Put the salad greens into a large salad bowl. Peel the oranges, removing the rind and pith, and separate into sections (page 430).

3 Halve, pit, and peel the avocados (page 336). Slice lengthwise and mix with the orange sections and pine nuts.

4 Make the dressing: combine the ingredients and pour over the salad. Toss gently and serve.

THREE-COLOR SALAD

 Serves 4

4 beefsteak tomatoes

salt and black pepper

1/2 lb (250 g) mozzarella cheese

2 avocados

2 tbsp lemon juice

3–4 tbsp olive oil

basil sprigs to garnish

1 Slice the tomatoes thinly, put into a bowl, and sprinkle with salt and pepper. Cut the mozzarella into thin slices.

2 Cut the avocados in half lengthwise. Twist to loosen the halves and pull them apart. Remove the pits (page 336), score and peel off the skin, then cut the halves in half again.

3 Cut the avocado quarters into slices lengthwise, then sprinkle with lemon juice to prevent discoloration.

4 Arrange the tomato, mozzarella, and avocado slices on a serving platter. Drizzle with the olive oil, garnish with basil sprigs, and serve immediately.

CUCUMBER & DILL SALAD

 Serves 4–6

1 cucumber, peeled and cut in half lengthwise

1 tbsp chopped fresh dill

DRESSING

2 tbsp hot water

2 tbsp white vinegar

1 tbsp sunflower or corn oil

2 tbsp sugar

salt and black pepper

1 Scoop out the cucumber seeds. Cut the flesh into thin slices and arrange in a serving dish.

2 Make the dressing: combine the measured water, vinegar, oil, sugar, and salt and pepper to taste.

3 Pour the dressing over the cucumber, sprinkle with dill, and serve immediately.

Cook's know-how
This Danish-style salad goes particularly well with cold fish.

GREEK SALAD

 Serves 4–6

4 beefsteak tomatoes

1 cucumber, sliced

1/2 lb (250 g) feta cheese, diced

24 pitted black olives

1/2 cup (125 ml) olive oil

1/4 cup (60 ml) lemon juice

salt and black pepper

2 tbsp chopped fresh oregano

1 Cut the tomatoes in half lengthwise, cut out the core, and cut each half into 4 wedges.

2 Put the tomatoes into a large salad bowl and add the cucumber, feta cheese, and olives.

3 Spoon on the olive oil, lemon juice, and add salt and black pepper to taste (do not use too much salt since feta is a salty cheese), then toss gently to mix.

4 Sprinkle the salad with the chopped oregano and serve immediately.

TOMATO & ONION SALAD

 Serves 6

1 mild onion, cut in half lengthwise and thinly sliced

1 1/2 lb (750 g) ripe firm tomatoes, peeled (page 39) and thinly sliced

1 tbsp snipped fresh chives

DRESSING

6 tbsp (90 ml) olive oil

2 tbsp red wine vinegar

1/4 tsp sugar

salt and black pepper

1 Separate the onion slices into half-rings. Overlap the tomato slices in circles of diminishing size in a large shallow dish. Arrange the onions on top.

2 Make the dressing: in a small bowl, combine the olive oil, red wine vinegar, sugar and add salt and pepper to taste.

3 Spoon the dressing over the tomatoes and onions, cover, and leave to chill for about 2 hours. Sprinkle with the snipped chives, and serve immediately.

TOMATO & BASIL SALAD

 Serves 4–6

2 beefsteak tomatoes

4 ripe salad tomatoes

1/4 pint (125 g) cherry tomatoes

1 yellow pepper, cored, seeded, and cut into chunks

2 tbsp shredded fresh basil

DRESSING

3 tbsp olive oil

2 tsp balsamic vinegar

1/4 tsp sugar

salt and black pepper

1 Make the dressing: combine the olive oil, vinegar, sugar, and salt and pepper to taste.

2 Cut the tomatoes in half lengthwise, cut out the core, and cut each half into 4 wedges. Thickly slice the salad tomatoes. Halve the cherry tomatoes.

3 Put all the tomatoes and the yellow pepper into a salad bowl and sprinkle with the dressing. Cover and leave to stand for 1 hour to let the flavors mingle. Sprinkle with the basil just before serving.

SALADE NIÇOISE

Serves 4

¹/2 lb (250 g) green beans, cut in half crosswise

salt and black pepper

2 hard-boiled eggs

1 romaine lettuce

¹/2 cucumber, sliced

4 tomatoes, peeled (page 39) and quartered

7 oz (200 g) canned tuna, drained

¹/2 mild onion, very thinly sliced

1³/4 oz (50 g) canned anchovy fillets, drained

12 pitted black olives

chopped parsley to garnish

DRESSING

²/3 cup (150 ml) olive oil

3 tbsp white vinegar

1 garlic clove, crushed

¹/2 tsp Dijon mustard

1 Cook the green beans in boiling salted water for 4–5 minutes, until just tender. Drain, rinse in cold water, and drain again.

2 Peel the shells from the eggs and cut the eggs into wedges lengthwise.

3 Make the dressing: combine the oil, vinegar, garlic, mustard, and salt and pepper to taste.

4 Tear the lettuce leaves into pieces and place on a large serving plate. Arrange the cucumber and beans on top of the lettuce.

5 Arrange the tomatoes and eggs on the serving plate. Coarsely flake the tuna with a fork and place in the middle. Arrange the onion, anchovy fillets, and olives over the tuna. Pour on the dressing, garnish with parsley, and serve immediately.

Salade niçoise

A great favorite from Nice in the south of France, there are many variations of this recipe and much debate about which particular ingredients are needed for an authentic Salade niçoise. *New potatoes are included in some versions.*

THREE-BEAN SALAD

Serves 4

¹/2 lb (250 g) green beans, cut in half crosswise

salt and black pepper

13 oz (400 g) canned garbanzo beans, drained and rinsed

13 oz (400 g) canned red kidney beans, drained and rinsed

10 pitted black olives, halved

chopped parsley to garnish

DRESSING

¹/4 cup (60 ml) plain yogurt

3 tbsp olive oil

3 tbsp red wine vinegar

2 tsp Dijon mustard

¹/4 tsp sugar

1 Cook the green beans in boiling salted water for 4–5 minutes, until just tender. Drain, rinse in cold water, and drain again.

2 Make the dressing: combine the plain yogurt, oil, red wine vinegar, mustard, sugar, and salt and pepper to taste.

3 Put the garbanzo beans, red kidney beans, and green beans into a large bowl. Pour the dressing on the beans and stir gently to mix. Cover and leave to stand for 1 hour. Add the olives, sprinkle with parsley, and serve immediately.

THREE-BEAN SALAD WITH BACON

Substitute ¹/2 lb (250 g) fava beans for the garbanzo beans and omit the olives. Cut 2 thick slices of bacon into strips and dry-fry until crisp and golden. Sprinkle on the salad just before serving.

TABBOULEH

 Serves 4

1 cup (175 g) bulgur wheat

1/4–1/3 cup (60–75 ml) vinaigrette dressing (page 338)

juice of 1 lemon

3 tomatoes, peeled (page 39), seeded, and diced

4 scallions, chopped

3 tbsp chopped parsley

3 tbsp chopped fresh mint

salt and black pepper

parsley sprigs to garnish

1 Put the bulgur wheat into a large bowl, cover with cold water, and leave to stand for 30 minutes.

2 Drain the bulgur wheat, pressing out as much of the liquid as possible. Transfer to a salad bowl and mix in the vinaigrette dressing, lemon juice, tomatoes, scallions, parsley, mint, and salt and pepper to taste. Garnish with parsley and serve immediately.

Bulgur wheat

Bulgur wheat is also known as burghul and is available from a variety of good supermarkets and health food stores.

COUSCOUS SALAD

 Serves 4–6

1/2 tsp hot red pepper flakes

6 tbsp (90 ml) olive oil

1 1/3 cups (250 g) couscous

2 cups (500 ml) boiling water

3–4 tbsp golden raisins

2-in (5 cm) piece of fresh ginger, peeled and chopped

pinch of salt

3–4 tbsp raspberry vinegar

5 ripe tomatoes, peeled (page 39), seeded, and diced

1 onion, chopped

3 scallions, thinly sliced

2 tbsp chopped fresh mint

mint sprigs to garnish

1 Combine the chilies and olive oil and set aside.

2 Put the couscous into a large saucepan. Stir in the measured water, golden raisins, ginger, and salt to taste and cook over medium-high heat for 5–10 minutes. Remove from the heat, cover, and leave to cool.

3 Stir in the chili oil, vinegar, tomatoes, onion, scallions, and mint. Garnish with mint sprigs, and serve.

WILD RICE SALAD

 Serves 4–6

1 1/4 cups (250 g) mixed long-grain and wild rice

salt and black pepper

2 cups (175 g) green beans, cut in half crosswise

2 tbsp chopped parsley

3/4 cup (60 g) thinly sliced mushrooms

1/2 cup (60 g) walnut pieces

DRESSING

1/4 cup (60 ml) sunflower oil

2 tbsp walnut oil

2 tbsp white vinegar

1 tsp Dijon mustard

1 Cook the rice in boiling salted water for about 20 minutes, or according to package instructions, until just tender. Drain, rinse in boiling water, and drain again. Transfer to a bowl.

2 Meanwhile, cook the beans in boiling salted water for 4–5 minutes, until just tender. Drain, rinse in cold water, and drain again.

3 Make the dressing: combine the oils, vinegar, mustard, and salt and pepper to taste. Pour over the rice while still warm, stir, and leave to cool.

4 Add the beans, parsley, mushrooms, and walnuts to the rice. Stir well, and serve immediately.

RICE SALAD

 Serves 4–6

1 1/4 cups (250 g) long-grain rice

salt and black pepper

1 cup (125 g) frozen peas, thawed

2/3 cup (125 g) frozen corn kernels, thawed

1 red pepper, cored, seeded, and diced

2 tbsp chopped fresh cilantro

DRESSING

6 tbsp (90 ml) olive oil

3 tbsp white vinegar

1 tsp Dijon mustard

1 garlic clove, crushed

1 Cook the rice in boiling salted water for 12–15 minutes, until just tender. Drain, rinse in boiling water, and drain again. Transfer to a salad bowl.

2 Make the dressing: combine the olive oil, wine vinegar, mustard, garlic, and salt and pepper to taste. Pour over the rice while still warm, stir gently, and leave to cool.

3 Add the peas, corn, red pepper, and cilantro to the rice, and stir gently to combine. Serve immediately.

PASTA & SMOKED FISH SALAD

 Serves 4–6

1 lb (500 g) pasta shells

salt and black pepper

2 zucchini, sliced

1 1/3 cups (125 g) green beans, cut in half crosswise

2 oranges

3/4 lb (375 g) peppered smoked mackerel or other fish fillets

1/4 cup (30 g) walnut pieces

DRESSING

juice of 1 orange

2 tbsp sunflower or corn oil

1 tbsp walnut oil

2 tbsp chopped parsley

1 Cook the pasta shells in a large saucepan of boiling salted water for 8–10 minutes, until just tender. Drain, rinse in cold water, and drain again.

2 Meanwhile, cook the zucchini and green beans in another pan of boiling salted water for 4–5 minutes, until tender. Drain, rinse in cold water, and drain again.

3 Peel and section the oranges (page 430) and set aside. Remove the skin and any bones from the mackerel, then flake the flesh into large pieces.

4 Make the dressing: combine the orange juice, sunflower and walnut oils, parsley, and salt and pepper to taste.

5 Put the pasta, zucchini, green beans, orange sections, flaked mackerel, and walnut pieces into a large salad bowl. Add the dressing and toss gently so that the fish does not break up. Leave to chill in the refrigerator for at least 30 minutes before serving.

Cook's know-how

Smoked mackerel is a rich, oily fish that goes well with citrus fruits such as oranges. If you prefer, replace the mackerel with smoked trout, which has a milder flavor.

PASTA SALAD WITH PEPPERS

 Serves 4–6

500 g (1 lb) pasta bows

salt and black pepper

1 red pepper, cored, seeded, and diced

1 green pepper, cored, seeded, and diced

3 scallions, sliced diagonally

1/4 cup (60 ml) mayonnaise (page 338)

scallion tops, sliced, to garnish

1 Cook the pasta bows in a large saucepan of boiling salted water for 8–10 minutes, until just tender.

2 Drain, rinse under cold running water, and drain again. Leave to cool.

3 Put the pasta into a salad bowl, add the peppers and scallions, and season. Add the mayonnaise, then stir well to coat all of the ingredients evenly. Chill for 30 minutes. Garnish with the scallion tops, and serve.

PASTA SALAD WITH SNOW PEAS & SESAME SEEDS

Substitute 1 1/2 cups (125 g) blanched snow peas for the red and green peppers. Omit the mayonnaise. Mix together 2 tbsp white vinegar, 3 tsp sunflower oil, 1 tsp sesame oil, and salt and pepper to taste and pour over the salad. Substitute 2 tbsp toasted sesame seeds for the scallion tops, and serve immediately.

Cook's know-how

If you are concerned about the raw eggs used in the mayonnaise, substitute the yolks from 3 hard-boiled eggs, and combine with 2/3 cup (150 ml) sour cream and 1 tbsp Dijon mustard.

10

YEAST
BAKING

OVER 60 MINUTES

FOCACCIA

Italian classic: flat pizzalike bread flavored with olive oil and fresh rosemary. Sprinkled with coarse sea salt.

MAKES 1 LOAF 2989 calories per loaf

Takes 35 minutes, plus rising   **PAGE 375**

HOT CROSS BUNS

Slightly sweet spiced buns studded with raisins and mixed peel, decorated with pastry crosses, and baked until golden.

MAKES 12 279 calories each

Takes 35 minutes, plus rising   **PAGE 386**

DINNER ROLLS

A simple dough shaped into rolls and baked until golden. Served warm or cool and spread with butter.

MAKES 18 95 calories each

Takes 40 minutes, plus rising   **PAGE 371**

BRIOCHES

Classic and rich: an egg- and butter-enriched dough baked until dark golden brown in characteristic fluted molds.

MAKES 12 149 calories each

Takes 35 minutes, plus rising   **PAGE 380**

WHOLE-WHEAT CROWN LOAF

Hearty and flavorful: a fine-textured loaf made from whole-wheat flour, shaped into a crown, and baked until golden.

MAKES 1 LOAF – 2975 calories per loaf

Takes 50 minutes, plus rising   **PAGE 372**

CINNAMON ROLLS

Breakfast treat: a plain dough enriched with egg, kneaded with cinnamon and raisins, rolled into spirals, baked, and glazed.

MAKES 16 450 calories each

Takes 60 minutes, plus rising   **PAGE 386**

SWEET BUNS

Sweetened dough with golden raisins and mixed peel. Shaped into buns, topped with sugar, and baked until golden.

MAKES 18 196 calories each

Takes 40 minutes, plus rising   **PAGE 385**

MILK ROLLS

Attractive rolls in a variety of shapes: knots, twists, and rosettes. Decorated with poppy seeds and sesame seeds and baked until golden.

MAKES 18 188 calories each

Takes 50 minutes, plus rising   **PAGE 371**

CROISSANTS

Classic French breakfast roll, made rich and flaky with butter. Shaped into crescents, glazed, and baked until golden.

MAKES 12 352 calories each

Takes 55 minutes, plus chilling   **PAGE 379**

⏱ OVER 60 MINUTES

ENGLISH MUFFINS

Golden and fresh from the griddle: a simple batter cooked until light and tender. Served warm spread with butter.

MAKES 20 73 calories each

Takes 50 minutes, plus rising   **PAGE 384**

SANDWICH ROLLS

Soft-crusted rolls made slightly sweet with the addition of honey. Dusted with flour and baked until golden.

MAKES 16 135 calories each

Takes 45 minutes, plus rising   **PAGE 370**

CHEESE & HERB BREAD

Hearty and flavorful: Cheddar and Parmesan cheeses, chopped parsley, and mustard flavor this crisp-crusted bread.

MAKES 1 LOAF 2707 calories per loaf

Takes 55 minutes, plus rising   **PAGE 374**

CALZONE

A delicious and aromatic mixture of Mediterranean ingredients wrapped in pizza dough and baked until golden.

MAKES 4 637 calories each

Takes 35 minutes, plus rising   **PAGE 378**

SPICY DEEP-DISH PIZZA

Thick, crisp-crusted pizza covered with tomatoes, pepperoni, and mozzarella and Parmesan cheeses. Spiked with green chilies.

MAKES 1 LARGE PIZZA 3596 calories

Takes 35 minutes, plus rising   **PAGE 378**

JELLY DOUGHNUTS

Old-fashioned favorite: doughnuts filled with raspberry jam, deep-fried, and sprinkled with cinnamon and sugar.

MAKES 16 269 calories each

Takes 40 minutes, plus rising   **PAGE 381**

WALNUT BREAD

Hearty and rustic: a coarse-textured loaf studded with chopped walnuts and parsley. Slashed in a crisscross pattern, dusted with flour, then baked until golden brown. This flavorful bread makes a classic accompaniment to any meal.

MAKES 2 LOAVES 1657 calories per loaf

Takes 55 minutes, plus rising   **PAGE 373**

COUNTRY BREAD

Simple to make: white flour loaf dusted with flour and baked until high and golden. It has a large and tender crumb.

MAKES 1 LOAF 2790 per loaf

Takes 50 minutes, plus rising   **PAGE 370**

⏱ OVER 60 MINUTES

STICKY BUNS
A plain dough rolled with a filling of golden raisins, currants, orange zest, and pie spices. Sliced, baked, and glazed with honey.
MAKES 12 298 calories each
Takes 60 minutes, plus rising   **PAGE 385**

CHALLAH
Tender and golden: an egg-enriched dough, shaped into a braid, and baked until golden. Excellent toasted or used to make French toast.
MAKES 2 LOAVES 1144 calories per loaf
Takes 60 minutes, plus rising   **PAGE 380**

OLIVE & SUN-DRIED TOMATO BREAD
The flavors of Provence: pungent olives and sun-dried tomatoes are kneaded into a dough darkened with buckwheat flour.
MAKES 2 LOAVES 1139 calories per loaf
Takes 60 minutes, plus rising   **PAGE 374**

POTATO BREAD
Old-fashioned favorite: mashed potato and butter enrich this simple bread. Makes 2 hearty, coarse-textured loaves.
MAKES 2 LOAVES 1002 calories per loaf
Takes 60 minutes, plus rising   **PAGE 373**

SOURDOUGH RYE BREAD
Sourdough starter gives a slightly tangy flavor to this hearty loaf. Studded with caraway seeds.
MAKES 2 LOAVES 3329 calories per loaf
Takes 1 hour 5 minutes, plus rising **PAGE 375**

SHORTENING BREAD
Traditional cake made tender and crisp with lard and studded with mixed fruit. Baked until dark golden brown.
MAKES 2 LOAVES 4093 calories per loaf
Takes 1 hour 5 minutes, plus rising **PAGE 381**

TRADITIONAL

WHOLE-WHEAT ENGLISH MUFFINS
Savory quick bread: whole-wheat flour is used to make these muffins. Cooked on a hot griddle. Served spread with butter and jam.
MAKES 12 158 calories each
Takes 60 minutes, plus rising   **PAGE 384**

HIGH FIBER

MULTIGRAIN LOAF
A nutritious, coarse-textured whole-wheat and white flour loaf studded with a combination of wheat flakes, linseed and sunflower seeds.
MAKES 2 LOAVES 1495 calories per loaf
Takes 60 minutes, plus rising

The loaves are lightly brushed with milk, sprinkled generously with wheat flakes, and baked until golden brown.

PAGE 372

YEAST BAKING KNOW-HOW

The PLEASURE of baking bread is legendary. From making and kneading the dough to slicing a freshly baked loaf, the experience is a thoroughly satisfying one that cooks the world over have shared for centuries. Indeed, yeast baking is perhaps the most popular of all kitchen crafts.

From this rich history comes a wide variety of recipes, both sweet and savory, some of which are easily made while others are more time-consuming to prepare. English muffins and hot cross buns, Danish pastries and croissants, whole-wheat bread and crispy, thin-crusted pizzas are all equally delicious.

Yeast know-how

Yeast is a living organism, activated by warmth and moisture. It converts natural sugars to gases and alcohol, causing dough to rise. Quick-acting dry yeast (also known as easy-blend) is used throughout this chapter. If you prefer, an equal quantity of ordinary dry yeast may be substituted, or fresh yeast may be used (see box, below).

FREEZING

Bread tends to dry out if stored in the refrigerator, so if you aren't going to use it quickly it should be frozen. Pack it in moisture-proof wrapping and seal well. Ordinary loaves can be frozen for up to 4 months; if enriched with milk or fruit, storage time is 3 months. Thaw the bread, still wrapped, at room temperature.

Successful home baking

The quantity of liquid given in a recipe is only a guide because the absorbency of flour can vary. The quantity of liquid that flour can absorb depends on temperature and humidity and how much hard wheat the flour contains (proportions vary from one brand to another). Add a small amount of liquid at first, then gradually add more if needed.

◆

Dough can be kneaded in a food processor or an electric mixer with a dough hook, as well as by hand.

◆

Dough rises fastest in a warm environment. The process slows as the temperature drops.

◆

To test whether the dough has risen sufficiently, press with a finger; an indentation should remain in the dough.

YEAST BAKING INGREDIENTS

There is a large range of flours to choose from, each one with its own unique texture and flavor.
The different types of yeast, on the other hand, vary simply in their method of preparation.

Flour
The best flours to use for yeast doughs are those labeled "bread flour." These are milled from hard wheat with a high gluten content that produces a good open-textured bread. Ordinary all-purpose flour, which contains a higher proportion of soft wheat, can be used for yeast doughs, but the result will be a much more close-textured and crumbly loaf.

The flour most commonly used for bread-making is white flour. Much bread is also made from whole-wheat flour, which is milled from the entire wheat kernel, including the bran and germ; health-food stores and specialty stores may carry variations on these two basic types of wheat flour.

Many other grains, such as barley, buckwheat, cornmeal, millet, oats, and rye may be milled and used to make bread. Soybeans are also ground into a flourlike powder. Many of these grains are low in gluten, so they are normally combined with stronger flours that have a much higher gluten content.

Fresh yeast
This form of yeast, which looks like creamy gray putty, is perishable and must be kept in the refrigerator in an airtight container for a maximum of 4–5 days. Fresh yeast should be almost odorless and have only a slightly yeasty smell; it should also break apart cleanly. Fresh yeast must be blended with warm liquid before mixing with flour. To substitute fresh yeast for quick-acting or for ordinary dry yeast, use double the weight; for example, $1/2$ oz (15 g) fresh yeast for $1/4$ oz (7 g) dried.

Dry yeast
If stored in a cool place, dry yeast will keep up to 6 months. Quick-acting dry yeast (also known as easy-blend) is added directly to flour with other dry ingredients. Ordinary dry yeast, however, must be blended with warm liquid and a little sugar before mixing with flour. After about 5 minutes, the yeast should dissolve and the mixture should be foamy. If this is not the result, discard the yeast and start again.

Lukewarm water (105–110°F/ 40–43°C) should be used to blend and dissolve fresh and ordinary dry yeast.

MAKING YEAST DOUGH

Making bread is not difficult, nor does it take up a lot of time – the most lengthy parts of the procedure, the rising and baking, are done by the bread itself.

1 Sift the flour into a large mixing bowl with the yeast and any other dry ingredients. Make a well in the middle and then gradually add the liquid ingredients.

2 Using your fingers, mix the liquid ingredients together and then gradually incorporate the flour. Mix thoroughly until a soft but not sticky dough is formed.

3 Turn the dough onto a floured work surface and knead: fold it over toward you, then push it down and away with the heel of your hand. Turn the dough, fold it, and push it away again. Continue kneading for 5–10 minutes, until the dough is elastic and smooth. Doughs made with bread flour take longer to knead than those made with all-purpose flour.

4 Shape the dough into a ball. Put the dough into an oiled bowl and turn to coat. Cover the bowl with oiled plastic wrap or a damp dish towel and leave in a warm, draft-free place to rise.

5 When the dough has doubled in size, turn it onto a lightly floured work surface and gently punch down the dough, using your fist. Knead the dough vigorously for 2–3 minutes, until smooth and elastic.

6 Shape the dough as directed. Cover loosely with plastic wrap or a dry dish towel and leave in a warm, draft-free place to rise until doubled in size again. Bake according to recipe.

SHAPING LOAVES

Because of the elastic quality of dough, it can very easily be formed into a variety of different shapes. Here are some of the more traditional shapes.

Cottage loaf
Cut off one-third of the dough. Roll each piece into a ball and put the small ball on top of the large ball. Push a forefinger through the middle to the bottom.

Pan loaf
Shape the dough into a cylinder a little longer than the pan and tuck the ends under to just fit into the pan. Place the dough in the pan, with the seams underneath.

Round loaf
Roll the dough into a ball, then fold the sides of the ball to the middle, to make a tight, round ball. Turn the ball over and put on a baking sheet.

Braided loaf
Divide and roll the dough into 3 strands. Place side by side and pinch together at one end. Braid the strands, pinching them together at the other end to secure.

GLAZES & TOPPINGS

Breads and rolls can be glazed before or after baking to add flavor and, depending on the glaze, to make the crust soft or shiny and crisp. Apply the glaze thinly, using a pastry brush. Here are a few suggestions for different glazes:

- water (before baking) for a crisp crust
- milk or cream (before baking) for a soft crust
- egg or egg yolk beaten with a pinch of salt (before baking) for a shiny, crisp crust
- butter (after baking) for a shiny crust
- sugar and water (after baking) for a shiny crust.

Toppings such as wheat or barley flakes, herbs, sunflower or sesame seeds, poppy seeds, grated cheese, chopped nuts, and coarse salt can be sprinkled over glazed breads and rolls before baking. Sweetened breads are often sprinkled with sugar or a spice and sugar mixture after cooking.

TESTING LOAVES

At the end of cooking, bread should be well risen, firm, and golden brown. To test whether it is thoroughly cooked, tip out of the pan or lift off the baking sheet and tap the bottom. The bread should make a hollow, drumlike sound. If it doesn't, return it to the oven for 5 minutes longer, then remove it and test again.

MAKING BUTTER SHAPES

Attractive butter shapes are perfect served with home-baked breads and rolls. They can be prepared in advance, tray frozen, then packed in freezer bags and thawed when needed. If you like, flavor them with herbs, garlic, or mustard for savory breads and spices, honey, or sugar for sweet breads.

Rose
1 Chill a block of butter in the refrigerator until firm. Using a vegetable peeler, shave a strip of butter from the block. Curl the strip, overlapping the ends, to form a cone. Stand the cone on the wide base on a work surface.

2 Using the vegetable peeler, shave off another strip of butter and wrap it about two thirds of the way around the cone. Carefully press the strip onto the cone at the bottom to secure it. Gently shape the butter strip so that it curves outward at the top.

3 Continue cutting strips from the butter block and wrapping them around the cone as before, overlapping each layer and pinching and curling the edges to imitate rose petals. The finished rose can be kept chilled in the refrigerator or frozen until required.

Disks
1 Use butter at room temperature. Beat the butter with a wooden spoon until it is soft, then beat in any flavorings. Put onto a sheet of waxed paper and roll it in the paper until it forms a neat sausage shape.

2 Wrap the roll of butter tightly in the waxed paper and twist the ends to seal. Chill in the refrigerator until firm. Unwrap and slice the butter crosswise into thin disks. Use immediately, leave to chill, or freeze until required.

Curls
Chill a block of butter. Warm a butter curler in hot water, then dry it. Pull the curler lengthwise along the surface of the block to shave off curls. Use immediately or keep the curls in ice water in the refrigerator until required.

COUNTRY BREAD

 Makes 1 large loaf

6 cups (750 g) unbleached white flour, plus extra for dusting

2 tbsp butter or margarine

2 tsp salt

1/4-oz (7-g) envelope quick-rise active dry yeast

about 13/4 cups (450 ml) lukewarm water

sunflower or corn oil for greasing

★ *2-lb (1-kg) loaf pan*

1 Put the flour into a bowl, rub in the butter with the fingertips until the mixture resembles bread crumbs, then stir in the salt and yeast. Make a well in the middle and pour in the water. Using a wooden spoon, mix to a soft but not sticky dough.

2 Lightly oil a large bowl. Knead the dough until smooth and elastic. Shape into a round and place in the bowl. Cover with oiled plastic wrap and leave in a warm place to rise for 1–1½ hours, until the dough has doubled in size.

3 Turn out the dough onto a lightly floured work surface and punch down with your fist. Knead vigorously for 2–3 minutes, until the dough is smooth and elastic.

4 Lightly oil the loaf pan. Shape the dough to fit the pan, tucking the ends underneath to give a smooth top, and place in the pan. Cover loosely with oiled plastic wrap and leave in a warm place to rise for about 30 minutes, until the dough reaches the top of the pan.

5 Lightly dust the top of the shaped dough with flour and bake in a 450°F (230°C) oven for 30–35 minutes, until well risen and golden. Turn the loaf out of the pan and tap the bottom to see if it is cooked; it should sound hollow. Leave the loaf to cool on a wire rack.

SANDWICH ROLLS

 Makes 16

4 cups (500 g) unbleached white flour, plus extra for dusting

2 tbsp butter

1 tsp salt

1 tsp quick-rise active dry yeast

about 2/3 cup (150 ml) lukewarm water

about 2/3 cup (150 ml) lukewarm milk

1 tsp honey

sunflower oil or corn for greasing

1 Put the flour into a large bowl. Add the butter and rub in with the fingertips until the mixture resembles fine bread crumbs. Stir in the salt and yeast. Make a well in the middle and pour in the water, milk, and honey. Using a wooden spoon, mix to a soft but not sticky dough.

2 Lightly oil a large bowl. Knead the dough until smooth and elastic. Shape into a round and place in the bowl. Cover with oiled plastic wrap and leave in a warm place to rise for 1–1½ hours, until the dough has doubled in size.

3 Turn out the dough onto a lightly floured work surface and punch down with your fist. Knead for 2–3 minutes, until the dough is smooth and elastic.

4 Lightly oil 2 baking sheets. Divide the dough into 16 even-sized pieces. Knead and roll into rounds and place far apart on the baking sheets. With the heel of your hand, flatten each round so that it measures 3 in (7 cm) across.

5 Cover loosely with oiled plastic wrap and leave in a warm place to rise for about 30 minutes, until the dough has doubled in size.

6 Lightly dust the rolls with flour and bake in a 400°F (200°C) oven for 15–20 minutes, until well risen and golden. Tap the bottoms to see if they are cooked; they should sound hollow. Leave the rolls to cool on a wire rack.

MILK ROLLS

 Makes 18

6 cups (750 g) unbleached white
flour, plus extra for dusting

4 tbsp butter or solid
vegetable shortening

2 tsp salt

1/4-oz (7-g) envelope
quick-rise active dry yeast

about 1 3/4 cups (425 ml)
lukewarm milk

sunflower or corn oil for greasing

1 egg, beaten

poppy seeds and sesame seeds
for sprinkling

1 Put the flour into a large
bowl, rub in the butter,
then stir in the salt and
yeast. Make a well in the
middle and pour in the
milk. Using a wooden
spoon, mix to a soft but
not sticky dough.

2 Lightly oil a large bowl.
Knead the dough until
smooth and elastic. Shape
into a round and place in
the bowl. Cover with oiled
plastic wrap and leave in a
warm place for 1–1 1/2 hours,
until doubled in size.

3 Turn out the dough
onto a lightly floured
work surface and punch
down with your fist. Knead
for 2–3 minutes, until the
dough is smooth and elastic.

4 Divide the dough into
18 even-sized pieces and
shape into balls, folding the
sides to the middles to form
tight round balls, or shape
as required (see box, right).

5 Lightly oil 2 or 3 baking
sheets. Arrange the rolls
on the baking sheets, leaving
enough room between them
for the dough to expand,
cover loosely with oiled
plastic wrap, and leave in
a warm place to rise for
15–20 minutes, until the
dough has doubled in size.

6 Brush the rolls with the
beaten egg to glaze and
sprinkle with poppy seeds
and sesame seeds. Bake in a
450°F (230°C) oven for
about 15 minutes, until they
are well risen and golden.
Tap the bottoms to see if the
rolls are cooked; they should
sound hollow. Leave to cool
on a wire rack.

Shaping milk rolls

Form each piece of
dough into a long rope
and tie into a single knot.

Roll each piece of dough
into a thin strand. Fold in
half and twist together,
sealing the ends well to
form a twist.

Shape each piece of dough
into a ball or an oval. Snip
tops with scissors.

DINNER ROLLS

 Makes 18

4 cups (500 g) unbleached white
flour

1 tsp salt

1 tsp quick-rise active dry yeast

about 1 1/2 cups (375 ml)
lukewarm water

sunflower or corn oil for greasing

1 Put the flour into a large
bowl, then stir in the salt
and yeast. Make a well in
the middle and pour in the
water. Work to a soft but not
sticky dough.

2 Lightly oil a large bowl.
Knead the dough until
smooth and elastic. Shape
into a round and place in
the bowl. Cover with oiled
plastic wrap and leave in a
warm place to rise for 1–1 1/2
hours, until doubled in size.

3 Lightly oil 2 or 3 baking
sheets. Divide the dough
into 18 even-sized pieces.
Fold the sides to the middles
to form balls. Arrange on the
sheets, leaving room for
the dough to expand,
cover loosely with oiled
plastic wrap, and leave in
a warm place to rise for
20 minutes or until
doubled in size.

4 Bake the rolls in a
375°F (190°C) oven for
20 minutes or until golden.
Tap the bottoms to see if
they are cooked; they should
sound hollow. Leave to cool.

WHOLE-WHEAT CROWN LOAF

 Makes 1 large loaf

6 cups (750 g) whole-wheat flour, plus extra for dusting

2 tbsp butter or margarine

1 tbsp sugar

2 tsp salt

1/4-oz (7-g) envelope quick-rise active dry yeast

about 1 3/4 cups (425 ml) lukewarm water

sunflower or corn oil for greasing

milk for glazing

cracked wheat for sprinkling

★ *8-in (20-cm) round cake pan*

1 Put the flour into a large bowl. Rub in the butter with the fingertips, then stir in the sugar, salt, and yeast and mix thoroughly. Make a well in the middle of the ingredients and pour in the water. Using a wooden spoon, mix to a soft but not sticky dough.

2 Lightly oil a large bowl. Knead the dough until smooth and elastic and shape into a round. Place the dough in the bowl, cover with oiled plastic wrap or a damp dish towel, and leave in a warm place to rise for 1–1 1/2 hours, until the dough has doubled in size.

3 Turn out the dough onto a lightly floured work surface and punch down with your fist. Knead for 2–3 minutes, until smooth.

4 Oil the cake pan. Shape the loaf (see box, below). Cover loosely with oiled plastic wrap or a dry dish towel and leave in a warm place to rise for 1–1 1/2 hours, until doubled in size.

5 Brush the loaf with milk to glaze and sprinkle with cracked wheat. Bake in a 450°F (230°C) oven for 20–25 minutes, until well risen. Tap the bottom to see if the loaf is cooked; it should sound hollow. Leave to cool on a wire rack.

Shaping a crown loaf

Divide the dough into 8 even-sized pieces, shape into rounds, and place in the cake pan to form a crown. The rounds will rise to fill the pan.

MULTIGRAIN LOAF

 Makes 2 small loaves

1 1/2 cups (150 g) wheat flakes

1 1/2 oz (45 g) linseed

1 1/4 cups (300 ml) boiling water

4 cups (500 g) unbleached white flour, plus extra for dusting

1 cup (125 g) whole-wheat flour

1/2 cup (60 g) sunflower seeds

2 1/4 tsp (20 g) salt

1/4-oz (7-g) envelope quick-rise active dry yeast

about 1 1/2 cups (350 ml) lukewarm water

sunflower or corn oil for greasing

milk for glazing

wheat flakes to decorate

★ *2 1-lb (500-g) loaf pans*

1 Put the wheat flakes and linseed into a large bowl, pour on the boiling water, and stir. Cover and set aside for 30 minutes or until the water has been absorbed.

2 Stir the flours, sunflower seeds, salt, and yeast into the wheat-flake mixture. Make a well in the middle of the ingredients and pour in the lukewarm water. Using a wooden spoon, mix to a soft but not sticky dough.

3 Lightly oil a large bowl. Knead the dough until smooth and elastic. Shape into a round and place in the bowl. Cover with oiled plastic wrap and leave in a warm place for 1–1 1/2 hours, until doubled in size.

4 Turn out the dough onto a floured work surface and punch down with your fist. Knead for 2–3 minutes, until smooth and elastic once again.

5 Oil the pans. Divide the dough in half, and shape into oblongs, tucking the ends underneath to give smooth tops. Place in the pans. Alternatively, shape into 2 rounds and place on oiled baking sheets. Cover loosely with oiled platic wrap and leave in a warm place to rise for 20–30 minutes.

6 Brush the loaves with milk to glaze and sprinkle with wheat flakes. Bake in a 450°F (230°C) oven for 10 minutes; reduce the oven temperature to 400°F (200°C) and bake for 20–25 minutes. Tap the bottoms to see if the loaves are cooked; they should sound hollow. Leave to cool on a wire rack.

WALNUT BREAD

 Makes 2 small loaves

5 1/4 cups (650 g) unbleached white flour, plus extra for dusting

2 tsp salt

2 tbsp butter or margarine

1 cup (125 g) walnut pieces, coarsely chopped

2 tbsp chopped parsley

1/4-oz (7-g) envelope quick-rise active dry yeast

about 1 2/3 cups (400 ml) lukewarm water

sunflower or corn oil for greasing

1 Put the flour and salt into a large bowl. Rub in the butter, then stir in the walnuts, parsley, and yeast. Make a well in the middle, pour in the water, and mix to a soft but not sticky dough.

2 Lightly oil a large bowl. Knead the dough until smooth and elastic, then shape into a round. Place the dough in the bowl, cover loosely with oiled plastic wrap, and leave in a warm place to rise for 1–1 1/2 hours, until doubled in size.

3 Lightly oil 2 baking sheets. Punch down the dough with your fist, then knead for 2–3 minutes, until smooth and elastic.

4 Divide the dough in half, shape each half into a round, and then place on a baking sheet.

5 Cover the rounds loosely with oiled plastic wrap, and leave in a warm place to rise for 20–30 minutes.

6 Dust each loaf with flour, slash the tops in a crisscross pattern, and bake in 425°F (220°C) oven for about 10 minutes; reduce the oven temperature to 375°F (190°C) and bake for 20 minutes or until the bread is well risen and golden brown.

7 Tap the bottoms to see if the loaves are cooked; they should sound hollow. Leave to cool on a wire rack.

POTATO BREAD

 Makes 2 small loaves

4 cups (500 g) unbleached white flour, plus extra for dusting

1 tsp salt

1 tbsp butter

1 tsp quick-rise active dry yeast

1 large potato, peeled, cooked, mashed, and cooled

about 1 cup (250 ml) lukewarm water

sunflower or corn oil for greasing

☆ 2 1-lb (500-g) loaf pans

1 Put the flour and salt into a large bowl, rub in the butter, then stir in the yeast. Add the potato, rubbing it loosely into the flour.

2 Make a well in the middle of the ingredients and pour in the lukewarm water. Using a wooden spoon, mix to form a soft dough.

3 Lightly oil a large bowl. Knead the dough until smooth and elastic, then shape into a round. Place in the bowl, cover with oiled plastic wrap, and leave in a warm place to rise for 1 hour.

4 Turn out the dough onto a lightly floured work surface and punch down with your fist. Knead until smooth and elastic.

5 Lightly oil the loaf pans. Divide the dough into 2 and shape to fit the pans, tucking the ends underneath. Place in the pans. Cover loosely with oiled plastic wrap and leave in a warm place to rise for 30 minutes or until the dough reaches the tops of the pans.

6 Bake in a 450°F (230°C) oven for 10 minutes; reduce the oven temperature to 400°F (200°C), and bake for 20–25 minutes, until well risen and golden. Tap the bottoms of the loaves to see if they are cooked; they should sound hollow. Leave to cool on a wire rack.

Cook's know-how

This recipe is ideal for using up leftover mashed potatoes. If you use freshly cooked and mashed potatoes, make sure that they are completely cold before use.

CHEESE & HERB BREAD

 Makes 1 medium loaf

4 cups (500 g) unbleached white flour, plus extra for dusting

³/4 cup (90 g) grated aged Cheddar cheese

¹/3 cup (30 g) grated Parmesan cheese

2 tsp dry mustard

2 tbsp chopped parsley

1¹/2 tsp salt

¹/4-oz (7-g) envelope quick-rise active dry yeast

about 1¹/2 cups (350 ml) lukewarm milk

sunflower or corn oil for greasing

beaten egg for glazing

2 tbsp grated Cheddar cheese for sprinkling

1 Put the flour into a large bowl and stir in the cheeses, dry mustard, parsley, salt, and yeast, mixing thoroughly. Make a well in the middle and pour in the lukewarm milk. Mix to a soft but not sticky dough.

2 Lightly oil a large bowl. Knead the dough until smooth and elastic, then shape into a round.

3 Place the dough in the bowl, cover with oiled plastic wrap, and leave in a warm place to rise for 1–1¹/2 hours, until doubled in size.

4 Turn out the dough onto a floured surface and punch down with your fist. Knead for 2–3 minutes, until smooth and elastic.

5 Lightly flour a baking sheet. Shape the dough into a 6-in (15-cm) round and place on the baking sheet. Cover loosely with oiled plastic wrap and leave in a warm place to rise for 20–30 minutes.

6 Brush the loaf with the egg to glaze, cut a shallow cross in the top, and sprinkle with the grated Cheddar cheese. Bake in a 450°F (230°C) oven for 10 minutes; reduce the oven temperature to 400°F (200°C), and bake for 20 minutes or until the loaf is well risen.

7 Cover with foil halfway through baking if the bread is browning too much. Leave to cool on a wire rack.

OLIVE & SUN-DRIED TOMATO BREAD

 Makes 2 small loaves

3¹/4 cups (400 g) unbleached white flour

¹/2 cup (60 g) buckwheat flour

1 tsp salt

¹/4-oz (7-g) envelope quick-rise active dry yeast

black pepper

about 1¹/4 cups (300 ml) lukewarm water

1 tbsp olive oil, plus extra for greasing

1 cup (125 g) coarsely chopped pitted black olives

3¹/2-oz (125-g) jar sun-dried tomatoes in oil, drained and chopped

1 tbsp chopped parsley

1 tbsp chopped fresh basil

1 tbsp coarse sea salt

1 Put the flours into a large bowl. Stir in the salt and yeast and season with black pepper. Make a well in the middle. Pour in the water and oil and mix to a soft but not sticky dough.

2 Lightly oil a large bowl. Knead until smooth and elastic, then shape into a round. Place the dough in the bowl, cover with oiled plastic wrap, and leave in a warm place to rise for 1–1¹/2 hours.

3 Lightly oil a baking sheet. Punch down the dough, then knead for 2–3 minutes. Divide the dough into 2 pieces. Roll out each piece to a 9- x 10-in (23- x 25-cm) rectangle. Spread one of the rectangles with the olives and the other with the sun-dried tomatoes, parsley, and basil.

4 Roll up each rectangle of dough from 1 long end and place, seam side down, on the sheet. Make 4–5 diagonal slashes on the top of each loaf, cover loosely with oiled plastic wrap, and leave in a warm place to rise for 20–30 minutes.

5 Brush the top of each loaf with water and lightly sprinkle with sea salt. Bake in a 450°F (230°C) oven for 15 minutes; reduce the oven temperature to 375°F (190°C), and bake the loaves for 15 minutes longer or until well risen and golden.

6 Tap the bottoms to see if the loaves are cooked; they should sound hollow. Leave to cool on a wire rack.

SOURDOUGH RYE BREAD

A satisfying and tasty country bread from Eastern Europe, this rye bread is not difficult to make but, because the starter has to be left to ferment for a couple of days, it does require a little advance planning.

 Makes 2 large loaves

12 cups (1.5 kg) unbleached white flour, plus extra for sprinkling

1/4-oz (7-g) envelope quick-rise active dry yeast

1 cup (250 ml) lukewarm water

3 tbsp caraway seeds (optional)

1 tbsp salt

sunflower or corn oil for greasing

cornmeal for sprinkling

SOURDOUGH STARTER

2 cups (250 g) unbleached white flour

1 tsp quick-rise active dry yeast

1 cup (250 ml) lukewarm water

SPONGE

1³/₄ cups (200 g) rye flour

1 cup (250 ml) lukewarm water

1 Make the starter: put the flour into a large bowl and stir in the yeast. Make a well, pour in the water, and mix.

2 Cover tightly and leave at room temperature for 2 days. Alternatively, leave the starter in the refrigerator for up to 1 week.

3 Make the sponge: put the rye flour into a large bowl, add the sourdough starter and the water, and stir to mix. Cover tightly and leave at room temperature for 8 hours or chill in the refrigerator for up to 2 days.

4 Put the flour into a bowl, add the sponge mixture, yeast, measured water, caraway seeds, if using, and salt, and mix to a soft and slightly sticky dough.

5 Turn the dough into a large ungreased bowl, sprinkle the top with flour, cover loosely with oiled plastic wrap, and leave in a warm place to rise for about 2 hours, until doubled in size.

6 Lightly sprinkle 2 baking sheets with cornmeal. Turn out the dough onto a lightly floured work surface and punch down with your fist. Knead for 3–4 minutes, until smooth and elastic. Halve the dough and form each half into a round. Score the tops with a sharp knife.

7 Place on the baking sheets, cover loosely with oiled plastic wrap, and leave in a warm place to rise for 45 minutes or until they have doubled in size.

8 Place the loaves in a 425°F (220°C) oven. Fill a roasting pan with boiling water and place at the bottom of the oven. Bake the loaves for about 35 minutes, until they are lightly browned. Tap the bottoms to see if the loaves are cooked; they should sound hollow. Leave to cool on wire racks.

FOCACCIA

 Makes 1 large loaf

6 cups (750 g) unbleached white flour, plus extra for dusting

1/4-oz (7-g) envelope quick-rise active dry yeast

3–4 tbsp chopped fresh rosemary

3 tbsp olive oil, plus extra for greasing

1 cup (250 ml) lukewarm water

2 tsp coarse sea salt

1 Put the flour into a bowl and add the yeast and rosemary. Make a well in the middle, add the oil and the water, and work to a soft but not sticky dough. Lightly oil a large bowl. Knead the dough until smooth and elastic, then shape into a round.

2 Place the dough in the bowl, cover loosely with oiled plastic wrap, and leave in a warm place to rise for about 1 hour, until the dough has doubled in size.

3 Turn out the dough onto a lightly floured work surface and punch down with your fist. Knead for 2–3 minutes, until smooth. Roll out the dough to form a round 2 in (5 cm) thick. Cover loosely with oiled plastic wrap and leave in a warm place to rise for 1 hour or until doubled in size.

4 Brush with olive oil and sprinkle with sea salt. Bake the loaf in a 375°F (190°C) oven for 20 minutes or until golden brown.

THIN-CRUST PIZZAS

Tomatoes, cheese, herbs, and olive oil are just a few characteristic pizza toppings, but there are endless combinations. In these recipes, imported strained tomatoes, from Italy, usually packaged in a box, are spread over the pizza crust.

TUNA & CAPER

 Makes 1 large pizza

6 tbsp (90 ml) strained tomatoes

1 pizza crust (see box, below)

7 oz (200 g) canned tuna in water, drained

2 tbsp capers

1 cup (125 g) grated mozzarella cheese

1 tsp dried oregano

2 tbsp olive oil

Spread the tomatoes in an even layer over the pizza crust. Top with the remaining ingredients.

NAPOLETANA

 Makes 1 large pizza

6 tbsp (90 ml) strained tomatoes

1 pizza crust (see box, below)

2 oz (60 g) canned anchovy fillets, drained

1 cup (125 g) grated mozzarella cheese

2 tbsp olive oil

Spread the tomatoes over the pizza crust. Halve the anchovies and arrange on top with the remaining ingredients.

FOUR SEASONS

 Makes 1 large pizza

6 tbsp (90 ml) strained tomatoes

1 pizza crust (see box, below)

salt and black pepper

1/2 cup (60 g) sliced pepperoni

1/2 tsp dried oregano

2/3 cup (45 g) sliced mushrooms

1/4 cup (30 g) grated mozzarella cheese

1 oz (30 g) anchovy fillets, drained

12 pitted black olives

1/2 red and 1/2 green pepper, thinly sliced

1 tbsp shredded fresh basil

2 tbsp olive oil

1 Spread the tomatoes over the pizza crust and season with salt and pepper to taste.

2 Arrange the pepperoni and oregano on 1 quarter, the sliced mushrooms and mozzarella on a second quarter, the anchovies and black olives on a third, and the red and green peppers and basil on the final quarter. Lightly sprinkle with olive oil.

MINI PIZZAS

 Makes 12

6 tbsp (90 ml) strained tomatoes

1 recipe pizza dough (see box, below), shaped into 12 3-in (7-cm) rounds

salt and black pepper

2 tbsp olive oil

SUN-DRIED TOMATO TOPPING

8 sun-dried tomatoes, diced

2 tbsp pitted black olives, diced

2 garlic cloves, chopped

1 tbsp shredded fresh basil

3 tbsp diced goat cheese

PROSCIUTTO TOPPING

1 oz (30 g) prosciutto, diced

1/2 6-oz (175-g) jar artichoke hearts in oil, drained and quartered

2/3 cup (60 g) grated Parmesan cheese

Spread the tomatoes over the rounds and season. Top half with the sun-dried tomatoes, olives, garlic, basil, and goat cheese, and half with the prosciutto, artichokes, and cheese. Sprinkle with oil.

Clockwise from top: *Napoletana Pizza, Mini Pizzas, Tuna & Caper Pizza, Four Seasons Pizza*

Making the thin-crust pizza crust

1 Sift *2 cups (250 g) unbleached white flour* onto a work surface and add *1/2 tsp quick-rise active dry yeast* and *1/2 tsp salt*. Make a well in the middle and add about *3/4 cup (175 ml) lukewarm water* and *1 tbsp olive oil*. Draw in the flour with your fingertips and work to form a smooth dough.

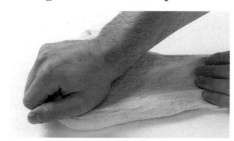

2 Lightly oil a large bowl. Knead the dough for 10 minutes until smooth. Shape into a round and put in the bowl. Cover loosely with oiled plastic wrap and leave in a warm place to rise for 1 hour or until doubled in size. Turn out of the bowl and knead for 2–3 minutes, until smooth.

3 Roll and stretch the dough until it forms a round 1/2 in (1 cm) thick and 14 in (35 cm) in diameter. Press around the edge to form a rim. Put on a baking sheet, add the topping, and bake in a 425°F (220°C) oven for 20–30 minutes. Bake the mini pizzas for 12–15 minutes.

CALZONE

Makes 4

1/2 cup (125 g) ricotta cheese

1 large tomato, peeled (page 39), seeded, and chopped

1/2 cup (60 g) grated mozzarella cheese

2 garlic cloves, chopped

1/4 cup (30 g) pitted black olives, chopped

1 scant cup (60 g) sliced mushrooms

1 green pepper, cored, seeded, and sliced

1/2 tsp dried oregano

salt and black pepper

beaten egg for glazing

DOUGH

1/4-oz (7-g) envelope quick-rise active dry yeast

1/2 tsp sugar

4 cups (500 g) unbleached white flour

1/2 tsp salt

2 tbsp olive oil, plus extra for greasing

about 1 cup plus 2 tbsp (275 ml) lukewarm water

1 Mix the dough ingredients to a soft dough. Oil a large bowl. Knead the dough for 5–10 minutes, until smooth.

2 Shape into a round and place in the bowl. Cover with oiled plastic wrap and leave in a warm place to rise.

3 Punch down the dough on a floured work surface, and shape into four 8-in (20-cm) rounds. Combine the ricotta, tomato, mozzarella, garlic, olives, mushrooms, green pepper, and oregano, and season. Fill the calzone (see box, below).

4 Put the calzone on an oiled baking sheet and bake in a 475°F (240°C) oven for 15 minutes.

Filling the calzone

Put one-quarter of the ricotta mixture onto half of each dough round.

Brush the edge of the dough with beaten egg and fold over to enclose the filling. Seal the edges and brush the top with egg.

SPICY DEEP-DISH PIZZA

Makes 1 large pizza

4 oz (125 g) tomato paste

13 oz (400 g) canned chopped tomatoes, drained

1/2 cup (60 g) sliced pepperoni sausage

2 1/2 cups (300 g) grated mozzarella cheese

2/3 cup (60 g) grated Parmesan cheese

2 tbsp sliced pickled green chilies

DOUGH

1/4-oz (7-g) envelope quick-rise active dry yeast

1/2 tsp sugar

4 cups (500 g) unbleached white flour

1/2 tsp salt

2 tbsp olive oil, plus extra for greasing

about 2/3 cup (150 ml) lukewarm water

✫ deep dish 14-in (35-cm) round pizza pan

1 Make the dough: mix the yeast, sugar, flour, and salt in a bowl. Add the oil and water and mix. Knead for 5–10 minutes, until smooth.

2 Put into an oiled bowl, turn to coat with the oil, cover with oiled plastic wrap, and leave in a warm place to rise for 1 hour or until doubled in size.

3 Lightly oil the pizza pan. Punch down the dough on a floured work surface and roll out and shape into a 14-in (35-cm) round. Put into the pan and shape the edge to form a rim.

4 Spread the tomato paste over the base. Top with the tomatoes and pepperoni. Sprinkle over the mozzarella, Parmesan, and green chilies.

5 Bake in a 475°F (240°C) oven for 10–15 minutes until the crust is golden and the cheese topping is and melted. Serve immediately.

Pickled green chilies

Jalapeño *peppers are pickled in strong and fruit vinegars and a variety of herbs and spices for a hot and zesty flavor.*

CROISSANTS

Croissant is the French word for crescent, the traditional shape for this classic breakfast roll. Delicious on their own, croissants are also good served warm with butter and jam or marmalade. Savory fillings, such as ham and cheese, make croissants into a delightful meal.

 Makes 12

4 cups (500 g) unbleached white flour

1/2 tsp salt

1¼ cups (300 g) butter, at room temperature

1 tsp quick-rise active dry yeast

2 tbsp sugar

about 2/3 cup (150 ml) lukewarm milk

about 2/3 cup (150 ml) lukewarm water

sunflower or corn oil for greasing

beaten egg for glazing

1 Put the flour and salt into a large bowl, add 4 tbsp of the butter, and rub in with your fingertips until the mixture resembles fine bread crumbs. Stir in the yeast and sugar.

2 Make a well in the middle of the dry ingredients and add the milk and water all at once. Mix together with a wooden spoon until smooth. Cover with oiled plastic wrap and chill the dough for 2 hours.

3 Meanwhile, on a sheet of baking parchment, spread out the remaining butter into a 5- x 8-in (12- x 20-cm) rectangle. Cover with another sheet of baking parchment and leave to chill.

4 Roll out the dough on a floured work surface into an 7- x 14-in (18- x 35-cm) rectangle, and place the chilled butter on top so that it covers the top two-thirds of the rectangle.

5 Fold the bottom third of the dough over the middle third, and fold the top third, with the butter, over the top to form a neat bundle. Seal the edges with the edge of your hand. Wrap and chill for 30 minutes.

6 Roll out the dough bundle into an 7- x 14-in (18- x 35-cm) rectangle, fold into 3 as before, and seal the edges of the bundles.

7 Wrap and chill for a few hours until firm enough to roll and shape.

8 Shape the croissants (see box, right). Place on 2 baking sheets and leave for about 30 minutes, until almost doubled in size.

9 Lightly brush the croissants with the beaten egg and bake in a 425°F (220°C) oven for 12–15 minutes, until crisp and golden brown. Leave the croissants to cool slightly before serving.

CHOCOLATE CROISSANTS

Make the dough as directed. Before rolling the triangles into sausage shapes, sprinkle them with 1/2 cup (90 g) semisweet chocolate chips. Roll the triangles and proceed as directed.

Shaping the croissants

Roll out the dough into a 14- x 21-in (35- x 53-cm) rectangle and cut into 12 triangles.

Roll each triangle into a sausage shape, starting from the long side and ending with the point of the triangle.

Bend the ends of each croissant to give the traditional shape.

CHALLAH

 Makes 2 small loaves

4 cups (500 g) unbleached white flour, plus extra for dusting

1 tbsp sugar

2 tsp salt

¹/₄-oz (7-g) envelope quick-rise active dry yeast

about 1 cup (250 ml) lukewarm water

2 eggs, beaten

2 tbsp sunflower or corn oil, plus extra for greasing

beaten egg for glazing

poppy seeds for sprinkling

1 Put the flour, sugar, and salt into a bowl. Stir in the yeast. Make a well in the middle. Combine the water, eggs, and oil and pour into the well. Mix to a soft but not sticky dough.

2 Lightly oil a large bowl. Knead the dough until firm and elastic. Shape into a round and place in the bowl. Cover with oiled plastic wrap and leave in a warm place to rise for 1–1¹/₂ hours, until doubled in size.

3 Turn out the dough onto a lightly floured work surface and punch down with your fist. Knead for 2–3 minutes, until smooth and elastic. Divide the dough into 2 pieces.

4 Lightly oil a baking sheet. Divide each piece of dough into 3 even-sized strands, and shape into a braid (page 368). Place on the baking sheet, cover loosely with oiled plastic wrap or a dry dish towel, and leave them in a warm place to rise for 30 minutes or until they are doubled in size.

5 Brush the loaves with the beaten egg and sprinkle generously with poppy seeds. Bake in a 450°F (230°C) oven for 10 minutes; reduce the oven temperature to 400°F (200°C), and bake for 20 minutes or until the loaves are well risen and a rich brown color. Tap the bottoms to see if the loaves are cooked; they should sound hollow. Leave to cool on a wire rack.

BRIOCHES

 Makes 12

2 ¹/₂ cups (275 g) unbleached white flour, plus extra for dusting

2 tbsp sugar

4 tbsp butter

¹/₄-oz (7-g) envelope quick-rise active dry yeast

2 eggs, beaten

about 3 tbsp lukewarm milk

sunflower or corn oil for greasing

beaten egg for glazing

★ 12 individual brioche molds

1 Sift the flour and sugar into a large bowl. Rub in the butter until the mixture resembles fine bread crumbs, then stir in the yeast. Make a well in the middle and pour in the eggs and milk. Mix to a soft but not sticky dough.

2 Lightly oil a large bowl. Knead the dough until smooth and elastic. Shape into a round and place in the bowl. Cover with oiled plastic wrap and leave in a warm place to rise for 1–1¹/₂ hours, until doubled in size.

3 Turn out the dough onto a lightly floured work surface and punch down with your fist. Knead the dough for 2–3 minutes, until smooth.

4 Lightly oil the brioche molds. Shape the brioches (see box, below).

5 Cover loosely with oiled plastic wrap or a dry dish towel and leave in a warm place for 20 minutes or until doubled in size.

6 Brush the brioches with a little beaten egg and bake in a 400°F (200°C) oven for 10–12 minutes, until well risen and golden brown. Tap the bottoms to see if the brioches are cooked through; they should sound hollow. Leave to cool on a wire rack.

Shaping brioches

Divide the dough into 12 pieces, cutting one-quarter from each. Shape each piece into a ball. Place the large balls in the molds, and press a hole in the middle of each. Place the small balls over the holes and press down to seal.

JELLY DOUGHNUTS

 Makes 16

4 cups (500 g) all-purpose white flour, plus extra for dusting

2 tbsp butter or margarine

1/3 cup (90 g) sugar

1/4-oz (7-g) envelope quick rise active dry yeast

2 eggs, beaten

6 tbsp (90 ml) lukewarm milk

6 tbsp (90 ml) lukewarm water

sunflower or corn oil for greasing and deep-frying

1/2 10-oz jar raspberry jam

1/2 cup (125 g) sugar

2 tsp ground cinnamon

1 Put the flour into a large bowl and rub in the butter with the fingertips until the mixture resembles fine bread crumbs. Stir in the sugar and yeast. Make a well in the middle of the dry ingredients, pour in the eggs, milk, and water, and mix to a smooth dough.

2 Lightly oil a large bowl. Knead the dough until smooth and elastic. Shape into a round and place in the bowl. Cover with oiled plastic wrap and leave in a warm place to rise for 1–1 1/2 hours, until doubled in size.

3 Turn out the dough onto a lightly floured work surface and punch down with your fist. Knead for 2–3 minutes, until smooth.

4 Divide the dough into 16 pieces. Shape each one into a ball, then flatten slightly. Fill the doughnuts (see box, below). Place the doughnuts on oiled baking sheets, cover with oiled plastic wrap and leave in a warm place to rise for 30 minutes.

5 Heat the oil to 325°F (160°C), and cook the doughnuts in batches for 5 minutes, until golden. Drain on paper towels. Combine the sugar and cinnamon and coat the doughnuts. Serve immediately.

Filling the doughnuts

Place 1 tsp raspberry jam in the middle of each doughnut. Gather the edges over the jam and pinch firmly to seal.

SHORTENING BREAD

 Makes 1 large loaf

4 cups (500 g) all-purpose white flour, plus extra for dusting

1 tsp salt

2 tbsp sugar

1/4-oz (7-g) envelope quick-rise active dry yeast

1 tbsp vegetable shortening

1 1/4 cups (300 ml) lukewarm water

sunflower or corn oil for greasing

FILLING

6 tbsp (90 g) shortening

4 tbsp butter, plus extra for greasing

1/3 cup (90 g) dried currants

1/2 cup (90 g) golden raisins

1/2 cup (60 g) chopped mixed candied peel

1/3 cup packed (90 g) dark brown sugar

GLAZE

1 tbsp sugar

1 tbsp boiling water

★ 9- x 12-in (23- x 30-cm) roasting pan

1 Mix the flour, salt, sugar, and yeast in a bowl. Rub in the fat. Make a well in the middle and pour in the water. Mix to a soft dough.

2 Knead until smooth and elastic, place in an oiled bowl, and cover with oiled plastic wrap. Leave to rise.

3 Turn out the dough onto a lightly floured work surface and roll out to a rectangle about 1/4 in (5 mm) thick. Dot with one-third each of the shortening and butter. Sprinkle over one-third each of the dried fruit, mixed peel, and sugar.

4 Fold into three, folding the bottom third up and the top third down on top of it. Seal the edges to trap the air, then give the dough a quarter turn. Repeat the rolling and folding twice more, with the remaining fat, fruit, peel, and sugar.

5 Lightly butter the roasting pan. Roll out the dough to fit the pan, and lift it into the pan. Cover with oiled plastic wrap and leave to rise in a warm place for about 30 minutes, until doubled in size.

6 Score the top of the dough in a crisscross pattern and bake in a 400°F (200°C) oven for about 30 minutes, until well risen and golden brown.

7 Leave to cool in the roasting pan for about 10 minutes. Meanwhile, make the glaze: dissolve the sugar in the measured water. Brush the glaze on top of the warm cake and leave to cool on a wire rack.

DANISH PASTRIES

These tender and flaky pastries are quick and easy to make and are particularly good for breakfast.
Vary the fillings, bake them ahead, and freeze. Warm the pastries, loosely covered with foil, in a low oven,
and serve for a special breakfast or brunch.

 Makes 16

4 cups (500 g) unbleached white flour,
* plus extra for dusting*

1/2 tsp salt

3/4 lb (375 g) butter, plus extra for greasing

1/4-oz (7-g) envelope quick-rise active dry yeast

1/4 cup (60 g) sugar

5/8 cup (150 ml) lukewarm milk

2 eggs, beaten

beaten egg to glaze

FILLING & TOPPING

1/2 lb (250 g) white almond paste

4 apricot halves, canned or fresh

about 2 tsp water

1 cup (125 g) confectioners' sugar

1/2 cup (60 g) slivered almonds

1/4 cup (60 g) glacé cherries

1 Put the flour and salt into a bowl and rub in 4 tbsp of the butter. Stir in the yeast and sugar. Make a well in the middle, add the lukewarm milk and eggs, and mix to a soft dough.

2 Turn out the dough onto a floured surface and knead for 10 minutes or until smooth. Shape into a round and place in an oiled bowl. Cover with oiled plastic wrap and leave in a warm place to rise for 1 hour or until doubled in size.

3 Turn out the dough onto a lightly floured work surface and knead for 2–3 minutes until smooth. Roll out into a 8- x 14-in (20- x 35-cm) rectangle. Dot the top two-thirds of the dough with half of the remaining butter. Fold the bottom third up and the top third down to form a bundle. Seal the edges, then give the dough a quarter turn so the folded side is to the left.

4 Roll out the dough into a 8- x 14-in (20- x 35-cm) rectangle as before. Dot with the remaining butter, fold, and chill for 15 minutes. Roll, fold, and chill twice more.

5 Divide the dough into 4 pieces. Shape and fill the pastries (see box, below). Arrange on buttered baking sheets and leave to rise in a warm place for 20 minutes. Brush with beaten egg and bake in a 425°F (220°C) oven for 15 minutes or until golden brown. Transfer to a wire rack.

6 Mix the water and confectioners' sugar and spoon a little over each pastry while still warm. Decorate kites with flaked almonds and pinwheels with glacé cherries. Leave to cool.

Clockwise from top: *Pinwheels, Kites, Crescents, Envelopes.*

Shaping Danish pastries

Crescents

1 Roll out the dough into a 9-in (23-cm) round. Cut into quarters. Place a small roll of almond paste at the wide end of each piece.

2 Starting from the wide end, roll up each dough quarter loosely around the almond paste, then curve the ends to form a crescent.

Kites

1 Roll out the dough into an 8-in (20-cm) square. Cut into 4 squares. Make cuts around 2 corners of each square, 1/2 in (1 cm) in from the edge.

2 Place a round of almond paste in the middle of each square. Lift each cut corner and cross it over the almond paste to the opposite corner.

Pinwheels & Envelopes

Pinwheels: roll out the dough. Cut into 4 squares as for kites. Put almond paste in middle. Cut from the corners almost to the middle. Fold in alternate points.

Envelopes: roll out the dough, cut into 4, and fill as for pinwheels. Fold 2 opposite corners into middle. Top with an apricot half, cut side down.

WHOLE-WHEAT ENGLISH MUFFINS

 Makes about 12

4 cups (500 g) whole-wheat flour, plus extra for dusting

1 tsp sugar

1 tsp salt

1 tsp quick-rise active dry yeast

about 1 cup (250 ml) lukewarm milk

about 1 cup (125 ml) lukewarm water

sunflower or corn oil for greasing

☆ 3-in (7-cm) pastry cutter

1 Put the flour and sugar into a large bowl and stir in the salt and yeast. Make a well in the middle, pour in the milk and water all at once, and mix to a soft but not sticky dough.

2 Knead the dough until smooth and elastic, then shape it into a round. Oil a large bowl. Place the dough in the bowl, cover with oiled plastic wrap, and leave in a warm place to rise for 45–60 minutes, until doubled in size.

3 Punch down the dough, then turn out onto a lightly floured work surface and knead for 2–3 minutes, until smooth and elastic.

4 Roll out the dough to a 1/2-in (1-cm) thickness and, using the cutter, cut into 12 rounds, rolling and kneading the dough as necessary.

5 Lightly dust 2 baking sheets with flour, arrange the rounds on the sheets, and cover loosely with oiled plastic wrap. Leave in a warm place to rise for 30 minutes or until doubled in size.

6 Lightly oil a griddle or skillet, and cook the muffins over medium heat, 3 or 4 at a time, for about 7 minutes on each side, until golden and cooked through. Do not allow the griddle to get too hot or the outside of the muffins will burn before the inside is cooked.

ENGLISH MUFFINS

 Makes 20

3 cups (375 g) unbleached white flour

1/2 tsp sugar

1/2 tsp salt

1 tsp quick-rise active dry yeast

about 1 1/4 cups (300 ml) lukewarm water

about 1 cup (250 ml) lukewarm milk

sunflower oil for greasing

☆ 4 3-in (7-cm) round pastry cutters

1 Put the flour and sugar into a large bowl and stir in the salt and yeast. Make a well in the middle, pour in the water and milk, and beat to form a smooth, thick batter.

2 Cover and leave in a warm place to rise for 1 hour or until the surface is bubbling.

3 Beat the batter mixture for 2 minutes, then pour into a pitcher.

4 Lightly oil the pastry cutters and oil a griddle or skillet. Place the pastry cutters on the griddle and then leave for 1–2 minutes to heat through.

5 Pour 3/4 in (2 cm) of batter into each cutter and cook for 5–7 minutes, until the surface is dry and full of holes and the muffins are shrinking away from the sides of the cutters.

6 Lift off the rings, turn the muffins over, and cook for 1 minute, until pale golden. Transfer the muffins to a wire rack and leave to cool.

7 Repeat with the remaining batter, lightly greasing the griddle and cutters between each batch. Serve warm.

Cook's know-how

Any leftover English muffins can be frozen successfully, but make sure they are fully cooled first. They can be toasted straight from the freezer.

STICKY BUNS

 Makes 12

4 cups (500 g) unbleached white flour

1 tsp salt

4 tbsp butter

1/4-oz (7-g) envelope quick-rise active dry yeast

2 tbsp sugar

about 7/8 cup (200 ml) lukewarm milk

1 large egg, beaten

sunflower or corn oil for greasing

1/4 cup honey

FILLING

4 tbsp butter

2 tbsp packed dark brown sugar

1/3 cup (60 g) golden raisins

1/4 cup (60 g) dried currants

grated zest of 1 orange

1 tsp ground pie spice

1 Put the flour into a large bowl and stir in the salt. Rub in the butter and yeast. Stir in the sugar. Make a well in the middle, pour in the milk and egg, and mix to a soft dough.

2 Oil a large bowl. Knead the dough until smooth and elastic, then shape into a round and place in the bowl. Cover with oiled plastic wrap and leave in a warm place to rise for 1–1 1/2 hours, until doubled in size.

3 Make the filling: cream the butter with the dark brown sugar. In another bowl, combine the golden raisins, currants, orange zest, and pie spice.

4 Lightly oil an 7- x 11-in (18 x 28 cm) roasting pan. Turn out the dough onto a lightly floured work surface, and punch down with your fist. Knead for 2–3 minutes, until smooth.

5 Roll out into a 12-in (30-cm) square and dot with the butter mixture. Fold in half and roll out into a 12-in (30-cm) square. Sprinkle with the fruit mixture, then roll up.

6 Cut the roll into 12 pieces and arrange cut side up in the roasting pan. Cover with oiled plastic wrap. Leave in a warm place to rise for 30 minutes or until the pieces are touching.

7 Bake in a 425°F (220°C) oven for 20–25 minutes, until well risen, covering the buns loosely with foil after about 15 minutes to prevent them from browning too much. Transfer the buns to a wire rack.

8 Warm the honey in a small pan and brush over the buns to glaze. Pull the buns apart and serve warm.

SWEET BUNS

 Makes 18

4 cups (500 g) unbleached white flour

1/4 cup (60 g) sugar

1 tsp salt

1/4 oz (7-g) envelope quick-rise active dry yeast

about 2/3 cup (150 ml) lukewarm milk

4 tbsp butter, melted and cooled slightly

1 egg and 2 egg yolks, beaten

1 cup (150 g) golden raisins

3/4 cup (90 g) chopped mixed peel

sunflower or corn oil for greasing

TOPPING

1 egg, beaten

2 tbsp crushed sugar cubes

1 Put the flour and sugar into a large bowl and stir in the salt and yeast. Make a well in the middle and add the milk, butter, egg and egg yolks, raisins, and mixed peel. Mix to a soft dough.

2 Knead the dough until smooth and elastic. Shape into a round and place in an oiled bowl.

3 Cover with oiled plastic wrap and leave in a warm place to rise for 1–1 1/2 hours until the dough has doubled in size.

4 Turn out the dough onto a lightly floured work surface and punch down with your fist. Knead the dough for 2–3 minutes, until smooth and elastic.

5 Lightly oil 2 or 3 baking sheets. Divide the dough into 18 pieces, shape into rolls, and place on the baking sheets. Cover loosely with oiled plastic wrap and leave in a warm place to rise for about 30 minutes, until doubled in size.

6 Brush the tops of the buns with the beaten egg and sprinkle with the sugar. Bake the buns in a 375°F (190°C) oven for 15 minutes or until they are well risen and golden brown.

7 Tap the bottoms of the buns to see if they are cooked through; they should sound hollow. Leave to cool on a wire rack.

CINNAMON ROLLS

 Makes 16

8 cups (1 kg) all-purpose flour

2 cups (425 g) sugar

¹/4-oz (7-g) envelope
quick-rise active dry yeast

1 tsp salt

about 1¹/2 cups (350 ml)
lukewarm milk

2 eggs, lightly beaten

2 tbsp butter, melted

1¹/2 cups (250 g) raisins

3 tbsp ground cinnamon

sunflower or corn oil for greasing

milk for glazing

GLAZE

1³/4 cups (200 g) confectioners'
sugar

¹/4 cup water

1 tsp vanilla extract

1 Sift the flour and 1²/3 cups (375 g) of the sugar into a bowl and stir in the yeast and salt. Make a well, pour in the milk, eggs, and butter, and stir to make a dough.

2 Knead the dough until smooth and elastic. Knead in the raisins and 1 tbsp of the cinnamon.

3 Divide the dough into 16 even-sized pieces. Shape each piece into an 8- to 10-in (20- to 25-cm) strand, then flatten.

4 Combine the remaining sugar and cinnamon, sprinkle the mixture over the strips of dough, then roll up tightly into spirals.

5 Lightly oil 2 baking sheets. Arrange the rolls on the trays, cover loosely with oiled plastic wrap, and leave in a warm place to rise for about 1 hour, until doubled in size.

6 Brush the rolls with milk to glaze, then bake them in a 375°F (190°C) oven for 30–40 minutes, until lightly browned. Transfer the rolls to a wire rack.

7 Meanwhile, make the glaze: in a small bowl, combine the confectioners' sugar, measured water, and vanilla extract. As soon as the cinnamon rolls come out of the oven, brush them with the glaze. Serve the rolls warm or cold.

HOT CROSS BUNS

 Makes 12

4 cups (500 g) unbleached
white flour

¹/4 cup (60 g) sugar

¹/4-oz (7-g) envelope
quick-rise active dry yeast

1 tsp salt

1 tsp ground pie spice

1 tsp ground cinnamon

¹/2 tsp grated nutmeg

4 tbsp butter, melted and cooled
slightly

²/3 cup (150 ml) lukewarm milk

5 tbsp (75 ml) lukewarm water

1 egg, beaten

¹/3 cup (90 g) raisins

¹/2 cup (60 g) chopped mixed
peel

sunflower or corn oil for greasing

2 oz (60 g) short crust pastry

GLAZE

2 tbsp sugar

2 tbsp water

1 Sift the flour into a large bowl and stir in the sugar, yeast, salt, pie spice, cinnamon, and nutmeg. Make a well in the middle and pour in the butter, milk, water, egg, raisins, and mixed peel. Mix to a soft dough.

2 Knead the dough on a floured work surface until smooth and elastic, then shape into a round.

3 Put into an oiled bowl, cover with oiled plastic wrap, and leave in a warm place to rise for 1–1¹/2 hours, until doubled in size.

4 Punch down the dough with your fist, then turn out onto a lightly floured work surface and knead for 2–3 minutes, until smooth and elastic. Divide the dough into 12 pieces and shape into round rolls.

5 Roll out the short crust pastry to ¹/4-in (5-mm) thickness, cut it into 24 narrow strips, and press 2 strips in the form of a cross on the top of each bun. Secure with a little water.

6 Lightly oil 2 baking sheets, arrange the buns on the sheets, and cover with oiled plastic wrap. Leave in a warm place to rise for 30 minutes or until they have doubled in size.

7 Bake the buns in a 425°F (220°C) oven for 15 minutes or until well risen and browned. Transfer to a wire rack.

8 Meanwhile, make the glaze: put the sugar and water into a pan and heat gently, stirring, until the sugar has dissolved. As soon as the buns come out of the oven, brush them with the glaze. Serve warm or cold.

11

PIES, TARTS, & HOT DESSERTS

Cherries Jubilee

Red cherries simmered in sugar and flavored with almond extract, then flambéed in brandy. Served with ice cream.

SERVES 4 162 calories per serving

Takes 20 minutes **PAGE 399**

French apricot pancakes

Small golden pancakes, baked, then folded over a filling of apricot jam, and sprinkled with sugar.

SERVES 4 378 calories per serving

Takes 35 minutes **PAGE 400**

FAMILY CHOICE

Saucy chocolate cake

Irresistible light chocolate cake flavored with cocoa and vanilla extract, and baked in a chocolate sauce.

SERVES 4 361 calories per serving

Takes 45 minutes **PAGE 404**

Warm Jamaican bananas

Banana halves coated in a rich caramel and cinnamon sauce and flambéed in rum. Served with vanilla ice cream.

SERVES 4 269 calories per serving

Takes 15 minutes **PAGE 398**

TRADITIONAL

Baked apples

Cooking apples filled with sugar and butter, then baked until soft and served hot with their juices spooned over.

SERVES 6 235 calories per serving

Takes 55 minutes **PAGE 397**

Apple brown Betty

Layers of spiced apple slices and buttered bread crumbs sprinkled with sugar, then baked until golden brown.

SERVES 4–6 426–284 calories per serving

Takes 55 minutes **PAGE 397**

Fruit fritters

Bite-sized pieces of apple and banana coated in batter and deep-fried until golden. Sprinkled with sugar and cinnamon.

SERVES 4 541 calories per serving

Takes 25 minutes **PAGE 399**

FRENCH CLASSIC

Crepes Suzette

Delicious crêpes coated with a sweet orange sauce. Flambéed in brandy and orange liqueur and served hot.

SERVES 4 604 calories per serving

Takes 55 minutes **PAGE 400**

Plum crumble

Sweet and crunchy: juicy plums sprinkled with sugar and cinnamon and baked beneath a golden brown topping.

SERVES 6 436 calories per serving

Takes 50 minutes **PAGE 398**

MAGIC LEMON PUDDING CAKE
Fresh and tangy: a light lemony mixture separates during cooking into a cake on top and a delicious lemon sauce underneath.
SERVES 4 295 calories per serving
Takes 1 hour 5 minutes **PAGE 401**

APPLE BREAD PUDDING
Slices of buttered bread covered with an apple and apricot jam mixture and topped with a layer of bread triangles.
SERVES 4–6 642–428 calories per serving
Takes 1 hour 5 minutes **PAGE 396**

DINNER PARTY

NAPOLEON
Melt-in-the-mouth puff pastry layered with whipped cream, jam, and pastry cream, and topped with icing.
SERVES 6 486 calories per serving
Takes 45 minutes, plus chilling **PAGE 422**

FLORIDA CLASSIC

KEY LIME PIE
Creamy, lime-flavored filling is baked in a pastry shell, then covered with whipped cream and decorated with lime slices.
SERVES 8 489 calories per serving
Takes 60 minutes, plus chilling **PAGE 418**

PINEAPPLE UPSIDE-DOWN CAKE
Pineapple rings and chopped apricots beneath a light and springy cake topping, turned out and served upside down.
SERVES 4–6 749–499 calories per serving
Takes 1 hour 5 minutes **PAGE 401**

SPECIAL SPONGE CAKE
Warming and filling: sweetened sliced cooking apples and lemon zest and juice are topped with a golden cake.
SERVES 6 414 calories per serving
Takes 1 hour 5 minutes **PAGE 396**

BANANA CREAM PIE
Rich and creamy: crushed cookie base with a caramel filling, topped with banana slices, whipped cream, and grated chocolate.
SERVES 6 1210–901 calories per serving
Takes 20 minutes, plus chilling **PAGE 418**

AUSTRIAN CLASSIC

APPLE STRUDEL
Sheets of phyllo pastry enclosing apples, lemon zest and juice, sugar, spices, and golden raisins, and sprinkled with almonds.
SERVES 8 278 calories per serving
Takes 1¼ hours **PAGE 411**

FRUITY CREAM PIE
Granola pastry shell filled with layers of creamy custard and fresh fruit and covered with whipped cream.
SERVES 6–8 787–590 calories per serving
Takes 60 minutes, plus chilling **PAGE 419**

OVER 60 MINUTES

QUEEN OF PUDDINGS

Old-fashioned English favorite: creamy custard is flavored with orange zest, spread with melted jam, and topped with meringue.

SERVES 6 386 calories per serving

Takes 60 minutes, plus standing **PAGE 405**

VERY CHOCOLATY

MISSISSIPPI MUD PIE

Popular dessert: pastry shell with a sweetened chocolate and coffee filling, decorated with whipped cream.

SERVES 8–10 692–553 calories per serving

Takes 1¼ hours, plus chilling **PAGE 419**

TREACLE TART

Rich and sweet: pastry shell filled with dark corn syrup, bread crumbs, and lemon zest and juice. Served warm.

SERVES 8 386 calories per serving

Takes 60 minutes, plus chilling **PAGE 414**

FAMILY CHOICE

STICKY DATE & WALNUT PUDDING

Rich pudding flavored with coffee extract, dates, and walnuts and served with a deliciously sticky toffee sauce.

SERVES 8 690 calories per serving

Takes 1 hour 5 minutes **PAGE 404**

HOT CHOCOLATE SOUFFLES

Light and airy: individual soufflés made from dark chocolate, baked until puffy, then dusted with confectioners' sugar.

SERVES 4 494 calories per serving

Takes 1¼ hours **PAGE 405**

GREEK CLASSIC

BAKLAVA

Traditional Greek pastry: layers of buttered phyllo pastry and walnuts soaked in honey and lemon juice and cut into squares.

MAKES 20 SQUARES 249 calories per serving

Takes 60 minutes, plus cooling **PAGE 422**

BAKED APPLE DUMPLINGS

Cooking apples filled with sugar and cinnamon, enclosed in decorative pastry case, and baked until golden.

SERVES 4 781 calories per serving

Takes 60 minutes, plus chilling **PAGE 409**

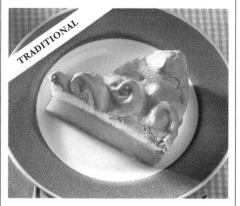

TRADITIONAL

LEMON MERINGUE PIE

Deliciously sweet: golden brown pastry with tangy lemon filling, topped with light and fluffy meringue.

SERVES 8–10 537–430 calories per serving

Takes 1¼ hours, plus chilling **PAGE 417**

APPLE PIE

Family favorite: light and golden puff pastry encases tender apple slices in this traditional apple pie.

SERVES 6 432 calories per serving

Takes 60 minutes, plus cooling **PAGE 410**

ALMOND TART

A favorite dessert: pastry shell spread with jam, topped with almond-flavored cake and a pastry lattice.

SERVES 6 560 calories per serving

Takes 1¼ hours, plus chilling   **PAGE 415**

BREAD & BUTTER PUDDING

Slices of white bread thickly spread with butter, layered with dried fruit, lemon zest, and sugar, and baked in a custard.

SERVES 6 516 calories per serving

Takes 60 minutes, plus standing   **PAGE 406**

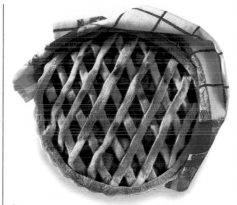

STRAWBERRY & RHUBARB PIE

Sweet strawberries and rhubarb are lightly spiced, then baked in a pastry shell with a lattice topping.

SERVES 6–8 371–278 calories per serving

Takes 1¼ hours, plus chilling   **PAGE 409**

FRENCH APRICOT & ALMOND TART

French classic: apricots in lemon juice on a bed of pastry cream in a pastry shell. Glazed with brandy and slivered almonds.

SERVES 10 398 calories per serving

Takes 45 minutes, plus chilling   **PAGE 416**

TARTE AU CITRON

Light and tangy: pastry shell with a cream and lemon filling, baked until set and lightly dusted with confectioners' sugar.

SERVES 10–12 572–476 calories per serving

Takes 1¼ hours, plus chilling   **PAGE 417**

RICE PUDDING

Rich and creamy: short-grain rice, milk, sugar, and lemon zest mixed together, then sprinkled with freshly grated nutmeg and

SERVES 4 210 calories per serving

Takes 2¾ hours, plus standing

dotted with small bits of butter. Baked slowly in the oven until the top turns golden brown.

PAGE 406

⏱ OVER 60 MINUTES

PECAN PIE

A twist on a traditional dessert: The buttery rich pecan kernels are toasted, mixed with lightly spiced corn syrup, and deliciously flavored with brandy and vanilla extract, then baked in a golden pastry shell.

SERVES 6–8 611–458 calories per serving

Takes 1¼ hours, plus chilling **PAGE 415**

FRENCH APPLE TART

Apple chunks, jam, sugar, and lemon zest, pureed and spooned into a pastry shell, and topped with apple slices and jam glaze.

SERVES 8–10 593–474 calories per serving

Takes 2 hours, plus chilling **PAGE 414**

STEAMED SYRUP PUDDING

Wonderfully sweet and sticky: a simple, traditional steamed pudding, deliciously sweetened with maple syrup.

SERVES 4–6 619–413 calories per serving

Takes 3¼ hours **PAGE 408**

TARTE TATIN

Rich and fruity: crisp pastry baked over caramel and apple slices, then turned out with the glazed apples on top.

SERVES 6 511 calories per serving

Takes 60 minutes, plus chilling **PAGE 411**

MINCEMEAT & ALMOND TART

A pastry shell filled with mincemeat and topped with a light, creamy almond mixture, then baked until golden.

SERVES 8–10 856–685 calories per serving

Takes 60 minutes, plus chilling **PAGE 408**

STEAMED JAM PUDDING

Traditional pudding: a temptingly light cake mixture is steamed over rich plum jam. A dessert-time classic.

SERVES 4–6 573–382 calories per serving

Takes 1¾ hours **PAGE 407**

CHRISTMAS PUDDING

Rich, dark and fruity traditional Christmas pudding: dried fruits are combined with nuts, and lemon zest and juice. Grated carrots ensure that the pudding stays deliciously moist. Once steamed, the pudding is liberally laced with rum.

SERVES 8–10 522–418 calories per serving

Takes 6¼ hours, plus storing **PAGE 407**

PIES, TARTS, & HOT DESSERTS KNOW-HOW

DESSERTS MAY NO longer be a feature of every family meal, but few people can say that they don't enjoy something sweet from time to time, especially to round off a special meal. From warming puddings to golden pastries filled with fresh fruit, there's a mouthwatering dessert for every season and occasion. Since a pie or tart made at home tastes so much better than a commercially made version, it's worth learning the art of pastry making – you'll find it surprisingly simple once you understand the basic principles.

TYPES OF PASTRY

*All pastries are based on a mixture of flour, fat, and a liquid to bind them.
All-purpose flour is usually used, although whole-wheat or a mixture of the
two gives a "nuttier" pastry. The liquid used for binding may be water, milk, or
egg; the fat may be butter, margarine, lard, shortening, or a combination.*

Short crust pastry
A blend of 2 parts flour, 1 part fat, and usually water, short crust pastry (page 394) is used for sweet and savory pies and tarts.

Pâte sucrée
Bound with egg yolks, pâte sucrée (page 394) is richer than short crust pastry and is used for sweet tarts and tartlets. The classic method for mixing the dough is on a flat marble work surface.

Puff pastry
A light, flaky pastry made by rolling and folding the dough, each time making more layers of dough and butter. Store-bought fresh or frozen pastry is very convenient, but is usually not made with butter. Puff pastry is often used as a top crust for sweet and savory pies, to wrap beef Wellington, and to make napoleons.

Flaky pastry
This is a shortcut version of puff pastry. The rolling and folding are repeated only a few times. It is used for pies and tarts.

Rough puff pastry
Like puff and flaky pastry, this is rolled and folded, but all the butter is added at once, in large cubes (page 394). Rough puff pastry can be used as flaky pastry and for dishes normally made with puff pastry.

Phyllo & strudel pastry
These are similar types of pastry made from a pliable dough that is stretched and rolled until extremely thin. It is then rolled around a filling or layered with melted butter. Phyllo and strudel pastries are difficult to make at home, but store-bought versions are available fresh and frozen. Common uses include strudel and baklava.

MICROWAVING

The microwave can be a helpful tool when preparing pies, tarts, and hot desserts. When it comes to baking pastry-based pies and tarts, however, there really is no substitute for the conventional oven.

The microwave is perfect for cooking fruit fillings for pies and tarts. The fruit remains plump and colorful. It can also be used to melt or soften butter and to heat liquids in which fruit is left to soak. Under careful watch, the microwave can be used to melt chocolate and make caramel.

FREEZING

Many desserts freeze well, particularly baked cakelike steamed puddings (before or after cooking), bread pudding (before cooking), crisps (before or after cooking), and crêpes.

Custard-based and milk puddings are not as successful because they tend to separate. Raw pastry can be frozen for up to 3 months, and baked pastries will keep for up to 6 months. Pastries baked before freezing will not be as crisp as those frozen unbaked. Thaw in wrappings at room temperature.

MAKING A PASTRY SHELL

Careful handling of pastry should ensure it doesn't shrink or distort when baking.

1 Put the pastry on a floured work surface and flour the rolling pin. Roll out from the middle outward, giving the pastry a quarter turn occasionally.

2 If lining a tart pan, roll the pastry to a round 2 in (5 cm) larger than the top of the dish. Roll it loosely around the rolling pin and unroll over the dish. A pastry lid should also be 2 in (5 cm) larger.

3 Gently ease the pastry into the tart pan, pressing it firmly but neatly into the bottom edge of the dish, being very careful not to overstretch the pastry. Carefully trim the excess pastry with a table knife.

ROUGH PUFF PASTRY

Ideal for both sweet and savory pies. These quantities make enough pastry for a 10-in (25-cm) double-crust pie.

1 Sift *2 cups (250 g) all-purpose flour* into a bowl. Add *6 tbsp (90 g) each of cubed butter and shortening*, then stir to coat in flour. Add *2/3 cup (150 ml) cold water* and *a squeeze of lemon juice*, and with a table knife bind to a dough.

2 Roll the dough into a rectangle 3 times as long as it is wide. Fold the bottom third up and the top third down. Press the edges with the side of your hand to seal. Wrap the dough and chill in the refrigerator for 15 minutes.

3 With the unfolded edges at top and bottom, roll the dough into a rectangle and fold as before. Turn the dough and repeat rolling, folding, and turning, twice more. Wrap the dough and chill in the refrigerator for 30 minutes.

PATE SUCREE

Traditionally made on a marble surface. These quantities make enough pastry to line a 10-in (25-cm) tart pan.

1 Sift *1 3/4 cups (200 g) all-purpose flour* and *a pinch of salt, if preferred*, onto a work surface. Make a well in the middle and add *6 tbsp (90 g) softened butter, 1/4 cup (60 g) sugar*, and *3 egg yolks*. With your fingertips, blend the butter, sugar, and egg yolks.

2 Using your fingertips, gradually work the sifted flour into the butter mixture until the mixture resembles coarse crumbs; if the butter mixture seems too sticky, work in a little more flour.

3 With your fingers or a pastry scraper, gather the dough into a ball, then knead until it is smooth and pliable. Shape the kneaded dough into a ball again, wrap, and chill in the refrigerator for 30 minutes or until just firm.

SHORT CRUST PASTRY

This basic recipe may be flavored or sweetened as preferred. For best results, the fat should be well chilled. Handle the dough as little as possible or the pastry will become tough. These quantities make enough pastry to line a 9- to 10-in (23- to 25-cm) tart pan.

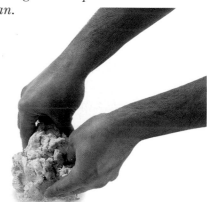

1 Sift *1 1/2 cups (175 g) all-purpose flour* and *a pinch of salt, if preferred*, into a bowl. Cut *6 tbsp (90 g) chilled butter, margarine, or other fat* into small pieces and add to the bowl. Stir to coat in the flour.

2 Using your fingertips, quickly and lightly rub the fat into the flour, lifting the mixture to incorporate air, until the mixture resembles fine bread crumbs. Sprinkle *about 2 tbsp cold water* over the mixture. Stir gently with a table knife to mix. If the mixture seems too dry, add a little more liquid.

3 Gather the mixture together and knead very briefly until smooth. If the dough feels at all sticky, add a little more flour. Shape into a ball, wrap, and chill for 30 minutes.

PREBAKING PASTRY

A pastry shell may be partly baked before adding a filling to help it stay crisp, or it may be fully baked if the filling itself does not need to be cooked. The shell is filled with pie weights to hold the pastry down.

1 Prick the pastry shell all over with a fork. Press a piece of foil or waxed paper into the pastry shell, smoothing it over the bottom and up the side of the shell.

2 Fill the shell with ceramic pie weights, dried beans, or uncooked rice and bake in a 400°F (200°C) oven for 10–15 minutes or until browning at the edges.

3 Remove the weights and foil and bake for 5 minutes for a partly baked shell or 15 minutes for a fully baked shell. If the pastry rises during baking, gently press it down with your hand.

STEAMED PUDDINGS

Light cakelike puddings and rich suet mixtures can both be gently cooked by steaming. Be sure to make the seal tight so that steam can't get in. It's important to keep the water in the saucepan replenished, so boil some water and keep it ready to add when needed.

1 Turn the mixture into a greased heatproof basin. Take a piece of buttered waxed paper, lay a piece of foil on top, and make a pleat across the middle, to allow for expansion.

3 Lower the basin into a saucepan containing enough simmering water to come halfway up the side of the basin. Cover tightly and steam for the required time. Make sure that the water stays at the simmering point and replenish with more boiling water when necessary.

2 Lay the paper and foil over the top of the basin. Secure by tying string under the rim of the basin. Form a handle with another piece of string. Trim away excess paper and foil.

DECORATIVE EDGES

Many decorative finishes can be given to the edge of a pastry lid. The simplest is to press all around the edge at regular intervals with the floured prongs of a fork. Alternatively, crimp the pastry with your fingers: place the thumb and forefinger of one hand just inside the edge of the pastry. With the forefinger of your other hand, push outward, and pinch the pastry between finger and thumb to make a rounded V shape. Repeat this action all around the pastry lid.

Decorating pies & tarts

A pastry lid can be given an attractive sheen by being brushed with a glaze before baking. A beaten egg or an egg yolk lightly mixed with 1 tsp water will give a golden finish. Milk or cream will give a shine. Brush with water, then sprinkle with sugar for a crisp, sweet glaze.

♦

Keep pastry trimmings to make small decorative shapes. Cut them freehand or use pastry cutters. They can be put on the edge of a pastry shell or arranged on a lid. If the pastry has a glaze, use it to attach the shapes or brush them with a little water.

APPLE BREAD PUDDING

 Serves 4–6

2 lb (1 kg) cooking apples, peeled, cored, and sliced

¹/₂ cup (125 g) sugar

3 tbsp water

2 tbsp apricot jam

¹/₂ cup (125 g) butter, softened, plus extra for greasing

12 medium slices of bread, crusts removed

✳ 6-in (15-cm) square cake pan

1 Put the apples into a large saucepan with the sugar and measured water. Cook gently until soft, then beat well with a wooden spoon until smooth. Add the apricot jam and heat gently to melt the jam, stirring occasionally to combine with the apples.

2 Spread the butter on one side of each slice of bread. Lightly butter the cake pan and assemble the pudding (see box, right).

3 Bake in a 400°F (200°C) oven for about 40 minutes until crisp and golden. Serve hot.

Assembling the pudding

Use 8 of the bread slices to line the pan, cutting them into strips or squares as necessary and placing them buttered side down. Spoon in the apple mixture.

Cut the remaining slices into quarters diagonally. Arrange the quarters on top of the apple mixture, buttered side up.

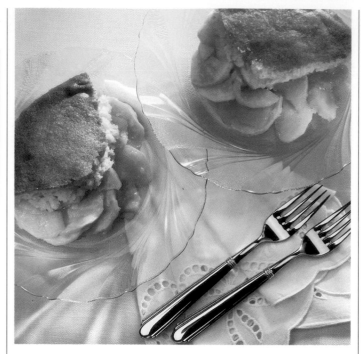

SPECIAL SPONGE CAKE

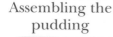 **Serves 6**

butter for greasing

2–3 cooking apples, peeled, cored, and sliced

³/₈ cup (90 g) light brown granulated sugar

grated zest and juice of 1 lemon

SPONGE CAKE TOPPING

¹/₂ cup (125 g) soft margarine

¹/₂ cup (125 g) sugar

2 eggs, beaten

1 cup (125 g) self-rising flour

1 tsp baking powder

✳ 5-cup (1.25 liter) ovenproof dish

1 Lightly butter the ovenproof dish and arrange the apples in the bottom. Sprinkle on the light brown sugar and the lemon zest and juice.

2 Make the sponge topping: put the margarine, sugar, eggs, flour, and baking powder into a large bowl and beat until smooth and well blended. Spoon the mixture on top of the apple slices and level the surface.

3 Bake in a 350°F (180°C) oven for about 45 minutes, until the sponge-cake topping is well risen, golden, and springy to the touch. Serve hot.

SPICED SPONGE CAKE

Add 1 tsp ground cinnamon to the sponge topping, and ¹/₃ cup (60g) raisins, 1 tsp ground cinnamon, and 1 tsp ground pie spice to the apple mixture. Proceed as directed.

Cook's know-how

Double the sponge-cake ingredients and use half to make a sponge cake or add some dried fruit and make buns to bake at the same time as this dessert. There will be enough cake mixture to make 2 7-in (18-cm) sponge cakes or about 18 fruit buns.

APPLE BROWN BETTY

Easy to prepare from ingredients often on hand, this dessert is deliciously satisfying and can be made with fruits other than apples if you prefer. Serve it with vanilla ice cream, vanilla frozen yogurt, or whipped cream.

 Serves 4–6

2–3 tbsp butter

3 cups (175 g) fresh bread crumbs

5–6 cooking apples, peeled, cored, and thinly sliced

1/2 cup (125 g) sugar, plus extra for sprinkling

1 tbsp lemon juice

1–2 tsp ground cinnamon

pinch of grated nutmeg

✿ deep 2-quart (1.5–2 liter) ovenproof dish

1 Melt the butter in a skillet. Add the bread crumbs and stir over medium heat for 5 minutes or until the crumbs are crisp and golden. Remove from the heat.

2 Toss the apples with the sugar, lemon juice, ground cinnamon, and grated nutmeg.

3 Press one-quarter of the crisp bread crumbs over the bottom of the dish. Spread half of the apple mixture over the bread crumbs and sprinkle another quarter of the bread crumbs over the top.

4 Arrange the remaining apple mixture on top of the bread crumbs, spoon over any juices, and cover with the remaining bread crumbs. Sprinkle the top of the dessert lightly with sugar.

5 Cover the dish with foil. Bake in a 400°F (200°C) oven for about 20 minutes.

6 Remove the foil and continue baking for 20 minutes longer or until the apples are tender and the top is golden brown. Serve warm.

APPLE & CRANBERRY BROWN BETTY

Add 1 1/2 cups (175 g) fresh or thawed frozen cranberries to the apple mixture. Add a little more sugar if necessary.

PEACH MELBA BROWN BETTY

Substitute 3 peeled and sliced peaches and 1 cup (250 g) raspberries for the apples. Omit the lemon juice, cinnamon, and nutmeg.

Cook's know-how

White or brown bread can be used for the bread crumbs. Whole-wheat gives a nutty flavor and whole-grain gives an interesting texture. For best results, the bread should be 2 days old.

BAKED APPLES

 Serves 6

6 cooking apples

1/2 cup (90 g) dark brown sugar

6 tbsp (90 g) butter, diced

3 tbsp water

1 Wipe the apples, and remove the cores using an apple corer. Make a shallow cut through the skin around the middle of each apple.

2 Put the apples into an ovenproof dish and fill the centers with the sugar and butter. Pour the water around the apples.

3 Bake in a 375°F (190°C) oven for 40–45 minutes, until the apples are soft. Serve hot, spooning all the juices from the dish over the apples.

CITRUS BAKED APPLES

Add the grated zest of 1 orange or 1 lemon to the brown sugar, and proceed as directed.

BAKED APPLES WITH MINCEMEAT

Use 1/2 cup (125 g) mincemeat instead of the sugar and butter, and proceed as directed.

PLUM CRUMBLE

Serves 6

2 lb (1 kg) prune plums,
halved and pitted

60 g dark brown sugar

1 tsp ground cinnamon

CRUMBLE TOPPING

2 cups (250 g) whole-wheat
flour

1 tsp baking powder

6 tbsp (90 g) butter

3/4 cup (150 g) dark brown
sugar

1 Put the plums into a
shallow ovenproof dish
and sprinkle with the sugar
and cinnamon.

2 Make the topping: put
the flour and baking
powder into a bowl and rub
in the butter with the
fingertips until the mixture
resembles fine bread
crumbs. Stir in the sugar.

3 Sprinkle the topping
evenly over the plums,
without pressing it down,
and bake in a 350°F (180°C)
oven for 30–40 minutes,
until golden. Serve hot.

CRUNCHY APPLE CRUMBLE

*Substitute 5–6 peeled, cored,
and sliced cooking apples for the
plums. Put into a saucepan
with the sugar and ground
cinnamon and 2 tbsp water.
Cook gently until the apples are
soft. Substitute oatmeal or
granola for half of the flour in
the crumble topping and proceed
as directed in the recipe.*

RHUBARB & GINGER CRUMBLE

*Substitute 2 lb (1 kg) rhubarb,
cut into 1-in (2.5-cm) pieces,
for the plums. Put into a
saucepan with the sugar, 2 tbsp
water, and 1 tsp ground ginger
instead of the cinnamon, and
cook gently until soft. Spoon
into the dish and proceed as
directed in the recipe.*

WARM JAMAICAN BANANAS

Serves 4

2–3 tbsp unsalted butter

2–3 tbsp packed dark brown
sugar

1/2 tsp ground cinnamon

4 firm but ripe bananas, cut in
half lengthwise

1/4 cup (60 ml) dark rum

vanilla ice cream to serve

1 Put the butter and sugar
into a large heavy skillet,
and heat gently until the
butter has melted and sugar
dissolved. Stir to blend
together, then cook, stirring
gently, for about 5 minutes.

2 Stir the cinnamon into
the caramel mixture, then
add the banana halves. Cook
for 3 minutes on each side,
to warm through. Remove
the skillet from the heat.

3 Gently warm the rum in
a saucepan, pour over
the banana halves, then light
it with a match.

4 When the flames have
died down, transfer the
bananas and hot sauce to
serving plates. Serve
immediately, with scoops of
vanilla ice cream.

Cook's know-how

*Great care must be taken when
flambéing food with alcohol.
Never pour the alcohol directly
from the bottle into a hot pan
because it may ignite and
flames can quickly lick back
up the bottle to your hand.
Use only a small amount of
alcohol, and warm it very
gently, removing it from the
heat before setting it alight.
Don't lean over the pan,
and keep young children
and pets well away from the
stove. Flames can leap
extremely high, so don't
attempt to do any flambéing
if you have a low hood or
cabinets over the top
of the stove.*

CHERRIES JUBILEE

 Serves 4

14 oz (425 g) canned red
cherries in syrup

2–3 tbsp sugar

few drops of almond extract

5 tbsp (75 ml) brandy

vanilla ice cream to serve

1 Drain the cherries,
reserving ½ cup (125 ml)
of the syrup. Put the cherries
into a saucepan with the
syrup and sugar. Heat gently,
stirring, until the sugar
dissolves, then bring to a
boil. Simmer for about
5 minutes, until the liquid
has thickened and reduced
by about half. Stir in the
almond extract.

2 Pour half of the brandy
over the cherries. Pour
the remainder of the brandy
into a small saucepan and
warm gently. Remove the
cherries from the heat, pour
the brandy over them, and
carefully light with a match.

3 When the flames have
died down, spoon the hot
cherries and syrup over
servings of vanilla ice cream,
and serve immediately.

FRESH CHERRIES JUBILEE

*Replace the canned cherries with
1 lb (500 g) fresh cherries. Pit
the cherries and poach them in
1 cup (250 ml) red wine and
a scant ½ cup (100 g) sugar
until tender. Substitute the
poaching liquid for the syrup,
and proceed as directed.*

Cherries

*These are classified as sweet or
sour. Morello cherries, which are
used to make jam or syrup, are a
sour variety. If you use fresh
cherries, make sure you choose
sweet dark ones.*

FRUIT FRITTERS

 Serves 4

2 apples, peeled and cored

3 bananas

juice of ½ lemon

sunflower oil for deep frying

¼ cup (60 g) sugar

1 tsp ground cinnamon

BATTER

1 cup (125 g) all-purpose flour

1 tbsp confectioners' sugar

1 egg, separated

⅔ cup (150 ml) mixed milk
and water

1 Cut the apples and
bananas into bite-sized
pieces. Toss the pieces in the
lemon juice to prevent
discoloration.

2 Make the batter: sift the
flour and confectioners'
sugar into a bowl and make
a well in the middle. Add
the egg yolk and a little of
the milk mixture and whisk
together. Whisk in half of
the remaining milk mixture,
drawing in the flour to form
a smooth batter. Add the
remaining milk mixture.

3 Beat the egg white until
stiff but not dry. Fold
into the batter.

4 Heat the oil in a deep-fat
fryer to 375°F (190°C).
Pat the fruit dry. Dip each
piece of fruit into the batter,
lower into the hot oil, and
cook in batches for 3–4
minutes, until golden and
crisp. Drain on paper towels
and keep warm while
cooking the remainder.

5 Combine the sugar and
cinnamon, sprinkle
generously over the fritters,
and serve immediately.

Cook's know-how

*For a light, crisp batter, the egg
white should be whisked and
folded in just before you are
ready to cook the fritters – don't
leave the batter to stand, or it
will lose its airy texture.*

FRENCH APRICOT PANCAKES

 Serves 4

4 tbsp butter, softened, plus
  extra for greasing

1/4 cup (60 g) sugar

2 eggs, beaten

1/2 cup (60 g) self-rising flour

1 1/4 cups (300 ml) milk

apricot jam and sugar
  to serve

★ 8-hole muffin pan with
  3-in (7-cm) cups or
  8 small soufflé dishes

1 Combine the butter and
sugar in a bowl and cream
together until soft. Beat in
the eggs, a little at a time,
then fold in the flour.

2 In a small saucepan, heat
the milk to just below the
boiling point. Stir into the
creamed mixture.

3 Lightly butter the muffin
pan cups, and divide the
batter equally among them.
Bake in a 375°F (190°C)
oven for about 20 minutes,
until the pancakes are well
risen and golden brown.

4 Slide the pancakes out
of the cups, and serve
with apricot jam and sugar.
To eat, place a little jam in
the middle of each pancake,
fold in half, and sprinkle
with sugar.

CREPES SUZETTE

 Serves 4

juice of 2 oranges

1/2 cup (125 g) unsalted butter

1/4 cup (60 g) sugar

1 tbsp orange liqueur

3 tbsp brandy

CREPES

1 cup (125 g) all-purpose flour

pinch of salt

1 egg

1 tbsp oil, plus extra for frying

1 1/4 cups (300 ml) milk

★ 7-in (18-cm) skillet

1 Make the crêpes: sift the
flour and salt into a bowl.
Make a well in the middle.
Mix together the egg, oil,
and milk and pour into well.
Gradually beat in the flour
to make a fairly thin batter.

2 Heat a little oil in the
skillet, then wipe away
the excess oil. Add about
2 tbsp batter to the pan,
tilting it to coat the skillet
evenly. Cook for about
1 minute, then turn over and
cook the other side for about
1 minute. Turn out onto a
warmed plate.

3 Repeat to make 7 more
crêpes. Stack the crêpes
with waxed paper between
the crêpes to prevent them
from sticking together.

4 Make the orange sauce
and add and fold the
crêpes (see box, below).
Heat to warm through.

5 Gently warm the liqueur
and brandy in a pan.
Remove from heat, set alight,
and pour over the crêpes.
When the flames have died
down, transfer to hot serving
dishes, and serve immediately.

Making the sauce and adding and folding the crêpes

Put the orange juice,
butter, and sugar into a
large skillet, and simmer
for 5 minutes.

Place 1 crêpe in the pan,
coat with sauce, fold in
half, then in half again.
Move to one side of pan.

Add another crêpe. Coat
with the sauce, and fold as
before. Repeat with the
remaining crêpes.

MAGIC LEMON PUDDING CAKE

 Serves 4

4 tbsp butter, softened, plus extra for greasing

grated zest and juice of 1 large lemon

³/₈ cup (90 g) sugar

2 eggs, separated

¹/₄ cup (30 g) all-purpose flour

³/₄ cup (175 ml) milk

lemon twists to decorate

★ 2 ¹/₂-cup (600-ml) shallow ovenproof dish

1 Put the butter, lemon zest, and sugar into a bowl and beat together until pale and fluffy.

2 Add the egg yolks, flour, and lemon juice and stir to combine. Gradually stir in the milk.

3 Beat the egg whites until stiff but not dry. Gradually fold into the lemon mixture.

4 Lightly butter the ovenproof dish. Pour the lemon mixture into the dish and put the dish into a roasting pan. Add enough hot water to the roasting pan to come almost to the rim of the dish. Bake in a 325°F (160°C) oven for 40 minutes or until the cake is springy to the touch. Serve immediately, decorated with lemon twists.

Cook's know-how

This "magic" pudding cake separates during cooking to form a sponge-cake topping with a tangy lemon sauce beneath.

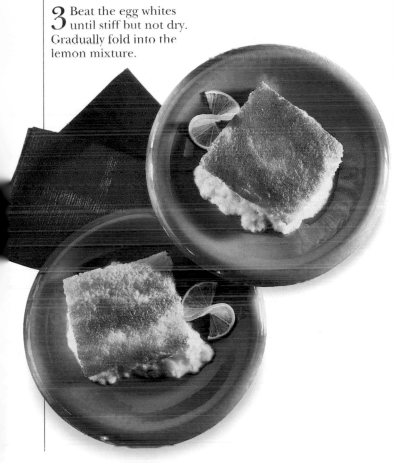

PINEAPPLE UPSIDE-DOWN CAKE

 Serves 4–6

4 tbsp butter, softened, plus extra for greasing

¹/₃ cup (60 g) sugar

7¹/₂ oz (225 g) canned pineapple rings in natural juice, drained, and juice reserved

4 dried apricots, coarsely chopped

CAKE

¹/₂ cup (125 g) butter, softened

¹/₂ cup (125 g) sugar

2 eggs, beaten

1¹/₂ cups (175 g) self rising flour

1 tsp baking powder

★ 7-in (18-cm) round cake pan

1 Lightly butter the pan and line the bottom with baking parchment. Cream together the butter and sugar and spread evenly over the baking parchment.

2 Arrange the pineapple rings on top of the butter and sugar mixture and sprinkle the chopped dried apricots between the pineapple rings.

3 Make the cake: put the butter, sugar, eggs, flour, and baking powder into a bowl with 2 tbsp of the reserved pineapple juice. Beat for 2 minutes or until smooth and well blended. Spoon the mixture on top of the pineapple rings and level the surface.

4 Bake in a 350°F (180°C) oven for about 45 minutes until the cake is well risen and springy to the touch. Carefully invert the cake onto a warmed serving plate and serve immediately.

APRICOT UPSIDE-DOWN CAKE

Substitute 13 oz (400 g) canned apricot halves for the pineapple and 2 tbsp chopped fresh ginger for the dried apricots and proceed as directed.

CHOCOLATE FONDUE

We're all familiar with savory fondues, but why not try a sweet one to finish a meal? Chocolate fondue is a rare treat that encourages conversation and conviviality. Choose a good selection of accompaniments and let everyone gather around to dip them into the luscious warm chocolate sauce.

 Serves 6

8-oz (250-g) package croissant dough

beaten egg for glazing

²/3 cup (60 g) sweetened flaked coconut

¹/2 cup (60 g) strawberries

2 oz (60 g) cape gooseberries (physalis) (optional)

1 star fruit

1 fresh fig

²/3 cup (125 g) cherries

¹/2 cup (60 g) blackberries

squares of plain cake

CHOCOLATE SAUCE

7 oz (200 g) baker's semisweet chocolate, chopped

¹/2 cup (125 ml) water

2 tbsp sugar

grated zest of 2 oranges (optional)

1 Cut each triangle of croissant dough into 3 smaller triangles. Roll up into 18 mini croissant shapes and glaze with beaten egg. Bake in a 375°F (190°C) oven for 10–15 minutes until golden. Set aside.

2 Spread the coconut on a baking sheet and toast in the oven, turning once, for a few minutes, until golden.

3 Rinse and dry the fruit. Halve any large strawberries. Peel back the papery covering from the gooseberries to reveal the fruit, if using. Cut the star fruit into slices crosswise. Cut the fig into 8 pieces.

4 Arrange the croissants and squares of cake on serving plates and set aside. Arrange the strawberries, gooseberries, star fruit, fig, cherries, and blackberries on another serving plate and set aside. Put the toasted coconut into a small bowl and set aside.

5 Make the sauce: put the chocolate into a heatproof bowl and put over a saucepan of hot water, making sure the bowl does not touch the water. Heat gently until the chocolate has melted. Remove from the heat, keeping the bowl over the water.

6 In another saucepan, combine the measured water and sugar and bring to a boil. Simmer for 5 minutes. Slowly stir the sugar syrup into the chocolate and whisk until smooth. Stir in the orange zest, if using.

7 Transfer the chocolate sauce to a fondue pot and place over a low flame to keep warm. Serve with the fruit, mini croissants, and cake for dipping and with the toasted coconut for sprinkling.

FONDUE SAUCES

WHITE CHOCOLATE SAUCE

Roughly chop *6 oz (175 g) good-quality white chocolate* and put the pieces into a heatproof bowl. Put the bowl over a saucepan of hot water, making sure the bowl does not touch the water, and heat gently until melted. Put *²/3 cup (150 ml) heavy cream* into a saucepan and bring almost to boiling point. Slowly pour the hot cream into the melted chocolate, stirring well. Transfer to a fondue pot or warmed serving bowl, and serve at once.

BLACK CHERRY SAUCE

Purée *13 oz (400 g) canned pitted black cherries, including the juice*. Make the white chocolate sauce as above. After adding the heavy cream, stir in the pureed cherries. Heat gently to warm. Transfer the sauce to a fondue pot or warmed serving bowl, and serve immediately.

CHOCOLATE FUDGE SAUCE

Roughly chop *4-oz (125-g) bar caramel and fudge chocolate* and *3 oz (90 g) baker's semisweet chocolate*. Put into a small saucepan with *¹/4 lb (125 g) butter* and *2 ¹/2 tbsp corn syrup* and cook over very low heat, stirring the mixture once or twice, for 10–12 minutes. Whisk together until smooth. Whisk in *¹/4 cup heavy cream*. Transfer to a fondue pot or warmed serving bowl and serve immediately.

Extra fondue accompaniments

A fondue can be served with a whole range of accompaniments other than those listed in the recipe above. Here are some suggestions.

- Sliced peaches and nectarines, which go particularly well with White Chocolate Sauce.
- Pieces of pineapple: either a fresh pineapple, peeled, sliced, and cut into wedges, or canned pineapple.
- Freeze whole bananas, then slice, peel, and serve still frozen.
- Chunks of nougat, fudge, or Turkish delight.
- Mini profiteroles; make the pastry (page 484) and shape into small rounds before baking.
- Seedless grapes.

- Finger-shaped cakes or cookies, such as shortcake, ladyfingers, or Viennese fingers.
- Kiwifruit, peeled and cut into pieces lengthwise.
- Apple and pear slices, which go well with Chocolate Fudge Sauce.

SAUCY CHOCOLATE CAKE

 Serves 4

1/4 cup (60 g) sugar

1/3 cup (60 g) fine semolina

1/4 cup (30 g) cocoa powder

1 tsp baking powder

2 tbsp butter, melted, plus extra for greasing

2 eggs, beaten

2–3 drops of vanilla extract

confectioners' sugar for dusting

SAUCE

1/2 cup (90 g) dark brown sugar

2 tbsp cocoa powder

1 1/4 cups (300 ml) hot water

✵ *1 quart (1 liter) ovenproof dish*

1 Mix together the sugar and semolina in a large bowl. Sift the cocoa powder and baking powder into the bowl and mix thoroughly.

2 In a separate bowl, whisk together the melted butter, eggs, and vanilla extract with an electric beater. Add this mixture to the dry ingredients and stir with a wooden spoon until well blended.

3 Lightly butter the ovenproof dish. Pour the mixture into the dish.

4 Make the sauce: mix together the dark brown sugar and cocoa powder and gradually stir in the measured hot water. Pour the liquid over the cake.

5 Bake the cake in a 350°F (180°C) oven for 30 minutes or until the liquid has sunk to the bottom and the cake is well risen and springy to the touch. Sprinkle with confectioners' sugar and serve immediately.

NUTTY CHOCOLATE CAKE

Add 1/2 cup (60 g) chopped pecan nuts or walnuts to the dry ingredients and proceed as directed.

STICKY DATE & WALNUT CAKE

 Serves 8

6 tbsp (90 g) butter, softened, plus extra for greasing

3/4 cup (150 g) dark brown sugar

2 eggs, beaten

1 tbsp coffee extract

1 1/2 cups (175 g) self-rising flour

1 tsp baking powder

1 cup (175 g) roughly chopped pitted dates

3/4 cup (90 g) roughly chopped walnuts

3/4 cup (175 ml) hot water

TOFFEE SAUCE

1/2 cup (125 g) butter

1 cup (175 g) dark brown sugar

6 tbsp (90 ml) heavy cream

1/2 cup (60 g) roughly chopped walnuts

✵ *deep 7-in (18-cm) square cake pan*

1 Butter the cake pan and line the bottom with baking parchment.

2 Put the butter, sugar, eggs, coffee extract, flour, and baking powder into a large bowl. Beat well until smooth and thoroughly blended.

3 Stir in the dates and walnuts and then the measured hot water. Pour the mixture into the pan.

4 Bake in a 350°F (180°C) oven for 45–50 minutes, until the cake is well risen, browned on top, and springy to the touch.

5 About 10 minutes before the cake is ready, make the toffee sauce: put the butter and sugar into a small saucepan and heat gently, stirring, until the butter has melted and the sugar dissolved. Stir in the cream and walnuts and heat gently to warm through.

6 Cut the cake into 8 even-sized squares and transfer to warmed serving plates. Spoon on the toffee sauce and serve immediately.

Cook's know-how

Serve the toffee sauce with other hot or cold desserts, such as gingerbread or ice cream.

QUEEN OF PUDDINGS

 Serves 6

4 egg yolks

2 1/3 cups (600 ml) milk

2 tbsp butter, plus extra for greasing

1/4 cup (60 g) sugar

grated zest of 1 orange

1 1/2 cups (90 g) fresh white bread crumbs

3 tbsp strawberry or raspberry jam

MERINGUE TOPPING

4 egg whites

3/4 cup (175 g) sugar

★ 5-cup (1.25 liter) shallow ovenproof dish

1 In a large bowl, lightly beat the egg yolks. Set aside. Heat the milk in a small saucepan until bubbles appear around the edge. Add the butter, sugar, and orange zest and heat gently until the butter has melted and the sugar dissolved.

2 Lightly butter the ovenproof dish and set aside. Gradually add the hot milk mixture to the egg yolks, whisking constantly.

3 Stir in the bread crumbs, then pour into the ovenproof dish. Leave to stand for 15 minutes.

4 Bake the pudding in a 350°F (180°C) oven for about 30 minutes, until just set. Remove the pudding from the oven and set aside.

5 Warm the jam in a small saucepan until melted. Spread the warmed jam evenly over the surface of the pudding.

6 Make the meringue topping: using an electric beater, beat the egg whites until stiff but not dry. Beat in the sugar, 1 tsp at a time, keeping the beater at high speed all the time.

7 Spoon the meringue on top of the pudding, spreading it to the edge and pulling it up to form peaks.

8 Return the pudding to the oven and bake for 10–15 minutes longer, until the top of the meringue is crisp and golden brown. Serve immediately.

HOT CHOCOLATE SOUFFLES

 Serves 4

1/4 lb (125 g) baker's semisweet chocolate, broken into pieces

2 tbsp water

1 1/4 cups (300 ml) milk

3 tbsp butter, plus extra for greasing

1/3 cup (45 g) all-purpose flour

2–3 drops of vanilla extract

1/4 cup (60 g) sugar

4 egg yolks

5 egg whites

sifted confectioners' sugar for dusting

★ 4 1 1/4-cup (300-ml) soufflé dishes

1 Put the chocolate into a small saucepan with the measured water and a few tablespoons of the milk. Heat gently, stirring, until the chocolate has melted. Add the remaining milk, stirring to blend.

2 Melt the butter in a pan, add the flour, and cook, stirring, for 1 minute. Remove from the heat and gradually add the chocolate mixture. Bring to a boil, stirring, until the sauce has thickened. Stir in the vanilla extract and sugar and leave to cool.

3 Beat the egg yolks into the cooled chocolate mixture. Lightly butter the individual soufflé dishes and set aside.

4 Beat the egg whites until stiff but not dry. Stir 1 large spoonful of the egg whites into the chocolate mixture, then carefully fold in the remainder. Divide the mixture between the 4 soufflé dishes.

5 Place the soufflé dishes on a hot baking sheet and bake in a 375°F (190°C) oven for 40–45 minutes, until the soufflés are well risen and firm. Dust with sifted confectioners' sugar. Serve the soufflés immediately.

Cook's know-how

If you prefer, you can make 1 large soufflé instead of individual soufflés. Simply use a 5-cup (1.25 liter) soufflé dish and bake for 45–50 minutes. You may need to tie a collar of waxed paper around the outside of the dish (page 429) to support the soufflé as it rises.

BREAD & BUTTER PUDDING

 Serves 6

12 thin slices of white bread, crusts removed

about 1/4 lb (125 g) butter, softened, plus extra for greasing

1 cup (175 g) mixed dried fruit

grated zest of 2 lemons

1/2 cup (125 g) light brown granulated sugar

2 1/3 cups (600 ml) milk

2 eggs

★ 7-cup (1.7-liter) ovenproof dish

1 Spread one side of each slice of bread with a thick layer of butter. Cut each slice of bread in half diagonally. Lightly butter the ovenproof dish and arrange 12 of the triangles, buttered side down, at the bottom.

2 Sprinkle on half of the dried fruit, lemon zest, and sugar. Top with the remaining bread, buttered side up. Sprinkle on the remaining dried fruit, lemon zest, and sugar.

3 Beat together the milk and eggs and strain over the bread. Leave for 1 hour so that the bread can absorb some of the liquid.

4 Bake in a 350°F (180°C) oven for about 40 minutes, until the bread slices on the top of the pudding are a golden brown color and crisp and the custard mixture has set completely. Serve the pudding immediately.

BREAD & BUTTER PUDDING WITH MARMALADE

Spread 6 of the slices of bread with thick-cut marmalade after spreading them with the butter. Halve the slices and arrange the triangles, buttered side down, in the dish. Sprinkle with the dried fruit, lemon zest, and sugar, then arrange the remaining triangles, marmalade side up, on top. Proceed as directed.

BREAD & BUTTER PUDDING WITH APRICOTS

Add 1/4 cup (60 g) roughly chopped dried apricots to the dried fruit and proceed as directed.

RICE PUDDING

 **Serves 4**

1 tbsp butter, plus extra for greasing

1/3 cup (60 g) Arborio rice

2 1/3 cups (600 ml) milk

2 tbsp sugar

1 strip of lemon zest

1/4 tsp grated nutmeg

★ 1-quart (1-liter) ovenproof dish

1 Lightly grease the ovenproof dish with butter. Rinse the rice under cold running water and drain well.

2 Put the rice into the ovenproof dish and stir in the milk. Leave for about 30 minutes to allow the rice to soften.

3 Add the sugar and lemon zest to the rice mixture and stir to mix together. Sprinkle the surface of the milk with freshly grated nutmeg and dot with small bits of butter.

4 Bake in a 300°F (150°C) oven for 2–2 1/2 hours, until the skin of the pudding is golden brown. Serve immediately.

Cook's know-how

Arborio rice has short, rounded grains that absorb a great deal of liquid and give a rich, creamy consistency. For the creamiest pudding, use whole milk.

CHILLED RICE WITH PEARS

Leave the rice pudding to cool. Remove and discard the skin. Chill the pudding in the refrigerator and serve with poached fresh pears or canned pear halves.

CHRISTMAS PUDDING

A steamed pudding, with its dried fruit, spices, and rum, is the traditional way to end a British Christmas meal. This is a rich, dark, heavily fruited version, delicious served with brandy butter.

 Serves 8–10

2/3 cup (90 g) self-rising flour

2/3 cup (125 g) chilled vegetable shortening, cut into cubes

1/4 cup (30 g) almonds, blanched and slivered

2 carrots, grated

1 1/3 cups (250 g) raisins

1/2 cup (125 g) currants

2/3 cup (125 g) golden raisins

2 cups (125 g) fresh white bread crumbs

1/4 tsp grated nutmeg

1/2 cup (60 g) mixed candied peel, chopped

1/2 cup (90 g) dark brown sugar

grated zest and juice of 1 lemon

2 eggs, beaten

butter for greasing

5 tbsp (75 ml) dark rum

brandy butter to serve

★ 5-cup (1.25 liter) pudding mold

1 In a large bowl, combine the flour, shortening, almonds, carrots, raisins, currants, golden raisins, bread crumbs, nutmeg, candied peel, sugar, and zest. Add the lemon juice and eggs and stir well.

2 Lightly butter the pudding mold. Spoon in the pudding mixture and level the surface.

3 Cover with buttered waxed paper, then foil, both pleated in the middle. Secure the paper and foil in place by tying string under the rim of the mold (page 395).

4 Put the mold into a steamer or saucepan of simmering water, making sure the water comes halfway up the side of the mold. Cover and steam, adding boiling water as necessary, for about 6 hours.

5 Remove the mold from the steamer or pan and leave to cool. Remove the paper and foil covering. Make a few holes in the pudding with a fine skewer and pour in the rum.

6 Cover the pudding with baking parchment and fresh foil. Store in a cool place for up to 3 months.

7 To reheat for serving, steam the pudding for 2–3 hours. Serve immediately with brandy butter.

Cook's know-how

Make your own brandy butter by creaming together 1/2 lb (250 g) unsalted butter, 1 cup (250 g) confectioners' sugar, and 6 tbsp (90 ml) brandy. The brandy butter can be frozen for up to 3 months.

STEAMED JAM PUDDING

 Serves 4–6

1/4 lb (125 g) soft margarine, plus extra for greasing

3 tbsp plum jam

1/2 cup (125 g) sugar

2 eggs, beaten

1 1/2 cups (175 g) self-rising flour

1 tsp baking powder

about 1 tbsp milk

★ 5-cup (1.25-liter) pudding mold

1 Lightly grease the pudding mold with margarine and spoon the jam into the bottom.

2 Put the margarine, sugar, eggs, flour, and baking powder into a large bowl and beat until smooth and thoroughly blended. Add enough milk to give a dropping consistency.

3 Spoon the mixture into the pudding mold and smooth the surface. Cover with greased waxed paper and foil, both pleated in the middle. Secure with string (page 395).

4 Put the mold into a steamer or saucepan of simmering water, making sure the water comes halfway up the side of the mold. Cover and steam, adding boiling water as needed, for about 1 1/2 hours. Turn the pudding out onto a warmed plate and serve immediately.

MINCEMEAT & ALMOND TART

This is a rich and spicy dessert, ideal for Christmas and during the cold winter months. If you prefer, you can use a little less mincemeat and add some stewed apple, which gives the tart a lighter, fruitier flavor.

 Serves 8–10

3/4 cup (175 g) butter, softened

3/4 cup (175 g) sugar

4 eggs

1 1/2 cups (175 g) ground almonds

1 tsp almond extract

about 1/2 cup (125 g) mincemeat

PASTRY

2 cups (250 g) all-purpose flour

1/4 lb (125 g) chilled butter, cubed

1/4 cup (60 g) sugar

1 egg, beaten

TOPPING

1 1/2 cups (175 g) confectioners' sugar, sifted

juice of 1/2 lemon

1–2 tbsp water

1/2 cup (60 g) slivered almonds

⋆ deep 11-in (28-cm) fluted tart pan with a removable ring

1 Make the pastry: put the flour into a large bowl. Add the butter and rub in with the fingertips until the mixture resembles fine bread crumbs. Stir in the sugar, then mix in the egg to bind to a soft pliable dough. Cover the dough in plastic wrap and chill for about 30 minutes.

2 Roll out the dough on a lightly floured work surface and use to line the pan. Prick the bottom with a fork. Cover and chill while preparing the filling.

3 Put the butter and sugar into a large bowl and cream together until pale and fluffy. Add the eggs one at a time, beating well after each addition, then mix in the ground almonds and almond extract.

4 Spread the mincemeat evenly over the bottom of the pastry shell. Pour the almond mixture over the mincemeat.

5 Bake the tart in a 375°F (190°C) oven for about 40 minutes, until the filling is golden and firm to the touch. Cover loosely with foil if it is browning too much.

6 Meanwhile, make the topping: stir together the confectioners' sugar, lemon juice, and enough water to make a thin glaze. Spread the mixture evenly over the tart, then sprinkle with the slivered almonds.

7 Return to the oven and bake for about 5 minutes until the glaze is shiny and the almonds lightly browned. Serve warm.

STEAMED SYRUP PUDDING

 Serves 4–6

butter for greasing

6 tbsp (90 ml) maple or golden syrup

1 cup (125 g) self-rising flour

2/3 cup (125 g) chilled vegetable shortening, cut into cubes

2 cups (125 g) fresh white bread crumbs

1/4 cup (60 g) sugar

about 1/2 cup (125 ml) milk

⋆ 1-quart (1-liter) pudding mold

1 Lightly butter the mold and spoon the maple syrup into the bottom.

2 Put the flour, shortening, bread crumbs, and sugar into a bowl and stir to mix. Add enough milk to give a dropping consistency. Spoon into the mold.

3 Cover the mold with buttered baking parchment and foil, both pleated in the middle. Secure by tying string under the rim of the mold (page 395).

4 Put the mold into a steamer or saucepan of simmering water, making sure the water comes halfway up the side of the mold if using a saucepan. Cover and steam, adding more boiling water as necessary, for about 3 hours. Turn out and serve.

STRAWBERRY & RHUBARB PIE

 **Serves 6–8**

2/3 cup (150 g) sugar, plus extra for sprinkling

4 1/2 tbsp cornstarch

1 1/2 lb (750 g) rhubarb, cut into 1/2-in (1-cm) slices

2 cinnamon sticks, halved

3 cups (375 g) strawberries, hulled and halved

SHORT CRUST PASTRY

1 1/2 cups (175 g) all purpose flour

6 tbsp (90 g) chilled butter, cut into cubes

about 2 tbsp cold water

* 9-in (23-cm) tart pan

1 Make the pastry: put the flour into a large bowl, add the butter, and rub in with the fingertips until the mixture resembles fine bread crumbs. Add enough water to bind to a soft but not sticky dough. Cover with plastic wrap and leave to chill for about 30 minutes.

2 Meanwhile, combine the sugar with the cornstarch and toss with the rhubarb, cinnamon, and strawberries. Leave to macerate for 15–20 minutes.

3 On a lightly floured work surface, divide the dough in half and roll out one half into a round to line the bottom and side of the tart pan.

4 Put the macerated fruit into the pastry shell, removing the cinnamon.

5 Roll out the second half of the pastry to the same size as the first round. Cut a 1/2-in (1-cm) strip from around the edge of the pastry.

6 Cut the remaining pastry into 1/2-in (1-cm) strips and arrange in a lattice on top of the pie. Brush the ends with water and attach the long strip around the rim of the pie. Sprinkle with 1–2 tbsp sugar.

7 Bake the pie in a 425°F (220°C) oven for 10 minutes; reduce the oven temperature to 350°F (180°C), and bake for 30–40 minutes longer, until the fruit is just cooked and the pastry golden.

8 Remove from the oven and leave to cool. Serve warm or cold.

BAKED APPLE DUMPLINGS

 Serves 4

4 cooking apples, peeled and cored

1/4 cup (60 g) light brown granulated sugar

1/2 tsp ground cinnamon

milk for glazing

SHORT CRUST PASTRY

3 cups (375 g) all-purpose flour

6 tbsp (90 g) chilled butter, cut into cubes, plus extra for greasing

6 tbsp (90 g) chilled vegetable shortening, cut into cubes

3–4 tbsp cold water

1 Make the pastry: put the flour into a large bowl. Add the butter and vegetable shortening, and rub in with the fingertips until the mixture resembles fine bread crumbs. Mix in enough water to make a soft, pliable dough. Cover the dough with plastic wrap and chill for about 30 minutes.

2 Divide the dough into 4 pieces. Roll out each piece on a lightly floured work surface and cut into a 7-in (18-cm) round. Reserve the trimmings. Put an apple in the center of each round and make 4 dumplings (see box, right).

Making the apple dumplings

Fill the apples with the brown sugar and cinnamon. Draw up a pastry round to enclose each apple, sealing the seams with a little water. Place, with the seams underneath, on a lightly buttered baking sheet.

3 Cut leaf shapes from the pastry trimmings and use to decorate the tops of the dumplings, attaching them with a little water. Make a hole in the top of each dumpling and lightly brush all over with milk.

4 Bake the dumplings in a 400°F (200°C) oven for 35–40 minutes, until the pastry is golden and the apples tender. Serve hot.

SWEET WHITE SAUCE

Blend *1 tbsp cornstarch* with *1 tbsp sugar* and a little milk taken from *1¹/4 cups (300 ml)*. Bring the remaining milk to a boil and stir into the cornstarch mixture. Return to the saucepan and heat gently, stirring, until thickened. If preferred, add flavorings such as *grated orange zest, brandy, rum,* or *vanilla extract* to the sauce. Serve warm.

CUSTARD SAUCE

Blend together *3 eggs, 2 tbsp sugar,* and *1 tsp cornstarch.* Heat *2 ¹/3 cups (600 ml) milk* to just below boiling and stir into the egg mixture. Return to the pan and heat gently, stirring, until thickened. Strain into a cold bowl to prevent further cooking and serve warm or cold.

APPLE PIE

For a successful pie, the pastry shell should be properly cooked. Putting the pie plate on a baking sheet ensures that the heat will be transferred to the base.

 Serves 6

1¹/2 lb (750 g) cooking apples, peeled, cored, and sliced

about 2 tbsp sugar or more to taste, plus extra for sprinkling

2 tbsp water

rough puff pastry (page 394)

milk for glazing

★ *9¹/2-in (24-cm) pie plate*

1 Put the apples into a large pan and add the sugar and water. Cover and cook gently, stirring, for about 10 minutes, until the apples are soft and fluffy. Taste for sweetness and add more sugar if necessary.

2 Transfer the apples to a bowl and leave to cool.

3 Divide the pastry into 2 portions, 1 portion slightly larger than the other. Roll out the larger portion on a lightly floured work surface and use to line the pie plate.

4 Spoon the apple filling onto the pastry shell, spreading it almost to the edge and then mounding the apples in the middle.

5 Roll out the remaining pastry. Brush the edge of the pastry shell with a little water, then lay the pastry lid over the apple filling. Trim the edge, then crimp to seal. Make a small hole in the pastry lid to allow the steam to escape.

6 Use the pastry trimmings to make leaves to decorate the pie, attaching them with milk. Brush the pastry lid with milk and sprinkle with sugar.

7 Put a baking sheet in the oven and preheat the oven to 425°F (220°C). Put the pie plate on the hot baking sheet (this helps ensure a crisp pastry base) and bake for 25–30 minutes, until the pastry is golden.

DUTCH APPLE PIE

When cooking the apples, substitute dark brown sugar for the white sugar and add ¹/2 cup (90 g) raisins, ¹/2 tsp ground cinnamon, ¹/4 tsp ground cloves, and ¹/4 tsp grated nutmeg to the apple filling. Proceed as directed in the recipe.

CITRUS APPLE PIE

When cooking the apples, add the grated zest and juice of 1 large lemon and 3 tbsp fine-cut orange marmalade to the apples.

SABAYON SAUCE

Put *4 egg yolks, ¹/4 cup (60 g) sugar,* and *²/3 cup (150 ml) dry white wine* into a bowl over a saucepan of gently simmering water. Whisk for 5–8 minutes or until the mixture is frothy and thick. Remove from the heat and whisk in the *grated zest of 1 orange.* Serve immediately or, to serve cool, continue whisking the mixture until cool.

TARTE TATIN

 Serves 6

6 tbsp (90 g) butter

1/2 cup (90 g) light brown granulated sugar

5–6 firm sweet apples

grated zest and juice of 1 lemon

PASTRY

1 1/2 cups (175 g) all-purpose flour

1/4 lb (125 g) chilled butter, cut into cubes

1/4 cup (30 g) confectioners' sugar

1 egg yolk

about 1 tbsp cold water

★ shallow 23-cm (9-in) round cake pan

1 Make the pastry: put the flour into a large bowl and add the butter. Rub in until the mixture resembles fine bread crumbs. Stir in the confectioners' sugar, then mix in the egg yolk and enough water to make a soft but not sticky dough. Wrap and chill for 30 minutes.

2 Put the butter and sugar into a pan and heat very gently until the sugar dissolves. Increase the heat and cook gently for 4–5 minutes, until the mixture turns dark golden brown and is thick but pourable. Pour evenly over the bottom of the pan.

3 Peel, core, and slice the apples. Toss them with the lemon zest and juice. Arrange in the cake pan (see box, below).

4 Roll out the pastry on a lightly floured work surface into a round slightly larger than the pan. Lay the pastry over the apples, tucking the excess down the side of the pan.

5 Bake in a 400°F (200°C) oven for 25–30 minutes, until the pastry is crisp and golden. Invert a serving plate on top of the pan, turn the pan and plate over, and lift the pan to reveal the caramelized apples. Serve the tart warm or cold.

Arranging the apples in the cake pan

Arrange a single layer of the best apple slices in a circular pattern on top of the caramel mixture. Cover evenly with the remaining apple slices.

APPLE STRUDEL

 Serves 8

4 10- x 18-in (25- x 45-cm) sheets of phyllo pastry

4 tbsp butter, melted

1/2 cup (30 g) fresh white bread crumbs

2 tbsp slivered almonds

confectioners' sugar for dusting

FILLING

1 1/2 lb (750 g) cooking apples, peeled, cored, and sliced

grated zest and juice of 1 lemon

3 tbsp dark brown sugar

1/2 tsp ground pie spice

1/2 tsp ground cinnamon

2/3 cup (125 g) golden raisins

1/2 cup (60 g) roughly chopped blanched almonds

1 Make the filling: mix together the apples, lemon zest and juice, sugar, pie spice, cinnamon, golden raisins, and almonds.

2 Lightly brush 1 sheet of phyllo pastry with melted butter. Cover with the remaining sheets, brushing each with butter. Add the filling and finish the strudel (see box, right).

3 Brush the strudel with melted butter and sprinkle with the almonds. Bake in a 375°F (190°C) oven for 40–45 minutes, until the pastry is crisp and golden. Dust with confectioners' sugar. Serve the strudel warm or cold.

Finishing the strudel

Sprinkle the bread crumbs over the pastry. Spoon the apple mixture along the middle of the pastry.

Fold the pastry to enclose the filling, turn over onto a baking sheet, and bend into a horseshoe shape.

FRUIT DESSERTS

Make the most of the fruits of all seasons with these delicious recipes. Just add an unusual topping, and any fruit can be turned into a dessert no one can resist. Here are 3 recipes, with a couple of extra toppings. If you're feeling really self-indulgent, serve these with custard, whipped cream, or ice cream.

NUTTY PEACH STREUSEL

 Serves 4

6 ripe peaches

1/2 tsp ground ginger

1/2 tsp ground cinnamon

1/4 cup (60 g) sugar

1/4 cup (60 ml) water

STREUSEL TOPPING

1/2 cup (60 g) all-purpose flour

1/4 cup (60 g) sugar

4 tbsp butter, diced

1 cup (125 g) chopped skinned hazelnuts

1 Score the bottoms of the peaches and immerse them in boiling water for a few seconds. Peel off the skins, remove the pits, and cut into quarters.

2 Put the peaches into a saucepan with the ginger, cinnamon, sugar, and water. Bring to a boil and simmer for 10 minutes. Remove from the heat.

3 Make the streusel: put the flour and sugar into a bowl and stir together. Add the butter and rub in with the fingertips. Stir in the hazelnuts.

4 Transfer the peaches to a shallow ovenproof dish and spoon on the topping: it should be no more than 1/2 in (1 cm) deep. Bake the streusel in a 400°F (200°C) oven for 20 minutes. Serve immediately.

NUTTY SHORTCAKE

Cream *6 tbsp (90 g) butter* and *5 tbsp (75 g) sugar* until very light and fluffy. Sift *2/3 cup (90 g) self-rising flour* and *4 1/2 tbsp cornstarch* and add to the mixture with *1/4 cup (30 g) chopped walnuts*. Mix to form a stiff dough. Knead the dough lightly for 3 minutes. Cut out rounds and arrange them on top of the fruit. Bake in a 375°F (190°C) oven for 45 minutes.

WINTER FRUIT WITH DUMPLINGS

 Serves 4–6

1 1/8 cups (250 g) sugar

7/8 cup (200 ml) water

1/2 cup (125 g) dried apricots

2/3 cup (125 g) raisins

1/4 lb (125 g) dried apple rings

1/2 cup (125 g) prunes

1 orange, sectioned

2 tbsp whiskey

DUMPLINGS

1 cup (60 g) fresh white bread crumbs

1 1/2 cups (175 g) self-rising flour

2/3 cup (125 g) vegetable shortening, in cubes

pinch of salt

about 2/3 cup (150 ml) water

pared orange zest to decorate

1 Put the sugar and water into a large saucepan and bring to a boil. Add the apricots, raisins, apple rings, prunes, orange, and whiskey. Cover and simmer for 10 minutes. Leave to stand for about 2 hours.

2 Make the dumplings: combine the bread crumbs, flour, shortening, and salt in a bowl. Add enough water to bind to a smooth dough. Knead briefly. Shape into 1-in (2.5-cm) dumplings.

3 Transfer the fruit to an ovenproof dish, arrange the dumplings on top, and bake in a 400°F (200°C) oven for 20 minutes. Serve hot.

CINNAMON CROUTONS

Melt *1/4 lb (125 g) butter* in a skillet over low heat. Add *1 tsp ground cinnamon* and triangles of crustless white bread, and fry for 1–2 minutes on each side, until lightly golden. Arrange on top of the fruit before serving.

BLACKBERRY & APPLE COBBLER

 Serves 4

2 cooking apples

3 cup (500 g) blackberries

1/4 cup (60 g) sugar

grated zest and juice of 1 lemon

TOPPING

2 cups (250 g) self-rising flour

4 tbsp butter

3/8 cup (90 g) sugar

6 tbsp (90 ml) milk, plus extra for glazing

★ star-shaped and crescent-shaped pastry cutters

1 Peel the apples and cut into large slices, about 1/2 in (1 cm) thick. Use the star-shaped cutter to cut shapes out of the apple slices.

2 Put the star-shaped pieces of apple as well as the trimmings into a pan with the blackberries, sugar, and lemon zest and juice. Cover and simmer gently for 10–15 minutes, until the apple pieces are tender but not broken up.

3 Meanwhile, make the topping: put the flour into a bowl, add the butter, and rub in with the fingertips until the mixture resembles fine bread crumbs. Stir in the sugar, add the milk, and mix to form a soft dough.

4 Roll out on a lightly floured surface until 1/2 in (1 cm) thick. Cut into shapes with the crescent pastry cutter.

5 Transfer the fruit to an ovenproof dish, arranging the star-shaped pieces of apple on the top. Arrange the pastry crescents on top of the fruit and brush with milk to glaze.

6 Bake the cobbler in a 425°F (220°C) oven for 15–20 minutes, until golden. Serve hot.

Clockwise from top: *Winter Fruit with Dumplings, Nutty Peach Streusel, Blackberry & Apple Cobbler.*

TREACLE TART

 Serves 8

*1 cup (375 g) dark corn syrup
or golden syrup*

3 1/2 cups (200 g) bread crumbs

*grated zest and juice of
1 large lemon*

PASTRY

*1 1/2 cups (175 g) all-purpose
flour*

*6 tbsp (90 g) chilled butter, cut
into cubes*

about 2 tbsp cold water

★ *10-in (25-cm) tart pan with a
removable bottom*

1 Make the pastry: put the
flour into a large bowl,
add the butter, and rub in
with the fingertips until the
mixture resembles fine bread
crumbs. Mix in enough water
to make a soft, pliable dough.

2 Cover the dough with
plastic wrap and leave to
chill in the refrigerator for
about 30 minutes.

3 Roll out the dough on a
lightly floured surface
and use to line the tart pan.

4 Gently heat the golden
syrup in a saucepan until
it has melted and stir in the
bread crumbs and lemon
zest and juice. Pour into the
pastry shell.

5 Bake the tart in a 400°F
(200°C) oven for
10 minutes; reduce the
oven temperature to 350°F
(180°C), and bake for
30 minutes longer or until
the pastry is golden and the
filling firm.

6 Leave to cool in the pan
for a few minutes. Serve
warm, cut into slices.

Golden syrup

*This is a common ingredient
in English desserts and
baked goods. Look for
it in specialty stores and
some supermarkets.*

FRENCH APPLE TART

 Serves 8–10

6 tbsp (90 g) butter

*3 lb (1.5 kg) cooking apples,
cored and cut into chunks*

3 tbsp water

6 tbsp apricot jam

1/2 cup (125 g) sugar

grated zest of 1 large lemon

APPLE TOPPING & GLAZE

*3/4 lb (375 g) sweet cooking
apples, peeled, cored, and sliced*

juice of 1 lemon

1 tbsp sugar

6 tbsp apricot jam

PASTRY

2 cups (250 g) all-purpose flour

1/4 lb (125 g) chilled butter, cubed

1/2 cup (125 g) sugar

4 egg yolks

★ *11-in (28-cm) tart pan with a
removable bottom*

★ *pie weights or dried beans*

1 Make the pastry: put the
flour into a large bowl.
Add the butter and rub in
until the mixture resembles
fine bread crumbs. Stir in the
sugar, then mix in the egg
yolks and a little cold water,
if necessary, to make a soft
dough. Cover with plastic
wrap and chill for 30 minutes.

2 Melt the butter in a large
saucepan and add the
cooking apples and water.
Cover and cook very gently
for 20–25 minutes, until the
apples are soft.

3 Rub the apples through a
nylon strainer into a
clean pan. Add the jam,
sugar, and lemon zest. Cook
over high heat for 15–20
minutes, stirring constantly,
until all the liquid has
evaporated and the apple
puree is thick. Leave to cool.

4 Roll out the pastry on a
lightly floured work
surface and use to line the
tart pan. Prebake with the
weights (page 395) in a
375°F (190°C) oven for
10–15 minutes. Remove the
weights and foil and bake
for 5 minutes. Leave to cool.

5 Spoon the apple puree
into the shell. Arrange
the apple slices on top,
brush with lemon juice, and
sprinkle with sugar. Return
to the oven and bake for
30–35 minutes, until the
apples are tender and their
edges lightly browned.

6 Heat the jam, work
through a strainer, then
brush over the apples.

ALMOND TART

 Serves 6

1/4 lb (125 g) butter

1/2 cup (125 g) sugar

1 egg, lightly beaten

2/3 cup (125 g) ground rice

1/2 tsp almond extract

2 tbsp raspberry jam

confectioners' sugar for
sprinkling

PASTRY

1 1/2 cups (175 g) all-purpose
flour

3 tbsp chilled butter, cubed

3 tbsp chilled vegetable
shortening, cut into cubes

about 2 tbsp cold water

milk for glazing

☆ 7 1/2-in (19-cm) tart pan with
a removable bottom

1 Make the pastry: put the
flour into a bowl. Add the
butter and shortening and
rub in until the mixture
resembles bread crumbs. Mix
in water to make a pliable
dough. Cover with plastic
wrap and chill for 30 minutes.

2 Roll out the pastry on a
lightly floured work
surface and use to line the
tart pan. Reserve trimmings.

3 Melt the butter in a
saucepan, stir in the
sugar, and cook for
about 1 minute. Remove
from the heat, leave to cool
a little, then gradually stir
in the egg, ground rice,
and almond extract.

4 Spread the jam over the
bottom of the pastry shell
and pour the almond
mixture on top.

5 Roll out the reserved
pastry trimmings and cut
into thin strips, long enough
to fit across the tart. Arrange
the strips on top of the
almond filling to form a
lattice, attaching them to the
edge of the pastry shell with
a little milk.

6 Bake in a 400°F (200°C)
oven for 45–50 minutes,
until the filling is well risen
and golden and springs
back when pressed lightly
with a finger. If the pastry
is browning too much,
cover the tart loosely with
a piece of foil

7 Remove the tart from
the oven. Sprinkle with
confectioners' sugar and
serve the tart warm or cold.

PECAN PIE

 Serves 6–8

1 1/4 cups (150 g) pecan halves

2 tbsp unsalted butter

1/2 cup (60 g) light brown sugar

2 tbsp sugar

1/3 cup (125 ml) dark corn syrup

3 tbsp brandy

1 tsp vanilla extract

2 tbsp light cream

1/4 tsp ground cinnamon

pinch of grated nutmeg

1 large egg, lightly beaten

2 egg yolks

PASTRY

1 1/2 cups (175 g) all-purpose
flour

6 tbsp (90 g) chilled butter, cubed

about 2 tbsp cold water

1 egg white, lightly beaten

☆ 9-in (23-cm) tart pan with a
removable bottom

☆ pie weights or dried beans

1 Make the pastry: put the
flour into a bowl, add the
butter, and rub in with the
fingertips until the mixture
resembles fine bread
crumbs. Add enough water
to make a soft dough. Leave
to chill for about 30 minutes.

2 Roll out the pastry on a
lightly floured work
surface and line the tart pan.
Prebake with the weights
(page 395) in a 350°F
(180°C) oven for 10 minutes.

3 Remove the weights and
foil, lightly brush the
pastry shell with egg white,
and return to the oven for
1–2 minutes.

4 Meanwhile, toast the
pecans in a 350°F
(180°C) oven, turning
occasionally, for 10–15
minutes. Reserve a few
pecan halves and coarsely
chop the remainder.

5 Put the butter into a
heavy saucepan and cook
over low heat until it turns
golden brown. Add both
sugars and the corn syrup
and heat gently until the
sugars dissolve. Add the
brandy, bring to a boil, and
cook for 5 minutes.

6 Remove from the heat
and stir in the vanilla
extract, cream, cinnamon,
and nutmeg.

7 Whisk together the egg
and egg yolks. Whisk a
little hot syrup into the eggs.
Add half of the syrup, little
by little, then add the
remainder. Leave to cool.

8 Arrange the chopped
pecans and pecan halves
in the pastry shell. Pour the
syrup and egg mixture over
them. Bake the pie in a
350°F (180°C) oven for
about 40 minutes, until
golden brown and set. Leave
to cool before serving.

FRENCH APRICOT & ALMOND TART

So often the star of French pâtisserie, this golden fruit tart is not too difficult to make at home. Fresh apricots really make it special, but if they are not available, canned apricots can be used instead.

 Serves 10

2 lb (1 kg) fresh apricots, halved and pitted

juice of 1 lemon

1/2 cup (125 ml) water

5 tbsp (75 g) sugar

pastry cream (see box, right)

1 tsp arrowroot

1 tbsp brandy

1/4 cup (30 g) slivered almonds, toasted

PASTRY

2 cups (250 g) all-purpose flour

1/4 lb (125 g) chilled butter, cubed

1/4 cup (60 g) sugar

1 egg, beaten

☆ 11-in (28-cm) tart pan with a removable bottom

☆ pie weights or dried beans

1 Sift the flour into a large bowl. Add the butter and rub in until the mixture resembles fine bread crumbs.

2 Stir in the sugar, then mix in the egg to make a soft, pliable dough. Cover with plastic wrap and chill for 30 minutes.

3 Roll out the pastry on a lightly floured work surface and use to line the tart pan. Prebake with the weights (page 395) in a 400°F (200°C) oven for 10 minutes, until the pastry shell is beginning to brown at the edge. Remove the weights and foil and bake for 5–10 minutes. Leave to cool.

4 Put the apricots, cut side down, in a shallow pan with the lemon juice, water, and sugar. Cover tightly and bring to a boil. Lower the heat and simmer gently for 3 minutes or until just soft.

5 Remove the apricots with a slotted spoon, reserving the juices. Drain on paper towels, and leave to cool.

6 Remove the pastry shell from the tart pan and put on a serving plate. Spread the pastry cream over the pastry shell and smooth the surface.

7 Arrange the apricots, cut side down, on the pastry cream. Combine the arrowroot and brandy in a small bowl and stir in the reserved apricot juices.

8 Return the mixture to the pan and bring to a boil, stirring until thick. Add the toasted slivered almonds.

9 Spoon the glaze over the apricots, making sure they are coated evenly. (Add a little water to the glaze if it is too thick.) Leave to stand until the glaze has cooled and set. Serve the tart cold.

Pastry cream

Put *3 eggs, 3/8 cup (90 g) vanilla sugar, and 1/2 cup (60 g) all-purpose flour* into a large bowl, add a little milk taken from *1 2/3 cups (400 ml)*, and mix until smooth. Pour the remaining milk into a heavy saucepan and bring almost to a boil. Pour onto the egg mixture, whisking well.

Rinse out the saucepan, return the egg mixture to the pan, and cook over low heat, stirring, for 15–20 minutes, until thickened.

Pour into a bowl and cover with plastic wrap, gently pressing it over the surface of the custard to prevent a skin from forming. Leave to cool.

LEMON MERINGUE PIE

 Serves 8–10

grated zest and juice of
  4 large lemons

1/2 cup (90 g) cornstarch

2 1/3 cups (600 ml) water

4 egg yolks

3/4 cup (175 g) sugar

MERINGUE

5 egg whites

1 1/8 cups (250 g) sugar

PASTRY

2 cups (250 g) all-purpose flour

1/4 cup (30 g) confectioners'
  sugar

1/4 lb (125 g) chilled butter, cut
  into cubes

1 egg yolk

2 tbsp cold water

✷ 10-in (25-cm) tart pan with a
  removable bottom

✷ pie weights or dried beans

1 Make the pastry: sift the flour and confectioners' sugar into a large bowl. Add the butter and rub in with the fingertips until the mixture resembles fine bread crumbs.

2 Mix in the egg yolk and enough cold water to make a soft, pliable dough. Cover with plastic wrap and chill in the refrigerator for about 30 minutes.

3 Roll out the dough on a lightly floured surface and use to line the tart pan. Prebake with the weights (page 395) in a 400°F (200°C) oven for 10 minutes.

4 Remove the pie weights and foil and bake the pastry shell for 5 minutes or until the base has dried out. Remove from the oven and reduce the temperature to 300°F (150°C).

5 Mix the lemon zest and juice with the cornstarch. Bring the water to a boil, then stir into the lemon mixture. Return to the pan and bring back to a boil, stirring, until the mixture thickens. Remove from heat.

6 Leave to cool slightly, then stir in the egg yolks and sugar. Return to low heat and cook, stirring, until just simmering. Pour into the pastry shell.

7 Beat the egg whites until stiff but not dry. Beat in the sugar 1 tsp at a time. Pile on top of the filling and spread over evenly. Bake for 45 minutes or until crisp and brown. Serve warm or cold.

TARTE AU CITRON

 Serves 10–12

9 eggs

1 1/4 cups (300 ml) heavy cream

grated zest and juice of
  5 large lemons

1 2/3 cups (375 g) sugar

confectioners' sugar for dusting

lemon twists to decorate

PASTRY

2 cups (250 g) all-purpose flour

1/4 lb (125 g) chilled butter, cut
  into cubes

1/4 cup (60 g) sugar

1 egg

✷ 11-in (28-cm) tart pan with a
  removable bottom

✷ pie weights or dried beans

1 Make the pastry: put the flour into a large bowl. Add the butter and rub in with the fingertips until the mixture resembles fine bread crumbs.

2 Stir in the sugar, then bind together with the egg to make a soft, pliable dough. Cover with plastic wrap and chill for 30 minutes.

3 Roll out the dough on a lightly floured work surface and use to line the tart pan. Prebake with the weights (page 395) in a 400°F (200°C) oven for 10 minutes

4 Remove the pie weights and foil and bake the pastry shell for 5 minutes or until the base has dried out. Remove from the oven and reduce the oven temperature to 350°F (180°C).

5 Beat the eggs in a bowl and add the cream, lemon zest and juice, and sugar. Stir until smooth, then pour the mixture into the pastry shell.

6 Bake for 35–40 minutes, until the lemon filling has set. Cover the tart loosely with foil if the pastry begins to brown too much.

7 Leave the tart to cool a little, then dust with confectioners' sugar. Decorate with lemon twists and serve warm or at room temperature.

KEY LIME PIE

 Serves 8

4 egg yolks

13 oz (400 g) canned sweetened condensed milk

grated zest and juice of 1 lime

1 cup (250 ml) heavy cream, chilled

2 tbsp superfine sugar

lime slices to decorate

PASTRY

1¹/₂ cups (175 g) all-purpose flour

6 tbsp (90 g) chilled butter, cubed

2 tbsp cold water

★ *9-in (23-cm) tart pan with a removable bottom*

★ *pie weights or dried beans*

1 Make the pastry: put the flour into a large bowl, add the butter, and rub in until the mixture resembles fine bread crumbs. Add enough cold water to make a soft, pliable dough.

2 Wrap the dough and chill for 30 minutes.

3 Roll out the dough on a lightly floured surface and use to line the tart pan.

4 Prebake the pastry shell with the weights (page 395) in a 400°F (200°C) oven for about 10 minutes. Remove the pie weights and foil and return the shell to the oven for 5 minutes. Cool slightly.

5 Mix together the egg yolks, condensed milk, and lime zest. Slowly stir in the lime juice. Pour the filling into the shell and bake for 15–20 minutes, until the filling has set and the pastry edge is a golden brown color.

6 Leave to cool, then chill in the refrigerator for at least 1 hour.

7 Whip the cream until it forms soft peaks and fold in the sugar. Spread decoratively over the pie. Serve chilled, decorated with lime slices.

BANANA CREAM PIE

 Serves 6

³/₄ cup (175 g) butter

³/₄ cup (175 g) sugar

13 oz (400 g) canned sweetened condensed milk

2 bananas, sliced

1¹/₄ cups (300 ml) heavy cream, lightly whipped

1 oz (30 g) baker's semisweet chocolate, grated, to decorate

COOKIE SHELL

¹/₄ lb (125 g) butter

9 oz (275 g) gingersnaps, crushed

★ *7-in (18-cm) tart pan with a removable base*

1 Make the cookie shell (see box, right).

2 Combine the butter and sugar in a nonstick pan. Heat, stirring occasionally, until the butter has melted and the sugar has dissolved.

3 Add the condensed milk and heat gently, stirring, until the mixture reaches the simmering point. Simmer, stirring occasionally, for about 5 minutes.

4 Pour the mixture into the cookie shell and leave to cool. Chill until the caramel filling is set.

5 Arrange the banana slices evenly over the caramel filling. Top with the whipped cream and decorate with the grated chocolate. Serve chilled.

Making the cookie shell

Melt the butter in a saucepan, add the crushed cookies, and stir well to combine. Press onto the bottom and side of the tart pan. Chill until set.

MISSISSIPPI MUD PIE

 Serves 8–10

7 oz (200 g) baker's semisweet chocolate

1/4 lb (125 g) butter

1 tbsp coffee extract

3 eggs

2/3 cup (150 ml) light cream

3/4 cup (175 g) packed dark brown sugar

2/3 cup (150 ml) heavy cream to decorate

PASTRY

2 cups (250 g) all-purpose flour

1/4 lb (125 g) chilled butter, cut into cubes

about 2–3 tbsp cold water

★ 10-in (25-cm) tart pan with a removable bottom

★ pie weights or dried beans

1 Make the pastry: put the flour into a large bowl. Add the butter and rub in until the mixture resembles fine bread crumbs. Add enough cold water to make a soft, pliable dough.

2 Wrap the dough and chill for 30 minutes.

3 Roll out the dough on a lightly floured surface and use to line the tart pan.

4 Prebake the pastry shell with the weights (page 395) in a 400°F (200°C) oven for about 10 minutes, until the pastry edge begins to brown.

5 Remove the pie weights and foil and bake for 5 minutes longer or until the base has dried out. Remove the pastry shell from the oven and reduce the oven temperature to 375°F (190°C).

6 Break the chocolate into pieces and place in a heavy pan with the butter and coffee extract. Heat gently, stirring occasionally, until the chocolate and butter have melted. Remove from the heat. Leave the mixture to cool slightly.

7 Beat the eggs, then add to the saucepan with the cream and sugar. Stir thoroughly to mix.

8 Pour the filling into the pastry shell. Bake for 30–35 minutes, until the filling has set. Leave to cool.

9 Pipe whipped cream rosettes around the edge of the pie before serving.

FRUITY CREAM PIE

 Serves 6–8

2 cups (200 g) sugar

3 tbsp cornstarch

1 tbsp all-purpose flour

pinch of salt

2 egg yolks, lightly beaten

3/4 cup (175 ml) milk

3/4 cup (175 ml) heavy cream

1 tsp vanilla extract

1 ripe banana, sliced

5 strawberries, sliced

1 ripe nectarine, sliced

1/2 cup (60 g) blackberries

1/3 cup (60 g) raspberries

1 cup (250 ml) heavy cream, chilled

2 tbsp superfine sugar

PASTRY

1 1/2 cups (175 g) all-purpose flour

6 tbsp (90 g) chilled butter, cubed

3 tbsp granola

about 2–3 tbsp cold water

★ 9-in (23-cm) tart pan with a removable bottom

★ pie weights or dried beans

1 Make the pastry: put the flour into a bowl, add the butter, and rub in until it resembles bread crumbs. Mix in the granola. Add enough cold water to make a soft dough. Chill for 30 minutes.

2 Roll out the pastry on a lightly floured work surface and use to line the pan (patch it with your fingers if the dough breaks).

3 Prebake with the weights (page 395) in a 400°F (200°C) oven for about 10 minutes. Remove the pie weights and foil and bake for 10–15 minutes longer.

4 Combine the sugar, cornstarch, flour, and salt. Mix together the egg yolks, milk, and cream, and whisk into the cornstarch mixture.

5 Cook over medium heat, stirring constantly, until the mixture boils and thickens. If the egg begins to curdle or stick, lower the heat. Remove from the heat, stir in the vanilla extract, and leave to cool.

6 Spread half of the custard over the pastry shell and arrange the fruit on top, reserving some berries for decoration. Spread with the remaining custard. Chill until serving time.

7 Before serving, whip the cream until it forms stiff peaks. Fold in the sugar, spread over the pie, and decorate with reserved fruit.

FRUIT TARTLETS

*A mouthwatering combination of crisp golden pastry, creamy filling, and refreshing fruits always makes
a special treat, whether served as a dessert or with coffee or tea. For convenience, use the same pastry
and filling, but vary the toppings for a stunning display.*

FRESH FRUIT TARTLETS

 Makes 16

¹/₂ lb (250 g) cream cheese

2 tsp lemon juice

2 tbsp sugar

2 kiwifruit, sliced

¹/₃ cup (60 g) seedless green grapes, halved

1 piece of ginger in syrup, chopped

2 ripe pears, cored, quartered, and sliced

apricot jam or ginger marmalade for glazing

PASTRY

2 cups (250 g) all-purpose flour

¹/₄ lb (125 g) chilled butter, cut into cubes

2 tbsp sugar

3–4 tbsp cold water

★ 3-in (7-cm) cookie cutter

★ 16 2¹/₂-in (6-cm) round tartlet pans

1 Make the pastry: put the flour into a bowl, add the butter, and rub in with the fingertips until the mixture resembles fine bread crumbs. Stir in the sugar, then add enough cold water to bind to a soft, pliable dough. Wrap and chill for at least 30 minutes.

2 On a lightly floured work surface, roll out the pastry thinly. Using the cookie cutter, cut out 16 rounds.

3 Gently press the rounds into the tartlet pans. Prick all over with a fork and bake in a 375°F (190°C) oven for 12–15 minutes, until golden. Leave the tartlets in the pans for 10 minutes, then remove and transfer to a wire rack. Leave to cool completely.

4 Beat together the cream cheese, lemon juice, and sugar. Divide half among 8 of the shells. Arrange kiwi slices and grapes on top and set aside. Add the ginger to the remaining cheese mixture and divide among the remaining shells. Top with pears.

5 Melt the jam or marmalade in a saucepan. Strain and brush over the fruits. Serve immediately.

FRUIT PUFFS

 Makes 8

1 lb (500 g) store-bought puff pastry

beaten egg

¹/₂ cup (60 g) strawberries, halved

¹/₂ cup (60 g) blueberries

²/₃ cup (150 ml) heavy cream

1 tbsp sugar

1 ripe nectarine, sliced

confectioners' sugar for dusting

1 Roll out the pastry until ¹/₄ in (5 mm) thick. Cut into strips 3 in (7 cm) wide, then cut the strips diagonally into 8 diamond shapes.

2 With a sharp knife, score each pastry diamond ¹/₂ in (1 cm) from the edge, taking care not to cut all the way through. Place on a dampened baking sheet and glaze with beaten egg.

3 Bake in a 450°F (230°C) oven for 10–15 minutes, until golden. Transfer to a wire rack. Remove the pastry centers, reserving them for lids if desired. Leave to cool.

4 Divide half of the strawberries and blueberries among the pastry shells. Whip the cream and sugar and divide among the shells. Top with nectarine slices and the remaining strawberries and blueberries. Dust the pastry lids with confectioners' sugar, replace, and serve.

Tartlet toppings

*Many other combinations of fruit work
equally well.*

- Cranberry puree and apple slices.
- Sections of orange and grapefruit.
- Raspberries and blackberries.
- Halved and pitted plums.
- Sliced star fruit.

TROPICAL TARTLETS

 Makes 10

3 tbsp sweetened flaked coconut

pastry cream (page 416)

*7 oz (200 g) canned mandarin oranges in
natural juice, drained*

*7 oz (200 g) canned pineapple slices in
natural juice, drained and cut into pieces*

ALMOND PASTRY

¹/₂ cup (60 g) ground almonds

1 cup (125 g) all-purpose flour

2 tbsp sugar

6 tbsp (90 g) chilled butter, cut into cubes

3 tbsp cold water

*★ 10 3-in (7-cm) round tartlet pans or boat-
shaped pans (barquette molds)*

1 Make the pastry: combine the ground almonds, flour, and sugar in a bowl. Add the butter and rub in with the fingertips until the mixture resembles fine bread crumbs. Add enough cold water to make a soft, pliable dough. Wrap and chill for 1 hour.

2 Put the pastry on a floured work surface and flatten slightly. Place a large sheet of waxed paper on top and roll out the pastry, beneath the waxed paper, until ¹/₈ in (3 mm) thick.

3 Line the tartlet pans with pastry and chill for 2 hours. Prick the pastry all over with a fork and bake in a 375°F (190°C) oven for 10 minutes.

4 Leave the shells to cool in the pans for 10 minutes. Remove and transfer to a wire rack. Leave to cool.

5 Toast the coconut under the broiler until golden. Spoon a little pastry cream into each shell. Top with the mandarin oranges and pineapple, sprinkle with the toasted coconut, and serve immediately.

Clockwise from top:
*Tropical Tartlets, Fresh Fruit
Tartlets, Fruit Puffs.*

NAPOLEON

Serves 6

8 oz (250 g) puff pastry, thawed if frozen

3 tbsp raspberry jam

2/3 cup (150 ml) heavy cream, whipped

PASTRY CREAM

2 eggs, beaten

1/3 cup (60 g) vanilla sugar

1/4 cup (30 g) all-purpose flour

1 1/4 cups (300 ml) milk

ICING

1 cup (125 g) confectioners' sugar

about 1 tbsp water

1 Make the pastry cream (page 416). Set aside.

2 Roll out the pastry on a floured surface to make a thin, 11- x 13-in (28- x 33-cm) rectangle. Lay it over a dampened baking sheet.

3 Prick the pastry with a fork. Bake in a 425°F (220°C) oven for 10–15 minutes, until the pastry is crisp and a deep brown color.

4 Remove from the oven and leave to cool. Reduce the oven temperature to 350°F (180°C).

5 Trim the edges of the pastry to a rectangle, then cut into 3 equal rectangles, 4 in (10 cm) wide. Crush the pastry trimmings and set aside.

6 Mix the confectioners' sugar and enough water to make a glacé icing. Spread over 1 of the rectangles, and place on a baking sheet.

7 Bake for 2 minutes or until the icing has just set and has a slight sheen. Leave to cool.

8 Place a second pastry rectangle on a serving plate. Spread evenly with the jam and then the whipped cream. Set the third rectangle on top and cover with the pastry cream.

9 Top with the iced pastry rectangle. Decorate the long edges of the rectangle with thin rows of crushed pastry trimmings.

10 Chill the napoleon in the refrigerator until ready to serve.

Cook's know-how

It doesn't matter if the edges of the pastry are uneven because they will be trimmed after cooking. To cut the napoleon, use a serrated knife, holding it almost vertically, and cut with a sawing action. If you prefer, cut the napoleon before cooking to provide individual servings.

BAKLAVA

Makes 20 squares

2 cups (250 g) walnut pieces, finely chopped

1/3 cup (60 g) dark brown sugar

1 tsp ground cinnamon

1 1/4 cups (175 g) butter, melted, plus extra for greasing

24 sheets of phyllo pastry, weighing about 1 lb (500 g)

6 tbsp (90 ml) honey

2 tbsp lemon juice

✱ shallow 7- x 9-in (18- x 23-cm) rectangular cake pan

1 Mix together the walnuts, sugar, and cinnamon.

2 Lightly butter the cake pan and lay 1 sheet of pastry in the bottom of the pan, allowing the pastry to come up the sides. (If necessary, cut the sheets in half to fit in the pan.) Brush the pastry with a little melted butter.

3 Repeat with 5 more phyllo sheets, layering and brushing each one with the butter. Sprinkle with one-third of the nut mixture.

4 Repeat this process twice, using 6 more sheets of phyllo pastry each time, brushing each sheet with butter and sprinkling the nut mixture on each sixth sheet. Finish with 6 buttered sheets of phyllo pastry and lightly brush the top with melted butter.

5 Trim the edges of the phyllo, then, using a sharp knife, cut about halfway through the pastry layers to make 20 squares.

6 Bake in a 425°F (220°C) oven for 15 minutes, then reduce the oven temperature to 350°F (180°C) and bake for 10–15 minutes, until the pastry is crisp and golden brown. Remove the baklava from the oven.

7 Heat the honey and lemon juice in a heavy saucepan until the honey has melted. Spoon over the hot baklava. Leave to cool in the pan for 1–2 hours. Cut into the marked squares, and serve the baklava at room temperature.

12

CHILLED
DESSERTS

⏱ UNDER 30 MINUTES

SCOTCH MIST

Rich heavy cream whipped with whiskey and crushed meringues, chilled, and sprinkled with toasted slivered almonds.

SERVES 6 446 calories per serving
Takes 10 minutes, plus chilling   **PAGE 436**

ITALIAN CLASSIC

ZABAGLIONE

Light dessert: egg yolks, sugar, and Marsala whisked until creamy and served with ladyfingers.

SERVES 6 114 calories per serving
Takes 20 minutes   **PAGE 447**

PEACH MELBA

Deliciously ripe peaches and raspberries, topped with a large scoop of vanilla ice cream and sweet raspberry sauce.

SERVES 4 273 calories per serving
Takes 15 minutes   **PAGE 454**

⏱ 30–60 MINUTES

DINNER PARTY

BAKED ALASKA

Stunning dessert: sponge cake shell filled with layers of raspberries and strawberries, topped with ice cream and meringue, and browned.

SERVES 8 256 calories per serving
Takes 30 minutes   **PAGE 455**

BERRY FOOL

Fresh gooseberries are lightly cooked with fragrant elderflowers until soft, mixed with whipped cream, and decorated with lime zest.

SERVES 6 396 calories per serving
Takes 30 minutes, plus chilling   **PAGE 433**

TRADITIONAL

LEMON SYLLABUB

Lemon zest and juice, whipped cream, sweet white wine, and whisked egg whites, folded together, and topped with lemon zest.

SERVES 4 470 calories per serving
Takes 20 minutes, plus standing   **PAGE 435**

⏱ OVER 60 MINUTES

MOCHA PUDDING

Easy and delicious: chocolate and coffee flavored bread crumbs are layered with whipped cream and sprinkled with chocolate.

SERVES 6 510 calories per serving
Takes 15 minutes, plus chilling   **PAGE 448**

LOW CALORIE

FRESH FRUIT SALAD

Light and refreshing: a variety of fruit including pink grapefruit, oranges, green grapes, pears, and bananas coated in syrup.

SERVES 6 173 calories per serving
Takes 25 minutes, plus chilling   **PAGE 432**

POTS AU CHOCOLAT

Rich and smooth: chocolate, coffee, butter, egg yolks, and vanilla extract mixed with egg whites and decorated with whipped cream.

SERVES 6 324 calories per serving
Takes 15 minutes, plus chilling   **PAGE 446**

OVER 60 MINUTES

FROZEN LEMON SHERBET

Whipped heavy cream, lemon zest and juice, sugar, and milk, frozen and decorated with strips of lemon zest.

SERVES 4 391 calories per serving

Takes 20 minutes, plus freezing   **PAGE 456**

CHOCOLATE & BRANDY MOUSSE

Smooth and delicious: an egg and whipped cream mousse flavored with chocolate and brandy. Topped with cream and chocolate.

SERVES 6 585 calories per serving

Takes 45 minutes, plus chilling   **PAGE 449**

RICH PEACHY TRIFLE

An elegant choice: cake layered with white peaches, crisp cookies, custard, and whipped cream. Decorated with toasted almonds.

SERVES 6–8 534–401 calories per serving

Takes 35 minutes, plus chilling   **PAGE 432**

LOW FAT

SUMMER FRUIT MOLD

Ripe and juicy strawberries, blueberries, blackberries, loganberries, raspberries, and cherries wrapped in juice-soaked bread.

SERVES 6 240 calories per serving

Takes 35 minutes, plus chilling   **PAGE 433**

FAMILY CHOICE

QUICK VANILLA ICE CREAM

Plain and simple: fresh eggs and heavy cream flavored with vanilla sugar, whisked until light and creamy, then frozen.

SERVES 4–6 799–533 calories per serving

Takes 20 minutes, plus freezing   **PAGE 451**

CHOCOLATE CHEESECAKE

Rich and delicious: a crunchy granola base is topped with a creamy mixture enriched with both melted chocolate and chocolate

SERVES 8 628 calories per serving

Takes 50 minutes, plus chilling

chips. The cheesecake is decorated with piped rosettes of whipped cream and chocolate curls for a luscious finish.

    PAGE 446

PAVLOVA WITH PINEAPPLE & GINGER

Crisp meringue case filled with whipped heavy cream and ginger and topped with pineapple rings and strips of ginger.

SERVES 6–8 504–378 calories per serving

Takes 2 1/2 hours, plus cooling **PAGE 436**

TIRAMISU

Traditional Italian dessert: a cake base layered with creamy mascarpone cheese flavored with brandy, chocolate, and coffee.

SERVES 12 556 calories per serving

Takes 45 minutes, plus chilling **PAGE 449**

CREME BRULEE

Simple and delicious: egg and cream custard baked until tender, finished with crisp, caramelized sugar on top.

SERVES 6 302 calories per serving

Takes 45 minutes, plus chilling **PAGE 450**

MANGO & LIME MOUSSE

Light and refreshing: mangoes and tangy lime zest and juice mixed with whipped cream. Decorated with lime slices and cream.

SERVES 6 354 calories per serving

Takes 40 minutes, plus chilling **PAGE 434**

CHOCOLATE ROULADE

Rich and creamy: a chocolate-flavored sponge cake with a deliciously rich cream and chocolate filling.

SERVES 6 677 calories per serving

Takes 60 minutes, plus cooling **PAGE 447**

TUTTI-FRUTTI BOMBE

Easy and different: dried fruit, apricots, cherries, and brandy combined with custard and whipped cream and frozen.

SERVES 8 437 calories per serving

Takes 20 minutes, plus freezing **PAGE 455**

CARAMELIZED ORANGES

Quick and easy: oranges caramelized and served in their own juices and decorated with strips of orange zest.

SERVES 4 388 calories per serving

Takes 30 minutes, plus chilling **PAGE 434**

CHILLED LEMON SOUFFLE

Light and fluffy: refreshing, smooth dessert with a citrus tang, decorated with whipped cream and toasted almonds.

SERVES 4 883 calories per serving

Takes 40 minutes, plus chilling **PAGE 435**

FLOATING ISLANDS

Fluffy oval-shaped meringues are served floating on a smooth and creamy vanilla custard. Decorated with almonds.

SERVES 4 412 calories per serving

Takes 40 minutes, plus cooling **PAGE 441**

AUSTRIAN CHEESECAKE

Smooth and creamy: cottage cheese, butter, egg, almonds, and semolina folded with golden raisins and lightened with egg whites.

SERVES 8 931 calories per serving

Takes 50 minutes, plus cooling **PAGE 443**

CHOCOLATE LAYERED TERRINE

Two chocolate and brandy mousselike layers sandwiched with white chocolate. Decorated with whipped cream and chocolate shavings.

SERVES 8–10 641–513 calories per serving

Takes 45 minutes, plus chilling **PAGE 448**

TROPICAL FRUIT CHEESECAKE

Crunchy coconut cookie base topped with a creamy mango mixture and decorated with tropical fruits.

SERVES 10 396 calories per serving

Takes 1 1/4 hours **PAGE 443**

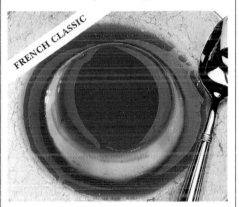

CREME CARAMEL

Easy and delicious: velvety vanilla-flavored custard coated with a tempting golden brown caramel sauce.

SERVES 6 255 calories per serving

Takes 60 minutes, plus chilling **PAGE 150**

CHERRY CHEESECAKE

Black cherries flavored with kirsch top a slightly sweet and creamy cheese filling with a crisp cookie base.

SERVES 8 530 calories per serving

Takes 60 minutes, plus chilling **PAGE 441**

RICH VANILLA ICE CREAM

Creamy and irresistible: rich egg custard mixed with heavy cream, flavored with vanilla extract, churned, and then frozen.

SERVES 4–6 577–385 calories per serving

Takes 30 minutes, plus freezing

A delicious and versatile recipe every cook should know. Colorful strawberry fans highlight each serving.

PAGE 454

MANGO & PASSION FRUIT MERINGUE

Two light and crunchy meringue rounds are sandwiched together with cream, mango slices, strawberries, and passion fruit.

SERVES 6 503 calories per serving

Takes 1 1/2 hours, plus cooling **PAGE 437**

CASSATA

Layers of ice cream, rum-soaked fruit, and sorbet are frozen to make this traditional Italian dessert.

SERVES 8 364 calories per serving

Takes 30 minutes, plus freezing **PAGE 456**

MARBLED RASPBERRY CHEESECAKE

Crunchy base of walnuts and oats is topped with a creamy raspberry and cheese filling. Decorated with whipped cream.

SERVES 10 439 calories per serving

Takes 45 minutes, plus chilling **PAGE 442**

CHOCOLATE & MERINGUE BOMBE

Delicious layers of vanilla and chocolate ice cream with a surprise center of whipped cream and meringue.

SERVES 8 413 calories per serving

Takes 45 minutes, plus freezing **PAGE 451**

HAZELNUT DACQUOISE

Toasted hazelnuts add a rich flavor to meringue rounds, which are sandwiched with cream and served with raspberry sauce.

SERVES 8 429 calories per serving

Takes 1 1/4 hours **PAGE 440**

STRAWBERRY MERINGUE ROULADE

A light meringue layer scattered with slivered almonds, spread with whipped heavy cream and strawberries, and rolled into a roulade.

SERVES 8 349 calories per serving

Takes 55 minutes, plus chilling

Chilled, then lightly dusted with confectioners' sugar before serving. A perfect and attractive end to a special dinner.

PAGE 437

CHILLED DESSERTS KNOW-HOW

CHILLED DESSERTS ARE ideal for family suppers as well as special entertaining because they can be made well in advance. Fruit salads and fools, trifles, creamy mousses, light chilled soufflés, meringue baskets, and cakes, luxurious cheesecakes, layered terrines, ice creams, sherbets, and sorbets – all can be kept in the refrigerator or freezer to be served when you're ready.

FREEZING

Many completed desserts, as well as ingredients and accompaniments for desserts, can be stored in the freezer. Freeze chocolate, caramel, or fruit sauces, then thaw at room temperature, or reheat from frozen if serving warm. Tray freeze piped rosettes of cream, pack in a freezer bag, and use frozen – they will thaw in minutes. Freeze citrus zest, then thaw, unwrapped, at room temperature. Chocolate decorations should be packed in rigid containers and used frozen. Tray freeze baked meringue shells, cake layers, and cheesecake. Unwrap and thaw in the refrigerator. Crème caramel should be frozen uncooked in the mold and baked from frozen, allowing extra time.

Warning

Some of the chilled desserts in this book, such as mousses and soufflés, contain uncooked eggs. Because of the risk of salmonella poisoning from raw eggs, these dishes should be avoided by vulnerable groups such as pregnant women, very young children, or the sick or elderly.

WHISKING EGG WHITES

Ensure all your equipment is clean, dry, and grease-free and that the egg whites are at room temperature. Use a balloon whisk and a glass, stainless steel, or copper bowl or an electric beater with a balloon beater.

Beat the whites slowly until they look foamy, then increase the beating speed, incorporating as much air as possible. Stop beating when the whites are just smooth and will stand in stiff peaks. Use immediately.

DISSOLVING GELATIN

Gelatin is a flavorless setting agent used in many chilled desserts, including mousses and fruit molds. It is most commonly available in a powdered form, which is usually sold in envelopes. However, if you prefer to use leaf gelatin, follow the package instructions, because sheets of gelatin vary in size.

1 Put the given quantity of cold water or other liquid into a small heatproof bowl and sprinkle the given quantity of gelatin over the surface. Leave for about 10 minutes until the gelatin has absorbed the liquid and become "spongy."

2 Put the bowl of gelatin into a pan of hot water and heat until the gelatin has dissolved and is clear. Use a metal spoon to check that there are no granules left. Use the gelatin at the same temperature as the mixture it is setting.

PREPARING A SOUFFLE DISH

To give a chilled soufflé the appearance of its baked counterpart, it is set in a dish with a raised collar.

Cut a piece of foil or waxed paper 2 in (5 cm) longer than the circumference of the dish and wide enough to stand 2 in (5 cm) above it when folded. Fold in half. Wrap around the dish and secure with tape or string. Remove before serving.

FOLDING EGG WHITES

Folding combines light and heavy mixtures. Work quickly and gently to keep in as much air as possible.

Mix a spoonful of the whites into the heavy mixture to lighten it. Using a rubber spatula or metal spoon, fold in the remaining whites using a figure-eight motion, cutting straight through the mixture, then turning it over until well blended.

PREPARING CITRUS FRUITS

When taking the zest from citrus fruits, first scrub the fruit with hot soapy water, rinse well, and dry. This will remove any wax coating on the skin.

Grating
Hold the grater on a plate. Rub the fruit over the medium holes of the grater, removing the zest and leaving behind the bitter white pith. Use a pastry brush to remove all the zest from the grater.

Paring
Use a vegetable peeler or small knife to pare strips of zest, trying not to take any of the white pith with the zest. Cut the pieces of zest lengthwise into very fine strips or "julienne."

Zesting
For speedy removal of zest, a special tool known as a "zester" is used.

Citrus tips

To get the maximum juice from citrus fruits, first roll the fruit gently on a work surface, pressing lightly. Or heat in the microwave, on **HIGH** (100% power) for 30 seconds, just until the fruit feels warm.

♦

If a recipe includes grated citrus zest, add it immediately after grating, preferably to any sugar in the recipe. Then the zest won't discolor or dry out, and all the flavorful oils from the zest will be absorbed by the sugar.

Peeling
Use a small sharp knife. Cut a slice across the top and the bottom, cutting through to the flesh. Hold the fruit upright on a cutting board and cut away the peel from top to bottom, following the curve of the fruit and cutting away the white pith as well.

Sectioning
Hold the peeled fruit over a bowl to catch the juice. With a sharp knife, cut down one side of a section, cutting it from the membrane. Cut away from the membrane on the other side and remove the section. Continue all around the fruit.

PREPARING A PINEAPPLE

When peeling pineapple, cut away the skin in strips, taking out all the eyes. If there are any left after peeling, cut them out with the tip of a knife.

Wedges or cubes
1 Cut off the green crown, then cut a slice from the bottom. Hold the pineapple upright on a cutting board and slice away strips of the skin.

2 To remove the core, cut the pineapple into quarters lengthwise. Cut the central core from each quarter. Cut the quarters into wedges or cubes as required.

Rings
Do not cut the pineapple lengthwise, but cut crosswise into 1/2-in (1-cm) slices. Stamp out the central core from each slice using a cookie cutter.

PREPARING MANGOES

Mangoes have a large, flat central pit and the flesh clings to it tightly. There are 2 methods of preparation, depending on how the flesh is to be used.

Slicing
For flesh to be sliced or pureed, cut the flesh from each side of the pit with a sharp knife. Cut the flesh from the edges of the pit, then peel and slice or puree.

Dicing
1 Cut the unpeeled fruit away from each side of the pit. With a sharp knife, score the flesh in a crisscross pattern, cutting through as far as the skin.

2 Press the middle of the skin to open out the cubes of flesh, then cut them away from the skin with a sharp knife.

DECORATING WITH CHOCOLATE

Chocolate decorations can transform a dessert, and you don't have to reserve them for desserts made only from chocolate; fruit fools and mousses can also benefit from a contrasting finishing touch.

Grating chocolate
Use chilled chocolate and hold it firmly in a piece of waxed paper. Hold the grater on a sheet of waxed paper and rub chocolate over the large holes of the grater.

Chocolate curls
With the chocolate at room temperature, use a vegetable peeler to shave off long curls onto a sheet of waxed paper. Use the paper to tip the curls onto the dessert.

Chocolate caraque
1 Spread a smooth, thin layer of melted chocolate, about 1/16 in (1.5 mm) thick, onto a cool work surface (preferably marble), and leave to cool until nearly set

2 Using a long, sharp knife held at an angle, push across the chocolate with a slight sawing action to shave it into "caraque" curls. Use a toothpick to pick up the caraque.

MELTING CHOCOLATE

A gentle touch is needed when melting chocolate, especially white chocolate. Don't allow it to overheat or come into contact with any steam or it may scorch or harden.

Chop the chocolate and put into a heatproof bowl over a pan of hot, not boiling, water. The bowl should not be touching the water. Heat gently, without stirring, until the chocolate becomes soft, then stir until very smooth and creamy. Remove from the heat, but leave over the water to keep the chocolate soft.

DECORATING WITH CREAM

Piping whipped cream adds a professional touch to desserts and cakes, and with a little practice and some confidence it's not so difficult to do. A star-shaped tip is the most useful one to have.

1 Drop the tip into the pastry bag and twist, then tuck the lower part of the pastry bag into the tip, to prevent the cream from leaking out when filling the bag.

2 Hold the bag in one hand, and fold the top of the bag over your hand. Spoon in the cream.

3 When the bag is full, twist the top until there is no air left. Pipe the cream as desired, gently squeezing the twisted end to force out the cream in a steady stream.

Rosette
Hold the bag upright, just above the surface of the cake. Squeeze, moving the bag in a small circle. Stop squeezing before you lift the tip away.

Swirl
Hold the bag upright, just above the surface of the cake. Squeeze the bag and pipe the cream in a steady stream, guiding the tip in an S shape.

Rope
Hold the bag at a 45° angle. Pipe a short length of cream to 1 side. Pipe another length of cream to the opposite side, overlapping the first one.

RICH PEACHY TRIFLE

 Serves 6–8

13 oz (400 g) canned peach halves

6 individual sponge cakes

1/4 cup (60 g) blueberry jam

2 oz (60 g) amaretti cookies

5 tbsp (75 ml) sherry

3 egg yolks

2 tbsp sugar

1 tsp cornstarch

1 1/4 cups (300 ml) milk

1 1/4 cups (300 ml) heavy cream

1/4 cup (30 g) slivered almonds, toasted, to decorate

1 Drain the peaches and reserve the juice. Slice and set aside.

2 Cut the individual sponge cakes in half horizontally and sandwich the halves together with the blueberry jam.

3 Use the sponge cakes to line the bottom of a glass serving bowl and arrange the peaches and amaretti cookies on top. Drizzle on the sherry and reserved peach juice and leave to soak while you make the custard.

4 In a bowl, mix together the egg yolks, sugar, and cornstarch. Warm the milk in a heavy saucepan, then pour it into the egg yolk mixture, stirring constantly. Return the mixture to the pan and cook over low heat, stirring constantly, until the custard thickens. Leave the custard to cool slightly.

5 Pour the custard over the sponge cakes, peaches, and cookies in the glass bowl. Cover the surface of the custard with a layer of plastic wrap, to prevent a skin from forming, and chill until set.

6 Whip the cream until thick and spread on the custard. Scatter the almonds over the top to decorate. Serve chilled.

APRICOT & GINGER TRIFLE

Substitute 13 oz (400 g) canned apricot halves for the peaches. Sandwich the sponge cakes with apricot jam and sprinkle with 1 piece of ginger in syrup, chopped, instead of the almonds.

FRESH FRUIT SALAD

 Serves 6

1/4 cup (60 g) sugar

6 tbsp (90 ml) water

zest of 1/2 lemon

2 pink grapefruit

2 oranges

1 cup (250 g) seedless green grapes, halved

2 ripe pears, peeled, cored, and sliced

2 bananas, sliced

1 Put the sugar and water into a saucepan and heat gently until the sugar has dissolved. Add the lemon zest and bring the syrup to a boil. Boil for 1 minute, then strain into a serving bowl. Leave to cool.

2 Using a sharp serrated knife, cut the peel and pith from each grapefruit and orange. Remove the sections by cutting between the membranes. Add the sections to the bowl.

3 Add the grapes, pears, and bananas to the serving bowl and gently mix to coat all of the fruit in the sugar syrup.

4 Cover and chill the fruit salad for up to 1 hour before serving.

FRESH BERRY SALAD

Halve 6 cups (750 g) strawberries, then mix them with 1 cup (250 g) raspberries and 2 cups (250 g) blueberries. Sift 3 tbsp confectioners' sugar over the fruit and pour the juice of 2 oranges on top. Stir gently, cover, and chill for 1 hour.

Cook's know-how

In order to prevent pears and bananas from discoloring when sliced and exposed to the air, toss the pieces in lemon juice.

SUMMER FRUIT MOLD

This classic summertime treat is as easy to make as it is delicious to eat, and not at all high in calories. Reserve half of the cooking juices and pour them over any pale patches of bread after turning out the mold for a perfect, evenly colored result.

 Serves 6

8 slices of stale medium-sliced white bread, crusts removed

1³/₄ lb (875 g) mixed summer fruits such as strawberries, blueberries, blackberries, loganberries, raspberries, and cherries

²/₃ cup (150 g) sugar

5 tbsp (75 ml) water

2 tbsp framboise or crème de cassis liqueur

light sour cream or plain yogurt to serve

★ 5-cup (1.25-liter) mold

1 Line the mold with the slices of stale white bread (see box, right).

2 Hull and halve the strawberries if they are very large, strip the berries from their stalks, pick them over, and wash them if they are dirty. Pit the cherries.

3 Place the blueberries and cherries in a saucepan with the sugar and measured water. Heat gently until the juices begin to run. Stir until the sugar has dissolved and cook until all of the fruit is just tender.

4 Remove from the heat and add the strawberries, blackberries, loganberries, raspberries, and liqueur.

5 Spoon the fruit and half of the juice into the bread-lined mold, reserving the remaining juice. Cover the top of the fruit with the 2 reserved slices of bread.

6 Stand the bowl in a shallow dish to catch any juices that may overflow, then put a saucer on top of the bread lid. Place a kitchen weight (a can of food will do) on top of the saucer. Leave to chill for 8 hours.

7 Remove the weight and saucer and invert the mold onto a serving plate. Spoon the reserved juices over the top, paying particular attention to any pale areas, and serve with either light sour cream or plain yogurt.

Lining the pudding mold

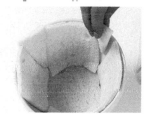

Reserve 2 slices of bread for the top of the mold, and use the remainder to line the mold, making sure that the bread fits snugly together, leaving no gaps.

BERRY FOOL

 Serves 6

1 lb (500 g) gooseberries or strawberries, trimmed and cleaned

4 tbsp butter

1 tbsp water

2 elderflower heads (optional)

sugar to taste

1¹/₄ cups (300 ml) heavy cream, whipped until thick

strips of blanched lime zest to decorate

1 Put the gooseberries into a pan with the butter, water, and elderflowers, if using. Cover and cook gently for 5–10 minutes, until the gooseberries are soft.

2 Beat with a wooden spoon until smooth and add sugar to taste. Leave to cool.

3 Fold mixture into cream. Turn into serving glasses and chill for 30 minutes. Decorate with lime zest.

RHUBARB & ORANGE FOOL

Substitute 1 lb (500 g) chopped rhubarb for the gooseberries. Omit the elderflower heads. Cook until soft with the grated zest and juice of 1 large orange. Sweeten and proceed as directed.

CARAMELIZED ORANGES

 Serves 4

1¹/8 cups (250 g) sugar

²/3 cup (150 ml) cold water

²/3 cup (150 ml) lukewarm water

3 tbsp orange liqueur

8 thin-skinned oranges

1 Put the sugar and measured cold water into a heavy pan and heat gently until the sugar dissolves.

2 When all the sugar has dissolved, bring to a boil and boil steadily until a rich brown color. (If the caramel is too light in color it will be very sweet, but be careful not to let it burn.)

3 Protect your hand with a mitt and remove the pan from the heat. Pour the measured lukewarm water into the caramel.

4 Return the pan to the heat and stir to melt the caramel. Pour the caramel into a heatproof serving dish. Leave to cool for 30 minutes. Stir in the orange liqueur.

5 Pare the zest from 1 of the oranges, using a vegetable peeler. Cut the zest into very thin strips (page 430). Cook for 1 minute in boiling water, drain, rinse thoroughly under cold running water, and set aside.

6 Using a sharp knife, remove the peel and pith from each orange, catching any juice to add to the caramel in the dish. Cut each orange into slices crosswise, then reassemble the oranges, holding the slices together with toothpicks.

7 Place the oranges in the dish of caramel and spoon the caramel over them. Scatter the strips of orange zest over the top. Chill for about 30 minutes. Remove the toothpicks before transferring the oranges to individual bowls to serve.

MANGO & LIME MOUSSE

 Serves 6

2 large ripe mangoes

grated zest and juice of 2 limes

2 tbsp powdered gelatin

3 eggs, plus 1 egg yolk

3 tbsp sugar

²/3 cup (150 ml) heavy cream, whipped until thick

DECORATION

²/3 cup (150 ml) heavy cream, whipped until thick

1 lime, thinly sliced

1 Slice the mango flesh away from the pits (page 430). Peel the flesh, then puree in a blender or food processor. Add the lime zest to the puree.

2 Put the lime juice into a small bowl, sprinkle the gelatin over the top, and leave for 10 minutes, until it becomes spongy. Stand the bowl in a pan of hot water and heat until the gelatin has dissolved.

3 Combine the eggs, egg yolk, and sugar in a large bowl and whisk vigorously for about 10 minutes, until the mixture is pale and very thick. Gradually add the mango puree, whisking between additions to keep the mixture thick.

4 Fold the whipped cream into the mango mixture. Add the dissolved gelatin in a steady stream, stirring gently to mix. Pour the mixture into a glass serving bowl and chill until set.

5 To decorate, pipe rosettes of whipped cream (page 431) on top of the mousse. Cut the lime slices in half, place 2 slices between the rosettes of cream, and serve chilled.

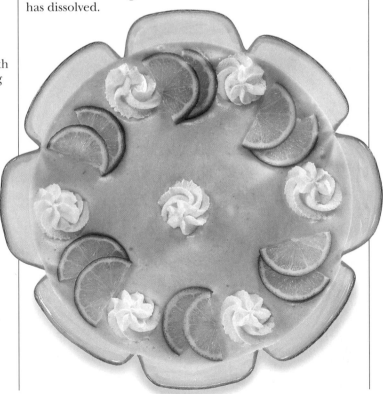

LEMON SYLLABUB

 Serves 4

²/₃ cup (150 ml) dessert wine or sweet white wine

2 large lemons

⅞ cup (90 g) sugar

1¼ cups (300 ml) heavy cream

2 egg whites

1 Put the wine into a bowl with the grated zest and juice of 1 of the lemons and the sugar. Stir to mix, then leave to stand for about 15 minutes, stirring occasionally, until the sugar has dissolved.

2 Meanwhile, pare the zest from the remaining lemon in long thin strips. Blanch the strips in a small saucepan of boiling water for 1 minute. Drain, rinse under cold running water, pat dry, and set aside.

3 In a medium bowl, whip the cream until it just holds its shape. Add the wine mixture very slowly, whisking well after additions to ensure that the mixture remains thick.

4 In a separate bowl, beat the egg whites until stiff but not dry. Carefully fold into the cream and wine mixture. Spoon into 4 tall syllabub glasses. Decorate the top of each syllabub with a strip of lemon zest and serve immediately.

Cook's know-how

For a less rich lemon syllabub, use half whipped heavy cream and half plain yogurt. Serve with shortbread cookies if desired.

CHILLED LEMON SOUFFLE

 Serves 4

3 tbsp cold water

2 tbsp powdered gelatin

3 jumbo eggs, separated

1⅛ cups (250 g) sugar

grated zest and juice of 3 lemons

1¼ cups (300 ml) heavy cream, whipped until thick

DECORATION

¼ cup (30 g) finely chopped almonds, lightly toasted

²/₃ cup (150 ml) heavy cream, whipped until stiff

★ 1-quart (1-liter) soufflé dish

1 Prepare the soufflé dish: tie a band of double-thickness waxed paper or foil around the outside so that it stands about 2 in (5 cm) above the top of the dish (page 429).

2 Put the water into a small bowl and sprinkle the gelatin over the top. Leave for about 10 minutes, until it becomes spongy. Stand in a pan of hot water and heat until dissolved.

3 Put the egg yolks and sugar into a heatproof bowl and put over a pan of gently simmering water. Do not let the bottom of the bowl touch the water. Using an electric hand-held beater, whisk together. Add the lemon zest and juice and whisk at full speed until the mixture is pale and thick.

4 Fold the whipped heavy cream into the lemon mixture, then fold in the dissolved gelatin.

5 In a separate large bowl, whisk the egg whites until stiff but not dry. Fold into the lemon mixture and carefully pour into the prepared soufflé dish. Level the surface, then chill for about 4 hours until set.

6 Carefully remove the paper collar. Decorate the outside edge of the soufflé with the lightly toasted almonds and sprinkle some in the middle. Pipe the cream (page 431) around the edge of the soufflé, and serve chilled.

SCOTCH MIST

 Serves 6

1³/4 cups (450 ml) heavy cream

¹/4 cup (60 ml) whiskey

3 oz (90 g) meringues, coarsely crushed

¹/4 cup (30 g) slivered almonds, toasted

1 Whip the cream with the whiskey until it just holds its shape. Fold in the crushed meringues.

2 Spoon the mixture into 6 glass serving bowls, cover, and chill for about 20 minutes or until firm.

3 Scatter the toasted slivered almonds over the desserts just before serving.

BERRY MIST

Substitute ¹/4 cup (60 ml) brandy for the whiskey and add 1 lb (500 g) chopped strawberries to the cream mixture. Decorate with strawberry halves and mint leaves instead of the almonds.

PAVLOVA WITH PINEAPPLE & GINGER

A light, delicate, and crisp meringue serves as the base for this delicious dessert. The meringue is crisp and golden on the outside but soft and chewy beneath. A pineapple and ginger topping provides the ideal complement.

 Serves 6–8

4 egg whites

1¹/8 cups (250 g) sugar

1¹/2 tsp cornstarch

1¹/2 tsp white vinegar

TOPPING

1¹/2 cups (375 ml) heavy cream

¹/4 cup (60 g) ginger in syrup, cut into matchsticks

13 oz (400 g) canned pineapple rings, drained

1 Preheat the oven to 325°F (160°C). Mark a 9-in (23-cm) circle on a sheet of nonstick baking parchment, turn the paper over, and line a baking sheet.

2 Beat the egg whites until stiff, then add the sugar, 1 tsp at a time, beating the mixture constantly.

3 Blend the cornstarch and vinegar and whisk into the egg white mixture.

4 Spread the mixture inside the circle on the baking parchment, building up the side so that it is higher than the middle. Place in the oven, then immediately reduce the heat to 300°F (150°C).

5 Bake the meringue for 1 hour or until firm to the touch. Turn off the oven and leave the meringue inside for another hour.

6 Peel the lining paper from the meringue and transfer the meringue to a serving plate. Leave to cool.

7 Before serving, whip the heavy cream until stiff and stir in half of the ginger strips. Spoon the mixture into the middle of the meringue. Top with the pineapple rings and the remaining ginger strips.

Cook's know-how

Keep the oven door closed when you leave the meringue to dry out. The meringue base can be made a day in advance and kept in an airtight container in a cool place until needed. Add the cream and pineapple and ginger topping just before serving the pavlova.

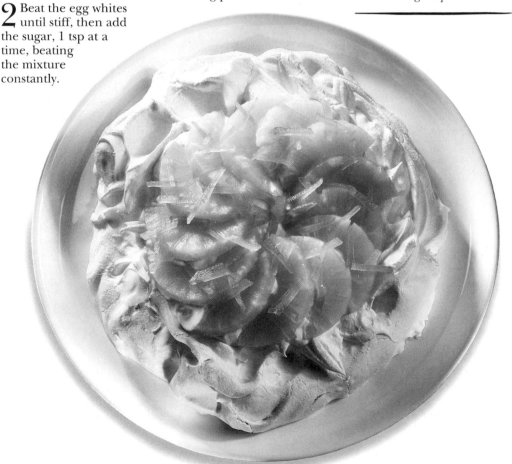

MANGO & PASSION FRUIT MERINGUE

 Serves 6

4 egg whites

1 1/8 cups (250 g) sugar

FILLING

1 ripe mango

1 passion fruit

1 1/4 cups (300 ml) heavy cream, whipped until thick

1 cup (125 g) strawberries, sliced

DECORATION

2/3 cup (150 ml) heavy cream, whipped until stiff

a few strawberries

1 Mark 2 8-in (20-cm) circles on 2 sheets of nonstick baking parchment, turn the paper over, and use to line 2 baking sheets.

2 Beat the egg whites with a hand held electric beater until stiff but not dry. Add the sugar, 1 tsp at a time, and continue to beat until all the sugar has been incorporated and the mixture is stiff and glossy.

3 Pipe the meringue, in concentric circles, inside the marked circles on the paper-lined baking sheets.

4 Bake the meringue rounds in a 275°F (140°C) oven for 1–1 1/4 hours, until crisp and dry. Leave to cool, then carefully peel off the paper.

5 Dice the mango very fine (page 430). Halve the passion fruit and scoop out the pulp.

6 Spread the whipped cream over 1 of the meringue rounds. Arrange the mango, passion fruit pulp, and strawberries on top and cover with the remaining meringue round.

7 Decorate with piped rosettes of cream (page 431), strawberry slices, and a whole strawberry.

PEACH MERINGUE

Substitute 2 peeled and sliced peaches for the mango, and 1/2 cup (125 g) raspberries for the strawberries. Proceed as directed in the recipe, decorating the top of the peach meringue with a few whole raspberries.

STRAWBERRY MERINGUE ROULADE

 Serves 8

sunflower or corn oil for greasing

4 egg whites

1 1/8 cups (250 g) sugar

3/8 cup (45 g) slivered almonds

confectioners' sugar for dusting

FILLING

1 1/4 cups (300 ml) heavy cream, whipped until thick

2 cups (250 g) strawberries, quartered

★ 9- x 13-in (23- x 33-cm) jelly roll pan

1 Lightly oil the jelly roll pan and line with a sheet of baking parchment.

2 Whisk the egg whites until stiff but not dry. Add the sugar, 1 tsp at a time, and continue to whisk until all the sugar has been incorporated and the mixture is stiff and glossy.

3 Spoon the meringue into the lined pan and tilt to level the surface. Sprinkle on the slivered almonds.

4 Bake near the top of a 425°F (220°C) oven for about 8 minutes, until the top of the meringue is golden brown.

5 Reduce the oven temperature to 325°F (160°C) and continue baking for 10 minutes or until the meringue is firm to the touch.

6 Remove the meringue from the oven and turn out onto a sheet of baking parchment. Peel the lining paper from the base and leave the meringue to cool for 10 minutes.

7 Spread the whipped cream evenly over the meringue and scatter the strawberries over the cream.

8 Roll up the meringue from a long end, using the lining paper to help lift it. Wrap the roulade in baking parchment and leave to chill in the refrigerator for about 30 minutes. Lightly dust with sifted confectioners' sugar before serving.

MERINGUES

Meringues are very quick and easy to prepare, and since they can be made weeks in advance and kept in the freezer, they're ideal for impromptu entertaining and special occasions of all kinds. Contrast their crisp, light texture with fillings and toppings of cream, chocolate, and fruit.

BASIC MERINGUE

4 egg whites

1 1/8 cups (250 g) superfine sugar

1 Beat the egg whites with an electric beater until firm. Add the sugar, 1 tsp at a time, and beat until the mixture is stiff and shiny.

2 Pipe the meringue as desired and bake as directed.

BERRY BASKETS

 Makes 8

1 recipe basic meringue (above)

1 cup (250 ml) heavy cream

selection of berries and mint sprigs to decorate

raspberry or peach sauce (page 440) to serve

1 Pipe 8 meringue baskets (see box, below). Bake in a 250°F (120°C) for 1–1 1/2 hours, until firm. Leave to cool.

2 Whip the cream until it forms stiff peaks. Fill the baskets with the cream and top with berries and mint sprigs. Serve with raspberry sauce.

COFFEE & ALMOND ROUNDS

 Makes 6

1 recipe basic meringue (left)

1 cup (125 g) slivered almonds

confectioners' sugar for dusting

COFFEE CHANTILLY CREAM

2 tbsp instant coffee powder

1 tbsp hot milk

1 cup (250 ml) heavy cream

2–3 tbsp sugar

1 Pipe 18 meringue rounds (see box, below). Sprinkle the almonds over the rounds. Bake the rounds in a 250°F (120°C) oven for 1–1 1/2 hours, until firm. Leave to cool.

2 Make the coffee Chantilly cream: dissolve the coffee in the milk and cool. Put the cream into a chilled bowl and whip until it forms soft peaks. Add the coffee mixture and sugar to the cream and whip until stiff peaks form.

3 Sandwich together the meringue rounds, 3 at a time, with the coffee Chantilly cream. Dust with a little confectioners' sugar before serving.

CHOCOLATE ROSETTES

 Makes 12

1 recipe basic meringue (left)

1/4 lb (125 g) baker's semisweet chocolate, chopped

CHOCOLATE GANACHE

1/4 lb (125 g) baker's semisweet chocolate, chopped

1/2 cup (125 ml) heavy cream

1 Pipe 24 rosettes (see box, below). Bake in a 120°C (250°F) oven for 1–1 1/2 hours, until firm. Leave to cool. Put the chocolate into a heatproof bowl over a pan of hot water and heat until melted. Drizzle over the meringues and leave to set.

2 Make the ganache: put the chocolate into a bowl. Put the cream into a pan and bring just to a boil. Pour it over the chocolate and stir until melted.

3 Whisk for about 5 minutes, until fluffy and cooled. Sandwich the meringues together with the ganache.

Clockwise from top: *Berry Baskets, Coffee & Almond Rounds, Chocolate Rosettes.*

Piping meringue shapes

Baskets

Mark 8 4-in (10-cm) circles on nonstick baking parchment; turn over. Put the meringue into a pastry bag fitted with a medium star tip, and pipe inside the circles, building up the sides to form baskets.

Rounds

Mark 18 3-in (7-cm) circles on nonstick baking parchment; turn over. Put the meringue into a pastry bag fitted with a medium plain tip. Pipe the meringue inside the circles, in concentric rings.

Rosettes

Put the meringue into a pastry bag fitted with a medium star tip. Pipe the meringue onto nonstick baking parchment to form 24 even-sized rosettes, about 2 in (5 cm) in diameter at the base.

SAUCES FOR DESSERTS

HOT CHOCOLATE SAUCE

Heat *6 oz (175 g) baker's semisweet chocolate, broken into pieces, 2 tsp instant coffee powder, 1/2 cup (125 ml) hot water* and *3/8 cup (90 g) sugar* in a pan until the chocolate has melted. Serve hot.

CHOCOLATE MARSHMALLOW SAUCE

Heat *2 oz (60 g) chopped baker's semisweet chocolate, 2 cups (100 g) marshmallows, 5 tbsp (75 ml) heavy cream,* and *5 tbsp (75 ml) honey* in a pan until the chocolate and marshmallows have melted. Serve hot.

BUTTERSCOTCH SAUCE

Heat *4 tbsp butter, 3/4 cup (150 g) dark brown sugar,* and *1/3 cup (150 g) corn syrup* in a pan until melted. Remove from the heat and add *2/3 cup (150 ml) heavy cream* and *a few drops of vanilla extract,* stirring until smooth. Serve hot.

PEACH SAUCE

Put *13 oz (400 g) canned peaches and their juice* into a food processor or blender with *1/4 tsp almond extract.* Work to a smooth puree. Serve chilled.

HAZELNUT DACQUOISE

Crisp meringues made with toasted hazelnuts are sandwiched with whipped cream. The decoration is easy to create: piped rosettes of cream are topped with hazelnuts and raspberries, and the dacquoise is accompanied by a raspberry sauce.

 Serves 8

1 cup (125 g) shelled hazelnuts

4 egg whites

1 1/4 cups (275 g) sugar

1/2 tsp white vinegar

1 1/4 cups (300 ml) heavy cream, whipped until thick

confectioners' sugar for dusting

RASPBERRY SAUCE

1 cup (250 g) raspberries

about 1/4 cup (60 g) confectioners' sugar, sifted

1 Mark 2 8-in (20-cm) circles on 2 sheets of nonstick baking parchment. Turn the paper over and use to line 2 baking sheets.

2 Spread the hazelnuts on another baking sheet and toast in a 375°F (190°C) oven for about 10 minutes. Continue to heat the oven.

3 Tip the hazelnuts onto a clean kitchen towel and rub together inside the towel to remove the skins. Reserve 8 whole nuts for decoration and grind the remaining nuts in a food processor.

4 Beat the egg whites until stiff but not dry (if using an electric mixer, turn it to high speed). Add the sugar, 1 tsp at a time, and continue to beat, still at high speed, until all of the sugar has been incorporated and the mixture is stiff and glossy.

5 Beat in the white vinegar, then fold in the ground hazelnuts.

6 Divide the hazelnut meringue mixture equally among the baking sheets, spreading it out evenly within the marked circles.

7 Bake in the oven for about 30 minutes, until the top of each meringue round is crisp and a pale beige color. The insides of the meringues should still be soft like marshmallow.

8 Lift the meringue rounds off the baking sheets and peel the lining paper from the bases. Leave to cool on a wire rack.

9 Make the raspberry sauce: reserve 8 whole raspberries for decoration and put the remainder of the raspberries into a food processor. Blend until smooth, then push through a nylon strainer to remove the seeds. Gradually beat in confectioners' sugar to taste.

10 Use two-thirds of the whipped cream to sandwich the meringue rounds together. Dust the top with sifted confectioners' sugar and decorate with piped rosettes (page 431) of the remaining whipped cream. Top the rosettes with the reserved whole hazelnuts and raspberries. Serve with the raspberry sauce.

Cook's know-how

This kind of raspberry sauce is known as raspberry coulis. It makes a colorful accompaniment to many chilled and frozen desserts.

FLOATING ISLANDS

 Serves 4

butter for greasing

3 eggs, separated

2 tbsp vanilla sugar (page 450)

1 tsp cornstarch

2 1/3 cups (600 ml) milk

3/4 cup (175 g) sugar

1/4 cup (30 g) slivered almonds, toasted

1 Butter 4 individual serving dishes. Line a baking sheet with a sheet of baking parchment.

2 In a large bowl, mix together the egg yolks, vanilla sugar, and cornstarch. In a heavy saucepan, bring the milk to a boil. Add the boiling milk to the egg yolk mixture, stirring constantly, then pour the mixture back into the pan.

3 Return to the heat and cook gently, stirring constantly, until the froth disappears and the custard is thickened. Pour the custard into the buttered dishes and leave to cool.

4 Beat the egg whites until stiff but not dry. Add the sugar, 1 tsp at a time, and continue to beat, still at full speed, until all the sugar has been incorporated and the mixture is stiff and glossy.

5 Shape the meringue (see box, below).

6 Cook in a 325°F (160°C) oven for 20 minutes, until the meringues are set and no longer sticky. Leave to cool, then arrange on top of the dishes of custard. Sprinkle with the almonds before serving.

Shaping the meringue

Shape the meringue into 8 ovals, using 2 tablespoons, and place the ovals on the baking sheet lined with baking parchment.

CHERRY CHEESECAKE

 Serves 8

3/4 lb (375 g) cream cheese

1/2 cup (125 g) sugar

2 eggs, beaten

a few drops of vanilla extract

1 tbsp lemon juice

COOKIE CRUST

3 cups (175 g) crushed graham cookies

6 tbsp (90 g) butter, melted

2 tbsp light brown sugar

TOPPING

1 tsp arrowroot

13 oz (400 g) canned pitted black cherries

a few drops of kirsch

✿ 9-in (23-cm) springform cake pan

1 Make the cookie crust: mix together the crushed cookies, melted butter, and sugar and press evenly over the bottom and up the side of the cake pan.

2 Put the cream cheese into a bowl and beat until smooth. Add the sugar and beat until well blended. Add the eggs, vanilla extract, and lemon juice. Mix until smooth and creamy.

3 Pour the filling into the cookie crust. Bake in a 350°F (180°C) oven for 25–30 minutes, until just set. Leave to cool completely, then transfer to the refrigerator and leave to chill.

4 Make the topping: dissolve the arrowroot in a little of the cherry juice. Put the cherries and their juice into a small pan and add the arrowroot mixture with the kirsch. Bring to a boil, stirring, until thick. Leave to cool completely.

5 Spoon the cherries on top of the cheesecake filling. Chill. Use a knife to loosen the side of the cheesecake from the pan, then remove the cheesecake from the pan. Serve chilled.

Cook's know-how

Cheesecakes freeze well but should always be frozen without the topping. Thaw in the refrigerator, then decorate. Fruit toppings may be prepared at the same time and frozen separately. Thaw and add to the cheesecake just before serving.

MARBLED RASPBERRY CHEESECAKE

The crunchy base of this cheesecake, made with crushed oatmeal cookies and walnuts, provides a delicious contrast to the creamy filling, marbled with streaks of fresh raspberry puree. It's a delicate cheesecake, so for best results be sure to chill it well before slicing and serving.

 Serves 10

3 tbsp cold water

2 tbsp powdered gelatin

2 cups (500 g) raspberries

1/4 cup (60 ml) framboise liqueur

1/2 lb (250 g) cream cheese, at room temperature

2/3 cup (150 ml) sour cream

2 eggs, separated

1/2 cup (125 g) sugar

COOKIE CRUST

1 1/3 cups (125 g) oatmeal cookies, coarsely crushed

4 tbsp butter, melted

2 tbsp light brown granulated sugar

1/3 cup (45 g) chopped walnuts

DECORATION

2/3 cup (150 ml) heavy cream, whipped until stiff

a few raspberries

mint sprigs

★ 9-in (23-cm) springform cake pan

1 Make the cookie crust: mix together the cookies, butter, light brown sugar, and walnuts and press evenly over the bottom of the pan.

2 Put the measured water into a heatproof bowl, sprinkle the gelatin over the top, and leave for about 10 minutes, until spongy.

3 Meanwhile, puree the raspberries in a food processor, then push them through a nylon strainer to remove the seeds. Stir in the framboise liqueur. Set aside.

4 Put the cream cheese into a large bowl and beat until soft and smooth. Add the sour cream and egg yolks and beat until well blended.

5 Stand the bowl of gelatin in a saucepan of hot water and heat gently until it dissolves. Stir the gelatin into the cheese mixture.

6 Make the filling (see box, right).

7 Use a knife to loosen the side of the cheesecake from the pan, then remove the cheesecake. Slide onto a serving plate. Pipe whipped cream (page 431) around the edge and decorate with raspberries and mint sprigs.

Cook's know-how

To achieve an attractive marbled effect, fold in the raspberry puree lightly but thoroughly so that it forms thin streaks. If there are large areas of raspberry puree, they will not set with the rest of the mixture.

Making the filling

Beat the egg whites until stiff but not dry. Add the sugar, 1 tsp at a time, and whisk until all the sugar is incorporated and the meringue mixture is stiff and glossy.

Turn the cheese mixture into the meringue and fold together, blending well. Leave the mixture to thicken slightly.

Fold in the raspberry puree, swirling it in just enough to give an attractive marbled effect.

Pour the mixture carefully onto the cookie base and chill until set.

AUSTRIAN CHEESECAKE

 Serves 8

6 tbsp (90 g) butter, at room temperature, plus extra for greasing

2/3 cup (150 g) sugar

1 1/4 cups (300 g) full-fat cottage cheese

2 eggs, separated

1/2 cup (60 g) ground almonds

2 tbsp semolina

grated zest and juice of 1 large lemon

1/3 cup (60 g) golden raisins

confectioners' sugar for dusting

★ 8 in (20 cm) springform cake pan

1 Lightly butter the pan and line the bottom with a round of baking parchment.

2 Beat the butter with the sugar and cottage cheese until light and creamy. Beat in the egg yolks, then stir in the almonds, semolina, and lemon zest and juice. Leave to stand for 10 minutes, then fold in the golden raisins.

3 In a separate bowl, beat the egg whites until stiff but not dry. Carefully fold into the cheese mixture.

4 Turn into the prepared pan and level the surface. Bake in a 375°F (190°C) oven for 30–35 minutes, until browned and firm to the touch. Turn off the oven and leave the cheesecake inside to cool for about 1 hour. Chill the cheesecake before serving.

5 Use a knife to loosen the side of the cheesecake from the pan, then remove the cheesecake. Slide onto a serving plate and dust with sifted confectioners' sugar (see below).

Cook's know-how

For a decorative pattern on top of a cake, place a doily on top, dust with confectioners' sugar, then carefully lift off the doily.

TROPICAL FRUIT CHEESECAKE

 Serves 10

2 ripe mangoes

2/3 cup (150 ml) mango and apple fruit juice blend

2 tbsp powdered gelatin

1/2 lb (250 g) cream cheese, at room temperature

1/2 cup (125 g) sugar

2 eggs, separated

2/3 cup (150 ml) heavy cream, whipped until thick

COOKIE CRUST

2 cups (125 g) crushed coconut cookies

4 tbsp butter, melted

2 tbsp light brown sugar

DECORATION

2 kiwifruit, peeled and sliced

8 oz (250 g) canned pineapple pieces in natural juice, drained

★ 9-in (23-cm) springform cake pan or pan with a removable bottom

1 Make the cookie crust: mix together the cookies, melted butter, and sugar, and press evenly over the bottom of the pan.

2 Slice the mango flesh away from the pits (page 430). Peel, then puree in a food processor.

3 Pour the fruit juice into a heatproof bowl and sprinkle the gelatin over the top. Leave for about 10 minutes, until it becomes spongy. Stand the bowl in a small pan of hot water, and heat gently until the gelatin has dissolved.

4 In a large bowl, beat the cheese until smooth and creamy. Beat in half of the sugar, the egg yolks, and the mango puree. Gradually beat in the gelatin mixture.

5 In a separate bowl, whisk the egg whites until stiff but not dry. Whisk in the remaining sugar, 1 tsp at a time, and continue to whisk at high speed until the sugar is incorporated and the mixture is stiff and glossy.

6 Fold the whipped cream into the cheese and mango mixture, then fold in the egg whites. Pour onto the cookie base and chill until set.

7 Use a knife to loosen the side of the cheesecake, then remove from the pan. Slide onto a serving plate. Decorate the top of the cheesecake with slices of kiwifruit and pieces of pineapple before serving.

GELATIN MOLDS

Gelatin molds are not just for children's birthday parties. Made from fresh fruits and fruit juices, they make a wonderfully light dessert worthy of any sophisticated dinner party. What's more, they can be prepared the day before and simply turned out, decorated, and served without too much last-minute fuss.

LAYERED FRUIT TERRINE

 Serves 4–6

2 oranges

1 cup (175 g) raspberries

1¹/₂ cups (175 g) strawberries

1 scant cup (175 g) seedless green grapes

²/₃ cup (150 ml) cold water

2 tbsp powdered unflavored gelatin

6 tbsp (90 g) sugar

2 cups (500 ml) dry white wine

juice of ¹/₂ lemon

★ 8¹/₂- x 4¹/₂- x 2¹/₂-in
(21.5- x 11.5- x 6-cm) terrine

1 Peel the oranges and cut out the sections (page 430). Pick over the raspberries. Hull the strawberries and cut in half if large. Reserve a few for decoration. Halve the grapes.

2 Put ¹/₄ cup (60 ml) of the measured water into a small heatproof bowl and sprinkle the gelatin over the top. Leave for 10 minutes or until spongy. Put the bowl into a pan of hot water and heat gently until the gelatin dissolves.

3 Put the remaining water into a large saucepan, add the sugar, and heat, stirring occasionally, until dissolved. Bring to a boil and simmer the syrup for 5 minutes.

4 While the gelatin is still warm, pour it into the sugar syrup and stir well. Add the wine and lemon juice and stir well to mix.

5 Pour a little of the mixture into the terrine to make a ¹/₂-in (1-cm) layer. Chill for about 30 minutes, until the gelatin is set.

6 Arrange the fruit in layers on top of the gelatin. Pour the remaining wine mixture into the terrine, a ladleful at a time, gently shaking the terrine to remove any air bubbles. Chill for about 6 hours until set. Turn out the gelatin, slice, then decorate with the reserved strawberries. Serve chilled.

STARBURST GELATIN

 Serves 6

7 tbsp (100 ml) cold water

2 tbsp powdered unflavored gelatin

13 oz (400 g) canned peach halves in syrup

6 passion fruit

6 slices of star fruit

1 pink grapefruit, peeled and sectioned

1 cup (125 ml) heavy cream

¹/₄ cup (30 g) confectioners' sugar

passion fruit to decorate

★ 6 1-cup (250-ml) gelatin molds

1 Put the water into a heatproof bowl and sprinkle the gelatin over the top. Leave for 10 minutes or until spongy. Put the bowl into a pan of hot water and heat gently until dissolved.

2 Puree the peaches and their syrup in a food processor or blender. Remove the pulp from the passion fruit, add to the puree, and process briefly to combine. Push through a nylon strainer. Stir in the gelatin.

3 Dip the star fruit slices into the peach mixture and place 1 in each mold. Arrange the grapefruit around the star fruit. Divide the peach mixture among the molds. Chill for 1–2 hours, until set.

4 Whip the cream until stiff. Sift the sugar and fold into the cream. Turn out the gelatins, pipe with whipped cream, and decorate with passion fruit.

ELDERFLOWER & GRAPE GELATIN

 Serves 4–6

⁷/₈ cup (200 ml) cold water

3 tbsp powdered unflavored gelatin

3 cups (750 ml) rosé wine

2 tbsp sugar

juice of ¹/₂ lemon

¹/₄ cup (60 ml) elderflower cordial

³/₄ cup (150 g) seedless red grapes, halved

lemon twists and mint sprigs to decorate

★ 4 wine glasses

1 Put the water into a heatproof bowl and sprinkle the gelatin over the top. Leave for 10 minutes or until spongy. Put the bowl into a pan of hot water and heat gently until dissolved.

2 Put half of the wine and the sugar into a saucepan. Heat gently until the sugar dissolves. Bring to a boil and simmer for 5 minutes. Add the lemon juice, elderflower cordial, and the remaining wine. Stir in the gelatin.

3 Arrange the grape halves in the glasses. Pour a little of the gelatin mixture into each glass. Chill for 10 minutes. Pour the remaining mixture into the glasses. Chill for 1–2 hours, until set. Decorate with lemon twists and mint sprigs before serving.

Clockwise from top: *Starburst Gelatin, Elderflower & Grape Gelatin, Layered Fruit Terrine.*

Successful gelatin molds

Almost all fruits make successful gelatins, with the exception of pineapples and kiwifruit, which contain an enzyme that keeps gelatin from setting.

- Wash and dry all fruit or the gelatin may turn cloudy or not set.
- To turn out, pull the edge of the gelatin away from the mold. Dip the mold in hot water for 2–3 seconds, then turn out onto a wet plate (this allows repositioning).

POTS AU CHOCOLAT

 Serves 6

6 oz (175 g) baker's semisweet
chocolate, broken into pieces

3 tbsp strong black coffee

1 tbsp butter

a few drops of vanilla extract

3 eggs, separated

²/₃ cup (150 ml) heavy cream,
whipped until stiff, to decorate

1 Put the chocolate pieces
into a saucepan with the
strong black coffee. Heat
gently, stirring, until the
chocolate melts.

2 Leave the chocolate
mixture to cool slightly,
then add the butter, vanilla
extract, and egg yolks and
stir until well blended.

3 Beat the egg whites until
stiff but not dry. Fold
gently but thoroughly into
the chocolate mixture.

4 Pour the mixture into
6 small custard cups,
ramekins, or other serving
dishes and leave to chill for
about 8 hours.

5 Decorate each cup of
chocolate with a piped
rosette of whipped cream
(page 431) before serving.

CHOCOLATE CHEESECAKE

*This delicious dessert, with its crunchy granola base and rich chocolate filling, is
ideal for parties. It can be prepared up to a month in advance and frozen in foil.
Thaw, wrapped, in the refrigerator for 8 hours, then decorate.*

 Serves 8

¹/₄ lb (125 g) baker's semisweet
chocolate, broken into pieces

3 tbsp cold water

2 tbsp powdered gelatin

¹/₂ lb (250 g) cream cheese

2 eggs, separated

¹/₄ cup (60 g) sugar

²/₃ cup (150 ml) sour cream

¹/₄ cup (30 g) baker's semisweet
chocolate chips

BASE

1 cup (125 g) granola

6 tbsp butter, melted

2 tbsp light brown sugar

DECORATION

1¹/₄ cups (300 ml) heavy cream,
whipped until stiff

chocolate curls or caraque
(page 431)

✳ 8-in (20-cm) springform
cake pan or pan with
a removable bottom

1 Make the base: mix
together the granola,
melted butter, and sugar and
press evenly over the bottom
of the pan. Chill.

2 Meanwhile, put the
chocolate into a small
heatproof bowl over a pan
of hot water. Heat gently to
melt the chocolate, stirring
occasionally. Leave to cool.

3 Put the measured water
into a heatproof bowl
and sprinkle the gelatin over
the top. Leave for 10 minutes,
until spongy. Stand the bowl
in a pan of hot water and
heat gently until the gelatin
has dissolved.

4 Beat the cheese until
smooth. Add the egg
yolks and sugar and beat
until blended. Stir in the
sour cream, melted
chocolate, chocolate chips,
and gelatin. Mix well.

5 In a separate bowl, beat
the egg whites until stiff
but not dry. Fold carefully
into the chocolate mixture.
Pour onto the granola base
and chill until set.

6 Use a knife to loosen the
side of the cheesecake
from the pan, then remove
the cheesecake. Slide onto a
serving plate. Pipe rosettes of
whipped cream (page 431)
on top and decorate with
chocolate curls or caraque.

Cook's know-how

*Chocolate chips are convenient,
but if you don't have any on
hand, chop squares taken from
a chocolate bar.*

CHOCOLATE ROULADE

This impressive dessert is made from a baked chocolate soufflé rolled around a cream and chocolate filling. It is important to cut the roulade cleanly, so use a long serrated knife and dip it in hot water before cutting each slice.

 Serves 6

sunflower or corn oil for greasing

6 oz (175 g) baker's semisweet chocolate, broken into pieces

6 jumbo eggs, separated

³/₄ cup (175 g) sugar

confectioners' sugar for dusting

FILLING

3 oz (90 g) baker's semisweet chocolate, broken into pieces

1¹/₄ cups (300 ml) heavy cream, whipped until thick

★ 9- x 13-in (23- x 33-cm) jelly roll pan

1 Lightly grease the pan with sunflower oil and line with baking parchment.

2 Put the chocolate into a small heatproof bowl over a pan of hot water and heat gently, stirring occasionally, to melt the chocolate. Leave to cool.

3 Combine the egg yolks and sugar in a large bowl and beat together until light and creamy. Add the cooled chocolate and stir to blend evenly.

4 In a separate bowl, beat the egg whites until stiff but not dry. Carefully fold into the chocolate mixture.

5 Turn the chocolate mixture into the pan, tilting it so that the mixture spreads evenly into the corners. Bake in a 350°F (180°C) oven for 20 minutes or until firm to the touch.

6 Remove the cake from the oven. Place a clean, dry dish towel on top of the cake and on top of this lay another dish towel that has been soaked in cold water and well wrung out. Leave the cake in a cool place for 8 hours.

7 Make the filling: put the chocolate into a heatproof bowl over a pan of hot water and heat gently, stirring occasionally, to melt the chocolate. Cool.

8 Remove the dish towels from the cake, and turn it out onto a piece of baking parchment sprinkled liberally with sifted confectioners' sugar. Peel off the lining paper.

9 Spread the melted chocolate over the cake, then spread the whipped cream evenly on top.

10 Roll up the cake from a long edge, using the sugared paper to help lift the cake and roll it forward.

11 Dust the roulade with sifted confectioners' sugar before serving.

ZABAGLIONE

 Serves 6

4 egg yolks

5 tbsp (75 g) sugar

¹/₂ cup (125 ml) Marsala

ladyfingers to serve

1 Put the egg yolks and sugar into a heatproof bowl. Whisk together until light and foamy, then add the Marsala. Whisk to blend.

2 Put the bowl over a pan of simmering water, making sure it does not touch the water. Heat gently, whisking the mixture until it becomes thick and creamy and stands in soft peaks.

3 Remove from the heat and continue whisking until the mixture is cool. Pour into 6 glass dishes and serve with ladyfingers.

Zabaglione

This Italian dessert may also be served warm. As soon as the mixture has thickened, remove from the heat and pour into serving dishes.

MOCHA PUDDING

 Serves 6

2 cups (125 g) fresh
whole-wheat bread crumbs

3/8 cup (90 g) light brown sugar

2/3 cup (75 g) sweetened cocoa
powder

2 tbsp instant coffee powder

1 1/4 cups (300 ml) heavy cream

2/3 cup (150 ml) light cream

2 oz (60 g) baker's semisweet
chocolate, grated

1 In a bowl, mix together
the bread crumbs, sugar,
cocoa powder, and coffee
powder. In another bowl,
whip together the heavy and
light creams until they form
soft peaks.

2 Spoon half of the cream
into 6 glass serving dishes.
Cover with the bread crumb
mixture and then with the
remaining cream. Chill for at
least 6 hours or 8 hours for
best results.

3 Sprinkle generously with
the grated chocolate just
before serving.

Cook's know-how

*For best results, make sure the
chocolate is well chilled before
you grate it. Use the large holes
on the grater.*

CHOCOLATE LAYERED TERRINE

*This rich and creamy dessert is ideal for a dinner party or special family treat.
A layer of white chocolate and heavy cream is sandwiched between layers of
semisweet chocolate and heavy cream flavored with brandy.*

 Serves 8–10

*SEMISWEET CHOCOLATE
LAYERS*

1/2 lb (250 g) baker's semisweet
chocolate

2 tbsp brandy

2 eggs

1 1/2 cups (375 ml) heavy cream

*WHITE CHOCOLATE
LAYER*

3 oz (90 g) white chocolate

1 egg

2/3 cup (150 ml) heavy cream

DECORATION

2/3 cup (150 ml) heavy cream,
whipped, grated chocolate,
and mint sprigs to decorate

★ 8 1/2- x 4 1/2- x 2 1/2-in (21.5-
x 11.5- x 6-cm) loaf pan

1 Make the semisweet
chocolate layers: break
the chocolate into pieces and
place in a heatproof bowl
with the brandy over a pan of
hot water. Melt, then cool.

2 Line the loaf pan with
plastic wrap. Set aside.

3 Put the eggs into a
heatproof bowl over a
pan of hot water. Beat until
the eggs are thick and
mousselike and leave a trail
when the beater is lifted.
Remove from the heat and
beat until the bowl is
completely cold.

4 Whip the cream until it
just holds its shape. Fold
the whisked eggs into the
cooled chocolate mixture,
then fold in the cream.

5 Pour half of the
semisweet chocolate
mixture into the prepared
pan, then place in the freezer
for about 15 minutes, until
firm. Reserve the remaining
semisweet chocolate mixture.

6 Meanwhile, make the
white chocolate mixture
in the same way as the
semisweet chocolate mixture.

7 Pour the white chocolate
mixture on top of the
firm layer in the pan, and
freeze for 15 minutes.

8 Spoon the reserved
semisweet chocolate
mixture on top of the white
chocolate layer and freeze
for about 30 minutes, until it
is firm enough to slice.

9 Invert the pan onto a
serving plate, and
remove the plastic wrap.
Decorate the terrine with
piped rosettes of whipped
cream (page 431), grated
chocolate, and mint sprigs.
Slice thinly to serve.

Cook's know-how

*Keep this terrine well chilled for
easy slicing and serving.
Substitute plain yogurt for one-
third of the heavy cream to give
a less rich flavor, if preferred.*

CHOCOLATE & BRANDY MOUSSE

 Serves 6

1/2 lb (250 g) baker's semisweet chocolate, broken into pieces

3 tbsp brandy

3 tbsp cold water

2 tbsp powdered gelatin

4 eggs, plus 2 egg yolks

3/8 cup (90 g) sugar

2/3 cup (150 ml) heavy cream, whipped until thick

DECORATION

2/3 cup (150 ml) heavy cream, whipped until stiff

chocolate curls or caraque (page 431) to decorate

1 Put the chocolate into a heatproof bowl with the brandy over a pan of hot water. Heat gently until melted. Leave to cool.

2 Put the cold water into a heatproof bowl and sprinkle the gelatin over the top. Leave for about 10 minutes, until spongy. Stand the bowl in a pan of hot water and heat gently until dissolved.

3 Combine the eggs, egg yolks, and sugar in a large heatproof bowl, and put over a saucepan of simmering water. Beat with a hand-held electric beater until the egg mixture is very thick and mousselike. Beat in the dissolved gelatin.

4 Fold the whipped cream into the cooled chocolate, then fold into the egg mixture. Carefully pour into a glass serving bowl, cover, and leave in the refrigerator until set.

5 Decorate with piped rosettes of cream and chocolate curls or caraque (page 431). Serve the mousse chilled.

Cook's know-how

Make sure you use good-quality chocolate. For the best flavor, look for the brand with the highest percentage of cocoa solids.

TIRAMISU

 Serves 12

1 1/2 tsp instant coffee powder

3/4 cup (175 ml) boiling water

2/3 cup (150 ml) brandy

3 eggs

1/2 cup (125 g) sugar

14 oz (425 g) mascarpone cheese

1 3/4 cups (450 ml) heavy cream

5 oz (150 g) baker's semisweet chocolate chips

16 slices plain cake or 1 package ladyfingers

2 oz (60 g) white chocolate, grated, to decorate

1 Dissolve the coffee in the measured boiling water and mix with the brandy.

2 Combine the eggs and sugar in a large bowl and whisk together until thick and light. The mixture should be thick enough to leave a trail on the surface.

3 Put the mascarpone cheese into a large bowl. Stir in a little of the egg mixture. Fold in the remaining egg mixture. Fold in the heavy cream.

4 Chop the chocolate chips in a food processor until they form a powder with some larger pieces of chocolate for texture.

5 Trim the cake slices and layer the tiramisu (see box, below).

6 Decorate the top of the tiramisu, making a pattern with the remaining semisweet chocolate and the white chocolate. Cover and chill for 4 hours.

Layering the tiramisu

Line the bottom of a large glass serving bowl with half of the cake pieces. Drizzle half of the coffee and brandy mixture over the cakes.

Scatter over one third of the chocolate, then spoon half of the mascarpone mixture on top. Level the surface. Repeat the layers.

CREME CARAMEL

 Serves 6

3/4 cup (175 g) sugar

2/3 cup (150 ml) water

4 eggs

*2 tbsp vanilla sugar
(see Cook's know-how, right)*

2 1/3 cups (600 ml) milk

☆ *6 small ramekins*

1 Combine the sugar and water in a saucepan and heat gently until all the sugar has dissolved. Bring to a boil, and cook without stirring, until golden. Pour into the ramekins.

2 Whisk the eggs and vanilla sugar in a bowl. Heat the milk until just warm, then pour into the egg mixture, stirring well. Strain into the ramekins.

3 Put the ramekins in a roasting pan and add enough hot water to come halfway up the sides of the ramekins. Bake in a 325°F (160°C) oven for about 40 minutes, until just set and firm to the touch but not solid. Cool, then chill in the refrigerator for about 8 hours.

4 Turn out onto individual plates to serve.

Cook's know-how

To make your own vanilla sugar, store a vanilla bean in a jar of sugar, and the sugar will absorb the vanilla flavor. You can then use the sugar when making custards and sauces.

CREME BRULEE

 Serves 6

butter for greasing

4 egg yolks

*2 tbsp vanilla sugar
(see Cook's know-how, left)*

2 1/3 cups (600 ml) light cream

1/4 cup (60 g) light brown sugar

☆ *6 small ramekins or 1 shallow 4-cup (900-ml) ovenproof dish*

1 Lightly butter the individual ramekins or ovenproof dish.

2 In a large bowl, beat the egg yolks with the vanilla sugar. Heat the cream to just below the boiling point, then pour into the egg yolk mixture, stirring well.

3 Pour the custard into the ramekins or the large ovenproof dish. Set in a roasting pan and add enough hot water to come halfway up the sides of the ramekins or dish.

4 Bake in a 325°F (160°C) oven for about 25 minutes for the individual ramekins or about 45 minutes for the large ovenproof dish, until just set and firm to the touch. Leave to cool.

5 Sprinkle the light brown sugar evenly over the top of the set custard. Place under a very hot broiler until the sugar melts and caramelizes to a rich golden brown color.

6 Chill the crème brûlée for no more than 2 hours before serving.

Cook's know-how

The caramel topping should be hard and crisp; don't chill crème brûlée for too long or the caramel will begin to soften. To reach the rich and creamy custard beneath, crack the hard caramel with the edge of a spoon.

QUICK VANILLA ICE CREAM

 Serves 4–6

6 eggs, separated

3/4 cup (175 g) vanilla sugar (see Cook's know-how, page 450)

1 3/4 cups (450 ml) heavy cream, whipped until thick

1 Beat the egg whites (at high speed if using an electric beater) until stiff but not dry. Add the vanilla sugar, 1 tsp at a time, and continue beating until the sugar has been incorporated and the egg white mixture is very stiff and glossy.

2 Put the egg yolks into a separate bowl and beat at high speed with an electric beater until the mixture is blended thoroughly.

3 Gently fold the whipped cream and egg yolks into the egg white mixture. Transfer to a large shallow freezer container, cover, and leave the mixture to freeze for 8 hours.

4 Transfer the ice cream to the refrigerator for about 10 minutes before serving so that it softens slightly.

COFFEE BRANDY ICE CREAM

Substitute plain sugar for the vanilla sugar and add 3 tbsp each coffee extract and brandy when folding the mixtures.

LEMON ICE CREAM

Substitute plain sugar for the vanilla sugar and add the grated zest and juice of 3 large lemons when folding.

STRAWBERRY ICE CREAM

Substitute plain sugar for the vanilla sugar. Puree 3 cups (375 g) strawberries and add when folding the mixtures.

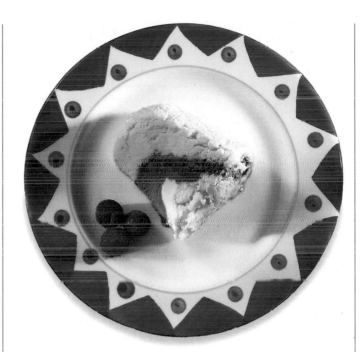

CHOCOLATE & MERINGUE BOMBE

 Serves 8

2 1/3 cups (600 ml) vanilla ice cream

2 1/3 cups (600 ml) chocolate ice cream

2/3 cup (150 ml) heavy cream

1 tbsp brandy

1/4 lb (125 g) meringues, coarsely crushed

✧ 6-cup (1.5-liter) bombe mold or dessert mold

1 Chill the mold in the freezer. Fill the mold with the vanilla and chocolate ice creams (see box, right).

2 Whip the cream with the brandy until it just holds its shape. Gently fold in the crushed meringues. Spoon the meringue mixture into the mold. Cover and freeze for 8 hours.

3 Dip the mold into cold water and invert the chocolate and meringue bombe onto a large serving plate. Slice and serve.

Filling the mold

Allow the vanilla ice cream to soften at room temperature for about 20 minutes. Spread it over the base and up the side of the mold. Chill in the freezer until solid.

Soften the chocolate ice cream, then spread it evenly over the vanilla ice cream to make a hollow inner layer. Return to the freezer until solid.

SORBETS

Light and refreshing, sorbets are the perfect ending to a rich meal. Flavored with fresh fruits and made from a basic mixture of sugar, water, and egg white, they're also low in fat. Decorate each sorbet with its key ingredient or with an ingredient complementary in flavor.

LIME

 Serves 6–8

$1^1/8$ cups (250 g) sugar

$2^1/3$ cups (600 ml) water

grated zest and juice of 6 limes

2 egg whites

strips of lime zest to decorate

1 Put the sugar and measured water into a saucepan and heat gently until the sugar dissolves. Bring to a boil and boil for 2 minutes. Remove from the heat, add the lime zest, and leave to cool completely. Stir in the lime juice.

2 Strain the lime syrup into a shallow freezer container and freeze for about 2 hours, until just mushy. Transfer the mixture to a bowl and whisk gently to break down any large crystals.

3 Beat the egg whites until stiff but not dry, then fold into the lime mixture. Return to the freezer and freeze until firm. Transfer the sorbet to the refrigerator to soften for about 30 minutes. Decorate before serving.

APRICOT

 Serves 6–8

$3/8$ cup (90 g) sugar

$1^1/4$ cups (300 ml) water

juice of 1 lemon

$1^1/2$ lb (750 g) apricots, halved and pitted

2 egg whites

1 Put the sugar, water, and lemon juice into a pan and heat gently until the sugar has dissolved. Bring to a boil, add the apricots, and simmer for 15 minutes or until very tender. Leave to cool.

2 Peel and slice a few apricots for decoration. Press the remainder through a nylon strainer. Pour with the syrup into a freezer container, then follow steps 2 and 3 of Lime Sorbet (above). Decorate before serving.

PEAR & GINGER

 Serves 6–8

$3/8$ cup (90 g) sugar

$1^1/4$ cups (300 ml) water

1 tbsp lemon juice

$1^1/2$ lb (750 g) pears, peeled and cored

1 piece of ginger in syrup, finely chopped

2 egg whites

strips of ginger to decorate

1 Put the sugar, measured water, and lemon juice into a saucepan and heat gently until the sugar dissolves. Bring to a boil, add the pears, and poach gently, basting occasionally with the sugar syrup, for 20–25 minutes, until the pears are tender. Cool, then puree in a food processor.

2 Add the chopped ginger to the pear puree. Pour the pear mixture into a freezer container, then follow steps 2 and 3 of Lime Sorbet (left). Decorate before serving.

RASPBERRY

 Serves 6–8

2 cups (500 g) raspberries

$3/4$ cup (175 g) sugar

$2^1/3$ cups (600 ml) water

juice of 1 orange

3 egg whites

raspberries and mint sprigs to decorate

1 Puree the raspberries in a food processor, then push through a nylon strainer to remove the seeds. Put the sugar and measured water into a saucepan and heat gently until the sugar dissolves. Bring to a boil, then boil for 5 minutes.

2 Pour into a bowl and cool. Stir in raspberry puree and orange juice. Pour into a freezer container, then follow steps 2 and 3 of Lime Sorbet (left). Decorate before serving.

GRANITAS

Granitas are similar to sorbets but even easier to make: they're simply flavored ice crystals.

COFFEE

Put *$1/4$ cup (60 g) sugar* and *4 tbsp instant coffee powder* into a pan with *3 cups (750 ml) water* and bring to a boil. Simmer for about 5 minutes. Leave to cool, then pour into a freezer container. Freeze, stirring occasionally, for 5 hours.

LEMON

Put *1 cup (200 g) sugar* into a saucepan, add *2 cups (500 ml) water*, and bring to a boil. Simmer for 5 minutes. Leave to cool. Add *2 tsp grated lemon zest* and the *juice of 4 lemons* to the sugar syrup. Pour into a freezer container and freeze, stirring occasionally, for 5 hours.

WATERMELON

Remove and discard the rind and seeds from *2 lb (1 kg) watermelon*. Puree the flesh in a food processor. Pour into a freezer container and mix in *$1/4$ cup (60 g) confectioners' sugar* and *$1^1/2$ tsp lemon juice*. Freeze, stirring occasionally, for 5 hours.

Clockwise from top: *Apricot, Pear & Ginger, Lime, and Raspberry Sorbets.*

PEACH MELBA

 Serves 4

4 ripe peaches, peeled, pitted, and sliced

8 scoops of vanilla ice cream

mint sprigs to decorate

MELBA SAUCE

1¹/₂ cups (375 g) raspberries

¹/₄ cup (60 g) confectioners' sugar

1 Make the Melba sauce (see box, below).

2 Arrange the peach slices in 4 glass serving dishes. Top with 2 scoops of ice cream each and some sauce. Decorate with the remaining raspberries and mint sprigs.

Making Melba sauce

Puree 1 cup (250 g) of the raspberries. Push through a nylon strainer to remove the seeds.

Sift confectioners' sugar over the puree and stir in.

RICH VANILLA ICE CREAM

Homemade ice cream tastes much better than any commercially made ice cream, and, despite its reputation, it is not at all difficult to make. It will keep for up to 1 month in the freezer.

 Serves 4–6

4 egg yolks

¹/₂ cup (125 g) sugar

1¹/₄ cups (300 ml) milk

1¹/₄ cups (300 ml) heavy cream

1¹/₂ tsp vanilla extract

strawberry fans to decorate

1 Put the egg yolks and sugar into a bowl and whisk until light in color.

2 Heat the milk in a heavy pan to just below boiling. Add a little of the hot milk to the egg yolk mixture and stir to blend, then pour in the remaining milk.

3 Pour back into the pan and heat gently, stirring, until the froth disappears and the mixture coats the back of a spoon. Do not boil.

4 Leave the custard to cool, then stir in the cream and vanilla extract.

5 Pour into a container and freeze for 3 hours. Tip into a bowl and stir. Return to the container. Freeze for 2 hours. Stir and freeze for 2 hours longer. Remove from the freezer 30 minutes before serving and decorate.

CHOCOLATE ICE CREAM

Heat the milk with ¹/₄ lb (125 g) pieces of baker's semisweet chocolate. Allow the chocolate to melt, then proceed as directed.

COCONUT ICE CREAM

Heat the milk with ³/₄ cup (175 g) unsweetened shredded coconut. Allow the coconut to soften, then proceed as directed.

CHOCOLATE CHIP ICE CREAM

Heat the milk with ¹/₄ lb (125 g) chopped white chocolate. Allow the chocolate to melt, then proceed as directed. Stir 2 oz (60 g) semisweet chocolate chips into the custard with the cream.

BANANA & HONEY ICE CREAM

Mash 4 bananas with 3 tbsp lemon juice and 2 tbsp honey. Add to the custard with the cream, then proceed as directed.

BAKED ALASKA

 Serves 8

8-in (20-cm) sponge cake case

1 cup (250 g) raspberries, 2 cups (8 oz) strawberries, sliced, or other summer fruits

1³/4 cups (450 ml) vanilla ice cream

2 egg whites

¹/2 cup (125 g) sugar

whole berries to decorate

1 Put the sponge cake case into a shallow ovenproof serving dish. Arrange the fruits in the case.

2 Put the ice cream on top of the fruits and put in the freezer to keep the ice cream frozen while making the meringue.

3 Beat the egg whites (an electric beater can be used) until stiff but not dry.

4 Add the sugar, 1 tsp at a time, and continue to beat until the sugar has been incorporated and the meringue mixture is stiff and glossy.

5 Pipe or spoon the meringue over the ice cream, covering it completely.

6 Bake immediately in a 450°F (230°C) oven for 3–4 minutes, until the meringue is tinged with brown. Serve immediately, decorated with raspberries and strawberries.

Cook's know-how

A hard block of deeply frozen ice cream is best for this recipe. Make sure the ice cream is completely covered by the egg white, which keeps the ice cream from melting.

TUTTI-FRUTTI BOMBE

 Serves 8

1 cup (175 g) mixed dried fruit

¹/4 cup (60 g) dried apricots, chopped

¹/4 cup (60 g) glacé cherries, halved

3 tbsp brandy

3 eggs

¹/2 cup (125 g) sugar

1³/4 cups (450 ml) milk

1³/4 cups (450 ml) heavy cream

²/3 cup (150 ml) light cream

★ 2-quart (1.7 liter) bombe mold or freezer-safe bowl

1 Combine the dried fruit, apricots, glacé cherries, and brandy. Cover and leave to soak for 8 hours.

2 In a large bowl, whisk together the eggs and sugar. Heat the milk in a heavy saucepan to just below the boiling point. Pour into the egg mixture, stirring.

3 Pour back into the pan. Cook gently, stirring with a wooden spoon, until the froth disappears and the mixture thickens. Do not boil. Remove from the heat and leave to cool.

4 Whip 1¹/4 cups (300 ml) heavy cream and the light cream together until they are just beginning to hold their shape. Fold into the custard with the fruit and brandy mixture.

5 Transfer to a shallow freezer container and freeze for 2 hours or until the mixture is beginning to set but still slightly soft.

6 Remove the pudding from the freezer and mix well to distribute the fruit evenly. Spoon into the bombe mold, cover, and return to the freezer. Freeze for 3 hours or until firm.

7 Remove from the freezer about 20 minutes before serving to soften. Turn out onto a serving plate, and spoon the remaining cream, lightly whipped, on top. Slice and serve immediately.

CASSATA

 Serves 8

1 oz (30 g) candied angelica, rinsed, dried, and chopped

2 tbsp glacé cherries, rinsed, dried, and chopped

1/4 cup (30 g) chopped mixed candied peel

2 tbsp dark rum

2 1/3 cups (600 ml) raspberry sorbet

2/3 cup (150 ml) heavy cream, whipped until thick

2 1/3 cups (600 ml) vanilla ice cream

★ 9- x 5- x 3-in (23- x 12- x 7.5-cm) terrine

1 Chill the terrine. Put the angelica, glacé cherries, and candied peel in a bowl.

2 Add the rum, stir well, then leave to soak.

3 Allow the sorbet to soften, then spread it evenly over the bottom of the chilled terrine. Chill in the freezer until solid.

4 Fold the fruit and rum mixture into the whipped cream. Spoon into the terrine and level the surface. Return to the freezer until firm.

5 Allow the vanilla ice cream to soften, then spread it evenly over the fruit layer. Cover and leave to freeze for 8 hours.

6 To turn out, dip the terrine into warm water and invert the cassata onto a large serving plate. Slice and serve immediately.

FROZEN LEMON SHERBET

 Serves 4

2/3 cup (150 ml) heavy cream

grated zest and juice of 1 large lemon

3/4 cup (175 g) sugar

1 1/4 cups (300 ml) milk

pared zest of 1 lemon, cut into strips, to decorate

1 Whip the cream until it forms soft peaks. Add the lemon zest and juice, sugar, and milk and mix until evenly blended.

2 Pour the mixture into a shallow freezer container, cover, and freeze for at least 6 hours, until firm.

3 Cut the mixture into chunks, then transfer to a food processor and work until smooth and creamy. Pour into 4 individual freezer dishes and freeze for about 8 hours.

4 Blanch the strips of lemon zest in boiling water for 1 minute. Drain, rinse, and pat dry.

5 Decorate the sherbet with the strips of lemon zest and serve.

FROZEN ORANGE SHERBET

Substitute the grated zest and juice of 1 orange for the lemon, reduce the sugar to 1/2 cup (125 g), and proceed directed. Decorate with blanched strips of orange zest.

13

CAKES & QUICK BREADS

WHOLE-WHEAT GRIDDLE CAKES

Family favorite: a simple batter made with whole-wheat flour for nutty flavor. Dropped onto a hot griddle and served with syrup.

MAKES 20 55 calories each

Takes 30 minutes **PAGE 481**

VICTORIA LAYER CAKE

Two light and golden layers of sponge sandwiched with jam and sprinkled generously with sugar.

SERVES 6–8 515–386 calories per serving

Takes 35 minutes, plus cooling **PAGE 472**

FORK COOKIES

Plain and simple: a butter-enriched dough imprinted with a fork pattern and baked until crisp and golden.

MAKES 32 104 calories each

Takes 30 minutes, plus cooling **PAGE 483**

BRANDY SNAPS

A delicate batter flavored with ground ginger and lemon juice, baked until golden, and rolled before crisp.

MAKES 15 107 calories each

Takes 40 minutes, plus cooling **PAGE 483**

CORN BREAD

An all-time favorite: a simple, slightly sweet batter made from cornmeal. Baked until golden and served warm.

MAKES 9 SQUARES 230 calories each

Takes 40 minutes, plus cooling **PAGE 478**

WALNUT COOKIES

Crisp and sweet: a walnut-studded dough, shaped into a roll, cut into thin slices, and baked until golden. Very easy to make.

MAKES 50 59 calories each

Takes 35 minutes, plus chilling **PAGE 486**

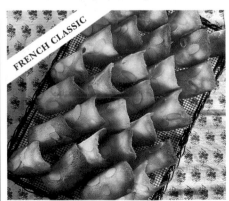

ALMOND TUILES

Crisp and delicate: a sweet, almond-flavored batter baked until golden brown, then shaped into curves before crisp.

MAKES 30 45 calories each

Takes 30 minutes, plus cooling **PAGE 482**

BISCUITS

Perfect at dinner time or anytime: a simple dough makes featherweight biscuits. Serve spread with butter and jam.

MAKES 12 133 calories each

Takes 30 minutes, plus cooling **PAGE 480**

MINCEMEAT MUFFINS

Rich and fruity: a miniature and quick version of mince pies. Baked in muffin pans to produce individual cakes.

MAKES 32 137 calories each

Takes 40 minutes, plus cooling **PAGE 474**

JELLY ROLL

An old favorite: a light golden cake spread generously with a layer of raspberry jam, rolled up, and decorated with sugar.

SERVES 6–8 260–195 calories per serving

Takes 45 minutes, plus cooling　　**PAGE 469**

VIENNESE FINGERS

Pretty and delicious: a rich butter dough piped into fingers, baked until golden brown, and each end dipped in chocolate.

MAKES 12 215 calories each

Takes 30 minutes, plus cooling　　**PAGE 482**

PINWHEEL COOKIES

Attractive and easy: vanilla and coffee doughs rolled together, cut into thin slices, and baked.

MAKES 18 98 calories each

Takes 45 minutes, plus chilling　　**PAGE 486**

COCONUT MACAROONS

Almonds and coconut flavor these macaroons. Crisp and golden on the outside and deliciously tender on the inside.

MAKES 26 116 calories each

Takes 40 minutes, plus cooling　　**PAGE 482**

POTATO ROLLS

An old-fashioned treat: a dough made with mashed potatoes and baked until crisp. Simple and delicious.

MAKES 12 113 calories each

Takes 40 minutes, plus cooling　　**PAGE 481**

FAMILY CHOICE

OAT BARS

Rich, chewy, and very easy to make: an oat-studded batter is spread into a roasting pan, baked, and cut into fingers.

MAKES 24 102 calories each

Takes 45 minutes, plus cooling　　**PAGE 486**

GINGERSNAPS

Crisp and spicy: ginger and cinnamon spice a dough enriched with butter and baked until dark golden brown.

MAKES 15 81 calories each

Takes 30 minutes, plus cooling　　**PAGE 483**

STRAWBERRY SHORTCAKE

Two layers of golden sponge cake filled with freshly whipped cream, sweet and juicy strawberries, and tropical passion fruit.

SERVES 8 260 calories per serving

Takes 60 minutes, plus cooling　　**PAGE 469**

ECONOMICAL

SWEET GRIDDLE CAKES

Old-fashioned griddle cakes studded with currants and flavored with mixed spice. Served hot from the pan or left to cool slightly.

MAKES 12 204 calories each

Takes 30 minutes, plus cooling　　**PAGE 480**

⏱ OVER 60 MINUTES

SHORTBREAD

Scottish classic: a dough made rich with butter, baked until golden, and sprinkled with sugar.

MAKES 8 WEDGES 233 calories each
Takes 55 minutes, plus cooling **PAGE 478**

DEVIL'S FOOD CAKE

Layers of moist, rich chocolate sponge cake spread with a sweet white frosting. Perfect for family gatherings.

SERVES 8–10 769–615 calories per serving
Takes 60 minutes, plus cooling **PAGE 466**

CARROT CAKE

Flavorful favorite: moist cake with chopped walnuts, mashed banana, and grated carrot. Cream cheese icing is spread on top.

SERVES 8–10 515–412 calories per serving
Takes 1¼ hours, plus cooling **PAGE 465**

MARBLED COFFEE RING CAKE

Two batters, one coffeee flavored and one plain, swirled together, baked, and topped with coffee icing and white chocolate.

SERVES 8–10 707–565 calories per serving
Takes 1¼ hours **PAGE 467**

IRISH SODA BREAD

A traditional bread made light and tasty with buttermilk. Scored and baked until golden brown.

MAKES 1 LOAF 1816 calories per loaf
Takes 45 minutes, plus cooling **PAGE 481**

GINGERBREAD

Moist and tasty: a batter made dark and delicious with molasses and spices. Best when baked ahead.

MAKES 15 SQUARES 349 calories each
Takes 1¼ hours, plus cooling **PAGE 478**

ICED LIME SHEET CAKE

Light and delicious: a lime-flavored cake batter baked in a rectangular pan, topped with tangy lime icing, and cut into squares.

MAKES 9 SQUARES 453 calories each
Takes 50 minutes, plus cooling **PAGE 472**

CHOCOLATE & ORANGE MOUSSE CAKE

Two layers of delicate chocolate cake filled with chocolate and orange flavored mousse.

SERVES 8–10 626–500 calories per serving
Takes 1¼ hours, plus chilling **PAGE 468**

WHITE CHOCOLATE CAKE

Rich and attractive: delicious whipped cream hides a cocoa-flavored sponge. Perfect for special occasions.

SERVES 8–10 684–547 calories per serving
Takes 1¼ hours, plus cooling **PAGE 467**

OVER 60 MINUTES

FRUITED BANANA LOAF

A hearty loaf made from a spiced fruit batter. Perfect use for ripe bananas. Serve sliced and spread with butter.

SERVES 8–10   501–401 calories per serving

Takes 1¹/₂ hours, plus cooling   **PAGE 475**

ZUCCHINI BREAD

American favorite: zucchini baked until sweet and tender in a deliciously spiced and walnut-studded batter.

SERVES 8–10   496–397 calories per serving

Takes 1¹/₂ hours, plus cooling   **PAGE 465**

DATE & WALNUT LOAF

Sweet dates and crunchy walnuts are baked in a lightly sweetened batter. Delicious sliced and spread with butter.

SERVES 8   404 calories per serving

Takes 1³/₄ hours, plus cooling   **PAGE 479**

CHOCOLATE & VANILLA BATTENBURG CAKE

Classic cake made from chocolate and vanilla batters wrapped with almond paste.

SERVES 8   425 calories per serving

Takes 60 minutes, plus cooling   **PAGE 473**

BARA BRITH

A Welsh favorite: A deliciously tender loaf studded with tea-soaked dried fruit. Serve sliced and spread with butter.

SERVES 8   385 calories per serving

Takes 2 hours, plus soaking   **PAGE 479**

SIMNEL CAKE

Moist and tender fruit cake, brushed with apricot jam, topped with almond paste, and decorated with balls of almond paste.

SERVES 8–10   742–593 calories per serving

Takes 2³/₄ hours, plus cooling   **PAGE 474**

DUNDEE CAKE

Rich and fruity: golden raisins, currants, cherries, and lemon, baked in a batter until golden and decorated with almonds.

SERVES 8–10   576–461 calories per serving

Takes 1³/₄ hours, plus cooling   **PAGE 475**

HEAVENLY CHOCOLATE CAKE

A rich chocolate and almond cake cut in half, filled and covered with fudge icing, and decorated with white chocolate curls.

SERVES 6   820 calories per serving

Takes 1¹/₂ hours, plus cooling   **PAGE 466**

FRUIT CAKE

Classic: raisins, golden raisins, glacé cherries, spices, and brandy flavor this moist cake. Best when baked ahead.

SERVES 8–10   712–570 calories per serving

Takes 6¹/₄ hours, plus cooling   **PAGE 473**

CAKES & QUICK BREADS KNOW-HOW

Cake making is often seen as the test of a cook's skills, but there are lots of cakes and quick breads, as well as biscuits, griddle cakes, cookies, and muffins that are really quite simple to make and just as delicious as more elaborate creations. If you are a beginner, remember to follow recipes carefully, and make sure your weighing and measuring is accurate. Use the right equipment and pans, and take the time to prepare cakes properly, and you'll achieve perfect results every time. You'll find that once you've gained confidence, you'll be able to experiment with more difficult recipes.

STORING

Most cakes are best eaten freshly made, particularly sponge cakes made without fat, but if you do want to keep a cake, be sure to store it in an airtight container. Use a metal cake tin with a lid. Put the cake on the upturned lid of the cake tin, then put the tin over the top. This makes it easy to remove the cake from the tin. Fruit cakes and cakes made by the melting method, such as gingerbread, will improve with age if kept in an airtight tin. Wrap fruit cake in waxed paper and then overwrap in foil. Don't put foil directly in contact with a fruit cake, or the acid in the fruit may react with the foil. Any cake that has a filling or icing of whipped cream, buttercream, or cream cheese should be kept in the refrigerator. Biscuits, muffins, and most quick breads are best eaten freshly made.

Most cookies can be stored in an airtight tin for a few days; if they soften, crisp them up in a warm oven. Allow cakes and cookies to cool completely on a wire rack before putting them into a tin. Do not store cakes and cookies together as the moisture from the cake will soften the cookies.

MICROWAVING

Microwave-baked cakes and cookies can be disappointingly pale in color and gluey in texture. In baking, the microwave oven comes into its own when used as an accessory to the conventional oven.

◆ Break chocolate into small pieces, put into a bowl, and cook on LOW for 3–5 minutes, until melted and shiny.
◆ Melt crystallized honey or syrup on HIGH for 1–2 minutes.
◆ Soften hardened, set sugar by cooking on HIGH for 30–40 seconds.
◆ Place hazelnuts on paper towels and cook on HIGH for 30 seconds; remove skins and cook until golden.

FREEZING

This is a good way of keeping cakes fresh if they are not eaten immediately. Cakes, quick breads, cookies, muffins, and biscuits freeze well. Wrap cakes and quick breads in foil or freezer paper. If a cake has been iced or decorated, tray freeze, then place in a rigid container or freezer bag. Fruit cakes can be stored for up to 12 months; uniced cakes for 4–6 months; iced cakes for 2–3 months. Unwrap decorated cakes before thawing, but leave other cakes in their wrapping. Layer cookies with foil or freezer wrap. Cookies, muffins, and biscuits can be stored for 6 months. Thaw at room temperature; biscuits can be successfully reheated or toasted from frozen.

BAKING INGREDIENTS

In baking it is important to use ingredients as they are specified. Choose the best quality available.

Butter and other fats
In simple cakes, cookies, and quick breads, where flavor is important, always use butter. In other cakes, margarine is acceptable. Soft margarine should be used in one-bowl mixtures since it is made up of 80% fat and blends easily. "Diet" spreads are not suitable for baking because of their high water content, so check before you buy. If oil is called for, use a mild one such as sunflower oil.

Flour
Both all-purpose and self-rising flours are used in baking. Self-rising flour includes leavening, so if you want to substitute all-purpose flour, add 2 tsp baking powder to each 2 cups (250 g) flour.

Rising agents
Baking powder and baking soda are used in cakes, quick breads, and cookies. When using baking powder, or self-rising flour, bake the mixture within 1 hour, while the chemicals are still active.

Sugar
For most mixtures, it is essential to use a sugar that dissolves easily, such as granulated or dark brown sugar. Light brown granulated sugar can be used in melted mixtures and is ideal for sprinkling on the top of cakes, quick breads, and muffins.

Eggs
Eggs at room temperature are more easily aerated than cold eggs taken from the refrigerator. Cold eggs can also cause some cake mixtures to curdle.

BAKING COOKIES

When arranging cookies on prepared baking sheets, leave enough space to allow for spreading if necessary. Since cookies cook quickly, they can easily be baked in batches if you don't have enough baking sheets.

At the end of the baking time, many cookies will still feel a little soft in the middle: they will continue to bake on the sheet after being removed from the oven. If the recipe directs, leave them to firm up for 1–2 minutes before transferring to a wire rack. Avoid letting cookies cool completely on the sheet or they may stick.

ONE-BOWL CAKES

Be sure to use a soft margarine for this quick, simple technique.

Put all the ingredients into a large bowl and beat together with a hand-held electric mixer until combined. You can also do this in a food processor or by hand.

BEATEN CAKES

This method is used for light, fat-free sponge cakes. Use a hand held or stand electric mixer. If using a hand-held mixer, set it at high speed.

1 Whisk the eggs or egg yolks with the sugar until the mixture is light, pale, and thick enough to leave a trail on the surface. This will take about 5 minutes.

2 Gently fold in the flour and any other ingredients. If the eggs have been separated, the beaten egg whites should be folded into the mixture last of all.

CREAMED CAKES

Creaming is used for both cakes and cookies. Use a wooden spoon, rubber spatula, or electric mixer, and soften the butter or margarine first.

1 Cream the fat and sugar together until the mixture is pale in color and fluffy in texture, scraping the side of the bowl with a wooden spoon to incorporate all of the mixture.

2 Lightly beat the eggs. Gradually add the eggs to the creamed mixture, beating well between additions. If the mixture curdles, which will result in a dense-textured cake, beat in a spoonful of the flour.

3 Sift on the flour and any other dry ingredients. Using a wooden spoon, gently fold the 2 mixtures together until well combined. Any liquid ingredients should also be added at this stage.

PREPARING CAKE PANS

Lightly greasing the pan makes it easier to turn the cake out. Some recipes also call for the pan to be floured or lined with either baking parchment or waxed paper.

Greasing and flouring
Use melted or softened butter or margarine, or oil, according to the recipe. Brush over the bottom and side of the pan using a pastry brush or paper towels. Add a spoonful of flour and tilt the pan to coat it with a thin layer. Shake out excess flour.

Lining
1 Set the cake pan on a sheet of waxed paper or parchment and mark around the base with a pencil or the tip of a knife.

2 Cut out the shape, cutting just inside the line, and press smoothly over the bottom of the pan. Lightly grease if directed in recipe.

BAKING, TESTING, & COOLING CAKES

Before baking cakes, quick breads, and cookies, be sure to preheat the oven to the correct temperature. If you need to, adjust the position of the racks before you turn on the oven.

1 As soon as the mixture is prepared, turn it into the pan and level the surface. Tap the pan on the work surface to break any large air bubbles. Transfer immediately to the oven.

2 When cooked, a cake will shrink slightly from the side of the pan. To test, lightly press the middle with a fingertip; the cake should spring back. Rich cakes should feel firm to the touch.

Testing dense cakes
For fruit cakes and fruited quick breads, insert a metal skewer or wooden toothpick into the middle: it should come out clean, without any crumbs sticking to it.

3 Set the pan on a wire rack and leave to cool for about 10 minutes. Run a knife around the side of the cake to free it from the pan.

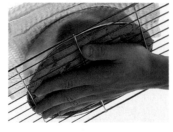

4 Hold a wire rack over the top of the pan, then invert the rack and pan so that the cake falls onto the rack. Carefully lift the pan away from the cake.

5 Peel off the lining paper. With a light-textured cake, turn it over again so the base is on the rack; this will prevent the rack from marking the top.

Baking know-how

To check the dimensions of a cake pan, measure inside the top rim. To work out the depth, measure from the bottom to the top rim on the inside of the pan. To check the capacity of a pan, measure how much water is needed to fill it to the brim.

◆

Bake for the minimum time given in the recipe before opening the oven door. If the door is opened too soon, it may cause some cakes to deflate.

◆

If a cake looks as though it is browning too quickly, cover the top loosely with foil.

◆

If baking several cake layers, stagger them on the oven racks so one is not directly beneath another.

◆

When measuring ingredients with a spoon, don't hold the spoon directly over the bowl, or you may accidentally add too much.

CUTTING A CAKE

A cake can be cut into layers and layered with cream or another filling. Use a long serrated knife.

Steady the cake by holding the top with one hand. Cut the cake horizontally, using a gentle sawing action.

FILLING & FROSTING

There are many simple ways to fill or decorate cakes. Whipped cream, jam, or chocolate frosting makes a quick and easy filling. Buttercream can be made in a variety of flavors to complement the flavor of the cake.

Chocolate buttercream
In a bowl, soften *10 tbsp (150 g) butter*, then add *¹/₄ cup (30 g) cocoa powder* and *2 cups (250 g) sifted confectioners' sugar*, and beat together until smooth. Add *a little milk* if necessary to give a spreading consistency. For a citrus icing, omit the cocoa powder and add *finely grated orange or lemon zest*.

Spreading frosting
Frost a cake only when it has cooled completely. Use a large narrow spatula and spread the frosting with long, smooth strokes over the top and side of the cake. Dip the spatula in warm water if the frosting sticks to it.

ZUCCHINI BREAD

 Serves 8–10

1 large zucchini

2 eggs

1/2 cup (125 ml) sunflower or corn oil, plus extra for greasing

1 1/8 cups (250 g) sugar

1/4 tsp vanilla extract

3 cups (375 g) self-rising flour

1 tsp ground cinnamon

1/2 tsp salt

1/2 cup (60 g) walnut pieces, coarsely chopped

★ 9- x 5- x 3-in (23- x 12- x 7.5-cm) loaf pan

1 Coarsely grate the zucchini into a strainer. Leave for 30 minutes to drain.

2 Beat the eggs until light and foamy. Add the sunflower oil, sugar, vanilla extract, and zucchini and mix lightly until combined.

3 Sift the flour, cinnamon, and salt into a large bowl. Make a well in the middle, pour in the zucchini mixture, and stir to mix thoroughly. Stir in the chopped walnuts.

4 Pour the mixture into the greased loaf pan and bake in a 350°F (180°C) oven for about 50 minutes, until firm. Turn out onto a wire rack and leave to cool.

Cook's know-how

For best results, the zucchini should be drained thoroughly. With your hand or the back of a spoon, press into the strainer to extract the excess juices.

CARROT CAKE

 Serves 8–10

2/3 cup (150 ml) sunflower or corn oil, plus extra for greasing

2 cups (250 g) whole-wheat self-rising flour

2 tsp baking powder

3/4 cup (150 g) dark brown sugar

1/2 cup (60 g) walnuts, coarsely chopped

2 carrots, grated

2 ripe bananas, mashed

2 eggs

1 tbsp milk

TOPPING

1/2 lb (250 g) low-fat cream cheese, at room temperature

2 tsp clear honey

1 tsp lemon juice

chopped walnuts to decorate

★ 8-in (20-cm) square cake pan

1 Lightly grease the pan and line the bottom with baking parchment.

2 Combine all the cake ingredients in a large bowl. Mix well until thoroughly blended. Turn into the prepared cake pan and level the surface.

3 Bake in a 350°F (180°C) oven for about 50 minutes, until the cake is well risen, firm to the touch, and beginning to shrink away from the sides of the pan

4 Leave the cake to cool in the pan for a few minutes. Turn out onto a wire rack, peel off the lining paper, and leave to cool completely.

5 Make the topping: mix together the cheese, honey, and lemon juice. Spread on top of the cake and sprinkle the walnuts over the top. Store the cake in the refrigerator until ready to serve.

Cook's know how

Spices enhance the flavor of all kinds of vegetable cakes; ground mace, cinnamon, coriander, and cloves and freshly grated nutmeg are particularly complementary. Add 1 tsp ground cinnamon to this cake if desired.

HEAVENLY CHOCOLATE CAKE

Serves 6

1/4 lb (125 g) butter, plus extra for greasing

7 oz (200 g) baker's semisweet chocolate, broken into pieces

2 tbsp water

3 eggs, separated

1/2 cup (125 g) sugar

2/3 cup (90 g) self-rising flour

1/2 cup (60 g) ground almonds

FUDGE ICING

4 tbsp butter

1/4 cup (30 g) cocoa powder

3 tbsp milk

2 cups (250 g) confectioner's sugar, sifted

white chocolate curls (page 431) to decorate

★ deep 8-in (20-cm) cake pan

1 Lightly butter the pan and line the bottom.

2 Put the chocolate into a heatproof bowl with the butter and water. Put the bowl over a pan of hot water and heat gently, stirring, until the mixture has melted. Leave to cool.

3 Combine the egg yolks and sugar in a large bowl and beat together with an electric beater until fluffy and very light in color. Stir in the cooled chocolate mixture. Carefully fold in the flour and ground almonds.

4 In a separate bowl, beat the egg whites until stiff but not dry. Fold into the cake mixture, gently but thoroughly. Pour the mixture into the prepared pan. Bake in a 350°F (180°C) oven for 50 minutes or until well risen and firm to the touch.

5 Leave the cake to cool in the pan for a few minutes, turn out onto a wire rack, and peel off the lining paper. Cool completely.

6 Make the fudge icing: melt the butter in a pan, add the cocoa powder, and cook, stirring, for 1 minute. Stir in the milk and confectioners' sugar. Beat well until smooth. Leave to cool until thickened.

7 Split the cake in half horizontally and sandwich the layers together with half of the fudge icing. With a narrow spatula, spread the remaining icing over the top and side of the cake. Decorate with white chocolate curls.

DEVIL'S FOOD CAKE

Serves 8–10

3/4 cup (175 g) soft margarine, plus extra for greasing

3 oz (90 g) baker's semisweet chocolate, broken into pieces

3/4 cup (175 ml) hot water

1 2/3 cups (300 g) dark brown sugar

3 eggs, beaten

2 1/2 cups (300 g) all-purpose flour

1 1/2 tsp baking soda

1 1/2 tsp baking powder

1 tsp vanilla extract

2/3 cup (150 ml) sour cream

DEVILISH FROSTING

1 3/4 cups (400 g) confectioners' sugar

2 egg whites

1/4 cup (60 ml) hot water

pinch of cream of tartar

★ 3 8-in (20-cm) layer cake pans

1 Grease the pans and line the bottoms with baking parchment.

2 Put the chocolate into a pan with the water. Heat gently, stirring, until the chocolate melts. Cool.

3 Combine the margarine and sugar in a bowl and beat until light and fluffy. Gradually beat in the eggs.

4 Stir in the melted chocolate. Sift together the flour, baking soda, and baking powder. Fold into the chocolate mixture until evenly blended, then fold in the vanilla extract and sour cream.

5 Divide the mixture evenly among the prepared pans. Bake in a 375°F (190°C) oven for about 25 minutes, until well risen, springy to the touch, and just shrinking away from the sides of the pans.

6 Turn out the cakes onto a wire rack, peel off the lining paper, and leave to cool thoroughly.

7 Make the Devilish Frosting: combine all the ingredients in a heatproof bowl. Set the bowl over a pan of hot water and beat with an electric mixer for 7–12 minutes, until the mixture is white, thick, and stands in peaks.

8 Use half of the Devilish Frosting to sandwich the 3 layers of cake together, then spread the remainder of the frosting over the top and side of the cake, swirling it decoratively and pulling it into peaks with a narrow spatula.

MARBLED COFFEE RING CAKE

 Serves 8–10

1 cup (250 g) soft margarine, plus extra for greasing

1¼ cups (250 g) sugar

4 eggs

2 cups (250 g) self-rising flour

2 tsp baking powder

2 tsp instant coffee powder

1 tbsp hot water

1 oz (30 g) white chocolate

ICING

4 tbsp butter, softened

3 tbsp milk

2 tbsp instant coffee powder

2 cups (250 g) confectioners' sugar, sifted

★ 7-cup (1.75 liter) ring mold

1 Lightly grease the ring mold with margarine.

2 Combine the margarine, sugar, eggs, flour, and baking powder in a large bowl. Beat until smooth.

3 Put half of the mixture into another bowl. Dissolve the instant coffee powder in the measured hot water and stir into one half of the cake mixture.

4 Drop tablespoonfuls of the plain mixture into the ring mold, then tablespoonfuls of the coffee mixture on top of the plain mixture. Marble by swirling together with a skewer.

5 Bake in a 350°F (180°C) oven for 40 minutes or until well risen and firm to the touch. Leave to cool for a few minutes, then turn out onto a wire rack set over a tray, and cool completely.

6 Make the icing: combine the butter, milk, and coffee in a pan and heat, stirring, until smooth. Remove from the heat and beat in the confectioners' sugar until the mixture is smooth and glossy.

7 Leave to cool, then pour over the cake, spreading it over the sides to cover completely. Leave to set.

8 Melt the white chocolate in a heatproof bowl over a pan of hot water. Leave to cool slightly, then spoon into a plastic bag. Snip off a corner of the bag and drizzle the chocolate over the cake. Leave to set.

WHITE CHOCOLATE CAKE

 Serves 8–10

6 tbsp (90 g) butter, melted and cooled slightly, plus extra for greasing

6 jumbo eggs

¾ cup (175 g) sugar

1 cup (125 g) self-rising flour

¼ cup (30 g) cocoa powder

2 tbsp cornstarch

FILLING AND TOPPING

1¼ cups (300 ml) heavy cream, whipped until thick

white chocolate curls (optional) (page 431)

★ deep 9-in (23-cm) round cake pan

1 Lightly butter the cake pan and line the bottom of the pan with a sheet of baking parchment.

2 Put the eggs and sugar into a large bowl and beat together with an electric beater at high speed until the mixture is pale and thick enough to leave a trail on itself when the beater is lifted out.

3 Sift together the flour, cocoa powder, and cornstarch and fold half into the egg mixture. Pour half of the cooled butter around the edge of the mixture and fold in gently.

4 Repeat with the remaining flour mixture and butter, folding gently.

5 Turn the mixture into the prepared cake pan and tilt the pan to level the surface. Bake in a 350°F (180°C) oven for 35–40 minutes, until the cake is well risen and firm to the touch. Turn out onto a wire rack, peel off the lining paper, and cool.

6 Cut the cake in half horizontally and sandwich the layers together with half of the whipped cream. Cover the cake with a thin layer of cream, then pipe the remainder around the top and bottom edges.

7 Press the chocolate curls over the top and side of the cake, if preferred.

CHOCOLATE & ORANGE MOUSSE CAKE

This cake is made of chocolate sponge layers sandwiched together with a deliciously fluffy chocolate and orange mousse. When making the mousse, don't overbeat the egg whites; when they just flop over at the tip of a peak they are ready to fold into the chocolate mixture.

 Serves 8–10

butter for greasing

4 eggs

1/2 cup (125 g) sugar

2/3 cup (90 g) self-rising flour

1/4 cup (30 g) cocoa powder

MOUSSE

6 oz (175 g) baker's semisweet chocolate, broken into pieces

grated zest and juice of 1 orange

1 tsp powdered gelatin

2 eggs, separated

1 1/4 cups (300 ml) heavy cream, whipped until thick

DECORATION

1 1/4 cups (300 ml) heavy cream, whipped until thick

strips of orange zest, blanched

✶ deep 9-in (23-cm) springform cake pan

1 Lightly butter the pan and line the bottom with baking parchment. Make the sponge cake (see box, right).

2 Bake the sponge in a 350°F (180°C) oven for 40–45 minutes, until the sponge cake is well risen and beginning to shrink away from the side of the pan. Turn the cake out onto a wire rack, peel off the lining paper, and leave to cool throughly.

3 Cut the cake in half horizontally. Put one half back into the clean pan.

4 Make the mousse: put the chocolate into a heatproof bowl set over a pan of hot water. Heat gently, stirring occasionally, until the chocolate has melted. Leave to cool slightly.

5 Strain the orange juice into a small heatproof bowl and sprinkle on the gelatin. Leave for 3 minutes or until spongy, then stand the bowl in a saucepan of gently simmering water for 3 minutes or until the gelatin has dissolved.

6 Stir the egg yolks and orange zest into the cooled chocolate. Slowly stir in the dissolved gelatin, then fold in the whipped cream. In a separate bowl, beat the egg whites until stiff but not dry, then gently fold into the chocolate mixture until they are well blended.

7 Pour the mousse on top of the cake layer in the pan. Put the remaining cake layer on top. Cover and chill in the refrigerator until the mousse filling is set.

8 Remove the side of the pan and slide the cake onto a plate. Decorate with cream and orange zest.

Making sponge cake

Combine the eggs and sugar in a large bowl and beat with an electric beater at high speed until the mixture is pale and thick enough to leave a trail on itself when the beater is lifted out.

Sift the flour and cocoa powder over the surface.

Fold in the flour and cocoa until blended.

Turn the mixture into the prepared pan and tilt to level the surface.

STRAWBERRY SHORTCAKE

 Serves 8

butter for greasing

3 eggs

3/8 cup (90 g) sugar

2/3 cup (90 g) self-rising flour

FILLING AND TOPPING

1 1/4 cups (300 ml) heavy cream, whipped until thick

1 cup (125 g) strawberries, sliced

1 passion fruit, halved

strawberries, halved, to decorate

★ 2 7-in (18-cm) layer cake pans

1 Lightly butter the cake pans, line the bottoms with baking parchment, then butter the parchment.

2 Put the eggs and sugar into a large bowl. Beat with an electric beater at high speed until the mixture is pale and thick enough to leave a trail when the beater is lifted out.

3 Sift in half of the flour and fold in gently. Repeat with the remaining flour.

4 Divide the mixture between the pans. Tilt to spread the mixture evenly.

5 Bake in a 375°F (190°C) oven for 20–25 minutes, until well risen, golden, and beginning to shrink away from the sides of the pans. Turn out onto a wire rack, peel off the lining paper, and leave to cool.

6 Spread half of the whipped cream over 1 of the cakes. Top with the sliced strawberries and passion fruit pulp. Put the other cake on top and press down gently.

7 Spread the remaining cream on top of the cake, smoothing it neatly with a narrow spatula. Decorate with strawberry halves.

Cook's know-how

Cakes made without fat do not keep well, so be sure to eat the cake on the day of baking.

JELLY ROLL

 Serves 6–8

butter for greasing

4 jumbo eggs

1/2 cup (125 ml) sugar, plus extra for sprinkling

1 cup (125 g) self-rising flour

confectioners' sugar for sprinkling

FILLING

1/4 cup (60 g) raspberry jam

★ 9- x 13-in (23- x 33-cm) jelly roll pan

1 Lightly butter the jelly roll pan, line with baking parchment, then lightly butter the parchment.

2 Put the eggs and sugar into a large bowl. Beat together with an electric mixer at high speed until the mixture is pale and thick enough to leave a trail when the beater is lifted out.

3 Sift the flour into the egg mixture and fold in gently but thoroughly. Turn the mixture into the prepared pan and tilt to spread the mixture evenly, particularly into the corners.

4 Bake in a 425°F (220°C) oven for 10 minutes, until the cake is golden and beginning to shrink away from the sides of the pan.

5 Invert the cake onto a large piece of baking parchment that has been sprinkled liberally with confectioners' sugar. Peel off the lining paper and trim the edges of the sponge with a sharp knife.

6 Roll up the cake and the baking parchment together. Leave to stand for 2–3 minutes.

7 Unroll the sponge and remove the baking parchment. Spread the cake with warmed jam and roll up again. Wrap tightly in baking parchment and leave to cool. Unwrap, dust with confectioners' sugar, and serve in slices.

Cook's know-how

Don't spread the cake batter in the pan with a spatula; that would knock the air out of the batter.

MUFFINS

Muffins are small, moist quick breads made with self-rising flour or flour and baking powder and flavored with endless combinations of ingredients. Here are 3 of the tastiest, together with some complementary butters for spreading while the muffins are still warm.

CRANBERRY & PECAN

 Makes 12

1 egg, lightly beaten

4 tbsp butter, melted, plus extra for greasing

1 cup (250 ml) orange juice

3 cups (375 g) self-rising flour, sifted

3/4 cup (175 g) sugar

3 tbsp oatmeal

pinch of salt

7 oz (200 g) pecan halves, coarsely chopped

1 cup (125 g) cranberries

☆ 12-cup muffin pan

1 Mix together the egg, butter, and orange juice. Combine the flour, sugar, oatmeal, and salt and stir into the orange juice mixture with the pecans and cranberries. Make sure the ingredients are just combined and that the mixture has a thick consistency.

2 Butter each cup of the muffin pan, then spoon in the muffin mixture, filling the cups almost to the tops.

3 Bake in a 400°F (200°C) oven for 10 minutes; reduce the oven temperature to 350°F (180°C), and bake for about 15 minutes, until the muffins are golden and firm. Serve the muffins warm.

APRICOT & BRAN

 Makes 12

1 cup (90 g) dried apricots, diced

1 egg, lightly beaten

2 tbsp (30 g) butter, melted, plus extra for greasing

2 tbsp honey

1/2 cup (125 ml) milk

1 tsp vanilla extract

1/2 cup (125 g) plain yogurt

1 2/3 cups (200 g) self-rising flour, sifted

2 1/2 cups (175 g) sugar

3/4 cup (125 g) raisin bran cereal

pinch of salt

☆ 12-cup muffin pan

1 Mix the apricots with the egg, butter, honey, milk, vanilla extract, and yogurt. Combine the flour, sugar, raisin bran, and salt, add to the milk mixture, and stir.

2 Butter each cup of the muffin pan, then spoon in the muffin mixture, filling the cups almost to the tops.

3 Bake the muffins in a 400°F (200°C) oven for 10 minutes; reduce the oven temperature to 350°F (180°C) and bake for 15 minutes or until golden and firm. Serve warm.

DOUBLE CHOCOLATE

 Makes 12

2 eggs, lightly beaten

1/2 cup (125 g) plain yogurt

1/2 cup (125 ml) strong brewed coffee

1/2 cup (125 ml) milk

2 cups (250 g) self-rising flour, sifted

1 1/8 cups (250 g) sugar

5/8 cup (75 g) cocoa powder

pinch of salt

1/2 cup (100 g) baker's semisweet chocolate chips

melted butter for greasing

☆ 12-cup muffin pan

1 Combine the eggs, yogurt, coffee, and milk in a large bowl.

2 Sift together the flour, sugar, cocoa powder, and salt, and stir into the milk mixture. Mix until just combined. Stir in the chocolate chips.

3 Butter each cup of the muffin pan, then spoon in the muffin mixture, filling the cups almost to the tops.

4 Bake the muffins in a 400°F (200°C) oven for about 10 minutes; reduce the oven temperature to 350°F (180°C) and continue to bake for about 15 minutes, until the muffins are golden and firm. Serve warm.

Clockwise from top: *Apricot & Bran Muffins, Double Chocolate Muffins, Double Chocolate Muffin served with Honey & Spice Butter, Apricot & Bran Muffin served with Chocolate & Nut Butter, Cranberry & Pecan Muffins.*

BUTTERS FOR MUFFINS

HONEY & SPICE

Put *1/4 lb (125 g) butter* into a bowl and beat with a wooden spoon until softened. Add *2 tbsp honey, 1/2 tsp ground cinnamon,* and *1/4 tsp grated nutmeg.* Stir until well combined. Roll the butter in plastic wrap to make a log shape and chill until firm. Remove the plastic wrap and cut into slices.

CHOCOLATE & NUT

Combine *3/4 oz (20 g) chopped baker's semisweet chocolate, 1 tsp sugar,* and *1 tbsp brandy* and heat over a pan of simmering water until melted. Cool. Soften *1/4 lb (125 g) butter* and stir in the chocolate mixture and *1/4 cup (30 g) ground hazelnuts.* Shape into a block and wrap in plastic wrap. Chill and slice.

VICTORIA LAYER CAKE

 Serves 6–8

3/4 cup (175 g) soft margarine, plus extra for greasing

3/4 cup (175 g) sugar

3 eggs

1 1/2 cups (175 g) self-rising flour

1 1/2 tsp baking powder

FILLING

1/4 cup (60 g) raspberry or strawberry jam

sugar for sprinkling

⋆ *2 7-in (18-cm) layer cake pans*

1 Lightly grease the pans and line the bottoms with baking parchment.

2 Combine all the cake ingredients in a large bowl. Beat well for about 2 minutes, until smooth.

3 Divide the mixture between the pans and level the surfaces. Bake in a 350°F (180°C) oven for about 25 minutes, until the cakes are well risen, golden, and springy to the touch.

4 Turn out onto a wire rack, peel off the lining paper, and leave to cool.

5 Sandwich the 2 cakes together with jam and sprinkle the top of the cake with sugar.

CHOCOLATE LAYER CAKE

Mix 2 tbsp cocoa powder with 3 tbsp boiling water and leave to cool. Add to the cake ingredients before beating. Sandwich together and cover with chocolate buttercream (page 464). Decorate the top of the cake with chocolate curls (page 431).

LEMON LAYER CAKE

Add the grated zest of 1 lemon to the cake ingredients before beating. Sandwich the cakes together with lemon curd and 2/3 cup (150 ml) whipping cream, whipped until thick.

ICED LIME SHEET CAKE

 Makes 9 squares

3/4 cup (175 g) soft margarine, plus extra for greasing

3/4 cup (175 g) sugar

2 cups (250 g) self-rising flour

1 1/2 tsp baking powder

3 eggs

3 tbsp milk

grated zest of 2 limes

ICING

2 cups (250 g) confectioners' sugar

juice of 2 limes

⋆ *9- x 12-in (23- x 30-cm) cake pan*

1 Lightly grease the pan and line the bottom with baking parchment.

2 Combine all the cake ingredients in a large bowl and beat well for about 2 minutes, until smooth and thoroughly blended.

3 Turn into the prepared tin and level the surface. Bake in 350°F (180°C) oven for 35–40 minutes, until the cake is well risen, springy to the touch, and beginning to shrink away from the sides of the cake pan.

4 Leave to cool slightly in the pan, then turn out onto a wire rack, peel off the lining paper, and cool.

5 Make the icing: sift the confectioners' sugar into a bowl. Mix in enough of the lime juice to give a runny consistency. Pour over the cake, spreading carefully with a narrow spatula, and leave to set. When cold, cut into squares and serve.

CHOCOLATE & MINT SHEET CAKE

Mix 1/4 cup (30 g) cocoa powder with 1/4 cup (60 ml) hot water and leave to cool. Add to the cake ingredients with 1/4 cup (30 g) chopped fresh mint. For the icing, break 1/2 lb (250 g) baker's semisweet chocolate into pieces and put into a heatproof bowl with 6 tbsp (90 g) margarine and 4 tbsp hot water. Put the bowl over a saucepan of hot water and heat gently until the chocolate has melted. Beat together until smooth and shiny. Spread over the top of the cake.

CHOCOLATE & VANILLA BATTENBURG CAKE

 Serves 8

*1/2 cup (125 g) soft margarine,
plus extra for greasing*

1/2 cup (125 g) sugar

2 jumbo eggs

1/3 cup (60 g) ground rice

1 cup (125 g) self-rising flour

1/2 tsp baking powder

a few drops of vanilla extract

1 1/2 tsp cocoa powder

3 tbsp apricot jam

1/2 lb (250 g) almond paste

*★ shallow 7-in (18-cm) square
cake pan*

1 Lightly grease the cake
pan with margarine and
line the bottom with
waxed paper.

2 Combine the margarine,
sugar, eggs, ground rice,
flour, baking powder, and
vanilla extract in a large
bowl. Beat well for 2 minutes
or until the mixture is smooth
and evenly combined.

3 Spoon half of the
mixture into one half of
the prepared pan. Dissolve
the cocoa in a little hot water
to make a thick paste and
add to the remaining cake
mixture in the bowl. Mix
well, then spoon into the
remaining half of the pan.

4 Bake the mixture in a
325°F (160°C) oven for
35 minutes or until the cake
is well risen and springy to
the touch. Turn out on to a
wire rack, peel off the lining
paper, and leave the cake to
cool thoroughly.

5 Trim the edges of the
cake. Cut it into 4 equal
strips down the length of the
2 colors.

6 Warm the apricot jam in
a small saucepan. Stack
the cake strips, alternating
the colors to give a
checkerboard effect and
sticking them together with
the apricot jam.

7 Roll out the almond
paste into an oblong
that is the same length as
the cake and wide enough to
wrap around it. Put the cake
on top, then brush with jam.
Wrap the paste around the
cake (see box, below).

8 Score the top with a
crisscross pattern and
crimp the edges with your
fingers to decorate.

Wrapping the cake

Wrap the almond paste
around the cake, pressing
it on gently and making
the seam in 1 corner.
Turn to hide the seam.

FRUIT CAKE

 Serves 8–10

*1 cup (250 g) soft margarine,
plus extra for greasing*

*1 1/3 cups (250 g) dark brown
sugar*

4 eggs

2 cups (250 g) self-rising flour

1 1/2 cups (250 g) raisins

1 1/2 cups (250 g) golden raisins

*1/2 cup (125 g) glacé cherries,
halved and rinsed*

1/2 tsp ground pie spice

1 tbsp brandy

*★ deep 8-in (20-cm) round
cake pan*

1 Lightly grease the pan
and line the bottom with
waxed paper.

2 Combine all the
ingredients in a large
bowl and mix well until
combined. Pour the mixture
into the prepared cake pan
and level the surface.

3 Bake in a 275°F (140°C)
oven for 2–2 1/4 hours.
Cover the top of the cake with
baking parchment after about
1 hour to prevent the top
from becoming too brown.

4 When cooked, the cake
should be firm to the
touch and a thin skewer
inserted in the middle of the
cake should come out clean.
Leave the cake to cool in the
pan before turning it out.
Store the cake in an airtight
container.

MINCEMEAT MUFFINS

 Makes 32

1 cup (375 g) mincemeat

1 cup (250 g) currants

2 eggs

2/3 cup (150 g) sugar

2/3 cup (150 g) soft margarine

2 cups (250 g) self-rising flour

★ 32 paper cupcake liners

★ 3 12-cup muffin pans

1 Combine all the ingredients in a bowl and beat well for about 2 minutes.

2 Divide the cake batter evenly among the paper liners inside muffin pans.

3 Bake in a 325°F (160°C) oven for 25–30 minutes, until golden and springy to the touch. Remove the muffins from the pans and cool on a wire rack.

Cook's know-how

Mincemeat is traditionally made with beef suet. If you want a vegetarian version, use vegetable shortening. Homemade mincemeat is best, but you can improve on commercial ones by adding a variety of different ingredients, such as chopped nuts, angelica, glacé cherries, or dried apricots, peaches, or pears.

SIMNEL CAKE

This is now a traditional Easter cake in England, but originally it was given by girls to their mothers on Mother's Day, or Mothering Sunday. The almond paste balls represent the 11 disciples of Christ, excluding Judas Iscariot.

 Serves 8–10

3/4 cup (175 g) soft margarine, plus extra for greasing

1 cup (175 g) dark brown sugar

3 eggs

1 1/2 cups (175 g) self-rising flour

1 cup (175 g) golden raisins

1/3 cup (90 g) currants

1/3 cup (90 g) glacé cherries, quartered, rinsed, and dried

1/4 cup (30 g) candied peel, roughly chopped

grated zest of 1 large lemon

1 tsp ground pie spice

FILLING AND DECORATION

1 lb (500 g) almond paste

2 tbsp apricot jam

1 egg white

★ deep 7-in (18-cm) round cake pan with a removable ring

1 Roll out one-third of the almond paste. Using the base of the cake pan as a guide, cut out a 7-in (18-cm) round.

2 Grease the cake pan and line the bottom and side with waxed paper.

3 Combine all the cake ingredients in a bowl. Beat well until thoroughly blended. Spoon half of the cake batter into the prepared pan and smooth the surface. Top with the round of almond paste.

4 Spoon the remaining cake batter on top and level the surface.

5 Bake in a 300°F (150°C) oven for 2 1/4 hours or until the cake is risen, golden brown, and firm to the touch.

6 Cover the top of the cake with baking parchment if it is browning too quickly. Leave to cool for 10 minutes, then remove from the pan, and leave to cool completely.

7 Warm the jam and use to brush the top of the cake.

8 To decorate the cake, roll out half of the remaining almond paste and use the pan to cut out a 7-in (18-cm) round. Put on top of the jam and crimp the edges. Roll the remaining almond paste into 11 even-sized balls. Place around the edge of the cake, using the egg white to attach them.

9 Brush the tops of the balls and the almond paste with egg white. Place under the broiler for 1–2 minutes, until the balls are golden.

DUNDEE CAKE

 Serves 8–10

10 tbsp (150 g) butter, at room temperature, plus extra for greasing

3/4 cup (150 g) dark brown sugar

3 eggs

2 cups (250 g) all-purpose flour

1 tsp baking powder

1 cup (175 g) golden raisins

1/3 cup (90 g) currants

1/2 cup (90 g) raisins

1/4 cup (60 g) glacé cherries, quartered, rinsed, and dried

1/2 cup (60 g) chopped mixed candied peel

2 tbsp ground almonds

grated zest of 1 large lemon

1/2 cup (60 g) whole almonds, blanched and halved, to decorate

★ deep 8 in (20 cm) round pan with a removable ring

1 Lightly butter the cake pan and line the bottom with waxed paper.

2 Combine the butter, sugar, eggs, flour, and baking powder in a bowl and beat for 2 minutes or until well blended. Stir in the fruit, mixed peel, ground almonds, and lemon zest.

3 Spoon the mixture into the prepared tin. Level the surface and arrange the halved almonds neatly in concentric circles on top.

4 Bake in a 325°F (160°C) oven for 1 1/2 hours or until well risen, golden, and firm to the touch. A thin skewer inserted into the middle of the cake should come out clean. Cover the cake with baking parchment halfway through baking if it is browning too quickly.

5 Leave the cake to cool in the pan for a few minutes, then turn out onto a wire rack and leave to cool completely. Store the cake in an airtight container for about 1 week before eating.

FRUITED BANANA LOAF

 Serves 8–10

1/4 lb (125 g) margarine, plus extra for greasing

2 cups (250 g) self rising flour

3/4 cup (175 g) sugar

2/3 cup (125 g) golden raisins

1/2 cup (60 g) walnuts, roughly chopped

1/2 cup (125 g) glacé cherries, quartered, rinsed, and dried

2 jumbo eggs, beaten

1 lb (500 g) bananas, peeled and mashed

★ 9- x 5- x 3-in (23- x 12- x 7.5 cm) loaf pan

1 Grease the loaf pan and line the bottom with waxed paper.

2 Put the flour into a bowl, add the margarine, and rub in until the mixture resembles fine bread crumbs. Add the sugar, golden raisins, walnuts, and glacé cherries and mix well.

3 Add the eggs and mashed bananas and beat the mixture until well blended. Spoon into the prepared pan.

4 Bake the mixture in a 325°F (160°C) oven for about 1 1/4 hours, until well risen and firm to the touch. A thin skewer inserted into the middle of the loaf should come out clean.

5 Leave the loaf to cool slightly in the pan, then turn out onto a wire rack, and peel off the lining paper. Leave the loaf to cool completely before slicing and serving.

Cook's know-how

If you like, you can add some grated lemon zest or 1 tsp ground pie spice to the mixture, for extra flavoring.

FESTIVE FRUIT CAKE

Celebrate the holidays with a specially decorated cake. Because rich fruit cake is usually eaten over a period of days, the decoration should be as attractive and long-lasting as possible. Here are 3 different presentation ideas, each of which is easy to adapt according to available ingredients and personal taste.

RICH FRUIT CAKE

Makes 1 9-in (23-cm) cake

1³/4 cups (425 g) currants

1¹/2 cups (250 g) golden raisins

1¹/2 cups (250 g) dark raisins

1¹/4 cups (300 g) glacé cherries, quartered, rinsed, and dried

²/3 cup (75 g) mixed candied peel, chopped

¹/4 cup (60 ml) brandy, plus extra for soaking

2¹/2 cups (300 g) all-purpose flour

1 tsp ground pie spice

¹/2 tsp grated nutmeg

1¹/4 cups (300 g) soft margarine, plus extra for greasing

1¹/4 cups (300 g) dark brown sugar

5 eggs

¹/2 cup (60 g) whole unblanched almonds, roughly chopped

1 tbsp molasses

grated zest of 1 large lemon

grated zest of 1 large orange

✶ deep 9-in (23-cm) round or 8-in (20-cm) square cake pan

1 Combine the fruit and candied peel in a large bowl. Add the brandy and stir to mix well. Cover and leave to macerate overnight.

2 Put the remaining ingredients into a large bowl and beat well with an electric mixer until thoroughly blended. Stir in the macerated fruits and any liquid.

3 Grease the cake pan with margarine, line the bottom and side with a double layer of waxed paper, and grease the paper. Spoon the mixture into the prepared tin. Smooth the surface and cover the top with baking parchment.

4 Bake in a 275°F (140°C) oven for 4³/4–5 hours, until firm to the touch and a skewer inserted into the middle of the cake comes out clean. Leave the cake to cool in the pan.

5 When the cake has cooled, pierce it in several places with a thin skewer and pour on a little brandy. Remove the cake from the pan, but leave the lining paper on. Wrap the cake in more waxed paper, then overwrap with foil. Store the cake in a cool place for up to 3 months, to mature, unwrapping and spooning over more brandy (1–2 tbsp) occasionally.

6 Decorate the cake with glacé fruit, almond paste, or ready-to-use icing (see box, right). Tie a ribbon around the cake, if desired.

Making holly leaves and berries

1 On a work surface lightly dusted with confectioners' sugar, thinly roll out the green icing. Cut the icing into diamond shapes with a small, sharp knife.

2 With a small pastry cutter or the tip of a small, sharp knife, cut a series of curves out of the edges of the diamond-shaped icing to form holly leaves.

3 Mold the holly leaves to form pointed tips. Roll the red icing into small balls to represent holly berries. Brush with water and attach to the cake.

CAKE DECORATIONS

Cakes can be decorated with a variety of items, many of which are available ready-made. These are a few of our favorites.

GLACE FRUIT CAKE

Put ¹/3 cup (90 g) apricot jam into a small saucepan and stir over low heat until melted. Brush the melted jam over the fruit cake with a pastry brush. Decorate the top of the cake with *glacé fruit* and *nuts* and glaze the topping with more apricot jam.

FESTIVE DRAGEE CAKE

Brush the cake with *3 tbsp melted apricot jam*. Roll out 1¹/2 lb (750 g) *almond paste* and use to cover the cake. Leave to dry for 1 week. Decorate with *gold and silver dragées*.

HOLLY BERRY CAKE

Brush the cake with *3 tbsp melted apricot jam*. Roll out 1¹/2 lb (750 g) *almond paste* to cover the cake. Leave for 1 week to dry. Roll out 1 lb (500 g) *fondant*. Brush the almond paste with *a little sherry*, then lift the icing onto the cake. Smooth and trim. Use green and red food colorings to color the trimmings. Make holly leaves and berries (see box, left).

Clockwise from top: *Glacé Fruit Cake, Holly Berry Cake, Festive Dragée Cake.*

CORN BREAD

 Makes 9 squares

sunflower or corn oil for greasing

1¹/₂ cups (175 g) fine yellow cornmeal

1 cup (125 g) all-purpose flour

2–3 tbsp brown sugar

2 tsp baking powder

1 tsp salt

1¹/₄ cups (300 ml) lukewarm milk

2 eggs, lightly beaten

4 tbsp butter, melted and cooled slightly

★ *7-in (18-cm) square cake pan*

1 Lightly oil the cake pan. Put the cornmeal, flour, sugar, baking powder, and salt into a large bowl and make a well in the middle. Pour in the milk, eggs, and butter and beat the ingredients to form a batter.

2 Pour the mixture into the cake pan and bake in a 400°F (200°C) oven for 25–30 minutes, until golden. Leave the corn bread to cool, then cut into squares.

CHILI & CHEESE CORN BREAD

For a savory variation to serve with Chili con Carne, add 1 cup (250 g) grated Cheddar cheese and 1 cored, seeded, and finely chopped fresh green chili to the corn bread mixture, and proceed as directed.

SHORTBREAD

 Makes 8 wedges

1 cup (125 g) all-purpose flour

¹/₈ cup (60 g) ground rice

1¹/₄ lb (125 g) butter, plus extra for greasing

¹/₄ cup (60 g) sugar, plus extra for sprinkling

1 Mix the flour with the ground rice in a bowl. Add the butter and rub in with the fingertips. Stir in the sugar. Knead the mixture lightly until it forms a smooth dough.

2 Lightly butter a baking sheet. Roll out the dough on a lightly floured work surface into a 7-in (18-cm) round. Lift onto the baking sheet. Crimp the edges to decorate, prick all over with a fork, and mark into 8 wedges with a sharp knife. Chill until firm.

3 Bake in a 325°F (160°C) oven for 35 minutes or until a pale golden brown color. Mark the wedges again and lightly sprinkle the shortbread with sugar.

4 Allow the shortbread to cool on the baking sheet for 5 minutes, then lift off carefully with a narrow spatula and transfer to a wire rack. Leave to cool completely. To serve, cut the shortbread into wedges along the marks.

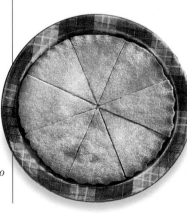

GINGERBREAD

 Makes 15 squares

¹/₂ lb (250 g) margarine or butter, plus extra for greasing

1 cup packed (250 g) dark brown sugar

²/₃ cup (250 g) molasses

3¹/₄ cups (375 g) all-purpose flour

5 tsp ground ginger

2 tsp ground cinnamon

2 eggs, beaten

3 pieces of ginger in syrup, drained and roughly chopped

1¹/₄ cups (300 ml) milk

2 tsp baking soda

★ *9- x 12-in (23- x 30-cm) cake pan*

1 Lightly grease the pan and line the bottom with waxed paper.

2 Combine the margarine, sugar, and molasses in a pan, stirring, and heat until smooth. Cool slightly.

3 Sift the flour and ground spices into the mixture. Stir well, then beat in the eggs and ginger.

4 Warm the milk in a small heavy saucepan, and add the baking soda. Pour into the gingerbread mixture and stir gently until thoroughly blended.

5 Pour the mixture into the prepared pan. Bake in a 325°F (160°C) oven for about 1 hour, until well risen and springy to the touch.

6 Leave to cool in the pan for a few minutes, then turn out onto a wire rack, and peel off the lining paper. Leave to cool completely. Cut into even-sized squares to serve.

Cook's know-how

Gingerbread improves with keeping and is best made 2–3 days before eating. Store in an airtight container to keep the gingerbread moist until serving.

BARA BRITH

 Serves 8

2 cups (375 g) mixed dried fruit

1 1/3 cups (250 g) dark brown sugar

1 1/4 cups (300 ml) strong hot tea, strained

butter for greasing

2 1/2 cups (300 g) self-rising flour

1 egg, beaten

★ 9- x 5- x 3-in (23- x 12- x 7.5-cm) loaf pan

1 Combine the fruit, sugar, and tea in a large bowl. Stir, then cover and leave to steep for at least 8 hours.

2 Lightly butter the loaf pan and line the bottom with waxed paper. Stir the flour and egg into the fruit mixture, mixing well. Transfer to the loaf pan and level the surface.

3 Bake in a 300°F (150°C) oven for 1 1/2–1 3/4 hours, until well risen and firm to the touch. A thin skewer inserted into the middle should come out clean.

4 Leave to cool in the pan for about 10 minutes, then turn out onto a wire rack, and peel off the lining paper. Leave to cool completely. Serve sliced and buttered, if desired.

Bara brith

This is a favorite fruit bread from Wales. "Bara" is the Welsh word for bread and "brith" means speckled.

DATE & WALNUT LOAF

 Serves 8

6 tbsp (90 g) soft margarine, plus extra for greasing

1 1/3 cups (250 g) roughly chopped pitted dates

2/3 cup (150 ml) boiling water

3/8 cup (90 g) sugar

1 egg

2 cups (250 g) self-rising flour

1 tsp baking powder

3/4 cup (90 g) walnuts, roughly chopped

★ 9- x 5- x 3-in (23- x 12- x 7.5-cm) loaf pan

1 Lightly grease the loaf pan with margarine and line with waxed paper.

2 Put the dates into a bowl, pour on the measured boiling water, and leave for about 15 minutes.

3 Combine the margarine, sugar, egg, flour, and baking powder in a large bowl and beat until well blended. Add the walnuts and dates, plus the soaking liquid, and stir to mix.

4 Spoon the mixture into the prepared loaf pan and bake in a 350°F (180°C) oven for 1 1/4–1 1/2 hours, until well risen and firm to the touch. A thin skewer inserted into the middle of the loaf should come out clean when it is cooked.

5 Leave to cool in the loaf pan for a few minutes, then turn out onto a wire rack, and peel off the lining paper. Leave to cool completely. Serve sliced and buttered, if desired.

CHERRY & BANANA LOAF

Omit the dates and walnuts and add 1/2 cup (125 g) quartered glacé cherries and 2 mashed large ripe bananas. Proceed as directed in the recipe.

SWEET GRIDDLE CAKES

 Makes 12

2 cups (250 g) self-rising flour

1 tsp baking powder

1/4 lb (125 g) butter

3/8 cup (90 g) sugar

1/3 cup (90 g) currants

1/2 tsp ground pie spice

1 egg, beaten

about 2 tbsp milk

sunflower or corn oil for greasing

★ 3-in (7-cm) cookie cutter

1 Sift the flour and baking powder into a large bowl. Add the butter and rub in with the fingertips until the mixture resembles fine bread crumbs.

2 Add the sugar, currants, and pie spice and stir to mix. Add the egg and enough milk to form a soft but not sticky dough.

3 On a lightly floured work surface, roll out the dough to a thickness of 1/4 in (5 mm). Cut into rounds with cookie cutter.

4 Heat a griddle or a heavy skillet and grease with a little oil. Cook the griddle cakes on the hot griddle or pan over low heat for about 3 minutes on each side until they are cooked through and golden brown.

5 Leave to cool on a wire rack. Serve on the day they are made, if possible.

Cook's know-how

If preferred, serve the sweet griddle cakes hot, lightly sprinkled with sugar, straight from the griddle or skillet.

BISCUITS

 Makes 12

4 tbsp butter, plus extra for greasing

2 cups (250 g) self-rising flour

2 tsp baking powder

2 tbsp sugar

1 egg

about 2/3 cup (150 ml) milk, plus extra for glazing

butter and jam to serve

★ 2-in (5-cm) cookie cutter

1 Lightly butter a large baking sheet.

2 Sift the flour and baking powder into a bowl. Rub in the butter with the fingertips until the mixture resembles fine bread crumbs. Stir in the sugar.

3 Break the egg into a measuring cup and add milk to make 2/3 cup (150 ml). Beat lightly to mix. Add to the bowl and mix to a soft dough.

4 Lightly knead the dough until smooth. Roll out until 1/2 in (1 cm) thick, cut into rounds with the cookie cutter, and put on the baking sheet. Brush with milk.

5 Bake in a 425°F (220°C) oven for about 10 minutes, until risen and golden. Cool on a wire rack. Serve the biscuits on the day made, if possible, with butter and jam.

CHEESE BISCUITS

Omit the sugar and add 1 cup (125 g) grated aged Cheddar cheese and 1/2 tsp dry mustard to the dry ingredients before mixing in the egg and milk. Roll out the dough into a 6-in (15-cm) round and cut it into wedges. Brush with milk and sprinkle with finely grated cheese. Bake as directed.

480

WHOLE-WHEAT GRIDDLE CAKES

 Makes 20

1 2/3 cups (175 g) whole-wheat self-rising flour

1 tsp baking powder

3 tbsp sugar

1 jumbo egg

7/8 cup (200 ml) milk

sunflower or corn oil for greasing

syrup or butter and jam to serve

1 Combine the flour, baking powder, and sugar in a bowl and stir to mix. Make a well in the middle and add the egg and half of the milk. Beat well to make a smooth, thick batter.

2 Add enough milk to give the batter the consistency of thick cream.

3 Heat a griddle or heavy skillet and grease with oil. Drop spoonfuls of batter onto the hot griddle or pan, spacing them well apart. When bubbles rise to the surface, turn the cakes over and cook until golden.

4 As each batch is cooked, wrap the cakes in a clean dish towel to keep them soft. Serve warm, with syrup or butter and jam.

PLAIN GRIDDLE CAKES

Substitute plain self-rising flour for the whole-wheat self-rising flour, use a little less milk, and proceed as directed.

Cook's know-how

In England these are also known as drop scones or Scotch pancakes. Leftovers freeze well. Stack with freezer wrap or waxed paper between layers and freeze for up to 6 months.

IRISH SODA BREAD

 Makes 1 loaf

4 cups (500 g) all-purpose white flour, plus extra for dusting

1 tsp baking soda

1 tsp salt

1 1/4 cups (300 ml) buttermilk, or half milk and half plain yogurt

6 tbsp (90 ml) lukewarm water

sunflower or corn oil for greasing

1 Sift the flour, baking soda, and salt into a large bowl. Pour in the buttermilk, or milk and yogurt, and the measured water. Mix with a wooden spoon or your hands to form a very soft dough.

2 Lightly oil a baking sheet. Turn out the dough onto a lightly floured work surface and shape into a round measuring 7 in (18 cm) in diameter.

3 Place the loaf on the prepared baking sheet and cut a deep cross in the top.

4 Bake the loaf in a 400°F (200°C) oven for 30 minutes. Turn the bread over and bake for 10 minutes longer or until the loaf sounds hollow when tapped on the bottom. Leave to cool on a wire rack. Serve the soda bread on the day made.

POTATO ROLLS

 Makes 12

1 1/2 cups (175 g) all-purpose flour

1 tbsp baking powder

4 tbsp butter, plus extra for greasing

3 tbsp sugar

1 1/3 cups (125 g) freshly boiled and mashed potato

3 tbsp milk

1 Sift the flour and baking powder into a bowl. Rub in the butter until the mixture resembles fine bread crumbs. Stir in the sugar and mashed potato. Add enough milk to bind to a soft but not sticky dough.

2 Turn out the dough onto a floured surface and knead lightly until blended. Roll out until 1/2 in (1 cm) thick and cut into rectangles.

3 Place the rectangles on a buttered baking sheet and bake in a 425°F (220°C) oven for 12–15 minutes, until risen and golden. Leave to cool on a wire rack. Serve on the day made.

Shapes

You can also make these rolls as triangles. Instead of rectangles as here, cut 12 triangles from the dough.

ALMOND TUILES

 Makes 30

2 egg whites

1/2 cup (125 g) sugar

1/2 cup (60 g) all-purpose
flour

1/2 tsp vanilla extract

4 tbsp butter, melted and cooled

1/4 cup (30 g) slivered almonds

1 Line a baking sheet with baking parchment. Put the egg whites into a bowl and beat in the sugar until frothy. Stir in the flour and vanilla extract, then add the melted butter.

2 Put 6 teaspoonfuls of the mixture onto the baking sheet, spacing them well apart to allow for spreading. Flatten each with a fork.

3 Sprinkle the mixture with the slivered almonds. Bake in a 350°F (180°C) oven for about 6 minutes, until golden brown around the edges but still pale in the middle.

4 Allow the cookies to cool on the baking sheet for a few seconds, then lift off with a spatula and gently lay them over a greased rolling pin to give the traditional curved shape.

5 Allow the cookies to set, then lift off onto a wire rack and leave to cool.

6 Cook and shape the remaining mixture in batches, cooking 1 batch while another is setting on the rolling pin.

Tuiles

These cookies take their name from the French word tuile, *meaning "roof tile," which they resemble in shape.*

VIENNESE FINGERS

 Makes 12

3/4 cup (175 g) butter, plus extra for greasing

1/4 cup (60 g) sugar

1 1/2 cups (175 g) self-rising flour

a few drops of vanilla extract

3 oz (90 g) baker's semisweet chocolate, broken into pieces

1 Lightly butter 2 baking sheets. Combine the butter and sugar in a bowl and cream together until pale and fluffy. Stir in the flour and vanilla extract and beat until well combined.

2 Spoon the mixture into a pastry bag with a medium star tip. Pipe into 3-in (7-cm) lengths on the baking sheets. Bake in a 325°F (160°C) oven for about 20 minutes, until golden. Transfer to a wire rack and leave to cool.

3 Put the chocolate into a heatproof bowl. Set the bowl over a pan of hot water and heat gently until the chocolate has melted. Dip both ends of each cookie into the chocolate. Leave to set on the wire rack.

COCONUT MACAROONS

 Makes 26

3 egg whites

1 1/2 cups (175 g) confectioners' sugar

1 1/2 cups (175 g) ground almonds

a few drops of almond extract

2 cups (175 g) sweetened flaked coconut

about 13 whole almonds, blanched and halved

1 Line 2 baking sheets with baking parchment.

2 Beat the egg whites until stiff but not dry. Sift in the sugar and fold it in gently. Fold in the ground almonds, almond extract, and flaked coconut.

3 Put teaspoonfuls of the coconut mixture onto the baking sheets. Top each with an almond half.

4 Bake in a 300°F (150°C) oven for 25 minutes or until golden brown and crisp on the outside and soft in the middle.

5 Cool on a wire rack. Best served on the day made.

BRANDY SNAPS

 Makes 15

6 tbsp (90 g) butter

³/₈ cup (90 g) light brown granulated sugar

¹/₄ cup (90 g) corn syrup

²/₃ cup (90 g) all-purpose flour

³/₄ tsp ground ginger

³/₄ tsp lemon juice

1 Line a baking sheet with baking parchment.

2 Combine the butter, sugar, and syrup in a saucepan and heat gently until the ingredients have melted and dissolved. Cool slightly, then sift in the flour and ginger. Add the lemon juice and stir to mix well.

3 Place 3–4 teaspoonfuls of the mixture onto the baking sheet, leaving plenty of room for the cookies to spread out.

4 Bake in a 325°F (160°C) oven for about 8 minutes, until the mixture spreads out to form large, thin, dark golden rounds. While the cookies are baking, oil the handles of 4 wooden spoons.

5 Remove the cookies from the oven and leave for 1–2 minutes to firm slightly. Shape the brandy snaps (see box, below).

6 Continue baking, shaping, and cooling the remaining mixture in batches until all is used.

Shaping the brandy snaps

Lift 1 cookie from the paper using a spatula, turn the cookie over so that the rough side is on the outside, and wrap around an oiled wooden spoon handle. Repeat with the remaining cookies. Transfer to a wire rack and cool until firm. Slip from the spoon handles.

GINGER-SNAPS

 Makes 15

4 tbsp butter, plus extra for greasing

¹/₄ cup (90 g) corn syrup

1 cup (125 g) self-rising flour

2 tsp ground ginger

1 tsp ground cinnamon

¹/₂ tsp baking soda

1 tbsp sugar

1 Lightly grease 2 baking sheets with butter.

2 Combine the butter and corn syrup in a small saucepan and heat gently until melted. Leave the mixture to cool slightly.

3 Sift the flour, spices, and baking soda into a bowl and stir in the sugar. Add the cooled syrup mixture and stir to mix to a soft but not sticky dough.

4 Roll the dough into balls about the size of walnuts and place well apart on the baking sheets. Flatten the dough balls slightly with the heel of your hand.

5 Bake in a 375°F (190°C) oven for about 15 minutes. Leave the cookies to cool on the baking sheets for a few minutes, then transfer them to a wire rack and leave to cool completely.

FORK COOKIES

Makes 32

¹/₂ lb (250 g) butter, at room temperature, plus extra for greasing

¹/₂ cup (125 g) sugar

2 ¹/₂ cups (300 g) self-rising flour

1 Lightly grease 2 baking sheets with butter.

2 Put the butter into a large bowl and beat with a wooden spoon to soften it. Gradually beat in the sugar, then stir in the flour. Use your hands to gather the mixture together into a soft but not sticky dough.

3 Roll the dough into balls about the size of walnuts and place well apart on the baking sheets. Dip a fork into cold water and press on top of each ball to flatten it and imprint the fork pattern.

4 Bake in batches in a 350°F (180°C) for 15–20 minutes, until the cookies are a very pale golden color. Transfer the cookies from the baking sheet to a wire rack and leave to cool.

PUFF PASTRIES

Quite unlike any other pastry, pâte à choux (puff pastry) is a thick paste that can be piped into any shape. Once baked, the light-as-air pastry can be served with sweet or savory fillings. Try ever-popular éclairs, cream puffs (profiteroles) filled with ice cream, or puff pastry hearts sandwiched with cream and tropical fruits.

COFFEE ECLAIRS

 Makes 8

butter for greasing

1 recipe puff pastry (see box, below)

1 egg, beaten

1 1/4 cups (300 ml) heavy cream

ground cinnamon for sprinkling

COFFEE ICING

1 tsp instant coffee powder

1 tbsp butter

2 tbsp water

3/4 cup (90 g) confectioners' sugar

1 Lightly butter a baking sheet and sprinkle with water. Spoon the puff pastry into a pastry bag fitted with a 1/2-in (1-cm) plain tip. Pipe the pastry into 3-in (7-cm) lengths, leaving enough space between them to spread. Brush with the beaten egg.

2 Bake in a 425°F (220°C) oven for 10 minutes; reduce the oven temperature to 375°F (190°C), and bake for 20 minutes longer, until golden brown. Split in half and leave to cool on a wire rack.

3 Whip the cream until stiff. Pipe into the bottom halves of the éclairs and sprinkle the cream with cinnamon.

4 Make the icing: put the coffee, butter, and measured water into a heatproof bowl over a pan of simmering water. Heat gently until the butter melts. Remove from the heat and beat in the confectioners' sugar. Dip the top half of each éclair into the icing, then place on top of the cream. Leave the icing to cool before serving.

CREAM PUFFS

 Makes 12

butter for greasing

1 recipe puff pastry (see box, below)

1 egg, beaten

vanilla ice cream and chocolate sauce (page 440) to serve

1 Lightly butter a baking sheet and sprinkle with water. Place 12 tablespoonfuls of choux pastry onto the sheet and brush with the beaten egg.

2 Bake in a 425°F (220°C) oven for 10 minutes; reduce the oven temperature to 375°F (190°C) and bake for 20 minutes, until golden brown. Split in half and leave to cool on a wire rack.

3 Fill the profiteroles with ice cream and serve with chocolate sauce.

PUFF PASTRY HEARTS

 Makes 4

butter for greasing

1 recipe puff pastry (see box, below)

1 egg, beaten

1 1/4 cups (300 ml) heavy cream

exotic fruits to serve

confectioners' sugar for dusting

1 Lightly butter a baking sheet and sprinkle with water. Spoon the puff pastry into a pastry bag fitted with a 1/2-in (1-cm) plain tip. Pipe 4 heart shapes, about 3 in (7 cm) across. Brush with the beaten egg.

2 Bake in a 425°F (220°C) oven for 10 minutes; reduce the oven temperature to 375°F (190°C) and bake the hearts for 20 minutes longer, until golden brown.

3 Cut in half horizontally and leave to cool on a wire rack. Whip the cream until stiff. Pipe the cream onto the bottom halves of the hearts and top with exotic fruits. Dust the top halves of the hearts with confectioners' sugar and replace on the bottom halves.

Clockwise from top: *Coffee Eclairs, Puff Pastry Hearts, Cream Puffs.*

Basic puff pastry

1 Put *4 tbsp butter, cut into cubes,* into a heavy saucepan with *2/3 cup (150 ml) water* and heat until the butter melts. Bring to a boil.

2 Remove from the heat and add *9 tbsp (75 g) sifted all-purpose flour* and *a pinch of salt, if desired.* Stir vigorously until the mixture forms a soft ball.

3 Leave to cool slightly, then gradually add *2 lightly beaten eggs,* beating well between additions, to form a smooth, shiny paste.

OAT BARS

 Makes 24

1/4 lb (125 g) butter, plus extra for greasing

1/4 cup (90 g) corn syrup

1/2 cup (90 g) dark brown sugar

2 1/4 cups (250 g) rolled oats

✶ roasting pan or shallow cake pan, about 8 x 12 in (20 x 30 cm)

1 Lightly butter the roasting pan or cake pan.

2 Combine the butter, syrup, and sugar in a saucepan and heat gently until the ingredients have melted and dissolved. Stir in the oats and mix well.

3 Spoon into the prepared pan and smooth the surface with a narrow spatula. Bake in a 350°F (180°C) oven for about 30 minutes.

4 Leave to cool in the pan for about 5 minutes, then mark into 24 fingers. Leave to cool completely, then cut and remove from the pan.

WALNUT COOKIES

 Makes 50

2 cups (250 g) all-purpose flour

1 tsp baking powder

1/4 lb (125 g) butter, plus extra for greasing

3/4 cup (175 g) sugar

1/2 cup (60 g) finely chopped walnuts

1 egg, beaten

1 tsp vanilla extract

1 Sift the flour and baking powder into a bowl. Rub in the butter with the fingertips until the mixture resembles bread crumbs. Mix in the sugar and walnuts. Add the beaten egg and vanilla extract, and stir to form a smooth dough.

2 Shape the dough into a long cylinder about 2 in (5 cm) in diameter. Wrap in foil, roll to give smooth sides, and chill for about 8 hours.

3 Lightly butter several baking sheets. Cut the cylinder into thin slices and place the cookies on the baking sheets. Bake in a 375°F (190°C) oven for 10–12 minutes, until golden.

PINWHEEL COOKIES

 Makes 18

VANILLA DOUGH

4 tbsp butter, at room temperature

2 tbsp sugar

2/3 cup (90 g) all-purpose flour

a few drops of vanilla extract

about 1 tbsp water

COFFEE DOUGH

4 tbsp butter, at room temperature

2 tbsp sugar

2/3 cup (90 g) all-purpose flour

1 tbsp coffee extract

milk for brushing

1 Combine the ingredients for the vanilla dough in a bowl and mix well, adding just enough water to bind. Knead lightly, then wrap and chill for at least 2 hours, until very firm.

2 Mix the ingredients for the coffee dough, using the coffee extract to bind. Wrap and chill for at least 2 hours, until very firm.

3 On a lightly floured work surface, roll out each dough to a rectangle about 7 x 10 in (18 x 25 cm).

4 Brush the coffee dough with a little milk, then place the vanilla dough on top. Roll up together like a jelly roll, starting at a narrow end.

5 Wrap the roll tightly in foil and leave to chill in the refrigerator for about 30 minutes or until firm.

6 Lightly grease 1–2 baking sheets. Cut the dough roll into about 18 thin slices and place them well apart on the baking sheets.

7 Bake the slices in a 350°F (180°C) oven for about 20 minutes, until the vanilla dough is a very pale golden color.

8 Leave the cookies to cool on the baking sheets for a few minutes, then lift off onto a wire rack and leave to cool completely.

Cook's know-how

If the doughs become too soft and difficult to roll out, put each piece of dough between sheets of waxed paper before rolling.

USEFUL INFORMATION

On the following pages you'll find practical information on Herbs, Spices, Microwaving, and Freezing, and advice on Healthy Eating. All of this will help you get more from the recipes in this book – and from all of your cooking.

HERBS

WITH THEIR WONDERFUL flavors, scents, and colors, herbs can transform even the simplest dish into something very special, accenting and enhancing other ingredients. Most savory dishes benefit from the inclusion of one or more herbs to add flavor during cooking or as a garnish to be sprinkled over the top of a dish just before serving. Sweet dishes, too, can be perfumed with herbs such as mint and lemon balm, and decorated with delicate herb flowers such as borage. Herbs are also used to make drinks known as infusions or tisanes, to be served hot or cold.

PRESERVING HERBS

You can preserve your own herbs by drying or freezing them. The best herbs for drying are bay, lovage, marjoram, oregano, mint, rosemary, spearmint, and thyme. When drying herbs, spread out the sprigs on trays or racks, cover with cheesecloth, and leave in a warm, airy place for about 24 hours. Alternatively, tie the stalks in bunches and hang them upside down in a warm, airy place. When dry, remove the leaves or sprigs from the stems, crumble them if they are large, pack into small jars, and seal tightly. The seeds of coriander, dill, and fennel are ideal for drying. If you have herbs with seedheads that are ripe (the seeds will have started to change from green to brown), pack the seedheads loosely in a paper bag. Leave to dry for 10–14 days, then shake out the seeds, and pack into small jars.

Herbs such as basil, chervil, dill, fennel, parsley, sorrel, and tarragon can be frozen successfully. Pack leaves or small sprigs in small plastic bags or mix chopped herbs with water and freeze in ice-cube trays. Freezing is generally considered to be a better method of preserving than drying as a fresher flavor is retained.

PREPARING HERBS

Rinse and dry the herbs, then remove the leaves or sprigs from the stems.

Chopping
Gather the leaves together on a cutting board. Chop the leaves with a sharp knife, rocking it back and forth, chopping as finely as necessary.

Snipping
A pair of scissors is best for snipping chives. Hold the stems in one hand and snip into short lengths, either into a bowl or directly into the dish you are flavoring.

GROWING YOUR OWN HERBS

The range of fresh herbs available in shops and supermarkets is extensive, but there are still some, such as the more unusual varieties of mint, that are more difficult to find. Also, buying fresh herbs is much more expensive than using those you grow yourself, particularly if you use large amounts.

The cultivation of herbs, indoors or out, is simple and satisfying. You can start from seed or from a small plant; the latter is the quicker and easier method. Herbs can be grown outdoors in the garden, in pots on a paved terrace or patio, in a rock garden, in a hanging basket, or simply in a window box. Inside the house, herbs will grow satisfactorily in a box or in pots on a windowsill.

Most herbs need as much sunshine as possible during the growing season, so they should be grown in a sunny spot that offers protection from cold winds. The only other requirement, for your own convenience, is to put them as close to the kitchen as possible.

STORING & USING FRESH HERBS

Buy or gather fresh herbs only when they are needed. If you have to store them for a day or so, keep them in a cool place or in the refrigerator. If they have stems, stand them in a glass of water, just as you would cut flowers. Herb leaves can be spread on damp paper towels, rolled up, and put into a plastic bag.

Most herbs should be chopped before being added to a dish, and this is usually best at the last possible moment. The volatile oils in herbs are released by heat or oxidation, so unless fresh herbs are used as soon as they are prepared, they will quickly lose their flavors and colors.

Bay leaves are among the few herbs that are best used whole. They should always be added at the start of cooking, and removed just before serving. Whole sprigs are also used if flavor is needed in a dish but not color – the herbs should be lifted out before serving. For easy removal, tie with string or wrap in cheesecloth.

HERB MIXTURES

There are certain combinations of herbs that are often used in dishes. The most common herb mixture is a bouquet garni (see box, right). *Herbes de Provence,* an aromatic mixture of sage, basil, savory, thyme, rosemary, and marjoram, is another popular combination, good in stews, but it should be used sparingly. *Fines herbes* combines equal quantities of tarragon, chervil, parsley, and chives and is good with omelets, fish, and poultry.

These mixtures can be made with fresh or dried herbs. Tie fresh herbs together with string or wrap dried herbs in a cheesecloth bag. Remember to remove the bundle or bag of herbs before serving.

MAKING A BOUQUET GARNI

A bouquet garni may vary, but always includes parsley stems, thyme, and a bay leaf. Remove before serving.

1 With a length of string, tie together 2–3 sprigs of thyme, 5–6 parsley stems, and 1 bay leaf.

2 Add to the saucepan or casserole – tie it to the handle for easy removal. Remove before serving.

STORING & USING DRIED HERBS

Whether they are store-bought or prepared at home, dried herbs must be stored correctly or they will quickly lose their flavor. Dark glass jars or earthenware pots with airtight lids are excellent for storage; if you use clear glass jars, keep them in a dark cabinet or drawer because light causes dried herbs to deteriorate. Make sure they are in a cool, dry place, away from kitchen heat and steam.

Dried herbs will not keep forever, even if they are stored correctly. Home-dried herbs should stay flavorful for 1 year, but store-bought ones will last only 6 months. It is best to buy dried herbs in small quantities from stores that have a rapid turnover.

Dried herbs can be substituted for fresh ones in most recipes. Dried herbs are more pungent than fresh, so a smaller quantity is required. Use 1/2 teaspoon finely powdered dried herb or 1 teaspoon crumbled dried herb to 1 tablespoon chopped fresh herb.

HERBS & THEIR USES

These are some of the most commonly used herbs, their flavors, and the foods or dishes they complement best.

HERB	FLAVOR	USE WITH
Basil	*sweet, spicy, aromatic*	beef, lamb, pork, and veal; whitefish; salad greens; tomatoes; eggs; pasta sauces
Bay	*aromatic, pungent*	soups and stocks; casseroles; sauces
Chervil	*delicate, fresh*	chicken; omelets; delicate sauces
Chives	*delicate, oniony*	fish; egg dishes; salads; garnish for creamy soups
Coriander	*aromatic, spicy*	curries; salsa; stir-fries; salads; yogurt; guacamole
Dill	*tangy, pungent*	salmon and herrings; veal; carrots, cucumber, and potatoes; eggs and cheese
Fennel	*aniselike*	pork; seafood; eggs
Lemon balm	*fragrant, lemonlike*	salads; eggs; soups; decoration for desserts
Lemon grass	*delicate, fresh, lemonlike*	Asian curries and soups, particularly Thai
Marjoram	*sweet, aromatic*	lamb, pork, and veal; chicken; tomatoes; Italian dishes; eggs and cheese; pasta dishes
Mint	*strong, sweet, cooling*	cucumber, new potatoes, and peas; melon; garnish for many savory and sweet dishes
Oregano	*sweet, aromatic*	as for marjoram
Parsley	*fresh, slightly spicy*	eggs; fish; almost every savory dish
Rosemary	*pungent, oily*	lamb and pork; chicken; breads; potatoes
Sage	*aromatic, slightly bitter*	pork and veal; duck, goose, and turkey; beans; eggs and cheese; risotto
Tarragon	*piquant, aniselike*	chicken; fish; eggs; béarnaise sauce

SPICES

THE USE OF SPICES in cooking has a very long history – they were often used to mask the taste of less-than-perfect food or to improve its keeping qualities. At one time, spices were so precious and expensive that even in the wealthiest of households they would be locked away in special spice boxes or cabinets. Today, most spices are no longer extravagant luxuries, and modern cooks use them to enhance flavors rather than to disguise them, as well as to provide vibrant colors and enticing aromas.

BUYING & STORING

Spices don't deteriorate as quickly as herbs, particularly if they are whole (which is why it's a good idea to buy them whole and grind them as you need them). When buying spices – whole or ground – sniff them if you can: the more pungent they smell, the fresher they are. Store spices in tightly sealed containers in a cool, dark, dry place. Whole spices can be kept for at least 1 year, often longer, and ground spices will keep for about 6 months.

COOKING WITH SPICES

Because spices need time to release their aromas and flavors, they are usually added near the start of cooking.

If the cooking process is prolonged, spices that are whole, cracked, or bruised are normally used rather than ground spices, which could become bitter. Large spices, such as cinnamon sticks and cloves, are best removed before serving.

In Asian cooking, whole spices are toasted in a heavy skillet until they smell aromatic, then ground. Toasting or warming in this way brings out the flavor of most spices, particularly if they are to be used in a dish that is cooked for only a short time. When toasting whole spices, cook them over low heat because they scorch easily. Use oil to prevent ground spices from scorching.

TYPES OF SPICES

Spicy food does not simply mean a fiery flavor – spices lend all kinds of qualities to dishes.

Hot spices
These spices stimulate the palate and sharpen the appetite as well as encouraging the body to produce perspiration – an excellent means of cooling down in a hot climate.

The best known of the hot spices include ground and crushed chilies, chili powder (which is usually a blend of chilies and other spices), cayenne (ground from red chili peppers), which is very strong and so should be used sparingly, and paprika (made from sweet peppers and very mild). Be careful to avoid contact with your eyes when using these spices because they can sting.

Peppercorns are a hot spice with a more aromatic flavor. Black, white, green, and pink varieties are available. If sold together, they are known as tropical or mixed peppercorns.

Fragrant spices
Spices such as allspice, cardamom, cloves, cinnamon, coriander, mace, juniper, and nutmeg add a pungent, sweet note to all kinds of dishes, both sweet and savory. Most can be used whole or ground and they are usually added at the beginning of cooking so that their flavor and perfume can permeate and enhance the dish.

Coloring spices
A dish can be colored as well as flavored by a spice. Saffron is the most expensive spice in the world, but only a pinch is needed to give a dish such as paella a vibrant yellow color. Turmeric is often used as an alternative and gives a rich yellow hue to many Indian dishes. The dark red color of goulash and chorizo sausages comes from paprika.

PREPARING SPICES

The way in which spices are prepared depends on the recipe in which they are used and the depth of flavor required.

Whole spices
When whole spices and herbs are to be removed before serving, tie them in a piece of cheesecloth, which will make it easier to lift them out of the dish.

Toasting spices
Heat a heavy skillet until hot. Add the spices and cook over low heat for 1–2 minutes, stirring occasionally, until the aromas are released. The spices can then be ground.

Grinding spices
Put the whole spices into a mortar and use a pestle to crush them to the required consistency. Electric spice grinders are also available.

SPICES & THEIR USES

Here are some of the most commonly used spices, their flavors, the forms in which they are sold,
and the foods or dishes they complement best.

SPICE	FLAVOR	FORM	USE WITH
Allspice	*sweet, like a mixture of cloves and cinnamon*	whole berries or ground	meat stews, particularly lamb; spiced vinegar; poached fruits; cakes, breads, and pies
Caraway	*aromatic, strong*	whole seeds	meat stews; sausages; cabbage and sauerkraut; breads; cheese
Cardamom	*pungent*	pods that contain whole seeds or ground	curries; pickled herrings; punches; pastries and cakes; fruit dishes
Cayenne	*spicy, very hot*	ground	Indian, Mexican, and Cajun dishes; eggs
Chili powder	*spicy, hot*	ground	Indian and Mexican dishes; eggs and cheese, soups and stews
Cinnamon	*sweet, aromatic*	sticks or ground	Middle Eastern dishes; curries; fruit desserts; cakes and breads; milk and rice puddings
Cloves	*sweet, strong*	whole or ground	ham and pork; sweet potatoes; pumpkin; spiced cakes; apples and other fruits
Coriander	*fragrant, lemony*	whole berries or ground	Indian dishes; meat; chicken; pickled fish; mushrooms; breads, cakes, and pastries; custards
Cumin	*pungent, slightly bitter*	whole seeds or ground	Indian and Mexican dishes; pork; chicken; cheese; soups
Curry powder	*mild to hot*	ground mixture of turmeric, fenugreek, coriander, cumin, cardamom, chili	poultry; fish; eggs; vegetables; sauces for meat
Garam masala	*aromatic*	ground mixture of spices such as cumin, coriander, cardamom, cinnamon, pepper, cloves, mace	Indian dishes
Ginger	*pungent, spicy*	fresh root or ground	Asian and Indian dishes; chicken; vegetables, particularly pumpkin and carrots; fruit such as melon and rhubarb; cakes and cookies
Juniper	*pungent*	berries	pork and pork sausage; pâtés and terrines; game, particularly venison; cabbage; stuffings
Mace	*sweet, fragrant*	whole blades or ground	as for nutmeg
Mixed spice	*sweet, aromatic*	ground mixture of cinnamon, allspice, cloves, nutmeg, ginger	Middle Eastern dishes; cakes, desserts, and cookies
Mustard	*pungent, hot*	whole seeds or ground	pork and beef; chicken; rabbit; vegetables; pickles and relishes; sauces and dressings
Nutmeg	*sweet, fragrant*	whole or ground	meat sauces; tomatoes, spinach, and potatoes; cakes and cookies; milk puddings and custards; mulled wine
Paprika	*pungent, mild or hot*	ground	meat stews; eggs and cream cheese
Pepper	*pungent, mild or hot*	berries (peppercorns) or ground	almost every savory dish and occasionally with strawberries

MICROWAVING

THE MICROWAVE OVEN has revolutionized cooking for many people. Those whose busy lifestyles don't allow time to devote to conventional cooking find it a boon. Vegetables and fish are quickly cooked to perfection, retaining vitamins, color, and texture. Stews and casseroles made with good cuts of meat are tender and succulent and stocks and steamed puddings can be made in a fraction of the time taken by the conventional method. For most cooks, however, the microwave is one tool among many, used to speed preparation, but not used to cook a dish from start to finish.

HOW A MICROWAVE OVEN WORKS

Cooking in a microwave oven is very different from cooking in a conventional oven, so an understanding of the basic principles is essential to achieve the best results. A microwave oven contains a device known as a magnetron. This converts electricity into microwaves, which pass through materials such as china, glass, and plastic and are absorbed by the moisture molecules in food. The microwaves penetrate food up to a depth of about 2 in (5 cm), where they cause the molecules to vibrate so quickly that they create heat. The heat created spreads to the rest of the food and cooks but does not brown it.

Most microwave ovens contain a turntable that rotates the food and exposes it evenly to the microwaves. Stirring foods also ensures even cooking. Because microwaves continue to produce heat when the power has been turned off, standing times are often given with recipes, to allow the food to finish cooking.

The microwave oven is ideal for cooking fish, vegetables, and other foods that are normally cooked using moisture methods such as steaming or poaching. Combination ovens also use conventional energy, similar to a broiler, which browns and crisps food.

Microwaving safety

A microwave oven is safe if used properly. The door of every oven has a special seal to ensure the waves do not escape. The oven will work only if the door is closed; if the door is accidentally opened during cooking, the power cuts off automatically. Always have the oven checked for leakage if it has been dropped or damaged.

◆

A microwave can be positioned wherever convenient, but make sure that any vents, which allow steam to escape, are not obstructed.

◆

Never switch on the microwave when it is empty; with nothing to absorb them, the waves will simply bounce back and damage the magnetron.

◆

Do not put metal into a microwave – it reflects the waves and causes "arcing," producing sparks that can damage the magnetron.

MICROWAVING EQUIPMENT

Special equipment is not essential for cooking in a microwave oven; many containers and implements used for conventional cooking are suitable.

Round or oval dishes are the most efficient for even heat distribution, particularly large containers with straight sides that allow the heat to spread in an even layer. Rectangular and square dishes are the least successful in a microwave because the corners cook faster than the middles.

Although metal should not be put in a microwave, small amounts of foil may be used, dull-side out, for shielding areas of food, but make sure its surface is smooth and keep it well away from the oven walls.

Paper towels are useful for soaking up moisture and covering foods, but make sure it is not recycled paper, which can contain impurities such as tiny fragments of metal. If cooking in a dish that does not have a lid, cover it with special microwave plastic wrap, or put the food directly into a roasting bag, fastened with a plastic tie.

Ovenproof glass and ceramic dishes are excellent, as are plastics specially made for the microwave. Plastic containers not specifically made for the microwave may soften and distort. Foods containing a high percentage of fat or sugar will get very hot and are not suitable for cooking in thin plastic containers. Wicker, wooden, or paper containers can be used for very short cooking times, such as for warming bread rolls, etc.

One special piece of equipment is a browning dish, which is usually made from a ceramic material that gets very hot when preheated and browns any food in contact with it.

Microwaving know-how

Remove eggs from their shells before cooking; otherwise, they will explode.

◆

Use large containers for liquids and keep stirring to avoid a buildup of hot spots that can cause the liquid to boil over.

◆

Foods with a skin or membrane, such as sausages or egg yolks, must be pierced before cooking.

◆

Don't use empty yogurt containers for heating foods – they will melt and collapse.

ARRANGING FOODS

The shape and texture of food determines how it is best cooked in a microwave oven. Remember that microwaves penetrate food from the outside toward the middle, so arrange foods properly to ensure even cooking.

Uneven shapes
Arrange unevenly shaped foods, such as broccoli, in a circle with the densest parts facing outwards. Chicken drumsticks should be arranged with the bones pointing toward the middle of the dish.

Delicate areas
The heads and tails of fish will cook too quickly and must be shielded with small pieces of smooth foil. Protruding bones on chops and chicken pieces should also be covered with smooth strips of foil.

Even shapes
Foods of the same size and shape, or small individual dishes, should be arranged in a circle, with plenty of space between them, to enable the microwaves to reach the food from all sides.

COVERING & WRAPPING

Covering food with plastic wrap keeps it from drying out during cooking and traps steam that helps to heat the food. A loose covering of waxed paper or paper towels prevents spattering.

1 Stretch microwave plastic wrap over the dish, then either pierce several times or peel back a small corner to allow some of the steam to escape.

2 After cooking, carefully remove the plastic wrap from the edge of the dish farthest away from you first, because the rush of steam is very hot and can scald.

POWER LEVELS

Most recipes are designed for 600- to 700-watt output ovens; smaller ovens may have an output of 400–600 watts. Cooking times are longer the lower the output, so some recipes may need to be adapted. Descriptions of the power levels of microwave ovens vary, but in general you can follow this guide:

HIGH = 100% of full power

MEDIUM = 50–60% of full power

DEFROST = 30–40% of full power

LOW = 10–20% of full power

THAWING & COOKING

A microwave oven can thaw frozen foods in a fraction of the time it normally takes. Thawing must be done slowly and gently – always use the defrost setting so that the outside does not begin to cook before the inside is thawed. Break up and stir the food as it thaws. Bread, pastry, and cakes are best thawed on paper towels that absorb moisture. Meat and poultry must be thawed completely before cooking to ensure they are at the same temperature all the way through. Cook food as soon as possible once thawed.

Quick cooking know-how

Soften a wedge of Brie on LOW or DEFROST for 20–30 seconds. A whole Camembert will take longer. Allow to stand for several minutes before serving.

◆

Use the microwave to gently warm bread and rolls; 4 rolls will take approximately 20–30 seconds on HIGH.

◆

Soften cold butter for 20–30 seconds on MEDIUM.

◆

Soften hard ice cream for 30–60 seconds on MEDIUM and leave to stand for 1 minute.

◆

To soften crystallized honey, remove the lid from the jar and microwave on HIGH for 30 seconds.

◆

To toast nuts, heat on HIGH for 2–4 minutes, stirring occasionally.

◆

Melt chocolate on HIGH for 2 minutes, stirring halfway.

FREEZING

HOME FREEZERS offer one of the most natural and economical methods of food preservation and storage and, when used in conjunction with a microwave oven, they are invaluable in a busy household. Fresh foods need no longer be bought every day – you can buy most of the food you need for a week, or even a month, in just one shopping trip and freeze it until needed. Follow the correct procedures and the food will lose none of the flavor, texture, and quality it had on the day you bought it.

FREEZING FOOD

Freezing halts the growth of bacteria, but only temporarily. It does not kill bacteria, so remember that when food thaws it will be in the same condition as it was before freezing, and the food must then be treated in the same way as any fresh produce. A temperature of 0°F (-18°C) is essential. A freezer thermometer will reassure you that your freezer is at the correct temperature. The freezer compartment of a refrigerator rarely reaches this temperature, so food can be stored there for only a few days. Turn the temperature to its coldest setting to speed the process several hours before freezing food. Quick freezing ensures that only small, round ice crystals form. In food frozen slowly, the ice crystals are larger and jagged; they puncture the cell walls, causing the loss of moisture, texture, and flavor.

SPECIAL EQUIPMENT

Use rigid plastic containers with lids, foil containers with lids, or freezer bags. Special freezer-quality plastic wrap or freezer paper is convenient for interleaving and wrapping foods. Freezer tape should be used for sealing packages because ordinary tape peels off. Color-coded labels are useful for indicating different types of food — it can be very difficult to identify unmarked packages once frozen.

Freezing know-how

Try to keep your freezer 75–100% full – this will keep the temperature down and make the freezer more economical to run. Bread is always a good space filler.

◆

Mark each item with details of the contents, weight or number of servings, and the date of freezing.

◆

Do not allow frozen foods to thaw partially when shopping. Immediately wrap them in newspaper or invest in an insulated bag.

BLACKOUTS

An unexpected power failure that causes the contents of your freezer to thaw can cause hundreds of dollars worth of damage.

If you have advance warning, fill any spaces in the freezer with towels, newspapers, or plastic boxes three-quarters filled with cold water. Switch on to the coldest setting. During the blackout, keep the door closed. Turn onto the coldest setting as soon as power is restored. Food in a chest freezer will be safe for about 48 hours and in an upright freezer for about 36 hours.

If you have no warning of a power failure, food, except for ice cream, in a chest freezer will be safe for 30–35 hours and in an upright freezer for about 30 hours.

PREPARING FOOD

Food should be packed in airtight, moisture-proof materials to avoid "freezer burn" – dry gray patches that form on the surface.

Tray freezing
Arrange items in a single layer, without touching, on a tray and freeze. Once frozen, transfer to a rigid container or freezer bag. Items can then be used individually.

Interleaving
Place a sheet of freezer paper or waxed paper between foods such as steaks and chops before wrapping them. This makes them easier to separate before thawing.

Liquids
Pour liquid into a rigid plastic container, leaving roughly 1/2 in (1 cm) headroom per 2 1/4 cups (600 ml) liquid to allow for expansion.

FOODS FOR FREEZING

The size, content, and texture of food largely determine how well it freezes, but you'll find that most foods can be frozen with great success as long as you follow the correct procedures.

Fruits and vegetables
Raw fruits tend to suffer a slight loss of quality when frozen and will always be softer once thawed. Soft fruits are best tray frozen. Treat pineapple and rhubarb in the same way. Freeze apples and pears in syrup, apple juice, or water and add lemon juice to prevent discoloring. Strawberries become soft when thawed so are best frozen as a puree.

Vegetables such as green beans, peas, carrots, Brussels sprouts, corn, and snow peas should be blanched first. Most vegetables freeze well in cooked dishes such as soups or casseroles. However, potatoes don't freeze particularly well; if uncooked, they will discolor; if part of a prepared dish, they will become floury.

Meat and poultry
Smaller pieces of meat give the best results. Poultry and larger pieces of meat are best bought frozen. Interleave individual items, then bag.

Fish and shellfish
Fish must be as fresh as possible when frozen. Whole fish should be scaled, gutted, rinsed, and dried, then wrapped in freezer paper or foil. Interleave fillets or steaks before wrapping. Crabs, lobsters, and shrimp are best if commercially frozen.

Pasta and rice
Fresh pasta, both filled and unfilled, freezes well. Pasta in sauces tends to turn soft when thawed. Rice dishes can be frozen, but there is no advantage in freezing plain cooked rice.

Dairy products
The higher the fat content, the better the product will freeze. Creams with over 40% fat freeze very well. Cheeses can be frozen, but they are best used in cooking; full-fat hard cheeses and grated cheeses are most successful. Lightly whisk uncooked eggs, then add 1/2 tsp salt or sugar per 6 eggs or yolks to prevent thickening. Hard-boiled eggs become rubbery but dishes such as quiches freeze well.

Breads, pastries, and cakes
Wrap bread in airtight plastic or foil. Thaw at room temperature. Sliced bread can be toasted when still frozen. Both cooked and uncooked pastry freezes well. Cakes can be frozen in individual portions, but for best results freeze before filling or frosting.

RECOMMENDED STORAGE TIMES

Some frozen foods are harmed if stored too long. Follow these guidelines to avoid loss of quality.

Food	Storage time
Bread	6 months
Butter	3 months
Cakes and pastries	3 months
Cheese	
Hard cheeses	6 months
Soft cheeses	6 weeks
Fish	
Whitefish	3 months
Oily fish and shellfish	2 months
Fruit and vegetables	12 months
Meat	
Beef	8 months
Lamb, veal, pork	6 months
Bacon, sausages	1 month
Milk, cream, and yogurt	1 month
Poultry	8 months
Soups and sauces	3 months

THAWING & REHEATING

For some foods, thawing before cooking is totally unnecessary. Vegetables and pasta can be added directly to boiling water. Put frozen sauces and soups into a saucepan and heat very gently until thawed. Thin pieces of meat, bacon, and breakfast sausages can be cooked straight from frozen, although thicker pieces of meat should be thawed first to ensure that they reach the right internal temperature. A meat thermometer can be used to check this at the end of cooking. If in doubt, simply thaw food before cooking.

It is vital that all poultry be thawed thoroughly before cooking. Thaw poultry and all other foods in the refrigerator: bacteria will soon begin to multiply if thawed at room temperature.

To thaw, remove food from wrappings and put on a plate with a rim or in a bowl, in order to prevent any juices from spilling. Cover loosely and then put in the refrigerator.

Frozen food must be cooked immediately after thawing to kill any bacteria. Use a food thermometer to check the temperature in the center of the food. Never refreeze foods that have already been thawed.

495

HEALTHY EATING

UNDER THE BANNER OF PROGRESS the food we eat has changed radically in the past few decades. Large amounts of money are being spent spreading the word that we can improve our general health and longevity if we improve our diets. Sorting through all of the research and nutritional trends can be difficult, but most experts agree on the basics behind a healthy diet: reduce the amount of fats in your diet; increase the complex carbohydrates by eating more whole-grain cereals, rice, pasta, and bread; and eat a wide variety of fruits and vegetables every day.

BALANCING YOUR DIET

A healthy, balanced diet need not mean excluding any particular foods, as long as they are eaten in the correct proportions.

Foods belong to different groups, depending on their properties and the nutrients they contain. A healthy diet includes a variety of foods, some from each group.

   The food pyramid is a very easy way to remember how to plan your diet. It shows the different food groups and the proportion of your diet they should make up.

Fats, oils, sugars

Dairy products, meat, fish, poultry, legumes, nuts

Fruits & vegetables

Potatoes, pasta, bread, cereals, rice

ARTIFICIAL ADDITIVES

Colorings, flavorings, and preservatives have gotten a very bad press in recent years, and many new products now claim to be completely free of them. It is important to be aware what this claim really means. Many foods still contain flavorings and colorings that, although natural (for example, beets are used to give a pink color) are still added ingredients. Nature-identical flavors and colors are artificially created, but with the same chemical makeup as the natural product. Read labels carefully before buying processed foods.

   Preservatives are necessary to maintain the shelf life of food. Antioxidants retard rancidity in fats and oils, and nitrites and

nitrates in cured meats such as bacon help to prevent food poisoning. Because they are potentially harmful, avoid eating too much of any single additive or preservative by eating a wide variety of foods.

   If you buy foods free from preservatives, you must remember that they will not keep for as long as other foods and therefore must be eaten or cooked as soon as possible after purchase.

   For foods that are as natural as possible, however, choose organic ones. Organic grains, fruits, and vegetables are grown without the use of chemical fertilizers or pesticides. Organic meats come from animals that have received no growth promoters or hormones.

HEALTHY COOKING TECHNIQUES

Changing the way we prepare food is one of the simplest ways to a healthier diet. Use one of the following cooking methods next time you prepare a meal.

Steaming
An ideal way to cook most vegetables. Arrange them in a single layer in a metal or bamboo steamer and put over a saucepan or wok of boiling water. Vegetables that are boiled lose many of their nutrients in the cooking water, whereas steaming ensures their goodness is retained.

Broiling
Cooking under a broiler is a good way to cook poultry, fish, tender cuts of meat, and even many vegetables. Some foods benefit from being lightly brushed with oil to prevent them drying out during cooking, but meats that already contain fat, such as bacon, need no added fat. As the food cooks, the fat melts and drips away.

Stir-frying
Meat, poultry, fish, and vegetables can all be stir-fried. The food is cooked quickly, only small amounts of fat are needed, and the fat is usually a light one, such as sunflower oil. Use a well-seasoned wok or skillet, or a nonstick one that requires even less oil.

Microwaving
Because microwave ovens often speed up the cooking process (pages 492–493), fewer essential nutrients are lost. Vegetables need only have a small amount of water in the cooking dish, and therefore many types of food can be successfully cooked with no added fat.

WEIGHT CONTROL

It is generally known that a healthy diet that results in a steady weight loss is much better than a very low-calorie diet that may promote a faster, but not always permanent weight loss.

To maintain the correct weight for your height and build you need to balance calorie intake with calorie output. If you take in more calories than you need to produce energy, that energy will be stored as fat. If you want to lose weight, you have to take in fewer calories than you need so that your body burns off some of the energy stored as fat. Very low-calorie diets can therefore be dangerous because they don't contain enough calories to produce the energy needed for basic body functions. You will feel ill, tired, and lacking in energy.

Reduce the total intake of fats and sugars, and replace some of the calories with complex carbohydrates, fruits, and vegetables. Together with an increase in the amount of exercise you do, this should not only make you feel healthier, but should also result in a steady weight loss.

CUTTING DOWN ON FAT

Advice on reducing the amount of fat in your diet can be confusing, and simply cutting down on all fats is not the answer. Generally, fats should make up no more than 30% of your total calorie intake, but bear in mind that there are different types of fat.

Saturated fat is usually of animal origin. Avoid saturated fat to reduce the risk of heart disease: it blocks the arteries and also increases the level of cholesterol in the blood. Unsaturated fats may be either poly-unsaturated, such as sunflower oil, or monounsaturated, such as olive oil. These fats, in small amounts, are actually beneficial to the health because they may help to prevent cholesterol building up in the arteries, thereby lowering the risk of heart disease.

It is important to be aware that when an unsaturated oil is treated or hydrogenated, it becomes a saturated fat. Read labels.

Quick ways to a healthier diet

Replace creams with yogurt – low-fat yogurts are the best, but even higher-fat yogurt contains much less fat than heavy cream. Fromage blanc is available in a low-fat form and is a good replacement for cream in cooked dishes.

◆

Eat less red meat.

◆

Increase the carbohydrates in your meals and reduce the proteins.

◆

Add salt or sugar sparingly to foods and avoid processed foods that often contain large quantities of salt and sugar.

◆

Eat fresh or frozen vegetables rather than canned. Vegetables lose nutrients from the moment they're picked, so frozen ones are often better than fresh.

◆

Buy whole-wheat bread and flour, and brown rice.

◆

Reduce the fat content of your meals wherever possible: remove any skin and fat from poultry and meat before cooking; skim any fat from the surface of casseroles, soups, or gravies; drain foods on paper towels before serving.

◆

Leave the nutritious skin on vegetables such as potatoes and carrots: simply scrub them before cooking.

◆

Instead of frying food, steam, broil, or stir-fry.

CALORIE COUNTS

The following calorific values are per 3½ oz (100 g) of each item.

Cereals
Bread, white	235
Bread, whole-wheat	215
Brown rice, boiled	141
Cornflakes	360
Granola	363
Spaghetti, boiled	104

Dairy products
Butter	737
Cheddar cheese	412
Cottage cheese, plain	98
Eggs, whole	147
Full-fat soft cheese	313
Heavy cream	449
Light cream	198
Margarine	739
Plain yogurt, low-fat	56
Skim milk	33
Whole milk	66

Fish
Cod, broiled	95
Mackerel, broiled	239
Tuna, canned in water	99
Tuna, canned in oil	189

Fruits
Apple, raw	47
Avocado, flesh only	190
Banana, flesh only	95
Kiwifruit, flesh only	49
Orange, flesh only	37
Pear, raw	40
Pineapple, raw	41
Strawberries, raw	27

Meats
Bacon, broiled lean and fat	405
Chicken, roast meat only	148
Ground beef, cooked	229
Ham, cooked	120
Hamburger, fried	264
Lamb chop, broiled lean only	222
Pork chop, grilled lean only	226
Pork sausage, broiled	318
Rump steak, broiled lean and fat	218

Vegetables
Broccoli, boiled	24
Carrots, boiled	24
Corn kernels, canned	122
French fries, deep-fried	183
Frozen peas, boiled	69
Potato, boiled	72
Tomatoes, canned	16
Zucchini, boiled	19

COOK'S NOTES

ALL THE RECIPES IN THIS BOOK have been carefully tested to ensure they produce successful results. It is important, however, to bear a few essential points in mind when shopping for and preparing any of the ingredients.

- Be sure to follow either all standard or all metric measurements in a recipe. They are not interchangeable, so don't combine the two.
- The tablespoons used throughout the book are 15 ml, the teaspoons are 5 ml. They are always level measurements.
- All eggs are large unless otherwise stated. Fruits and vegetables are medium-sized unless otherwise specified in a recipe.

- If you want to replace fresh herbs with dried in any of the recipes, use 1 teaspoon dried herbs for 1 tablespoon fresh.
- When a dish is cooked in the oven, always use the middle shelf unless otherwise stated.
- Because ingredients can vary, calorie counts are approximate only.
- Any serving suggestions given with the recipes are not included in the calorie counts.

MEASUREMENTS

STANDARD	METRIC
1/4 in	5 mm
1/2 in	1 cm
1 in	2.5 cm
2 in	5 cm
3 in	7 cm
4 in	10 cm
5 in	12 cm
6 in	15 cm
7 in	18 cm
8 in	20 cm
9 in	23 cm
10 in	25 cm
11 in	28 cm
12 in	30 cm

LIQUID MEASURE

STANDARD	METRIC
1/2 cup	125 ml
2/3 cup	150 ml
3/4 cup	175 ml
1 cup	250 ml
1 1/4 cups	300 ml
1 1/2 cups	375 ml
1 2/3 cups	400 ml
1 3/4 cups	450 ml
2 cups	500 ml
2 1/2 cups	600 ml
3 cups	750 ml
1 quart (4 cups)	1 liter
1 1/4 quarts	1.25 liters

WEIGHT

STANDARD	METRIC
1/2 oz	15 g
1 oz	30 g
2 oz	60 g
3 oz	90 g
4 oz	125 g
6 oz	175 g
8 oz	250 g
10 oz	300 g
12 oz	375 g
13 oz	400 g
14 oz	425 g
1 lb	500 g
1 1/2 lb	750 g
2 lb	1 kg

OVEN TEMPERATURES

FAHRENHEIT	CELSIUS	DESCRIPTION
225°F	110°C	Cool
250°F	120°C	Cool
275°F	140°C	Very slow
300°F	150°C	Very slow
325°F	160°C	Slow
350°F	180°C	Moderate
375°F	190°C	Moderate
400°F	200°C	Moderately hot
425°F	220°C	Hot
450°F	230°C	Hot
475°F	240°C	Very hot

INDEX

Page numbers in *italic* type refer to illustrations.

ACKNOWLEDGMENTS

◆

Food preparation
Eric Treuille
Annie Nichols
Cara Hobday
Sandra Baddeley
Elaine Ngan

◆

Assisted by
Maddalena Bastianelli
Sarah Lowman

◆

Photographers' assistants
Nick Allen
Sid Sideris

◆

Additional recipes/Contributors
Sue Ashworth
Louise Pickford
Cara Hobday
Norma MacMillan
Anne Gains

◆

US Editors
Christine M. Benton
Laaren Brown
Ray Rogers

◆

Nutritional Consultant
Anne Sheasby

◆

Index
Madeline Weston
Anne Crane

◆

Typesetting
Axis Design (DTP)

◆

Production Consultant
Lorraine Baird